Exploring Women's Studies
Looking Forward, Looking Back

Edited by

Carol Berkin

Judith L. Pinch

Carole S. Appel

Introduction by

Anne Firor Scott

PEARSON
Prentice
Hall

Upper Saddle River, New Jersey 07458

Library of Congress Cataloging-in-Publication Data

Exploring women's studies : looking forward, looking back / edited by Carol
Berkin, Judith L. Pinch, Carole S. Appel.
    p. cm.
    Includes bibliographical references and index.
    ISBN 0-13-185088-1 (alk. paper)
    1. Women's studies. 2. Women--Research. 3. Women scholars. I. Berkin,
Carol. II. Pinch, Judith L. III. Appel, Carole S.
    HQ1180.E87   2006
    305.4--dc22

                                                2005042955

VP, Editorial Director: Charlyce Jones Owen
Executive Editor: Charles Cavaliere
Editorial Assistant: Shannon Corliss
Executive Marketing Manager: Heather Shelstad
Senior Marketing Assistant: Cherron Gardner
Managing Editor: Joanne Riker
Production Editor: Jan H. Schwartz
Manufacturing Buyer: Ben Smith
Interior Designer: Preparé, Inc.
Cover Designer: Bruce Kenselaar ·
Cover Art: Getty Images Inc. – Hulton Archive Photos

Director, Image Resource Center: Melinda Reo
Manager, Rights and Permission:
    Zina Arabia
Manager, Visual Research: Beth Brenzel
Manager, Cover Visual Research & Permission:
    Karen Sanatar
Image Permission Coordinator/Researcher:
    Robert Farrell
Composition/Full-Service Management:
    Preparé, Inc.
Printer/Binder: Courier

Credits and aknowledgments borrowed from other sources and reproduced, with permission,
in this textbook appear on appropriate page within text.

Pearson Education LTD.
Pearson Education Singapore, Pte. Ltd
Pearson Education Canada, Ltd
Pearson Education — Japan

Pearson Education Australia PTY, Limited
Pearson Education North Asia Ltd
Pearson Educación de Mexico, S.A. de C.V.
Pearson Education Malaysia, Pte. Ltd

10 9 8 7 6 5 4 3 2 1

ISBN 0-13-185088-1

Contents

Preface

Exploring Women's Studies: Looking Forward, Looking Back is a reunion, in a sense, for all its contributors were assisted at a critical phase of their own work by a Women's Studies Dissertation Grant from the Woodrow Wilson National Fellowship Foundation. Many have gone on to become leaders in their fields and each has continued her commitment to exploring women's experiences, the representation of women, and the gender ideologies that define both female and male members of a society. The contributors were selected to represent a range of fields and the first thirty years of the program. This, then, is both a celebration of success and a reflection on the challenges and, we believe, the adventures that lie ahead for feminist and gender studies.

The editors put two tasks before each contributor. The first of these tasks focused on their work as scholars. We asked them to discuss any significant changes in the theories and methodologies that have guided them and to demonstrate through their own research how those theories can be applied to enrich our knowledge of history, sociology, literature, anthropology, political science, film studies, or art history. For some, this meant guiding the reader through feminist and gender theory from the first, powerful insights through the challenges, debates, and yes, even heated arguments that led to greater insights and subtleties in both theories and applications. For others, it meant narrating the struggle to integrate class, race, religion, and region of the world into their studies of women, as feminist scholars began to recognize that gender was not a dichotomy but a multiplicity of identifications. And for still others, this meant examining the impact of new tools and technologies for research that have made women's studies a more complicated, but richer, field. However, no matter which of these issues they grappled with, we asked that each of these talented scholars serve as a model for younger scholars working in the field by writing an essay that exemplified the current state of their discipline and their field of study.

The second task we put to these scholars was to reflect on their own careers, for we believe that the history of the field of women's studies might be glimpsed in such autobiographical reflections. Thus, each essay begins with answers to critical questions such as how did you become interested in women's studies? What questions so intrigued you that you chose to focus your training and skills on finding their answers? What goals did you set for yourself? What hurdles did you face? How has your understanding of the field changed over the years? And, finally, what impact do you believe three decades of women's studies has had on the way the young women and men of today view the world? These questions have no single or correct answer. But in their responses, the contributors have the opportunity to speak directly to the readers, to begin a dialogue with the next generation of students and scholars, and to provide them with a rare insight into the human beings behind the essays, articles, and books that they encounter in works like *Exploring Women's Studies: Looking Forward, Looking Back.*

Despite the rich variety of approaches and topics in the essays we received, a set of five natural groupings emerged and these shaped the organization of the book. Following an introduction by Professor Anne Firor Scott, one of the most distinguished pioneers in the field of American women's history and a mentor to many who followed, the book has five distinct sections. In the first, "The Evolution of Economic and Political Citizenship for Women," three scholars look back on the evolution of their fields and look forward, setting ambitious agendas for themselves and for their colleagues. In the second, "Gender Construction in Action," historians, anthropologists, and scholars of literature illustrate the new paths being taken by those who examine gender as relational and as a historical construct rather than a fixed, unchanging reality. In the third section, "Labor, Class, and Space," our contributors offer case studies that illuminate the intersection of class and gender in defining work roles, family roles, and women's responses to social and psychological pressures such as idealized happiness and the anxieties of modern life. In the fourth section, "Rights, Reforms, and Welfare," four scholars turn their attention to specific moments in modern women's experience in which gender and political issues are inextricably joined. Finally, in the fifth section, "Knowledge Production," contributors take a hard look at the world of literary and artistic criticism as well as recent technology and remind us that the production of knowledge is never free of gendered bias.

Exploring Women's Studies: Looking Forward, Looking Back thus introduces readers to the troublesome but exciting problems of evidence and methodology, to the heated debates and serious dialogues that refine every field of academic endeavor, and to the challenges ahead that will face the next generation of scholars in the field. It also introduces readers to a remarkable set of scholars whose ongoing engagement with the task of uncovering, analyzing, and narrating women's experiences and the complexities of gender ensures future reunions of feminist scholars in the years to come.

Acknowledgments

The editors would like to acknowledge Carolyn Q. Wilson, who directed the Woodrow Wilson Dissertation Grants in Women's Studies between 1980 and 1993; Shelia Walker, whose technical support has been invaluable; Charles Cavaliere, our editor at Prentice Hall; and the Woodrow Wilson National Fellowship Foundation for providing time and space for this publication.

The editors would like to thank the following people for comments and helpful critiques of the manuscript: Mary Beth Norton, Cornell University; Barbara Winslow, Brooklyn College/CUNY; Bess Beatty, Oregon State University; Mari Jo Buhle, Brown University; Susan Hartmann, The Ohio State University; Karen Manners Smith, Emporia State University; Terry Murphy, George Washington University; Susan Van Dyne, Smith College; and Tracey Weis, Millersville University.

In the contributors' biographies at the beginning of each essay is listed the year in which they were awarded a Woodrow Wilson Dissertation Grant in Women's Studies.

About the Editors

Carol Berkin   is a Professor of History at Baruch College and The Graduate Center, City University of New York, and the author of *Women in America: A History* (1980); *First Generations: Women of Colonial America* (1996); *A Brilliant Solution: Inventing the American Constitution* (2002); *Revolutionary Mothers: Women in the Struggle for America's Independence* (2005) and other works. She has served on the selection committee for Woodrow Wilson Dissertation Grants in Women's Studies.

Judith L. Pinch   is a Senior Fellow and former Vice President and Secretary of The Woodrow Wilson National Fellowship Foundation. She is longtime director of the Woodrow Wilson Dissertation Grants in Women's Studies and other graduate fellowships.

Carole S. Appel   is an Affiliated Scholar in the Connors Writing Center, University of New Hampshire, and a former Women's Studies Editor at the University of Illinois Press. Her publications include "University Press Editing and Publishing," in *Editors as Gatekeepers: Getting Published in the Social Sciences*, ed. Rita J. Simon and James J. Fyfe (1994). She held a Woodrow Wilson Fellowship for graduate study in 1958.

**THE WOODROW WILSON
NATIONAL FELLOWSHIP FOUNDATION**

The Woodrow Wilson National Fellowship Foundation began in 1945 with graduate fellowships that helped to create a great generation of college teachers and intellectual leaders. In the 1960s and 70s, the Foundation broadened its commitment to opportunities in higher education for the best students, regardless of sex or race. Its national programs now include fellowships for graduate education and professional and intellectual development for teachers. It is also committed to strengthening American education through partnerships with universities, public schools, other nonprofit organizations, and government agencies.

Dating back to 1974, the Woodrow Wilson Dissertation Grants in Women's Studies was the first program to support doctoral work in women's studies and remains the only national program of its kind. Since its inception, the Women's Studies program has supported more than 450 scholars in various fields who are doing research and writing on topics concerning women and gender.

This collection of notable feminists includes, clockwise from the top, abolitionist and woman suffrage advocate Lucretia Mott; organizer of the Seneca Falls convention and founder of the National Woman Suffrage Association Elizabeth Cady Stanton; journalist, philanthropist, temperance advocate, and editor of the feminist journal, "The Agitator," Mary A. Livermore; novelist, editor, journalist, abolitionist, and suffragist Lydia Maria Child; temperance advocate and co-founder of the National Woman Suffrage Association Susan B. Anthony; poet, essayist and women's rights advocate Grace Greenwood (Sarah Jane Clark Lippincott); and in the center, lecturer, reformer and abolitionist Anna E. Dickinson.

(Courtesy of the Library of Congress)

Introduction

by Anne Firor Scott

It is difficult to remember now just how little scholarly attention women attracted only half a century ago. From Helen of Troy to Anna Karenina, Madame Bovary to Dorothea Brooke, Scarlett O'Hara to Nancy Drew, poets and novelists have always created interesting women. But in 1946, when Mary Beard published *Woman as Force in History*, it caused hardly a ripple in the scholarly world.[1] The diversity and the dedication to scholarship of the authors in this volume, over a range of topics from literature to art to history and sociology bear witness to the great changes that have taken place since that time.

In 1950, a scholar searching for the history, psychology, or sociology of women had to look hard to find much that was relevant. My perspective is necessarily through the lens of American women's history, my own field. With some effort I bring to my mind's eye the meager two or three shelves devoted to the history of women found in a major university library in 1960. Even in 1971 when I began to teach a course labeled "The Social History of American Women," the assigned reading was, perforce, nearly all in primary sources.

To be sure there were a handful of biographies and biographical collections (but most relied heavily on myth and legend) and half a dozen serious history books published between 1914 and 1945. In England, Alice Clark and Eileen Power had shown just how revealing women's history could be. In the United States, Eleanor Flexner's *Century of Struggle* had come out in 1958. Freud and others less notable had a good deal to say about the female psyche. A few anthropologists had paid attention to women in their field research. Here and there a sociologist had included women in a community study. Some women's voluntary associations paid attention to their own history and, by extension, to that of American women generally. But that was about the sum of what was available.

Even as a tiny group of would-be scholars were bemoaning the absence of data, a revolution was beginning. By the first decade of the twenty-first century, whole stacks in university libraries were devoted to history, psychology, politics, economics, anthropology, biology, philosophy, and sociology related to women, or to gender. Courses, programs, and occasionally departments appeared in most colleges and universities and an umbrella field labeled "women's studies" grew with astonishing speed.

1

How do we account for this remarkable, and seemingly sudden, shift in the intellectual landscape? As with most such changes, this one was a long time in the making.

Identifying beginnings is an uncertain affair, but we know that significant changes in the ordinary life experiences of free American women began to accelerate shortly after the adoption of the Constitution. While the country would remain predominantly rural for most of another century, already in some places, artisan workshops were giving way to factories. Over time, more and more independent artisans became wage workers and no longer worked at home. As men left plowing, planting and harvesting, or blacksmithing and shoemaking in favor of working for factory owners, mothers, wives, and daughters were less likely to be an integral part of the family economy. Some young women and widows went into the first textile mills to support themselves and often to help their families. For wives and mothers, there was plenty of work to be done in what the census takers would call "keeping home," but as husbands or fathers earned enough for a comfortable living, here and there little groups of women began to meet together, first for prayer and religious discussion, and then in what came to be called "benevolent societies" to provide necessities to the poor women and children who were so visibly a part of rapidly growing towns and cities. From these small beginnings, it was not long before some women—seeing inebriated men as depriving women and children of food and clothes—began to join together in temperance associations.

Free black women, as well as white women, were discovering the power of association. Very early they began to gather in literary societies for their own education.[2] They were first to organize female antislavery associations. White women soon followed their example and, finding themselves not much respected in the male dominated antislavery societies, formed their own. The experiences of opposing slavery and alcohol made women aware of their more general disabilities, and by the middle of the nineteenth century, the most courageous were ready to issue a ringing Declaration of Sentiments, modeled on the Declaration of Independence, detailing women's grievances. "Women's rights" became a subject for debates, editorials, sarcasm, and cartoons. Susan B. Anthony's name became a household word. Elizabeth Cady Stanton, at home with her numerous children, forged verbal thunderbolts for Anthony to launch at opponents. An impressive array of capable women joined the cause.

Then came the Civil War, and many crusaders for women's rights turned their energy to war work. South and North, women organized thousands of Soldier's Aid societies whose collective efforts made vital contributions to the health and welfare of soldiers. Steadfast supporters of women's rights organized the Women's Loyal National League with the overt purpose of lobbying for a constitutional amendment abolishing slavery and the covert purpose of keeping their movement together and ready for action once the war was over.[3] These women gathered half a million signatures on a petition to the Congress. In a population in the North of approximately twenty million, this was an impressive figure.

After all this, it was predictable that women who had been so active would not vanish into obscurity after the war ended, but would go on to volunteer or professional careers. Though the numbers, compared to the total female population were small, they represented a forecast of what was to come. Through the nineteenth century, a handful of intellectually ambitious young women braved considerable ridicule to enroll in female seminaries—of which the most demanding were those at Troy and Mt. Holyoke. There were thousands of others, some quite rigorous, others less so. In 1865, the founding of Vassar marked the beginning of colleges for women with standards equal to those of the leading male colleges. Some midwestern state universities that had kept themselves alive during the Civil War by admitting women found that the female scholars were there to stay. The number of women college graduates grew steadily.

While more and more young women were emboldened to venture into academic waters, their mothers expanded the possibilities of all-female voluntary associations for purposes ranging from traditional philanthropy to the demand for the right to vote. Black women confronted with the multiple challenges of freedom began to organize groups focused on their communities.[4] The Atlanta Neighborhood Union founded by the wife of the president of Morehouse College was the model for many others.[5] In the process, a rapidly increasing number of women learned how to stand before an audience and speak their minds. By the 1890s, black women's clubs and white women's clubs had each decided to set up a national federation.

By the first decade of the twentieth century, some bemused observers noted that while men ran the country, in many cases women's organizations were telling them how to do it. In 1906, women persuaded Congress to adopt pure food and drug legislation. In 1911, under prodding from the women of Hull House and other notable settlements, Congress created a Children's Bureau, and with women watching his every move, President Taft appointed a woman to head it. For roughly a decade, the Children's Bureau, with the truly extraordinary help of thousands of volunteers, brought dramatic improvement in the health and welfare of children all over the country.[6] The influence of such women on the development of child labor laws and aid to mothers' programs, along with their motivations and strategies, is described by Miriam Cohen in her chapter in this book.

As women were becoming more visible every day, a major change in academic life was also under way. In the 1870s, the Ph.D. degree came to the United States by way of Johns Hopkins University. By the 1880s, the scholarly disciplines we know today began to develop. One after another, the historians, the economists, the sociologists, the anthropologists began to form professional associations and a number of both private and public universities began to offer Ph.D. degrees. For the most part the newly defined disciplines were overwhelmingly male and the academic atmosphere was far from welcoming to women. Even so, a new kind of scholar came on the scene, the woman with an advanced degree and an aspiration to teach in a college or university. A few women found ways to become lawyers, medical doctors, ministers, and professors.

All this ferment, known as the woman movement, culminated in the United States in 1920 when the Constitution was amended to assure white women the right to vote. (In many parts of the country black women, like black men, were not included in the electorate for another forty years.) In the decades of the twenties and thirties, the absence of a single agreed-upon goal appeared to diminish women's public activity, but this was more appearance than reality. After 1920, the number of women in college equaled the number of men; newly enfranchised women struck out in new directions to change public policy, and experiments with new kinds of marriages were rife.[7]

Telling the story now makes it all sound easy—and perhaps inevitable— but there were many bumps along the way and a good deal of backsliding. In a remarkable speech at the University of Michigan in 1937, Marjorie Hope Nicolson, a distinguished literary scholar, suggested that hers was "the only generation of women which ever really found itself," coming late enough to take education for granted and early enough to secure professional positions. "The millennium had come," she wrote, and "it did not occur to us that life could be different. But . . . the glory is departed. Within a decade shades of the prison house began to close . . . upon the emancipated girl. . . . In the higher professions women reached their peak about 1926, and since that time a decline has set in."[8] The decline was no doubt partly due to the Depression, which set in in earnest in 1929 and challenged all Americans of whatever sex. While opportunities for professional women shrank, for many others the survival of their families became the first order of business.

The New Deal brought unprecedented numbers of women into the government, and Eleanor Roosevelt achieved visibility usually reserved for great singers and actresses. She inspired a generation of ambitious young women, including myself. Then came Pearl Harbor and barriers that had hitherto limited women's economic opportunities were suddenly breached. WACS, WAVES, and women who ferried bombers were there for all to see. Other women found work in a wide variety of war industries or war-created businesses. For a few years, women born in the 1920s could do whatever they could envision and had the courage to try.

The impression that once the war was over, women happily retired to their homes to have numerous children and create a so-called baby boom, we know now, was an overly simple view of things. No sooner were those babies ready for first grade than their mothers were going off to Continuing Education programs or looking for jobs. Some began creating their own independent businesses or running for public office. Many wage-earning women had enjoyed having their own paychecks, and looked for ways to continue work.

As the children, white and black, born in the 1940s reached their twenties, a good many took matters into their hands; the Civil Rights Movement, the anti-war movement, and the feminist movement emerged. If one asks why feminism appeared, part of the answer is that the cumulative developments outlined here had prepared the way. Women were no longer invisible. Young women began to ask all kinds of questions and to try out all kinds of new lives.

A notable part of the multifaceted movement, which for short we call "the sixties," was the number of college women who chose to go on to advanced work and to aim for academic careers. A growing number battered their way into graduate programs where—because they were generally held to a higher standard than male applicants—many turned out to be outstanding students. Translating their observations and experience into intellectual interest, a considerable number of these new scholars decided to concentrate on matters to do with their own sex. So it was that by the early 1970s, an unprecedented number of women, minority and white, were searching for dissertation subjects, and looking for support once those topics had been chosen.

The first university courses in women's studies grew out of the women's liberation movement as students sought classes they considered relevant to their political and personal interests, and instructors began to realize how male-centered the standard college curriculum was. Scholars in the disciplines began to address the huge gaps that existed in consideration of women's role in every aspect of human endeavor. Underlying the new scholarship were precepts that could be summed up in two words: gender matters. Some of the other basic premises for women's studies were that until recently the history of women throughout the world has largely been ignored; that works by women were omitted from the literary canon; that gender may be constructed differently across cultures; that gender, class, and race are interwoven; that people who left no record still have a history; and that queer theory derives from but sometimes overturns central insights of feminist theory. These are some of the issues our contributors address.

Already well known for the support it had given to traditional graduate study, in 1974, with the support of The Ford Foundation, The Woodrow Wilson National Fellowship Foundation inaugurated a program specifically for Ph.D. candidates who wanted to do research about women. In the ensuing thirty years, more than four hundred young scholars qualified for grants; many of them have gone on to forge distinguished careers in history, literature, anthropology, sociology, economics, linguistics, and computer science.[9] Several major foundations have supported women's studies in various ways, but the Woodrow Wilson program has gone on steadily for more than thirty years, modifying its criteria as the intellectual world has changed, and opening doors for promising young people, many of whom, such as those represented in this volume, have become preeminent scholars in their fields. The program continues to flourish and attracts several hundred applicants a year, testimony to continued strong interest in studies concerning women.

The authors of the chapters in this book all held Woodrow Wilson Dissertation Grants in Women's Studies. As one way of taking stock, of asking where the study of women has come and where it may be going, each was persuaded to present an example of her mature work and some personal reflections on the process by which she had come to that work. Taken together, their essays make clear just how complicated the process of knowledge creation can be.

In the early years of the 1960s and '70s, the framework and the assumptions for most studies were fairly simple. Women were often examined without much attention to men; there were assumed to be two sexes, and a straightforward narrative report of research findings was the prevailing mode. Those assumptions are now viewed as too simple. The number of sexes (or, maybe, genders) has increased considerably; historians of women are expected to offer explicit theoretical foundations for their work, and the concept of "feminist history" has developed alongside Marxist history, Freudian history, and other variations. Similar changes have occurred in the social sciences and in literary studies. New technology has vastly expanded the resources for scholarship; first came microfilm, and then, as Martha Nell Smith recounts, the digital revolution brought far flung archives into one's own study.

None of the chapters in this volume could have been written thirty years ago.[10] The subjects are wide ranging and properly treat the whole world as their territory. The editors have tried to tame the diversity of subjects by devising categories and providing a road map to help the reader know where each essay is going. Diverse as they are, these essays exhibit a conscious effort to put data into a theoretical framework. All the authors are aware, as earlier scholars were not always, of the uses of theory as an organizing principle and as a heuristic device. Many share the recognition, so cogently argued by Jacqueline Jones, that women cannot be studied without attention to men. Others, for example Beverly Guy-Sheftall, argue that it is not possible to understand white women without reference to black women. A corollary, evident in a number of these chapters, especially those by Myra Marx Ferree and Shanshan Du, is an awareness of a need to view the whole spectrum of women around the world, not just those who live in the in the United States or in the Western Hemisphere. Beyond that there is a heightened awareness of context—the realization, spelled out by Estelle Freedman—that not all women's experiences, not all feminisms are alike. Most of these authors see traditional sources differently from the way they were viewed by the pioneers. Laurel Ulrich, for example, has found new insight into what had once seemed a thoroughly studied period of American history by examining the records of women. Antoinette Burton and Sharon Marcus demonstrate approaches to the study of Victorian Britain that would have been hard to find in the literature before 1970, and equally absent then would have been the methods Susan Casteras tells us she used to examine images of Victorian womanhood in British art through the lens of the period's social practices. Adela Pinch's chapter on women in Georgian England is an example of the interdisciplinary nature of a great deal of current scholarship in women's studies. Caroline Brettell's review of theoretical debates in anthropology since 1974 proves that the renewed interest in narrative reveals much hitherto hidden about women's lives, while Felicity Callard's chapter on agoraphobia demonstrates the great influence that psychoanalytical theory has had on all fields of study. Michele Barale, Sabrina Barton, and Deborah Nord all exemplify in their work the insights being brought to cultural studies by scholars versed in the perspectives of women's studies.

The chapters exhibit a search for new methods, new sources, as well as new theoretical structures. Leila Rupp shows just how imaginative a historian of women can be in searching for new data. The authors also share the assumption that things once seen as fixed or inevitable must be understood as unstable, subject to change. It is worth noting, too, that not one author among those who exhibit a clear political position apologizes for doing so. The reader will have no doubt of the political views of Felicia Kornbluh or Ellen Reese. For them, the objectivity debate is over—there is no such thing.

All in all there is enough food for thought here to fuel several seminars, and some scholarly soul searching. The Woodrow Wilson National Fellowship Foundation has done a fine thing in bringing these essays to fruition and publishing them.

Anne Firor Scott, W. K. Boyd Professor of History, Emerita, Duke University, is author of *The Southern Lady* (1970); *Making the Invisible Woman Visible* (1984); *Natural Allies* (1991); *Unheard Voices: The First Historians of Southern Women* (1993); and other works.

Notes

1. Mary R. Beard, *Woman as Force in History: A Study in Traditions and Realities* (New York: Macmillan, 1946). Beard took issue with the assumption that women had always and everywhere been subjects of discrimination. The evidence of the indifference to her work was reinforced when she wrote as an equal partner with her husband what may still be the most widely read textbook in American history—*The Rise of American Civilization*—it was reviewed as if only Charles Beard had written it. Charles Beard himself insisted that the general form of that book had been her idea. Along with her other books, *Women's Work in the Municipalities* (1914), *On Understanding Women* (1931), and *America through Women's Eyes* (1933), *Woman as Force* was enthusiastically rediscovered in the 1970s.

2. Dorothy Sterling, ed., *We Are Your Sisters: Black Women in the Nineteenth Century* (New York: W. W. Norton, 1984), 85–234.

3. The dramatic story of women's war work is covered in detail in Chapter 3 of Anne F. Scott, *Natural Allies: Women's Associations in American Life* (Urbana: University of Illinois Press, 1991), 59–83.

4. Anne Firor Scott, "Most Invisible of All: Black Women's Voluntary Associations," *Journal of Southern History* LVI, No. 1, February 1990, 3–22.

5. Deborah Gray White, *Too Heavy a Load: Black Women in Defense of Themselves 1894–1994* (New York: W. W. Norton, 1999).

6. Robin Muncy, *Creating a Female Dominion in American Reform 1890–1935* (New York: Oxford University Press, 1991) is an excellent study of this phenomenon.

7. Anne Firor Scott, "After Suffrage: Southern Women in the 1920s," *Journal of Southern History* XXX, 3 August 1964, 208–318.

8. "The Rights and Privileges Pertaining Thereto . . ." in Wilfred B. Shaw, ed., *A University between Two Centuries*: The Proceedings of the 1937 Celebration of the University of Michigan (Ann Arbor, 1937), 414.

9. The total number of grants made as of 2004 is 469. Of these 153 were in history, 73 in literature, 46 in anthropology, 46 in sociology, and 31 in psychology. The rest were scattered from art and economics to area studies and a variety of other fields. Other major donors to the Woodrow Wilson Dissertation Grants in Women's Studies include the Helena Rubinstein Foundation, the Philip Morris Companies, and many individuals.

10. When I collected my early essays written in the 1960s and 1970s in a volume called *Making the Invisible Woman Visible* (Urbana: University of Illinois Press, 1984), a kind younger colleague wrote that this was the "best of old-fashioned history." In two decades, one could go from being *avant garde* to being old fashioned—a lesson for our times.

Woman suffrage parades became a popular means of applying political pressure in the second decade of the 20th century. This parade, organized by New York City activists on May 6, 1912, came in the midst of both a presidential election year and debates in several states over amendments to their constitutions that would grant women the vote. That year, Michigan, Kansas, Oregon, and Arizona approved woman suffrage and both Teddy Roosevelt's Progressive Party and Eugene V. Debs's Socialist party endorsed a national woman suffrage amendment. Although the largest woman suffrage marches took place in 1913 and 1915, the May 6, 1912, march reflected the heightened national interest in the debate over women's rights.

(Courtesy of the Library of Congress)

part 1

The Evolution of Economic and Political Citizenship for Women

The essays in this section deal with the challenges and opportunities women's studies scholars face as they continue to redefine feminism as a political and social movement as well as a theoretical tool of analysis. Two of these essays chart the intellectual history of feminism, as scholars abandoned older definitions that linked feminism simplistically to white, middle class women of European and American backgrounds and came to see it as a complex, multifaceted consciousness among women of all regions, races, and social classes. Scholars acknowledge this complexity by speaking of "feminisms" rather than a single feminism.

In her essay "Beyond the Waves: Rethinking the History of Feminisms," Estelle Freedman argues for the necessity of placing feminist movements in their historical setting, or context, and determining what is essential for such movements to emerge. Freedman argues that two broad historical forces— democratic politics and free wage labor systems—produced the conflicts that propelled feminists to mobilize. She finds that the exclusion of women from a full voice in representative government and their exclusion from equal economic opportunities and rewards initially prompted the rise of feminist movements. Freedman is careful to point out that, although the preconditions are similar, the forms that political and labor systems take vary from country to country. Therefore, a variety of feminisms arise. Each is devoted to expanding the rights of women yet each takes its distinctive form from the particular mix of race, ethnicity, and culture in which they arise. In each case, however, feminist demands for equality and self-determination challenge the political structures, the labor system, and the traditions of sexual violence against women that their society tolerates.

In "African Feminisms: the Struggle Continues," Beverly Guy-Sheftall forcefully reminds us of the tensions between particular and universal forms of feminism. She traces the development of African-based feminist theory and organizations and demonstrates their differences and similarities to western feminism. African-based feminism is not monolithic, but takes a variety of forms as it develops in the diverse cultural settings of Africa, the Caribbean, or Britain. Guy-Sheftall stresses the need for women's studies scholarship to embrace the insights provided by black feminisms and to incorporate these feminisms into the complex portrait of women's experience we are attempting to create. Antoinette Burton's essay, "Feminism, Empire and National Histories: The Case of Victorian Britain," examines the role feminist historians have played in shaping a new imperial scholarship that transcends national boundaries. She believes that feminist scholarship has challenged the older tradition of writing self-contained national histories. It has not only added women to the stories being told; it has led the way for the inclusion of children, "natives," and other once-invisible social groups. Burton uses the history of Victorian Britain to illustrate her point that feminist scholars have opened up fruitful debates around the meaning of citizenship and the representation of national identity in the arts, literature, and the discipline of history itself.

Beyond the Waves: Rethinking the History of Feminisms

Estelle B. Freedman

Estelle B. Freedman (1974) is the Edgar E. Robinson Professor in U.S. History at Stanford University. She is currently studying the history of sexual violence and the politics of rape. Her books include *Intimate Matters: A History of Sexuality in America*, with John D'Emilio (1988); *Maternal Justice: Miriam Van Waters and the Female Reform Tradition* (1996); and *No Turning Back: The History of Feminism and the Future of Women* (2002).

The critical questions in women's studies at the beginning of her career, Estelle Freedman writes, concerned the sources of women's oppression and the identification of women's historical agency. By the 1980s, questions about the racial, sexual, and national diversity of women's identities, raised both outside and within the academy, had transformed feminist scholarship. Tensions over deconstructing the category of woman as well as the internationalization of feminist studies continued to challenge earlier scholarly assumptions. "In my own intellectual development, both writing about the history of sexuality and teaching the introductory course in feminist studies deepened my appreciation of the intersection of gender with other forms of social hierarchy. I continue to be intrigued by historical patterns in feminist movements, but my conceptual frameworks have shifted markedly." In her earlier work, she tried to link organizational strategies with continuities and discontinuities in nineteenth- and twentieth-century U.S. feminist history. In the past few years, she has taken a much longer view and tried as well to place the U.S. within a cross-cultural and transnational history of feminism.

The questions we ask in the early years of our training as scholars may continue to haunt us throughout our careers; our answers reveal much about changes in our disciplines and in our intellectual trajectories. In this chapter,

I want to reflect on my career-long engagement with questions of feminist periodization. In the early 1970s, when I began to study women's history, the metaphor of "the waves" was taking root. The image of recurrent oceanic swells that crest and recede differentiated the "first wave" of women's rights activism—from Seneca Falls in 1848 to the ratification of the Nineteenth Amendment in 1920—and the recent "second wave" that began in the 1960s. Beginning in graduate school, I became curious about the eras before, or in between, these standard periods; over time I have returned to this issue through different research projects. In early essays and monographs, I adopted "the waves," but teaching interdisciplinary women's studies contributed to a shift in my framework. Eventually I came to subsume the waves within a more comprehensive argument about historical momentum. Rather than endorsing a new metaphor, I offer here an account of how my periodization of feminism has changed as both women's studies and my own historical vantage points have expanded their scope.

WATERSHEDS AND BENCHMARKS IN U.S. WOMEN'S HISTORY

Personal history no doubt inspired my recurrent curiosity about the waves of U.S. feminist history. Coming of age intellectually and politically just as the "second wave" washed over American culture, I could not imagine where all that energy had been stored for so long, why it had revived just then, and why it had seemingly stopped, with so much unfinished business, a generation before I encountered it. What little I had read of U.S. women's history portrayed the slow but steady march of women's rights from Seneca Falls to suffrage, always ending in 1920. Yet entering graduate studies in U.S. history at Columbia University in 1970, I sorely wanted feminism back. I was keenly aware of the absence of women faculty, in contrast to their abundance at Barnard College, where I had been an undergraduate. And like many women of my generation, I found feminist insights were daily changing my world, my worldview, and my personal life. Perhaps, I thought, I could learn what had happened to that earlier movement, why it had effectively disappeared, and why this new "wave" was gathering enough force to make me value my intellectual instincts and to sustain my commitment to becoming an historian.

The question of "what happened to the women's movement" has been at the heart of at least half of my scholarship since that time. Beginning in a graduate seminar on the 1920s and 1930s, I approached the question historiographically. How had scholars explained the post-suffrage era, and what were their interpretations of women's status and politics after 1920? What struck me most from my survey was that historians themselves had contributed to the silencing of feminism by declaring its irrelevance after suffrage. American society, most of them pronounced, had achieved gender equality with the stroke of a constitutional amendment (aided and abetted, perhaps, by a revolution in manners and morals).[1] Ever since writing that essay on "The New Woman," I have been suspicious about historical periodization and concerned about the implications of the benchmarks we create.

Frustrated by the limits of a suffrage-centered history, I wanted my scholarship to contribute to a more complex understanding of feminism. Like other women's studies scholars of the 1970s, I was intrigued by the contours of women's politics. As a historian, I wanted to explore social movements in which women mobilized before or after suffrage. From the 1870s to enfranchisement, middle-class American women built an expansive organizational world, addressing issues from temperance and moral reform to support for working women's housing and labor union organizing. We now know that white, African-American, Latina, and Asian-American women formed associations, usually distinct from each other but occasionally in alliance, in the WCTU or YWCA, for example. In an early article, which reflected the separatist politics of the 1970s, I argued that a major strength of the women's movement between 1870 and 1920 was what I called its *separatist* strategy— evidenced by women-run schools, clubs, clinics, and even prisons. After suffrage, I argued, those premature pronouncements of equality had encouraged a dismantling of the separatist infrastructure, which depleted the strength of the movement. "When women tried to assimilate into male-dominated institutions," I wrote, ". . . they lost the momentum and the networks which had made the suffrage movement possible."[2] Clearly, I was still working within the framework of the waves: 1920 marked the crest of the first wave and the turn away from a separate women's culture helped explain the subsequent neap tide.

Because I was so intrigued by the separate organizational life women created, I explored in depth a particular movement, women's prison reform, for clues to both periodization and strategies. In *Their Sisters' Keepers*, I asked why and how religiously motivated, white middle-class women in the late-nineteenth century had successfully lobbied to create a sexually segregated correctional system, run largely by and for women only.[3] By the 1920s, they had succeeded in establishing separate institutions in most states and influencing the creation of the first federal women's prison. But the original reformers' vision of maternal, rather than punitive, institutions had not survived. In most states, the reform impulse had been supplanted by equally punitive and bureaucratic prisons. Even well-intended social critics, I learned, had to conform in order to retain state funding. Like other historians restoring agency to women (via temperance, anti-prostitution, or Americanization efforts, for example), I learned that the results of reform were not always pretty.

Looking back on my early explorations of women's reform and feminist movements, I can see how I had fallen into a periodization I intended to question. In each case, I assumed that 1920 was the watershed and then tried to explain why. Two things would push me beyond this framework: teaching women's history and women's studies, and writing a biography.

Periodization helps historians organize our courses, and suffrage initially appeared as a major benchmark on my syllabi, demarcating an earlier era of separate spheres and social reform from a later one of sexual revolution and wage labor. But as I incorporated a growing literature on twentieth-century women's history into my teaching, the weaker that benchmark seemed.

For example, Nancy Cott's important study, *The Grounding of Modern Feminism*, nicely complicated the periodization.[4] She identified the earlier origins of equal rights feminism in the U.S. around 1910 and showed the proliferation of women's organizations after 1920. Other scholarship also convinced me that throughout the post-suffrage years, women's movements had not necessarily eroded. They had taken different shapes, often supporting varied social justice causes, and they rarely called themselves feminist. Yet when the YWCA or the National Council of Negro Women tackled racism, or the Women's International League for Peace and Freedom (WILPF) protested war, they sustained the separatist strategy.

The vantage point of writing a biography further revised my ideas about periodization and separatism. In the 1990s, I returned to the history of women's prisons to write about a twentieth-century reformer, Miriam Van Waters. From the 1930s through the 1950s, Van Waters championed a redemptive and educational approach as superintendent of the Massachusetts Reformatory for Women. She refused to capitulate to repeated demands that she make the reformatory more penal, although it almost cost her job. She may have been exceptional in the world of prisons, but like her contemporaries Eleanor Roosevelt and Molly Dewson, Van Waters relied on women's networks to support her quest for public authority. These qualities forced me to modify my separatism argument. "Where separatism in some form persisted," I now wrote, "women continued to influence social reform and politics to an extent that earlier histories have underestimated."[5]

In my teaching and my scholarship, I increasingly treated American feminism as a continuous and building current, rather than a series of waves. While the explosion of women's liberation after the mid-1960s did look a bit like a tsunami, it was much less sudden than usually portrayed.[6] Nor was it distinctive to the U.S., for throughout Europe and North America, women's movements had erupted against the backdrop of social protest. Partly in light of the international feminist dialogues of the 1970s and 1980s, women's studies broadened its perspectives. Political scientists theorized about comparative feminisms; post-colonial scholars such as Chandra Mohanty questioned the western monopoly on feminist politics; historians such as Leila Rupp explored international feminist organizing in the past.[7] The significance of periodization on a U.S. timeline diminished in light of a rich scholarship that revealed a centuries-long intellectual history of feminism, the transatlantic dynamics of women's rights activism after the 1840s, and the histories of nineteenth- and twentieth-century women's organizing in countries such as Brazil, Chile, Egypt, and India.[8]

When I began to teach FS101, Introduction to Feminist Studies, in 1988, women's studies was in the process of internationalizing, and I had the opportunity to revise my historical and geographical frameworks. To place women's experiences and feminist politics in both interdisciplinary and international perspective, I had to think further about the historical motors driving diverse women's movements. Where and when did feminist ideas appear outside of the U.S.? How did colonialism complicate women's movements?

Do national and local distinctions preclude overarching historical interpretations? Teaching about feminism from these perspectives required so much new knowledge that I once joked that I could have written a book, given the time I spent preparing for this course. In retrospect, I think that if I had known how much additional work it would actually take to turn that course into a book, I might never have done so. But after a decade of teaching FS101, I decided that the expansive scholarship in women's history and feminist studies would allow me to provide a synthetic account of feminist history.

HISTORICAL FRAMEWORKS FOR FEMINISM

The title of the book I wrote based on my course, *No Turning Back*, refers to the historical momentum that has propelled movements that seek women's full political and economic citizenship.[9] Before feminism (and since, as well), women regularly resisted or modified patriarchy, but they usually did so as individuals. Political critiques of gender hierarchy did not appear until the convergence of two historical transformations made them both possible and necessary: democratic politics and wage labor systems. The rejection of hierarchical rule allowed women and their male allies to question patriarchy; the transition from a family to a market economy created unique dilemmas for women as mothers and as workers.

Because these political and economic processes occurred at different times throughout the world, the U.S. model of two feminist waves could not contain them. Feminism unfolded over space as well as time. In parts of Europe and North America, where these political and economic processes first converged after 1800, feminists began to agitate for education, property rights, and full citizenship. By 1900, an international women's movement was beginning to advance these goals in urban areas of Latin America, the Middle East, and Asia, as well. In the twentieth century, post-colonial and democratization movements, as well as a global economy, repeatedly extended these historical processes. Today, transnational communications have brought women's rights to regions that have neither democratized nor industrialized. While no single narrative can do justice to the complexities of unique regional histories, a framework that emphasized the recurrent effects of democratization and wage labor, along with international communications, helped me synthesize the new scholarship on multiple feminisms.

The first element in this framework, the roots of feminism in democratic political theory, has long been recognized by historians. Since the eighteenth century, the shift from hierarchical rule by elites to representative government—based on the natural rights of man—has inspired demands for self-representation and full citizenship that go well beyond the Western, propertied, white males who first articulated the ideal. Like movements to abolish slavery in the Americas or to emancipate serfs and Jews in Europe, arguments for women's rights rested upon these democratic principles. As more European and American men gained the right to vote and run for office in the nineteenth and twentieth centuries, the exclusion of women from voting, office holding, and jury duty stood out as signs of incomplete democracy, vulnerable to feminist critiques. In other world regions, such as parts of Latin America and post-colonial Africa and Asia, when educational opportunities exposed women to democratic ideals, they, too, expected full citizenship.

But even democratic societies resisted the extension of self-determination to women, for both the Enlightenment and the revolutionary political ideas that gave birth to women's longings for emancipation rested upon contradictory views. Universal rights promised emancipation from the Old Regime of inherited status; simultaneously, however, the principle of *natural law* drew biological distinctions between the sexes and among races. The flip side of natural *rights* was natural *sex* and natural *race*. Thus when women or Africans or Asians claimed universal rights, critics could respond that their biological differences disqualified them from inclusion as citizens. This contradiction within modern political thought, as Joan Scott has pointed out, required a dual strategy on the part of feminists.[10] On the one hand they emphasized universalism and demanded inclusion in the language of rights; on the other hand, they pointed to particularistic, biologically rooted, female claims to political authority.

The exclusion of women from the body politic, a staple of Western democracy since the classical era, required these paradoxical strategies for achieving inclusion. How else could women claim full citizenship, when their reproductive roles in families created the kind of dependency that seemed antithetical to exercising democratic rights? Thus a balancing act between universalism and maternalism recurred throughout Western feminist history. For example, when Mary Wollstonecraft called for women's education in eighteenth-century England, she insisted it would better fit them as "sensible mothers"; Flora Tristan pressed for education for French working women in the nineteenth century in part "because women have the responsibility for educating male and female children"; in 1890 the Brazilian feminist Francisca Diniz wrote that the sanctity of maternal love and wifely fidelity proved women's superiority, rather than inferiority, and required equal treatment by men. Early twentieth-century American suffragists echoed these particularistic arguments when they insisted that women voters would insure a more peaceful and nurturing society. For Charlotte Perkins Gilman, life-giving women (preferably, in her view, those of Teutonic stock) would improve on the man-made world.[11]

The expanding definition of citizenship proved a necessary but not sufficient cause for feminist movements to form. An economic motor reinforced ideas: the transition from agricultural, family-based economies to commercial, and later industrial, market economies based on wage labor. This process, too, occurred at different times throughout the world. The initial transition to industrial production in Europe and North America excluded most women, reinforcing maternal identities within the middle class and employing working-class women largely to perform domestic labor outside their own homes. Over the twentieth century, however, light manufacturing, clerical and service jobs, and later information economies, would draw women of all classes and ages into formal labor markets. In industrializing societies, the pool of available female workers grew as women's reproductive labor declined. In the U.S., for example, average marital fertility rates dropped from around eight children in 1800 to under two children in 2000. Whenever an expanding sector of the economy sought cheap labor, women, who now had fewer reproductive labors, filled the jobs.

As a result of worker availability and employer demand, female labor changed from exceptional to commonplace in most Western cultures. First younger and single women, later older and married women, and then mothers of small children spent longer periods of their lives earning wages. By 1999, 70 percent of married women with children were working for wages in the U.S. By then, 46 percent of the U.S. and 42 percent of western European workers were women. Given the global reach of market economies, the process was not limited to the West. By the 1990s, women constituted 43 percent of the wage labor force in Sub Saharan Africa, East Asia, and the Caribbean. Significantly, their jobs clustered in "female" sectors of the economy: light manufacturing, clerical and sales, or providing services once offered in private homes, such as preparing and serving food, cleaning, caring for children, and sex work. During every transition from agricultural to industrial economies, sexual commerce has drawn women from rural areas into cities, where the restrictions on women's jobs keeps the pool of sex workers full.

It was not wage earning *per se* that fomented feminism. Whether in the realm of citizenship or labor, it has been the discrepancies between male and female opportunities that ignited feminist critiques. Female wage earning potentially weakened the patriarchal family by providing women a measure of economic independence or, at the least, greater leverage at home. But the lingering ideology of female dependency—the fiction of the "private woman" supported in the home—survived the demographic and economic transition to female wage labor. Lower wages and a sexually segregated job market (as well as limited rights to property and access to credit) meant that women could not support themselves, which in turn ensured their dependence on fathers and husbands, thus reinforcing patriarchy.

In another legacy of the private home, even when women earned wages they continued to have primary responsibility for caring for family members. This unpaid work in the home perpetuated labor force economic inequality at every stage of economic development. For one, association as primarily unpaid caregivers masked women's full economic contributions, just as it masked men's capacity for familial labors. In addition, it created the double day for most women workers, who continue to absorb the social costs of family care. Data on the division of housework throughout the world, even for dual earning couples, document this disparity. Working women do most of the caring work within families. Even when socialist states have provided some relief, such as child care, women's domestic responsibility remains powerful. The domestic legacy has also led to employer biases that women are not dedicated to their jobs, simply by virtue of being potential or actual mothers.

Because of this dual economic burden, along with their secondary political status, women began to chafe against the limitations on their full participation as workers and as citizens.

FEMINIST STRATEGIES AND AGENDAS

One of the problems with dividing feminist history into two waves has been the lack of a single political analysis in each period. At every mobilization, competing strategies have emerged. Just as the paradox of female citizenship required a dual strategy that balanced universal and maternal claims to authority, so too labor inequalities inspired multiple responses.

Historians of Western feminism have identified at least three dominant strategies that recurred in the nineteenth and twentieth centuries. In the nineteenth century, *liberal* feminists in the U.S., England, Chile, Japan, and elsewhere emphasized women's access to education, property rights, and jobs. European *socialists* like Clara Zetkin in Germany, organized working women within leftist parties, while Alexandra Kollontai, Commissar of Social Welfare in the early Soviet Union, tried to address family as well as workplace dilemmas, decreeing free maternity care, for example. A third strain, since labeled *maternalism* by historians, built upon family needs. Amanda Labarca of Chile reported to a U.S. women's group in 1922 that she expected "a new feminist creed" to arise in the southern continent, one "more domestic, more closely linked to the future of the home, the family, and the children," than that marked by the "exaggerated individualism" of what she called "Saxon feminism."[12]

Yet liberal, socialist, and maternalist strategies always overlapped, coexisted, and constantly influenced each other. In the nineteenth and early twentieth centuries, when most women worked within their own families, even liberal feminists recognized that as long as women remained economically *dependent* on men, motherhood provided a powerful argument for protecting and empowering women. By the mid-twentieth century, following the surge in Western women's wage labor, the universalist, equal rights strategy effectively expanded women's economic *independence*, but it left most familial labor in women's hands as well. Viewed from outside the West, or from communist countries that had mobilized women's labor, the freedom to work for wages could look unrewarding. By the twenty-first century, more feminists had begun to articulate a new model of *interdependence*, in which women and men share care-giving and bread-winning tasks, but with the support of employers and the state.[13] Unlike maternalism, this strategy avoids gender essentialism, and unlike the autonomous individualism of Western liberalism, it addresses familial needs and community responsibility.

In addition to its strategic malleability, feminism has also redefined its agendas in response to recurrent, often painful, internal conflicts. Two kinds of challenges to the white, middle-class, Western composition of feminism reflected the legacies of colonial relations. The first concerned racial justice: Would feminism subsume race to gender concerns or recognize racism as central to its politics? The second concerned national liberation from European dominance: Would feminism reject the "white woman's burden" of "civilized morality"—Gilman's Teutonic bias, for example—and recognize the political integrity of non-Western and former colonial subjects? These questions have continuously redefined feminism, not only during crests in Western feminism but in the interludes as well. Indeed, the historical strength of feminism often correlates with its attention to broader social justice concerns, while its weak periods are often those in which feminism is isolated from other critiques of social hierarchies.

Within the U.S., for example, ties between movements for gender and racial justice ran deep within the antislavery and early women's rights movements. Yet the initial alliance of abolitionists and feminists before the Civil War largely crumbled during the post-war rise of Jim Crow segregation, which was also a lean period for the suffrage movement. African-American activists, however, never stopped pressuring white feminists to reject the racial hierarchy that relegated black women to the back of the suffrage parades and the margins of the political agenda. Tentative interracial coalitions reemerged in the twentieth-century civil rights movement, which in turn helped revive feminist politics.

By the 1960s, with a more diverse U.S. population, not only African-American but also Mexican, Native American, and Asian-American women—as well those who identified as lesbian and disabled—insisted that feminism dismantle all social hierarchies that impeded women's full citizenship. In the words of activist Barbara Smith, speaking in 1979, "Feminism is the political theory and practice that struggles to free *all* women: . . . Anything less than this vision of total freedom is not feminism, but merely female self-aggrandizement."[14] A repeated process of naming differences, organizing separately, and working toward political coalitions challenged U.S. feminism, but rather than splintering, much of the movement has tried to learn, in Audre Lorde's phrase, "how to take our differences and make them strengths."[15]

Racial inclusion meant that the U.S. feminist agenda had to change. Reproductive rights, for example, came to include not only contraception and abortion, but also an end to sterilization abuse. The women's health movement had to address the particular concerns of women of color and make health care available in their communities. With so many women of color living in poverty, welfare reform had to become a feminist issue. While large swaths of American feminism still reflect a white and middle class membership, at its best the movement now works in alliance, rather than in competition, with movements for universal civil and human rights.

Internationally, colonialism set the stage for most global encounters among women, leaving a powerful legacy of unequal relations across regions. In India and Egypt, anti-colonial and nationalist politics mobilized women such as Huda Sha'arawi to claim citizenship rights. In other countries, such as Turkey or Iran, top-down modernization movements enacted some women's rights but precluded feminist political organizing. Many national liberation movements—in Algeria, for example—associated feminism with Western imperialism and called for a nationalistic return to one version of local "tradition," namely, patriarchy.

Not surprisingly, given European dominance and anticolonial rejection of the West, the international feminist organizations of the early twentieth century remained international largely in name only. In addition, what has been termed "feminist orientalism" on the part of European women hampered their outreach efforts. Women of color continually protested these attitudes. At an international conference in 1935, for example, Shareefeh Hamid Ali of India spoke for women of "the East" when she explained to women "of the West" that "any arrogant assumption of superiority or of patronage on the part of Europe or America" would alienate "the womanhood of Asia and Africa."[16]

Growing internationalism after World War II provided new opportunities for communication across cultures. The founding of the United Nations may provide a more important benchmark for feminist history than any national enfranchisement. From its charter in 1945, the U.N. declared "the equal rights of men and women." The organization has been instrumental in facilitating transnational feminist organizing, particularly during the Decade for Women (1975–1985), which produced three international conferences, with concurrent non-governmental organization (NGO) forums, as well as the Convention to Eliminate All Forms of Discrimination Against Women (CEDAW). These interactions forced Western feminists to begin to de-center their priorities in the light of multiple strategies for empowering women. As the Forum newspaper in Copenhagen reported in 1980, "To talk feminism to a woman who has no water, no food and no home is to talk nonsense."[17] Poverty, illiteracy, and homelessness—critical women's issues throughout the world—had to become central to international feminist movements.

By the time of the U.N. conference in Beijing in 1995, both NGOs and states had created feminist infrastructures concerned with women's economic inequality, physical vulnerability, political representation, and creative opportunities. A broad range of projects now address women's issues: Organizing domestic workers in Latin America; monitoring the treatment of migrant domestics internationally; exposing domestic violence in India; expanding micro-enterprise in South Asia; grass-roots health movements to eradicate female genital cutting in Africa; female literacy campaigns; marriage and divorce reform in Egypt and Turkey; and women's arts, theater, publishing, and performance spaces internationally.

In addition to addressing the particular needs of women, international feminism has insisted that human rights be understood from women's perspective. In a sense, this strategic move helps to resolve the Western tension between universal and particularist claims by redefining the universal as the female. In some cases, the impact on world and local politics has been transformative. For example, in response to a campaign by the Women's Caucus for Gender Justice, the 1998 Rome Statute creating the International Criminal Court outlawed gender-based violence in wartime. Despite strong opposition, the Caucus succeeded in including as war crimes rape, sexual slavery, enforced prostitution, forced pregnancy, and enforced sterilization. Equally transformative, the statute required that the

Court include both female and male judges who had expertise on violence against women or children.

Similarly, electoral reforms, such as the French system of *parité*, which withholds state funding for political parties that do not nominate equal numbers of male and female candidates, can go far beyond merely increasing female office holding. In India, where seats are reserved on municipal councils for female and lower caste candidates, close to a million poor, rural women now hold village offices. One study has found that once elected, these women try to allocate village resources to create better water and sewage infrastructure.[18] This structural reform is critical to feminist goals, for it allows girls to spend less time hauling water and more time going to school. Along with helping to close the literacy gap (two-thirds of those who are illiterate throughout the world are female), female education correlates highly with family planning. Both literacy and family planning enable not only women but entire families to escape poverty. In a world in which 70 percent of those living in poverty are female, these structural reforms can help narrow the global gap between the wealthy and the poor. In short, the particularist strategy of empowering women can have universal consequences; instead of a justification for exclusion from rights, women's difference has become a basis for redefining rights, with implications for all.

FEMINIST FUTURES?

I began this essay by tracing the origins of my career-long fascination with periodization in feminist history. From an exploration of one decade, the 1920s, I moved backward and forward to place the U.S. within a much longer and wider history. I have learned that the continuous, varied, and malleable history of feminism cannot be contained in one nation or region, cannot be defined by a dominant strategy, and cannot be mapped on a two-dimensional timeline. The broader our vantage point, the harder it becomes to contain this history within the metaphor of cresting oceanic waves. At any given moment, high and low tides are reaching different shorelines around the world. Perhaps the image of a rising global sea level better captures this history. Deep economic and political currents, as well as changing atmospheric conditions, contribute to the process, but human agency also shapes its contours.

The future of this process also depends largely on human will. Despite the predictive value implied by my title *No Turning Back*, I am well aware that a feminist future is by no means inevitable. For one, no form of feminism has gone without opposition, including formidable backlash at every era in which women have gained public authority. In addition, my argument about momentum rests upon the expanding influence of democratic rights and wage labor throughout the world. Cultures where only one or neither of these conditions prevails are particularly resistant to feminist critiques of gender hierarchy. Afghanistan under the Taliban represented an extreme case, but elsewhere, authoritarian states or ravished economies deepen patriarchal values.

Even where feminism has flourished it faces continuous challenges. Fundamentalism represents one powerful counterforce. Some Christian churches in the U.S. have revived an ideal of wifely obedience in the home, while a coalition of the religious right mobilizes to restrict reproductive rights. The political right also effectively deploys gender nostalgia to win votes and then reverses feminist gains once elected. For example, one platform of the right-wing French presidential candidate Jean-Marie LePen in 2002 was to repeal *parité*. And in both academic and popular culture, the resurgence of deterministic biological theories threatens a feminist project that is deeply grounded in social constructionist—indeed, politically utopian—values.

For all of these caveats and complications, I still believe that the historical momentum for achieving full economic and political citizenship for women is powerful, and strong enough to go beyond the waves. Despite widespread discomfort with the term, despite repeated media proclamations of its death, feminism has become central to contemporary politics. While resisted and contested, it will likely be central to political histories of the next century, especially if human rights expand rather than contract, if caring and bread-winning tasks can be disentangled from gender, and if the legacies of colonialism are vigilantly refused. As Gertrude Mongella, Secretary General of the 1995 U.N. conference on women, told the gathering in Beijing: "A revolution has begun and there is no going back. There will be no unraveling of commitments—not today's commitments, not last year's commitments, and not the last decade's commitments. This revolution is too just, too important, and too long overdue."[19] In my view, the historical record supports her prediction.

Notes

1. "The New Woman: Changing Views of Women in the 1920s," *Journal of American History* (September, 1974), 373–93.
2. "Separatism as Strategy: Female Institution Building and American Feminism, 1870–1930," *Feminist Studies* 5 (Fall, 1979), 512–29.
3. Estelle B. Freedman, *Their Sisters' Keepers: Women's Prison Reform in America, 1830–1930* (Ann Arbor: University of Michigan Press, 1981).
4. Nancy Cott, *The Grounding of Modern Feminism* (New Haven: Yale University Press, 1987).
5. Estelle B. Freedman, "Separatism Revisited: Women's Institutions, Social Reform, and the Career of Miriam Van Waters," in *U.S. History as Women's History: New Feminist Essays*, Linda Kerber, Alice Kessler-Harris, Kathryn Kish Sklar, eds. (University of North Carolina Press, 1995), 173; Estelle B. Freedman, *Maternal Justice: Miriam Van Waters and the Female Reform Tradition* (Chicago: University of Chicago Press, 1996).
6. Several recent histories of modern American feminism treat its antecedents and aftereffects: Susan Hartmann, *The Other Feminists: Activists in the Liberal Establishment* (New Haven: Yale University Press, 1998); Ruth Rosen, *The World Split Open: How the Modern Women's Movement Changed America* (New York: Viking, 2000); Sara Evans, *Tidal Wave: How Women Changed America at Century's End* (New York: The Free Press, 2003).

7. Mary Fainsod Katzenstein and Carol McClurg Mueller, eds., *The Women's Movements of the United States and Western Europe: Consciousness, Political Opportunity, and Public Policy* (Philadelphia: Temple University Press, 1987); Maxine Molyneux, "Mobilization Without Emancipation? Women's Interests, State, and Evolution," in Richard R. Fagen, Carmen Diana Deere, and Jose Luis Coraggio, eds., *Transition and Development: Problems of Third World Socialism* (Boston: Monthly Review Press, 1986), 280–302; Chandra Mohanty, "Under Western Eyes: Feminist Scholarship and Colonial Discourses," *Feminist Review* 30 (Autumn, 1988), 61–85; Leila Rupp, *Worlds of Women: The Making of An International Women's Movement* (Princeton: Princeton University Press, 1997); Ellen Carol DuBois, "Woman Suffrage around the World: Three Phases of Suffragist Internationalism," in *Suffrage and Beyond: International Feminist Perspectives*, Caroline Daley and Melanie Nolan, eds., (New York: New York University Press, 1994), 252–74; Bonnie G. Smith, ed., *Global Feminisms Since 1945: Rewriting Histories*, (London: Routledge, 2000). See also, Amrita Basu, ed., *The Challenge of Local Feminisms: Women's Movements in Global Perspective* (Boulder: Westview Press, 1995); and Barbara J. Nelson and Majma Chowdhury, eds., *Women and Politics Worldwide* (New Haven: Yale University Press, 1994).

8. On the long history of feminist ideas, see Gerda Lerner, *The Creation of Feminist Consciousness: From the Middle Ages to 1870* (New York: Oxford University Press, 1993); on transatlantic communication, see Bonnie S. Anderson, *Joyous Greetings: The First International Women's Movement, 1830–1860* (Oxford: Oxford University Press, 2000); on international feminist histories, see for example, Margot Badran, *Feminists, Islam, and the Nation: Gender and the Making of Modern Egypt* (Princeton: Princeton University Press, 1995); and Margot Badran and Miriam Cook, eds., *Opening the Gates: A Century of Arab Feminist Writing* (London: Virago, 1990); June E. Hahner, *Emancipating the Female Sex: The Struggle for Women's Rights in Brazil, 1850–1940* (Durham: Duke University Press, 1990); Radha Kumar, *The History of Doing: An Illustrated Account of Movements for Women's Rights and Feminism in India, 1800–1990* (London: Verso, 1993); and Corinne A. Pernet, "Chilean Feminists, The International Women's Movement, and Suffrage, 1915–1950," *Pacific Historical Review* 69:4 (2000), 663–88.

9. Estelle B. Freedman, *No Turning Back: The History of Feminism and the Future of Women* (New York: Ballantine Books, 2002). In the book, as in this essay, I use *feminism* ahistorically—that is, as an umbrella term for any movements to achieve full economic and political citizenship for women, whether or not the term was used at the time, although I identify the historical specificity of the term at the outset.

10. Joan Scott, *Only Paradoxes to Offer: French Feminists and the Rights of Man* (Cambridge: Harvard University Press, 1996).

11. Mary Wollstonecraft, *A Vindication of the Rights of Women*, excerpted in *Women, the Family, and Freedom: The Debate in Documents, Volume I: 1750–1880*, Susan Groag Bell and Karen M. Offen, eds. (Stanford: Stanford University Press, 1983), 62; Flora Tristan, *L'Union Ouvrière*, in Bell and Offen, *Women, the Family, and Freedom*, vol. I, 212–15; Francisca Diniz, "Equality of Rights" (1890) in June E. Hahner, *Emancipating the Female Sex: The Struggle for Women's Rights in Brazil, 1850–1940* (Durham: Duke University Press, 1990), Appendix B, 214; on Gilman, see Gail Bederman, *Manliness and Civilization: A Cultural History of Gender and Race in the U.S., 1880–1917* (Chicago: University of Chicago Press, 1995).

12. Quoted in Pernet, "Chilean Feminists," 668–69.

13. See, for example, Joan Williams, *Unbending Gender: Why Family and Work Conflict and What to Do About It* (New York: Oxford University Press, 2000).

14. Barbara Smith, "Racism and Women's Studies," in *The Truth That Never Hurts: Writings on Race, Gender, and Freedom* (New Brunswick: Rutgers University Press, 1998), 96.

15. Audre Lorde, "The Master's Tools Will Never Dismantle the Master's House," *Sister Outsider* (Freedom, CA: Crossing Press, 1984), 112.

16. Quoted in Rupp, *Worlds of Women*, 80.

17. NGO Forum' 80 newsletter (Copenhagen), quoted in Charlotte Bunch, *Passionate Politics: Feminist Theory in Action* (New York: St. Martin's Press, 1987), 299.

18. Chetna Gala, "Empowering Women in Villages: All-Women Village Councils in Maharashtra, India," *Bulletin of Concerned Asian Scholars* 29:2 (1997), 35.

19. Gertrude Mongella, "A Revolution Has Begun," 4 September, 1995, excerpted in *Women's Studies Quarterly: Beijing and Beyond, Toward the Twenty-First Century of Women* XXIV:1-2 (Spring/Summer, 1996), 116.

Suggestions for Further Reading

Basu, Amrita, ed. *The Challenge of Local Feminisms: Women's Movements in Global Perspective*. Boulder, CO: Westview Press, 1995.

Burton, Antoinette M. *Burdens of History: British Feminists, Indian Women, and Imperial Culture, 1865–1915*. Chapel Hill: University of North Carolina Press, 1994.

Cott, Nancy. *The Grounding of Modern Feminism*. New Haven: Yale University Press, 1987.

Evans, Sara M. *Tidal Wave: How Women Changed America at Century's End*. New York: Free Press, 2003.

Freedman, Estelle B. *No Turning Back: The History of Feminism and the Future of Women*. New York: Ballantine Books, 2002.

García, Alma M., ed. *Chicana Feminist Thought: The Basic Historical Writings*. New York: Routledge, 1997.

Grewal, Inderpal, and Caren Kaplan, eds., *Scattered Hegemonies: Postmodernity and Transnational Feminist Practices*. Minneapolis: University of Minnesota Press, 1994.

Mohanty, Chandra Talpade. *Feminism without Borders: Decolonizing Theory, Practicing Solidarity*. Durham: Duke University Press, 2003.

Newman, Louise Michelle. *White Women's Rights: The Racial Origins of Feminism in the United States*. New York: Oxford University Press, 1999.

Rosen, Ruth. *The World Split Open: How the Modern Women's Movement Changed America*. New York: Viking, 2000.

Rupp, Leila. *Worlds of Women: The Making of An International Women's Movement*. Princeton: Princeton University Press, 1997.

Smith, Barbara. *The Truth That Never Hurts: Writings on Race, Gender, and Freedom*. New Brunswick: Rutgers University Press, 1998.

Smith, Bonnie, ed. *Global Feminisms Since 1945*. London: Routledge, 2000.

Williams, Joan. *Unbending Gender: Why Family and Work Conflict and What to Do About It*. New York: Oxford University Press, 2000.

African Feminisms: The Struggle Continues

Beverly Guy-Sheftall

Beverly Guy-Sheftall (1982) is the Anna Julia Cooper Professor of Women's Studies and Director of the Women's Research and Resource Center at Spelman College. She is the editor of *Words of Fire: African American Feminist Thought* (1995); and, with Rudoph P. Byrd, *Traps: African American Men on Gender and Sexuality* (2001); and author, with Johnnetta Cole, of *Gender Talk: The Struggle for Women's Equality in African American Communities* (2003).

> *For Beverly Guy-Sheftall, the critical questions in women's studies today have to do with how the field deals with the global realities of women; how race, class, gender, and sexuality intersect in the lives of all women; how the field deals with constructions of masculinity; and finally, how women's studies interacts with other discourses such as queer theory, cultural studies, and ethnic studies. "I'm not sure that women's studies has had the same impact on young women and men in all settings— non-college students, for example, or among all racial/ethnic groups, or women and men around the globe. It is probably fair to say, though, that for young women and men who have enrolled in women's studies classes it has had an important impact. It is also the case that women's studies has enabled the average young woman or man to be familiar with terms and concepts such as sexual harassment, marital rape, choice, reproductive rights, gay and lesbian rights, domestic violence, and the sexual abuse of children."*

> To present African women simply as destitute
> and in need of charity from the West is to do an
> injustice to women with a rich history of authentic
> leadership skills, economic enterprise and strategies
> of resistance to oppression.
>
> Ifi Amadiume[1]

Despite the hegemony of Western feminist theory and gender discourses, a growing body of creative (fiction, visual art, film), scholarly, and political work by African women[2] can be placed under the rubric of "African feminism."[3] These discursive, imaginative, and activist works are important examples of resistance among women of African descent in various cultural contexts and compel us to reimagine what is meant by "feminism" in a global context. While a comprehensive examination of African feminisms would take into consideration this broad range of work throughout the continent and the African diaspora, including the U.S., Canada, Latin America, and Britain, I focus here on the analytical prose of women from sub-Saharan Africa.[4]

Despite its potential contributions to women's studies, African feminist thought has generally been ignored by Western scholars, highly contested on the continent, and often misunderstood.[5] Though this discourse is complex and addresses a range of topics from many different perspectives and disciplinary locations, there are common themes: the negative impact of colonialism and neo-colonialism on gender roles; the impact of gender oppression or patriarchal structures in various African cultural contexts before and after the arrival of Europeans and Islam; the necessity for transformation in gender relations and interventions in the lives of African women and girls, especially in the wake of globalization, structural adjustment, and state-sanctioned abuses in post-colonial governments; discrimination against women in the public sphere, including government and education; the involvement of African women in policy-making at the local, national, and international levels; the eradication of gender-based violence, and other cultural practices including child marriage, forced marriage, female circumcision, inheritance laws, and land rights that privilege men.[6] While many African scholars reject Western feminism because of its exclusionary practices, ethnocentric biases, cultural imperialist tendencies, unexamined universalist claims, and misrepresentations of Third World women, self-defined African feminist scholars are also making important contributions to our understanding of the challenges that confront Africa and other developing nations in the twenty-first century. This essay focuses on the work of these African women scholars, largely unknown within mainstream higher education circles in the U.S.

At a conference on "Women in the African Diaspora" at Howard University in 1983, the Sierra Leonian anthropologist Filomena Chioma Steady delivered a keynote address, "African Feminism: A Worldwide Perspective," that was an expansion of the introductory essay in her pioneering anthology, *The Black Woman Cross-Culturally* (1981). It provided a conceptual framework for the comparative study of black women in Africa, the Caribbean, Latin America, and the United States. Despite Steady's assertion about problematic relationships between women of African descent and the mainstream women's movement in the West, she argued that African women have evolved their own brand of feminism and that for them the struggle against gender oppression has always been "fused with liberation from other forms of oppression, namely slavery, colonialism, neo-colonialism, racism, poverty, illiteracy, and disease."[7] Steady amplified this concept of the simultaneity of oppressions in the lives of black women during her keynote address by calling for a theory of African feminism in the study of women throughout the African diaspora. Her concept of African feminism is radically different from Euro-American feminism. For Steady, it is more holistic and humanistic than Western feminism because it has been nurtured in agricultural cultures that are more communal, and in which women play significant roles. She also argues that the impact of patriarchy before colonialism was more benign in traditional West African societies because of women's autonomous economic roles and their centrality in the maintenance of lineage groups.[8]

Nearly a decade later, the prominent Ghanaian writer Ama Ata Aidoo engaged the debate about African women and feminism at another historic conference, "Women in Africa and the African Diaspora," held in Nsukka, Nigeria, in 1992. In her keynote address, she was unequivocal in her assertion about the value of this politic for a new Africa:

> When people ask me rather bluntly every now and then whether I am a feminist, I not only answer yes, but I go on to insist that every woman and every man should be a feminist—especially if they believe that Africans should take charge of African land, African wealth, African lives, and the burden of African development. It is not possible to advocate independence for the African continent without also believing that African women must have the best that the environment can offer. For some of us this is the crucial element in our feminism.[9]

Despite a broad range of feminist theory, including by women of color, having been critical to the development of women's studies, the work of African feminist scholar/activists has been largely ignored, even among those who stress the importance of transnational perspectives.[10] Trinidadian literary critic and scholar Carole Boyce Davies articulated one of the most cogent definitions of African feminism in her pioneering introduction to *Ngambika*, the first anthology of critical essays on women in African literature:

> African feminism ... recognizes a common struggle with African men for the removal of the yokes of foreign domination and European/American exploitation. It is not antagonistic to African men but challenges them to be aware of certain salient aspects of women's subjugation which differ from the generalized oppression of all African peoples ... [it] recognizes that certain inequities and limitations existed/exist in traditional societies and that colonialism reinforced them and introduced others. ... It acknowledges its affinities with international feminism, but delineates a specific African feminism with certain specific needs and goals arising out of the concrete realities of women's lives in African societies ... [it] examines African societies for institutions which are of value to women and rejects those which work to their detriment and does not simply import Western women's agendas. Thus, it respects African woman's status as mother but questions obligatory motherhood and the traditional favoring of sons. ... It respects African women's self-reliance and the penchant to cooperative work and social organization ... [it] understands the interconnectedness of race, class, and sex oppression.[11]

One of the earliest non-fiction texts written from an African feminist perspective is Awa Thiam's *Black Sisters Speak Out: Feminism and Oppression in Black Africa* (1978).[12] In her scathing critique of oppressive, patriarchal African traditions, such as polygamy, forced marriages, and female circumcision, she asserts that "black women have been silent for too long. ... Women must assume their own voices—speak out for themselves."[13] What distinguishes this text from subsequent examples of African feminist thought is its inclusion of the voices of various African women who speak about their personal experiences in patriarchal West African societies, mainly Senegal. She also discusses the negative impact of colonialism on African women and articulates the concept of multiple jeopardy, a familiar theme in African-American feminist thought as well: ". . . the Black woman of Africa suffers a threefold oppression: by virtue of her sex, she is dominated by man in a patriarchal society; by virtue of her class she is at the mercy of capitalist exploitation; by virtue of her race she suffers from the appropriation of her country by colonial or neo-colonial powers. Sexism, racism, class division; three plagues!" (118)

Any discussion of African feminism must include the work of scholars such as Molara Ogundipe-Leslie, a Yoruba writer, critic, intellectual, and scholar who has been writing about the issue of gender politics and social transformation within the African context for over three decades.[14] Her essay, "African Women, Culture, and Another Development," is explicit about the nature of African women's oppression in her discussion of the six mountains on their backs, which includes oppression from the outside, ravages of colonialism, and some African cultural traditions. One of the most compelling treatises in her collection, *Re-Creating Ourselves: African Women and Critical Transformations* (1994), is "Stiwanism: Feminism in an African Context." I would compare this statement with the Combahee River Collective statement, which captures the essence of African-American feminism.[15] The Combahee River Collective was an important black feminist group that began in 1974 as the Boston chapter of the National Black Feminist Organization (NBFO), founded in 1973. A river in South Carolina where Harriet Tubman had mounted a military campaign during the Civil War to free 750 slaves inspired the name. NBFO's statement of purpose emphasized the importance of the much-maligned women's liberation movement to black and other Third World women. In 1977, three members of the collective— Barbara Smith, Beverly Smith, and Demita Frazier—wrote a statement documenting the activities of the collective and articulating their philosophy. This black feminist manifesto is a clear articulation of the evolution of contemporary African-American feminism and the concept of the simultaneity of oppressions that black women suffer. An examination of feminist thought in Africa and throughout the diaspora reveals the influence of African-American women's scholarship and activism on black women globally.

Ogundipe-Leslie was a founding member of WIN (Women in Nigeria), a feminist women's research and activist group, and another African feminist organization, AAWORD (the Association of African Women for Research and Development) that is located in Dakar, Senegal. A leading African woman intellectual, Ogundipe-Leslie argues that gender asymmetry was an integral part of many precolonial societies, even though African women's position relative to men certainly deteriorated under colonialism. She also argues, as do African-American feminists, that there are also traditions of resistance and activism among African women going back to precolonial times. In other words, there were indigenous "feminisms" prior to contact with Europeans, just as there were indigenous modes of rebellion and resistance throughout the period of colonial domination. What this means is that the struggle for women's rights is not the simple imitation by African women of Euro-American values. She reminds us that there have always been indigenous manifestations of "feminism" that take very different forms in particular cultural contexts. An important task, therefore, for African scholars has been identifying, excavating, and analyzing these indigenous forms of feminist resistance.

As is the case among feminist intellectuals within the same geographic region in other parts of the world, African women scholars also have serious disagreements among themselves with respect to gender matters. Professor Oyeronke Oyewumi, also Yoruba, accuses Ogundipe-Leslie of misrepresenting certain aspects of Yoruba culture and its treatment of women in her book, *The Invention of Women: Making an African Sense of Western Gender Discourses.* She especially takes issue with Ogundipe-Leslie's characterization of Yoruba culture as patriarchal and accuses her of "importing Western concepts and categories into African studies and societies."[16] Male scholars, such as Omah Tsatsaku Ojior, have been particularly critical of feminists, including black Americans, because of their alleged assaults on traditional family structures and African family values. Emphasizing African women's important political roles in his dissertation, "African Women and Political Development," he also espouses pro-natalist and Christian perspectives: "Man is the leader or head of the home in Etsako, and the woman complements the man's efforts to lead the home. . . . Motherhood is the greatest status of womanhood."[17] Leopold Senghor, poet and the first Senegalese president, voices a common anti-feminist position because he believes that gender oppression is not an African reality: "Contrary to what is often thought today, the African woman does not need to be liberated. She has been free for many thousands of years."[18] Oriaku Nwosu attempts a more middle-of-the road position: while she discusses the importance of complementary gender roles in the traditional West African context and affirms the importance of motherhood and wifehood, she also argues that much has been lost in African societies as a result of colonialism. She is also less suspicious about the usefulness of feminist approaches to development in the contemporary African context: "The removal of religious and traditional barriers to equality for women, will not be easy. . . . As we approach the twenty-first century everyone is invited to join in the movement towards the total eradication of the impediments to Nigerian women's full and equal participation in all aspects of national life."[19] She even articulates the value of women's studies and the elimination of sex role stereotypes, and argues that African societies have something to teach the West with respect to more egalitarian gender roles if they would return to their earlier practices:

> Traditional African communities have lived under well-established systems of co-leadership, co-rulership, co-governance between MAN and WOMAN. Collectively and individually, they participated and contributed to the overall well-being of their members. . . . The march towards restoring or reinstating the dignity of women has long begun. . . . It becomes disturbing to most African women of today

to see men tremble or feel threatened by what they refer to as "women's war on society," "women's liberation movements," "feminist movements," "women's emancipation" and other similar slogans.[20]

Despite the marginalization of African women and the controversial nature of gender discourses, Oblama Mnaemeka, founding president of the Association of African Women Scholars (AAWS), makes visible a broad range of feminist scholarship produced by African women that challenges masculinist paradigms within African diaspora studies and ethnocentric constructs within women's studies. She believes that using the word *feminism* is not an endorsement of white, middle-class feminism and that, in fact, feminism speaks different languages worldwide.[21] She also argues, like Ogundipe-Leslie, that while *feminism* is a Western term, "the feminist spirit and ideals are indigenous to the African environment; we do not need to look too far into the annals of African history to see the inscription of feminist engagements."[22]

In an analysis of African feminism, it is important to examine the activist work of contemporary women's organizations without which it is impossible, I would argue, to understand the ways in which scholars are conceptualizing it. For example, WIN (which includes women and men) emphasizes the importance of understanding both class and gender systems in Nigeria and asserts that the majority of women and men suffer from the exploitative and oppressive character of many aspects of Nigerian society under military dictatorships, though women are doubly victimized as members of subordinate classes and as women. "Nigerian women are subordinate to men as a group," Ogundipe-Leslie argues, despite other alleviating variables such as age, status, or wealth.[23] Despite the critical contribution of women to the Nigerian economy, she asserts, "their indispensable labour is unacknowledged, unpaid-for and poorly taken into account in national development plans" (129).

In another cultural context, there is the important political work of Akina Mama wa Africa (AMWA), a nongovernmental organization for African women based in the United Kingdom and founded in 1985. A major premise of this African feminist organization is that African women living outside the continent face struggles on two fronts: in a predominantly white society, they face racial discrimination, and within their own communities they suffer gender-based oppression. AMWA is also concerned about the deteriorating economic, political, and social systems in Africa and human rights abuses of African women and children both in Europe and Africa. It maintains strong links with progressive women's movements in Africa and around the world and is committed to helping African women articulate their own development needs. AMWA documents racial abuse, trafficking of African women in England, some of whom are lured there as domestic workers and then exploited by pimps;[24] the treatment of African women prisoners, many of whom had been tricked into an involvement with the illegal international drug trade; the treatment of migrant workers; domestic violence; and female genital surgeries on young girls. It also provides training to women activists about how to deal with gender-related human rights abuses. The organization publishes a biannual journal, *African Woman*, which has focused on issues such as African Women and Conflict (1995), African Women and Health (1995), and African Feminism (1996).

Another site for the production of African feminist scholarship has been research organizations such as CODESRIA, the Council for the Development of Social Science Research in Africa, headquartered in Senegal. It publishes *Africa Development*, the longest standing Africa-based journal, and organizes workshops and other forums that facilitate the exchange of ideas and information among African researchers. CODESRIA sponsored a pivotal workshop in 1996 to advance knowledge about gender, particularly in and for Africa. The conference proceedings, *Engendering African Sciences* (1997), represents the state of the art in gender-sensitive scholarship about Africa, employs African feminist frameworks, and includes some of the most productive African women scholars such as Ayesha M. Imam, Fatou Sow, Amina Mama, Ndri Therese Assie-Lumumba, and Rudo B. Gaidzanwa.[25]

Southern Africa is another critically important place for the production of African feminist thought. One of the most prolific and compelling African woman intellectuals and activists is the sociologist Patricia McFadden, who was born in Swaziland, spent much of her professional life in Zimbabwe and is completing a book on feminism and nationalism. She has been associated with AAWORD (executive secretary in 1988); the Southern Africa Political Economy Series (SAPES) Trust, its journal, *Southern African Feminist Review* (SAFERE), and its Gender Project;[26] and the Southern African Research Institute for Policy Studies (SARIPS), whose journal *South African Political Economy Monthly* she edited. She was also Director of the Feminist Studies Center in Zimbabwe, an important, though short-lived organization in the African women's movement. Because of its progressive views and stances with respect to sexual orientation and choice, it came under attack by the Mugabe government and was closed down in July 1997. Her pioneering scholarship can be characterized as radical African feminist theory and includes analyses of sexuality in the African context, a taboo topic, especially before the ravages of HIV/AIDS.[27] In a lecture delivered at the Feminist Institute of the African Women's Leadership Institute, she offered a challenge to African women at the dawn of the twenty-first century. After discussing African women's legacy of struggle, HIV/AIDS, gender violence, bodily integrity, indigenous women's movements in Africa, reproductive rights, female circumcision, sexuality, the rise of religious fundamentalisms, civil strife, and the insensitivity of the Organization of African Unity (OAU) to the plight of women, she asserted: "We bring the African feminist tradition of thinking and problem solving to the global women's movement and participate in the formulation of new theories and methodologies. . . . We must write about ourselves and speak for ourselves. We have nothing to lose by envisioning and crafting a new future, and we have every reason to want something different for Africa in the twenty-first century."

South Africa is also home for several feminist publications including *Agenda: Empowering Women for Gender Equity*, based in Durban, South Africa.

There are three special issues on "African Feminisms" (No. 50, 2001; No. 54, 2002; and No. 58, 2003, guest edited by Bahati Kuumba of the Women's Center, Spelman College). There is also *Southern African Feminist Review*, published by the Southern African Institute for Policy Studies, Harare, Zimbabwe, and *Feminist Africa*, founded in 2002 and based at the African Gender Institute, University of Cape Town, South Africa.[28]

A comprehensive examination of African feminisms, both scholarship and activism, is long overdue. This study would help to dismantle the dominance of Western, white feminist analytical frameworks and broaden our knowledge about a region of the world that continues to be misunderstood, devalued, and in some cases both romanticized and demonized with respect to its gender constructs and cultural practices. Certainly, the long history of African women and their resistance to both external and internal oppressions is instructive for women everywhere. I have tried to show the richness and complexity of African feminist politics and its potential for profound social change on the continent and throughout the diaspora. These emerging and evolving gender discourses outside the West have the potential as well for invigorating women's studies and providing compelling analyses of the diverse meanings of feminism around the globe.

Notes

1. Ifi Amadiume, *Daughters of the Goddess, Daughters of Imperialism: African Women Struggle for Culture, Power and Democracy* (London: Zed Books, 2000), 21.

2. I am including women whose family of origin would have been sub-Saharan Africa, though they may now reside in various parts of the African diaspora, especially the U.S. and Britain.

3. The earliest scholarship related to African feminism or "womanism" dealt with the fiction of African women writers such as Buchi Emecheta (*Joys of Motherhood* and *Second Class Citizen*); Flora Nwapa (*Efuru*); Mariama Ba (*So Long a Letter*); and Bessie Head (*The Collector of Treasures*). Useful feminist literary criticism by African women scholars includes Irene Assiba D'Almeida, *Francophone African Women Writers: Destroying the Emptiness of Silence* (Gainesville: University Press of Florida, 1994); Helen Chukwuma, ed., *Feminism in African Literature: Essays on Criticism* (Enuga, Nigeria: New Generation Books, 1994); Oblama Mnaemeka, ed., *The Politics of (M) othering: Womanhood, Identity, and Resistance in African Literature* (London: Routledge, 1997); Juliana Makuchi Nfah-Abbenyi, *Gender in African Women's Writing: Identity, Sexuality and Difference* (Bloomington: Indiana University Press, 1997); Mary E. Modupe Kolawole, *Womanism and African Consciousness* (Trenton, NJ: Africa World Press, 1997); and Chikwenje Okonjo Ogunyemi, *Africa Wo/Man Palava: The Nigerian Novel by Women* (Chicago: University of Chicago Press, 1996). The literary critic Ogunyemi also articulated the concept of African womanism and indicates that she arrived at the term "womanism" independently of Alice Walker, who conceptualized "womanism" in the African-American context and popularized this alternative conception of feminism in *In Search of Our Mothers' Gardens: Womanist Prose* (New York: Harcourt Brace Jovanovich,

1983); see Ogunyemi's essay, "Womanism: The Dynamics of the Contemporary Black Female Novel in English," *Signs* 11(1985–1986), 63–80.

4. This essay is an expanded version of earlier articles, "Shifting Contexts: Lessons from Integrating Black, Gender, and African Diaspora Studies," which appeared in *Women's Studies Quarterly* 36, nos. 3 & 4 (Fall/Winter 1998), 17–24, and "Speaking For Ourselves: Feminisms in the African Diaspora," in *Decolonizing the Academy: Diaspora Theory and African New-World Studies*, ed. Carole Boyce Davies (Trenton, NJ: Africa World Press, Inc., 2004). The African Diaspora was defined by Joseph E. Harris in *Global Dimensions of the African Diaspora* (Washington, D.C.: Howard University Press, 1982) as "the voluntary and forced dispersion of Africans at different periods in history and in several directions; the emergence of a cultural identity abroad without losing the African base, either spiritually or physically; the psychological return to the homeland, Africa." The largest migration of Africans during the transatlantic slave trade was to the Americas, most notably Brazil, the U.S., and the Caribbean.

5. There is considerable disagreement among African women scholars concerning the contemporary status of African women, many of whom are suspicious of feminist approaches to the scholarship on Africa. They would include Oyeronke Oyewumi, who questions the relevance of gender as an analytical category for African realities, and Olufemi Taiwo. See *African Women and Feminism: Reflecting on the Politics of Sisterhood*, Oyeronke Oyewumi, ed. (Trenton, NJ: Africa World Press, 2003).

6. Rancorous debates have ensued about the treatment of female circumcision (also referred to as female genital mutilation, female genital surgeries) in Africa by Western feminists (European/American and African-American). Texts by African women/men on the subject include: Asthma El Dareer, *Woman, Why Do You Weep?: Circumcision and Its Consequences* (London: Zed Press, 1982); Raquiya Haji Abdallah, *Sisters in Affliction: Circumcision and Infibulation in Women in Africa* (London: Zed Press, 1997); Nahid Toubia, *Female Genital Mutilation: A Call for Action* (New York: Rainbo, 1995); Amna Elsadik Badri, *Female Circumcision in the Sudan: Change and Continuity* (Omduran, Sudan, 1984); Olayinka Koso Thomas, *The Circumcision of Women: A Strategy for Education* (London: Zed Books, 1987); Efua Korkenoo, *Cutting the Rose: Female Genital Mutilation: The Practice and its Prevention* (London: Minority Rights Group, 1994); Emmanuel Babatunde, *Women's Rights versus Women's Rites: A Study of Circumcision among the Ketu Yoruba of South Western Nigeria* (Trenton, NJ: Africa World Press, 1998). See also the special issue of *Case Western Reserve Law Review* 47, 2 (1997) which includes a special colloquium on the issue, especially Leslie Amede Obiora's article, "Bridges and Barricades: Rethinking Polemics and Intransigence in the Campaign against Female Circumcision," 441–21. See also Stanlie M. James and Claire C. Robertson, eds., *Genital Cutting and Transnational Sisterhood: Disputing U.S. Polemics* (Urbana: University of Illinois Press, 2002) for its critiques of Eurocentric approaches to FGM.

7. Filomena Chioma Steady, ed., *The Black Woman Cross-Culturally* (Cambridge, MA: Schenkman, 1981), 34. For the entire conference proceedings see, *Women in Africa and the African Diaspora*, edited by Rosalyn Terborg-Penn, Sharon Harley, and Andrea Benton Rushing (Washington, DC: Howard University Press, 1987).

8. See Deborah Fahy Bryceson, ed., *Women Wielding the Hoe: Lessons from Rural Africa for Feminist Theory and Development Practice* (Oxford: Berg Publishers, 1995).

9. Ama Ata Aidoo, "The African Woman Today," in *Sisterhood, Feminisms, and Power: From Africa to the Diapora*, Oblama Mnaemeka, ed. (Trenton, NJ: Africa World Press, 1998), 47. This international women's conference took place in Nsukka, Nigeria in 1992.

10. See *Meridians: Feminism, Race, Transnationalism*, founded in 2002 at Smith College, which is an interdisciplinary journal that provides a forum for scholarship and creative work by and about women of color in North American and international contexts, and *Encompassing Gender: Integrating International Studies and Women's Studies*, Mary M. Lay, Janice Monk, and Deborah S. Rosenfelt, eds. (New York: The Feminist Press, 2002).

11. Carole Boyce Davies and Anne Adams Graves, eds., *Ngambika: Studies of Women in African Literature* (Trenton, NJ: Africa World Press, 1986), 8–10.

12. Awa Thiam, *Black Sisters, Speak Out: Feminism and Oppression in Black Africa* (London: Pluto Press, 1986). Editions Denoel as La Parole aux Negresses first published Thiam's text in 1978 in Paris.

13. Ibid., 11.

14. See also the work of other Nigerian feminist scholars (including Oblama Mnaemeka), such as Ifi Amadiume, *Male Daughters, Female Husbands: Gender and Sex in an African Society* (London: Zed Books, 1987); Theodora Akachi Ezeigbo, *Gender Issues in Nigeria: A Feminine Perspective* (Lagos: Vista Books, 1996) or African women scholars writing about gender issues, such as Catherine O. Acholonu, *Motherism: The Afrocentric Alternative to Feminism* (Lagos: NIIA, 1991); Oyeronke Oyewumi, *The Invention of Women: Making an African Sense of Western Gender Discourses* (Minneapolis: University of Minnesota Press, 1997) and her edited collection, *African Women and Feminism: Reflecting on the Politics of Sisterhood* (Trenton, NJ: Africa World Press, 1993). A useful analysis of African feminism by a German scholar of African literatures is Susan Arndt, *The Dynamics of African Feminism: Defining and Classifying African Feminist Literature* (Trenton, NJ: Africa World Press, 2002).

15. The Combahee River Collective document is included in Beverly Guy-Sheftall, ed., *Words of Fire: African American Feminist Thought* (New York: New Press, 1995).

16. Oyeronke Oyewumi, *The Invention of Women: Making an African Sense of Western Gender Discourses* (Minneapolis: University of Minnesota Press, 1997), 20.

17. Omoh Tsatsaku Ojior, *African Women and Political Development: A Case Study of Etsako Women in Edo State, Nigeria* (Bloomington, IN: First Books Library, 2002), 408–409.

18. Quoted in Florence Stratton, *Contemporary African Literature and the Politics of Gender* (New York: Routledge, 1994), 54.

19. Oriaku Nwosu, *The African Woman: Nigerian Perspective* (Lagos: Bima Publications, 1993), 117–18.

20. Ibid., 8–9.

21. Oblama Mnaemeka, *Sisterhood, Feminisms and Power: From Africa to the Diaspora* (Trenton, NJ: Africa World Press, 1998), 22.

22. Ibid.

23. Ogundipe-Leslie, *Re-creating Ourselves*, 129.

24. See Marian Douglas's Web site, *www.authorsden.com/Marian Douglas*, for her discussion of international trafficking in African women, especially in Italy where she observed in 1999 large numbers of black women working as prostitutes on the streets

of Rome. See also Temitope Ogunjinmi's article, "Girls for Sale" (*www.AllAfrica.com*), which focuses on trafficking of Nigerian women in Europe, especially Italy.

25. See *Engendering African Social Sciences*, Ayesha Imam, Amina Mama, and Fatou Sow, eds. (Dakar: CODESRIA, 1997).

26. See *Gender in Southern Africa: Conceptual and Theoretical Issues*, Ruth Meena, ed. (Harare: SAPES Books, 1992), 157–95, which is the result of a Gender Planning Workshop organized by the SAPES Gender Project in July 1991.

27. Her long essay, "Sex, Sexuality and the Problems of AIDS in Africa," in *Conceptualising Gender in Southern Africa* ed. Ruth Meena (Harare: SAPES Trust, 1992), remains useful. More recent analyses of the gendered aspects of HIV/AIDS in the African context include *Aids, Sexuality, and Gender in Africa: Collective Strategies and Struggles in Tanzania and Zambia*, Carolyn Baylies and Janet Bujra, eds. (New York: Routledge, 2000). An important site for up-to-date information on issues of sexuality in Africa is Behind the Mask: A Website on gay and lesbian affairs in Africa, launched in 2000 in Johannesburg, South Africa: *www.mask.org.za*; email: *info@mask.org.za*. A number of gender-focused African AIDS organizations include the Society for Women Against AIDS in Africa (SWAA), founded in 1988 and based in Dakar, Senegal; it has offices in over 35 African countries. In the August 18, 2003 issue of the *Washington Post*, "Kenyan Women Reject Sex 'Cleanser'," Emily Wax reports on a heretofore hidden cultural practice in various African countries that is exacerbating the AIDS crisis. Ritual "cleansers," men in rural villages, are paid by community elders to have sex with widows and unmarried women (without condoms) in order to dispel evil spirits. She says, "In Africa, women are six times as likely to contract HIV as men, mostly because of rape and customs like cleansing, in which one man can spread the disease to hundreds of women." According to Wax, the tradition is centuries old and springs from the belief that women are haunted by spirits after their husbands die and thought to be unholy if they remain unmarried and celibate.

28. See also *Sauti Ya Siti*, the official publication of the Tanzania Media Women's Association (TAMWA), based in Dar es Salaam; the *African Journal of Reproductive Health*, based in Benin City, Nigeria, at the Women's Health and Action Research Centre; *Echo: Bilingual Quarterly Newsletter of the Association of African Women for Research and Development*, based in Dakar, Senegal; and *Jenda: A Journal of Culture and African Women Studies* (*www.jendajournal.com*); *Fippu*, founded in 1987, based in Dakar, Senegal, and the magazine of the feminist organization which bears its name.

Suggestions for Further Reading

Abdallah, Raquiya Haji. *Sisters in Affliction: Circumcision and its Consequences.* London: Zed Press, 1997.

Allan, Tuzyline Jita. *Womanist and Feminist Aesthetics: A Comparative Review.* Athens: Ohio University Press, 1995.

Amadiume, Ifi. *Daughters of the Goddess, Daughters of Imperialism: African Women Struggle for Culture, Power, and Democracy.* London: Zed Books, 2000.

———. *Male Daughters, Female Husbands: Gender and Sex in an African Society.* London: Zed Books, 1990.

Arndt, Susan. *The Dynamics of African Feminism: Defining and Classifying African Feminist Literatures.* Trenton, NJ: Africa World Press, 2002.

Bryceson, Deborah Fahy, ed. *Women Wielding the Hoe: Lessons from Rural Africa for Feminist Theory and Development Practice.* Oxford: Berg Publishers, 1995.

Chukwuma, Helen, ed. *Feminism in African Literature: Essays on Criticism.* Enuga, Nigeria: New Generation Books, 1994.

D'Almeida, Irene Assiba. *Francophone African Women Writers: Destroying the Emptiness of Silence.* Gainesville: University Press of Florida, 1994.

Davies, Carole Boyce, ed. *Ngambika: Studies of Women in African Literature.* Trenton, NJ: Africa World Press, 1986.

Dolphyne, Florence Abena. *The Emancipation of Women: An African Perspective.* Accra: Ghana University Press, 1991.

El Dareer, Asthma. *Woman, Why Do You Weep?: Circumcision and Its Consequences.* London: Zed Press, 1982.

Ezeigbo, Theodora. *Gender Issues in Nigeria: A Feminine Perspective.* Lagos: Vista Books, 1996.

Green, December. *Gender Violence in Africa: African Women's Responses.* New York: St. Martin's Press, 1999.

Imam, Ayesha, Amina Mama, and Fatou Sow, eds. *Engendering African Social Sciences.* Dakar: CODESRIA, 1997.

Johnson-Odim, Cheryl, and Nina Emma Mba. *Funmilayo Ransome-Kuti of Nigeria.* Urbana: University of Illinois Press, 1997.

Kanyoro, Musimbi R. A. *Introducing Feminist Cultural Hermeneutics: An African Perspective.* Cleveland: Pilgrim Press, 2002.

Kolawole, Mary E. Modupe. *Womanism and African Consciousness.* Trenton, NJ: Africa World Press, 1997.

Mikell, Gwendolyn, ed. *African Feminism: The Politics of Survival in Sub-Saharan Africa.* Philadelphia: University of Pennsylvania Press, 1997.

Newell, Stephanie, ed. *Writing African Women: Gender, Popular Culture and Literature in West Africa.* London: Zed Books, 1997.

Nfah-Abbenyi, Juliana Makuchi. *Gender in African Women's Writing.* Bloomington: Indiana University Press, 1997.

Mnaemeka, Oblama, ed. *Sisterhood, Feminisms, and Power: From Africa to the Diaspora.* Trenton, NJ: Africa World Press, 1998.

———, ed. *The Politics of (M)othering: Womanhood, Identity, and Resistance in African Literature.* London: Routledge, 1997.

Obbo, Christine. *African Women: Their Struggle for Economic Independence.* London: Zed Books, 1980.

Oduyoye, Mercy Amba. *Daughters of Anowa: African Women and Patriarchy.* Maryknoll: Orbis Books, 1995.

Ogundipe-Leslie, Molara. *Re-creating Ourselves: African Women and Critical Transformations.* Trenton, NJ: Africa World Press, 1994.

Ogunyemi, Chikwenye Okonjo. *Africa Wo/Man Palava: The Nigerian Novel by Women.* Chicago: University of Chicago Press, 1996.

Ojior, Omoh Tsatsaku. *African Women and Political Development: A Case Study of Etsako Women.* Bloomington: First Books Library, 2002.

Oyewumi, Oyeronke, ed. *African Women and Feminism: Reflecting on the Politics of Sisterhood.* Trenton, NJ: Africa World Press, 2003.

Steady, Filomena Chioma, ed. *The Black Woman Cross-Culturally.* Cambridge, MA: Schenkman, 1981.

————. "African Women, Industrialization, and Another Development: A Global Perspective," *Development Dialogue: A Journal of International Development*. (1982), 1–2.

Toubia, Nahid. *Female Genital Mutilation: A Call for Global Action*. New York: Rainbo, 1995.

Thiam, Awa. *Black Sisters, Speak Out: Feminism and Oppression in Black Africa*. London: Pluto Press, 1986. First published in 1978 in Paris.

Journals

African Journal of Reproductive Health
Agenda: Empowering Women for Gender Equity
Echo: Bilingual Quarterly Newsletter of the Association of African Women for Research and Development
Feminist Africa
Fippu
Jenda: A Journal of Culture and African Women Studies (*www.jendajournal.com*)
Southern African Feminist Review

Feminism, Empire, and the Fate of National Histories: The Case of Victorian Britain

Antoinette Burton

Antoinette Burton (1988) is a Professor of History at the University of Illinois at Urbana-Champaign, where she is also affiliated with the Women's and Gender Studies Program. Her most recent books are *Dwelling in the Archive: Women Writing House, Home, and History in Late Colonial India* (2003) and *After the Imperial Turn: Thinking with and through the Nation* (2003).

When Antoinette Burton was a graduate student at the University of Chicago in the 1980s working on a study of women in the British Empire, there were few women faculty members and little encouragement for her. The arrival of a feminist historian in her last year "literally saved my life. I had never seen a feminist historian embodied; I didn't know what one looked like, that there was such a thing in reality, this thing I was trying to become." Twenty years later, now a faculty member and scholar of imperialism, she finds that "national histories can no longer be written as if they are self-contained, self-evident stories. The question of race and the historical legacy of imperialism, in tandem with more 'traditional' feminist concerns, have exerted tremendous pressure for a new narrative in national histories, with ramifications for teaching as well as scholarship. The challenge that remains is how to channel these insights back into traditional texts as well as new research so that the historical significance of the new imperial history in Britain—and the role of feminist scholars in shaping it—can be fully appreciated."

When I was a graduate student at the University of Chicago in the 1980s, women's history—let alone the history of feminism—was not considered a legitimate topic for research among many faculty members there. My dissertation proposal on the relationship between the British Empire and the

Victorian women's movement was met with skepticism and even derision.[1] What in the world did women have to do with the grand narratives of imperialism? I was often asked. To be sure, the University of Chicago was a very particular place, and quite different than it is now, when Gender Studies is an established program and the ratio of men to women professors and men to women students is markedly better than it was in my day. My advisor, for his part, was a staunch empiricist as well as a historian of Irish Catholicism with an appreciation, shall we say, for the power of patriarchy. After he read my 500-page dissertation in draft he called me on the phone and said that he had just one question. "This Michel Foucault—who is she?" That anecdote always gets a laugh, and probably says as much about my own path toward feminism as it does about my thesis director. It is also an instructive reminder of the kinds of changes which women and feminists in the academy have brought about in the last quarter of a century, not simply by insisting that women and gender should occupy a central place in teaching and scholarship, but also by bringing new theoretical and analytical models to bear on problems old and new—and by compelling historians to engage with questions that were considered unimaginable as *historical* subjects not so long ago.

At the same time, historians of women, gender, and feminism of the 1980s were slow to recognize and fully embrace the ways in which gender was and is entangled in systems of racial domination. This was manifest in responses to my study of the impact of empire on nineteenth-century British feminism—a set of movements sympathetic to imperial values that produced a highly racialized, exclusionary discourse about the world of women and a concept of "global sisterhood" rooted in a consistently hierarchical outlook. I was literally shouted down at a panel at the annual American Historical Association meeting in Washington, D.C. in 1987 for arguing that British suffragists had shared in and helped to promote the imperial ideologies of their day. One audience member actually accused me of tarnishing the reputation of "our feminist foremothers." There are a number of explanations for this contretemps. It has in part to do with the fact that England "at home" has long been seen as a place unmarked by racial strife—despite the continual presence of people of color in Great Britain since the seventeenth century, and of course, despite the persistence of racial conflict in the post-World War II period (itself a legacy of empire) as well. But such reactions—which dogged my project until its completion and beyond—were also the result of a largely white Western feminist triumphalism which tended to exempt "the cause" from critique and to view its past as a story of emancipation and progress. That this emancipatory narrative applied only to white women, and even then only to some of them, is a point that it has taken overlong to make in both monographs and classroom contexts. Significantly, this has been true even (and especially) in the United States, where the story of women's suffrage was always bound up with abolition and anti-slavery politics, and not always in ways flattering to the women's movement, as Ellen DuBois's early work was at pains to tell.[2] So that if my discipline has been transformed by the institutionalization of women's studies, feminism, and women's and gender history, feminist ideologies and practices in the North American academy have also been challenged by the intellectual and political currents generated by critical race theory, cultural studies, and postcolonialism since the 1960s. In this essay, I focus on the impact of those convergences on my field, modern Britain, in an attempt to assess the role of feminist historiographical practice on one national history.

To say that modern British history has been a conservative field with respect to women's history and its cognate concerns is a tremendous understatement. In part because of the work of E. P. Thompson, the historiography of modern Britain has had longstanding transnational appeal as a model of the new social history, an appeal which endures in a variety of forms today.[3] And yet the very strength of Marxist paradigms—which arguably pioneered the concept of "history from below" and made possible, at least in theory, an expanded view of what counts as an historical subject—meant that attempts made by the first generation of feminist scholars of Britain to place women and gender at the center were often rejected, parried, or simply ignored. This is a story whose details are too complex to rehearse fully here. Nor would I like to suggest that the challenges that historians of Britain have faced were any more difficult than those experienced by feminist scholars working on the United States, Europe, Latin America, Africa, or Asia—or that the struggles of the 1980s have not resulted in "success," in terms of the integration of women and gender into many if not most historical narratives. But if women and gender are now givens for most social historians of Britain, the battle between class and gender was nonetheless a very real and at times an acrimonious one, and was carried on in the work and through the careers of a number of feminist historians—historians who, incidentally, did not wish to dispense with class, but rather to complicate it, to put "sex and class" together in the same analytical field.[4] Indeed, those early practitioners strove to retain a variety of structural and materialist analyses even as they tried to account for female agency, gendered experience, and a variety of historically specific social and cultural systems that shaped women's lives.

On questions of women and empire, the field has proven even more resistant. Until very recently, historically speaking, the history of the British empire has traditionally been a high political affair which has tended to disaggregate "domestic" events from "colonial" narratives, thereby implicitly gendering that divide (men went off to empire, women stayed home), while for all practical purposes sidelining women and gender altogether as categories of historical analysis. Although Victorians generally felt that empire was no place for a white woman, after two decades of feminist scholarship we now know that British women wandered all over imperial territories, making their presence known and bringing back a whole host of representations of colonial rule and culture to an avid public at home. And although in most instances, they were excluded from the formal mechanisms of power, white women who traveled to and lived in empire contributed to empire-building by setting up homes, recreating English gardens, establishing educational institutions based on British models, and generally acting as agents of imperialism in a variety of subtle and not-so-subtle ways.[5] This is in part because empire seemed to many white women to be the most natural thing in the world: belief in the right-eousness of the British empire, its capacity for doing good and bringing civilization to "native" peoples and societies, was such a commonplace for Victorians that few questioned it. But empire also provided a much-needed, much sought-after outlet for many middle-class British women, who were often unable to find the kinds of opportunities or support for their profession-al endeavors at home that were available to them in India, Africa, and other colonial possessions and dominions. In this sense, British women's investment in empire-building was not merely the result of patriotism, but reflected the contradictions of being "imperial women" in Britain's imperial century.

The role of women of color, "native" women, and indigenous communi-ties in imperial and colonial histories has an even more complex and elusive history—some of which has been recovered by historians, some by anthropol-ogists, and some by scholars working at the intersection of both disciplines. Imperial and colonial archives have been notoriously silent on—or, alternately, moralistic about—colonized women, compelling students of the gendered colonial experience to be extraordinarily creative about sources, methods, and interpretive approaches. Recent work on sati, bio-medicine, sexuality, repro-duction, and sentiment has joined already rich literatures on slavery, labor, missionaries, and migration, making the field of "gender and colonialism" broadly conceived one of the most vibrant and promising in the twenty-first century.[6] Here again, feminist historians and anti-imperialist scholars more generally have been at the forefront, opening up new geographies of power and knowledge, and centralizing stories about women and gender at the in-tersection of histories of race, class, sexuality, work, ethnicity, nation, and reli-gion under colonial and postcolonial regimes.[7]

What remains striking to me is that the dichotomy of "home" and "away" still tends to structure much imperial and colonial history, even after nearly three decades of work by feminist scholars. It doesn't take a huge imaginative leap to realize that cordoning off British history from imperial history is a pro-foundly ahistorical move. Empire was present, and visible, "at home" in a range of spaces: in high politics and popular culture; in the Houses of Parlia-ment and the homes of middle- and working-class people; in fiction and on the streets; in economic policy and the popular imagination. Goods and people from India, China, Africa, Australia, New Zealand, and the Caribbean were constantly on the move to and through the British Isles, crossing the paths and entering the lives of native Britons in ways that shaped their attitudes about national identity, their consumption practices, their experience of entertain-ment and above all, their convictions about what it meant to be an imperial cit-izen. Tea and sugar are just the most familiar examples of how commodities extracted from colonial possessions infiltrated the daily lives and national imagination of Victorian Britons. Metropolitan life was so saturated by im-ages, ideas, and peoples of empire that it is right to speak of the Victorian peri-od as an era of "imperial culture."[8]

The false dichotomy persists despite Britain's being a full-fledged multi-cultural nation in which evidence of imperial legacies is everywhere in the post-colonial present, not least in the historic populations of native-born "black British" (Caribbean, African, and South Asian) communities, many of whom have been contesting the putative whiteness of "English identity" since the 1950s. Attachments to the presumptive whiteness of Britain "at home" have helped to perpetuate, and to naturalize, this division between the domestic and the imperial—a whiteness whose invisibility feminists, in their preoccupation with gender, have tended to reinforce, again until very recently. Catherine Hall calls this "historical amnesia," and the introduction to her 2002 book, *Civilising Subjects*, offers a thoughtful autobiographical reflection on the limits of feminist politics with respect to race and empire in pre-1990s Britain, as well as a rigorous self-critique where the costs of such blindness is concerned.[9] Hall's work has, in fact, been instrumental in opening up the insular national narratives of British history and accounting for the constitutive impact of gender, empire, and race on the so-called "domestic story." In a series of articles in the 1990s and then in her aforementioned monograph, she has tracked the impact of empire on metropolitan politics and society with a specifically feminist purpose: to relocate both race and gender, simultaneously and interdependently, at the heart of histories of Englishness. This she has done at the high political level by demonstrating the role of Jamaica in the political settlements of the early Victorian period. The significance of this intervention cannot be underestimated, for it takes aim at the chief guarantor of white, male, and middle-class identity: the Whig narrative of history, which envisions Britain's racial and civilizational superiority based on its march toward progress and prosperity through gradual (and apparently predestined) democratization. By insisting that the political reforms of 1832 and 1867 that engendered this "democracy" were both gendered and raced—that is, that the men and women who participated in them saw the stakes in gendered and racialized terms, *and* that events like the Christmas Riot (1831) and the Eyre affair (1865) in Jamaica shaped the terms of political debate in Britain—Hall has effectively rewritten the traditional story of English national greatness from a feminist and anti-imperial perspective. Equally important, she tackles the ultimately artificial divide between empire and home at the level of the social as well as the political. By following the movements of missionary men back and forth between metropole and colony—as well as more circuitously through a variety of imperial sites—she succeeds in demonstrating quite concretely how ostensibly "domestic" discourses about evangelicalism and nation were shaped inexorably by imperial concerns, gendered anxieties, and racialized experiences.

As I have discussed elsewhere, such interpretations of "English" and "British" history have been afoot at least since the beginning of the last decade, thanks in part to Hall's own work and also to scholars both of Britain and of other imperial experiences.[10] Mrinalini Sinha's 1995 *Colonial Masculinity* was and remains an important intervention in this regard, arguing as it did for a discursive and material space ("imperial social formation") that is neither exclusively metropolitan nor colonial and offering one way out of the binaries of empire and home that had long undergirded both "national" and "imperial" histories.[11] Frederick Cooper and Ann Stoler's 1996 collection, *Tensions of*

Empire, brought together essays by historians and anthropologists working in a wide array of imperial and colonial landscapes under the auspices of their much-quoted and much-taught theme, "Between Metropole and Colony: Rethinking a Research Agenda," the title of their introductory essay.[12] Madhavi Kale's 1998 *Fragments of Empire* has taken direct aim at the metropole/colony dichotomy by tracking labor migration from India to the Caribbean to Britain and back again—thereby disrupting facile distinctions between "home" and "empire" and offering an eminently usable model for a transnational imperial history.[13] And finally, Stoler's work on Dutch colonial rule in the East Indies— much of which is collected in her 2002 book, *Carnal Knowledge and Imperial Power*—not only makes protocols of sexuality and reproduction crucial to the story of colonial politics at the micro- and macro levels, but advances the notion that "domestic" ideas and ideals were hardly original, having been made and remade in response to colonial encounters, whether literal or figurative.[14] Although Stoler's research is not about the British Empire per se, it offers important insights about European imperial and colonial forms which can and should be tested against the British experience (a process which will, incidentally, help to de-exceptionalize that experience in salutary ways).

Thanks to the accumulation of research upon which recent work is based, then, Britain (and England within it) can no longer be understood simply as an "island story." It has been opened up in ways that make crystal clear not just the enduring impact of empire on "national" politics and society, but the geopolitical stakes of "splendid isolationism" for a declining post-war, post-colonial power as well. It has made available, in short, new narratives of Victorian Britain, ones that foreground imperial culture as an analytical concept and insist on the centrality of women, gender, race, and people of color to a new kind of "domestic" narrative. So, for example, the years 1820 to 1857 can now be read as a period of imperially minded rather than simply constitutional change, in part because the parliamentary reforms of the period were shaped by officials who had one eye on metropolitan concerns and the other on colonial economic interests. Whether the issue was Catholic Emancipation, the abolition of the slave trade, or the extension of democracy to the new middle class, parliamentary statesmen and social reformers understood the link between domestic concerns and imperial problems. Blacks were involved in Chartist agitations, whose spokesmen drew in turn on metaphors of slavery to inform their political demands. White English middle-class women were drawn into debates about citizenship through their interest in the plight of slaves and colonial peoples—an interest which laid the groundwork for later Victorian feminism. Events like the Don Pacifico incident and the Crimean war also brought imperial questions home, gendering citizenship as masculine and coding it implicitly as white, the very public work of Florence Nightingale (the famous "Lady with the Lamp") and Mary Seacole (a mixed-race nurse who was also in the Crimea) notwithstanding. The Indian Mutiny of 1857—in many ways a defining moment for metropolitan consciousness of empire, its costs and its burdens in the mid-Victorian period—must also be seen as a gendered affair, given the way that images of endangered and violated English women dominated accounts of the siege of Lucknow and other "rebellion" events relayed to a reading public by an ever-expanding metropolitan press.[15]

The possibilities for re-periodization continue for 1860 to 1886, when all manner of high political dramas were enmeshed in imperial developments. The Eyre controversy, Irish nationalism, and the scramble for Africa all helped to shape the terms of parliamentary debate, as well as to reestablish white male suffrage as the true standard of democracy in Britain, albeit in expanded ways. English women's attempts to participate in political reform, to vote and to run as members of Parliament—together with the rise of Indian National Congress activity in Britain in the 1880s—helped solidify the terms upon which liberal democracy was managed in the late-Victorian period. Renewed attention must now be paid to the ways in which Benjamin Disraeli and William Gladstone tried to manipulate the concept of imperialism for party political purposes, even as Britain's imperial commitments grew under their respective premierships. These powerful statesmen, in turn, articulated new forms of imperial manliness on the world stage, performing imperial masculinity in new and newly visible ways. Imperial culture in all its *fin-de-siècle* variety has also come into focus thanks to the work of a variety of feminist historians. By the 1890s traces of empire were to be found everywhere on the Victorian "domestic" scene—on biscuit tins and in Bovril advertisements, in female suffrage tracts and international exhibitions, at universities like Oxford and Cambridge, and in urban landscapes like London and Glasgow. Through missionary societies, school textbooks, penny dreadfuls, and all manner of commercial and artistic productions, the average Briton (male and female) was not just exposed to imperialism, but experienced empire as part of the very fabric of social and cultural life. Colonial "natives" were among those who peopled the metropole in this period, coming in search of work or education or professional improvement—a diasporic movement which culminated in the election of two Indian men to the Parliament at Westminster in the 1890s.[16] The Boer War which closed the century (1899–1902) is further evidence of how imperial preoccupations shaped metropolitan society, politics, and culture. The end of the sieges at Ladysmith and Mafeking prompted dancing in the streets at home as well as a sobering reassessment of Victorian culture and progress in the wake of the military debacles in South Africa—much of which was carried out through debates about the gendered character of Boers and "native" Africans alike.[17] Largely thanks to the early work of Anna Davin on maternalism, empire, and motherhood, the new meta-narratives which work like Hall's inaugurates also allow us to make important and overlooked connections between the Boer War and the outbreak of hostilities in Europe in 1914, keeping the complex relationship between Britain, Germany, and their respective imperial ambitions always in view.[18] Events in Ireland as well as the campaign for women's suffrage—both of which had imperial resonances—must be examined anew as emerging from a decidedly Victorian imperial cultural complex rather than simply as inaugurating a "modern" post-war settlement.[19]

Numerous others scholars, both feminist and otherwise, have worked and continue to work to detail how and to what extent imperial commodities—

whether in the form of human capital, material goods, ideas, or ideological systems—circulated through Great Britain in the modern period. That scholarship is too prodigious and too varied to do more than footnote here.[20] In any case, it would be difficult to deny that imperial expansion, colonial policy-making, and the rhetoric of the civilizing mission all helped to shape "domestic" society in the age of Victoria in ways inexorably entailed by, and generative of, gender and its entanglements with race and class. The empirical research of at least two generations of feminists has been critical in showcasing how and why imperial culture at home sponsored a variety of colonial encounters on British soil, thereby illustrating that empire was as highly visible to Victorians as it should be now, to us. What I have sketched should not, of course, be taken as any kind of definitive new narrative. It represents one of many possibilities enabled by students of women and gender, some of whom are now refocusing our attention on the role of Britain's white settler colonies (South Africa, Canada, Australia, New Zealand) in ways that recontextualize and may in the end mitigate our emphasis on the role of India and Africa, long considered the dominant colonial influences at home and in the empire.[21] This work, together with the explosion of visual culture projects in a variety of British metropolitan and provincial museums in recent years, provides the basis for a number of different, and perhaps even competing, paradigms for the study of imperial Britain in the nineteenth and twentieth centuries, thus throwing into bold relief one of the defining characteristics of feminist practice: pluralities of interpretive and analytical vision.[22]

In keeping with this multi-sited, multifaceted national-imperial history, recent feminist work on Britain has not simply made women and gender visible in the new imperial history. As crucially, it has drawn our attention to the imperial nation-state in its various forms as an object of feminist analysis—something which feminist scholars in political science and sociology were attuned to early on but which feminist historians are only now fully countenancing in and for Britain. The point is emphatically *not* to re-center Britain in an already nationalist and insular historiography. It is, rather, to make clear the ways in which the nation is not an original or fixed political form, but is shaped by a historically specific set of forces, empire among them. Let me be absolutely clear on the stakes of such a project for feminist historiography, which has long targeted separate spheres as an object of criticism and has, in its Joan Scott/Judith Butler manifestations, emphasized the constructedness of all political, social, and cultural formations. First and foremost, by refusing the binary of Home (domestic/feminine) and Away (imperial/masculine), feminist historians have interrogated the gendered logic of the imperial nation-state in Britain. They have also, in the process, attempted to reverse the typical trajectory through which historians have imagined the ideological and material flow of power: rather than viewing it as one-directional (from home to empire), they are suggesting, with some powerful and evocative evidence, that the reverse was also true (from empire back to home). In many respects this is a direct application of a separate spheres critique (women at home, men at work) to the domain of "imperial culture" writ large. And yet such a maneuver does more, in the end, than simply critique separate spheres: it demonstrates the untenability of separating home from empire or empire from home, and insists that Britain was as much made by empire as empire was made by Britain. Britannia (that quintessentially female icon of Britain and of Englishness) is, in other words, not a purely national symbol, but is always already constituted by the power, political economies, and cultural imaginaries of British imperial rule—making her an unstable, rather than a foundational, figure in and of "British" history.

This is not to say that such work has been accepted or even noticed in more than a cursory way by the historical establishment in Britain. The five-volume *Oxford History of the British Empire*—edited by William Roger Louis (1999–2000) and comprising nearly 80 essays across four centuries—scarcely mentions women or gender, and those authors who do address gender and feminist history do so quite dismissively, on the grounds that it is not "fiercely empirical" in the way that "real" history is.[23] And while the body responsible for overseeing British Studies in North America does not reject the new imperial history, and its conferences reflect new work in the field, officially it has expressed unease about the "imperial turn."[24] Such postures stem from a suspicion of "extra-archival" sources and an anxiety about the "infiltration" of theoretical influences like postcolonialism or feminism, as well as from a negative view of the kind of interdisciplinary analysis which has been a hallmark of feminist practice since the 1970s. Most revealing of all, as Hall would be the first to tell you, by far the most popular historian of empire in Britain is Linda Colley. Colley's work on empire does not deal with women and gender at all, and her 2002 book *Captives* offers what can only be called retrogressive account of the racial underpinnings of the early British imperial experience.[25] The same is true of David Cannadine's 2001 *Ornamentalism: How the British Saw their Empire*, which forecloses discussions of race in favor of class and scarcely acknowledges the work of feminist scholarship of the past two decades.[26] Both books have been rapturously reviewed in the American press as well.[27] Rather than lament these developments, I prefer to read them as evidence of the truly subversive power of feminist histories of Britain. For even when it goes unnoticed and especially when it is characterized as "undisciplinary" (as contributors to the *Oxford History* have done), feminist work strikes at the heart of conservative political and empirical conventions embedded in the historiography of Britain, which have a tenacity and resilience found in few other national traditions.

The Oxford project is, arguably, the heart of the historiographical empire of modern Britain—an intellectual and political space where one would not perhaps expect the challenges of women's and gender history to be embraced, or its stakes to be fully grasped. Interestingly, the reaction to the first five volumes' exclusion of gender (as well as race and a number of other "overlooked" topics) has prompted William Roger Louis to commission a series of "companion" books, including one on gender in the British empire, edited by Philippa Levine.[28] This turn of events raises larger questions of impact for feminist scholarship, especially because the *Oxford History of the British Empire* volumes are written to sell to a literate, non-academic audience as well as to specialists in the field. This is an especially pressing question in light of contemporary debates about globalization, neo-imperialism, and the specter of a British-inspired American imperialism generated by the events of September 11, 2001, the war in Iraq, and American aspirations to world hegemony more generally. It is undoubtedly a good sign that Hall's book—which as I have suggested, documents some of the most crucial interconnections between empire and home in the pre-1867 period—won the 2003 Forkosch Prize, given to the best book on British history by the American Historical Association. On the other hand, the lure of the unadulterated nation—especially in the globalizing, neocolonial present—is extremely powerful, not least because almost all historical traditions (whether social, imperial, or indeed, colonial) have long been built on its foundational presumptions. Anyone who doubts this need only have followed the initial reception of Niall Ferguson's 2003 book (and BBC series), *Empire: How Britain Made the Modern World*, in the British mainstream press, where it was lauded as the savior of "the empire was a good thing" thesis and Ferguson as the "Errol Flynn of British historians."[29] At the core of Ferguson's argument is that British imperialism was not only good, but better than Dutch, German, or Japanese imperialisms would have been had they been destined to rule the world. That such chauvinism (in both senses of the term) lies at the heart of this historical account of global empire should give us pause, particularly in an age of resurgent Anglo-American nationalism/imperialism. That it ranks high as entertainment—at least in its BBC TV incarnation—and low as serious scholarship is also a sobering thought.[30] At the very least, it should remind us of the sensational and above all, the sentimental power of national allegiances and modes of historical investigation, despite the many innovations of a book like Hall's *Civilising Subjects*.

Given the acceleration of neo-imperial power and pro-imperial scholarship in the new millennium, the challenges facing a new generation of feminist historians in British history are in many respects more daunting than they would have been even a few years ago. Women and gender have become mainstays in the writing of history, and most graduate students acknowledge gender as a dimension of historical experience and women as historical actors. But whether we fully appreciate, even now, the power that gender—in concert with systems of hierarchy and domination like class and race and ethnicity and nationality, to name a few—has to shape and actively to (re)produce historically contingent forms of political coercion, violence, and hegemony remains for me an open question. Lip service is often paid to these issues, but the truly radical, revolutionary potential of a feminist agenda for history and historical writing is rarely countenanced. In this sense feminism, like women and gender, has been incorporated and I would even say, domesticated by a North American media and an academic establishment committed to multiculturalism and other liberal regimes of recognition and containment.

For many, this registers as progress, and perhaps rightly so. It is important to remember, however, that among women in the American academy, white women still dominate even as demographically, colleges and universities draw on and serve increasingly diverse student populations. Hence a full-scale democratization of the profession, and all that that entails in terms of changing curricular initiatives, alternative methodological approaches, and new subjects of history, still awaits. Those of us dedicated to the kinds of feminist politics and feminist histories that the institutionalization of women's and gender studies in the North American academy has the potential to foster cannot afford to be sanguine about the long-term security of our achievements. The corporatization of the university in an era of aggressive global capital and neocolonial Western hegemony at home and abroad should make us cautious about our "success" and ever alert to the ways in which our priorities may be sidelined or eradicated altogether, especially in the context of current ideological and fiscal conservatisms. As in the 1980s, we must see to it that feminism responds actively and pro-actively to the challenges posed to it in new forms, such as the technological juggernaut (which has produced a highly gendered asymmetry of access and hence power across the world); discourses and practices of globalization (which both erase and appropriate women, especially those made vulnerable by caste, class and capital "development"); and, not least, blatantly imperial ideologies (which in the U.S. have attempted to co-opt "the Afghan woman" in the name of American "liberty"). North American feminisms (for there are many variants and constituencies) must expect to be changed in the process, and must seek out agendas and coalitions which will galvanize that transformation—particularly by women who operate from outside the West and by allies who may have different priorities and ways of seeing. Such flexibility, openness, and commitment to self-critique has never been more urgent than at this particular geopolitical juncture if North American feminists are not to replicate the colonizing impulses of late-Victorian "global sisterhood" or, for that matter, its imperial historical perspectives.

The "imperial turn" in British history is an excellent and timely example of the intellectual opportunities that are available to students of the past who wish to demonstrate the ongoing relevance—and indeed, the enduring necessity—of feminist historical work for "national" histories in a new imperial age. Some questions remain to be asked. What are the costs and benefits of re-imagining the Whig narrative, as Hall has done, rather than doing away with it altogether? What role did women of classes other than the bourgeoisie play in shaping imperial ideologies at home? What does it mean to de-center Africa and especially India in narratives of imperial culture in order to account for, say, Irish political and cultural influences, or the transnational flow of goods, people and gendered forms of modernity from the Antipodes to Britain? What would a history of imperial domesticity look like that did not parse metropole and colony, but took seriously Mrinalini Sinha's concept of imperial social formation? How have regimes of sexuality, both normative and "deviant," shaped the making of modern British imperial culture, especially where questions of whiteness and racial mixture are concerned? How can histories of the body (whether Foucauldian or not) help to map the transnational webs of imperial and colonial power at both the level of high politics and in daily life? What did ordinary men and women—and especially in communities of color—do to participate in, conform to, and/or contest empire-building regimes in the Victorian period and after? What does feminist historical work on imperial Britain contribute to contemporary understandings of globalization in the profession and in the classroom? How and for whom does feminist history still matter in a putatively post-feminist world? And last but not least, how has feminist historiographical practice changed (or not) under the pressure of these new questions?

As with all bold intellectual agendas, feminist research on Britain has raised more questions than it has yet answered, not least by making the stakes of transnational history indubitably clear for the nation and the discipline. If, as a number of critics have suggested, the colonial age is not over, "and is in fact still unfolding in the present global logic of modernity," the ramifications of this project cannot be ignored, either in our work or in those classroom contexts where we take up and presumably experiment with the ongoing problem of national time, nation-bounded histories, and the exigencies of a globalizing present.[31] And if, as the postcolonial critic Salman Rushdie has suggested, "the trouble with the English is that their history happened overseas, so they don't know what it means,"[32] feminist historians still have much to contribute to the project of determining how and why Britain's "domestic" history has been shaped by empire.

Notes

1. With help from a Fulbright grant and a Woodrow Wilson scholarship, the dissertation became *Burdens of History: British Feminism, Indian Women and Imperial Culture 1865–1915* (Chapel Hill: University of North Carolina Press, 1994).

2. Ellen Carol DuBois, *Feminism and Suffrage* (Ithaca: Cornell University Press, 1978).

3. As witnessed by the session, "The Making of the English Working Class at Forty: A Roundtable on the Global Impact of a Local Study," at the annual meeting of the American Historical Society, Chicago, January 2003.

4. Among the most important books in this contest were Judith Walkowitz, *Prostitution and Victorian Society* (Cambridge: Cambridge University Press, 1980) and Leonore Davidoff and Catherine Hall, *Family Fortunes* (Chicago: University of Chicago Press, 1987).

5. See for example Nupur Chaudhuri and Margaret Strobel, *Western Women and Imperialism* (Bloomington: Indiana University Press, 1992) and Mary Procida, *Married to The Empire: Gender, Politics and Imperialism in India, 1883–1947* (Manchester: Manchester University Press, 2002).

6. In this first category, I am thinking specifically of Lata Mani, *Contentious Traditions: The Debate on Sati in Colonial India* (Berkeley: University of California Press, 1998); Laura Briggs, *Reproducing Empire: Race, Sex, Science, and U.S. Imperialism in Puerto Rico* (Berkeley: University of California Press, 2002); Philippa Levine, *Prostitution, Race and Politics: Policing Venereal Disease in the British Empire* (London: Routledge, 2003); Lynn Thomas, *The Politics of the Womb: Women, Reproduction and the State in Kenya* (Berkeley: University of California Press, 2003) and Ann

L. Stoler, *Carnal Knowledge and Imperial Power* (Berkeley: University of California Press, 2002). For a variety of bibliographic perspectives on these subjects for the British empire and beyond, see Marysa Navarro, Decia Ali, and Virginia Sanchez Korrol, *Women in Latin America and the Caribbean* (Bloomington: Indiana University Press, 1999); Guity Nashat and Judith E. Tucker, *Women in the Middle East and North Africa* (Bloomington: Indiana University Press, 1999); Barbara N. Ramusack and Sharon Sievers, *Women in Asia* (Bloomington: Indiana University Press, 1999); Iris Berger, E. Frances White, and Cathy Skidmore-Hess, *Women in Sub-Saharan Africa* (Bloomington: Indiana University Press, 1999) and the essays on India (Geraldine Forbes), China (Tani E. Barlow), Latin America (Sarah Chambers), the Middle East (Marilyn Booth) and Africa (Iris Berger) in Jean Allman and Antoinette Burton, eds., "Destination Globalization? Women, Gender and Comparative Colonial Histories in the New Millennium," *Journal of Colonialism and Colonial History* 4, 1 (2003): *http://muse.jhu.edu/journals/cch/*.

7. Here I borrow from the essay I wrote with Jean Allman, "Destination Globalization," cited above.

8. For an elaboration of this theme see my essay, "The Visible Empire and the Empire at Home, 1832–1905," for Empire On-Line (Adam Matthew, Ltd.'s virtual archive: *www.adam-matthew-publications.co.uk*).

9. See Catherine Hall, *White, Male and Middle Class: Explorations in Feminism and History* (London: Routledge, 1992) and her *Civilising Subjects* (Chicago: University of Chicago Press, 2002).

10. See Antoinette Burton, "Imperial Weights and Measures: Evaluating Empire in Catherine Hall's *Civilising Subjects,*" *Victorian Studies*, 45, 4 (2003): 699–707.

11. Mrinalini Sinha, *Colonial Masculinity: The 'Manly Englishman' and the 'Effeminate Bengali' in the Late Nineteenth Century* (Manchester: Manchester University Press, 1995).

12. Frederick Cooper and Ann Stoler, "Between Metropole and Colony: Rethinking a Research Agenda" in their collection, *Tensions of Empire: Colonial Cultures in a Bourgeois World* (Berkeley: University of California Press, 1996), 1–58.

13. Madhavi Kale, *Fragments of Empire: Capital, Slavery, and Indian Indentured Labor in the British Caribbean* (Philadelphia: University of Pennsylvania Press, 1998).

14. Ann Stoler, *Race and the Education of Desire* (Durham: Duke University Press, 1995) and *Carnal Knowledge and Imperial Power.*

15. For English women and Mutiny stories see Jenny Sharpe, *Allegories of Empire: the Figure of Woman in the Colonial Text* (Minneapolis: University of Minnesota Press, 1993).

16. See Rozina Visram's *Ayahs, Lascars and Princes: Indians in Britain, 1700–1947* (London: Pluto Press, 1986) and her *Asians in Britain: 400 Years of History* (London: Pluto Press, 2002).

17. See Paula Krebs, "'The Last of the Gentlemen's Wars': Women in the Boer War Concentration Camp Controversy," *History Workshop Journal* 33 (1992): 38–56 and her *Gender, Race and the Writing of Empire* (Cambridge, 1999).

18. Anna Davin, "Imperialism and Motherhood," *History Workshop Journal* 5 (Spring 1978): 9–65.

19. For an important essay on the networks of imperial activity in this period see Ian Fletcher, "Double Meanings: Nation and Empire in the Edwardian Era" in An-

toinette Burton, ed., *After the Imperial Turn: Thinking with and through the Nation* (Durham: Duke University Press, 2003), pp. 246–59.

20. For an extensive though by no means exhaustive bibliography see my essay "On the Inadequacy and the Indispensability of the Nation" in my edited collection, *After the Imperial Turn*, 1–26.

21. See for example Pamela Scully, *Liberating the Family? Gender and British Slave Emancipation in the Rural Western Cape, S. Africa, 1823–1853* (London: Heinemann, 1997); Adele Perry, *On the Edge of Empire: Gender, Race, and the Making of British Columbia, 1849–1871* (Toronto: University of Toronto Press, 2000); Cecilia Morgan, "A Wigwam to Westminster: Performing Mohawk Identities in Imperial Britain, 1890s–1900s," *Gender and History* 15, 2 (2003): 319–41; and Angela Woollacott, *To Try Her Fortune in London: Australian Women, Colonialism, and Modernity* (Oxford: Oxford University Press, 2001). Though they do not emphasize gender, see also Tony Ballantyne, *Orientalism and Race: Aryanism in the British Empire* (London: Palgrave, 2002) and Alan Lester, *Imperial Networks: Creating Identities in Nineteenth-century South Africa and Britain* (London: Routledge, 2001) for models of how to do transnational history that does not privilege empire or metropole.

22. See for example the Merseyside Maritime Museum's collections on slavery at *www.liverpoolmuseums.org.uk/maritime/slavery/slavery.asp*; press coverage of plans for a museum of slavery in Liverpool in 2007: *www.guardian.co.uk/arts/news/story/0,11711,905368,00.html*; and Durba Ghosh, "Exhibiting Asia in Britain: Commerce, Consumption, and Globalization," provided courtesy of author. For two rather different narratives of imperial culture at home that I have tried to work out, see Antoinette Burton, "Women and 'Domestic' Imperial Culture: The Case of Victorian Britain," in Marilyn J. Boxer and Jean H. Quataert, eds., *Connecting Spheres: Women in a Globalizing World, 1500 to the Present*, (2nd ed., Oxford: Oxford University Press, 2000) 174–84 and my essay, with primary text links, "The Visible Empire" (cited in full above).

23. Robin Winks, ed. *The Oxford History of the British Empire, v. V: Historiography* (Oxford: Oxford University Press, 1999), 659.

24. See Peter Stansky et al., *NACBS Report on the State and Future of British Studies in North America* (November 1999) and my collection, *After the Imperial Turn*.

25. Linda Colley, *Captives: The Story of Britain's Pursuit of Empire and How its Soldiers were Held Captive by the Dream of Global Supremacy, 1600–1850* (New York: Pantheon, 2002).

26. David Cannadine, *Ornamentalism: How the British Saw their Empire* (Oxford: Oxford University Press, 2001).

27. For Cannadine see Sarah Lyall, "Provocative Book Says Class System, Not Racial Pride, Ruled Britannia," *New York Times*, August 25, 2001; Fouad Ajami, "Ornamentalism: Married to the Raj," *The New York Times Book Review*, August 26, 2001. For Colley see Adam Hochschild, "Captivity Nation," *New York Times Book Review* (January 5, 2003): 10. For a critical, albeit academic, take on *Ornamentalism* see the special issue of the *Journal of Colonialism and Colonial History* (April 2002) edited by Tony Ballantyne which features a roundtable forum on the book: *http://euterpe-muse.press.jhu.edu/journals/jcch/*.

28. Philippa Levine, ed., *Gender and Empire* (Oxford: Oxford University Press, 2004).

29. Niall Ferguson, *Empire: How Britain Made the Modern World* (Allen Lane, 2003); and Andrew Roberts, "Errol Flynn's Empire," *The Times* (January 8, 2003).

30. See Gerard DeGroot's review of the book and TV series, "A Lesson Worth Forgetting," *Scotland on Sunday*, January 19, 2003. "Beautiful people are entertaining,
and so are contentious ideas," says DeGroot. "When ideas and presenter are both
hot, that spells blockbuster."

31. See David Bunn, "Comaroff Country," *Interventions* 31, 1 (2001): 6.

32. Quoted in Homi K. Bhabha, "Dissemination: Time, Narrative and the Margins
of the Modern State," in Bhabha, ed., *Nation and Narration* (London: Routledge,
1990), 317.

Suggestions for Further Reading

Briggs, Laura. *Reproducing Empire: Race, Sex, Science, and U.S. Imperialism in Puerto
Rico*. Berkeley: University of California Press, 2002.

Burton, Antoinette. *Burdens of History: British Feminism, Indian Women and Imperial
Culture 1865–1915*. Chapel Hill: University of North Carolina Press, 1994.

———. "The Visible Empire and the Empire at Home, 1832–1905," for Empire On-Line,
Adam Matthew, Ltd.'s virtual archive: *www.adam-matthew-publications.co.uk*.

———, ed. *After the Imperial Turn: Thinking with and through the Nation*. Durham: Duke
University Press, 2003.

Chaudhuri, Nupur, and Margaret Strobel. *Western Women and Imperialism*. Bloomington: Indiana University Press, 1992.

Davidoff, Leonore, and Catherine Hall. *Family Fortunes*. Chicago: University of Chicago
Press, 1987.

Davin, Anna. "Imperialism and Motherhood," *History Workshop Journal* 5 (Spring 1978):
9–65.

DuBois, Ellen Carol. *Feminism and Suffrage*. Ithaca: Cornell University Press, 1978.

Hall, Catherine. *Civilising Subjects*. Chicago: University of Chicago Press, 2002.

———. *White, Male and Middle Class: Explorations in Feminism and History*. London:
Routledge, 1992.

Kale, Madhavi. *Fragments of Empire: Capital, Slavery, and Indian Indentured Labor in the
British Caribbean*. Philadelphia: University of Pennsylvania Press, 1998.

Krebs, Paula. *Gender, Race and the Writing of Empire*. Cambridge: Cambridge University
Press, 1999.

Levine, Philippa. *Prostitution, Race and Politics: Policing Venereal Disease in the British
Empire*. London: Routledge, 2003.

———, ed. *Gender and Empire*. Oxford: Oxford University Press, 2004.

Mani, Lata. *Contentious Traditions: The Debate on Sati in Colonial India*. Berkeley: University of California Press, 1998.

Procida, Mary. *Married to The Empire: Gender, Politics and Imperialism in India, 1883–1947*.
Manchester: Manchester University Press, 2002.

Sinha, Mrinalini. *Colonial Masculinity: The 'Manly Englishman' and the 'Effeminate Bengali' in the Late Nineteenth Century*. Manchester: Manchester University Press, 1995.

Stoler, Ann L. *Carnal Knowledge and Imperial Power*. Berkeley: University of California
Press, 2002.

Thomas, Lynn. *The Politics of the Womb: Women, Reproduction and the State in Kenya*.
Berkeley: University of California Press, 2003.

Walkowitz, Judith. *Prostitution and Victorian Society*. Cambridge: Cambridge University Press, 1980.

Visram, Rozina. *Asians in Britain: 400 Years of History*. London: Pluto Press, 2002.

———. *Ayahs, Lascars and Princes: Indians in Britain, 1700–1947*. London: Pluto Press, 1986.

Study Questions

1. Estelle Freedman recounts her efforts to approach the women's movement historiographically in a seminar on the 1920s and 1930s. How would you define the difference between "history" and "historiography"? What do you consider the value of examining the changing interpretations of an event of a movement before you write your own account of it?

2. If you counterpose Freedman'conditions for feminism with Guy-Sheftall's finding of "indigenous feminisms," do you arrive at a deeper understanding of what feminism is?

3. Antoinette Burton argues that feminist historians have opened the way for other, once ignored groups to be included in the writing of an empire's history. Do you think that the introduction of women into the traditional narrative of history prompts an interest in other groups as well? Whose story do you feel remains to be written? What group or groups do you feel have been left out in the history you have studied?

"IT STANDS AT THE HEAD"   "THE LIGHT RUNNING"
DOMESTIC SEWING MACHINE.

By the 1870s, illustrated trade cards had become a popular means of advertising new household products. The Domestic Sewing Machine Company created a series of these cards that told the story of the courtship of a young Victorian woman and her devoted beau. In an earlier card, the young man had proposed; the young woman's response was conditional. "Yes," said the bride to be, "on condition that you buy me a DOMESTIC with new wood work and attachments." In the card shown above, the happy bride and groom look down admiringly at the sewing machine that sealed their relationship.

(Courtesy of the Library of Congress)

part 2

Gender Construction in Action

The essays in this section demonstrate the malleable nature of gender and the ways in which cultures and subcultures construct it. Two contributors focus on marginal groups who create new gender behavior and ideals and, in doing so, blur the rigid lines that the dominant society draws between genders and the rigid rules it tries to enforce regarding sexuality. The other two contributors focus on the techniques feminist scholars employ in order to uncover and analyze the ways in which societies go about gendering themselves and their institutions.

Leila Rupp's "When Women's Studies Isn't about Women: Writing about Drag Queens" challenges the notion that there are only two genders. In her examination of the performances of drag queens in Key West, Florida, Rupp introduces us to an alternative sexuality and gender identity. She shows us how the performances at the 801 Cabaret educate straight people about gay life and invite audience members—and us—to question traditional ideas about gender and sexuality. Rupp's study of drag queens reinforces the notion that gender is socially constructed and suggests that sexual desire is too complex to be rigidly categorized.

In "Anthropology, Gender, and Narrative," Caroline Brettell looks at the revival of life history and narrative by feminist anthropologists, viewing this technique as a means to emphasize the agency, that is, the active choices made by their female subjects. Using the body of work on women migrants, Brettell evaluates the degree to which the concept of gender has been fully integrated into the field by comparing what scholars thought they knew when she first began her research and what they believe they know now about these women.

Sharon Marcus's "The Queerness of Victorian Marriage Reform" explores "female marriage" and "contractual marriage" in mid-century England. In her examination of legal, religious, and anthropological literature, Marcus finds evidence of arguments rather than agreements on what constituted marriage and family among Victorians. In their debates, experts questioned whether heterosexual marriage was a mark of civilization, challenged the notion that same-sex relationships were primitive arrangements, and explored female sexuality with a frankness modern readers might find surprising.

In " 'Return from Exile': Community, Nation, and Gender in George Eliot's Fiction," Deborah Nord uses a feminist perspective to produce new insights on a much-studied topic. Through an examination of several of George Eliot's works, Nord reveals the reoccurring theme of individualism versus community. Eliot's individualistic characters are often the disinherited, the racially alien, and the non-English. As Jews or gypsies, they are members of a "disinherited race." But characters like Maggie Tulliver in *The Mill on the Floss* are also different because of their failure to conform to gender norms in appearance or actions. The female characters who tame their individualism in order to avoid being outcasts are, in Nord's words, "imprisoned heroines."

When Women's Studies Isn't about Women: Writing about Drag Queens

Leila J. Rupp

Leila J. Rupp (1975) is Professor and Chair of the Women's Studies Program at the University of California, Santa Barbara. Her current work focuses on sexuality and women's movements. Among her publications are *Worlds of Women: The Making of an International Women's Movement* (1997); *A Desired Past: A Short History of Same-Sex Love in America* (1999); and *Drag Queens at the 801 Cabaret*, with Verta Taylor (2003).

For Leila Rupp, "the resurgence of the women's movement gave shape to everything I had felt since I was a young girl. As a child, I devoured those biographies of famous people written for young readers, and I always sought out any about women, though they were few and far between." Now, she believes, the field of history is more open to feminist thinking. "I think women's studies has had an enormous impact on the way young women (I'm less sure about young men) view their world, but there is still a long way to go. First, students still have to choose to enroll in women's studies classes. Those who do are usually changed in profound ways, but they sometimes come with negative ideas about feminism and are pleasantly surprised to learn what feminisms are really about. I think that sometimes young women are resistant until they get out in the work world on a permanent basis and deal with things like having children (or not)—and then my hope is that what they learned in women's studies will help them to see that what they are experiencing is not personal but societal and that there are political solutions worth fighting for."

When I completed my dissertation in 1976, I never dreamed I would ever write about men. I fell in love with women's history in the context of the resurgence of the women's movement in the late 1960s, and from then on, everything I wrote in college and graduate school focused on women. I began to specialize in German women's history, but in the course of my graduate training developed an interest in U.S. women's history as well. I wrote a comparative dissertation, which is in truth what launched me into women's studies proper.[1] Applying for jobs in both German and U.S. history (there were no comparative jobs advertised), I found that my unconventional interests presented an obstacle to finding work. "How wonderful that you do comparative history, but we're looking for a Germanist/Americanist," my rejection letters repeated over and over again.

And then I encountered a novel job advertisement, one that made my heart beat faster. Ohio State University was searching for a women's historian, "European or American," for a joint appointment between the Department of History and the Office of Women's Studies (not even yet an academic unit). I applied, interviewed, and to my great excitement, received the offer. That was the true beginning of my career in women's studies.

Over the last twenty-seven years, my work has ranged from women, war, and propaganda to women's movements to the history of sexuality. I spent my first years between history and women's studies, the next sixteen in a department of history, and now I am chair of the Women's Studies Program at the University of California, Santa Barbara. It is from this perspective that I approach the questions of the trajectory of women's studies scholarship over time.

In my opinion, the three biggest challenges facing women's studies are making scholarship accessible, figuring out what it means to be an interdisciplinary discipline, and holding together the field in the face of our deconstruction of the category "woman." In the 1970s, it was possible to be well-versed in the entire body of women's studies scholarship. Not so today, as the blossoming of the field has meant an enormous increase in both the quantity and complexity of scholarship. Teaching even an introductory women's studies course is a challenge. Furthermore, at the beginning, students could rather easily find an appropriate level of entry into the field. Now that is much more difficult. Compare reading, say, Adrienne Rich's *Of Woman Born* to Judith Butler's *Gender Trouble*.[2] Rich's exploration of the experience and institution of motherhood does not require the theoretical sophistication or knowledge of a specialized vocabulary that Butler's transformative contribution to understanding gender does. We know so much more about women, genders, feminisms, and the plurality of all of those things, and both the range of our knowledge and the expertise needed to read some of the theoretical work in women's studies has multiplied exponentially.

One of my most important commitments—and my passion—is to write compelling and moving scholarship that can reach people where they live. Yet I also want that scholarship to be conceptually sophisticated and cognizant of the major theoretical developments in the field. That was my goal in writing *A Desired Past: A Short History of Same-Sex Love in America* and, with my partner and sociologist coauthor, Verta Taylor, *Drag Queens at the 801 Cabaret*.[3]

Women's studies began as a kind of joining of disciplinary perspectives, but it has developed into its own discipline at the same time that the various traditional disciplines—to different degrees—have incorporated the insights of women's studies. Gender is, indeed, a necessary category of analysis in the field of history these days. As the field of women's studies becomes more autonomous intellectually and institutionally, it is important to keep both kinds of connections to other disciplines as well. This, too, is a challenge for the future. Part of what has always defined women's studies for me, and what I think will continue to define the field in the future, is the connection to women's movements. Feminist activism has pushed women's studies in the direction of confronting differences among women and the intersectionality of gender, race, class, and sexuality, and it has opened academic eyes to the ways that the forces of globalization require us to think globally and act locally. Women's studies is about making the world a better place, one idea and one act at a time.

Confronting difference has led to a progressive deconstructing of the category "woman." First came recognition of the implicit whiteness and middle-classness of the term in much of our scholarship, and then expansion to include butch lesbians, male-to-female transsexuals, transgendered biological men, and others who push the boundaries of sex and gender. Queer theory, which posits both the fluidity of gender and sexuality and the social construction of identities, desires, and even bodies, poses a challenge for women's studies. Is our subject women? Or genders? In my program, we will house a queer studies minor. Should we change our name? On the most basic level, queer studies is not just about women, and those who teach about masculinities—including female masculinities—might feel as if "women's studies" is not capacious enough a term to encompass what they do. On a deeper level, although queer theory and queer studies developed out of the interest in feminist theory and women's studies in the complexities of gender and sexuality, the very term "queer" is intended to destabilize our understandings of such basic concepts as "woman," "female," "lesbian," "heterosexual," and even "sexual." Can women's studies continue to hold together if we are uncertain what our central concepts mean? Or if they exist at all?

The questions of the naming of women's studies and our relationship to queer studies are, of course, hotly debated issues on the national scene. I think I come down on the side of remaining as we are, "women's studies," but opening our conception of "women" and living with ambiguity and contradiction: tittie queens with breasts and penises, transgendered men with male chests and no bottom surgery having penis-in-vagina gay sex with gay men.

Which brings me back to the odd position of writing about men, or, more accurately, drag queens, for one of the central arguments of our book is that "drag queen" is a kind of gender category of its own. And another is that drag is itself the performance of protest, an intentional (and successful) way not only of building community among gay, lesbian, bisexual, and transgendered people and educating straight audiences but also, as scholars would put it, "troubling" gender and sexuality. One of the things I found in undertaking this study is that studying men—specifically gay men—has a great deal to offer the field of women's studies.

So, first, a word about the study. When we first wandered into the drag show at the 801 Cabaret, in Key West, Florida, having already met Sushi, the house queen, we were entranced. This was a style of drag we had not encountered before, very different from the female impersonation with which we were more familiar. The drag queens didn't pretend to be women. Rather, they spoke in their own male voices, in some cases didn't shave their underarms and legs, referred to their male genitals tucked away (or not), identified as gay men, flashed their male chests, even stripped entirely, and in multiple other ways tore away the illusion of femaleness. It was as if right before our eyes, we were seeing an enactment of queer theory. Describing what we hoped to accomplish ourselves, they were clothing the theoretical bones of the scholarship in the finery of drag queen life.

As a result of meeting Sushi and seeing the show over and over, we decided to write about the drag queens. From the very beginning, Sushi trusted us and told us to "tell the truth" about them. We began by interviewing the members of the troupe, all full-time drag queens, sometimes over dinner at our house. We attended weekly drag queen meetings and practice sessions, went to social events, and kept going to the shows. Ultimately, we interviewed twelve drag queens, the co-owner of the bar, two mothers of the "girls," as they call each other, and two boyfriends. We taped and transcribed fifty shows and scoured the gay and mainstream media in Key West for stories about the drag queens, of which there were many. Verta had a wonderful idea that made the study especially unique: we ran focus groups with audience members the afternoon after the show, no mean feat in a bar in a tourist town. We would recruit people to come back, the bar owner offered them a free drink, and we ended up with a group of forty diverse respondents who shared their reasons for going to the show and their reactions.

A word about Key West is also in order. The "Conch Republic," as it is known, is only tenuously attached to the rest of the United States, perched on the end of a chain of islets, closer to Cuba than Miami. In 1982, as a result of a drug-enforcement blockade across the only road into and out of the keys, Key West seceded from the United States, declared war, surrendered, and appealed for foreign aid. That independence and sense of humor says a lot about the place. Home to Cuban, Bahamian, gay, and hippie communities, Key West is diverse, mostly tolerant, and tries hard to live up to its official policy, that we are all "One Human Family." Tourism is the main business, the gay community has a big presence, and there are probably more drag queens per capita than anywhere else in the world. They hold a revered place in Key West as celebrities, but at the same time they sometimes feel like freaks.

The 801 girls perform every night of the year, at eleven o'clock, no cover, upstairs in the Cabaret, which sits atop a gay bar in the heart of the gay end of town. For forty-five minutes beginning at ten o'clock, they stand on the street outside the bar, the main road that runs for a mile from the Gulf of Mexico to the Atlantic, and drum up business. That's how most tourists come to the show: they see the girls, towering over everyone else in their five-inch heels, they gawk a bit, sometimes stop for a chat, and they get interested. It's known as the best show in town. There are also a lot of regulars, mostly gay men, but also straight men (who find it a wonderful place to pick up women—no competition and women find the show arousing) and women, both straight and lesbian, who know and love the girls.

The shows themselves have a different host and theme every night of the week. They range from "A Night in Havana," emceed by Gugi Gomez, who is actually Puerto Rican, to the Saturday night "Sex Show," at the end of which the host, Kylie Jean Lucille, strips to "Queen of the Night," leaving on her heels, wig, and makeup. The drag queens lip synch their numbers, most of which are nothing like impersonations of the great female icons. Even when Scabola Feces (whose name expresses well her in-your-face critique of conventional femininity) does a Karen Carpenter number, she ends by spewing water out of her mouth onto the stage in reference to Carpenter's eating disorder. The songs express pride in gay identity, pain at their treatment by men, ethnic identity, solidarity with women, and a wide range of emotions and political positions.

This is a style of drag, we now know, that can be found throughout the country, but the one way that this show differs a bit is in the extent of interaction with the audience. This involves the drag queens moving out into the cabaret to grope and fondle men and women, bringing volunteers on stage to participate in a segment known as "doing shots," and all sorts of random exchanges. In the bar, there are tables up front by the stage where tourists, and especially straight couples, serve as props for the drag queens' antics. Sometimes audience members get into the act themselves, jumping up on stage to dance with the girls or even to mimic sex acts with them. It's a bawdy show, with lots of talk about sex and lots of use of slang terms for body parts and sex acts.

One of the things we learned about women's studies from studying men in drag was how complicated gender and sexual categories can be. On the surface, it might seem that the drag queens reify existing gender and sexual categories. At the beginning of the show, they routinely ask people in the audience to identify themselves as heterosexual, lesbian, or gay, encouraging heterosexuals to keep breeding and raising more gay sons; calling lesbians by their "politically correct" name, "vagitarians," "because you are what you eat," and then exulting because "all the rest are beautiful homosexual men." "Doing shots" involves calling for a volunteer from what they call "each sexual category," by which they mean a straight man, gay man, straight woman, and lesbian, sometimes a bisexual or transsexual. Sometimes they define the categories by sex acts. When a lesbian, gay man, straight man, and straight woman come up to the stage, Sushi might announce, "Now we have the whole world here."

At first glance, this strategy seems to make concrete and distinct categories of sexuality and gender, but the girls (and the audience) are fanciful enough to make the point just the opposite. First of all, the girls invite people to be creative. "Who wants to be a lesbian tonight?" asks Margo, at sixty-something introduced as "the oldest living drag queen in captivity." A burly gay man one night volunteered, offering, "My name is Lisa, I'm a policewoman." Another night a gay man in drag as a lesbian came up, introduced by Kylie as "our gay man-woman." In addition, once the volunteers are up there, the drag queens play with their sexuality. They order the straight man to lie down on his back and invite the gay man to sit across his pelvis. The women they position on their backs, feet facing one another, and then have them intertwine their legs. While each pair is in position, the others pour a shot of some awful liquor down their throats, to much banter about fellatio and cunnilingus. It's vulgar and rather shocking, but that is intentional. By crossing the lines of respectability, and involving the audience in that process, the drag queens blur the boundaries between themselves as marginal people and the audience as respectable in the same ways that they encourage people to act, if only for a moment, outside their sexual categories.

They do the same thing in other less structured interactions as well. Kylie tells of having once "licked a pussy" and invites a lesbian to pretend to do that to her. "You'd have to, I don't really have one." Another time she drags a woman on stage, pretends to hump her, then asks if she is a lesbian. When the woman says she's straight, Kylie feigns astonishment. "Even after being with me?" R.V. Beaumont tells the audience Kylie could be taken for a female strip-per at the straight end of town "until they find out that her clitoris is larger than the average clitoris and goes all the way back to her ass." Kylie and R.V. also touch their genitals and announce, "You're making me moist." Sushi refers to her "man-pussy" or "mangina," and asks a lesbian to feel her clitoris. "It's big tonight. I was born with a big clitoris."

The drag queens intend to trouble gender, sexuality, and even bodies in these ways. "What we're gonna do is try to open these people's minds," Kylie announces in her "Sex Show," which opens with a group rendition of En Vogue's "Free Your Mind." "I intend to challenge people," Kylie tells us an-other time. "I'm not just doing a number," says Sushi. "I have a platform now to teach the world." To a reporter for the Key West *Citizen*, the mainstream paper, Sushi proclaimed, "We're not just lip-synching up here, we're chang-ing lives." They know that they make it impossible to think of the categories of man/woman and gay/straight in any simple way. And the audience mem-bers confirmed it. A straight woman tourist loved when the girls fondled her husband, finding it the sexiest part of the show, "there was something crack-ling the most. . . . The line was crossed the most at that moment." Her hus-band found himself sexually excited, then thought, "Wait a minute, don't do this. You're not supposed to be sexually excited, this is a man, you know." Both straight and lesbian women found themselves aroused by Milla, who describes herself as a black women in a white gay male body and "omnisexu-al," attractive to everyone. A straight woman "felt like kissing her. And I'm not gay at all." A lesbian woman described finding Milla "very sexy."

As a result of such feelings, many audience members concluded that the labels don't fit. A straight male tourist put it best: "I think that one of the beau-ties of attending a show like this is that you do realize that you . . . shouldn't walk out and say, 'I only like men,' and you shouldn't say, 'I only like women,' and it all kind of blends together a lot more so that maybe what we want to live in our normal lives." Others agreed, concluding that the categories in the end just don't matter. One young gay man put it this way: "we all have these differences but here we are all together within this small space. . . . Once we all leave this bar, if we can all see four different people that are different and commune together, or at least respect each other, then when we leave this bar, wouldn't the world be a little bit better place?"

All of this made concrete for us the need to think more creatively about sexual and gender categories, although we concluded that, rather than attempt to eliminate them altogether, we need to expand the possibilities. Like Liz Kennedy and Madeline Davis and Joan Nestle, expanding "lesbian" into "butch" and "fem" and further into "stone butch" and other variations, and like Judith Halberstam defining "female masculinity," and like Don Kulick portraying "travesti" as a category neither female nor male, we see "drag queenness" as something different from either femininity or masculinity.[4] And we see in practice the social constructedness of gender and sexuality and what it might mean to blur the boundaries of the existing categories of man and woman, heterosexual and homosexual.

Perhaps nothing brought that home more than the night that Sushi announced we would never truly understand drag until we experienced it directly. So, after a brief lesson on the standard procedure for devising a drag name (the name of your first pet and the street where you lived), Jinxie Dogwood and Blackie (which almost immediately morphed into Blackée) Warner were born. Sushi took about half an hour to make up each one of us, making our faces look bigger so we could pass as men dressed as women. And we did. Before even donning her wig (which looked just like the shag she sported in college), Verta went out of the dressing room with her hair slicked back, in shorts and a silk tank top, and although she is short even for a woman, no one would believe that she wasn't a man wearing makeup. We learned a lot about what makes a man a man and a woman a woman.

After the drag names came a lesson in walking. Sushi brought out a pair of heels for me to try at a drag queen meeting. They must have had five-inch heels, and when I put them on, I couldn't walk at all. "Come on, darling, walk," said Sushi, who then shouted, "*Oh no*, don't walk on the heels, girl! Walk on your toes! Walk like this! Walk on your toes!" Everyone else started calling out advice too. Sushi explained, patiently, "The only time you put weight on your heels is when you stand, to balance. Walk like this." I tried, holding on to the back of the bar stools for support. Gugi started to imitate my wobbly stride and called out, "Stop walking like that! Move your hips! Small steps, girl!" Kylie couldn't believe they had to teach us how to walk in heels. "You don't have any high heels? Not even at home? You wear Doc Martens?!"

Sushi wanted us to perform a number—the lesbian duet from "Rent" that she and Milla performed so erotically—but we begged off. "You teach, don't you?" Sushi demanded, as if teaching and lip-synching while dancing involve the same kind of performance. So we volunteered to go on the street before the show and help them out with whatever they needed—mostly going around with the tip bucket and getting drinks—during the show. We'd spent a lot of time observing them on the street, but it wasn't until we joined them that we really understood the gender and sexual dynamics of their interactions. We had quite different responses that seem to mirror both sides of the experience. Verta felt vulnerable, afraid that men staring at her would come up and touch her, as often happens. People touch the drag queens all the time, in ways that they never would anyone else, and the girls, in turn, grope them. They aren't at all feminine on the street, they are aggressively sexual, which comes off as profoundly masculine in the sense, ironically, that female prostitutes are masculine. So it's not all vulnerability either. In contrast to Verta, I felt powerful disguised as a man dressing as a woman. I felt freed to say and do things I wouldn't ordinarily, to enjoy the freedom of being a man (if in drag) in command on the street, and I enjoyed the in-your-face nature of the performance in front of straight tourists. We both came to experience what we had already noted, that drag queens are neither feminine nor masculine in any conventional sense, that they are, in fact, simply drag-queenish.

If we learned a lot about the fluidity of gender and sexuality, we also learned something about their rigidity in practice in U.S. society. For some of the girls, being effeminate and feeling more comfortable in women's clothes led them to think for a while that they wanted to be women. Both Sushi and Milla lived as women for a time. When Sushi was young, he thought, "Oh my god, I look like such a woman, maybe I am a woman." Then he realized, "I'm a drag queen. . . . That's who I am." Then recently, Sushi told us of watching a television program about transgendered people and realizing, with great pain, "I'm not a drag queen. I'm a closeted transsexual-transgendered person." When we asked the difference, Sushi explained, "A drag queen is someone like Kylie who never has ever thought about cutting her dick off." But Sushi says she will never seek surgery, in part because "I've been a drag queen for so long, and my whole persona—I don't want to try to change my whole personality again into Susie." About her previous revelation that she was a drag queen, Sushi says, "But now I'm realizing that it's not that I realized I was a drag queen; I learned how to become a drag queen."

Gugi, too, has a sense of herself as transgendered in some ways. She likes the femininity in herself and also links her desire to be a woman to her attraction to men. "Out of drag, I feel like I'm acting. In drag, I feel like myself." Like Milla, she took hormones for a time and grew breasts. Both enjoyed having men falling all over them when they went out dressed as women. Milla, however, came to love himself and pull away "from that whole effeminate side . . . and I became a man."

It is in their relationships with men that we can see mostly clearly the ways that gender and sexuality are often experienced as rigid, even for those like the drag queens who transgress the boundaries in some ways. For whether they identify sexually as tops or bottoms (and they call attention in their shows to the fact that lots of drag queens are tops, contrary to what their audiences might think), they are invariably attracted to what they call "masculine" and often presumably straight or at least bisexual men. "I go out to seduce masculine men," Milla says. "I would never be attracted by a drag queen," exclaims Inga, the towering blonde "Swedish bombshell." "I like masculine men," affirms Sushi. "Yeah, exactly," adds Margo.

That leads to a lot of heartache, which prompts them to express in their shows a great deal of hostility to men and masculine domination. Because many masculine gay men are not interested in drag queens. "Why is it that so many guys will not go out with a drag queen?" asks Margo in her newspaper-column-writing persona as David Felstein. Sushi says gay men aren't attracted to drag queens, that she finds "these straight, bisexual boys." The girls see this as a challenge and set out to win over gay men they find attractive. But they often find that straight or presumably straight men are the easiest conquests.

We sometimes found it hard to understand why gender difference was so eroticized for them. More than once we talked about the lesbian feminist ideal and sometimes practice of loving and sleeping with your friends, but the idea of being erotically attracted to someone like them in gender style seemed incomprehensible, despite their intense friendships. Kylie and Sushi, for example, have been best friends since high school and have a deep and abiding friendship. "I think that if I could find someone that I was as close to as Sushi and had that kind of relationship with and be sexually attracted to them, then that would be a really good lover for me," Kylie tells us. Milla and Scabby were also really close, but Scabby made clear the limits. Having seen Milla one day with her newly hairy legs, Scabby commented, "I saw her yesterday, I said, 'You know what, bitch, if I didn't know you so well, I'd fuck you.'" It was a lesson to us in distinctions between love and friendship, and the gendering of desire, that seemed foreign to us as women. All of this made me think differently about historical interpretations of gender differentiation in same-sex attractions and, especially, assumptions that heterosexual men sometimes, in different cultures and contexts, have sex with gay men because they don't care where they insert their penises. Because the drag queens insist (and this is borne out in Don Kulick's work on the Brazilian travesti) that straight men often want not to be the inserter, but rather the encloser (to use a term—although I didn't know it when I first began to use it—proposed in *Our Bodies, Ourselves*) in same-sex encounters.[5]

This tension between the fluidity of gender and sexuality and the rigidity as sometimes experienced in the lives of drag queens made me realize, if I had not before, how complex these deeply felt aspects of our identities can be. I had already been struck, teaching a course on the history of same-sex sexuality in the Western world, how difficult it is to teach undergraduates, especially gay male undergraduates who feel as if they were "born gay," about social constructionist interpretations of sexuality. Ideas about cultural influences on our understandings of same-sex attractions and societal differences in defining categories of sexuality give way to a simpler notion that social construction is about "choice" of one's sexuality or social pressures that cause one to define oneself a particular way. Learning about drag queen sexual and gender identity helped me to understand that it might help to teach concepts of social constructionism through such identities and categories as "drag-queenness."

Returning to the issues with which I began, writing about drag queens has been an eye-opening experience. It was my first encounter with a research project focused on living people. I must admit I sometimes dreaded the consequences, no more so than when Sushi's mother, who had moved to Key West after the book appeared, lambasted Verta and me and cried for hours because we had shamed her family by writing honestly about Sushi's experiences as a prostitute on the streets of L.A. It was interdisciplinary because I brought my historical perspective and mode of analysis to what was fundamentally a sociological ethnography, Verta's area of expertise. Our central arguments engage with gender theory, sexuality studies/queer theory, and social movement theory (the latter because of the long tradition of drag in the lesbian, gay, bisexual, and transgendered movement). Thus this was an interdisciplinary project in the tradition of women's studies, despite its focus on men. It is perhaps unnecessary to note that a number of the major theorists in women's studies focus on men, following the notion of gender as relational, something that I am sure helped us to win financial support from the Department of Women's Studies at Ohio State. This was also a project profoundly shaped by the women's and gay/lesbian movements.

Studying men, or at least drag queens, has, ironically, made me realize how much my real intellectual home is women's studies. This is not a book about history or women's history, but it does fit perfectly with my renewed commitment to teaching and scholarship in women's studies. For the expansion of women's studies, the centrality of intersectionality, the incorporation of queer theory, have all made the interdisciplinary discipline seem a welcoming place. One review called us, as lesbian academics studying drag queens, "strangers in a strange land," but in fact I feel in some fundamental way that I have come home.[6]

Notes

1. My dissertation was published as *Mobilizing Women for War: German and American Propaganda, 1939–1945* (Princeton: Princeton University Press, 1978).
2. Adrienne Rich, *Of Woman Born: Motherhood as Experience and Institution* (New York: W.W. Norton, 1976); Judith Butler, *Gender Trouble: Feminism and the Subversion of Identity* (New York: Routledge, 1990).
3. *A Desired Past: A Short History of Same-Sex Love in America* (Chicago: University of Chicago Press, 1999); *Drag Queens at the 801 Cabaret* (Chicago: University of Chicago Press, 2003).
4. Elizabeth Lapovsky Kennedy and Madeline Davis, *Boots of Leather, Slippers of Gold: The History of a Lesbian Community* (New York: Routledge, 1993); Joan Nestle, "Butch-Fem Relationships: Sexual courage in the 1950s," *Heresies* 3, no. 4 (1981): 21–24; Judith Halberstam, *Female Masculinity* (Durham, N.C.: Duke University Press, 1998); Don Kulick, *Travesti: Sex, Gender and Culture among Brazilian Transgendered Prostitutes* (Chicago: University of Chicago Press, 1998).
5. Boston Women's Health Book Collective, *Our Bodies, Ourselves* (New York: Simon and Schuster, 1984), 178. I am grateful to Estelle Freedman for pointing out this usage; see her *No Turning Back: The History of Feminism and the Future of Women* (New York: Ballantine Books, 2002).
6. Syndicated review by Richard Labonte, 2003.

Suggestions for Further Reading

Bloom, Amy. *Normal: Transsexual CEOs, Crossdressing Cops, and Hermaphrodites with Attitude*. New York: Random House, 2002.

Brevard, Aleshia. *The Woman I Was Not Born to Be: A Transsexual Journey*. Philadelphia: Temple University Press, 2001.

Brubach, Holly, and Michael James O'Brien. *Girlfriend: Men, Women, and Drag*. New York: Random House, 1999.

Garber, Marjorie. *Vested Interests: Cross-Dressing and Cultural Anxiety*. New York: Routledge, 1992.

Halberstam, Judith. *Female Masculinity*. Durham, N.C.: Duke University Press, 1998.

Meyerowitz, Joanne. *How Sex Changed: A History of Transsexuality in the U.S.* Cambridge: Harvard University Press, 2002.

Newton, Esther. *Mother Camp: Female Impersonators in America*. Chicago: University of Chicago Press, 1972.

Paulson, Don, with Roger Simpson. *An Evening at the Garden of Allah: A Gay Cabaret in Seattle*. New York: Columbia University Press, 1996.

Rupp, Leila J., and Verta Taylor. *Drag Queens at the 801 Cabaret*. Chicago: University of Chicago Press, 2003.

Schacht, Steven P., with Lisa Underwood, eds. *The Drag Queen Anthology: The Absolutely Fabulous but Flawlessly Customary World of Female Impersonators*. Binghamton, NY: Haworth Press, 2004.

Senelick, Laurence. *The Changing Room: Sex, Drag and Theatre*. New York: Routledge, 2000.

Anthropology, Gender, and Narrative

Caroline B. Brettell

Caroline B. Brettell (1974) is Dedman Family Distinguished Professor and Chair of the Department of Anthropology at Southern Methodist University. Her research interests are in the areas of immigration, feminist anthropology, and U.S. and European culture and society. Among her publications are *Anthropology and Migration: Essays on Transnationalism, Ethnicity and Identity* (2003); *Writing against the Wind: A Mother's Life History* (1999); *We Have Already Cried Many Tears: The Stories of Three Portuguese Migrant Women* (1982/1995); and *Men Who Migrate, Women Who Wait: Population and History in a Portuguese Parish* (1986). She is also coeditor of *Gender in Cross-Cultural Perspective*, 4th edition (2004), *Migration Theory: Talking Across Disciplines* (2000), *Gender and Health* (1996), *and International Migration: The Female Experience* (1986), and editor of *When They Read What We Write: The Politics of Ethnography* (1993).

> *When Caroline Brettell began her graduate studies, the critical questions in women's studies and anthropology concerned the nature of patriarchy and its universality and the patterns of equality and inequality between men and women. "We were concerned with issues of power and with the difference between the private sphere and the public sphere and the power and authority accorded to men and women in each. Many of these questions have been tackled and answered in a sophisticated fashion. The acknowledgment of the social construction of gender has become universal in academic research but perhaps more so by women scholars than by male scholars. Within anthropology there remains an ongoing tension between scientific and humanistic approaches to knowledge and between biological models and cultural models."*

In 1974, the anthropologists Michelle Rosaldo and Louise Lamphere published a book titled *Woman, Culture, and Society*. Although inspired by Margaret Mead's book *Male and Female* and Simone de Beauvoir's *The Second Sex*, this book broke new ground in its effort to bring consideration of the position and roles of women in society to a central place within the discipline and, ultimately, to set an agenda for a new field of feminist anthropology that studies how gender is socially, culturally, and historically constructed.[1] Two important essays in that volume, one by Rosaldo and another by Sherry Ortner, laid out a set of issues that shaped theoretical debates for several years and became the springboard for new perspectives and approaches.[2] These essays posed the broad question of whether or not sexual asymmetry was universal and, by extension, where in the cross-cultural record one might find relative equality in gender relations. These were appropriate questions for anthropology, a discipline that attempts to explain cultural variation over time and across space, as well as human universals broadly conceived.

Beginning with a discussion of the essays in *Woman, Culture, and Society*, I review here the development of key theoretical debates in feminist anthropology since 1974 using specific ethnographic monographs to illustrate key questions and concerns. I then focus on the role that feminist anthropology has played in the renewed interest in narrative and life history in anthropology and discuss my own work in this area. I have been particularly interested in the relationship between gender and migration and hence I spend some time addressing how narratives that emphasize voice and agency have expanded our understanding of the experience of immigrant women in particular. In the final section of this chapter, I adopt a broader women's studies perspective. I examine the relationship between fiction and ethnography and briefly explore the literature of migration.

TOWARD A FEMINIST ANTHROPOLOGY
AND FEMINIST ETHNOGRAPHY

Michelle Rosaldo's opening essay in *Woman, Culture, and Society* began with the assumption that sexual asymmetry is widespread. Rosaldo argued that this was because women are relegated to the domestic sphere and that this sphere and the activities associated with it are universally devalued by comparison with the public sphere, the domain where the political, economic, and religious activities of men take place. Sherry Ortner's essay made a similar assumption about universal male dominance but, drawing on the work of the French anthropologist Claude Levi-Strauss, explained it in relation to the universal symbolic equation of males with culture and females with nature. Things cultural are superior to things natural and hence, by analogy, men and the things that men do are more highly valued than women and the things that women do, including reproduction.[3]

Fairly quickly the claims to universality and to the "singular narrative of subordination" formulated in these two essays were challenged. For example, several of the essays in Carol MacCormack and Marilyn Strathern's edited volume *Nature, Culture and Gender* suggested that the nature-culture dichotomy emerged from categories that are characteristic of Western societies, but not necessarily of non-Western peoples. Further, one of the editors argued that "the ethnographic literature does not justify the extreme position of defining women but not men as mediators between nature and culture, nor does it uniformly equate women's attributes exclusively with those of nature."[4] A number of the essays in the volume also substantiated this claim.

A second counterargument suggested that while there is little evidence for the existence of a truly matriarchal society at any time and in any place, societies exist that have achieved some semblance of gender equality or complementarity in the roles of men and women. This position was presented most powerfully by those studying pre-contact Native American societies, by those studying other hunting and gathering societies, and even by some anthropologists studying peasant societies.[5] Indeed, ethnographers suggested that in some cultures women hold a great deal of power in relation to men.

> In both academic and non-academic discourse, parts of Galician Spain and northern Portugal have been constructed as territories in which women are relatively autonomous and hold unusual positions of dominance over men in both their own households and to some extent in the "public" space of their neighborhoods and local communities.[6]

Finally, Michelle Rosaldo herself, in a thoughtful essay written in 1980, conceded that the dichotomy between the domestic and the public might not be universal and that the rigid division between the two domains owes much to nineteenth-century social theory:

> The turn-of-the century social theorists whose writings are the basis of most modern social thinking tended without exception to assume that women's place was in the home. In fact, the Victorian doctrine of separate male and female spheres was, I would suggest, quite central to their sociology. Some of these thinkers recognized that modern women suffered from their association with domestic life, but none questioned the pervasiveness (or necessity) of a split between the family and society.[7]

Rosaldo concluded this essay by suggesting that in specific cultural contexts the distinction between domestic and public spheres might indeed be significant to female subordination and to the construction of gender. It was just not necessarily universal. Indeed more recently Henrietta Moore has suggested that the domestic/public model "has been and remains a very powerful one in social anthropology because it provides a way of linking the cultural valuations given to the category 'woman' to the organization of women's activities in society."[8]

The theoretical debates generated by *Woman, Culture and Society* were accompanied by the publication of a host of monographs, based on detailed ethnographic research, that incorporated previously muted women's voices and hence offered more nuanced understandings of the status and roles of women in various societies around the world. Let me briefly mention three such works, one representing a hunting and gathering society, the second a horticultural society, and the third a farming society.

Diane Bell's study of Australian aboriginal women reported in her book *Daughters of the Dreaming* offers a revision to prior representations of women in this culture who had been described by earlier anthropologists as pawns in a game of kinship, marriage, and ritual managed and controlled by men:

> Within Australia the tendency has been for male fieldworkers to study male institutions and subsequently to offer analyses which purport to examine the totality of Aboriginal society. Evaluation of female institutions has been based too often on

male informants' opinions, refracted through the eyes of male ethnographers and explained by means of the concepts of a male-oriented anthropology. Thus statements concerning the role and status of women are formulated within the context of a male ideology, which means they can only rarely be reconciled with the behavioral patterns of Aboriginal women in desert society.[9]

Bell clearly demonstrates how Australian aboriginal women are "social actors in their own right" who have clear structural importance in their society and control of an extremely important body of ritual knowledge that gives them a good deal of power in relation to men. She suggests that this understanding of women only emerges when women are allowed to speak for themselves. In Bell's view, it is the settlement lifestyle and contact with the wider society of Northern Australia that has served to undermine women's power:

> In Northern Australia the incoming whites have brought new ideas and resources. These have been differently exploited by Aboriginal men and women. Women were disadvantaged from the outset because of the white male perception of them as domestic workers and sex objects. Aboriginal men have been able to take real political advantage of certain aspects of frontier society, while Aboriginal women have been seen by whites as peripheral to the political process.[10]

Bell's work reflects the growing trend in feminist anthropology to explore the agency of women as well as to explore how women's lives have been impacted by culture contact. She concludes her monograph by describing three different frameworks that have been applied, over time, to the analysis of Australian aboriginal society. The first she labels the "Man Equals Culture" framework. This framework casts women "as the profane, the 'other,' the devalued, the wild, the feared and the excluded, the substance of symbols but never the makers of their own social reality, the exploited and dominated but never the decision-making adults." The second she labels the "Anthropology of Women" framework that attended to the roles of women, suggesting that "women have rights, opinions and values that are not exactly coincidental with those of the men." This was a complementary model that added rich ethnographic data to the pot. Finally, the "Toward a Feminist Perspective" framework went beyond the "just add women and stir" approach to wrestle critically with why gender hierarchies exist and why cultural ideologies about sexually asymmetry persist. Interestingly, the trajectory that Bell describes for the ethnography of the Australian aborigines is one that has often been described for the field of Women's Studies more broadly as it grew to maturity.[11]

In *Fruit of the Motherland*, Maria Lepowsky's reports on her research in an island society in New Guinea characterized by matrilineal descent and an absence of an ideology of male dominance that has been described as pervasive in so many other societies in Melanesia. Lepowsky argues that

> males and females on Vanatinai have equivalent autonomy at each life cycle stage. As adults they have similar opportunities to influence the actions of others. There is a large amount of overlap between the roles and activities of women and men, with women occupying public, prestige-generating roles. Women share control of the production and the distribution of value goods, and they inherit property . . .

Women's role as nurturing parent is highly valued and is the dominant metaphor for the generous men and women who gain renown and influence over others by accumulating and then giving away valuable goods.[12]

Women's power in Vanatinai derives not only from their control of land and other economic resources but also from the symbolic capital that they acquire through their participation in exchange and in mortuary ritual. By contrast with much of the rest of Melanesia, there are no men's houses, male initiation rituals, or other male cult activities on Vanatinai. There are both "big men" and "big women" (*gia*).[13]

On Vanatinai the title of gia is awarded to any woman or man who is, as the islanders say, "strong, wise, and generous" enough to build a reputation through traditional exchange and acquisition of supernatural knowledge. The institution of the giagia, in a society with no chiefs, is part of an autonomous cultural tradition that is inherently democratic. It provides an avenue to prestige, renown, and influence over others to any adult of either sex and from any kin group, who desires to exceed the minimum demands of custom for participation in exchange and mortuary ritual.[14]

One arena of difference between men and women is in the practice of witchcraft and sorcery. Sorcery is almost entirely the province of males and men are generally symbolically associated with death and war while women are associated with healing and life-giving. Knowledge of sorcery, according to Lepowsky, gives men a certain political ascendancy over other men and women. However, women do practice witchcraft and ultimately Lepowsky concludes that the waters are murky and "that there is no overall division of positive and negative supernatural powers into male and female domains."[15]

Evelyn Blackwood has also studied a matrilineal society, the Minangkabau of Sumatra. While matriliny "empowers women as controllers of land and houses" it also creates a "dissonance with the masculinist discourses of the state, Islam, and capitalism."[16] Blackwood's book is about how women negotiate their identities in relation to the forces of economic, political, and social change as well as the hegemonic forces of a state that defines men as household heads. It is also an effort to dislodge previous "narratives of Minangkabau gender and power [that have fallen] prey to the Western binary terms of domestic/public and official/practical, leaving the definition of power uncontested." Blackwood describes the various ways in which Minangkabau women sustain their position as heads of household, heirs to land, key players in the network of kin relations, and hence, as powerful local actors who control the labor of sons, daughters, and husbands. She further demonstrates how elite women control the meanings of ceremonial practices to preserve their position of dominance. Blackwood recognizes that ritual events are key sites of power and in the case of the Minagkabau, women have important roles to play that help them maintain the status and reputation of their families.

Much of Minangkabau women's power in this group is sustained by *adat*, local custom. Blackwood argues that "while men's authority at the village level is substantiated by the state, within clan deliberations *adat*-inscribed notions of authority underwrite women's authority as senior women."[17] Even daughters who are moving away from the matrihouses controlled by their mothers toward a nuclear family system of households still work to sustain the matrilineal practices that give them clear advantage within both their kin groups and their communities.

The works of Blackwood and Lepowsky ask us to think more carefully about what we mean by gender equality and to be more precise in our definitions of concepts such as status and power. Status refers to a person's position in society and it can be shaped by ideology. Hence, no matter how much control over economic resources women may have, their status may be undermined in a society that accords more value to what men do. However, equally, there may be competing ideologies and it is the task of the anthropologist to determine what those may be as well as their significance for gender relations. Power refers to the ability to make other people do what you want them to do in order to achieve your own ends. In this context, anthropologists have demonstrated that often women have more informal than formal power, but that this power is quite effective in shaping the activities of the group and the nature of social relations. Blackwood adopts an approach that looks at how power is expressed in the creation and negotiation of social identities. "From the angle of social identities, power operates in a number of ways: in the ability 1) to name someone or the services they may or must provide, or the material resources they can or cannot claim; 2) to determine how human energy will be spent, for whose benefit and return; 3) to make decisions on behalf of a group; 4) to define a need and what would satisfy it; 5) to define issues as nonissues; 6) or to define one's rights (or the rights of all others in the same category) as fore-ordained or normative." It should also be noted that some anthropologists have cautioned us against a purely coercive understanding of power, suggesting that this too is a Western fixation.[18]

Blackwood's monograph also introduces a range of other questions that have occupied the attention of feminist anthropology in more recent years—the impact of postcolonialism and the global economy on gender roles, as well as forms of women's resistance. In the case of the Minangkabau, Blackwood argues that transformations in the agrarian structure have resulted in "an increasing complexity of peasant relations—without, however, undermining women's control of land. . . . As rural farmers, women act as manipulators as well as resistors of changing production relations. Some wealthy elite women have taken advantage of wage labor to increase their profits, while poorer client and elite women have used collective labor as a tool to assure reliable work and income and increase wages."[19] In the cross-cultural literature this is not always the outcome—indeed many studies have demonstrated the erosion of women's power and status in the face of agrarian transformation or the increasing incursion of the global economy.

While many anthropologists have strived to present a more nuanced understanding of women's status and roles in various societies around the world and to explore the impact of the broad forces of global transformation on their lives, others have taken the analytical frameworks emerging from feminist anthropology and used them to explore more fully men's roles and the meaning of masculinity. As Matthew Gutmann has observed, "anthropology has always involved men talking to men about men. Until recently, however, very few within the discipline of the 'study of man' had truly examined men *as men*. . . . It is the new examinations of men as engendered and engendering subjects that comprise the anthropology of masculinity today."[20]

Anthropologists such as David Gilmore, Stanley Brandes, and Gilbert Herdt have addressed the question of how men are "made" in various cultures. Gilmore has also written about the "male malady of misogyny," a set of beliefs that he argues is widespread in space and across time with its origins deep in the male psyche. Other anthropologists have studied male fatherhood in hunting and gathering societies and closer to home. In his study of a group of white middle-class men in California, Nicholas Townsend shows how masculine gender ideology in America "excludes and oppresses many men," not only those whose particular circumstances make it impossible for them to live up to the ideal, but also those who feel trapped in the struggle to attain what Townsend labels "the package deal"—having children, being married, holding a steady job, and owning a home."[21]

A second ethnography that explores masculinity in a specific cultural context is Matthew Gutmann's study of machismo in Mexico. Like Townsend's, his method is to allow the men to talk about themselves and their roles as husbands and parents. In so doing, we, as readers of his ethnography, come to understand much more profoundly what it means to be a man in Mexican culture and society. Gutmann argues quite convincingly that machismo is not a homogenous category, but rather one filled with ambiguity and contradiction. "Nationalism . . . class, ethnicity, generation, and other factors deeply brand Mexican male identities. Mexican machos are not dead any more than are their North American or Russian counterparts, but claims about a uniform character of Mexican masculinity, a ubiquitous macho mexicano, should be put to rest."[22]

Gutmann's emphasis on the heterogenous meanings of masculinity in Mexico incorporates the concept of social location—that is, that people see the world and speak from a particular position defined by class or race or ethnicity as well as by gender. Thus, the predominant question has become how gender, *together with race/ethnicity and class*, shapes identity and creates difference. Henrietta Moore has noted that this "passion for difference" and the emphasis on location or positionality are important developments in feminist anthropological writing. Inspired by post-structuralist theories of the subject, Moore calls for greater focus on the individual and on various discourses that are generated by different individual subject positions.[23]

Post-structuralist theory, the new interest in discourse, and subaltern critiques that emphasize the perspective and voice of the insider have turned feminist anthropologists toward more reflexive and experimental modes of writing. They have asked themselves if there can even be a feminist ethnography given the inherently hierarchical relationship between fieldworker and subject. Thus Margery Wolf writes in *A Thrice Told Tale*,

> As third-world feminists have found their own voices, feminist anthropologists internationally have become painfully aware of the remnants of a colonial mind-set

in their research. We have begun to search for a way to do ethnographic research that not only will not exploit other women but will have positive effects on their lives. Feminist anthropologists are struggling with ways of transforming the objects of research into subjects.[24]

It is this concern with accountability to the subject that has generated a new interest in narrative among feminist anthropologists as well as the call for what Lila Abu-Lughod has labeled "ethnographies of the particular" within the discipline of anthropology more broadly. Ethnographies of the particular eschew generalization both within and across cultures. In feminist ethnography they accord women even greater voice and recover their agency.[25]

LIFE HISTORY, LIFE STORIES, AND NARRATIVES

Narratives have always been part of the theoretical and methodological tool kit of anthropology. One of the oldest forms was the life history, a method used to record, if not really recapture, the cultures of Native American populations that were being threatened by westward expansion in the continental United States. The emphasis in these works was on how the life of a single individual reflected a culture or a social group. The aim, in Paul Radin's words was "not to obtain autobiographical details about some definite personage, but to have some representative middle-aged individual of moderate ability describe his life in relation to the social group in which he had grown up."[26] It was a form of salvage ethnography aided by individual memory. But as the use of life history developed, it became a method by which to exemplify. The underlying assumption was that "the life story of an individual who was somehow representative of his or her culture—a story in that individual's own words—would be illustrative of the way in which a typical member of that group passed through the life cycle, for some attention to the distinctive features of the life cycle within particular cultures has often been the aim of ethnography."[27]

Kamala Visweswaran points out that some of the earliest anthropological works with women as their main subject used the mediums of life history and autobiography. She cites Ruth Landes's *Ojibwa Woman* and Ruth Underhill's *Papago Woman* as prime examples, noting that these authors attempted to emphasize both the uniqueness and the typicality of their subjects. Visweswaran goes on to discuss how autobiography, biography, and life history were often conflated in these works "to erase the narratorial presence of the white woman anthropologist, while her authorship was paradoxically underscored. Some saw themselves as neither editors nor elicitors of the life stories gathered; others were more cognizant of their role in shaping the narrative."[28]

Scorned for its lack of scientific rigor, the life history went into decline after World War II, particularly as a period of new empiricism emerged in the discipline of anthropology. But more recently, the life history and the life story, together with what Ruth Behar labels "hybrid genres" such as self-ethnography and ethnobiography, have been reinvented, largely by feminist anthropologists searching for another voice that captures the complexity of the I's and

We's engaged in cross-cultural interchange. As mentioned above, feminist anthropologists are equally searching for a method of representation that allows other women to be "the subjects of their gaze without objectifying them and thus ultimately betraying them."[29] The results are a range of books that, curiously, have had enormous success precisely because they do tell a story—Marjorie Shostak's *Nisa: The Life and Words of a !Kung Woman*, Ruth Behar's *Translated Woman: Crossing the Border with Esperanza's Story*, Sharon Gmelch's *Nan: The Life of an Irish Travelling Woman*, Karen McCarthy Brown's *Mama Lola* and Margaret Blackman's *During My Time: Florence Edenshaw Davidson, a Haida Woman*, to list but a few.[30] These books are quite different from one another: in the way the anthropologist—Marjorie, Ruth, Sharon, Karen, or Margaret—chooses to situate (or not situate) herself in the work; and in the decisions that are made about where to discuss, if at all, the meaning of the elements of the story that is being told by the ethnographic subject—Nisa, Esperanza, Nan, Lola, or Florence. Two further examples illustrate these varying approaches to the role of the feminist anthropologist as interlocutor.

In her book *Women of Belize*, Irma McClaurin explores the diverse strategies used by individual women "to achieve personal, community and institutional change."[31] Although she interviewed more than fifty women, her book is structured around the narratives of three of these women—Rose (a Garifuna), Zola (an East Indian), and Evelyn (a Creole). While the voices of these three women are central to the ethnography, McClaurin intervenes in their narratives to reveal the commonalities in their lives despite their different social locations and personal circumstances. Indeed McClaurin suggests that collectively these narratives

> provide personal insights into important aspects of Belize's culture of gender, which include, but are not limited to, the cultural view of women as minors and property; the reasons for the economic-sexual dynamics that underlie many heterosexual relationships in Belize; the degree to which the physical and mental abuse of women by men reveals strategies to elicit the former's compliance; the process of gender enculturation for women; and the role of women's groups in changing attitudes and behaviors in various communities.[32]

McClaurin moves back and forth between the "ethnography of the particular" and the broader historical and cultural processes that shape these individual lives and the lives of women of Belize in general.

Lila Abu Lughod's *Writing Women's Worlds*, by contrast, focuses not on a single individual, or on three individuals, but on several related Bedouin women. It self-consciously moves away from the life history format to one of broader and interconnected story-telling. Abu Lughod restricts her own voice to the preface and introduction where she tells us that her book is a critique of ethnographic typification and generalization. In the remainder of *Writing Women's Worlds*, the Bedouin women themselves speak with authorial voice about how they live and experience the institutions of patrilineality, polygyny, reproduction, patrilateral parallel cousin marriage, and honor and shame that have been described as characteristic of the Middle East. What these stories demonstrate is that while the Awlad Ali Bedouin are patrilineal, with tribal affiliation, descent, and inheritance reckoned through the male line, patrilineality "does not foreclose women's opportunities or desires to shape their own lives or those of their sons and daughters, or to oppose the decisions of their fathers."[33] Unlike McClaurin, Abu Lughod offers no conclusion and no comment on the culture of Bedouin gender roles:

> Such a concluding commentary, pronouncing the lessons of all these rich and complex stories, would have restored the superiority of the interpretive/analytical mode being questioned by the very construction of narratives, would have reestablished the familiar authority of the expert's voice, and, most troubling, would inevitably have contained the stories. That I selected and organized them according to the themes designated by the chapter headings seemed limiting enough to their meaning.[34]

In short, Abu-Lughod resists the homogenizing tendency that McClaurin accepts. This is indeed a book that manifests a passion for difference.

My own forays into life history and narrative, in my books *Writing Against the Wind* and *We Have Already Cried Many Tears*, find a path between these two approaches.[35] *Writing Against the Wind*, the more recent work, is the life story of my mother and her career as a journalist in Canada. As a book by a daughter about a mother who was a writer, the text involves a blending of voices and, by extension, a blurring of narrative genres. It is both biography and autobiography, not only because it weaves my words with those of my mother, but also because the lives of a mother and a daughter are inextricably intertwined. Although I draw a good deal on my own memories and those of others who knew my mother, much of what I know about her comes from the written words and images that she left behind in the form of an adolescent diary, a travel memoir, a college scrapbook, letters, photographs, and her professional oeuvre. Thus, the words in this text are my words about my mother's words; but they are also her words chosen by me because they help to compose her life. They are, furthermore, her words about herself, as well as her words about the world she lived in and particularly about the worlds of women that she observed and commented upon throughout a career spanning from 1942 to the early 1980s. She often used her own experiences as a prism through which to view the lives of those she incorporated into her journalism.

Periodically, I situate myself in this text. Indeed each chapter opens with a personal memory included in a prologue that provides a context or emphasizes a more general point about what follows in the life narrative. When set into a broader social and historical framework, my mother's life is indeed illustrative of women who were ahead of their time, who juggled a career and family before anyone ever thought about superwomen, the glass ceiling, or the second shift. In her role as editor of the Women's Pages of *The Montreal Star*, she nurtured younger women who were following in her footsteps well before the word mentoring became a recognized strategy by which women could help other women to succeed in a man's world. I was not afraid to generalize from the particular for that was indeed what she did as she wrote women's worlds in her newspaper articles.

We Have Already Cried Many Tears also uses the narrative format to engage the relationship between the general and the particular. It presents the stories of Ana, Ricardina, and Virginia, three women whom I interviewed as part of a larger and more traditional ethnographic study of Portuguese migrant women in France. When I wrote this book, my goal was to show the diversity of lived experiences of Portuguese migrant women through the lives of three individuals, each of whom represented a different pattern of migration. Ricardina was a young single woman at the time of her departure for France. Ana followed a husband abroad, leaving her two children in Portugal in the care of their maternal grandmother. Virginia, unmarried mother to a teenage boy who had been born in the mid-1950s, left for France with a married sister who was joining her husband. Before her departure she had been working as a domestic servant in Lisbon. These three women also came from different social and economic backgrounds—Ricardina from a small village in the central interior of Portugal; Ana from the city of Porto and hence, a working-class background; Virginia from a village not far from the Atlantic coast that for centuries had been affected by emigration. They each had different reasons for choosing to emigrate, but all were shaped by the gendered contexts of their lives within Portuguese culture and society.

At the time that I published *We Have Already Cried Many Tears*, I acknowledged my editorial hand in organizing their stories into chronological order. I edited out redundancies and created a balance between the three accounts that would permit systematic analysis as a unit as well as separately. However, I also tried to maintain the impression of their spoken language, using their phrases and adages, and the short expressive sentences that are so much a part of conversational autobiography. Rather than insert myself into their texts, I limited my comments to the introductions to each of the narrative chapters where I noted matters of more general ethnographic significance that could be learned from each of their lives. In the general introduction to the book, I addressed the broader historical context of Portuguese emigration as well as legal, religious, and structural constraints on the status and roles of women in Portuguese society during the Salazar period between 1930 and 1974. While some contemporary proponents of a life history or narrative method would consider the editorial authority that I used in this volume too intrusive, I remain comfortable with it because it suits the purpose for which the narratives were collected and written. I mediated the words of Ana, Ricardina, and Virginia in order to illustrate the similarities and differences in how women experience migration.

The narrative or life history genre, although not widely used, is clearly well suited to the study of migration because much of the storytelling is necessarily retrospective, an account of decisions and events in the past that explain the present. Nicole Constable uses this genre quite successfully to write about Filipina workers in Hong Kong, as do George Gmelch and Mary Chamberlain to write about people from the Caribbean who have migrated to Britain and sometimes returned. Indeed, Gmelch suggests that drawing on life narratives helps to "get beneath the abstractions of migration theory and to understand migration from the insiders perspective." And Chamberlain observes that it is family stories and memories that reveal the complexity, ambiguity, and cultural specificity of motives for migration. Indeed, in an extremely insightful chapter of her book, Chamberlain reveals the gendered discourse of migration narratives. Her male subjects emphasized impulse and autonomy, casualness, and transience. Their migration narratives exonerate failure and highlight success. Her female subjects, by contrast, while often as autonomous as the men, emphasize family context and calculation rather than adventure and heroism:

> They did not stress casualness as a hedge against disappointment, or monitor their progress as a metaphor of achievement. Nor did women always have a clear model of return which would have lessened the pain of departure, however much they anticipated return. What they stressed in the style and content of their accounts was the enormity of the move, an implicit acknowledgement that migration contained the potential for permanent absence, stressing within this the emotional wrench of leaving children, the compulsion to be reunited with them.[36]

The gendered aspect of the migration narrative is also quite apparent in Dianne Walta Hart's record of the life of Yamileth Lopez, an undocumented Latina from Nicaragua who arrived in Los Angeles in January of 1989.[37] On the surface Yamileth's migration was economically motivated—to make money and return to a better life in her own country—and shaped by the political context of her home country. But Yamileth also says that she left because she wanted to escape "el qué dirán" (what people would say about her sexual choices). One of the women in my own study, *We Have Already Cried Many Tears*, told a similar story. As a young woman she had migrated to the local provincial town to work as a domestic. People in her village began to gossip about her, saying that she had lost her virginity while she was away. Although the gossip had no foundation, it became too much for her to bear and she decided to leave for France. Yamileth gave Hart one additional reason for her departure. She had been involved in the Sandinista movement, but the male leadership empowered women in words but not in actions. These are all significant statements about the way in which gender ideology and patriarchal oppression figure into the decisions that women make with respect to migration. They are often omitted from broader theoretical discussions of the causes of migration, but they emerge quite clearly in individual narratives. Narratives lend agency to migrant women but also demonstrate how their lives are constrained by the structures of local labor markets, by the structures of immigration policy in both sending and receiving societies and by gender ideologies both at home and abroad.

NARRATIVE, ETHNOGRAPHY, AND THE FICTION OF MIGRATION

In an essay on feminist ethnography, Kamala Visweswaran points out that at the same time that anthropologists of the 1930s and 1940s were experimenting with the genre of life history they were also experimenting with fiction. She cites Gladys Reichard's *Dezba: Woman of the Desert* (1939) as an early example. Both Margaret Mead and Phyllis Kaberry, Visweswaran observes, likened the anthropological narrative to works of fiction and the anthropologist's eye to the novelist's eye. "Ethnographies of women," she concludes, "reveal considerable forethought and reflexivity about the conditions of textual production, often deliberately using 'fiction' as a strategic narrative device to relay a 'woman's point of view'."[38]

The relationship between fiction and ethnography is one that has captured the attention of feminist anthropologists in recent years although they are by no means of uniform mind about how distinct or different the two genres are. Henrietta Moore, for example, explores anthropological novels that address questions similar to those that concern anthropologists, and argues that the popular and the fictive "provide the imaginative impetus for the academic models and discourses of feminism and anthropology." Visweswaran argues that "if we agree that one of the traditional ways of thinking about fiction is that it builds a believable world, but one that the reader rejects as factual, then we can say of ethnography that it, too, sets out to build a believable world, but one that the reader will accept as factual." But, she continues, "even this distinction breaks down if we consider that ethnography, like fiction, constructs existing or possible worlds, all the while retaining the idea of an alternate 'made' world. Ethnography, like fiction, no matter its pretense to present a self contained narrative or cultural whole, remains incomplete and detached from the realms to which it points."[39]

Margery Wolf takes a different tack from Visweswaran and Moore in *A Thrice Told Tale*.[40] Wolf juxtaposes three different accounts, one raw field notes, a second an academic article, and the third a fictional short story ("The Hot Spell"), of the same incident that occurred in the 1960s in the village in Taiwan where she and her husband Arthur Wolf were conducting their field research. Wolf recognizes that there are different goals in these various genres of writing, and she ends up arguing that one is certainly not a substitute for the other and that a fictional story, while evocative, is no substitute for the analysis and understanding that emerges from a careful ethnographic account.

While I tend to agree with Wolf that there are differences between works of fiction and works of ethnography, I have nevertheless been stimulated sufficiently by the interdisciplinary enterprise of women's studies to find inspiration in novels written by first-generation immigrant women. Of particular interest to me is how the voice and agency of immigrant women have been represented and portrayed in these novels and, in some cases, how the authors veil autobiography in fiction to create works of ethnographic realism that address important questions about the immigrant experience, about identity, assimilation, discrimination, and gender and generational relations. Let me briefly mention two examples.

Cristina García's novel *Dreaming in Cuban* tells the story of three generations of Cuban women in a transnational family: a grandmother, Celia, who remains in Cuba, loyal to the revolution and to Castro; a daughter, Lourdes, a small entrepreneur who owns the "Yankee Doodle Bakery" in Brooklyn; another daughter, Felicia, who has remained behind in Cuba and is unhappy in her life; and a granddaughter (Lourdes's daughter), Pilar, an artist searching for her roots and dreaming of returning to Cuba. At the opening of the novel, which moves back and forth in both space and time, Lourdes has owned the bakery for five years, having bought it from a French-Austrian Jew who migrated to Brooklyn after the war. Just as the name of her bakery is patriotic, so too are the pastries and the decor, including custom-made signs in red, white, and blue with her name printed at the bottom right-hand corner. Lourdes's dreaming is the American Dream:

> She envisioned a chain of Yankee Doodle bakeries stretching across America to St. Louis, Dallas, Los Angeles, her apple pies and cupcakes on main streets and in suburban shopping malls everywhere.

Garcia contrasts Lourdes's adaptability with that of her husband Rufino, thereby addressing differences that have sometimes been noted by social scientists writing about gender and migration:

> It became clear to Lourdes shortly after she and Rufino moved to New York that he would never adapt. Something came unhinged in his brain that would make him incapable of working in a conventional way. There was a part of him that could never leave the *finca* or the comfort of its cycles, and this diminished him for any other life. He couldn't be transplanted. So Lourdes got a job. Cuban women of a certain age and a certain class consider working outside the home to be beneath them. But Lourdes never believed that.

Lourdes has been redefined by immigration and is grateful for it. "Unlike her husband, she welcomes her adopted language, its possibilities for reinvention."[41]

If Lourdes is a fictional character who represents the immigrant women who have come to the United States and become moderately successful as small entrepreneurs, América Gonzalez, the central character in Esmeralda Santiago's novel *América's Dream*, tells the more common story of an immigrant woman who becomes a live-in domestic. América leaves Puerto Rico to escape an abusive boyfriend, settling into the Westchester County home of a couple whom she met while they were vacationing at the hotel where she worked in Puerto Rico. She quickly learns the routine of an American family, and masters all the machines that are used to run a household:

> There are three machines for getting a cup of coffee. One to grind the beans, and depending on whether she wants cappuccino or regular coffee, two to make it. There are machines for baking bread, making pasta, steaming rice, pressing and browning sandwiches, chopping vegetables, juicing fruit, slicing potatoes. There are two regular ovens, plus a toaster oven and a microwave, an enormous refrigerator in the kitchen, a smaller one in the sports den, a freezer. There are machines for washing and drying dishes and clothes. Machines for sweeping rugs, waxing floors, vacuuming furniture. Machines for brushing teeth, curling hair, shaving legs, rowing, walking, climbing stairs.[42]

A similar scene is captured in the film *El Norte*, a film about a Guatemalan brother and sister who migrate illegally to Los Angeles, and both offer an immigrant woman's view of the superficial yet telling differences between the United States and other places. Rarely is it more sharply portrayed.

América recognizes that her situation is different from other live-in maids whom she meets because, as a Puerto Rican national, she has citizenship. She meets immigrant women from other countries who are all in the United States illegally and who must work as maids—Liana from El Salvador who is a bank teller; Frida from Paraguay who is a schoolteacher; Mercedes from the Dominican Republic who is a telephone operator. None of them can understand why she would take a maid's job when, as a citizen, she could do something else. These conversations lead América to wonder why her dreams and ambitions are not as big as theirs. In the parks, these women exchange stories about their experiences of discrimination, about being watched closely in stores, about people avoiding them on buses and trains. América reflects on how in Puerto Rico, American tourists treated her as part of the tropical landscape, "something to be stared at with curiosity and forgotten the moment they returned home":

> But here, she says to herself, they can't forget us. We're everywhere, and they resent us for it. It's incomprehensible. If it weren't for us, none of these women would be able to work. And their husbands wouldn't have it so easy, either. If we weren't here, who would clear the tables at their restaurants? Who would mow their lawns and build the stone fences around their properties? Who would clear their offices, restock store shelves, disinfect hospital rooms, make their beds, wash their laundry, cook their meals?[43]

América is speaking from her own social location, as an insider looking out, and as a subaltern looking up.

CONCLUSION

Women's studies challenges us to transgress disciplinary boundaries. I have spent a good deal of my career studying migration, and particularly the impact of migration on the lives of women, both those who migrate themselves and those who stay behind. On this intellectual journey, I have found it particularly useful to engage with narratives, whether they are narratives that are part of the dialogical work of ethnography or narratives that are part of immigrant fiction. In either case, these narratives allow women to speak for themselves, in their own voice, in a different voice, and in a positioned voice. As such they represent one of the turns that feminist anthropology and feminist ethnography has taken as it has grown to maturity during the past thirty years.

Notes

1. Michelle Zimbalist Rosaldo and Louise Lamphere, eds., *Woman, Culture and Society* (Stanford, CA: Stanford University Press, 1974); Margaret Mead, *Male and Female* (New York: William Morrow, 1949); Simone de Beauvoir, *The Second Sex* (New York: Alfred A. Knopf., 1952; orig. French edition 1949).

2. The Rosaldo and Lamphere book also included an essay by Nancy Chodorow that explored the impact of the maternal roles of women on childhood develop-

ment; another by Lamphere that addressed how women gain informal power through the formation of strategic domestic group alliances; and an essay by Joan Bamberger that illustrated how a myth of matriarchy is used in some societies to legitimate male authority. Chodorow, "Family Structure and Feminine Personality," 43–66; Lamphere, "Strategies, Cooperation, and Conflict among Women in Domestic Groups," 97–112; Bamberger, "The Myth of Matriarchy: When Men Rule in Primitive Society," 263–80.

3. Michelle Zimbalist Rosaldo, "Woman, Culture and Society: A Theoretical Overview," in *Woman, Culture and Society*, 17–42; Sherry Ortner, "Is Female to Male as Nature is to Culture?" in *Woman, Culture and Society*, 67–88; Claude Levi-Strauss, *The Elementary Structures of Kinship* (Boston: Beacon Press, 1974; orig. French publication 1949).

4. Evelyn Blackwood, *Webs of Power: Women, Kin and Community in a Sumatran Village* (Lanham, MD: Rowman and Littlefield Publishers, 2000), 7; Carol MacCormack and Marilyn Strathern, eds., *Nature, Culture and Gender* (Cambridge: Cambridge University Press, 1980); Carol MacCormack, "Nature, Culture and Gender: A Critique," in *Nature, Culture and Gender*, 10–11. Ortner eventually modified her own one-dimensional form of analysis.

5. Mona Etienne and Eleanor Leacock, eds., *Women and Colonization* (New York: Praeger, 1980); Eleanor Leacock, "Women's Status in Egalitarian Society: Implications for Social Evolution," *Current Anthropology* 19 (1978), 247–75; Eleanor Leacock, *Myths of Male Dominance* (New York: Monthly Review, 1981); Jane Collier and Michelle Rosaldo, "Politics and Gender in Simple Societies," in *Sexual Meanings*, Sherry Ortner and Harriet Whitehead, eds. (Cambridge: Cambridge University Press, 1981), 275–329; Marjorie Shostak, *Nisa: The Life and Words of a !Kung Woman* (Cambridge: Harvard University Press, 1981); Caroline B. Brettell, *Men Who Migrate, Women Who Wait: Population and History in a Portuguese Parish* (Princeton: Princeton University Press, 1986); Sally Cole, *Women of the Praia* (Princeton: Princeton University Press, 1991); Rayna Reiter, "Men and Women in the South of France: Public and Private Domains," in *Toward an Anthropology of Women*, Rayna Reiter, ed. (New York: Monthly Review Press, 1975), 252–82; Susan Carol Rogers, "Female Forms of Power and the Myth of Male Dominance: A Model of Female-Male Interaction in Peasant Society," *American Ethnologist* 2 (1975), 727–57.

6. Sharon Roseman and Heidi Kelley, "Introduction: Ethnographic Explorations of Gender and Power in Rural Northwestern Iberia," *Anthropologica* 41 (1999), 89.

7. Michelle Zimbalist Rosaldo, "The Use and Abuse of Anthropology: Reflections on Feminism and Cross-Cultural Understanding," *Signs* 5 (1980), 401–402.

8. Henrietta Moore, *Feminism and Anthropology* (Minneapolis: University of Minnesota Press, 1988), 21. See also Louise Lamphere, "The Domestic Sphere of Women and the Public World of Men: The Strengths and Limitations of an Anthropological Dichotomy," in *Gender in Cross-Cultural Perspective* (third edition), Caroline B. Brettell and Carolyn F. Sargent, eds. (Upper Saddle River, NJ: Prentice-Hall, 2001; orig 1993), 100–109; Michel Rolph-Trouillot, "The Caribbean Region: An Open Frontier in Anthropological Theory," *Annual Review of Anthropology* 21 (1992), 19–42.

9. Diane Bell, *Daughters of the Dreaming* (Melbourne: McPhee Gribble, 1983), 241.

10. Ibid., 250.

11. Ibid., 230, 250.

12. Maria Lepowsky, *Fruit of the Motherland: Gender in an Egalitarian Society* (New York: Columbia University Press, 1993), 306; See also Thomas A. Gregor and Donald Tuzin, *Gender in Amazonia and Melanesia: An Exploration of the Comparative Method* (Berkeley: University of California Press, 2003).

13. A Big Man is an informal leader whose power depends on the influence that he exerts on his followers rather than the authority of a political office. There is an emerging literature on big women in some Melanesian societies, but in general Big Men are more widespread and taken to be characteristic of a part of the world where male dominance is pervasive. See Ann Chowning, "'Women Are Our Business': Women, Exchange and Prestige in Kove," in *Dealing with Inequality: Analysing Gender Relations in Melanesia and Beyond*, Marilyn Strathern, ed. (Cambridge: Cambridge University Press, 1987), 130–49; Maurice Godelier, *The Making of Great Men* (Cambridge: Cambridge University Press, 1986); Rena Lederman, "Big Men, Large and Small? Towards a Comparative Perspective," *Ethnology* 19 (1990), 3–15.

14. Lepowsky, *Fruit of the Motherland*, 78.

15. Ibid., 205.

16. Blackwood, 1.

17. Ibid., 41.

18. Ibid., 14; Nigel Rapport and Joanna Overing, *Social and Cultural Anthropology: The Key Concepts* (London and New York: Routledge, 2000), 149.

19. Blackwood, *Webs of Power*, 180.

20. Matthew Gutmann, "Trafficking in Men: The Anthropology of Masculinity," *Annual Review of Anthropology* 26 (1997), 385.

21. Stanley Brandes, *Metaphors of Masculinity: Sex and Status in Andalusian Folklore.* (Philadelphia: University of Pennsylvania Press, 1980); David Gilmore, *Manhood in the Making: Cultural Concepts of Masculinity* (New Haven: Yale University Press, 1990); David Gilmore, *Misogyny: The Male Malady* (Philadelphia: University of Pennsylvania Press, 2001); Gilbert Herdt, ed., *Rituals of Manhood* (Berkeley: University of California Press, 1982); Michael Herzfeld, *The Poetics of Manhood: Context and Identity in a Cretan Mountain Village* (Princeton: Princeton University Press, 1985); Barry S. Hewlett, *Intimate Fathers: The Nature and Context of Aka Pygmy Paternal-Infant Care* (Ann Arbor: University of Michigan Press, 1991); Nicholas W. Townsend, *The Package Deal: Marriage, Work and Fatherhood in Men's Lives* (Philadelphia: Temple University Press, 2002), 203.

22. Matthew C. Gutmann, *The Meanings of Macho: Being a Man in Mexico City* (Berkeley: University of California Press, 1996), 263.

23. Henrietta L. Moore, *A Passion for Difference: Essays in Anthropology and Gender* (Bloomington: Indiana University Press, 1994).

24. Margery Wolf, *A Thrice Told Tale* (Stanford: Stanford University Press, 1992), 52. See also Judith Stacey, "Can There Be a Feminist Ethnography?" *Women's Studies International Forum* 11 (1988), 21–27; Lila Abu-Lughod, "Can There Be a Feminist Ethnography?" *Women's Performance* 5 (1990), 7–27; Ruth Behar and Deborah Gordon, eds., *Women Writing Culture* (Berkeley: University of California Press, 1995); Pat Caplan, "Engendering Knowledge: the Politics of Ethnography," in *Persons and Powers of Women in Diverse Cultures*, ed. Shirley Ardener (Oxford: Berg Publishers, 1992), 65–87; Kamala Visweswaran, "Histories of Feminist Ethnography," *Annual Review of Anthropology* 26 (1997), 591–621.

25. Lila Abu-Lughod, "Writing against Culture," in *Recapturing Anthropology*, Richard Fox, ed. (Santa Fe, N.M: School of American Research, 1991), 149; Sherry Ortner, *Making Gender: The Politics and Erotics of Culture* (Boston: Beacon Press, 1996).

26. Paul Radin, ed., *Crashing Thunder, The Autobiography of an American Indian* (New York: Appleton, 1926), 384.

27. Michael Angrosino, "The Use of Autobiography as Life History: The Case of Albert Gomes," *Ethos* 4 (1976), 133. For further discussion of the use of the life history in anthropology see L. L. Langness and Geyla Frank, *Lives: An Anthropological Approach to Biography* (Novato, CA: Chandler and Sharp Publishers, 1985), and Lawrence C. Watson and Maria-Barbara Watson-Franke, *Interpreting Life Histories: An Anthropological Inquiry* (New Brunswick, NJ: Rutgers University Press, 1985).

28. Visweswaran, "Histories of Feminist Ethnography," 602.

29. Ruth Behar, *The Vulnerable Observer: Anthropology That Breaks Your Heart* (Boston: Beacon Press, 1996), 26, 28.

30. Ruth Behar, *Translated Woman: Crossing the Border with Esperanza's Story* (New Brunswick, NJ: Rutgers University Press, 1993); Margaret Blackman, *During My Time: Florence Edenshaw Davidson, a Haida Woman* (Seattle: University of Washington Press, 1992, rev. ed.); Sharon Gmelch, *Nan: The Life of an Irish Travelling Woman* (Prospect Heights, IL: Waveland Press, 1986); Marjorie Shostak, *Nisa: The Life and Words of a !Kung Woman* (Cambridge: Harvard University Press 1981).

31. Irma McClaurin, *Women of Belize: Gender and Change in Central America* (New Brunswick, NJ: Rutgers University Press, 1996), 7.

32. Ibid., 8.

33. Lila Abu-Lughod, *Writing Women's Worlds* (Berkeley: University of California Press, 1993), 19.

34. Ibid., xvii-xviii.

35. Caroline B. Brettell, *We Have Already Cried Many Tears: The Stories of Three Portuguese Migrant Women* (Prospect Heights, IL: Waveland Press, 1995; revised edition, orig. publ. 1982 by Schenkman) and Caroline B. Brettell, *Writing against the Wind: A Mother's Life Story* (Wilmington, DE: Scholarly Resources, Inc., 1999).

36. George Gmelch, *Double Passage: The Lives of Caribbean Migrants Abroad and Back Home* (Ann Arbor: University of Michigan Press, 1992), 311; Mary Chamberlain, *Narratives of Exile and Return* (London: MacMillan, 1997), 102, 104; Nicole Constable, *Maid to Order in Hong Kong: Stories of Filipina Workers* (Ithaca: Cornell University Press, 1997).

37. Dianne Walta Hart, *Undocumented in L.A.: An Immigrant's Story* (Wilmington: Scholarly Resources Inc., 1997).

38. Visweswaran, "Histories of Feminist Ethnography," 603.

39. Moore, *A Passion for Difference*, 135; Kamala Visweswaran, *Fictions of Feminist Ethnography* (Minneapolis: University of Minnesota Press, 1994), 1; Visweswaran notes in "Histories of Feminist Ethnography" (614) that feminist anthropologists who have recently reengaged with life history have been very careful to distance themselves from fiction, insisting that the stories included in their monographs are "true ethnographic accounts" and that even where authors have used "the devices of fiction to highlight their ethnographic reporting [they] juxtapose it with more ethnographic accounts."

40. Wolf, *A Thrice Told Tale*.

41. Cristina Garcia, *Dreaming in Cuban* (New York: Ballantine Books, 1992), 170–71, 129, 73.

42. Esmeralda Santiago, *América's Dream.* (New York: Harper Collins, 1996), 152–53.

43. Ibid., 228.

Suggestions for Further Reading

Bell, Diane, Pat Caplan and Wazir Jahan Karim, eds. *Gendered Fields: Women, Men and Ethnography.* London and New York: Routledge, 1993.

Brettell, Caroline B., and Carolyn Sargent. *Gender in Cross-Cultural Perspective*, 4th Edition. Upper Saddle River, NJ: Prentice Hall Inc., 2005.

di Leonardo, Micaela. *Gender at the Crossroads of Knowledge: Feminist Anthropology in the Postmodern Era.* Berkeley: University of California Press, 1991.

Miller, Barbara Diane. *Sex and Gender Hierarchies.* Cambridge: Cambridge University Press, 1993.

Moore, Henrietta. *Feminism and Anthropology.* Minneapolis: University of Minnesota Press, 1988.

———. *A Passion for Difference: Essays in Anthropology and Gender.* Bloomington: Indiana University Press, 1994.

Mukhopadhyay, Carol C., and Patricia J. Higgins. "Anthropological Studies of Women's Status Revisited: 1977–1987," *Annual Review of Anthropology* 17 (1988), 461–95.

Ortner, Sherry. *Making Gender: The Politics and Erotics of Culture.* Boston: Beacon Press, 1996.

Visweswaran, Kamala. *Fictions of Feminist Ethnography.* Minneapolis: University of Minnesota Press, 1994.

Wolf, Diane L. ed. *Feminist Dilemmas in Fieldwork.* Boulder, CO: Westview Press, 1996.

The Queerness of Victorian Marriage Reform

Sharon Marcus

Sharon Marcus (1991) is an Associate Professor in the Department of English and Comparative Literature at Columbia University. She is completing a book on female homoeroticism and the Victorian family. Her publications include "Fighting Bodies, Fighting Words: A Theory and Politics of Rape Prevention" (1992); "Placing Rosemary's Baby" (1995); *Apartment Stories: City and Home in Nineteenth-Century Paris and London* (1999); and "Have a Nice Day: The City as Joke" (2003). Recent articles drawn from her forthcoming book include "Comparative Sapphism" (2002), and "Reflections on Victorian Fashion Plates" (2003).

Sharon Marcus was inspired to begin feminist studies by the example of feminist faculty on her college campus. Originally, she was especially interested in how gender difference inflects education. Later, she considered how public/private boundaries define gender, and how different relationships to the body, to violence, and to action define gender difference. In the last decade she has become more interested in how gender and sexuality define each other. Among other subjects she teaches queer theory and, though pleased that such subjects are now staples of higher education, she is also continually surprised and disappointed that so many people are still uncomfortable discussing homosexuality, even in women's studies classes.

When announcing his support for a constitutional amendment banning gay marriage in February 2004, President Bush characterized same-sex nuptials as a threat to civilized life: "After more than two centuries of American jurisprudence and millenia of human experience, a few judges and local authorities are presuming to change the most fundamental institution of civilization."[1] Opponents of an 1857 law that made civil divorce available for the first time in England issued similarly apocalyptic warnings that to change marriage would destroy civilization. As we now know, Victorians who opposed changes to marriage law in 1857 were wrong: civilization did not end when divorce became legal. When overstating their concerns about the future, opponents of legal reform also distort the past. Scholarship that shows that for almost a thousand years, from 500-1500 C.E., there were Christian ceremonies formalizing same-sex unions.[2] The roots of same-sex marriage run deeper than we often assume; indeed, when Victorians changed the laws governing marriage between men and women one hundred and fifty years ago, same-sex marriage was also in the air.

When President Bush says, "marriage cannot be severed from its cultural, religious, and natural roots without weakening the good influence of society," he asserts that no matter what changes marriage has undergone, its "roots" have always been exclusively heterosexual. Even proponents of gay marriage sometimes collude in this assumption by viewing gay marriage primarily in terms of gay liberation, with its stages of separatist identity formation, coming out, decriminalization, and demands for civil rights. But gay marriage also emerges from the history of marriage, feminism, and heterosexuality. When Victorian feminists fought to make marriage between men and women more egalitarian, they also demanded that marriage be less defined by sexual difference. It is an interesting and neglected historical fact that many of those Victorians who struggled to change the meaning of marriage were in same-sex relationships, knew people who were, or thought about the role same-sex relationships played in the history of marriage. Marriage has always included heterosexuality, but marriage has almost never been exclusively heterosexual. For some Victorians, quasi-marital relationships between women were not the antithesis of marriage but an implicit model for reformed marriage.

The equation of heterosexual marriage with millenia of civilization also evokes an association between homosexuality and primitivism that originated when late-nineteenth-century anthropologists manufactured the idea of the primitive and sexologists invented the homosexual. Anthropologists attributed hypersexuality to savages, while sexologists portrayed inverts as immature, unevolved, and degenerate.[3] In the early twenty-first century, opponents of gay marriage perpetuate the association between homosexuality and primitivism by asserting that as enemies of civilization, same-sex couples must be forbidden access to an institution that symbolizes civilization. Nineteenth-century anthropologists produced elaborate conjectural histories to explain how monogamous marriage had emerged from an original state of incest, polygamy, and matriarchy. Conservatives today warn that gay marriage will reverse that narrative, returning us to an undifferentiated presocial state in which anything goes. In 2002, for example, United States Senator Rick Santorum declared his support for the Texas sodomy law that would be overturned by the Supreme Court a year later by warning that if the right to privacy were extended to gay sex, then "you have the right to bigamy, you have the right to polygamy, you have the right to incest . . . you have the right to adultery. You have the right to anything."[4]

Gay rights activists might want to steer Santorum away from *When Romeo Was a Woman*, Lisa Merrill's brilliant biography of the United States actress Charlotte Cushman, who lived her life well outside what Santorum calls "traditional heterosexual relationships."[5] Best known for playing Romeo, Cushman was one of the most acclaimed and financially successful American actresses of the nineteenth century. She lived outside the United States for most of her life, first in England and then in Italy, often returning to the U.S. to play sold-out national tours. Cushman was involved in two long-term relationships with women: one with Matilda Hays, an author, translator, and feminist activist, and another with the sculptor Emma Stebbins, whom she met in 1857. Stebbins remains known today for her sculpture "Angel of the Waters," which stands in Central Park's Bethesda Terrace and features prominently in Tony Kushner's *Angels in America*. Until her death in 1876, Cushman cultivated a public persona as a respectable artist and lived openly with Emma Stebbins in an elegant Roman apartment brimming with friends and pets.

As we will see, the lesson those who oppose gay marriage should take from Cushman's life is how little her relationships with women interfered with her reputation for propriety; Cushman's society readily adopted her understanding of her same-sex relationships as marriages. However, those who oppose gay marriage might instead latch onto Cushman's secret life—suggestive of adultery, polygamy, and incest—to misconstrue it as an essential consequence of her sexuality. Merrill's biography reveals that Cushman, who had always cultivated primary relationships with accomplished women close to her in age while encouraging her many worshipful female fans, began a clandestine relationship with one such young woman in 1858, soon after she began living with Emma Stebbins.[6] Cushman met Emma Crow while touring the United States. Their affair lasted years, spanned continents, and is documented in Cushman's many letters to Crow, which Crow preserved and bequeathed to the Library of Congress, despite Cushman's many anxious requests that she burn them.

In that correspondence, Cushman frequently tries to naturalize her adultery—she considered herself married to Stebbins—by describing the younger Emma as her daughter, niece, and baby, as though to soften her betrayal of Stebbins by suggesting that Crow was not Stebbins's rival but simply an addition to the family. "'Never did a mother love her child so dearly. Never did Auntie think so sweetly so yearningly of her Niece. Never did Ladie love her lover so intensely," Cushman wrote.[7] Cushman took the incestuous fantasy of sex as kinship to its literal limits when she encouraged Emma Crow to marry Cushman's nephew and adopted son Ned Cushman. Cushman devised this plan for informal polygamy because she believed it would allow Crow to live near her as her daughter-in-law, a situation to which Emma Stebbins could not object. Crow was so in love with Cushman that she agreed to this arrangement, and she and Cushman continued their affair well after Crow's marriage to Ned made Charlotte Cushman young Emma's mother-in-law. After Crow married Ned Cushman, Charlotte addressed Emma as her "dear new daughter," one who had, in taking the Cushman name, also become in some sense Cushman's wife. Cushman called Emma's marriage with Ned her own "ultimate entire union" with Emma, and her later letters to a pregnant Emma "convey . . . the impression that she and her 'little lover' were having this baby together." With a grandiosity that came easily to a rich and famous actress, Cushman arrogated to herself the roles of husband, wife, father, mother, aunt, and lover, saluting Emma as "Dearest and Sweetest daughter[,] niece, friend and lover," and referring to herself in other letters as "Big Mamma."[8]

Cushman's matrilineal, incestuous, adulterous, polygamous, homosexual household seems to realize the conservative fantasy of the primitive family in which no distinctions are made, no restrictions imposed, and patriarchal monogamy has yet to overcome the promiscuity that results when women reign unfettered. For that very reason, Cushman provides an excellent point of departure for interrogating the equation of homosexuality with primitive sexual anarchy. Her affair with Emma Crow shows not that those who disregard the taboo on homosexuality will also flout the prohibitions on incest and polygamy but that, like most Victorians, Cushman's desires were shaped by taboos that incited the very desires they prohibited. As Foucault shows in the first volume of the *History of Sexuality*, nothing in the Victorian family was more normative than its intensive sexualization of family relationships.[9] Heterosexual couples were as prone as lesbian ones to take clandestine pleasure in breaking sexual rules. Victorian pornographic plots obsessively depicted incest of every variety and in every possible gender configuration, and Henry James easily translated Cushman's and Crow's story into the heterosexual plot of his novel *The Golden Bowl*, in which a father marries his daughter's husband's lover, also named Charlotte.[10] Cushman's letters to Emma Crow blur the lines between lover and family member in the same way as a mainstream 1850 novel blurred those lines when describing a wife's love for her husband: "She loved him at once with the love of mother, sister, friend, and wife."[11]

The normative cast of even Cushman's most hidden desires may help explain why she was not univocally branded as deviant in her lifetime and why her relationships with women were so unremarkable to those surrounding her. Cushman was a recognized and often admired type: a nineteenth-century woman who supported herself as an artist and whose financial independence made it relatively easy for her to form a couple with another woman. Although Cushman sometimes dressed as a man on stage, she was not like the working-class women who passed as men to marry other women and were, if caught, legally censured for seizing male privileges.[12] Instead, like most middle-class and wealthy women in female couples, Cushman presented herself as a woman *and* used the language of marriage to describe her more committed sexual relationships. Just as Eleanor Butler referred to her beloved Sarah Ponsonby in her journals as "my better half," Cushman called the woman she lived with her "other and better half."[13]

Because middle-class women in relationships with other women carefully managed their displays of masculinity, they mingled easily with legally married couples. The social circle Cushman helped to create in Rome and Florence was neither a separatist subculture nor an underground community, although it did form a meeting ground for women in or hoping to be in female couples. Journalist Kate Field, for example, came to Rome to recover from what her biographer called "an absorbing affection . . . akin to romantic love" for her aunt; once in Italy, she merrily flirted with everyone around her, dubbing her hostess

Isa Blagden "Hubby."[14] Those homoerotic energies circulated in a community that also included legal spouses such as Blagden's close friends the Brownings, now famous figures of heterosexual romance and conjugal passion. Robert and Elizabeth Barrett Browning spent much of their time with women whose charged relationships included tempestuous infatuations, short-term love affairs, and long-term partnerships. The Brownings' letters recount numerous dinners, picnics, and excursions with women like Harriet Hosmer, Isa Blagden, Charlotte Cushman, Emma Stebbins, Kate Field, and Frances Power Cobbe. In some cases, the ties were deep: Blagden was one of Robert Browning's chief correspondents, Hosmer made a famous cast of the Brownings' hands, and after his wife's death, Robert gave Field a chain and locket Elizabeth had worn since childhood, adding to it some of his wife's hair.[15]

It is hard to know what the Brownings made of their friends' erotic lives, in part because relevant passages in the Brownings' respective correspondence suggest that they themselves had no clear vocabulary for their friends' relationships. The notion of the open secret—what everyone knows but cannot say aloud—comes to mind but is not quite apt, because in the regime of the open secret, everyone knows *exactly* what cannot be said. The notion of reticence better describes a climate in which same-sex relationships were acknowledged only perfunctorily in public documents such as newspaper articles or published biographies but were dissected in private exchanges.[16] Letters reveal correspondents grasping for a vocabulary to describe what was at once familiar and unknown. Elizabeth Barrett Browning wrote to her sister Arabel in 1852 about meeting Matilda Hays and Charlotte Cushman: "I understand that she & Miss Hayes [sic] have made vows of celibacy & of eternal attachment to each other—they live together, dress alike . . . it is a female marriage. I happened to say, 'Well, I never heard of such a thing before.' 'Haven't you,?' said Mrs Corkrane, '. . . oh, it is by no means uncommon.' They are on their way to Rome, so I dare say we shall see a good deal of them. Though an actress . . . Miss Cushman has an unimpeachable character."[17] Barrett Browning's reference to vows of celibacy suggests an equation of female marriage with sexual renunciation. But the conjunction of the women's celibacy with their "eternal attachment" redefines celibacy as a mutual vow never to leave one another to marry men, one way of predicating Barrett Browning's next term, "a female marriage." The offhandedness of Barrett Browning's "I happened to say" sits uneasily with the emphatic nature of what she does say—"Well, I have never heard of such a thing"—but suggests her desire to demonstrate that she has already learned the lesson in urbanity imparted by her married interlocutor, Mrs. Corkrane, who remarks "it is by no means uncommon." Far from suggesting that she might want to avoid Cushman and Hays, Browning writes that she will see a good deal of them—and she did, often bringing along her husband and their young son. Browning ends with a comment on Cushman's reputation for respectability that makes no connection, positive or negative, between Cushman's female marriage and her "unimpeachable character."

The Browning circle consisted of eminently respectable artists who lived in Italy not because they were social outcasts but to get a liberating distance from immediate family, access to a warmer climate, and exposure to Italy's historic culture. Charlotte Cushman's integration into that circle shows how easily same-sex relationships between women were assimilated to the model of marriage. Hence Cushman's relationship with Stebbins did not detract from but augmented the actress's aura of propriety and respectability.[18] In the 1860s and 1870s, a period when few knew of the sexological idea of inversion and many still associated sodomy with sexual acts absolutely opposed to nature and virtue, the female couple was accepted as a variation on legal marriage, not treated as a separate species. This suggests that Lillian Faderman and Carroll Smith-Rosenberg were absolutely right that Victorians considered love between women to be perfectly normal, whether that love involved intense, sensual friendships that ran parallel to marriage to men (Smith-Rosenberg) or lifelong partnerships that replaced marriage to men (Faderman).[19] It also shows how they were wrong. Smith-Rosenberg erred in identifying the separation between men and women as the reason why Victorians accepted intimacy between women as a supplement to male-female marriage. Many female couples did not supplement marriage but appropriated it, and women in such couples never lacked contact with men. Faderman was absolutely wrong to argue that acceptance of female couples depended on the perceived asexuality of their relationships, since there is ample evidence that individuals who knew women in female marriages assumed that sexual desire was involved. Indeed, marriage itself (unlike friendship) was never an asexual term; for Victorians, marriage meant the union of sexual and spiritual impulses, the reconciliation of sexuality with propriety.

The idea of female marriage was not simply a private metaphor used by women in same-sex relationships; Barrett Browning's letter shows that it was a term used by legally married women as well. This suggests that even among middle-class Victorians, marriages were not defined by law alone, and for couples with no legal status, social acceptance provided legitimation and established rules for beginning and ending relationships.[20] For example, after Cushman met Emma Stebbins and her relationship with Matilda Hays began to fray in 1857, Hays threatened to sue Cushman for damages on the grounds that she had sacrificed a literary career to follow Cushman to Italy. Hays's demand that Cushman pay some form of alimony was both an assertion of the marital nature of their relationship and a subtle form of blackmail. The threat Hays wielded was not, however, the revelation of their relationship, which was open enough to be mentioned in newspapers and which had garnered more approval than scorn. Rather, the *rupture* of their relationship due to Cushman's adultery was the potential source of scandal, although evidently not a very troubling one, since Cushman ultimately placated Hays with a moderate sum of money.[21]

After her relationship with Cushman ended, Hays returned to her feminist circle in London, where she helped run the *English Woman's Journal* and the Society for Promoting the Employment of Women and eventually formed another relationship with Theodosia, Dowager Lady Monson.[22] Once there, Hays renewed contact with the women who in 1856 had developed a petition to change married women's property laws which Barbara Leigh Smith submitted to Parliament in 1856. Although that petition's immediate success was only partial, it influenced politicians to create a civil divorce law the following year. Matilda Hays and Charlotte Cushman had both signed that petition, along with many other women who were not married to men and were therefore considered objective, disinterested supporters of marriage reform.

The number of women more interested in relationships with women than marriages to men who signed a petition calling for a Married Women's Property Act suggests an affinity between same-sex relationships and marriage reform. To understand why women like Hays and Cushman found legal marriage reform so compelling requires a closer look at the Victorian marriage debates—at the milieu in which they were conducted and at the issues they comprised: divorce, attitudes about single women, and conflicting accounts of the history of marriage.

To begin with divorce: marriage initally became a hotly debated topic in mid-Victorian England because of the 1857 Divorce and Matrimonial Causes Act. The 1857 Act was passed when liberal utilitarians interested in rationalizing the law and transferring authority from church to state joined forces with feminists seeking to end coverture, the doctrine that husband and wife were one person, the husband. Despite the double standard of the new law, which made it more difficult for wives to sue for divorce than husbands, the law made divorce available to many more people than ever before in England by creating England's first *civil* divorce law and court. Statistics give some sense of the law's effects: When divorce could be granted solely by Parliamentary petition, only 190 divorces were granted between 1801 and 1857, while in the 10 years between 1858 and 1868, the divorce court granted 1,279 decrees.[23] The 1857 legislation provided an appealing new option for ending marriage, especially for women: Before its passage, only four women had ever obtained a Parliamentary divorce decree, but between 1858 and 1868, wives initiated 40 percent of divorce court petitions and were successful about as often as husbands in obtaining divorces.[24]

The 1857 Act had cultural ramifications that went far beyond its legal ones because the publicity given to divorce trials increased public awareness of marital breakdown and exposed the variability of marriage as a lived institution. Divorces were granted to hundreds of spouses, but divorce trials were followed by many thousands of readers.[25] The general public discovered through trial reports that violence, adultery, incestuous adultery, bigamy, and even sex between women (an issue in two notorious divorce trials, the 1864 Codrington trial and the 1885 Dilke-Crawford trial) were often part of married life in Britain. A spate of novels about bigamy, adultery, and divorce, mostly published between 1857 and 1865, also fed the appetite for reading about how marriages failed to conform to social rules.

The 1857 law of divorce also changed the terms of celibacy, producing much journalistic discussion about whether marriage was necessary at all, especially in light of census figures that showed an increasing number of men and women never marrying. Victorian feminists charged that the social compulsion to marry consolidated male domination, claiming that women sought and accepted marriages that made them inferiors only because the unmarried state entailed economic dependence and social death. For marriage between men and women to be equal, they argued, it would be necessary to make life practicable and pleasurable for women who never married. The demand to reform marriage, which began as a quest to make marriage more equal and more flexible, evolved into a demand to make heterosexuality less obligatory for women.

Even passionate advocates of marriage hostile to feminism began to accept that some women would never marry. As an example of this, take the most famous Victorian article about single women, W. R. Greg's "Why Are Women Redundant?" (1862).[26] Greg's article has been cited as evidence of the stigma Victorians attached to unmarried women, because his strong commitment to marriage led him to propose sending "redundant" Englishwomen who could not find husbands to colonies where men outnumbered women. But Greg's article also demonstrates the growing acceptance of single women; although he pleads that every woman who can be paired with a man should be, he assumes that because adult women outnumber adult men, single women are as natural as monogamy. Nature rules that "marriage, the union of one man with one woman, is unmistakably . . . the despotic law of life," but "she not only proclaims the *rule*, she distinctly lays down the precise amount and limits of the *exception*." Greg quantifies the natural exception in terms of census figures showing 106 women over twenty for every 100 men in the same age group. What Greg calls a "startling anomaly" is the census finding that *30 percent of women over twenty are unmarried*. The "redundant six per cent for whom equivalent men do not exist" are, he writes, a normal exception consonant with "a thoroughly natural, sound, and satisfactory state of society" and proportionate to the "precise percentage of women whom Nature designed for single life." So natural is the single woman for Greg that in his personification, Nature is herself a single woman, busily laying down the law with no husband to guide her. In a footnote Greg even suggests that single life may be the happier choice for many women: "In thousands of instances [maiden ladies] are, *after a time*, more happy [than wives and mothers]. In our day, if a lady is possessed of a very moderate competence, and a well-stored and well-regulated mind, she may have infinitely less care and infinitely more enjoyment than if she had drawn any of the numerous blanks which beset the lottery of marriage."[27] Greg's acceptance of single life as natural transforms marriage from a fatal necessity into a lottery, a game of chance whose risks women can rationally choose not to incur.

Across the political and rhetorical spectrum, writers in the 1860s testified to the growing acceptance of single women and growing awareness that marriage between men and women was not a universal element of social life. In "What Shall We Do with Our Old Maids?" (1862) Frances Power Cobbe used the same statistics as Greg to show that single women were becoming a constitutive and transformative element of England's social reality.[28] Cobbe and others argued that single women were happier than they had ever been, and that when unmarried women enjoyed the good life, marriage itself would also change. Furthermore, the rise of companionate marriage as an ideal, in addition to changing the relationship between husband and wife, also changed the status of unmarried people. The belief that without love it was better not to marry elevated those who decided not to marry for expediency into spiritually superior beings.

The suggestion that people could survive independently of marriage also undid the notion of marriage as the union of opposite sexes, each requiring the other in order to supplement a lack, and harmonized with a modern understanding of companionate marriage based on similarity and friendship. Feminist John Stuart Mill, for example, wrote that "likeness," not difference, should be the foundation of true unions, and that marriage should be modeled on what "happens between two friends of the same sex."[29] If marriage was defined by love and patterned on same-sex friendship, then what happened between two friends of the same sex could also be understood as a marriage. Frances Power Cobbe argued that women would marry for love only if the single state were "so free and happy that [women] shall have not one temptation to change it save the only temptation which *ought* to determine them—namely, love."[30] Her reasoning shrewdly framed her rejection of compulsory heterosexuality as a desire to improve marriage and called on defenders of virtuous marriage to support the unmarried woman's right to happiness. Implicitly, she also rallied them to ratify any union based on love.

Cobbe may have had in mind a union like her own. Although she never legally married, for over thirty years she lived with the woman she wrote of openly as her "beloved friend," sculptor Mary Lloyd.[31] Cobbe and her partner were well known to many people who directly advocated marriage reform, such as Barbara Leigh Smith, Charlotte Cushman, Geraldine Jewsbury, and John Stuart Mill. Cobbe and Lloyd were also acquainted with those who supported marriage reform indirectly, by developing historical frameworks that represented changes in marriage as either positive outcomes of progress or continuous with a prestigious past. Cobbe, for example, knew Henry Sumner Maine, one of the nineteenth-century writers whom intellectual historians now call Victorian anthropologists. In her autobiography Cobbe wrote that Maine's "interest in the claims of women and his strong statements on the subject, made me regard him with much gratitude."[32] Both Cobbe and Maine were involved in Victorian marriage reform, Cobbe through her advocacy of single women and battered wives, Maine as a legal historian who showed that the hierarchical marriage supported by traditionalists was antiquated and inconsistent with liberal individualism. Many of the authors George Stocking includes in his book *Victorian Anthropology* were trained as lawyers and their interest in cross-cultural studies of marriage and kinship was inspired by their engagement with contemporary legal codes. To Stocking's list of male professional jurists one can add an autodidact like Edith Simcox, a feminist labor activist and professional writer whose lifelong romantic obsession with George Eliot earns her an entry in a recent encyclopedia of lesbianism. Simcox also wrote two erudite studies, one called *Natural Law*, the other *Primitive*

Civilizations (1894).[33] The latter work used the study of the past to reflect on the present, asserting that no aspect of "modern family life . . . can be put forward as so pre-eminently and absolutely natural as to be universal."[34] Simcox emphasized that primitive civilization was not only as natural as modern life, it was in some respects superior. Demonstrating that wives in the past had owned property, had rights over their children, and enjoyed legal autonomy, Simcox implied that wives could also enjoy the same independence in the present without undermining the social fabric.

Many scholars have suggested a connection between the 1857 Matrimonial Causes Act and the anthropological studies of kinship and marriage written in the 1860s and after, but few agree whether anthropology was a reaction against feminist changes to marriage laws or an extension of them.[35] Contemporary scholars all assume, however, that when Victorian anthropologists discussed marriage, they discussed heterosexuality. Yet as we have seen, the reformist network in which many anthropologists were situated was surprisingly queer, and one way that some Victorian anthropologists contributed to marriage reform was to challenge the very idea that marriage was exclusively heterosexual. For some anthropologists, this meant showing that marriage did not depend on sexual difference for its definition, and therefore that marriage was not essentially defined as occurring between a man and a woman. For others, this meant explicitly discussing the role that same-sex relationships played in narratives of social progress.

In their histories of marriage and kinship, Victorian anthropologists attempted to account for the development of primitive into civilized societies. Most anthropologists concurred that the modern state was superior to the primitive one, so that in the broadest sense "primitive" and "civilized" functioned simply as negative and positive signs. More specifically, most anthropologists defined primitive societies as based on myth, force, enslavement, the assignment of fixed status, and the equation of political authority with the family or clan. Conversely, anthropologists defined modernity in terms of the rule of law, equality, promises, and consent, as well as the emergence of science, abstract symbolization, and state formations distinct from family clans. A few contrarians argued that primitive society was in some respects superior to Christianity and capitalism: examples include Friedrich Engels, Edith Simcox, and Nietzsche, whose *Genealogy of Morals* was an explicit polemic against English moral history. Even Engels, however, agreed with Henry Sumner Maine's influential statement in *Ancient Law* (1861) that primitive society was "an aggregation of families," modern civilization "a collection of individuals," although unlike Maine, Engels did not admire modern individualism.[36]

Anthropologists also made sexuality a crucial factor in defining degrees of civilization. Under the influence of a Darwinian emphasis on variation, anthropologists represented monogamous marriage as only one of many possible organizations of sexuality, and in the spirit of Darwin's concept of evolution, depicted monogamous marriage not as timeless but as developing from an earlier stage of promiscuity. For some, that earlier stage remained operative or legible in modern life; for others, it represented what modern civilization had overcome; and for others, the fact that primitive societies accommodated divorce or female ownership of property questioned the inevitability and superiority of Victorian marriage laws. There was less agreement, however, about what was primitive or modern about the family and marriage with respect to women. Then, as now, primitive society was equated with the degradation of women, but some anthropologists thought that civilized societies also degraded women. Depending on an author's politics, degradation was associated with almost every type of marriage and kinship: polygyny and polyandry, promiscuity and monogamy, hierarchical marriage and egalitarian marriage, marriage with divorce and marriage without divorce. Anthropologists agreed that civilization meant the rise of individuals, but like everyone around them, they could not agree whether women were already part of civilization's increasing emphasis on the individual, a saving exception to that rule, or unjustly excluded from it.

Other scholars have shown how this confusion surfaced first as an argument about whether matriarchy preceded patriarchy, and then as a related argument about how to explain the transition from primitive promiscuity to modern monogamy. Because anthropologists were unusual in acknowledging that forms of marriage other than monogamy could constitute a cultural and social system, they were put in the extraordinary position of having to *explain* why monogamous marriage represented an advance in civilization over primordial promiscuity, and in particular what features of monogamous marriage made it more civilized than its antecedents. Here again, their explanations were often discordant. In *Kinship and Marriage in Early Arabia* (1885), for example, W. Robertson Smith wrote that patrilineal monogamy advanced "progress towards civilised ideas of conjugal fidelity" because it placed a woman "specially under the protection of one man."[37] For others, polygamy was primitive because it depended on force, on primitive marriage's violent basis in male capture of women; conversely, monogamy was civilized because it was more likely to involve the woman's consent. Others extended that view to argue that monogamy was more civilized because less violence meant less inequality, and increasing equality of persons was another marker of civilization. Thus William Lecky, in his *History of European Morals* (1869), wrote "the whole tendency of civilisation is to diminish the disparity between the different members of the family"; in the shift to monogamy "the wife from a simple slave becomes the companion and equal of her husband." Only with the end of wife purchase, the establishment of monogamous marriage, and the institution of female dowries did the wife "cease to be [the husband's] slave, and become in some degree a contracting party."[38]

Lecky's reference to contract alludes to one of the key terms in Victorian debates about marriage and divorce and one of the key points of intersection between legal reform and anthropology. Defining marriage as monogamy and associating monogamous marriage with civilization were uncontroversial propositions that provided a moral justification for British superiority to polygamous societies.[39] But the question of whether marriage was or was not a contract, and if it was a contract, what that should mean, was one of the most intractable conflicts in the mid-Victorian marriage debates. For some writers, contractual marriage meant that husbands and wives were understood as formal, equal individuals consenting to an agreement that either party could terminate. Many feminists argued that marriage should be a contract because contract represented a voluntary, consensual agreement between equals. Feminists also argued that marriage was not yet truly contractual, because in marrying under English law, women gave away equality (wives were not equal to husbands), autonomy (wives were absorbed into their husband's legal personality), and freedom (wives could obtain a divorce only under very limited conditions).[40]

Those who advocated contractual marriage expressed strong support for divorce, arguing that a key feature of contracts was that they could be terminated. Even before 1857, in an 1830s essay on marriage laws, John Stuart Mill asserted that the "indissolubility of marriage is the keystone of woman's present lot, and the whole comes down and must be reconstructed if that is removed."[41] Dissolubility, the term that described the possibility that marriages might end, became a container for the freedom, consent, and equality that feminists believed should define marriage as an ongoing condition. Mill wrote that marriage, "like the other relations voluntarily contracted by human beings . . . [should] depend for its continuance upon the wishes of the contracting parties." Mill situated contractual marriage in an anthropological schema when he asserted that "When women are merely slaves, to give them a permanent hold upon their masters was a first step towards their evolution. That step is now complete: and in the progress of civilization, the time has come when women may aspire to something more than merely to find a protector. . . . [Woman] is now ripe for equality. But it is absurd to talk of equality while marriage is an indissoluble tie."[42] In a series of rhetorical elisions, Mill associated women's equality with divorce, divorce with contract, and contract with the highest degree of "civilization."

In a later work, *The Subjection of Women* (1869), Mill continued to employ what we might call a feminist civilizational framework that grafted cultural and social differences onto temporal narratives of development. Translating his liberal belief in unfettered individual development into the anthropological idiom of social plasticity, Mill dismissed attempts to fix women's nature; no such generalizations were possible, he wrote, given "the extreme variableness of those of [human nature's] manifestations which are supposed to be most universal and uniform."[43] In addition to anthropology's emphasis on variability, Mill adopted its progress narrative, in which the move from primitivism to civilization depended crucially on women's position in marriage. Over and over again, Mill stated that married women's inequality in the present was a "relic of the past," an instance of "the primitive state of slavery lasting on," a survival that seemed compatibile with "modern civilization" but in fact contradicted progress toward a society based on consent, freedom, equality, and unconstrained self-development.[44] For Mill, modernity begins when superiors make and keep promises to inferiors and thus create a realm of equals who make contracts with one another. Thus for Mill, for marriage to be modern means that it must become contractual—egalitarian and dissoluble. One of marriage's inequities is that a wife "vows a life-long obedience to [her husband] at the altar, and is held to it all through her life by law." In a business contract, Mill writes, one partner "is free to cancel the power [of the other] by withdrawing from the connexion. The wife has no such power"—but should.[45]

Mill and Maine suggested that the progress of civilization depended on an equal distribution of individual rights that ultimately would make an institution like marriage a union of equals. The queerness of their reforming definition of marriage inheres in the fact that marriage as dissoluble contract bypasses and even contradicts the idea that marriage depends on, fixes, and reproduces the sexual difference between man and woman. Equality became so compelling a value that even those who opposed divorce and contractual marriage began to do so by claiming that dissolubility militated against equality. For those who believed that Christian monogamous marriage made wives equal to husbands because it made the marriage bond equally permanent for husband and wife, dissoluble marriage threatened to undo that equality by making it possible for husbands to repudiate wives at will. Thinkers who equated civilization with restraint rather than with autonomy considered indissoluble monogamous marriage civilizing because it created a negative equality by placing similar limits on male and female sexuality. As late as 1901, in an article on "Marriage and Modern Civilization," W. S. Lilly called Christian marriage "the Magna Charta of woman in modern civilisation" because it established marriage as the "lifelong union of two equal personalities," resulting from "the free consent of the man and woman contracting it." Even as Lilly exalted contract, he also belittled it, arguing that Christian marriage was also "something more than a contract" and thus superior to Roman marriage which could be dissolved by mutual consent. In his present day, Lilly noted, only the Catholic Church remained to warn men "that to degrade indissoluble marriage to a *mere* dissoluble contract . . . will be to throw back modern civilisation to that wallowing in the mire from which she rescued it."[46]

In invoking the threat of historical regression to a state of savagery, Lilly referred to the idea of primitive sexuality discussed earlier, although it is unclear what he believed was in that primordial "mire." As we have seen, marriage reformers and anthropologists writing histories of marriage knew of same-sex relationships modeled on marriage. We have also seen that arguments in favor of divorce and contractual marriage implicitly grounded conjugality in equality and argued against sexual difference as the basis of marriage. What remains to be seen is whether Victorian anthropology ever explicitly discussed homosexuality. Those of us who approach this question with Gayle Rubin's influential reading of anthropological theory in mind might anticipate that Victorian anthropologists either never discussed homosexuality at all or did so only to associate it with presocial, precultural savagery. In "The Traffic in Women," Rubin famously pointed out that "the incest taboo presupposes a prior, less articulate taboo on homosexuality. A prohibition against *some* heterosexual unions assumes a taboo against *non*heterosexual unions." It follows that anthropological theories of kinship that posit the incest taboo and male exchange of women as universal or necessary for the emergence of culture and civilization designate not only incest but also homosexuality as antithetical to civilization.[47]

Homosexuality does indeed haunt one of Rubin's key texts, Levi-Strauss's *The Elementary Structures of Kinship* (1949), but interestingly, Levi-Strauss does not associate homosexuality with incest or with the pre-cultural. One can see the case for Rubin's argument that Levi-Strauss's concept of the incest taboo assumes a prior taboo on homosexuality, because Levi-Strauss's theory is not overtly hospitable to the possibility of formalized same-sex relationships. "[T]he rules of kinship and marriage," Levi-Strauss writes, "are not made necessary by the social state. They are the social state itself."[48] The rule of marriage is the prohibition on incest, which regulates the relation between the sexes as a dictate that men must exchange women (23). It would thus follow that sexual relationships that do not involve male exchange of women could not be part of the social state. Levi-Strauss accordingly dismisses any theory of kinship that depends on what he calls "feminism"—by which he means explanations that assign agency and autonomy to women. In this sense, 1940s structuralist anthropology proves less willing to recognize the possibility of female autonomy than Victorian anthropology, with its accounts of early matriarchy and claims that primitive societies lacked incest taboos. By asserting that the incest taboo is universal, Levi-Strauss confers structure and sociality on primitive society, but he also aligns "the social state" with marriage, defined as male authority over women, and with culture, posited as a set of rules that require men to exchange women.

Surprisingly, however, Levi-Strauss is also willing to recognize the sociality of homosexuality. He notes that homosexuality and fraternal polyandry are both "solutions" to the scarcity of wives (38). Responding to Brenda Seligman's argument that blood-brotherhood "disputes that the woman is the sole or predominant instrument of alliance," Levi-Strauss concedes that "[i]t is far from our mind to claim that the exchange or gift of women is the only way to establish an alliance in primitive societies" (483). He even asserts that before Seligman did so, he himself had already shown that among some groups, the cross-cousin and potential brother-in-law "is the one with whom, as an adolescent, one indulges in homosexual activities" (484). That is, he glosses, brothers-in-law are the same "whether they play the role of the opposite sex in the erotic games of childhood, or whether their masculine alliance as adults is confirmed by each providing the other with what he does not have—a wife—through their simultaneous renunciation of what they both do have—a sister" (484). Levi-Strauss recognizes homosexuality only to the extent that he can subsume it within heterosexuality, but that also means that he recognizes homosexuality as social, as a form of alliance. For Levi-Strauss, the universality of the incest taboo means not that homosexuality is equally taboo but rather that even homosexuality is ultimately governed by the prohibition on incest and the imperative to exogamy. Hence at another point when Levi-Strauss mentions homosexual relationships, he asserts that they are governed by the rules of alliance: "marriage serves as model for that artificial and temporary 'conjugality' between young people of the same sex in some schools and on which Balzac makes the profound remark that it is never superimposed upon blood ties but replaces them" (480). An artificial, temporary, imitative conjugality—Levi-Strauss is barely willing to concede the existence of homosexuality as such. But precisely because he can barely see it as different from heterosexuality, he does not distinguish between heterosexuality and same-sex alliances, nor does he locate homosexuality in a primordial state of nature before incest was prohibited.[49]

Unlike Levi-Strauss, Victorian anthropologists believed that some societies lacked an incest taboo, and those who identified civilization with monogamous marriage often viewed homosexuality as a variation on primitive promiscuity. Lecky, for example, equated polygamy and pederasty. But those who argued that the primitive family did constitute a form of kinship, or that hierarchical monogamy was not the only legitimate form of marriage, sometimes suggested that the absence of an incest taboo also meant the absence of any prohibition on homosexuality. Thus Engels, who explicitly shared Lecky's negative view of Athenian pederasty, inadvertently proposed that same-sex marriage was an element of kinship systems that evolved "[b]efore incest was invented," when "the principle of promiscuity—the absence of any restriction imposed by custom on sexual intercourse" governed the family.[50] Engels described an early form he calls the the consanguine family, in which "[b]rothers and sisters, male and female cousins of the first, second, and more remote degrees, are all brothers and sisters of one another, and *precisely for that reason* are all husbands and wives of one another" (102). "All husbands and wives of one another"—Engels takes it for granted that only men can be husbands to women, only women wives to men. Precisely for that reason he produces a phrase that literally states that in the primitive family, everyone is *both* husband and wife to everyone else, without regard to sex. When Engels writes "brothers and sisters . . . are all brothers and sisters of one another," he deploys kinship terms that are not limited by the sex of their object: women are sisters of both women and men. That gender inclusiveness extends grammatically to the sentence's final clause, which turns to sexual relationships; syntax transforms semantics, so that "husbands and wives" can be defined like the siblinghood that determines them. Women are the wives of their sisters and brothers, men the husbands of their brothers and sisters. Engels makes the same grammatical slip when he comments on the punaluan family, in which several sisters are the common wives of common husbands, who unlike those in consanguine marriages are not each other's brothers or brothers of the sisters whom they marry. The term *punalua* refers not to different-sex relationships but to same-sex ones: "husbands . . . no longer called themselves brothers, for they were no longer necessarily brothers but punalua—that is, intimate companion, or partner. Similarly, a line of natural or collateral brothers had a number of women, *not* their sisters, as common wives, and these wives called one another *punalua*" (104). In this "classic form of family structure . . . whose essential feature was the mutually common possession of husbands and wives within a definite family circle" wives are the intimate partners of other wives, husbands the intimate partners of other husbands (104), and marriage establishes relationships between women and between men as well as between men and women.

Where Engels unwittingly suggested that same-sex relationships were a component of primitive group marriage, Johann Bachofen explicitly described formal same-sex unions as features of civilization and modernity. In Bachofen's *Mother-Right* (1861), the sexual relations that prevail in primordial nature are reproductive, fecundating, fulfilling the needs of the material world alone, and exclusively heterosexual. A corollary of civilization thus becomes the move away from the primitive state Bachofen calls hetairism, in which sexuality is violent and concerned only with biological reproduction. In a lengthy discussion of Sappho, unusual in its day for its frankness about her sexual relationships with women, Bachofen calls Sappho chaste, but defines chastity not as sexuality's absence but as its idealizing regulation. "The love of women for their own sex [in Lesbian poetry] was equivalent to Orphic [male homosexuality]. . . . Sappho's striving to elevate her sex was the source of all her sorrows and joys, and it was Eros who inspired her in this attempt. Her ardent words flowed not from maternal solicitude but from amorous passion, and yet this enthusiasm, which seized upon the sensuous and the transcendent, the physical and the psychic, with equal vigor, had its ultimate and richest source in religion. Love and identity of sex, which had seemed exclusive, were now united."[51] For Bachofen, lesbianism, like monogamous marriage, is a form of culture that represents an advance over materialist lust without abandoning sensuality. By interpreting Sapphic love as an advanced stage of civilization, Bachofen implicitly argued against any absolute equation of civilization with heterosexual monogamy and reproduction.

Those who have praised and criticized Victorians for equating civilization with what we now call heterosexual monogamy have been equally mistaken in attributing a nonexistent homogeneity to Victorian institutions and public opinion. The 1850s and 1860s were defined by arguments, not agreement, over what constituted marriage and family, and same-sex relationships informed those debates. Arguments about marriage and divorce law and histories of marriage were not exclusively about heterosexuality. Participants in those debates had varying degrees of familiarity with women in female marriages, and some considered same-sex relationships compatible with Victorian values such as respectability, civilization, and progress. Charlotte Cushman was an international star much beloved by a community of artistic and intellectual luminaries who treated her and her partner as a couple. Frances Power Cobbe never feared that her open relationship with Mary Lloyd might compromise her status as a champion of women's rights inside and outside marriage. Writers like Maine and Mill advocated definitions of marriage that asserted the benefits of equality and likeness between spouses. Bachofen explicitly linked lesbianism to modern enlightenment. The varied stances Victorians adopted unsettle the idea that until very recently, there has been an unbroken consensus that marital relationships can exist only between a man and a woman. Whether one sees gay marriage as modern or primitive has always been a question of politics, and the terms "primitive" and "civilized" remain as incoherent, contested and arbitrary today as they were for Victorians debating the legitimacy of divorce and the meaning of marriage.

Notes

1. *www.cnn.com/2004/ALLPOLITICS/02/24/elec04.prez.bush.transcript/index.html.*

2. John Boswell, *Same-Sex Unions in Premodern Europe* (New York: Villard Books, 1994).

3. On the ways that sexual norms informed the notion of the primitive, see Elizabeth Povinelli, "Sexual Savages/Sexual Sovereignty: Australian Colonial Texts and the Postcolonial Politics of Nationalism" *diacritics* 24.2–3 (1994): 122–50. For discussions of primitivism and homosexuality, see Siobhan Somerville, *Queering the Color Line: Race and the Invention of Homosexuality in American Culture* (Durham: Duke University Press, 2000), 3–37 and Jennifer Terry, *An American Obsession: Science, Medicine, and Homosexuality in Modern Society* (Chicago: University of Chicago Press, 1999), 27, 30, 46, 61.

4. Hendrik Hertzberg, "Dog Bites Man," *New Yorker*, 5 (May 2003), 33.

5. Hertzberg, "Dog Bites Man," 34. Lisa Merrill, *When Romeo Was a Woman: Charlotte Cushman and Her Circle of Female Spectators* (Ann Arbor: University of Michigan Press, 1999). See also Julie Crawford, "Charlotte Cushman," in Bonnie Zimmerman, ed., *Lesbian Histories and Cultures: An Encyclopedia* (New York: Garland Publishing, 2000), 217.

6. Merrill, *When Romeo Was a Woman*, 150.

7. Cited in Julia Markus, *Across an Untried Sea: Discovering Lives Hidden in the Shadow of Convention and Time* (New York: Knopf, 2000), 175.

8. See Merrill, *When Romeo Was a Woman*, 223, 217, 226, 231, 230.

9. Foucault writes: "In a society such as ours, where the family is the most active site of sexuality . . . incest occupies a central place; it is constantly being solicited and refused; it is an object of obsession and attraction, a dreadful secret and an indispensable pivot. It is manifested as a thing that is strictly forbidden . . . but it is also a thing that is continuously demanded in order for the family to be a hotbed of constant sexual incitement." *The History of Sexuality: Volume I: An Introduction* (New York: Vintage, 1980), 109.

10. Markus notes the connection between James's acquaintance with Cushman's circle and the plot of *The Golden Bowl*, 72–73. Markus also notes that Emma Crow Cushman, while married to Ned and after his death, continued to have intimate relationships with other women (231, 282).

11. Dinah Mulock Craik, *Olive* (New York: Oxford University Press, 1999 [1850]), 314.

12. See Gretchen van Slyke, "Who Wears the Pants Here? The Policing of Women's Dress in Nineteenth-Century England, Germany and France," *Nineteenth-Century Contexts* 17.1 (1993), 17–33; Camilla Townsend, "'I Am the Woman for Spirit': A Working Woman's Gender Transgression in Victorian London," in Andrew H. Miller and James Eli Adams, eds., *Sexualities in Victorian Britain* (Bloomington: Indiana University Press, 1996), 214–33; Julie Wheelright, *Amazons and Military Maids: Women Who Dressed as Men in Pursuit of Life, Liberty and Happiness* (London: Pandora, 1989); and "Cross-dressing Women" in Alison Oram and Annmarie Turnbull, *The Lesbian History Sourcebook: Love and Sex Between Women in Britain from 1780 to 1970* (London: Routledge, 2001), 11–34.

13. Butler cited in Rick Incorvati, "Introduction: Women's Friendships and Lesbian Sexuality," *Nineteenth-Century Contexts* 23.2 (2001), 176; Cushman cited in Merrill, *When Romeo Was a Woman*, 9, 195.

14. On Field's affection for her aunt, see Lilian Whiting, *Kate Field: A Record* (Boston: Little, Brown & Co., 1900), 46. On Field's nickname for Blagden, see Merrill, 195.

15. Hosmer later gave Kate Field's companion and biographer Lilian Whiting a cast of the Brownings' hands; see Jessie Rittenhouse, *Lilian Whiting: Essayist, Critic, and Poet* [n.d.], 10. Whiting records Robert Browning's gift to Field in *The Brownings: Their Life and Art* (Boston: Little, Brown & Co., 1911), 153–4, and notes that later it came into her own possession, since Field left Whiting all her property and papers.

16. Elizabeth Lapovsky Kennedy, "'But we would never talk about it': The Structures of Lesbian Discretion in South Dakota, 1928–1933," discusses how discretion on the part of lesbians and complicit heterosexuals allowed high levels of lesbian activity that never became public; in Ellen Lewin, ed., *Inventing Lesbian Cultures in America* (Boston: Beacon Press, 1996), 16–33. What is striking about the women the Brownings knew, by contrast, is how public their private lives could be, with few negative results, and how willing their heterosexual friends were to discuss their relationships.

17. Cited in Robert Browning, *Dearest Isa: Robert Browning's Letters to Isabella Blagden*, ed. Edward C. McAleer (Austin: University of Texas Press, 1951), p. 27, n. 12; my attention was drawn to this quotation by its partial citation in Merrill, *When Romeo Was a Woman*, 160.

18. Merrill, *When Romeo Was a Woman*, 190.

19. Carroll Smith-Rosenberg, "The Female World of Love and Ritual: Relations between Women in Nineteenth-Century America," in Joan Wallach Scott, ed., *Feminism and History* (Oxford: Oxford University Press, 1996), 366–97. Lillian Faderman, *Surpassing the Love of Men: Romantic Friendship and Love Between Women from the Renaissance to the Present* (New York: William Morrow, 1981).

20. Like bigamous working-class heterosexual couples, female couples in middle-class society lived in non-legal alliances that were socially regulated: governed by informal rules, marked by some form of wedding ritual, and recognized by the couple's milieu, if not by the state or the church. On working-class couples who were technically bigamous but were considered properly married by their peers, see Ginger Frost, "Bigamy and Cohabitation in Victorian England," *Journal of Family History* 22.3 (July 1997), 286, 294, 295.

21. See Merrill, *When Romeo Was a Woman*, 185.

22. On Hays's "ardent friendship" with Monson, see Lee Holcombe, *Wives and Property: Reform of the Married Women's Property Law in Nineteenth-Century England* (Toronto: University of Toronto Press, 1983), 85.

23. The figures for divorce between 1801 and 1857 come from Allen Horstman, who writes that "slowly Victorians came to accept that 200 or 300 marriages would be dissolved yearly" and compares that figure to the roughly 170,000 marriages contracted annually; *Victorian Divorce* (London: Croom Helm, 1985), 32, 85.

24. Savage, "'Intended Only for the Husband': Gender, Class, and the Provision for Divorce in England, 1858–1868," in Kristine Ottesen Garrigan, ed. *Victorian Scandals: Representations of Gender and Class* (Athens: Ohio University Press, 1992), 26.

25. See Barbara Leckie, *Culture and Adultery: The Novel, the Newspaper, and the Law, 1857–1914* (Philadelphia: University of Pennsylvania Press, 1999), 68, and Jeanne Fahnestock, "Bigamy: The Rise and Fall of a Convention," *Nineteenth-Century Fiction* 36 (1981), 47–71.

26. W. R. Greg, "Why Are Women Redundant?" reprinted in *Literary and Social Judgements* (Boston: James R. Osgood, 1873), 274–308.

27. Ibid., 279, 282, 299.

28. Frances Power Cobbe, "What Shall We Do with Our Old Maids?" in Andrea Broomfield and Sally Mitchell, eds., *Prose by Victorian Women: An Anthology* (New York: Garland, 1996), 236–61; first published in *Fraser's Magazine* (November 1862).

29. John Stuart Mill, "The Subjection of Women," [1869], in Alice S. Rossi, ed., *Essays on Sex Equality: John Stuart Mill and Harriet Taylor Mill* (Chicago: University of Chicago Press, 1970), 233.

30. Cobbe, "What Shall We Do," 239.

31. Frances Power Cobbe, *Life of Frances Power Cobbe*, vol. 2 (Boston: Houghton, Mifflin & Co., 1895), 645.

32. Ibid., vol. 2, 436.

33. Constance M. Fulmer, "Edith Jemima Simcox (1844–1901)," Bonnie Zimmerman, ed., *Lesbian Histories and Cultures* (New York: Garland Publishing Co., 2000), 699–700.

34. E[dith] J. Simcox, *Primitive Civilizations or Outlines of the History of Ownership in Archaic Communities* (London: Swan Sonnenschein, 1894), 9.

35. Elizabeth Fee and Elazar Barkan argue that anthropological texts reacted against feminism by invidiously associating marriage reform with reversion to a promiscuous primitive state. Kathy Psomiades sees anthropology as reinventing heterosexuality at a time when sexual difference was breaking down. George Stocking perceives continuity between the 1850s reformers who encouraged Victorians to imagine marriage differently and the 1860s anthropologists who recorded diversity in marriage customs and kinship systems. See Elizabeth Fee, "The Sexual Politics of Victorian Social Anthropology," in *Clio's Consciousness Raised: New Perspectives on the History of Women*, Mary S. Hartman and Lois Banner, eds. (New York: Harper Colophon, 1974), 87, 89, 100; Elazar Barkan, "Victorian Promiscuity: Greek Ethics and Primitive Exemplars," in *Prehistories of the Future: The Primitivist Project and the Culture of Modernism*, Elazar Barkan and Ronald Bush, eds. (Stanford: Stanford University Press, 1995), 62; Kathy Psomiades, "Heterosexual Exchange and Other Victorian Fictions: *The Eustace Diamonds* and Victorian Anthropology," *Novel* 33.1 (Fall 1999), 94; George W. Stocking, Jr., *Victorian Anthropology* (New York: The Free Press, 1987), 207.

36. Henry Sumner Maine, *Ancient Law: Its Connection with the Early History of Society and Its Relation to Modern Ideas* [1861] (Boston: Beacon Press, 1963), 121.

37. W. Robertson Smith, *Kinship and Marriage in Early Arabia* [first published 1885] (Boston: Beacon Press, reprint of 1903 edition), 166, 146.

38. William Lecky, *History of European Morals from Augustus to Charlemagne* [1869] (London: Longmans, Green, 1902 [based on revised 1877 edition]), vol. 2, 297–8, 277.

39. On the ways that sexuality was used to promote the imperial project, see Povinelli "Sexual Savages."

40. See Wendy Jones, "Feminism, Fiction and Contract Theory: Trollope's *He Knew He Was Right*," *Criticism* 36.3 (1994), 401–405.

41. John Stuart Mill, "Early Essays on Marriage and Divorce," in *Essays on Sex Equality*, 73.

42. Ibid., 83.

43. Mill, "Subjection of Women," 149.

44. Ibid., 136, 132.

45. Ibid., 133, 158, 169.

46. W. S. Lilly, "Marriage and Modern Civilization," *Nineteenth Century and After* 50.298 (December 1901), 908, 909–10, 919.

47. Gayle Rubin, "The Traffic in Women: Notes Toward a Political Economy of Sex," in *Toward an Anthropology of Women*, Rayna Reiter, ed. (New York: Monthly Review Press, 1975) 180. In *Gender Trouble: Feminism and the Subversion of Identity* (New York: Routledge, 1990), Judith Butler developed Rubin's argument into a critique of what she calls the "heterosexual matrix," which charges the incest prohibition with producing gender identity as heterosexuality. In *Antigone's Claim: Kinship between Life and Death* (New York: Columbia University Press, 2000), Butler reconfigures that insight to argue that the incest taboo should not be understood as leading inevitably to heterosexuality, that one must distinguish between prohibitions on incest and prohibitions on homosexuality. It thus becomes possible to decouple kinship from heterosexuality: "from the presumption that one cannot—or ought not to—choose one's closest family members as one's lovers and marital partners, it does not follow that the bonds of kinship that *are* possible assume any particular form" (66).

48. Claude Lévi-Strauss, *The Elementary Structures of Kinship*, rev. ed., trans. James Harle Bell, John Richard von Sturmer, and Rodney Needham [1949] (Boston: Beacon Press, 1969), 490. All further references to this text will appear as page numbers cited in the body of the essay.

49. It is perhaps because Levi-Strauss comes so close to acknowledging that homosexuality is not asocial, like incest, but as social as marriage, that he also concedes the converse proposition, that marriage approaches incest: "marriage is an arbitration between two loves, parental and conjugal . . . and the instant the marriage takes place, considered in isolation, the two meet and merge" (489). For conjugal love to replace parental love, there must be a moment when they are "momentarily . . . joined . . . At this moment, all marriage verges on incest. More than that, it is incest, at least social incest, if it is true that incest, in the broadest sense of the word, consists in obtaining by oneself, and for oneself, instead of by another, and for another" (489).

50. Frederick Engels, *The Origin of the Family, Private Property and the State*, ed. Eleanor Burke Leacock [1884; first English edition 1888] (New York: International Publishers, 1972), 101. All further references to this text will appear as page numbers cited in the body of the essay.

51. J. J. Bachofen, *Myth, Religion, and Mother Right: Selected Writings of J.J. Bachofen*, trans. Ralph Mannheim (Princeton: Princeton University Press, 1967), 204–205.

Suggestions for Further Reading

Boswell, John. *Same-Sex Unions in Premodern Europe*. New York: Villard Books, 1994.

Butler, Judith. *Gender Trouble: Feminism and the Subversion of Identity*. New York: Routledge, 1990.

————. *Antigone's Claim: Kinship Between Life and Death.* New York: Columbia University Press, 2000.

Faderman, Lillian. *Surpassing the Love of Men: Romantic Friendship and Love Between Women from the Renaissance to the Present.* New York: William Morrow, 1981.

Foucault, Michel. *The History of Sexuality: Volume I: An Introduction.* New York: Vintage, 1980.

Holcombe, Lee. *Wives and Property: Reform of the Married Women's Property Law in Nineteenth-Century England.* Toronto: University of Toronto Press, 1983.

Merrill, Lisa. *When Romeo Was a Woman: Charlotte Cushman and Her Circle of Female Spectators.* Ann Arbor: University of Michigan Press, 1999.

Oram, Alison, and Annmarie Turnbull. *The Lesbian History Sourcebook: Love and Sex Between Women in Britain from 1780 to 1970.* London: Routledge, 2001.

Poovey, Mary. *Uneven Developments: The Ideological Work of Gender in Mid-Victorian England.* Chicago: University of Chicago Press, 1988.

Rubin, Gayle. "The Traffic in Women: Notes Toward a Political Economy of Sex." In *Toward an Anthropology of Women*, ed. Rayna Reiter. New York: Monthly Review Press, 1975.

Shanley, Mary. " 'One Must Ride Behind': Married Women's Rights and the Divorce Act of 1857." *Victorian Studies* 25 (1982): 355–76.

Smith-Rosenberg, Carroll. "The Female World of Love and Ritual: Relations between Women in Nineteenth-Century America." In Joan Wallach Scott, ed., *Feminism and History.* Oxford: Oxford University Press, 1996: 366–97.

Stetson, Dorothy M. *A Woman's Issue: The Politics of Family Law Reform in England.* Westport, CT: Greenwood Press, 1982.

"Return from exile": Community, Nation, and Gender in George Eliot's Fiction

Deborah Epstein Nord

Deborah Epstein Nord (1976) is Professor of English and former Director of the Program in the Study of Women and Gender at Princeton University. The focus of her work is nineteenth-century British literature and culture, with an emphasis on gender and women writers. Her publications include *The Apprenticeship of Beatrice Webb* (1985); *Walking the Victorian Streets: Women, Representation, and the City* (1995); and an edition of John Ruskin's *Sesame and Lilies* (2002). She is currently completing a book on Gypsies in the nineteenth-century British imagination, from Walter Scott to Augustus John.

> *In the 1970s, when Deborah Nord was writing her dissertation on the British socialist Beatrice Webb, an important figure largely neglected by scholars, "we were intent on adding women to the canon—or upon rewriting the canon—and were attracted to those texts and figures that seemed to epitomize feminist struggle. Twenty-five years later, the individual writer has ceased to hold the fascination for feminist scholarship she once did. We are now less concerned with revising the canon and rediscovering 'lost' women; and gender, rather than woman, is our object of study." She still believes, however, that the nature of individual women's lived experience and its transmutation into literary expression are crucial and enduring elements of feminist scholarship.*

This essay reflects some, though surely not all, of the changes that feminist literary studies has undergone over the past thirty years. Just as there are a variety of "feminisms," so too are there varying histories of feminist criticism. My own began in the 1970s, when I emerged from graduate school as a fairly typical student of the founding feminist critics: Ellen Moers, Kate Millett, Elaine Showalter, Sandra Gilbert and Susan Gubar, to name only the most visible. Behind these late-twentieth-century pioneers stood Mary Wollstonecraft, who marshaled a lengthy critique of Rousseau's fiction in her *Vindication of the*

Rights of Woman (1792); Virginia Woolf, who inaugurated the modern tradition of what Showalter called "gynocriticism" (the study of women writers) in *A Room of One's Own* (1929) but also in her brilliant occasional essays on literary precursors; and Simone de Beauvoir, who devoted a section of *The Second Sex* (1949) to "Myths"—really literary texts.[1] In the '70s we focused our critical energies on the recovery of lost women writers, the revaluation of others, the constitution of a female literary tradition, and the unveiling of patriarchal paradigms in men's writing. Feminist work in that period was informed by many other critical approaches as well: psychoanalytic, exemplified by the neo-Freudianism of Juliet Mitchell and Nancy Chodorow and the work of film theorist Laura Mulvey; Lacanian-inflected theories of *écriture feminine*, as practiced by Hélène Cixous and others; and Marxist, evident in Cora Kaplan's insistence on class as a primary consideration in the analysis of writers like Charlotte Brontë and Virginia Woolf.[2]

The 1980s saw a gradual movement away from "women's studies" in the direction of "gender studies" and away from the study of individual women writers toward an examination of discourses of femininity and masculinity. Objections to the heterosexist bias of feminist scholarship of the '70s were answered, in part, by a deepening emphasis on sexuality in general and by gay, lesbian, and queer studies in particular. Eve Sedgwick's work formed a bridge from feminism to queer theory and demonstrated the important distinction between gender and sexuality.[3] Of particular salience for my own field of Victorian Studies was the influence of postcolonial theory, which put its stamp on literary criticism throughout the 1990s. Critics began to explore the relationship of British writers, both female and male, to the experience of Empire and to the colonized peoples they encountered both abroad and at home.[4] Just as African-American feminist criticism had earlier had an impact on the study of American literature, postcolonial studies—as well as identity politics—helped to introduce race as an important term in the analysis of British texts. My interest in the representation of race, Gypsies, Jews, nationalism, femininity, and masculinity in Eliot's work has been shaped by these expansions of feminist critical concerns over the last few decades.

* * * * *

Some twenty-five years ago, in the heyday of feminist literary criticism, Gillian Beer wrote a few lines about George Eliot's heroines that struck a chord with the novelist's fervent but frustrated readers. "George Eliot chose always," Beer wrote, "to imprison her most favored women—Dinah, Maggie, Dorothea. She does not allow them to share her own extraordinary flight from St. Oggs and from Middlemarch. She needs them to endure their own typicality."[5] Here Beer was commenting on the inevitable constraints faced by Eliot's most compelling and most defiant heroines. Dinah Morris, the itinerant Methodist preacher of *Adam Bede* (1859), gives up preaching and settles down with her carpenter husband; Maggie Tulliver's fierce childhood rebellion and adult bid for love end in premature death in *The Mill on the Floss* (1860); and

Dorothea Brooke's aspirations to reform the world in the manner of a latter-day St. Theresa in *Middlemarch* (1871–72) are ultimately subsumed within the political ambitions of her husband, Will Ladislaw. Unlike their creator, who left her family and community in provincial England and established an unconventional life and an extraordinary career in London, these heroines "endured" unexceptional lives. Indeed, Eliot's narratives would have us believe, they had no other choice, no way out.

In this chapter, I want to consider the pattern of imprisoned heroines in the context of Eliot's interest in community, in race (both as a matter of identity and as a metaphor for individual eccentricities), and in the possibilities and complexities of female heroism through the project of nationalism.[6] The crucial text for this last interest is Eliot's dramatic poem *The Spanish Gypsy* (1868), set in fifteenth-century Spain, which culminates in the heroine Fedalma's discovery of her Gypsy birth, assumption of the leadership of her people after her father's death, and departure from Spain in search of a Gypsy homeland in Africa. What happens, we might ask, when the heroine escapes typicality altogether and assumes the political role ordinarily occupied by the husbands of Eliot's heroines? What role does the difference of race play in the heroine's fate? And how does her relationship to both the known community of her upbringing and the imagined community of her "nation" figure in the trajectory of her life and in the unfolding of her femininity? Along the way, I will touch on the interplay between gender, race, and community in a number of Eliot's novels, most importantly *Daniel Deronda* (1874–76). In *Deronda*, the eponymous hero discovers that he is not the illegitimate son of an English aristocrat but the offspring of a Jewish mother who abandoned him and arranged for him to be raised as a non-Jew. By the story's end, he has left England for the Levant in the company of his Jewish wife to "restor[e] a political existence to my people, making them a nation again."[7] Because *Deronda* is, in many respects, a revision of *The Spanish Gypsy* that replaces Gypsy with Jew and female leader with male, it allows us to return in interesting and comparative ways to Beer's statement about gender and escape in Eliot's oeuvre.

KNOWABLE COMMUNITY

In trying to delineate George Eliot's passionate and longstanding commitment to representing the provincial communities of England's recent past, Raymond Williams used the phrase "knowable communities."[8] St. Oggs, Middlemarch, the Raveloe of *Silas Marner* (1861), the Hayslope of *Adam Bede*—these are the fictional communities that draw Eliot's novelistic interest and constitute the great achievements of her sociological imagination. Each can be fully known because, in Steven Marcus's words, "the world [they] represent has already been defined and in some sense closed off; things in it . . . *have already happened.*"[9] But these places are knowable as well because of the homogeneity, despite class differences, of the social experiences of their inhabitants and because of the presumed familiarity—the knowability—of each inhabitant to his or her neighbors.

Williams locates the dramatic tension of Eliot's novels in the conflict between the knowable community and what he calls the "separated individual." "It is part of a crucial history of the development of the novel," he writes, "in which the knowable community . . . comes to be known primarily as a problem of ambivalent relationship: of how the separated individual, with a divided consciousness of belonging and not belonging, makes his own moral history."[10] Suzanne Graver, in *George Eliot and Community*, defines this tension slightly differently. In her terms, Eliot searches for a new understanding of community, one that combines elements of *Gemeinschaft*, or local, traditional community rooted in the family, and *Gesellschaft*, or urban-influenced, industrial society that fosters individualism.[11] Eliot's separated individual, who struggles against traditional ways of being and yearns toward a modernity that frees individual desire, is very often a woman and often at risk of going beyond separateness to the condition of being a pariah. Williams argues that Eliot finds it nearly impossible to imagine or to represent a satisfying resolution to the conflict between traditional community and individual aspiration—or, between the values of *Gemeinschaft* and *Gesellschaft*—and that, more often than not, she settles on "sad resignation" rather than personal transcendence for her hero or heroine.[12] Rather than becoming a pariah—or running off to London—and risking an irrevocable break with family and home, Maggie Tulliver will tame her own wildness, suppress desire, and cling to the community that judges her a ruined woman. Williams's sad resignation and Beer's endurance of typicality are much the same thing. As Beer understands, however, resignation is almost always sadder and more limiting for Eliot's heroines than for her heroes, no matter how marginal or how outcast. Or, put differently, the claims of *Gemeinschaft* are more pressing—and the values of *Gesellschaft* riskier—for women than for men.

In Eliot's fiction, the separated individual is often figured as disinherited, either literally or metaphorically. We think of Will Ladislaw, object of a double disinheritance, of Silas Marner, who has been robbed of both love and wealth, of Daniel Deronda, whose Jewish inheritance has been denied him, of Dorothea Brooke, in danger of being written out of her husband's will, of Tom and Maggie Tulliver, ejected from childhood happiness and economic stability like Adam and Eve from Eden. Indeed, the theme of disinheritance informs a good deal of eighteenth- and nineteenth-century fiction, beginning but certainly not ending with *Tom Jones*, *Jane Eyre*, and *David Copperfield*. The orphan's plight, unanswered questions of origin, and the fantasy of noble or at least salutary birth—what Freud called the family romance—are central to the development of the novel.[13] But for Eliot the phenomenon of disinheritance is always linked not only to relations between child and parents and to fortune or property but also—and what is more important—to the individual's vexed relation to community and often to race or nation.

Critics like Michael Ragussis and Bernard Semmel have emphasized Eliot's extensive debt to Walter Scott, in whose works the theme of disinheritance is ubiquitous.[14] The debt to Scott is particularly instructive in trying to establish the contours of Eliot's interest in the disinherited ones. If we look, for example, at *Ivanhoe* (1819), we see that Scott has given the "Disinherited Knight," the novel's hero, an analogue in the Jews, whom Isaac of York describes to his daughter, Rebecca, as "disinherited and wandering."[15] Scott had used this kind of analogous relation as well in *Guy Mannering* (1815), in which a disinherited Scottish laird is juxtaposed with a tribe of Gypsies banished from their home on that same laird's property. Eliot takes up Scott's fascination with dispossessed groups, deepening the connection between estranged individual and disinherited nation, evoking characters metaphorically as marked by race or giving them a distinct but hidden racial identity. Even *Silas Marner*, a novel in which no racial or national group figures or is overtly mentioned, opens with a meditation on the figures of displaced linen weavers, "emigrants from the town into the country," who make their way among the "brawny country-folk" looking like "the remnants of *a disinherited race*." These weavers, of whom Silas Marner will emerge as one, are marked physically—they are "pallid undersized men," "alien-looking"—and exist in a "state of wandering."[16] Eliot, in other words, uses the precise language to identify the likes of Silas that Scott puts in the mouth of Isaac to describe the Jews. An outsider, a pariah, a "separated individual," is almost always imagined in Eliot's fiction in relation to an alien group, even in a novel that includes no actual instance of such a group. Silas, then, is conjured as if a Jew or a Gypsy, an implicit comparison underscored later in the novel when the community of Raveloe suspects that a swarthy peddler, with curly black hair and earrings, has stolen Silas's gold.[17] Just as the superstitious inhabitants of Raveloe had initially suspected and shunned Silas, they now invent another outsider, a peripatetic of a different sort (presumably a Gypsy) and an ironic double for Silas, to blame for this crime.

DISINHERITED RACES

Imagined as the remnant of a "disinherited race," a wanderer whose origins, home, and parentage are unknown to those among whom he comes to dwell, Silas himself is evoked only obliquely as an alien. Both Maggie Tulliver and Will Ladislaw, however, are outsiders whose difference is characterized through persistent association with racially or nationally distinct groups. Maggie Tulliver's parents lament her anomalous femininity—her dark looks and unruly hair, her tomboy ways and lack of decorousness—as signs of insanity, genetic mutation, or racial otherness. In the second chapter of *The Mill on the Floss*, Mrs. Tulliver frets about Maggie's resemblance to "a Bedlam creatur'" and about the "brown skin as makes her look like a mulatter," while Mr. Tulliver explains that his daughter's inheritance of his, rather than her mother's, mental and physical characteristics makes her a casualty of "the crossing o'breeds," a freak of nature like a "long-tailed sheep."[18]

Eliot marks Maggie's difference through metaphor but also through a sense that she is physically, even genetically idiosyncratic. Though she is not, of course, of a different race, something in her bodily constitution destines her for a fate that does not conform to the conventional plot of femininity. Later in the novel Maggie, disgraced by an incident with her brother and acceptably feminine cousin Lucy, decides to run off to join the Gypsies, having been told so often that she was like a Gypsy and "half wild." Impulsively in search of her "unknown kindred," she follows the familiar plot of the family romance. Imagining herself a changeling and fueled by motives of revenge, Maggie seeks her true parentage and kin. Although she will discover that her fantasy of Gypsy life bears no resemblance to the reality she discovers in a Gypsy camp on the edge of St. Oggs, she does glimpse the face of a "gypsy-mother" who resembles her: "Maggie looked up in the new face rather tremblingly as it approached, and was reassured by the thought that . . . the rest were right when they called her a gypsy, for this face with the bright dark eyes and the long hair was really something like what she used to see in the glass."[19] This moment of recognition is eclipsed by Maggie's ultimate fear of the Gypsies and her desire to return home, the chastised child who has foolishly run away. But in the course of *Mill on the Floss*, Maggie never does discover her true kin, either by escape or by marriage. Although her waifishness turns into a dark and voluptuous beauty as she grows older, her racially marked body changing from freakish to exotic, Maggie's ability to attract the love of men fails utterly to ensure her happiness or even her survival.[20] As she had run off, with unhappy results, to the Gypsies, she later leaves home, with even more disastrous consequences, with a man she can never marry. She resumes the status of pariah, this time irrevocably, and is "rescued" from a life of isolation, disgrace, and celibacy by regression and death.

With Will Ladislaw, Dorothea Brooke's lover and second husband in *Middlemarch*, Eliot makes actual the foreignness that remained largely figurative in *Mill on the Floss*. Ladislaw's identity in the provincial, midlands town of Middlemarch is never separable from the foreignness of his surname, his appearance, and his ancestry. Neither is his foreignness separable from his bohemianism, his relationship to the arts, his reformist politics, and his heterodox masculinity. The nephew of Dorothea's punitive and dry-as-dust first husband Casaubon, Will is descended from a Polish grandfather—a patriot and musician—on one side and a pawnbroker and his high-spirited actress-daughter on the other. ("You see," he tells Dorothea, "I come of rebellious blood on both sides."[21]) On both sides, as I have indicated, he has been disinherited: his paternal grandmother had been disowned upon running off with the Pole, Ladislaw, and his mother ostensibly forfeited the inheritance that ought to have come to her from her father when she went on the stage.

Although Will's Polish ancestry remains his only real claim to foreignness, he is alluded to by numerous characters in the novel as an alien of various sorts. His peripatetic ways, uninhibited manner, and social promiscuity inspire Lydgate, an outsider of a different kind, to refer to Ladislaw as "a sort of gypsy."[22] The narrator cites this comment of Lydgate's a number of pages later and corroborates that Will "rather enjoy[s] the sense of belonging to no class" and has a "feeling of romance in his position, and a pleasant consciousness of creating a little surprise wherever he went."[23] The narrator, continuing to emphasize the benign aspects of Will's unconventional behavior, remarks on his delight in taking the town's children "on a gypsy excursion to Halsell Wood at nutting time" and on his habit of stretching out full length on the floor of those he visits. But the narrator sounds a more ominous note by referring to the way in which this recumbent posture confirms for other visitors "the notions of his dangerously mixed blood."[24] When rumors begin to circulate in Middlemarch about the possibility of a love match between Dorothea and her late husband's nephew, the epithets directed at Will begin to accrue. No longer just a Pole or a Gypsy, he becomes, in the words of his detractors, an "Italian with white mice," then the possessor of "any cursed alien blood, Jew, Corsican, or Gypsy," and finally, when news of his maternal grandfather's occupation becomes a matter of common knowledge, "the grandson of a thieving Jew pawnbroker."[25]

Although critics have disagreed about whether Eliot intended to suggest that Will's grandfather was indeed a Jew and whether Will was, therefore, an early version of Daniel Deronda, the novelist's point here seems to be that Will's status as an outsider is both salutary and an incitement to the bigotry of those around him in the "knowable community" to which he has attached himself.[26] He is an ideal husband for Dorothea, Eliot suggests, because of his foreignness, which is inseparable from his artistic spirit, political liberalism, and lack of social snobbery. But his identity is also a flashpoint for the insularity and narrow-mindedness of Middlemarchers, a way of exposing the liabilities of existence in a community that insists on homogeneity, or at least on its appearance. Dorothea's friends and relations imagine Ladislaw's "bad origin"—as Sir James Chettam, Dorothea's brother-in-law, refers to his birth—to be inextricably connected to the lack of principle and "light character" they attribute to him.[27] But the resolution of Dorothea's and Will's story suggests that this persistent prejudice is only a minor impediment to happiness and success. Will, we learn, "became an ardent public man, working well in those times when reforms were begun with a young hopefulness," and his marriage to Dorothea is loving and reproductive. Dorothea may be prevented from becoming a new St. Theresa or an Antigone because of the "imperfect social state" into which she had been born, but her happiness is not marred by the convictions of others that her marriage is a mistake.[28] The doubly disinherited outsider, Will Ladislaw, prospers.

NATIONALISM AND THE IMAGINED COMMUNITY

With Fedalma and with Daniel Deronda, Eliot's "separated individual" moves from pariah to exile. No mere metaphorical aliens or foreigners capable of a satisfactory, if resigned, integration into English society, these characters are members of a disinherited and displaced nation and implicit exiles from a home or place of origin to which they will ultimately try to return. Although it would be a mistake to attribute to Eliot's fiction an absolute teleology from disinherited individual to disinherited nation, it seems nonetheless the case that, by the latter part of her career, she is attracted to the idea of permanent separateness—or separation—as a solution to the problem of the outcast. The mechanism for this imagined solution is "racial" difference, not as a metaphor for temperamental difference or marginal social position, but rather as a total and irreducible identity. Racial or national identity is offered as the reason, perhaps the occasion, for severing ties to a seemingly temporary or at least tenuous British home. Furthermore, identity in both *The Spanish Gypsy* and *Daniel Deronda* is a hidden reality, a secret fact of birth to be discovered by the protagonist. Maggie Tulliver may imagine that she is a foundling, born to parents other than those who raised her, but, in the cases of Fedalma and Daniel Deronda, this daydream—or nightmare—comes true. The Freudian fantasy of family romance becomes the plot of family romance, and the discovery of true parentage brings with it the confirmation and reification of difference. The trauma of disinheritance and ostracism is ostensibly to be overcome by inheriting an unknown lineage and a distant land.

Influenced by mid-nineteenth century discussions of nationalism and inspired by the case of Italy, Eliot valued the persistence and cultivation of national identities.[29] In an essay entitled "The Modern Hep! Hep! Hep!," published in 1879 as part of *Impressions of Theophrastus Such*, Eliot laments a tendency toward the "fusion of races" and counsels "moderation" in the "effacement of those national traditions and customs which are the language of the national genius":

> Such moderating and guidance of inevitable movement [she continues] is worthy of all effort. And it is in this sense that the modern insistence on the idea of Nationalities has value. That any people at once distinct and coherent enough to form a state should be held in subjection by an alien antipathetic government has been becoming more and more a ground of sympathetic indignation; and, in virtue of this, at least one great State has been added to European councils.[30]

The essay speaks generally about the virtues of what she calls the "spirit of separateness" and about its relationship to memory and to the "national life" that dwells "in our veins," but she pays special attention to the case of the Jews, an "expatriated, denationalised race."[31] It is not simply, then, that she prizes the Jews' survival as a distinct group with a set of traditions, rituals, and cultural characteristics but that she imagines the Jews as exiles awaiting return to "a native country, the birthplace of common memories and habits of mind, *existing like a parental hearth quitted but loved.*"[32] Like the Italians, the Jews merit a state of their own, and the state is imagined here as the wellspring, the "parent," of group identity. In *Daniel Deronda* the visionary Mordecai, who acts as Deronda's spiritual and political guide, speaks of reviving the Jews' "organic centre," a community that will, like Italy, be a "republic" and the realization of a people's connection to its ancient land.[33] Using the metaphor of the parental hearth in "The Modern Hep! Hep! Hep!," Eliot brings into relief what her fictions imply: that individual inheritance and identity find their analogue, perhaps their extension, in the contours and vicissitudes of national identity.

The knowable communities that form the heart of Eliot's fiction constrain and yet hold most of the individuals—separated, marginal, outcast—who find themselves in a struggle with convention and tradition. Fedalma and Daniel Deronda, however, outsiders who discover that their separateness derives from a biological tie to an alien group, leave their countries of exile—Spain and England respectively—to seek a homeland, a nation. Nationalism, then, provides an answer to the separated individual's conflict with knowable community, a conflict that, in these two cases, does not become acute until the protagonists discover the true stories of their birth. Difference from community can be transcended through the creation of a community of fellow outsiders, in which difference itself constitutes the basis for citizenship. Eliot's sympathy with subject groups and her desire to invent at least a novelistic solution to their oppression coalesce here, one imagines, with her own fantasy of an alternative community that is both knowable and hospitable to the alien and the outcast.

Benedict Anderson uses the term "imagined communities" to define the idea of nation: imagined because, in some instances, not yet realized and because, even when realized, the nation contains individuals who nurture the "image of their communion" with an array of compatriots they will never know.[34] As Mordecai declares in *Deronda*, "Community was felt before it was called good," even before it was imagined in the form of a nation.[35] Anderson also emphasizes the way the state within a nationalist imagination "loom[s] out of an immemorial past . . . and glide[s] into a limitless future."[36] Here he sounds a note very similar to Eliot's account of the role of memory in "The Modern Hep! Hep! Hep!" In both Eliot and Anderson, the individual's memory ties him or her to something the person cannot remember but locates in some very distant, primordial past and takes as the basis of identity, as well as fate. "It is the magic of nationalism to turn chance [the chance of birth] into destiny," writes Anderson, crafting a line that could stand as the synopsis of both *The Spanish Gypsy* and *Daniel Deronda*.[37] These works add another meaning to "imagined community" by refusing to represent—how could they?—the imagined homelands toward which they merely gesture at narrative's end.[38]

THE DIFFERENCE OF GENDER

As I have already suggested in my brief discussions of *The Mill on the Floss*, *Silas Marner*, and *Middlemarch*, Eliot's pariah-heroes fare better than her pariah-heroines. The male characters associated with foreignness and racial difference in these novels not only achieve a kind of social integration and acceptance but, perhaps more significantly for the purposes of this discussion, they secure for themselves—or are blessed with—procreative futures. Ladislaw, though still suspect in the eyes of some hidebound Middlemarchers, realizes his political ambitions as an English reformer and produces a family with Dorothea. Even Silas Marner becomes a father, not through marriage and biological paternity but through the fortuitous adoption of Eppie.[39] His fatherhood helps not only to redeem him as a moral being but also to bind him to his community. Maggie Tulliver—mulatto, Bedlamite, Gypsy—perishes, barred from marriage because of her romantic failures and destined for a premature death as an estranged member of her community. Her male counterpart in the novel, Philip Wakem, who as a hunchback is bodily though not "racially" marked, remains celibate but survives. Maggie's victory, if she can be said to have one, is in the grave, where both of her lovers in life come to visit and mourn her and where she is permanently reunited with her brother Tom. Nonetheless, because her sex makes her vulnerable to public disgrace, it precludes both generativity and survival.

What, then, of Fedalma, the Spanish Gypsy? Eliot's long dramatic poem, set in Spain during the time of the Inquisition, has attracted attention of late from critics interested in issues of race, conversion, and nationalism in Eliot's fiction. The most cogent way of identifying the philosophical debate of the poem would employ the terms that Bernard Semmel uses to analyze Eliot's novel *Romola*. According to him, Eliot struggles between two powerful and competing beliefs: on the one hand, the Comtean sense of an individual's need to sacrifice his or her will to the "general good" and, on the other, the liberal individualist critique of Comte, best represented by John Stuart Mill—and, not incidentally, by George Henry Lewes, Eliot's companion—that emphasizes the paramount importance of individual liberty.[40] In the *Spanish Gypsy*, Eliot dramatizes this struggle in the heroine Fedalma, raised as a Spanish princess and torn between her love for the Castilian knight Duke Silva, to whom she is betrothed, and her duty to the people, the Gypsies, the Zincala, she discovers to be her own. Her father, Zarca, leader of a tribe of Zincala who have been brutally captured by Silva's people and are destined for annihilation by Silva's uncle, the Prior, demands of Fedalma that she become his second-in-command, "the angel of a homeless tribe":

> To help me bless a race taught by no prophet
> And make their name, now but a badge of scorn.
> . . . .
> I'll guide my brethren forth to their new land,
> Where they shall plant and sow and reap their own,
> . . . .
> Where we may kindle our first altar-fire
> From settled hearths, *and call our Holy Place*
> *The hearth that binds us in one family.*
> That land awaits them: they await their chief—
> Me, who am imprisoned. All depends on you.[41]

Fedalma must dedicate herself to a project of nationalism, imagined here much as it is in *Theophrastus Such* as an effort to build a "birthplace of common memories and habits of mind, existing like a parental hearth."

Silva, Fedalma's lover and, by association, the inevitable enemy of her people, argues for the Millite position: the primitive tie of blood and the call of birth must not be given primacy and "Love [must come] to cancel all ancestral hate,/ Subdue[ ] all heritage, prove[ ] that in mankind/ Union is deeper than division."[42] Liberty in choosing one's destiny is essential for Silva and, to demonstrate this, he decides to join the Zincala, to become a Gypsy, so that he can marry Fedalma and support her people's just cause. Eliot stages a refutation of Silva's belief in individual liberty when the Zincala hang his uncle, the evil Prior, and Silva, feeling betrayed and enraged by the people to whom he has chosen to ally himself, murders Zarca, the father of his beloved Fedalma. This establishes a permanent enmity between the lovers, demonstrates the impossibility of choosing identity and ignoring birth, and bestows the leadership of Fedalma's people wholly on her. Obliged to take her father's place, she haltingly but dutifully proceeds to set sail with her people for an unknown homeland in Africa. Not dead like Maggie Tulliver, her sacrifice is only partial: she will keep faith with her father's dream and "plant / His sacred hope within the sanctuary," but she will die a "priestess," a "hoary [white-haired] woman on the altar-step" who has become the "funeral urn," the "temple" of her father's remains.[43] Heroic but celibate, she will not achieve the synthesis of personal happiness and vocational success that Will Ladislaw enjoys, or even the surrogate parenthood and communal integration of Silas Marner.

Fedalma is linked to the other "imprisoned" heroines of Eliot's works not because of her typicality or her ties to knowable community but because she is denied individual liberty and the fulfillment of personal desire, in her case through her dedication to the imagined community of nation. Gender, then, complicates the philosophical debate that informs the *Spanish Gypsy*. For women, the two poles of individual liberty and devotion to the general good seem farther apart than they ever do for men in Eliot's fiction; indeed, they seem always to be at odds. What has confounded readers and critics of the *Spanish Gypsy*, however, is that the general good and allegiance to community are aligned with a heroic and public role rather than with fealty to the customs of St. Oggs and the imperative to marry and procreate. Indeed, in Eliot's own extensive and striking comments on the poem in her journal, she writes that she "required the opposition of race to give the need for renouncing marriage."[44] Inspired by a Titian painting of the Annunciation, she seeks a subject that will reproduce the idea of a woman's separation from "the ordinary lot of womanhood" and her call "to fulfil a great destiny."[45] She settles on race—or what she calls a "hereditary condition"—to pry her heroine loose from love, marriage, and desire. That Eliot means these circumstances to inspire ambivalence is clear: "It is the individual with whom we sympathise," she continues in the journal, "and the general of which we recognize the irresistible power."[46]

In *Figures of Conversion* Michael Ragussis places Fedalma, along with the daughter-heroines of Bulwer-Lytton's *Leila* (1838) and Grace Aguilar's *The Vale of Cedars; or the Martyr* (1850), in the literary tradition of Scott's Rebecca.[47] These heroines of what Ragussis calls "racial plots" (as opposed to marriage plots) are paired with an apparently widowed father who tries to prohibit their intermarriage to a non-Gypsy or non-Jew. Fedalma, Ragussis writes, faces "an exile based in the sacrifice of the erotic," and her body "becomes no more than a kind of grave for the memorialization of the dead father."[48]

Although Ragussis concedes that Fedalma's dismal fate does not override what he calls "the central ideology of the text," the poem's rejection of assimilation or "conversion," he emphasizes the cruelty of the daughter's sacrifice to the father's will. If Ragussis stresses the denial of individual desire—or liberty—in his reading of the poem, Alicia Carroll finds in Fedalma's acquiescence to the needs of the "general" a decidedly sanguine meaning. Far from seeing Fedalma as sacrificial or the conclusion of the poem as funereal, she argues that Fedalma represents "a technically chaste maternal subjectivity that nonetheless resonates with erotic meaning."[49] Carroll finds in Fedalma a type of queenly presence that, combined with her elevated role as mother to her people, makes her a triumphant and resplendent figure.

It may be difficult to reconcile these two views—a young woman denied an erotic and procreative future on the one hand and a leader of her people whose symbolic motherhood has an erotic tinge on the other. But it is not, I think, difficult to see that these contradictory readings are the result of the mixed signals Eliot leaves us with at the poem's end. Although the association Eliot herself makes between the Virgin Mary and Fedalma might tend to support Carroll's interpretation, it also seems clear from the poem's imagery ("I am but the funeral urn that bears the ashes of a leader. . . . A hoary woman on the altar-step . . .") that Fedalma faces celibacy and sterility and has been masculinized at her father's bidding. Before Zarca dies he refers to his daughter, now turbaned, wearing Moorish dress, and bearing a dagger, as "my younger self."[50] Earlier, Zarca had dared Fedalma to deny her Gypsy inheritance, using language that conflates an exaggerated femininity with "passing" as a Spaniard and a Christian:

> Unmake yourself, then, from a Zincala—
> Unmake yourself from being a child of mine!
> Take holy water, cross your dark skin white;
> Round your proud eyes to foolish kitten looks;
> Walk mincingly, and smirk, and twitch your robe;
> Unmake yourself—doff all the eagle plumes
> And be a parrot. . . .[51]

To remain a Spanish princess is to remain inauthentic and a coquette. To be what she really is—a Gypsy—is to strip herself of both Christian and feminine pretenses, to leave behind what Zarca calls "the petty round of circumstance . . . [t]hat makes a woman's lot." The poem also suggests that the nationalist project Fedalma is about to undertake is likely doomed: "her father's hope,/ Which she must plant and see it wither only—/ Wither and die. She saw the end begun."[52] Without the "invisible passion" of Zarca, the "great force" that held the Zincali together, the voyage from Spain takes on a melancholy, enervated air. And Fedalma is just as "resigned" to her fate as the celibate leader of her people as other Eliot heroines are to their lives of typicality and conventional domesticity. As Ragussis implies, the grimness of the poem's conclusion makes it difficult for the reader to muster enthusiasm for what ought to be Fedalma's heroic mission.

A moment much earlier in the poem, however, dramatically prefigures Fedalma's role as leader of her people and lets us glimpse her genuine yearning toward community and the experience of collective identity. Before she has learned the secret of her birth, she ventures into the Plaça Santiago and is swept up in the joy of the crowd. She dances before the common people in the square, tambourine in hand. But this is not simply a frivolous moment of pleasure. Fedalma, as Eliot describes her, "[m]oves as, in dance religious, Miriam,/ When, on the Red Sea shore she raised her voice/ And led the chorus of the people's joy."[53] Fedalma is evoked as a type of Miriam, the sister of Moses, who helped to lead the Israelites out of exile in Egypt to journey to the Promised Land. Later, Fedalma will lead the Zincali in just this way, although by then she will combine the role of Miriam with that of Aaron, the brother of Moses who led the people into Canaan after their great leader's death.[54] At this point the poem celebrates, through prefiguration and biblical allusion, the full and transcendent meaning of Fedalma's role in the Zincalis' exodus. When Prince Silva admonishes her, shocked that she should display herself by dancing in a public square, Fedalma argues that the dance, far from separating her out from the crowd as a spectacle to be gawked at, had brought her into communion with the people: "I seemed new-waked/ To life in unison with a multitude—/ Feeling my soul upbourne by all their souls . . . Soon I lost/ All sense of separateness."[55] Here, merging with the general will and with communal purpose takes on a joyous and spiritually uplifting cast. That this should almost wholly evaporate by the end of the poem, as joy is replaced with sacrifice and devotion to community with the apparent suppression of individual liberty and desire, perplexes the reader and confounds easy interpretation. What does seem clear, however, is that this poem, like Eliot's novels, cannot find a way to reconcile public heroism with an acceptable feminine destiny, the leadership of community with "a woman's lot." When Eliot tries a second time to write the story of hidden parentage, alien identity, and nationalist idealism, she makes her protagonist a man.

THE DIFFERENCE OF GENDER, AGAIN

It might be said that when George Eliot wrote *Daniel Deronda*, her last novel, she rewrote the figure of Fedalma by dispersing her qualities among at least three different characters, two of them women and one a man. Eliot transforms the "Rebecca" figure, the beautiful, nubile young woman who ends the narrative unmarried and bereft of the man she has loved, into an Englishwoman, Gwendolyn Harleth. As the Jewish Rebecca loses Ivanhoe to the golden-haired Rowena, the golden-haired Gwendolyn loses Daniel Deronda to the Jewish, raven-haired Mirah. Gwendolyn, then, is the "imprisoned" heroine, although she is imprisoned, like Fedalma, in celibacy rather than, like Dinah and Dorothea, in domesticity. Eliot restages the conflict that Fedalma faces between faithfulness to her people and her personal desires in the history of the Alcharisi, Daniel's mother, a Jewish woman who gave up her son and hid her identity in order to practice her art and escape the moral strictures and obligations of her religion. Judaism to her is simply "bondage," obedience to the ideals of Jewish womanhood "slavery."[56] The Alcharisi chooses desire over community, and, through the perspective and grief of her abandoned son, she is vilified. The power that "racial" inheritance holds for Eliot helps, I think, to explain why this woman, who pursues her vocation and her longing for "the wide world," receives such brutal treatment within the novel.

Fedalma's most important double in this novel, however, is Deronda himself. Like Fedalma, he discovers the secret of his birth and ends by leaving his erstwhile homeland to explore a national home for his people, to become, *avant la lettre*, a Zionist. Deronda, however, leaves England in an aura of hopefulness, idealism, and nobility, and he leaves with a Jewish wife, Mirah. Further, Daniel fulfills the dream of the scholarly and gentle Mordecai, Mirah's brother, rather than the legacy of an exigent father who stands in determined opposition to the person he loves. Put simply, love and mission merge for Deronda, while they split disastrously apart for Fedalma. To some degree, the subdued, not to say, defeatist rhetoric of the end of the *Spanish Gypsy* reflects a difference of history as well as a difference of the protagonist's sex. The idea of a Gypsy homeland in Africa seems to have been Eliot's alone, and she could barely manage to represent this fantastical aspiration convincingly in a work set in fifteenth–century Spain. The Jews had not only an established link to a specific homeland but the beginnings of a modern ideology of return.[57] Jews also possessed a written tradition and, what she referred to in "The Modern Hep! Hep! Hep!" as "a sense of separateness unique in its intensity," "an organized memory of a national consciousness," that was inseparable from its religion and its holy texts.[58] In the *Spanish Gypsy*, Eliot places in Zarca's mouth the case for the Gypsies' difference from other alien groups—Jews and Moors in particular—who inhabit Spain: the Zincali are "wanderers whom no God took knowledge of/ To give them laws, to fight for them, or blight/ Another race to give them ampler room;/ Who have no Whence or Whither in their souls,/ No dimmest lore of glorious ancestors."[59] Even their faith, Zarca remarks, is taught not by a priest but by "their beating hearts." All they have to bind them together is their loyalty to one another—"the fidelity of fellow-wanderers"—and their susceptibility to the "mystic stirring of a common life."[60] In terms of the demands of literary realism, the Jews offer Eliot a historical subject that suits the plot of exile and nationalism and that holds a place of religious and intellectual importance in the Christian tradition and in contemporary English life.

The impasse of the *Spanish Gypsy*—a heroine too bereft and too uncertain to embrace with passion the mission she nonetheless accepts—may have given Eliot the impetus to re-imagine her story differently. Crucial to this re-imagining are the question of choice and the evolution, rather than the imposition, of identity. Deronda can be said to have slowly *become* a Jew even before he discovers the religion (or "race") of his parents and, once he makes this discovery, to have chosen an identity with the full exercise of his will. Unlike Fedalma—and more like Maggie Tulliver—Deronda feels certain that his birth had been an anomalous one. He possesses a keen sense of "entailed disadvantage—the deformed foot doubtfully hidden by the shoe" that makes him sympathetic to the outcasts, "the Hagars and the Ishmaels."[61] His rescue of Mirah draws him first to a Jewish love object and then to the idea of Judaism as something "still throbbing in human lives."[62] Refusing the path of a conventional English gentleman he wanders abroad, not knowing precisely what he is looking for, and enters a synagogue in Frankfurt. Looking for Mirah's lost brother in the East End of London he encounters Mordecai, who takes Deronda under his tutelage and decides to regard him as a Jew for his own quixotic reasons. By the time Deronda meets his mother and learns the story of his birth, he is primed to be a Jew; a Jewish sensibility, we are to understand, has developed within him. As if to emphasize that he actively chooses, as well as inherits, Jewishness and does not, like Fedalma, simply regard it as a worthy though inescapable duty, he declares "I shall call myself a Jew. . . . But I will not say that I shall profess to believe exactly as my fathers have believed."[63]

The identity of difference, of otherness, that Fedalma had briefly sensed and reveled in during her dance in the town square ultimately becomes her burden, her legacy of responsibility. Although the moment in the square suggests the possibility of a Deronda-like evolution of identity, it is not fulfilled, in part because her national inheritance and her lover are irrevocably at odds. So, unlike Deronda, she does not choose her fate, nor does she enjoy a perfect synthesis of love and mission, of personal desire and devotion to community. In *Deronda*, Eliot is not interested in staging a struggle between the individual will and "the general" and, for this reason, she shifts to a male protagonist who does not face the conflict, habitual to women in Eliot's fiction and Eliot's time, between private and public desire. Women's ability to choose their destinies, in Eliot's works, is suppressed: their will remains subject to the demand that they fulfill, first and foremost, a woman's lot and the will of the community. In the case of Fedalma, her inheritance separates her from the private pleasures of "woman's lot" and determines that her obligation to the community—her community—be a life of public heroism and private denial. Indeed, she all but ceases to be a woman at the poem's end, as if to underscore the necessarily masculine nature of a political leader's public role and its irreconcilability with conventional femininity.

CONCLUSION: "MARKS OF RACE" AND MASCULINITY

I began this essay with Gillian Beer's statement about George Eliot's need to have her heroines endure their typicality and with a number of questions about the relationship between gender, race, and community in Eliot's works. My discussion of the *Spanish Gypsy* makes clear, I hope, that escape from typicality, from "knowable" to "imagined" community, has the effect of nullifying the heroine's sexuality and femininity. The strictures of imagined community turn out to be just as confining, in their own way, as the demands of knowable community: each inhibits female choice and exacts a price for woman's expression of desire. Imagined community offers Daniel Deronda refuge and transcendence, as it might be expected to do for Fedalma who, as a Gypsy during the period of the Inquisition, would be denied a life of liberty in Spain, or perhaps a life at all. Fedalma's return from exile turns out, however, to be a highly equivocal fate.

The heroine's difference of race in *Spanish Gypsy* acts much as the sexual transgression attributed to Maggie Tulliver in *The Mill on the Floss* does: as bodily stigma, as a physical marking that short-circuits the resolution of the marriage plot. In her notes on the *Spanish Gypsy*, Eliot defines the "inherited organisation" that would necessarily prevent a woman from attaining personal happiness: "she may be lame, she may inherit a disease, or what is tantamount to a disease: she may be a negress, or have other marks of race repulsive in the community where she is born."[64] This striking statement, revealing as it is of Eliot's equation of race with deformity or disease, also raises the slightly different question with which I would like to end this essay. Does "race" mark the male body as it does the female? And does anomalous masculinity carry with it a bodily stigma similar to Maggie's embodied sexual sinfulness and Fedalma's dark skin? Are favored men also imprisoned in Eliot's fiction?

We have already seen that anomalous masculinity expressed as foreignness, as in the case of Will Ladislaw, or as actual "racial" difference, as in the case of Daniel Deronda, does not bar Eliot's heroes from private satisfactions and public efficaciousness. But do such men carry with them an enduring mark, a physical stigma of difference? And if so, can they compensate for bodily stigma or, perhaps, obscure it in some way that enables them to mask their alien identities? Eliot represents Philip Wakem's difference of temperament and sensibility as a literal physical deformity in *Mill on the Floss*. She associates his crippled frame with his sensitivity and his acute ability to understand the most complicated motives of others. But his marked body is also associated with his femininity. The narrator repeatedly refers to Philip, who blushes more often than any other character in the novel, as being or looking like a girl. This is true not only in Philip's childhood but in his young adulthood as well. At the very moment Philip declares his love for Maggie and she hesitantly but hopefully reciprocates, we read: "Maggie smiled . . . and then stooped her tall head to kiss the low pale face that was full of pleading, timid love—like a woman's."[65] Even before Maggie runs off with another man and her death precludes the possibility that she and Philip will marry, we know that this union will not happen. In the erotic economy of Victorian romance, Philip's girlishness and vulnerability make him an object of pity and tenderness but not of heterosexual love. Philip's curved spine, like the wound of Philoctetes, with whom the text aligns him, makes the young man a pariah.[66] The narrator's last words about Philip describe him as "always solitary," a being whose "great companionship" after Maggie's death remains the trees among which they had walked. Philip survives while Maggie perishes, but he is destined for celibacy and noble isolation.

Daniel Deronda's stigma—his wound—is a more complicated and a more hidden business. Inevitably, critics have been fascinated by the question of circumcision in a novel about a young Jewish man who cannot tell that he is a Jew. If, in the nineteenth century, all Jewish boys were circumcised and non-Jews were not, then Deronda had only to look at his own body and compare it to those of his fellow students at Eton and Cambridge to know his identity.[67] It is possible that Deronda's mother contrived not to have her baby circumcised because she was determined that he not be raised a Jew. Her devout father died before Daniel's birth, and Daniel's father was entirely subject to his wife's will ("he went against his conscience for me," she says of him), so she may have been able to avoid this most basic of Jewish rituals. I would argue that Eliot leaves this matter obscure out of necessity but refers to it a number of times indirectly in the text. I have already quoted the passage in which Deronda thinks of the stigma of his "hidden birth" as "the *deformed foot doubtfully hidden by the shoe*" (emphasis added). Unlike Philip Wakem's wound (which is also displaced to the foot in the comparison with Philoctetes), Deronda's can be covered over and temporarily obscured: he can pass as an Englishman, at least up to a point. Toward the end of the novel the Alcahrisi, Daniel's mother, also equates Jewishness with bodily stigma. "I rid myself of the Jewish tatters and gibberish that make people nudge each other at sight of us," she tells her son, "as if we were *tattooed under our clothes, though our faces are as whole as theirs.*"[68] The tattoo, like the deformed foot and like circumcision, is both a literal and a metaphorical mark of difference. The body is invisibly marked, cut, beneath clothing, and yet the mark is somehow visible, a sign of something that is not "whole." For Eliot, I would argue, the body of the alien, anomalous and, to some degree, feminized male is also marked. And, as in the case of Fedalma, race joins a profound physical difference to an unconventional destiny. Deronda's body is, however, marked in a way that allows him to marry Mirah or, put slightly differently, that allows him to marry only Mirah. Deronda, whose hidden circumcision is a "mark of race," proves able to survive the physical marks of difference in a way that is unavailable to Eliot's favored but doomed women. In Eliot's universe, a wound to masculinity is endurable, while a wound to femininity is not.

Notes

1. Elaine Showalter coined the term "gynocriticism" in "Feminist Criticism in the Wilderness," *Critical Inquiry* 8 (Winter 1981). She used it to distinguish the study of women's writing from what she called "feminist critique," the analysis of men's writing.

2. Juliet Mitchell, *Feminism and Psychoanalysis: Freud, Reich, Laing, and Women* (New York: Pantheon, 1974); Nancy Chodorow, *The Reproduction of Mothering: Psychoanalysis and the Sociology of Gender* (Berkeley: University of California Press, 1978); Laura Mulvey, "Visual Pleasure and Narrative Cinema," *Screen* 16:3 (Autumn 1975); Elaine Marks and Isabelle de Courtivron, eds., *New French Feminisms: An Anthology* (Amherst: University of Massachusetts Press, 1980); Hélène Cixous, "The Laugh of the Medusa," trans. Keith Cohen and Paula Cohen, *Signs* 1

(Summer 1976); and Cora Kaplan, "Pandora's Box" in *Sea Changes: Essays on Culture and Feminism* (London: Verso, 1986).

3. Eve Kosofsky Sedgwick, *Between Men: English Literature and Male Homosocial Desire* (New York: Columbia University Press, 1985) and *The Epistemology of the Closet* (Berkeley: University of California Press, 1990).

4. One of the places where feminist criticism and postcolonial studies first came together was Gayatri Chakravorty Spivak's "Three Women's Texts and a Critique of Imperialism," *Critical Inquiry* 12 (1985). Spivak's reading of Charlotte Brontë's *Jane Eyre* was particularly influential.

5. Gillian Beer, "Beyond Determinism: George Eliot and Virginia Woolf," in *Women Writing and Writing About Women*, Mary Jacobus, ed. (London: Croom Helm, 1979), 88.

6. The terms "race" and "nation" were used loosely and often interchangeably in the Victorian period. Religious, national, linguistic, cultural or geographically coherent groups could all be understood as "races." As George Stocking explains, "given the belief that the habitual behavior of human groups in different environments might become part of their hereditary physical makeup, cultural phenomena were readily translatable into 'racial' tendencies." See George W. Stocking, Jr., *Victorian Anthropology* (New York: The Free Press, 1987), 64.

7. George Eliot, *Daniel Deronda* (Harmondsworth, Middlesex: Penguin, 1967), 875.

8. Raymond Williams, *The Country and the City* (London: Chatto and Windus, 1973), chapter 16.

9. Steven Marcus, "Literature and Social Theory: Starting in with George Eliot," in *Representations: Essays on Literature and Society* (New York: Random House, 1975), 190.

10. Williams, *The Country and the City*, 174.

11. Suzanne Graver, *George Eliot and Community: A Study in Social Theory and Fictional Form* (Berkeley: University of California Press, 1984), 14–25. Graver uses the work of the late-nineteenth-century German theorist Ferdinand Tönnies as the starting point for her analysis.

12. Williams, *The Country and the City*, 176.

13. Sigmund Freud, "Family Romances," *The Standard Edition of the Complete Psychological Works of Sigmund Freud*, vol. 9, trans. James Strachey (London: Hogarth Press, 1953), 237–41.

14. Michael Ragussis, *Figures of Conversion: "The Jewish Question" and English National Identity* (Durham and London: Duke University Press, 1995) especially chapters 4 and 6; and Bernard Semmel, *George Eliot and the Politics of National Inheritance* (New York: Oxford University Press, 1994), especially chapter 5, "The Disinherited Races." I am indebted to Semmel's excellent book, which suggests that Eliot's emphasis on nationality and "national inheritance" in *The Spanish Gypsy* and *Daniel Deronda* is the final phase in her longstanding concern with the problem of disinheritance.

15. Sir Walter Scott, *Ivanhoe* (London: Penguin, 1986), 117.

16. George Eliot, *Silas Marner* (London: Penguin, 1996), 5–6 (emphasis added).

17. Ibid., 61–62, 75. It is worth noting in this context that Eliot never identifies this peddler, who turns out to be a figment of the collective imaginations of Raveloe's inhabitants, as a Gypsy, even though the description of hair, jewelry, and complexion more than suggest this.

18. George Eliot, *The Mill on the Floss* (London: Penguin, 1985), 59–60.

19. Ibid., 171–72. For a fuller discussion of this episode and of Eliot's Gypsy references in relation to other women writers, see Deborah Epstein Nord, "Marks of Race": Gypsy Figures and Eccentric Femininity in Nineteenth-Century Women's Writing," *Victorian Studies* 41, no. 2 (1998): 190–210.

20. It is interesting to note that Maggie's bodily anomalousness, understood by those around her in childhood as a sign of madness or an aberrant racial affiliation, is reinterpreted by the female gossips of St. Oggs ("the world's wife," in Eliot's phrase) as a sign of her inevitable sexual immorality: "to the world's wife there had always been something in Miss Tulliver's very physique that a refined instinct felt to be prophetic of harm" (621).

21. George Eliot, *Middlemarch* (New York: Penguin, 1994), 366.

22. Ibid., 436.

23. Ibid., 461–62.

24. Ibid., 463.

25. Eliot, *Middlemarch*, 490, 719, 772.

26. See Thomas Pinney, "Another Note on the Forgotten Past of Will Ladislaw," *Nineteenth-Century Fiction* 17 (June 1962): 69–73. Pinney takes issue with the position of Jerome Beatty, who regarded Will as at least partly Jewish, and believes that "genetic speculation" is unnecessary in light of what is really important here: that Eliot created a series of characters all "cut off from their rightful inheritances" (72–73). While I think that Pinney is right to stress that Will's ostensible Jewishness is attributed to him by unreliable and small-minded gossips, I also think that the fact of Daniel Deronda's and Fedalma's actual genetic—or "racial" —difference is crucial to Eliot's representation of their respective inheritances.

27. Eliot, *Middlemarch*, 816.

28. Ibid., 836, 838.

29. See Semmel, *George Eliot*, especially 103–104.

30. George Eliot, *Impressions of Theophrastus Such* (Edinburgh and London: Blackwood and Sons, 1879), 347. The "State" to which the text refers is Italy. Eliot was an admirer of Giuseppe Mazzini, leader of the movement to reunite Italy as a republican state, who was a refugee in London for a number of years. See Gordon S. Haight, *George Eliot, A Biography* (London: Oxford University Press, 1968), 99.

31. Eliot, *Theophrastus Such*, 348, 338.

32. Ibid., 338 (emphasis added). A good deal of critical debate about the "imperialist" politics of Eliot's notion of a Jewish state has occurred. Current views of the Israeli-Palestinian conflict have colored and, I believe, distorted much of this debate. I refer the reader to the intelligent discussion of this matter in Nancy Henry, *George Eliot and the British Empire* (Cambridge: Cambridge University Press, 2002), chapter 4.

33. Eliot, *Daniel Deronda*, 592. Daniel himself mentions Mazzini and his vision for a reunited Italy just after Mordecai's declaration. Shortly thereafter, Mordecai's sister Mirah, Deronda's future wife, sings Leopardi's "*O patria mia*," an ode to Italy (619).

34. Benedict Anderson, *Imagined Communities* (London: Verso, 1991), 5–6.

35. Eliot, *Daniel Deronda*, 594.

36. Anderson, *Imagined Communities*, 11.

37. Ibid., 12.

38. In her recent book, Irene Tucker argues that in *Daniel Deronda* Eliot redefines what it means to read a novel by inviting us to imagine a place that does not yet exist—a utopia—and a "world that she has not yet *written*" at the novel's conclusion. This is a large claim, but it adds an interesting new gloss to the idea of an "imagined" community. See Tucker, *A Probable State: The Novel, the Contract, and the Jews* (Chicago: University of Chicago Press, 2000), 119.

39. It is interesting to note that Eppie rejects her biological inheritance—and the prosperity and status it would bring her—in favor of remaining the daughter of Silas. Fedalma and Daniel Deronda do the opposite, severing filial ties to those who had raised them and answering the call of blood. In their cases, of course, biological inheritance is associated with a national cause and a people to help redeem. See Semmel's discussion of *Silas Marner*, 24–26.

40. Ibid., 75.

41. George Eliot, *The Spanish Gypsy* (Edinburgh: Blackwood's, 1868), 147 (emphasis added).

42. Ibid., 288.

43. Ibid., 370.

44. J. W. Cross, *George Eliot's Life as Related in her Letters and Journals* (Boston: Dana Esters, n.d.), 3:32.

45. Ibid. Mary is a somewhat confusing model for this drama, given that she sacrifices "ordinary . . . womanhood" but for a very special form of motherhood.

46. Ibid., 3:33.

47. Ragussis, *Figures of Conversion*, 136–59.

48. Ibid., 155.

49. Alicia Carroll, *Dark Smiles: Race and Desire in George Eliot* (Athens: Ohio University Press, 2003), 51.

50. Eliot, *The Spanish Gypsy*, 272.

51. Ibid., 157.

52. Ibid., 360.

53. Ibid., 64.

54. One can imagine that Eliot meant to stress this parallel: Zarca is denied entry into the Promised Land as Moses is, and both are punished in some way for their excesses and replaced by more temperate leaders.

55. Eliot, *The Spanish Gypsy*, 92.

56. George Eliot, *Daniel Deronda* (Harmondsworth, Middlesex: Penguin, 1967), 689, 694.

57. For Eliot's knowledge of a variety of aspects of Judaism and Jewish life, including proto-Zionist aspirations to return to a homeland in Palestine, see William Baker, *George Eliot and Judaism* (Salzburg: Institut fur Englische Sprache und Literatur, Universitat Salzburg, 1975), 134–42.

58. Eliot, *Theophrastus Such*, 140, 153.

59. Eliot, *The Spanish Gypsy*, 142.

60. Ibid., 145.

61. Eliot, *Daniel Deronda*, 215, 489.

62. Ibid., 411.

63. Ibid., 792.

64. Cross, *George Eliot's Life*, 3:35.

65. Eliot, *The Mill on the Floss*, 438.

66. For Philip's affinity with Philoctetes, see *The Mill on the Floss*, Book II, chapter 6.

67. The first mention of this appears in the 1974 essay by Steven Marcus that I have quoted above. Marcus attributes this observation about Deronda to Lennard Davis, then his graduate student. "In order for the plot to work, Deronda's circumcised penis must be invisible, or nonexistent—which is one more demonstration in detail of why the plot does not in fact work." See Marcus, "Literature and Social Theory," 212.

68. Eliot, *Daniel Deronda*, 698 (emphasis added).

Suggestions for Further Reading

Anderson, Amanda. *The Powers of Distance: Cosmopolitanism and the Cultivation of Detachment*. Princeton: Princeton University Press, 2001.

Anderson, Benedict. *Imagined Communities*. London and New York: Verso, 1991.

Baker, William. *George Eliot and Judaism*. Salzburg: Institut für Englishe Sprache und Literatur, 1975.

Boyarin, Jonathan. "The Other Within and the Other Without." In *The Other in Jewish Thought and History*, ed. Laurence J. Silberstein and Robert L. Cohen. New York: New York University Press, 1994, 424–49.

Carroll, Alicia. *Dark Smiles: Race and Desire in George Eliot*. Athens: Ohio University Press, 2003.

Cross, J.W. *George Eliot's Life as Related in her Letters and Journals*. Boston: Dana Estes, n.d.

Eliot, George. *Daniel Deronda*. Harmondsworth, Middlesex: Penguin, 1967.

———. *Impressions of Theophrastus Such*. Edinburgh and London: Blackwood and Sons, 1879.

———. *Middlemarch*. New York and London: Penguin, 1994.

———. *Silas Marner*. London and New York: Penguin, 1996.

———. *The Mill on the Floss*. London and New York: Penguin, 1985.

———. *The Spanish Gypsy*. Edinburgh and London: Blackwood's, 1868.

Graver, Susan. *George Eliot and Community: A Study in Social Theory and Fictional Form*. Berkeley: University of California Press, 1984.

Haight, Gordon S. *George Eliot, A Biography*. London: Oxford University Press, 1968.

Henry, Nancy. *George Eliot and the British Empire*. Cambridge: Cambridge University Press, 2002.

Meyer, Susan. *Imperialism at Home: Race and Victorian Women's Fiction*. Ithaca: Cornell University Press, 1996.

Nord, Deborah Epstein. "'Marks of Race': Gypsy Figures and Eccentric Femininity in Ninetieth-Century Women's Writing." *Victorian Studies* 41 (1998): 189–210.

Paxton, Nancy L. *George Eliot and Herbert Spencer: Feminism, Evolutionism, and the Reconstruction of Gender*. Princeton: Princeton University Press, 1991.

Ragussis, Michael. *Figures of Conversion: "The Jewish Question" and English National Identity*. Durham: Duke University Press, 1995.

Semmel, Bernard. *George Eliot and the Politics of National Inheritance*. New York and Oxford: Oxford University Press, 1994.

Sharpe, Jenny. *Allegories of Empire: The Figure of the Woman in the Colonial Text*. Minneapolis: University of Minnesota Press, 1993.

Stocking Jr., George W. *Victorian Anthropology*. New York: The Free Press, 1987.

Trumpener, Katie. "The Time of the Gypsies: A 'People without History.'" In *Identities*, ed. Kwame Anthony Appiah and Henry Louis Gates, Jr. Chicago: University of Chicago Press, 1995, 338–80.

Tucker, Irene. *A Probable State: The Novel, the Contract, and the Jews*. Chicago: University of Chicago Press, 2000.

Williams, Raymond. *The Country and the City*. London: Chatto and Windus, 1973.

Study Questions

1. Leila Rupp's essay uses evidence from real life to examine our conceptions of women, gender, and sexuality. How would you design a project in which students, individually or in pairs, used such evidence? What type of public life—such as college students in campus hangouts, older people at a coffee shop, comedians on television, workers at a union meeting, or clerks in a college administration office—would you select in order to observe gender constructions in action? What questions would you pose in your study?

2. Caroline Brettell believes that feminist anthropology has prompted a renewed interest in the techniques of narrative and life histories in her discipline. Do you see evidence that feminist scholarship in other fields—history, sociology, psychology, for example—has revived certain traditional techniques or generated new ones?

3. The right of gay couples to legal marriage is a controversial political and cultural issue in America today. But, as Sharon Marcus shows, debates over the role of marriage as a critical social institution are not new, nor are debates over the impact of any changes to that institution. How does Sharon Marcus's in-depth examination of the nineteenth-century debate over English marriage laws help us set the modern controversy in historical perspective? How does the application of queer theory shape the questions Marcus asks about the debate?

4. How do Deborah Nord in this Part, Adela Pinch in Part 3, and Michèle Barale in Part 4 relate literature to real life? Are there differences in the way they understand this relationship?

A Lahu couple (joined by a relative) threshing wheat in their field. The Lahu people live in a village in Southwest China in which gender sharing of labor is the norm.

(Photo by Shanshan Du)

Labor, Class, and Space

The essays in this section drive home the necessity of writing the story of women not simply as a gender narrative but as a narrative that incorporates other key variables such as social class, work roles, and psychological factors.

In "Writing Women's History: What's Feminism Got to Do with It?" Jacqueline Jones examines the nature of gender and the complex identities of women. Like race, gender is a socially constructed category rather than a biological fact. Both are products of a particular time and place and thus their characteristics, behaviors, and social roles are not fixed but changeable. The goal of feminist movements has been to change gender ideology and the gendered division of labor in ways that are favorable to women. One of the problems for feminist movements, however, is that women have multiple identities and loyalties that cross-cut and often compete with their gender identity. Because women are not simply women but are also members of racial, religious, ethnic, class, and regional groups, the creation of a universal feminist is a difficult challenge. When women unite to improve their conditions, the issues they focus on are often defined in local or specific terms rather than in universal, or feminist, terms. This can be seen clearly, Jones notes, in the agenda put forward by white women's rights activists that ignored the needs of other American women.

In "'Independence Herself': A New Spin on Old Stories about Household Production in Early New England," Laurel Ulrich examines the role of cloth production in shaping the identity of white colonial New England women. Although these women were legal dependents of their fathers or husbands, household production afforded them a measure of independence, both of activity and identity. While the men in their families engaged in production for the market, women engaged in vital production for the home. Their ability to manufacture clothing for domestic use was an economic contribution to the family, and, during the revolutionary era, it was hailed as a contribution to American resistance to British taxation policy. The skills involved in cloth production were a source of pride and personal achievement for these New England women. At the same time, cloth production distinguished them from the Native Americans they considered to be "savages," and the use of their products by their own families separated them from the enslaved women who produced for their masters. In this sense, weaving, spinning, and sewing became a vital element in their identity as white women. Ulrich's essay demonstrates the importance of using material artifacts in the recreation of women's lives.

Adela Pinch's "Stealing Happiness: Women Shoplifters in Georgian England" looks at an activity of wealthy nineteenth-century women which seems to contradict our image of the proper, domestic lady. Through the examination of several court cases involving well-to-do shoplifters, including the trial of Mrs. Jane Leigh-Perrot for the theft of a piece of lace, Pinch exposes important tensions between class and gender. These shoplifters received public sympathy, she argues, because their actions could be viewed as a form of class warfare directed against the urban, male shopkeeper. Having established the historical context, Pinch next turns to a literary text based on the Leigh-Perrot case, Thomas De Quincey's novella, "The Household Wreck." Through a critique of this work, Pinch explores the relationship of gender ideology and the new consumer culture.

Shanshan Du's essay, "Gender Sharing of Labor: A Cross Cultural Perspective," challenges our assumption that there is a necessary link between feminist concerns and an exclusive focus on women. Using four ethnographic cases, she suggests that viewing women as a separate social category may limit an anthropologist's analytic abilities. The concept of the sexual division of labor, Du argues, implies a biological determinism; in her studies, Du finds a gender-sharing of labor. For example, among the Lahu of Southwest China, husband and wife share all child-related tasks, and among the Orang Suku Laut of Indonesia, men and women work together in a single, undifferentiated space, sharing in most domestic tasks. Although Du acknowledges that these are extreme examples, she persuasively argues that they challenge the presumed association of domestic work with women and subsistence work with men as well as the "naturalness" of the mother-child bond.

In "Understanding Agoraphobia: Women, Men, and the Historical Geography of Urban Anxiety," Felicity Callard argues that psychic and social phenomena are distinct and must not be conflated by feminist scholars. Agoraphobia is associated in the professional literature and in the popular mind with women, and is seen linked to real conditions such as domestication and restriction to private space. However, Callard points out that the earliest cases reported are of males rather than females. Agoraphobia is not, Callard concludes, a product of actual conditions, for example, of women's confinement to the home or fear of public space. Instead, it is a manifestation of phobic anxiety and thus it is not necessarily connected to a particular thing, place, event, person—or gender.

Writing Women's History: What's Feminism Got to Do with It?

Jacqueline Jones

Jacqueline Jones (1974) is Harry S. Truman Professor of American History at Brandeis University, where she teaches American social history. She is currently working on a history of Savannah, Georgia, during the Civil War and Reconstruction. Among her publications are *American Work: Four Centuries of Black and White Labor* (1998) and *Creek Walking: Growing Up in Delaware in the 1950s* (2001).

Jacqueline Jones identifies herself not as a "feminist historian" but as a historian of American social history, interested in the struggles of many different groups. "I came to women's history from African-American history, a field that opened up whole new areas of scholarly inquiry: How can we redefine human achievement and notions of success and failure? What is the significance of the routines of everyday life, as factors shaping the historical drama? How can we explore ideologies of social difference based on race, gender, class, and marital status?"

For the students in "Problems in American Women's History," the first class meeting of the fall, 2002, semester was coming to a predictable end. The instructor had outlined the major themes of the seminar, and she was now ticking off the course requirements. The sixteen students—a mix of undergraduates and graduate students—paged through the syllabus and dutifully noted reading and paper assignments. After exchanging personal introductions they anticipated a swift end to a perfunctory session related to course-administrative matters.

Oh, and one final point. The instructor announced that, for the entire semester, she wanted everyone in the class to avoid using the words "feminist" or "feminism"—*unless we encountered those words in a specific text.*

Over the years, I have prepared myself for the inevitable reaction that greets this mandate for collective and individual self-censorship—the glances the students exchange among themselves, the raised eyebrows and downcast eyes, the nervous giggles, the general "What the . . .?" looks. As a group, students respond the same way every time I make this announcement the first day of my women's history classes.

I know that I owe the class an explanation, so I proceed to offer my objections to the word feminism in a course on United States women's history—again noting that we would be freed from this restriction once we found people in the past invoking the term (probably after 1900 or so). Even then, however, we would focus on the way people used the term rather than apply it ourselves to a particular group or individual.

I enlist the students in my attempt to justify this particular course policy. I begin by asking for a definition of feminism. Students free-associate and respond with any number of ideas—the notion that women should be equal to men under the law, that women possess special affective or temperamental qualities that set them apart from men, that women should be strong and independent of men ("empowered"), that the key to a more just society is organized resistance to patriarchal authority, and so on. The multiple meanings attached to the word suggest that it lacks precision; we cannot even agree upon a definition. Therefore, I suggest, the term will not be very useful as a tool of historical analysis.

This brief discussion usually yields an additional insight—that the term itself carries a great deal of cultural baggage: People often react to it in a visceral way, but not everyone reacts the same way. Some students consider themselves feminists while others think of the beliefs associated with the term as relics of the 1960s—old-fashioned and irrelevant today. Some students associate feminists with militant, strident, and slightly off-balance women's rights activists, and these younger women and men find that style of self-presentation to be unappealing. Still others, who hold conservative political views, shy away from the radical political implications of feminism; for them, the term conjures up other unpleasant corollaries of "liberalism" (another term we use without much precision). In any case, these divergent responses suggest we must be especially careful in the way we use the word feminism; some folks simply will not be able to get beyond the word and think historically.

Our discussion continues. What are the problems with using a word to describe people and events at a particular point in the past if the people living at the time did not use the word themselves? Do we not risk imposing modern assumptions about gender relations, about social relations in general, on time periods and places that are best studied on their own terms? I go on to make a prediction: When reading historical monographs or primary documents, students will be tempted to label any particularly outspoken, feisty, or even eccentric women they encounter as "feminists" on the assumption that anyone who challenged conventional gender roles deserves the title.

We talk about the concentric circles of communities that we all inhabit—kin networks; workplaces; neighborhoods; and associations and allegiances based on religion, ethnicity, and politics, for example. Many notable women (famous or not) often acted out of various forms of self-interest: They saw themselves as members of faith communities, as activists in the struggle against racial ideologies, as supporters of labor unions or political parties—and not necessarily as advocates of all women everywhere.

Indeed, one of the greatest liabilities of the term feminism flows from the ways that various groups of women have advanced their own interests throughout American history. Most women found common ground with the women they knew best—mothers, sisters, aunts, and other kin relations first, and then co-religionists or co-workers next. Most women lived and organized within relatively bounded communities—their own families, religious institutions, and workplaces. Concerned first and foremost with their own immediate interests, they rarely thought about the plight of women outside their circle. To cite one example: The history of the organized women's movement in the United States reveals the uneasy relationship between women's rights on the one hand and black civil rights on the other. Delegates to the Seneca Falls convention in 1848 and founders of the National Organization for Women in 1966 derived inspiration from the great black liberation movements of the day—abolitionism in the antebellum period and grassroots civil-rights protests in the 1950s and 1960s. Yet both groups of women activists tended to highlight the peculiar liabilities of relatively well-to-do women and avoid public pronouncements about the unique legal and political liabilities of poor women and people of color. This sort of exclusivity is best illustrated by the mainstream woman's suffragists from 1890 to 1919, when national activists took pains to distance themselves from immigrant and working-class women, and even shunned the public support of African-American women.

In other words, the American experience leaves us with the distinct impression that a person might favor "women's rights" in a most narrow, self-interested sense of the term, and still remain committed to the mechanisms of discrimination that shaped the lives of less privileged groups of women. Slaveholding women of the antebellum planter elite possessed a strong sense of "sisterhood" with the women who shared their peculiar responsibilities and worldview—members of their inner kin circles and church congregations. Yet precisely because their social bonds were based upon the unique status they had in common with each other, they could not and would not extend that fellow feeling to other women they lived with and saw every day, enslaved workers on the plantation.

I suggest an additional issue that makes problematic our careless use of the word feminism in American women's history courses—the fact that some African-American scholars and writers have rejected the term altogether, arguing that it connotes white, middle-class, self-absorbed activists and their narrow definition of "women's issues." About the time I began my own work as a historian, I read Alice Walker's collection of essays, *In Search of My Mother's Gardens*. In the book she proposes using the word "womanist" to describe "A Black feminist or feminist of color . . . Usually referring to outrageous, audacious, or courageous or *willful* behavior . . . Responsible. In charge. *Serious.*" She adds a second definition: "A woman who loves other women, sexually and/or nonsexually. Appreciates and prefers women's culture, women's emotional flexibility (values tears as natural counterbalance of laughter), and women's strength."[1] Setting aside the problem of whether or not there exists a single "women's culture" within the African-American (or any other) community, we can appreciate the way history and culture together have shaped the peculiar uses and meanings of feminism. It is a messy, loaded term.

As part of a first-day introduction to American women's history, this discussion of feminism—as a word, an analytical tool, a historical reality—would seem to offer a pretty strong, concentrated dose of correction to prevailing practice and conventional wisdom. Yet my in-class experience over the years suggests that the initial shock to the students is well worth the effort. They are receptive to the idea that the purpose of the course is to make it ever more difficult for them to generalize about "women" or "all American women." Gender ideologies are fluid ideas, part of a larger matrix of other equally fluid notions about class, racial, regional, and age differences, for example. If we take each time, place, and community on its own terms, then we are free to explore the many factors that shaped women's lives, and the many ways women responded to their individual circumstances, without feeling bound by present-day convictions about what the world should look like and what women and men should do to make it look that way.

As a college student (at the University of Delaware, 1966–1970) and as a graduate student (at the University of Wisconsin, 1970–1976), my first encounters with the modern women's (or "feminist") movement had a profound, but a profoundly ambivalent, effect upon me. I came of age during a time when many seemingly discrete groups of young people were seeking and finding their public voices—anti-war and Black Power activists, Marxists, feminists, and environmentalists, to name a few. At the time, it was obvious that these groups overlapped with each other in terms of both their adherents and their overall message calling upon young people to challenge established forms of authority, whether lodged in corporate boardrooms, the halls of Congress, the defense industry, or even our parents' households. And yet few people were wondering out loud how all of these different perspectives, whether overtly political or based on some sort of vague cultural impulse, fit together and reinforced each other. Each group of activists remained jealous of the media attention captured by other groups. And certainly we knew that it was possible to protest against the war in Vietnam and at the same time adhere to racist ideas, that environmentalists and Marxists were not necessarily concerned about the rights of women, and that you could flout authority by smoking pot without thinking about the struggles of the working class or the desperate plight of poor folks in the projects. Like the Progressive reformers of the early twentieth century, young people in the 1960s often compartmentalized themselves; they worked for a particular "cause" without necessarily granting the legitimacy or worthiness of other causes we usually associate with the same general historical impulse.

Out of this rich stew of 1960s activism, emerging ideologies, and political sensibilities, my own interest in women's issues emerged only gradually. As an undergraduate, I sat through more than my share of history courses that left me bored, even enervated; at the time it never occurred to me to consider why I found the study of the past so dull, why all the meaningful debates and hard questions and colorful dramas were taking place outside the classroom and not inside. Most of my professors seemed almost principled in their refusal to acknowledge the multiple revolutions swirling around them. As for the content of history courses, I never even questioned the absence of the vast majority of people from the pages of textbooks; I remained in a state of obliviousness, blind to the possibility that the story of the past could capture the everyday experiences of people who were not monarchs, generals, philosophers, or religious leaders.

My intellectual awakening came in 1969, when I took a brand-new course, an undergraduate survey of African-American history. This course made me think about history in new ways, and question conventional notions of power and achievement. The study of African-American history offered a compelling window into all of American history; through this one subject were revealed the contours of the American paradox—the great moral burden of slavery that an otherwise relatively free and open society simultaneously embraced and inflicted upon itself. And yet of course thirty-five years ago it was possible to read widely and deeply in African-American history and still not learn much about the experiences of women.

While I was a graduate student at the University of Wisconsin I joined a women's cooperative called the Women's Transit Service. Nighttime drivers used university vehicles to transport women students who needed after-hours rides in and around Madison. The potluck dinners and fundraisers sponsored by this group provided me with a stereotypical early 1970s "consciousness raising" experience. Too, I was intrigued by the academic politics surrounding the hiring of the first female history faculty member on tenure track in the University's history; though trained in economic history; she graciously accepted an assignment from the department that she offer a course in the new field of women's history. As a teaching assistant for that course, I began to build on the insights I had learned in my course on black history—most significantly, the idea that any self-respecting social historian needed to find new research methodologies and sources, and needed to appreciate the multiple ways that ordinary people expressed themselves throughout history. African-American history encouraged me to think about the past in terms of everyday experience, with all its mundane routines and small trials and triumphs, and to place that experience within the larger context of particular political economies. This, then, was the complex pattern of history—the warp and woof of individual lives that formed the fabric of the human past.

My first major research project fit squarely within the "We Were There" category of American women's history.[2] Focusing on the northern women who went south after the Civil War to teach former slaves in Georgia, I was able to inject women (at least northern middle-class women) into the conventional narrative of the Civil War, a narrative dominated by men as legislators and soldiers. The women I studied considered themselves "soldiers of light and love"; they believed that now that the invasion with the bayonet was over, women must conquer the benighted South with their benevolence.

In the course of researching this project, I took note of the way the teachers devoted themselves wholeheartedly to their work. In an era when large numbers of middle-class women suffered from nervous disorders, many of the teachers reported that they had never experienced such energy, such good health, as when they were in the classroom contending with large numbers of restless, eager pupils. The women found the challenges of living and laboring within a hostile white society to be exhilarating because those challenges were morally purposeful. As well-educated professionals (most had attended teacher training, or normal, schools), they at times banded together in opposition to overweening male school superintendents, usually clergymen who had never taught a class of "abecedarians."

The teachers shared with other northern government officials the conviction that the former slaves needed only to return to the cotton fields, now as freed people, and to practice the virtues of thrift, temperance, and punctuality, in order to achieve economic self-sufficiency; after a while black families would be able to buy land (so the reasoning went) and transform themselves into an independent peasantry. The Northerners failed to understand that, within a staple-crop agricultural system, financial credit is the key to economic well-being. In the postbellum South, whites retained control of credit institutions and almost all farmland. Furthermore, many embittered former rebels engaged in persistent, unchecked violence toward blacks who tried to vote and resist the depredations of white landowners and employers. Moreover, the substantial class and cultural differences that separated northern aid workers from rural southern blacks meant that the daughters of Yankee clergymen, craftsmen, lawyers, and farmers found it difficult to consider impoverished black people their equals in any meaningful sense of the word. The teachers were idealistic but ultimately naïve about the structural realities of the postbellum South.

When I began teaching at Wellesley College in the mid-1970s, I was struck by my students' conviction that the world of work was intrinsically liberating. Their notions of "working women" were based upon a tiny subset of women in the paid labor force—the well-educated, highly compensated, high-profile professionals featured on newscasts and in popular magazines. At the same time, the students seemed not to notice the cafeteria workers and custodians, the librarians and the secretaries, who kept the campus going day in and out. I wrote *Labor of Love, Labor of Sorrow* to show my students that for African- American women, the work they performed for whites was more often demeaning and dangerous than liberating.[3] In contrast, the work black women performed for their own families and communities provided them with a measure of pride and satisfaction. In this story, white women appear as slave owners and as employers of black maids and cooks; as haughty reformers and intrusive social workers; as class-conscious suffragists and as activists for a variety of other causes, indifferent to the historic vulnerabilities of women of color. By the time the book was published in the mid-1980s, it was part of a larger trend that focused on the rich diversity of women's lives in American history—the context shaping the lives of seamstresses and domestic servants in New York City during the Early National period; Lowell mill girls in the vanguard of the Industrial Revolution; plantation mistresses in the South and the free women of Petersburg, Virginia before the Civil War; Mexican migrants in the Southwest; Hispanic cannery workers in California; North Carolina Piedmont textile mill employees during the 1920s and 1930s.[4] More particularly, my work was also part of a broader effort to highlight the divergent life experiences of white women and African-American women workers and activists.[5]

By the late 1980s, historians of women had achieved a measure of success to the extent that the field had become fully enmeshed within the profession; at the same time, women historians had succeeded to the extent that they now played a prominent role in what had previously been a male-dominated profession. Departments set aside tenure-track lines in women's history, and books on women's history won prestigious scholarly prizes. Women were serving as officers and committee members of all the major professional organizations. I remember a specific conversation I had with two other women historians around this time. The three of us were serving as members of a history-association program committee. We congratulated ourselves on the remarkable scholarly progress of women's history scholars. We noted that, unlike other disciplines, history seemed not to be wracked by bitter feuds and principled disagreements over what constituted a good piece of scholarship. As a profession we shared broad agreement about standards of scholarship, and those standards encouraged the kind of innovation that produced works on women.

I realize now that this heartfelt moment of self-congratulation was not only premature, it was also misguided. Certainly not all instructors of American history in the academy incorporate material about women into their courses, and a fair number of instructors simply do not care about women's history at all. Some departments confine women's history to a single identified slot, refusing to consider scholars who study women for positions in the general fields of labor, intellectual, or political history (for example). And by the early 1990s, some scholars were claiming bitterly that women's history was just one more effort to fracture and distort the story of the American past, a story that (they argued) revealed that most Americans had shared a common experience and set of values, broadly defined. These scholars objected to what they considered a disjointed, contentious tale of separate and distinct ethnic, racial, gender, and class groups.

In fact, I was having my own doubts about women's history, though my reasons differed from those who found the field objectionable for political reasons. My work on African-American's women's history had alerted me to several potential and real problems emanating from studies focusing on women exclusively. First, many times in the course of my own research I found myself downplaying the role of African American men—as co-workers, fathers, husbands, and preachers, for example—in order to write a story about women. The result was (at least in certain sections of *Labor of Love*) a rather arbitrary and ultimately artificial view of women, one that failed to consider them fully as members of households and communities. Second, an analysis of census data for the late nineteenth century cotton South revealed that black women as sharecropping wives, mothers, daughters, and sisters had much in common with their poor-white counterparts. Women of both groups tended to marry older men, to bear large numbers of children, and to alternate between the home and the cotton fields according to the agricultural season and the life cycle of their families. Certainly class factors played a dramatic role in the lives of African-American women. To sort out the complex tangle of racial, gender, and class ideologies that shaped their lives, I would have to give serious attention to the history of poor white men and women in the same time and place.

In a book published in 1992, *The Dispossessed*, I pursued the idea that the household is a particularly revealing and useful unit of analysis for the study of ordinary women throughout American history.[6] Focusing on black and white rural southerners, two distinct groups that eventually migrated north in the twentieth century, I was struck by the resourcefulness of nuclear and extended kin members determined to care for other family members. In some cases, fathers and sons and brothers left the plantation or farm to seek wage-work in coal mines, sawmills, or lumber camps. Families orchestrated their own productive energies in the fields according to the ages and abilities of the children. Economic distress placed immense burdens on women not only to earn extra money as domestic servants, but also to stretch meager family budgets and to rely on kin and neighbors. Layers of kin and community, ranging from the nuclear family to the extended family and into the local neighborhood, provided evidence of the symbiotic relationships between husbands and wives, parents and children, young and old, kin and neighbors. In telling this story, to single out women was to miss these larger networks that were so crucial in shaping the everyday lives of all household members.

Women's historians in particular and social historians in general often invoke the "race-class-gender" mantra: the guiding question seems to be, given a certain standard experience shared by white men of privilege and property, how do the experiences of women, people of color, and the property-less depart from that standard? Class issues too often do get short shrift in works of historical scholarship. It is not difficult to pinpoint dramatic contrasts between the lives of slaveholding women and those of enslaved women. However, comparing the lives of enslaved women with those of the daughters and wives of antebellum white tenant farmers and squatters proves to be a much greater challenge.

As a work in American women's history *The Dispossessed* carried distinct liabilities. The word "women" did not appear in the title, and the book's cover consisted of an evocative, but female-free photograph—of a migrant Mexican cotton picker from the 1930s. No women's history journals reviewed the book. Gradually, I began to think of myself and call myself a labor historian and not a women's historian. The former term seemed more inclusive and ultimately more accurate considering the work I did.

I became more interested in the history of work, paid and unpaid, because I believe that racial, gender, and class ideologies are socially constructed ideas that reach their most concrete expression *via* the social division of labor. Throughout American history, elites have used various means, including violence and manipulation of the legal system, to ensure the subordination of overlapping groups of people of color, women, and the laboring classes. Gradually, the use of state-sanctioned and extralegal violence against these groups has subsided, at least in public venues (of course domestic violence against women continues unabated). Beginning in the 1960s, the federal government took steps to eliminate formal structures of discrimination that targeted women and minorities. In the early twenty-first century, we do not deny impoverished citizens the right to vote, and employers cannot advertise "whites only" or "no women need apply" when they seek out potential employees.

Despite this seemingly "level playing field" for women, people of color, and the poor, the structure of the labor force reveals enduring patterns of discrimination and inequality. Most women still work in traditional "women's jobs"—as clerical workers, store clerks, beauticians, teachers, and nurses, and at home they perform a disproportionate share of childcare and housework. Women have not achieved parity with their male peers in a whole host of professions—law, medicine, academia—or in Congress or other elected positions, the offices of high-powered law firms, and the executive suites of Fortune Five Hundred companies. It is not law that shapes the gender division of labor, but inbred, workplace-based white male cultures that hinder openness and diversity. Cultural expectations dictate that women will devote much of their adult years to raising children; the presumption is that wives and mothers lack the stamina and emotional resources to commit to a demanding job outside the home.

In a similar vein, black people no longer encounter blatant discriminatory laws that keep them out of certain colleges, jobs, or neighborhoods. Still, to a disproportionate degree compared to whites, black men and women work in the areas of food services, health care, manual labor, and service. Even professionals and managers more often are assigned jobs in the "human resources" division of a company. Poor people toil at the dirtiest, most arduous, least-paying jobs the economy has to offer—again, not because we have a caste system enforced by the federal government, but because poor people are unlikely to have the formal education necessary to succeed in our increasingly credentials-conscious society. For the laboring classes, the United States today resembles an aristocracy, with the poor confined to impoverished neighborhoods, forced to send their children to inferior schools, thereby producing a generation that will recapitulate the cycle. In other words, jobs are never just jobs; they are social markers of great real and symbolic value.[7]

By taking patterns of labor as our departure point, we can begin to trace the change in those patterns over time. From this vantage point, we can see that ideologies of social difference have served specific purposes at specific points in time. To state the matter more boldly: white men have often employed such ideologies as political strategies in order to enforce a certain social division of labor that relegates women, blacks, and the poor to the margins of the body politic.

Racism, sexism, and contempt for the poor are not static structures, but rather fluid and often internally inconsistent ideologies. During the colonial period, many propertied white men believed all subordinate laborers shared certain dangerous characteristics. Masters and employers often lumped together Indian wage earners, young English indentured servants, and black slaves because elites believed that members of these groups (men and women) were sexually promiscuous, resistant to discipline, and prone to running away. Advertisements for fugitive slaves describe them as cunning, sly, and potentially dangerous, skilled at concocting poisons and applying the arsonist's torch. Not until the late eighteenth century did whites such as Thomas Jefferson begin to think in "racial" terms, identifying Africans and their descendants as a group apart from other Americans no matter how poor.

By the antebellum period, southern slaveholders were justifying their "peculiar institution" by claiming that all black people were inherently dependent and childlike. The years of Civil War brought a new twist to the story; now once again black people were labeled as incendiary, dangerous to white people and their communities. Postbellum observers described blacks as part of a dying race, unable to fend for themselves, useful to whites as field hands but immoral and subversive of the social order. These ideas had real consequences for real people. For example, before the Civil War, southern textile mill owners eagerly used black people—enslaved and free—as operatives. When the destruction of slavery left southern poor whites jealous of their privileges, mill owners began to hire white work forces exclusively, claiming that black people lacked a "mechanical sense." Racial ideologies shaped the jobs that blacks could or could not do, but those ideologies changed over time in response to shifting military, economic, and political conditions.[8]

Ideologies of social difference are often internally inconsistent and contradictory. In the early nineteenth-century North, members of the white laboring classes labeled black people simultaneously as lazy, dependent on the public dole, and as predatory, determined to wrest good jobs and educational opportunities from whites. Whites claimed that for every black person who got a good job or a chance to go to school, a white man would be deprived of such advantages. These views foreshadow modern notions suggesting that black people as beneficiaries of programs such as housing subsidies and food stamps remain inveterate dependents on the government, while black people as advocates of affirmative action seem bent on pursuing good educational and employment opportunities—again, to the detriment of the "rights" and well-being of white people.

Ideologies of gender difference are similarly complex, ever shifting, and inconsistent. In some cases, those ideologies are rigorously class-specific; the supposedly widely held idea that women should stay home and devote themselves to their families full time never applied to African-American women or to poor women (and still do not today). In the 1930s, the white wife who worked for wages out side the home found herself publicly criticized for supposedly depriving a man of a job; a few years later, during World War II, the country hailed white working wives and mothers for their patriotism and heroic contributions in the fight against fascism.

I would suggest that it is difficult to isolate gender ideologies from other systems of labor and social control. Ideas about womanhood are contingent upon and reflect ideas about manhood; the duties performed by wives are contingent upon and reflect the work responsibilities of their husbands. All systems of oppression—justified by ideologies of social differences but bolstered by custom and particular political economies—are interlocking and reinforcing. Trying to separate those systems, to study them in isolation, illustrates a scholarly variation on the Heisenberg principle; the very act of examination alters the conditions we are observing. Gender, racial, class ideologies derive their power from their interconnectedness within any particular time and place. One way to approach these issues is to ask, who benefits from a certain ideology of social or biological difference, why, and in what way? By considering ideologies of difference as political strategies wielded by specific groups of people, rather than as transcendent, historical prejudices, we can begin to understand the dynamics of power throughout American history.

What does this analysis have to say about the problem of feminism? First, it reminds us of the compartmentalization of activist and reform movements throughout history. Consider late nineteenth-century southern white suffragists who scorned the claims of African-Americans, immigrants, and workers to a robust citizenship. Can we label racist suffragists as feminists? Consider some of the pioneers of the 1960s women's movement and their indifference toward lesbians and members of the National Welfare Rights Organization. Were those pioneers feminists? The term itself leaves unanswered a whole host of questions about a person's way of looking at the world; historically, American mainstream feminism has advanced a relatively narrow, exclusive agenda.

Perhaps some people would suspect that I am in the process of arguing myself out of teaching my women's history courses. And yet I (and my students) find women's history to be intellectually stimulating. Though too often adopting a celebratory tone, monographs in the field are worthwhile talking about and arguing over. I end the seminar with Estelle Freedman's book *No Turning Back: The History of Feminism and the Future of Women*,[9] a powerful indictment of patriarchal ideas and structures as they affect women all over the world, and a moving account of the forms of resistance used by women to subvert and destroy those ideas and structures. I shall continue to teach and write about women's history—but no one should expect me to make contributions to "feminist scholarship" anytime soon.

Notes

1. Alice Walker, *In Search of Our Mothers' Gardens: Womanist Prose* (New York: Harcourt Brace Jovanovich, 1983), xi.

2. Jacqueline Jones, *Soldiers of Light and Love: Northern Teachers and Georgia Blacks, 1865–1873* (Chapel Hill: University of North Carolina Press, 1980). I began work on the dissertation in 1972 and finished it in 1976. Other examples of this same

impulse around the same time include Linda Kerber, *Women of the Republic: Intellect and Ideology in Revolutionary America* (Chapel Hill: University of North Carolina Press, 1980); Mary Beth Norton, *Liberty's Daughters: the Revolutionary Experience of American Women, 1750–1800* (Boston: Little, Brown, 1980); Thomas Dublin, *Women at Work: The Transformation of Work and Community in Lowell, Massachusetts, 1826–1860* (New York: Columbia University Press, 1979); Barbara Wertheimer, *We Were There: The Story of Working Women in America* (New York: Pantheon, 1977).

3. *Labor of Love, Labor of Sorrow: Black Women, Work and the Family from Slavery to the Present* (New York: Basic Books, 1985; second ed., 1995).

4. Christine Stansell, *City of Women: Sex and Class in New York, 1789–1860* (Urbana: University of Illinois Press, 1986); Catherine Clinton, *The Plantation Mistress: Women's Work in the Old South* (New York: Pantheon, 1982); Suzanne Lebsock, *The Free Women of Petersburg: Status and Culture in a Southern Town, 1784–1860* (New York: W. W. Norton, 1984); Sarah Deutsch, *No Separate Refuge: Culture, Class, and Gender on an Anglo-Hispanic Frontier, 1880–1940* (New York: Oxford University Press, 1987); Vicki Ruiz, *Cannery Women, Cannery Lives: Mexican Women, Unionization, and the California Food Processing Industry, 1930–1950* (Albuquerque: University of New Mexico Press, 1987).

5. Deborah Gray White, *Ar'n't I a Woman: Female Slaves in the Plantation South* (New York: W. W. Norton, 1987); Darlene Clark Hine, *Black Women in White: Racial Conflict and Cooperation in the Nursing Profession, 1890–1950* (Bloomington: Indiana University Press, 1989); Rosalyn Terborg-Penn, *The Afro-American Woman: Struggles and Images* (Port Washington, NY: National Universities Publications, 1978); Paula Giddings, *When and Where I Enter: The Impact of Black Women on Race and Sex in America* (New York: Bantam Books, 1985).

6. Jacqueline Jones, *The Dispossessed: America's Underclasses from the Civil War to the Present* (New York: Basic Books, 1992).

7. See Jacqueline Jones, *American Work: Four Centuries of Black and White Labor* (New York: W. W. Norton, 1998).

8. For an overview, see Jacqueline Jones, *Social History of the Laboring Classes from Colonial Times to the Present* (New York: Blackwell, 1999).

9. Published in New York by Ballantine in 2002.

Suggestions for Further Reading

Bederman, Gail. *Manliness and Civilization: A Cultural History of Gender and Race in the United States, 1880–1917*. Chicago: University of Chicago Press, 1995.

Brown, Kathleen M. *Good Wives, Nasty Wenches, and Anxious Patriarchs: Gender, Race, and Power in Colonial Virginia*. Chapel Hill: University of North Carolina Press, 1996.

Cott, Nancy F. *The Grounding of Modern Feminism*. New Haven: Yale University Press, 1987.

Deutsch, Sarah. *Women and the City: Gender, Space, and Power in Boston, 1870–1940*. New York: Oxford University Press, 2000.

Dublin, Thomas. *Women at Work: The Transformation of Work and Community in Lowell, Massachusetts, 1826–1860*. New York: Columbia University Press, 1979.

Faderman, Lillian. *Odd Girls and Twilight Lovers: A History of Lesbian Life in Twentieth Century America*. New York: Columbia University Press, 1991.

Gilmore, Glenda Elizabeth. *Gender and Jim Crow: Women and the Politics of White Supremacy in North Carolina, 1896–1920*. Chapel Hill: University of North Carolina Press, 1996.

Hall, Jacquelyn Dowd, et al. *Like a Family: The Making of a Southern Cotton Mill World*. Chapel Hill: University of North Carolina Press, 1987.

Hewitt, Nancy. *Southern Discomfort: Women's Activism in Tampa, Florida, 1880s–1920s*. Urbana: University of Illinois Press, 2001.

Hine, Darlene Clark. *A Shining Thread of Hope: The History of Black Women in America*. New York: Broadway Books, 1998.

Hunter, Tera. *To 'Joy My Freedom: Southern Black Women's Lives and Labors After the Civil War*. Cambridge: Harvard University Press, 1997.

Jones, Jacqueline. *American Work: Four Centuries of Black and White Labor*. New York: W. W. Norton, 1998.

———. *Labor of Love, Labor of Sorrow: Black Women, Work and the Family from Slavery to the Present*. New York: Basic Books, 1985; rev. ed. 1995.

Kamensky, Jane. *Governing the Tongue: The Politics of Speech in Early New England*. New York: Oxford University Press, 1997.

Norton, Mary Beth. *In the Devil's Snare: The Salem Witchcraft Crisis of 1692*. New York: Knopf, 2002.

Orleck, Annelise. *Common Sense and a Little Fire: Women and Working Class Politics in the United States, 1900–1965*. Chapel Hill: University of North Carolina Press, 1995.

Pascoe, Peggy. *Relations of Rescue: The Search for Female Moral Authority in the American West, 1874–1939*. New York: Oxford, 1990.

Ruiz, Vicki. *From Out of the Shadows: Mexican Women in Twentieth-Century America*. New York: Oxford, 1998.

Stanley, Amy Dru. *From Bondage to Contract: Wage Labor, Marriage and the Market in the Age of Slave Emancipation*. Cambridge: Cambridge University Press, 1998.

Ulrich, Laurel Thatcher. *A Midwife's Tale: The Life of Martha Ballard, Based on Her Dairy, 1785–1812*. New York: Knopf, 1990.

Yung, Judy. *Unbound Feet: A Social History of Chinese Women in San Francisco*. Berkeley: University of California Press, 1995.

"Independence Herself:"
A New Spin on Old Stories about Household Production in Early New England

Laurel Thatcher Ulrich

Laurel Thatcher Ulrich (1978) is Phillips Professor of Early American History at Harvard University. She is the author of many books and articles on early American history, including *A Midwife's Tale*, which won the Pulitzer Prize for History in 1991. Her latest book, *The Age of Homespun: Objects and Stories in the Creation of an American Myth* (2001), focuses on fourteen domestic items from early New England. She is currently at work on a book-length essay called *Well-Behaved Women Seldom Make History*.

The title of Laurel Ulrich's forthcoming book, "Well-Behaved Women Seldom Make History," came originally from an article she published in American Quarterly *in 1976. Twenty years later, it had escaped into popular culture and could be found on T-shirts, mugs, and bumper stickers. She writes, "My new book is a response to the popularization of the slogan. My original meaning had more to do with giving invisible women a history—the objective of most of my work over the past thirty years. In popular culture the same words have become a rallying cry for activism or, in some cases, for conventional misbehavior. Seeing my own words reinterpreted in this way makes me wary of defining what impact women's studies has had on the current generation. Each generation will define feminism for itself. Historians don't own history."*

In *The Tale of the Spinning Wheel*, published in 1903, Elisabeth Barney Buel celebrated colonial women as prodigious producers. Early New England housewives, she believed, made soap, candles, butter and cheese, brewed beer, raised hens and geese, and even manufactured bullets, but their supreme achievement was in textiles. Despite all their other duties, they spun flax and wool, "knitted every pair of stockings and mittens, wove every inch of linen and woolen cloth, and cut and made every stitch of clothing worn by a family which generally numbered ten or a dozen Johns and Hezekiahs and Josiahs and Hepzibahs and Mehitable Anns. No wonder a man could go to the war for his country's independence, when he left Independence herself at home in the person of his wife."[1]

Few historians today would use the term *independence* to describe the lives of early American women. Feminist scholarship has taught us that a married woman might work hard to feed and clothe her family yet have little power over the disposition of her own assets. Under the English common law, a wife not only lost her name but the right to own property. Nor did the American Revolution do anything to alter that status. Despite Abigail Adams's injunction, the men who wrote the nation's first code of laws did not "Remember the Ladies."

Yet in the context of a broader Atlantic history, Buel's notion of "independence" rings true. In comparison with impoverished outworkers in Europe or the British Isles or enslaved spinners in the plantation south, household producers in New England enjoyed many freedoms. Farmer's wives managed production, and in the process created female property that they handed on to their daughters. Young women worked at home and in their neighbors' houses, and through a practice called "changing works" combined production with pleasure. In the build-up to the Revolution and again in the early Republic, their work won public praise. Technically, of course, everything a woman accumulated was subject to a husband's or father's authority. In practice, household manufacturing allowed white women considerable control over their own labor.

Elisabeth Barney Buel to the contrary, however, they did not make every inch of cloth and every stitch of clothing their families required. Homemade and imported fabrics appeared in the same households and sometimes in the same objects. Family subsistence was achieved through a patchwork of enterprises, including men's work in commercial lumbering, farming, and fishing. New England vessels carried flax seed to Ireland, house frames to Portugal, and African slaves to ports all along the Atlantic seaboard, returning with a wide range of manufactured goods, including English cloth. Women were able to work for themselves in part because their husbands and brothers were engaged in market production. The key to their independence was the limited commercial value of their cloth. Cloth making was a part-time, locally based, seemingly haphazard, yet culturally and economically significant enterprise.

Elsewhere, I have written at length about New England's textile economy, including the important basketry traditions of New England Indians.[2] This essay summarizes aspects of my earlier scholarship by revisiting the stories Elisabeth Barney Buel and her contemporaries told about intrepid colonial women. My interpretation of these stories reflect three changes in my own scholarship and in the field of women's history since I began my work thirty years ago.

First, it takes colonial revival writers like Buel more seriously than most of us did in the past. In *Good Wives*, for example, I debunked the spinning wheel as a symbol of women's work, dismissing it as a nostalgic invention of the nineteenth century. My study of the diary of Martha Moore Ballard helped to change that, but so did greater attention to the power of "memory," the term historians use to describe widely shared public perceptions of the past. Colonial revival writers like Buel exaggerated New Englander's productive prowess, but they captured attitudes toward work and an ethos of independence that more conventional sources missed.

Second, this essay and the larger work from which it draws would not have been possible without the assistance and, in some cases, the tutoring of museum curators, conservators, and interpreters. Over the past twenty years, an interest in women's work and in the history of American Indians stimulated serious attention to seemingly ephemeral objects like wood splint baskets and household linens. Working with these materials I was able to see how textile production created female property, enlarged skills, structured consumption, strengthened networks of work and exchange, and nurtured pride.

Finally, this essay reflects more recent scholarship in gender history by emphasizing continuity as well as change. Many of the landmark books of the 1970s and 1980s emphasized the emergence of middle-class New England women from patriarchal domination in the early nineteenth century through membership in voluntary societies, wage work in textile mills, and engagement with abolition and women's rights. In such studies, the colonial economy was often a hazily glimpsed backdrop to later change. Paying close attention to the actual processes of household work and to the ways women used material goods to transmit their own values from one generation to another, reveals the preindustrial roots of female activism. In the nation's first industrial strikes, memories of household production defined worker's rights. Unfortunately, in a nation still sustained by slavery and in a region shaped by two centuries of Indian war, textile production also ratified white identity. In the rhetoric of the strikes, as in the domestic fiction that followed, New England women contrasted independence with both slavery and savagery. Read alongside period documents, colonial revival stories help us to see how and why this happened.

CLOTH MAKING CREATED FEMALE PROPERTY

The same story appears over and over again on scraps of paper attached to old blankets, coverlets, towels, and sheets displayed in museums or treasured in family collections. Sometimes the labels are pinned to the fabric. Sometimes they are sewn. "My great-great-grandmother raised the flax, spun the thread, and wove the cloth," they read, or "The wool in this blanket was raised, spun, and woven on my grandfather's farm." Although the names and objects change, the story remains the same. Like pieces of the true cross, old fabrics confirm the existence of an imagined world in which American families grew or manufactured almost everything they needed.

It is easy to dismiss these labels, especially when they are attached to articles that were clearly imported. But the stories they tell are powerful evidence of the capacity of American women to create their own history. An affidavit now at the New Hampshire Historical Society in Concord is an especially interesting example. Dated February 20, 1890, it accompanies two fragments of linen that were once part of a towel.

> The Warp of this Towel was spun by Mary (Wilson) Wallace, known in family history as "Ocean born Mary." The Filling was spun by Elisabeth (Wallace) Patterson, and the towel was woven by Peter Patterson.
> This towel was given to Jane Duncan (Patterson) Mack, by Mrs. Elisabeth Patterson (Duncan) Baker, daughter of Elisabeth (Wallace) Patterson, who received it from her Mother, "Ocean born Mary."

Beneath the date, the memorialist's husband, "Robert C. Mack, Justice of Peace," attested to the truthfulness of the story.[3]

The affidavit is less about the linen than the family history. Jane Mack was obviously proud of her descent from "Ocean born Mary," a woman famous in New Hampshire folklore for having been born in 1725 on a ship attacked by pirates on its journey from northern Ireland. She was also proud of the fact that her great-grandfather, Peter Patterson, also an Irish immigrant, was a weaver. But the larger story is in the parenthetical succession of names that traces the linen's lineage from Mary Wallace to her daughter Elisabeth Patterson to her grand-daughter Elisabeth Baker to her great-granddaughter Jane Mack.[4] Here was a lineage in linen.

This well-documented towel is one of several legacies from the same family. A linen sheet that came to the New Hampshire Historical Society from another descendant has the initials E.W. neatly embroidered at the top in gold silk typical of the late eighteenth century and, upside-down and just beneath the embroidery, the name Elisabeth Patterson stamped in India ink in a manner typical of the early nineteenth century.[5] "E.W." was Elisabeth Wallace Patterson, who embroidered the sheet before her own marriage, then many years later passed it on to her daughter, the Elisabeth Patterson Duncan Baker mentioned in Jane Mack's affidavit.

It was probably this Elisabeth who, in 1842, began distributing family linens to nieces living across New Hampshire and in upstate New York. By the end of the nineteenth century, some of these objects reached Canada, where another descendant attached labels attesting to their origins.[6] At some point, Baker began subdividing whole textiles. The two pieces to which Mack attached her affidavit are neatly hemmed fragments of the top half of a towel. Presumably the rest of it ended up in another Patterson trunk—or in a rag bag.

Multiple examples of the same phenomenon survive in museums all across the United States. Because household goods—or "movables"—formed the core of widow's portions and the bulk of goods that young women took into marriage, it is not surprising that bed coverings, sheets, towels, and table-cloths ended up many generations later in the hands of female descendants. Women's "independence," like that of property-owning white men, had less to do with personal autonomy than with the ability to transmit property and identity to future generations. They passed on imported as well as home made textiles, and cooking pots and furniture as well as coverlets. Through household manufacturing, they enlarged the meaning of certain goods, transmitting skills as well as products.

In the nineteenth century, household linens marked with women's initials—and stories—moved across the continent. As factories took over the work of production, old-fashioned fabrics became relics. A fragment of a New England bed curtain, embroidered in silk, ended up in a collection of textiles at the University of Washington of Seattle. Although the donor's name has been forgotten, the little note attached to the corner supplied its story:

> This is the work of Charity Bryant, great aunt of Wm Cullen Bryant: about 1750. The flax was raised, spun & woven in the family; the silk was from China, & dyed in the home; the design was original.
> This piece was cut from a set of curtains, bed spread & valance.[7]

The details of this account may or may not be accurate; there is no evidence that New England women were home-dyeing Chinese silk. Without question, however, the fabric became a carrier of family history; the story attached to the corner conveyed a lineage that not only included a famous male poet but his Great Aunt Charity. The bed curtain with its brittle label is part of a larger story about the creation and transmission of female property in early New England.

CLOTH MAKING ENLARGED WOMEN'S SKILLS

Some stories about cloth making fully qualify as "tall tales." In Northfield, Vermont, for example, people told about a man called to fight in the Revolution who didn't have warm clothes to wear. The day before he left, his wife went to the pasture with her scissors and cut some white and some black from the back of the sheep. She carded, spun, and wove the cloth, and then before she slept, stitched a pair of sturdy gray pants.[8] The story is fantastic, but it suggests a larger truth—subsistence cloth making did enlarge skills.

The most dramatic example of this concerns a shift in the gender division of labor. Women had always been spinners, but in commercial cloth-making areas of Europe and the British Isles, weaving was a male occupation. In the new world, weaving became first a marginal enterprise and then a female occupation. In textile production, the New England economy, like a woman at a wool wheel, walked backward. Even if English mercantilism had allowed large-scale manufacturing, there was too much other work for men to do, too many fields to develop and trees to cut down. Although some men, including the Scots-Irish immigrant Peter Patterson, continued to weave, by the second quarter of the eighteenth century, they were already far outnumbered by women. The shift from male to female weavers marked a transformation in the nature of production. Commercial manufacturing subdivided the many steps in production. In the putting-out system that dominated English production, spinning often took place in one village, weaving and finishing in others. In contrast, New England's small-scale manufacturing offered little specialization, though it encouraged astonishing variety.

The diary of Eliza Wildes of Kennebunk, Maine, shows household production in its most conventional form. She spun flax (both long-fibered linen and short, stubby tow), linen, cotton, worsted, and wool; knitted mittens, gloves, stockings, and hose; turned tow into towels and linen into handkerchiefs; and wove webs of wool for bedding and clothing. The vocabulary of her diary shows how subsistence manufacturing compressed steps that were subdivided in commercial production. Eliza recorded breaking, washing, and carding wool; spinning, doubling, twisting, and winding yarn; and bleaching, boiling, scouring, and dyeing thread and cloth. She didn't just write of weaving, but of "making harness," "spooling," "warping," "striking harness," "putting in" and "getting out" her cloth. Like other New England housewives, she was multiskilled rather than unskilled, an experimenter rather than a specialist. She did not shear sheep—that was men's work, nor did she try to perform every task on her own. She turned to skilled neighbors for instruction, carried woolen cloth to a fulling mill for finishing, and employed her younger sisters and occasional hired girls in spinning. Still, the range of her skills was impressive. Twenty years later, with the help of factory-spun yarn and three grown daughters, she was weaving and marketing raised-weft cotton coverlets that were credible imitations of those imported from Lancashire. Her story demonstrates the skill-building possibilities in a seemingly retrograde household production system.[9]

In the early Republic, Americans celebrated household producers like Eliza, believing that through their work, the new nation would escape the indignities of England's manufacturing system. Still, throughout the colonial period and into the nineteenth century, New Englanders happily purchased manufactured cloth as well.

CLOTH MAKING STRUCTURED CONSUMPTION

A speaker at the annual meeting of the Pocumtuck Valley Memorial Association in Massachusetts in 1871 acknowledged that there were some things early American women could not manufacture. He said that his grandmother, "anxious to increase her stock of household articles by the addition of an iron dinner pot, and lacking the needful money, industriously carded and spun her carefully gathered wool, and taking the rolls upon her back, walked to Deerfield and effected an exchange, and shouldering the heavy iron pot, walked triumphantly home. These were the days of 'women's rights'."[10] His reference to "women's rights" was probably a subtle criticism of nineteenth-century movements to expand women's political rights. He seemed to be saying that any woman capable of providing her own kettles had all the rights she needed.

The ability to buy things without the intervention of a husband or father does seem like an essential component of women's rights. Yet an eighteenth-century observer might have turned that story upside down, wondering why the speaker's grandfather had not provided the pot. Was he too poor or too stingy? Until the early nineteenth century, most storekeepers were less interested in yarn than in the lumber, shingles, flax seed, fish, or grain that formed the foundation of the public economy. Although wives were probably the active agents in many purchases, legally, household heads were responsible for any debt contracted. Even if a wife brought in her own butter or homespun, it would be entered under her husband's name. Most purchases were on credit, so debits and credits accumulated over months and sometimes years. The ability to purchase things depended on a good reputation in the community and on harmonious relations between husbands and wives.

When there was conflict, female purchases became a dangerous thing. Hence, those curious advertisements in early newspapers where husbands warn storekeepers that since their wives have "eloped from their bed and board" they will not longer be responsible for any debts they might contract. In a few cases, wives published their own rejoinders, letting the world know that they had been forced to abandon adulterous or stingy husbands. Not surprisingly, some aggrieved wives invoked their hard work in spinning and weaving. One Vermont woman complained that she had left her husband because he had not only refused to support her but had taken away her cloth "& all my yarn that I had spinned." Defending herself against the charge of having "eloped" from her husband, another wife wrote, "I never left your house only to set up my loom at your son Edgcoms to weave for you to pay a debt." A third complained that the family had already been living "by the Fruit of my industry principally." [11]

In fact, every woman's work was essential to family support even though only a tiny part of it appeared in storekeeper's accounts. Producing some of their own fabrics allowed families to spend precious store credits on true luxuries, like tea pots, table forks, and East Indian calico. They used their own fabrics to extend British goods, attaching collars of Irish linen to shirts made of local flax or backing quilts made from imported calimanco with their own onion-dyed wool. The primary producers of cloth—unmarried women between the ages of sixteen and twenty-five—were also the major consumers. In a society with a rapidly expanding population, setting up new households was an enormous drain on available resources. Daughters' portions required a wide array of textiles in addition to pots, kettles, and crockery. If a girl could make at least some of that cloth, she simultaneously helped her self and eased her family's burden.

To encourage female enterprise many families gave young women in their late teens almost complete control over their own labor. Girls worked in and out of their parents' household, spinning for one neighbor, doing housework or nursing for another. Although most of this work was within a largely undocumented female economy, hints of the expansion of female responsibility appear in the changing proportion of women's names in New England store accounts, from 3.8 percent in the years before 1674 to 11.4 percent in the 1765–1774 period. After the opening of water-powered spinning mills in the 1790s, there were even more opportunities for purchasing store goods as mill owners put out yarn to storekeepers who acted as middle-men to outwork weavers. Rural women were wary about becoming dependent on such work, however. In 1815, one Rhode Island manufacturer wrote in exasperation to his New Hampshire factor:

> I did not expect but that your weavers would take from you such yarn as you had to put out. You will on a little reflection see, that if the weavers are to weave just such kind of goods as they chuse and those only, that we are in but a sorry way, what advantage shall we derive from putting out yarn in large quantities, if it is to be selected by the weavers & that which they do not like is to be returned unwoven.[12]

Spinning mills eventually learned that they could make more money by selling thread directly to home weavers who integrated it with their own flax and wool. Twenty years after the opening of the first water-power spinning factories, New England had the highest per capita household production in the United States. Most factory yarn was destined for household use, but some of it, once woven, found its way back to stores were it was exchanged for other goods. Through weaving, rural women provided themselves with teapots and calico aprons as well as homespun sheets and towels.

CLOTH MAKING CREATED NETWORKS OF WORK AND EXCHANGE

New England had an abundance of looms but few trained weavers capable of constructing and maintaining specialized equipment. As a consequence, household weavers were constantly borrowing the slatted implements called "reeds" or "sleys" that they used to regulate the distribution of threads on a loom. A memoir published in New Hampshire in the late nineteenth century turned this necessity into a celebration of female fortitude:

> But there were heroes then—men who went to the wars or fought the elements at home, and women of wonderful fortitude to bear and courage to do. One instance must suffice: my grandfather Sanborn lived between the Square and East Tilton— then Union Bridge. At one time his wife had occasion to use in weaving a certain reed and harness which could not be obtained nearer than the west part of the town—now East Franklin—in the Cate neighborhood. They owned it was said, "the smartest four-year-old colt in town." My grandmother mounted this animal, and, with a baby in her arms and another child on a pillion behind her, she started off on her ride of five miles over some of the worst hills in town. Soon after her arrival there were signs of a coming tempest, and she had to hasten. The reed and harness, at least four feet long, were bound to the colt and she turned toward home. My great, great uncle Cate said that when she passed his house she was going like the wind, the sky was black with the coming storm, and the thunder and lightning were terrible. As soon as it cleared off he saddled his horse and followed, "expecting," he said, "to find Tabitha and the children dead in the road. But I went *clean* over, and there she was, getting supper and singing as lively as a cricket." She had kept ahead of the shower which came from the west and reached home without getting wet.[13]

Tabitha's lightning-like ride through the countryside may have been heroic, but her errand was commonplace. New England diaries document the same sort of borrowing in more prosaic language. In Maine, Martha Ballard borrowed a "40 sleigh of the widow Coburn" to weave one kind of cloth and a "64 twenty slay" from her neighbor Merriam Pollard to weave another. In rural new Hampshire, Abner Sanger went to "Daniel Gleason's [to] get my wife's weaving sley and said Gleason's wife's harness to weave with."[14] The two women obviously had a long-standing habit of cooperation.

Women traded work as well as equipment. They called it "changing works." One woman spun or carded at another's house until the work was done; her friend repaid the favor with the same or similar work a later day. "Spun and sang songs," Ruth Henshaw wrote in her diary two days after a friend arrived to help with spinning. Sociability did indeed change the nature of work, though in New England parlance "changing" was actually a contraction of "exchanging." Workers expected to be repaid. "At night I went to Mr. Otis's to work & they ow'd me 2 Run of Linnen towards changing works," Elisabeth Foote of Colchester, Connecticut wrote. "They" were the Otis sisters, girls who spent almost as much time in the Foote house as in their own. On July 10, 1775, for example, Mercy Otis "handed ends" while Elisabeth's sister Abigail warped her loom. Three days later, Abigail returned the favor, going to the Otis house to help card tow.[15]

Cooperative work was a foundation for skill-building. When Mary Palmer Tyler's family moved from Boston to rural Massachusetts, she and her sisters "learned to spin, borrowing wheels of our good-natured neighbors who seemed pleased to teach the city ladies their craft." A young woman named Zerniah Price taught the Palmer girls to card wool, cotton, and tow and hetchel flax. Meanwhile Mary's mother "would change work with Zerniah's mother and other women, knitting and sewing for them while they would weave cotton and flax into cloth."[16] Such exchanges were the foundation of a cloth making system without apprenticeship, markets, or disgruntled manufacturers. As long as farmers could hold on to the land they had taken from the Indians, their wives and daughters had the liberty of working for themselves. New Englanders resisted outwork because they could.

CLOTH MAKING EARNED PUBLIC PRAISE

In the centennial celebration at Goshen, Connecticut, in 1838, a speaker told about a spinning match that took place in the town in 1771. During the first round of competition, the winner spun yarn "equal to two and a half days labour when on hire." Her success inspired a young woman named Lydia Beach to "come forward and take up the gauntlet. She spun from early dawn to nine-o-clock in the evening. She had her distaffs prepared, her yarn reeled, and her food put into her mouth. She spun in this time seven runs, three and half days' labour, and took the wreath from the brow of the other spinner." Fortunately for Beach, the husband of a third challenger forbad her to work beyond sunset. The centennial speaker approved of this intervention, agreeing that the woman's health was more important than success in a spinning bee.

He obviously believed that women were delicate creatures, entitled to a little pampering. If any one in his audience doubted it, he added a somber footnote to the story. The triumphant spinner married "while her garland was yet fresh upon her brow, but her doting husband was destined to see it wither down to the grave, for Lydia never enjoyed health from the hour of her triumph." There was such a thing as too much work.[17]

In an 1838 speech, public spinning was a curious practice of a bygone age. In 1771, it was a form of recreation, a way of providing support for Congregational ministers, and an acknowledged method of political participation. Between 1769 and 1770, New England newspapers reported more than sixty spinning meetings held in towns from Maine to Long Island. There were no doubt dozens of others, including the one in Goshen, that weren't reported in the papers. Many took place in the homes of Congregational ministers who had long received part of their compensation in the form of community work parties in their behalf. It gave the women of the congregation, often the majority of the membership, an opportunity to contribute collectively. The yarn contributed at a typical spinning meeting could amount to a full month's salary. In a period when radical Whigs were protesting taxation through boycotts of British goods, the spinning meetings also had political meaning. Some writers described the young women as "Daughters of Liberty," extolling self-sacrifice and household industry.

Spinning matches continued through the Revolution and into the early republic. In the autumn of 1810, newspapers across the Northeast reported a vicarious spinning match that began in New York State when a Miss Triphosa Butler spun and reeled more than eleven skeins of woolen yarn in fifteen hours and ten minutes. Soon, the papers were reporting the triumph of two Massachusetts women who outdid Miss Butler. That victory did not last. Two weeks later, an "Eye Witness" from Winthrop, Maine, reported that two young ladies in his neighborhood had done even better. Surely, if more women would imitate these spinners, "they would be relieved from the odious dun of the shop keeper, and the curse of foreign gew gaws and fashions, and their Country become emphatically Independent."[18] In the next decade, agricultural fairs or "Cattle Shows" took up the cause, offering prizes for the best woven blankets, flannel, or patterned linen.

Women's diaries suggest that most women worked, not for public praise or even for charity, but to supply their own households. "I spun one Black stocking Cleane my West room and Scoure the Pewter" Eliza Wildes wrote on October 5, 1789. Obviously she wasn't spinning the stocking, but the yarn she would use to knit it. Her way of describing her work shows how she saw it. Only on days of unusual productivity did she use the language of measurement employed in newspaper stories. Six or seven skeins, a good days work at a spinning match, was the usual entry, though she was proud of having produced two skeins on a washday.[19] Most of the time, however, she described her work in objects imagined—"I spoold my aprons at Night" or "wove some on the Children coats."[20] Yet the fact that she recorded it at all suggests that the ethic of productivity that underlay public spinning was formed in the household.

In the early nineteenth century, prizes offered at the agricultural fairs sure-ly induced some women to work better if not harder. Persis Sibley Andrews, a country lawyer's wife who had studied art in school before marriage, spun and dyed the yarn for a homemade hearth rug, stitching from a design of her own creation. When family obligations interrupted her work, she salved her disappointment with humor, telling her diary that she intended to finish it but "*not* at the expense of duty to my husband or daughter, but for this latter I shall get no great name, for the rug I shall be famous thro' out the County."[21] Spinning and weaving were duties, but from the 1760s onward, such work also earned public praise, and some women knew it.

CLOTH MAKING RATIFIED WHITE IDENTITY

Candace, the central African-American character in Harriet Beecher Stowe's New England anti-slavery novel *The Minister's Wooing*, is a cook rather than a spinner. Though she sometimes knits in the chimney corner at the end of the day, as Stowe portrays her one can hardly imagine this "tropical specimen of humanity" engaged in the delicate work of spinning. In Stowe's characteriza-tion, Candace's immense body and large heart belong in the kitchen. In con-trast, the winsome Mary Scudder, the white heroine of Stowe's novel, spends hour after hour at the little flax wheel kept near an upper window in her moth-er's house. She "could not waltz, or polka, or speak bad French, or sing Italian songs," but she "could spin both on the little and the great wheel; and there were numberless towels, napkins, sheets, and pillow-cases in the household store that could attest the skill of her pretty fingers."[22] Lydia Sigourney em-ployed a similar contrast in her description of a kind-hearted Mohegan woman who adopted a sickly white girl. The orphan repaid the kindness by bringing neatness and artistry to the Mohegan cottage.[23]

These nineteenth-century stories are a seemingly benign manifestation of racial definitions of work that long preceded them. From early settlement on-ward, New Englanders situated themselves between the bondage of slavery and the dangerous freedom of the forest. They described the heaviest, dirtiest, and least pleasant household labor as "slavish work, whether or not it was done by slaves." In contrast, American Indian women exemplified work's op-posite. Living without discipline, they were either degraded "savages" given to excessive drink or, in more sympathetic stories, perpetual children living in uncultivated woods and meadows.

In early New England, a few women of color surely knew how to spin and weave. In Plymouth County, an investigating minister was surprised to dis-cover an American Indian woman who lived in "a high House of the English Fashion" with "2 Loomes in it." In Boston, shopkeeper John Osborne kept his spinning wheels upstairs in the "Negro's Chamber" presumably because his unnamed slave used them.[24] But the prototypical cloth maker in early New England was the wife or daughter of a property-owning white man.

New England Indians had their own textile traditions. In June of 1791, a Rhode Island farmer noted in his diary, "I Setled with the three Squors that boutoumd my Cheers, and paid them all but one bushel of Corn."[25] The three women were presumably weaving rush seats on common chairs. Over the course of the colonial period, racial boundaries blurred as African Americans, enslaved or free, intermarried with New England Indians. Those who identified with their Indian heritage frequently became basket makers, a practice that in white eyes reinforced their identity as children of nature. Rather than working with cultivated crops like flax or domestic animals like sheep, they drew their raw materials from swamps and woods.

Indian baskets were ethnic crafts, self-consciously marketed to a rural clientele no longer fearful of a presumably "dying race." Although designed for hard use on farms and in kitchens, they were also decorative objects treasured today for their artistry. Yet none were displayed at the agricultural fairs, even though by the 1820s, white women were receiving prizes for items made of weeds or grass. One exhibition of The Rhode Island Society for the Encouragement of Domestic Industry included a carpet made of grass and rushes, window blinds of rushes, and "a vandyke of milk weed down."[26] For white women, these constituted "fancy work." For Indian women, working with found materials evidenced to the others an undeveloped capacity for labor. One New Hampshire weaver even changed her name to avoid being associated with a family of basket makers who had the same surname.[27]

THE FIRST STRIKE

When Elisabeth Barney Buel described the colonial New England housewife as "Independence herself," she was building on cherished myths about household self-sufficiency in early America. She and her contemporaries imagined intrepid wives who heroically—or sometimes comically—rose to every occasion. They could shoulder heavy kettles, shear sheep with their household scissors, spin flax from sun-up to candle-light without pausing to eat, and when necessary ride like lightning on the fastest colt in town. There was no room in these stories for rebellion. Yet surprisingly, it was hard-working and presumably obedient rural women like these who launched the first industrial strikes in New England.

In the 1820s, New England industrialists finally succeeded in drawing all the steps of production of cotton cloth into new water-powered factories. Although Lowell, Massachusetts, is the best known of the new industrial cities, there were important installations in other settings, including Dover, New Hampshire. The new mills at Dover were barely in operation before the manager began reporting trouble with his workers, who were mostly New Hampshire farm girls in their teens or early twenties. There were small disruptions, then a full-fledged strike in 1828, purportedly the first in the United States led entirely by women. Many years later an anonymous eyewitness recalled, "on a fine morning the mills were idle. Every operative was out, leaving the overseers to run them alone. They met at some convenient square, and forming a procession, with a band, and bearing the American flag, they paraded the town."[28]

Contemporary sources confirm this account. In an article entitled "Oppressions," a writer for a workingman's paper published in Philadelphia said that though "half the newspapers from Maine to Georgia had noticed the strike, none had given a full account of its causes."[29] He then proceeded to do so. This document, and a broadside published in 1834 in Dover during a second walk-out, shows the many ways in which household production shaped worker consciousness.

Although wages were an issue in later strikes, the 1828 strike at Dover focused on broader conditions of employment. The mill workers were annoyed by rigid rules and insulted by attempts to monitor their behavior. They had explicit goals in coming to the mills, and they expected to achieve them. A few months earlier they had threatened to boycott the downtown stores when they proposed to cut costs by closing early two evenings a week and stop giving free patterns and trimming with each sale of fabric.[30] These were young women in the business of accumulating clothing and household goods needed in marriage. If denied the opportunity to acquire store goods at a decent price, they might just as well have remained in their rural households. There was certainly nothing particularly appealing about the work. In the words of the 1828 essay, the lords of industry seemed content to see "a portion of their fellow creatures grow up as mere machines . . . with all the dignified attributes of the human soul merged in the exalted art of tying a knot in a thread of cotton."[31]

Today, it hardly seems surprising that manufacturers wanted workers to show up on time. But to the rural workers, the punctiliousness of the managers seemed excessive. Girls were fined if they failed to enter the factory within five minutes of the ringing of the bell. "What would the good people of this city say, to see 3 or 400 girls running, like hunted deer, on the ringing of a bell?" exclaimed the writer in the *Mechanics Free Press*. The "unkindest cut of all" was a rule against talking to fellow workers "except on business." There was no opportunity here to spin and sing songs.

Finally, the workers were outraged by clumsy attempts to legislate moral behavior. Once work had been a source of pride, a mark of piety and patriotism. Now, in the eyes of the imperious manufacturer, working girls were potential libertines. There were rules against smoking and drinking, and demands that they attend Divine Worship on Sundays. "Surely it is not necessary to tell 3 or 400 young women, that if they were guilty of any *debauchery* they would be dismissed! It is but a few years since these large cotton factories had an existence in this country—did they find a vulgar population, or have they had a debasing influence?"[32] In the words of their advocates, the young women of New England were too proud, too independent to submit to such insults. Better that "Cocheco falls should again be the abode of the 'four-footed denizen' of the forest, and the haunt of savage nations, that that the 'Bell of No 2' at each successive peal should call together hundreds of willing and obedient slaves."[33]

These early strikes were an integral part of a broader workers' movement in Jacksonian America, and they were no doubt influenced by labor activism in England, but the women who marched through the streets of Dover and other New England towns did not get their ideas secondhand. They came to the factory with notions of independence acquired in the household economies of rural New England. When New England mill girls sang "Oh! I cannot be a slave,/ I will not be a slave,/ For I'm so fond of liberty,/ That I cannot be a slave," they were building on generations of experience in a textile economy that gave women property, skills, access to consumer goods, public praise, and a sense of their own superiority as wives and daughters of property-owning white men. Women who made their own cloth could be neither savages nor slaves.

When I began my work in early American history thirty years ago, I hoped to rescue women's work from the haze of nineteenth-century sentimentality. Today I see history as well as nostalgia in the sometimes comical, usually exaggerated, and often racist stories preserved in town histories, novels, family chronicles, and on the cracked labels attached to old cloth. The romance of the spinning wheel not only reveals the values of the nineteenth century, it points to cultural patterns grounded in the household economies of early America.

Notes

1. Elisabeth Cynthia Barney Buel, *The Tale of the Spinning-Wheel* (Litchfield, CT, 1903), 30–31.
2. See especially, Laurel Thatcher Ulrich, "Wheels, Looms, and the Gender Division of Labor in Eighteenth-Century New England," *William & Mary Quarterly*, 3d Ser. LV (1998): 3–38 and Laurel Thatcher Ulrich, *The Age of Homespun: Objects and Stories in the Creation of An American Myth* (New York: Alfred A. Knopf, 2001; Vintage paperback, 2002).
3. New Hampshire Historical Society, Accession Files, 65.29.
4. Elisabeth Baker, who had no children of her own, was Jane Mack's aunt. Robert Mack, the Justice of the Peace, was Jane's husband.
5. Linen Sheet, New Hampshire Historical Society, 1965.38.2. Family tradition attributes the sheet to Elisabeth's mother, "Ocean born Mary." Since it is marked with "W" rather than a "P," it was likely made before Elisabeth Wallace's marriage to Thomas Patterson in 1776.
6. These eventually came to the Royal Ontario Museum in Toronto. For more on the Patterson textiles, see "In the Garrets and Ratholes of Old Houses," in *Textiles in New England: Four Centuries of Material Life*, ed. Peter Benes, The Dublin Seminar for New England Folklife: Annual Proceedings, 1999 (Boston: Boston University, 2001), 6–15.
7. Henry Art Gallery, University of Washington in Seattle. I would like to thank Liz Bless of the Sheldon Museum, Middlebury, Vermont, for helping me identify Charity Bryant. The papers of her niece and namesake are at the Sheldon Museum; the diary of William Cullen Bryant's mother is at the Houghton Library, Harvard University. These papers document the importance of household production in Charity Bryant's family as well as the aspiration toward gentility evident in her embroidery.

8. *Green Mountain Heritage: The Chronicle of Northfield, Vermont* (Canaan:NH Phoenix Publishing, 1974), 33.

9. For more on Eliza Wildes Bourne, see Sandra S. Armentrout, "Eliza Bourne of Kennebunk: Professional Fancy Weaver, 1800-1820," in *House and Home*, ed. Peter Benes (Dublin Seminar for New England Folklife, Annual Proceedings, 1988), 101–15, and Ulrich, *The Age of Homespun*, chapters 8 and 9.

10. *History and Proceedings of the Pocumtuck Valley Memorial Association, 1870–1879*, vol. 1 (Deerfield, MA, 1890), 17.

11. *Rutland Herald*, December 3, 1821, *American Register*, September 15, 1821, *Vermont Journal*, August 5, 1811, quoted in Mary Beth Sievens, "Stray Wives: Marital Conflict and Gender Relations in Vermont, 1790–1830," Ph.D. Dissertation, Boston University, 1996, 96, 102, 95.

12. Dublin, *Transforming Women's Work*, 33–40, quote on p. 40 and Gail Fowler Mohanty, "Putting Up with Putting-Out: Power Loom Diffusion and Outwork for Rhode Island Mills, 1821–1829," *Journal of the Early Republic*, 9 (1989), 191–216. For efforts to establish factories and employ artisan weavers see Mohanty, "Experimentation in Textile Technology, 1788–1790, and Its Impact on Handloom Weaving and Weavers in Rhode Island," *Technology and Culture* 19 (January 1988), 1–31, and Barbara M. Tucker, *Samuel Slater and the Origins of the American Textile Industry, 1790–1860* (Ithaca: Cornell University Press, 1984), 47–66.

13. Hannah Sanborn Philbrook, "A Few Memories and Traditions of Sanbornton," *The Granite Monthly* 32 (March 1902), 181–82.

14. Martha Moore Ballard Diary, April 20, 1790, October 15, 1792, Maine State Museum, Augusta; *Very Poor and of a Lo Make: The Journal of Abner Sanger*, Lois K. Stabler, ed. (Portsmouth, NH: Peter Randall, 1986), 500.

15. See Ulrich, "Wheels, Looms, and the Gender Division of Labor," 17–18.

16. *Grandmother Tyler's Book: The Recollections of Mary Palmer Tyler, 1775–1866*, Frederick Tupper and Helen Tyler Brown, eds. (New York: G. P. Putnam, 1925), 141.

17. Quoted in Buel, *Tale of the Spinning Wheel*, 41–42.

18. *Columbia Phoenix*, Providence, Rhode Island, Sept. 1, 1810; *American Advocate*, Augusta, Maine, Oct. 11 and 24, 1810.

19. Diary of Eliza Wildes, July 1, 1789, October 26, 1791, April 12, 1793, manuscript, Maine Historical Society, Portland.

20. Diary of Eliza Wildes, July 1, 1789, October 26, 1791, April 12, 1793.

21. Persis Sibley Andrews Diary, October 23, November 16, December 14, 1845, typed transcription, Maine State Museum, Augusta.

22. Harriet Beecher Stowe, *The Minister's Wooing* (Boston: Tickner & Fields, 1866), 20, 109–113.

23. [Lydia Huntley Sigourney], *Sketch of Connecticut Forty Years Since* (Hartford, CT: Cooke, 1824), 55–59.

24. Josiah Cotton, "Some Inquiries Made among ye Indians in the General Visitation begun Septr. 4: 1726," Curwen papers, American Antiquarian Society, Worcester, MA; Suffolk County Probate Records, Massachusetts State Archives, 44:517.

25. Caroline Hazard, ed., *Nailer Tom's Diary: Otherwise the Journal of Thomas B. Hazard of Kingstown, Rhode Island* (Boston: Merrymount, 1930), 300, 323, 326, 346.

26. *Rutland Herald*, October 22, 1821, *New England Farmer*, V (1827): 110, 101.

27. For the story of Hannah Wilson see Donna-Belle Garvin, "The Warp and Weft of a Lifetime: The Discovery of a New Hampshire Weaver and Her Work," in *Textiles in Early New England*, ed. Peter Benes, Dublin Seminar for New England Folklife, Annual proceedings, 1997 (Boston: Boston University Press, 1999), 29–47 and Ulrich, *The Age of Homespun*, 309–401.

28. "The First Strike," *New York Times*, February 6, 1886, 3.

29. *Mechanics Free Press*, January 17, 1829.

30. For more on the strikes, see Ulrich, *The Age of Homespun*, 390–95.

31. *Mechanics Free Press*, January 17, 1829.

32. Ibid.

33. "To the Factory Girls," Broadside, March 1834, Woodman Institute, Dover, New Hampshire.

Suggestions for Further Reading

Barber, Elisabeth Wayland. *Women's Work: The First 20,000 Years*. New York: W. W. Norton, 1994.

Blewett, Mary H. *We Will Rise in Our Might: Workingwomen's Voices from Nineteenth-Century New England*. Ithaca: Cornell University Press, 1991.

Dublin, Thomas. *Transforming Women's Work: New England Lives in the Industrial Revolution*. Ithaca: Cornell University Press, 1994.

Hill, Sarah Hill. *Weaving New Worlds: Southeastern Cherokee Women and Their Basketry*. Chapel Hill: University of North Carolina Press, 1997.

Hood, Adrienne. *The Weaver's Craft: Cloth, Commerce, and Industry in Early Pennsylvania*. Philadelphia: University of Pennsylvania Press, 2003.

McMullen, Ann, and Russell G. Handsman, eds. *A Key to the Language of Woodsplint Baskets*. Washington, CT: American Indian Archeological Institute, 1987.

Nylander, Jane C. *Our Own Snug Fireside: Images of the New England Home, 1760–1860*. New York: Alfred A. Knopf, 1993.

Ulrich, Laurel Thatcher. *The Age of Homespun: Objects and Stories in the Creation of An American Myth*. New York: Alfred A. Knopf, 2001.

———. "Wheels, Looms, and the Gender Division of Labor in Eighteenth-Century New England." *William & Mary Quarterly*, 3d Ser. LV (1998): 3–38.

Weiner, Annette B., and Jane Schneider, eds., *Cloth and Human Experience*. Washington: Smithsonian Institution Press, 1989.

Stealing Happiness:
Women Shoplifters
in Georgian England

Adela Pinch

Adela Pinch (1987) is Associate Professor of English and Women's Studies at the University of Michigan. She is the author of *Strange Fits of Passion: Epistemologies of Emotion, Hume to Austen* (1996) and numerous essays on eighteenth- and nineteenth-century English literature and culture. She edited Jane Austen's *Emma* for Oxford University Press (2003).

Adela Pinch writes, "I was motivated to think of the study of women as an important, exciting endeavor relatively early in life because of my great good fortune in having been a teenager in the 1970s when my mother, Judith Pinch, was helping to launch the WWNFF's Women's Studies Program." Of the impact of feminist scholarship on students, she says, "Students in my survey class on British Romantic Literature don't seem to find it odd that there are so many women writers in the syllabus, nor do they seem averse to discussing gender. I hope this is a sign of the place of gender and feminist thinking in their lives in general, and that this demonstrates the effectiveness of more than three decades of women's studies."

Why would a feminist scholar be interested in nineteenth-century English shoplifters? The path that led me to this research topic speaks volumes about how women's studies has transformed scholarship in the humanities over the past thirty years. Since the origins of academic women's studies programs in the 1970s, feminist scholars in literature and in history have done groundbreaking work on nineteenth-century British culture. Important work from the early years typically focused on the great woman writers of the era—Jane Austen, the Brontes, George Eliot—or on valiant crusaders for women's rights. Nineteenth-century England, the birthplace of liberalism, often seemed full of precursors to twentieth-century feminist struggles. But the era also seemed to represent a not-so-distant dark age, from which twentieth-century women had just recently escaped: Nineteenth-century British literature and historical documents were scoured for evidence of the ideologies and customs that had kept women in their place—to "suffer and be still"—for so long. In the years since, feminist scholarship of nineteenth-century British literature and culture has exploded with outstanding studies of women who never fit into the dominant, middle-class cult of domesticity: prostitutes, working-class mothers, women of different ethnic and national origins who traversed the borders of the British empire.[1]

But feminist scholarship on nineteenth-century England—like feminist scholarship everywhere—has not simply focused on kinds of women; it has transformed the scholarly methods of the traditional disciplines such as literature and history. By transgressing the boundaries of the disciplines, and by looking at cultural and social life through the lens of gender, women's studies has opened up new areas of human experience for scholarship. One such area is the study of consumption and consumerism: the study of how consumerism plays a role, not just in economics, but in cultural and social life; the study of how and why people shop; the study of the intense relations people have with the material things of this world. The causes of the last twenty years' efflorescence of scholarship on consumption, in fields ranging from anthropology and archaeology, to psychology, to economic history, to social history, literary studies, and cultural studies, are many. But within British studies, the role of feminist scholarship has been central. Scholars generally recognize eighteenth-and early nineteenth-century England as the birthplace of modern consumer society: the place and time where consumerism got stamped with its modern identity by being associated with femininity. In particular, during the first few decades of the nineteenth-century—the end of the reign of George III and the Regency and reign of George IV—the upper classes of English society achieved an affluence, a fashion consciousness, and a culture of conspicuous consumption in which it appeared, to visitors from all over Europe, that "the usual morning employment of English ladies [was to] go a-shopping."[2]

My own interest in women shop*lifters* emerged about ten years ago, in part through an undergraduate women's studies class on Gender and Consumerism that I taught several times at the University of Michigan during the early 1990s—another era of conspicuous consumption. I discovered that some very interesting research had been done on the history and meaning of female shoplifting, as a symptom of the dangers and excesses that consumer society puts on women. In the course of the class itself, I found that my students had a lot to say on this topic. At one point, they all spontaneously confessed that they had themselves—mostly as preteens or teenagers, and often, they stressed, under peer pressure—committed at least one act of petty retail theft. They mentioned lipstick, nail polish, costume jewelry, and small items of clothing such as swimsuits as the prime objects of adolescent theft, and they had very smart things to say about the ways in which shoplifting represents perhaps not so much a violation of the norms of consumer society, but its logical extension.[3]

Some feminist theorists of the 1990s corroborated my students' views. Leslie Camhi, for example, writing about the literature on the late nineteenth-century department store, described female kleptomania as a critical, subversive activity, lifting the cover off the fraud of femininity itself:

> It is an entire social order that the female kleptomaniac calls into question by her actions. It is, perhaps, this very gamble with an entire social identity that compels her, the unconscious need to establish the fraudulence of inherited wealth and social position. . . . Thus the difference between buying and stealing, or between normal women and thieves, becomes increasingly attenuated, because the commodities that are bought or stolen are used to produce and maintain the permanent fraud of feminine sexuality, the deception of the feminine masquerade. . . . Femininity is always already stolen, a dissimulated mask, veil, or fiction of difference.[4]

Camhi—as well as other feminist scholars of thieving—redefined theft not as a transgression against the world of consumption but as that which discloses its true meaning. By shopping the wrong way, the shoplifter gets it right.

From the point of view of our current, less affluent and less confident moment, it may not make sense to glamorize the female shoplifter as a feminist heroine. And further historical research suggests, as we shall see, that the gendered meanings of shoplifting can be quite complex. However, I do maintain that studying shoplifting can teach us a great deal about gender and consumerism. Focusing on stories about shoplifting can teach us about how affluent women in Georgian England may have used the public space of the luxury shop to negotiate a perplexing set of contradictions about their place in society—did they belong in the private realm in the home? Or out in public?—and about who their allies and enemies were—members of their own social class? Or gender? These stories can also teach us how ordinary women as well as writers, both men and women, may have used stories about women taking desirable things out of stores to raise some important questions about the role of things in our lives: the way seemingly inanimate objects can bring us happiness or misery. I describe in these pages a context in which the stolen good—most prominently a piece of lace—attracted to itself and to the players in its drama a range of emotions: sympathy, anxiety, contempt, dread. I go back and forth between things and persons, between shoplifters, shopkeepers, and the goods themselves, and between real and fictional people. The first section of this chapter analyzes the classification of genteel female theft in early nineteenth-century England, and the second section examines a particular case from 1799 of peculiar interest to scholars of early nineteenth-century literature: the trial of Jane Austen's aunt, Mrs. Jane Leigh Perrot. The third section explores a literary text by Thomas de Quincey, the brilliant writer best known now for his own excessive consumptions, described deliriously in his *Confessions of An English Opium Eater* (first edition, 1821). His crazy, beautiful novella, "The Household Wreck," treats the story a woman accused of stealing a piece of lace as a matter of life and death, and explores the miseries and joys that material things can bring us.

I

Feminist historians such as Elaine Abelson and Patricia O'Brien have written about the emergence of the kleptomania diagnosis in the context of the rise of the *fin-de-siècle* department store. However, the notion that a propensity to shoplift among those who can legitimately afford to pay might be a moral disorder rather than a crime, a compulsion rather than a choice, goes back at least to the early nineteenth century. A stealing mania was codified by a Swiss doctor, Andre Matthey, as *klopémanie* in 1816, and by 1830 the concept of klep-tomania was current enough that the British literary periodical the *New Monthly Magazine* could note in passing that "instances of this cleptomania are well known to have happened in this country, even among the rich and noble" (1830: 15). (The term "shop-lift" itself appeared in slang dictionaries as early as the 1670s). Early to mid-nineteenth-century medical literature categorized such instances as species of moral insanity—perplexing cases, in that they often seemed to occur in persons who seemed otherwise neither mad nor criminal. The subjects of the medical narratives—often, though not always, women, but always well-to-do—often lamented their unaccountable propensity: things simply seemed to follow them home. For example,

> A gentleman, having an independent income of £2,000 a year, was at Scarborough. In passing through one of the streets, he saw a friend with his daughter, in a shop; he joined them. The party then left the shop together. In a short time the mercer waited on the father of the lady, and regretted much to state, that his daughter had, no doubt by mistake, taken a silk shawl from the counter of his shop. The father contradicted the charge, and inquired who was in the shop during the time when the shawls were exposed. The reply was "no one but himself, the lady, and gentle-man." The shopkeeper accompanied the gentleman to his friend's residence, in the hall of which he found the great coat worn in the morning, and in one of the pock-ets was the lost shawl. . . . This theft could not have been committed for the purpose of gain, nor could he have stolen it for use.[5]

So common were tales of this kind that the *Times* asserted in 1855 that "everyone who is acquainted with London society could at once furnish a dozen names of ladies who have been notorious for abstracting articles of trifling value from the shops where they habitually dealt."[6]

Such anecdotes were most often in the service of the growing field of foren-sic medicine, which was charged with helping justices determine whether these cases deserved criminal prosecution—a particularly vexing issue, be-cause the penalties for conviction for shoplifting were severe. Until 1820, the punishment for stealing any goods valued at five shillings or more from a shop was execution. Throughout the first decades of the century, humanitarians led by Sir Samuel Romilly campaigned to reform the draconian Shop-lifting Acts, but a bitter opposition successfully blocked attempts to abolish capital punish-ment in shoplifting cases in the House of Lords in 1810, 1813, and 1816. After 1820 (and after 1826, when further reforms were instituted), the penalty for shoplifting even goods of small value was still imprisonment or transportation.

The enforcement of these laws was highly variable, often tempered by the leniency or sympathy of the jury, who could, for example, render a defendant guilty of a lesser charge by simply declaring that the actual value of the goods stolen was in their view less than five shillings.[7]

It was, predictably, the cases of genteel thieves that were most likely to attract a diagnosis of moral mania rather than a criminal conviction. Contemporaries murmured that the rich and feminine got diagnosed while the poor hung. However, genteel shoplifters did get convicted, to the pained ambivalence of middle-class onlookers. Here is Harriet Martineau on a convict of the 1820s:

> It should appear to a stranger from another hemisphere a strange thing that we should boast of our Christian civilization, while we had such a spectacle as was seen even at a later time than this.—An elderly lady, of good station and fortune, might be seen on the tread-wheel in Cold Bath Fields prison, in the jail-dress, and with her hair cut close—for the offense of shoplifting. It is difficult to write this fact; and it must be painful to read it; but the truths of the time must be told.[8]

"Justice," she moralizes, was sometimes "brought to persons of property and standing as well as the poor":

> A lady was convicted for shoplifting, who actually carried on her person, at the moment of the theft, the sum of £8,000 in bank-notes and India bonds. She underwent her punishment. In this case, if insanity had existed, it must have been proved. All parties would have been too happy to admit the plea. It was no doubt one of those cases of strong propensity for which neither our education, law, nor justice makes provision. It is a case which makes the heart bleed; . . . the wretched woman of wealth suffered as if she had been a hungry mother, snatching a loaf for famishing children at home.

In Martineau's accounts of the convictions of genteel shoplifters, we hear an uneasy assent. She is indignant when two respectable young ladies collude with the prosecution and are acquitted; yet in the cases of successful prosecution she is mournfully at a loss: neither education, law, nor justice makes provisions for such cases. Genteel lady shoplifters posed an interpretive dilemma.[9]

There are ways, of course, that we can interpret shoplifting in nineteenth-century England as occupying a space somewhere outside of crime and madness. We might begin by following the lead of physician John Bucknill who started to describe that space in his own terms in an article on the abuse of the kleptomania defense in 1863. Surveying the literature on kleptomania, weighing it against the purported frequency of shoplifting-addiction among English ladies, Bucknill has difficulty consigning most cases either to crime or to insanity. "But there is another aspect to this matter," he argues: "The struggle for existence in the middle, and even in the upper classes of our complex social system, combined with the prevailing fashion of an emulative and showy expenditure, make the sense of want felt keenly in many an English home, where no traces of vulgar poverty are discernable." Shoplifting of this kind has nothing to do with vulgar poverty, but it speaks to other kinds of felt indigence, other needs. Pinpointing the pressures of "emulative . . . expenditure," Bucknill lays the blame at the doorstep of a society of conspicuous consumption. He goes on with a series of rhetorical questions:

> And how are they tempted? How are women, whose education has been one system of skillful parade, who have been trained to derive a vast proportion of their daily happiness from that most personal of the aesthetic arts, the cultivation of dress, how are they tempted to possess themselves of its material? Are they not stimulated to covet its possession by every ingenious device which the mind of man or of woman can devise, by streets of gorgeous shops, touted in every possible manner by the most pertinacious inducements, and almost persecutions to buy, buy, buy; so that it has at last become the custom of the town-bred English-woman of the present day to spend no inconsiderable portion of her time . . . in the new and peculiar duty of life called "shopping." Can we be surprized that when the means fail to gratify the desires thus stimulated . . . that in some instances the desire of the eye should prove too strong for the moral sense? It is painful and humiliating if these things are so, but it is not wonderful that they should be so; and on the whole we can find more pity for the poor woman who purloins a piece of lace, without which she thinks she will be absolutely not fit to be seen, than for the smirking fellow who has caught her in his haberdashery trap.[10]

The doctor's sympathy, his refusal to pathologize "the shop-lifting ladies" his insistence on a social context that turns women into thieves and fetishists are all striking; and all the more so for the ways he anticipates the explanations of feminist historians of shopping, who similarly point to the burdens and restrictions consumer culture places on women.[11] But it is precisely such echoes that should make us pay attention to where Bucknill's sympathies do *not* lie: the "smirking" figure of the shopkeeper. For it is with this figure that some of the meaning of women's shoplifting in early nineteenth-century England can be found.

Shoplifting was—as we shall see in the following sections—a very intimate crime. A shopper could not easily lift items off the shelves herself. Open shelves were unknown until the invention of the department store in the later nineteenth century; a customer's access to all goods, in shops large and small, was mediated by the shopkeeper behind his (and it often was, even in women's shops, *his*) counter. Thus shoplifting involved not a magical encounter between shopper and object of desire, but a triangle of desire between shopper, object, and shopkeeper. Professional thieves of Regency England such as James Hardy Vaux prided themselves on their ingenious tricks for outwitting the shopkeeper; female shoplifts often pretended to order goods, arranged for their delivery to a false address, and dexterously swiped stuff off the counter as the clerk busied himself or herself with the transaction. Shoplifting was an engagement with a shopkeeper.[12]

Another aspect of genteel shopping that made relations between shopkeeper and customer particularly intimate was the credit system. Cash rarely changed hands; the prestige of the haberdasher, draper, dry-goods purveyor to the well-to-do depended on his willingness to extend credit to customers. The wealthier or more prestigious the customer, the longer the leash of his or her credit. According to one historian, "a year was the normal time for high-class tradesmen or shopkeepers to be kept waiting for the settlement of accounts. Few indeed, if they wished to keep custom, would dare to send out their bills inside a year."[13] One implication of the credit system was that in early nineteenth-century shops, walking out of stores with merchandise one hadn't actually payed for was the norm, rather than the exception. In this context, the difference between shoplifting and shopping indeed appears to be a difference of degree rather than of kind. Genteel shoppers constantly pushed at the boundaries of the credit system. Thomas De Quincey was caught up in a constant cycle of "buying and yet not paying for." A familiar figure of early nineteenth-century culture is that of the fashionable male "Dandy" who neglected to pay his bills, and in so doing, expressed a complex, intimate contempt for the shopkeeper who depended on the Dandy for his status as a fashionable tradesman, and who in turn the Dandy himself depended for his own prestige. The genteel lady shoplifter may thus be seen as engaging in an odd combination of intimacy, privilege, and resentment similar to that of the era's Dandies and courtesans who refused to pay their bills.[14] The notorious, high-class whore Hariette Wilson recorded in her *Memoirs* her pleasure in deliberately withholding her debts owed to one "Smith, the haberdasher of Oxford Street": "Not that I was in any sort of difficulty during the whole period I remained with Lord Ponsonby, who always took care of me, and for me, but Smith's scolding furnished me with so much entertainment, that I purposely neglected his bills, knowing his high charges, and how well he could afford to give long credit."[15]

Why contempt for shopkeepers? While the answer to this question might seem obvious, we need to note that the shopkeeper was a crucial figure in early nineteenth-century political discourse. Napoleon's epithet for England—a "nation of shopkeepers"—resonated even with his worst enemies. (Another French observer of the period, social reformer Flora Tristan, thought the English were a nation of shop*lifters*—she was astonished by the existence of an entire branch of London commerce devoted to the sale of stolen silk handkerchiefs.[16]) The same political party that fought successfully for years against Romilly's campaign to abolish capital punishment for shoplifting by championing the shopkeepers' right to protect their property, also demonized the shopkeeper as a force for democracy and revolution. Foes of the Reform Bill of 1832, which enfranchised large and petty shopkeepers, feared that reform would give the "shopocracy" unprecedented political power. Thomas De Quincey's conservative diatribes in the pages of *Blackwood's Magazine* raged against their ascendancy. In an article on "The Progress of Social Disorganization," De Quincey sought to determine who is to blame for the social ills he itemizes: "We shall give the answer in the words of our bitterest enemy; of one who knows us in many respects better than we did ourselves. . . . "The English," says Napoleon, 'are a nation of SHOPKEEPERS.' In this single expression is to be found the true secret of the pecuniary difficulties in which all classes have been involved for the last fifteen years."[17]

For De Quincey, the battle against the shopocracy was the new domestic war that replaced the war against Napoleon. In "The Approaching

Revolution in Great Britain" he positioned himself as spy on the trading classes, on their ways and their tendencies: "No symptom from which their predominant inclinations can be collected, has escaped me for the last sixteen years—that is, since the general close of the European wars has left men entirely free and undisturbed for the consideration of domestic politics." The result of his observations, is definitive proof that "this order of men is purely Jacobinical, and disposed to revolutionary courses, as any that existed in France at the period of their worst convulsions." Shopkeepers, for De Quincey and his *Blackwood's* colleagues, are driven by revenge, resentment, and desperation. Close to the bottom of the social scale, they have nothing to fear and will take any risks: "but their prospectus in the opposite direction, so naturally suggested by each man's ambition and vanity, seem altogether indefinite. The single step which they can lose, is soon reascended; and for the many which they can gain, new chances seem opened . . . by the confusions of revolution."[18]

In this context we can make a little bit more sense of Bucknill's sympathy for the shoplifting ladies. The contempt for shopkeepers that both Bucknill and De Quincey express indicates how resonant this particular class border was in early nineteenth-century England. The shopkeeper represented not only a particular political force, but also a new world in which at least the external markers of distinction were truly available to anyone who could pay. Like the bizarre Georgian Dandy who both flaunted and flouted the rules of consumer society, the genteel lady who walked out of shops with stolen goods may have been asserting her privilege to imagine herself entitled to a luxury beyond price. She was also, perhaps, finding a way to participate in a public, political debate—the growing upper-class fear of political reform—in an era when her formal political power was limited.[19] Both the temptation to shoplift and the different languages addressing this temptation—debates about legal reform, about forensic diagnosis, both sympathy for and outrage at the genteel female shoplifters, confusion over victimage—spell out a rich context for understanding how a culture interpreted women's actions.

II

In August of 1799, Mrs. Jane Leigh Perrot, a 53–year–old gentlewoman, was arrested for stealing a card of lace from a shop in Bath. Her trial in March 1800, watched closely by her contemporaries, is best known to us today because Mrs. Perrot happens to have been Jane Austen's aunt.[20] Here is her account of what happened:

> It is now five Weeks since I went into *Smith's*, a Haberdasher in Bath St; to buy some black Lace to trim a Cloak; when I had bought it the Shopman took it into the further part of the shop to put it up—this might have struck me as something particular had I not given the man a 5-pound note to pay himself and bring me the difference—when he left me I turned from the Counter to the door to catch my Goodman [i.e. her husband, who was in Bath to drink its healing waters] who in going to drink his Water generally passed that way. When the Man brought me my

Change and the Parcel I left the Shop carrying the Parcel in my hand. I went homewards the same way that Perrot usually came and had not gone far before I met him, we went together to the Cross Bath, stopt to pay a tradesman's bill, and as we had a letter to put into the Post Office were going through Bath St; where I had an hour before bought my Lace, and when we came opposite the Shop the Woman who had sold me the Lace came across the Street and accosted me with these words "I beg pardon, Madam, but was there by mistake a card of white lace put up with the black you bought?" I answered I could not tell as I had not been home but she might satisfye herself as the parcel had never been out of my hand—on saying which I gave it to her, She open'd it, and there was a Card of White Edging which She took out saying "Oh here it is" and returned to the Shop. This did not surprise me as I thought it might have proceeded from Shop hurry or Negligence, but before we had gotten to the Abbey Church Yard the Man who had taken my Lace away to fold up, came after us to desire my Name and place of Abode as he never had put up that card of White Edging. This alarmed me a good deal because I had neither asked for White Lace nor had I seen any such thing in the Shop. . . . On Wednesday following (the 14th) I was sitting up in my dear Perrot's Bed Chamber when my Maid came up and said a Gentleman in the Parlour wanted to speak to me. Judge my horror upon going down to find he was a Constable with a Warrant from the Mayor for my immediate appearance. I went up to Perrot . . . who forgetting everything but my danger got up and attended me to the Mayor where we found these two Wretches had sworn solemnly the One to seeing me take the Lace, the Other to finding her Lace to the value of 20/- in my possession—this She certainly did, but how it came to be there they best can tell as the first I ever saw of it was on the Woman's unfolding the paper with my Black Lace. The Mayor and Magistrates, to whom we were well known, lamented their being obliged to commit me to prison on the oaths of these People—they could only act in the capacity of Magistrates whatever their own private opinions might be—to prison I was sent. . . .[21]

Mrs. Perrot endured over seven months in a jailor's house, was brought to trial, and acquitted: the jury, deliberating for only fifteen minutes, brought back a verdict of not guilty. In doing so, they—along with the crowd of onlookers both male and female who wept openly at the spectacle of such innocence on trial—affirmed her version of the event. The judge directed the jury to consider the character of a lady of Mrs. Perrot's social standing and the characters of the genteel witnesses on her behalf, and the prosecution urged that they consider the likelihood that a wealthy woman like Mrs. Perrot would stoop to steal such a trifle. The shopman, Mr. Filby, and the shopwoman, Mrs. Gregory, were painted by the prosecution as adulterous lovers with shady pasts, who hoped to shore up an insolvent shop by blackmailing the well-to-do Perrots.

Mrs. Perrot's letters are extraordinary. Those dating from her days in custody before her trial are ladylike and long-suffering; the letters written after her vindication bristle with an overwhelmingly unladylike rage at her accusers. She repeatedly stresses her regret that Filby and his associates cannot be persecuted within an inch of their lives; not enough can be said about their villainy to satisfy her. Once free she indulges in fantasies of Gregory and Filby's humiliation: "I own what partly consoled me for what I had undergone was the delightful Idea of the *Pillory Exhibition* for my *pretty pair of Lovers*—but my Solicitor says," she laments, "that nothing can be done" (she was legally prohibited from prosecuting them). Through her account of her resentment of the judge—whom she felt hadn't said nearly enough about Filby's "vile" and "vicious" nature—one can hear the judge's protestations that indeed he had said enough to liberate her and thus his alarm at her excessiveness—and perhaps at least a doubt about her innocence. She crudely expresses her wish that her accusers should be hung: "The more I reflect on the diabolical Set that *swore* such abominable Falsehoods the less I wonder at the Numbers that *swing* every Year. . . . Query did he not richly deserve the Gallows?" And she desires to know "how can *we* blacken those People more than they have blacken'd themselves—*the Man is off* and the Shop I hear must be ruin'd," she reports with evident satisfaction.[22] That Mrs. Perrot's evident desire for Filby and Gregory's humiliation and extermination might indeed suggest her own guilt is for my purposes immaterial. Skepticism about the evidence of emotion should not prevent us from hypothesizing about the stability of the emotional ratio of aggression to aggrieved victimization that would seem to pertain either way. Innocent, that is, Mrs. Perrot utilizes her arrest as an occasion for exploring the depths of contempt; if guilty, one suspects, the same balance of aggression and victimization that her letters express might have played some role in the deed itself.

But what about the piece of lace that sits at the center of this episode and crosses the border—whether legitimately or illegitimately—between shop and street? For what is at issue in Perrot's trial is not her possession of the lace, but competing accounts of its travels: "how it came to be there they best can tell," as she insists. In this regard, the trial of Jane Leigh Perrot can be seen as the story of lace writ small, for lace in early nineteenth-century England had everything to do with borders and border crossings. Borders between England and France, for example: the Napoleonic Wars suspended the importing of French lace—"real" lace—during much of the period 1799–1815, which, while aiding the domestic lace industry, made an attachment to good lace an example invocation of the tensions among luxury, trade, and politics.[23] Itself a border, moreover, lace is a classic feminine object of desire. Mrs. Perrot bought the black lace to "trim a cloak"; the white lace that attaches itself to her is "white edging." Diaphanous, barely there, both concealing and revealing what lies beneath, lace always has mysterious, even erotic meanings.

On the eve of her trial, Mrs. Perrot lamented the expense of her case and professed her innocence once more: "This ruinous Expense is what we shall long feel—but we are not expensive People, and believe me, *Lace* is not necessary to my happiness."[24] Her joking protestation—"believe me"—that she needs lace neither as something to steal nor as something to buy in her new economically straighted circumstances after her expensive trial demonstrates the moral anxiety that causes us to banish the material good from the calculus of happiness. Rejecting lace's necessity to her happiness seems, for Perrot, to be incontrovertible evidence of her innocence of the crime. In her own defense she places this piece of lace squarely in the context of Enlightenment rhetoric about luxury, value, necessity, and the pursuit of happiness. Her use of the word "necessary" here, for example, invokes an important piece of legislation that governed English married women's access to luxury goods: the "law of necessaries." This law stipulated that a husband was bound to supply his wife with "necessaries suitable to his station in life," and well-to-do women (and sympathetic juries) used this law to justify all kinds of conspicuous consumption. Who was to say, for example, that fine lace was *not* "necessary" to a middle-class lady's status?[25] Nevertheless, Mrs. Perrot's declaration has the effect of both challenging and enforcing our ideas about what a lady's needs and desires are: Shouldn't it be a truth universally acknowledged that a lady in possession of a good fortune, must not be in want of lace? Thus she expresses an uneasiness that haunts modern consumer society: that happiness might in fact be found in the material thing.

III

The narrator of Thomas De Quincey's extravagant and extravagantly titled novella, "The Household Wreck," worries that happiness can steal from itself. A suburban gentleman fondly anxious about his too perfect, too happy young wife, he finds his own happiness a self-consuming burden. "I lived," he confides,

> under the constant presence of a feeling which only that great observer of human nature [Shakespeare] . . . has ever noticed; viz, that merely the excess of my happiness made me jealous of its ability to last, and in that extent less capable of enjoying it; that, in fact, the prelibation of my tears, as a homage to its fragility, was drawn forth by my very sense that my felicity was too exquisite; or, in the words of the great master,—"I wept to have (absolutely, by anticipation, shed tears in possessing) what I so feared to lose."[26]

The misquoted Shakespearean phrase, "weep to have," stresses the fragility of happiness when it is conceived of as a kind of possession. It suggests that the objects of our affections cause us sorrow even in their presence; the mind's wayward motions lead us indiscriminately forward to their loss. Once you start "weeping to have," there's no end to weeping. Thus, although Jane Leigh Perrot's account of happiness could invoke the rationality of needs, in De Quincey's understanding, needs and desires eat away at themselves. The paradox of having which is also a not-having is revealed by the narrator's comparison of his "restless distrust" of happiness to that which "in ancient times often led men to throw valuable gems into the sea, in the hope of thus propitiating the dire deity of misfortune by voluntarily breaking the fearful chain of prosperity, and led some of them to weep and groan when the gems thus sacrificed were afterwards brought back to their hand by simple fishermen, who had recovered them in the intestines of fishes."[27]

The possession of goods is terrifying; it is a fearful chain one must break. One can see why this narrator is haunted by shoplifting: his fear is not simply that things may be lost; rather, it is that they may attach themselves to us in unfortunate ways. The things of this world have a deadly force to them: in their very innocence, the gems seem worse not when they've been gotten in worldly ways, but when they return, purified by the sea, in the guts of fish. De Quincey was a writer who was haunted by the possibility that, like the Shakespearean phrase he misquotes, many of his own writerly "gems" were derived from other authors—that is, plagiarized. Highly self-conscious about literary possession and theft, De Quincey solved the matter by embracing— both in his literary and in his real life—a perpetual state of debt. At the time of the writing of "The Household Wreck," he was hiding from his creditors, living apart from his children and concealing his lodgings. Happiness never got too close; it was always on borrowed time.[28]

The nameless narrator's fears are realized when his angelic wife, Agnes, is arrested for shoplifting. Agnes is falsely accused of stealing a piece of valuable French lace: the malevolent shopkeeper, Mr. Barratt, has slipped a piece of it into her muff, in hopes of blackmailing her into sex. The case in "The House- hold Wreck" thus resembles that of Jane Leigh Perrot, and W. J. B. Owen has convincingly demonstrated that De Quincey would have known her story.[29] The narrator himself acknowledges that Agnes's story is not an unfamiliar one. At his long-delayed first meeting with Agnes in prison, his faith in her innocence wavers as he racks his brain with accounts of genteel shoplifting:

> A horrid thought came into my mind. Could it, might it, have been possible that my noble-minded wife . . . was open to temptations of this nature? Could it have been that in some moment of infirmity, when her better angel was away from her side, she had yielded to a sudden impulse of frailty . . .? I had heard of such things. Cases there were in our own times . . . when irregular impulses of this sort were known to have haunted and besieged natures not otherwise noble and base. I ran over some of the names amongst those which were taxed with this propensity. More than one were the names of people in a technical sense held noble.[30]

Shoplifting is a violation so troubling, for this narrator, that it can only be spoken of in the most euphemistic language: it is an "infirmity," a "frailty," an "irregular impulse." It is an alien thing that haunts and besieges its hap- less victims. So awful is it that to have committed a bloody or murderous act would have been better, "because more compatible with elevation of mind." Though Agnes ultimately vindicates herself before her husband (who is stricken ill and unconscious throughout her trial, during which time their infant son also dies of the same infection), the incontrovertible evidence of the lace "secreted in her muff" convicts and sentences her to hard labor. Her husband and friends liberate her from prison and take her into hiding, but just as the police come to take her back, she dies.[31]

As this plot summary, together with the overwrought, emotional rhetoric of the passages I've quoted might suggest, "The Household Wreck" is characterized by striking disproportions both stylistic and thematic: dis- proportions between the story's "source" in the real life of Jane Leigh Perrot and its fictionalized tragic weightiness; between the story's suburban, do- mestic theme and its doomed, gothic tone; between the slimness of its narra- tive incident—one shopping trip, one piece of lace—and its awkward length. Incurably digressive, it is too long to be called a short story, too thin to be a novella. The slimness of its incident seems barely able to bear the weight of its baroque prose just as the narrator can scarcely bear his own happiness: it is, in one critic's words, an "elephantine dilation."[32] We might see these disjunctions as De Quincey's way of articulating the problem of what feminine luxury goods mean to us. "The Household Wreck" testifies to the power of the "low plane reality" of material things to disturb our sense of time and proportion. This weird story enacts a literary analogue to modern commodity culture's crisis concerning the understanding of things, a crisis that speaks in the overlapping languages of luxury, necessity, overproduction, impoverishment, and entitlement.[33]

The story's narrator ponders this crisis at the beginning when he muses on how one might fit ordinary, modern crimes of property—such as an allegation of shop-theft—into a sense of the tragic. His meditations on the fragility of human happiness revolve around this question. He notes that the "class of hasty tragedies and sudden desolations" of a commercial society seem to fall with a sudden, unprecedented speed ("often indeed it happens that the desolation is accomplished within the course of one revolving sun; often the whole dire catastrophe . . . is accomplished and made known . . . within one and the same hour"). Contemplating the effects of this new kind of calamity both requires and defies calculations of probability. It requires a consideration of the stage on which we see them, for modern society in its enormity conceals the very tragedies it produces:

> The increasing grandeur and magnitude of the social system, the more it multiplies and extends its victims, the more it conceals them, and for the very same reason; just as in the Roman ampitheatres, when they grew to the magnitude of mighty cities (in some instances accomodating four hundred thousand spectators . . .), births and death became ordinary events, which in a small modern theatre are rare and memorable; and, exactly as these prodigious accidents multiplied, *pari passu* they were disregarded and easily concealed; for curiosity was no longer excited; the sensation attached to them was little or none.[34]

Like an optical effect, the lens of modernity exponentially multiplies and diminishes its calamities. What the writer has to do, this passage suggests, is focus an inverted lens on the incident, one that will blow it up out of all proportion and make it stand alone. That is the only way to reattach "sensation" to such tales. In order to become visible and meaningful, what the story of the piece of lace requires is neither the scale of a normative realism, nor Mrs. Perrot's normalizing invocations of necessity and non-necessity, nor Harriet Martineau's pained moralizings—but a mode of representation that defies all proportion.

It may seem perverse to insist on "The Household Wreck" as a story of a piece of lace. The incriminating frill barely appears; the encounter in the store, plus the trial itself, take place offstage. Though only minimally "represented" (in the sense of being named, described, kept before the reader's eyes), it is the center of the text, serving as the point from which it spins out centrifugally. In this respect "The Household Wreck" is typical of De Quincey's prose, which usually leaves hard facts behind. J. Hillis Miller's phenomenological descriptions of the disorienting, infinitely expanding inner space of De Quincey's sentences, his preference for a thickening spiral over a narrative line, stands up especially well with regard to "The Household Wreck." Speaking of De Quincey's aversion to discontinuity, Miller likens the imperative embodied in his prose to the making of lace:

> Each man must go, like the lace-maker, with the utmost care over every bit of the space between "here" and "there," connecting every point with every other point, and never for a moment allowing the thread to break. If necessary, he must go over the same area repeatedly, recapitulating it, seeing it from slightly different angles, making sure he has not missed anything. He must be certain he is "filling up all those chasms which else are likely to remain as permanent disfigurations of [the] work."[35]

Describing an endless covering over and filling in of gaps, Miller diagnoses De Quincey's lace-like prose as both a supplement to and substitution for reality. His assessment allows us to hypothesize that for De Quincey, the sheer verbal excessiveness of the novella is in a sense a substitute for the thing itself. Just as the wealth of the rich men is most reassuring when buried under the ocean—and most terrifying when it returns to the surface—the valuable piece of lace that sticks too close to Agnes makes its sense when sunk in an ocean of words. Wealth and representation do not only function as cognate terms; the latter can stand in for and stabilize anxieties attendant upon the former.[36]

Let me return from the style of "The Household Wreck" to its plot. Although I have allowed myself to construe the piece of lace as the prime mover of the text, the lace is merely a pawn in a human conspiracy: the evil shopkeeper plants the lace in Agnes's muff, and the muff is procured by a corrupt housemaid. In its human drama, "The Household Wreck" exhibits some of the attitudes toward the players in the shoplifting scenario that have appeared in the writings examined earlier in this essay. De Quincey's treatment of Agnes embodies intense ambivalence about the shopping/shoplifting lady. She is a wavering figure: in spite of his great love for her, the narrator literally can't see her straight;[37] and though the story insists on her innocence, everything about this creepy narration conspires to make her seem guilty. Agnes, the suburban shopping lady (the narrator dwells on her fashionable yet transcendent perfection as she sets off on the shopping trip to the metropolis where she meets her downfall), is connected to at least one other lady in De Quincey's writings. She is a distant cousin of the title figure in his armchair-archaeology piece, "The Toilette of the Hebrew Lady." There, the Hebrew lady, increasingly decked out with luxury ornaments, represents "ages of excessive luxury," both cultural advance and cultural decline.[38] And De Quincey's treatment of the lecherous shopkeeper, Barratt, violently dramatizes the venemous attacks of his political journalism. Discovered to be setting the same trap for another innocent woman, Barratt ultimately receives at the hands of a popular uprising what the law could not do. He is dragged into the street, and, as the police stand by, beaten to a pulp: "the mob had so used or so abused the opportunity they had long wished for that he remained the mere disfigured wreck of what had once been a man, rather than a creature with any resemblance to humanity." Barratt lives just long enough to confess his crime against Agnes. "My revenge was perfect," are the novella's last words.[39]

But there is a sense in which Barratt's guilt seems strangely besides the point, and not simply because he is so obviously being scapegoated. Rather, his criminality is rendered a non-issue by the way in which De Quincey distributes guilt across all of the principle characters. As I've noted, the weirdly morphing Agnes (now she looks like a child, now like a woman; now she looks very tall, but really she's of average height; now she is utterly distinctive-looking, now she could be confused with anyone you see in the street) seems guilty of some complicity in her demise. Her husband disingenuously refers to her as a "double character." And he is constantly indicting himself in our eyes, not only in his own self-incriminations and protestations, but more and more covertly. His relationship to Agnes comes to seem simultaneously sinisterly overprotective, domineering, and irresponsible. And his absolute paralysis throughout most of the story seems to indicate his moral turpitude. He gets fixed to spots; frozen by icy terrors; struck speechless; blanks out. He shrinks from sight like a guilty man when the policeman first bearing news of Agnes's arrest comes to his door; immures himself in the house while a faithful servant looks into Agnes's case; decides both his and her life are over before he even knows what's happened, and of course becomes sick and unconscious throughout her trial. This is an unreliable narrator who is truly *unreliable*.[40]

In making everyone guilty in "The Household Wreck," De Quincey has made everyone the same. The characters bleed into each other. One slight hint of these floating identifications can be found in the way the word "wreck" circulates throughout. Does the title phrase "household wreck" refer to Agnes herself? Or does it come to attach itself to the totally wrecked narrator? In the last pages, the shopkeeper Barratt becomes the wreck: "he remained the mere disfigured wreck of what had once been a man." At the end of her life, Agnes and her husband turn out to be actually having each other's dreams at night.[41] Elsewhere in this chapter, I've noted ways in which the stolen luxury good— the transgressive piece of lace—serves to police borders, enforcing the differences (of class, gender, privilege) among the several actors in the shoplifting drama. But in "The Household Wreck," it is as if the consumable, stealable thing makes everyone the same. As its human partners become more and more corrupt in relation to it, the piece of lace at the center is rendered more and more innocent, like the gems washed up on the rich men's shores. Like those rich men who dread the very purity of the gems to which they're in thrall, it seems that literature's perception of things' social density, their ability to explain a social world, is inseparable from a perception of their asocial purity and deadliness. De Quincey's gothic shoplifting tale discovers the uncanniness of things in a society that is simultaneously consumerist and fundamentally antimaterialist, afraid of locating happiness in things: the more happiness one invests in them, the more they resist the human, sucking the life out of their human partners and enduring with an innocent, inhuman persistence.[42]

IV

Like Mrs. Perrot's odd, loaded remark—"Believe me, Lace is not necessary to my happiness," "The Household Wreck" unpacks some rich philosophical questions about the meanings of material things. What would it mean for a woman to say that lace *was* necessary to her happiness? Why does that seem so scary, make us feel so guilty? Why does admitting the essence of things seem in itself like a kind of theft, a cheating of our own identities? How can we, as persons in a consumer society, come to a clearer understanding of what we do value? Thus, both Mrs. Perrot's real-life story and De Quincey's work of fiction show us that feminist scholarship's concern with class and gender in a case of seemingly limited historical interest can open up larger issues of concern to all people interested in the humanities. While women's studies scholarship has certainly achieved legitimacy and authority in many fields in the humanities, we must still work to clarify how central the topics of feminism are to the basic goals of the humanities—the study of human rights, human values, and human happiness.

The shoplifting ladies of Georgian England were certainly not feminist heroines. Some of them, like Jane Leigh Perrot, were probably unpleasant, snobby people with whose politics we might vehemently disagree (Mrs. Perrot's niece, Jane Austen, always dreaded spending time with her). But if we consider their actions and their words in context, in light of the changing social circumstances of their day, we can see them articulating some important issues. I would argue, moreover, that a more complex picture of the shoplifting ladies, their world, and the meaning of their actions emerges from the interdisciplinary research materials this essay employs. The mixing together of real-life stories and literary texts demonstrates one of the important methodological principles of women's studies scholarship since its beginnings: its interdisciplinary nature. In this essay, for example, I used Thomas De Quincey to crucially open up both the political and the philosophical dimensions of the shoplifters' acts and objects, both through his political essays and his literary writings. Feminist scholarship demands that we use the methodologies we've learned from the traditional disciplines—the close reading methods of literary criticism, for example—while recognizing that studying gender involves defying the boundaries that the traditional fields of knowledge put in place over a century ago.[43] We must acknowledge the methodological acts of theft that produce new forms of knowledge, as well as new forms of (scholarly) happiness.

Notes

An earlier version of this essay was presented at a conference on "Border Fetishisms" at the Research Centre for Religion and Society at the University of Amsterdam and published as "Stealing Happiness: Shoplifting in Early Nineteenth Century England" in *Border Fetishisms: Material Objects in Unstable Spaces*, edited by Patricia Spyer (London: Routledge, 1998, 122–49), reprinted by permission of Routledge/Taylor and Francis Books, Inc.

My thanks to Austin Booth for her research assistance; to the Program in Women's Studies, University of Michigan, for funding this research; and to William Galperin, Deidre Lynch, and Patricia Spyer for their comments.

1. Important work on nineteenth-century British women from the first generation of Women's Studies scholars includes Elaine Showalter, *A Literature of Their Own* (Princeton: Princeton University Press, 1977); Ellen Moers, *Literary Women* (New York: Anchor Books, 1977; Martha Vicinus, ed., *Suffer and Be Still: Women in the Victorian Age* (1972) and *A Widening Sphere: Changing Roles of Victorian Women* (1977), both Bloomington: Indiana University Press. More recent studies that have focused on a more diverse range of nineteenth-century British women include Judith Walkowitz, *Prostitution and Victorian Society* (Cambridge: Cambridge University Press, 1980); Ellen Ross, *Love and Toil: Motherhood in Outcast London 1870–1918* (New York: Oxford University Press, 1993); Antoinette Burton, *Burdens of History: British Feminists, Indian Women, and Imperial Culture, 1865–1915* (Chapel Hill: University of North Carolina Press, 1994); and Deborah Nord, *Walking the Victorian Streets: Women, Representation, and the City* (Ithaca: Cornell University Press, 1995). See also the essays by Burton and Nord in this volume.

2. Useful guides to the interdisciplinary study of consumption include Daniel Miller, ed., *Acknowledging Consumption: A Review of New Studies* (1995) and *Consumption: Critical Concepts in the Social Sciences*, 4 vols. (2001), both London: Routledge. Feminist studies of consumerism include Anne Friedberg, *Window Shopping* (Berkeley: University of California Press, 1993); Victoria De Grazia, *The Sex of Things: Gender and Consumption in Historical Perspective* (Berkeley: University of California Press, 1996); and Meaghan Morris, *How to Do Things with Shopping Centers* (Milwaukee: University of Wisconsin Center for Twentieth-Century Studies, 1988). Important studies of consumerism in eighteenth- and nineteenth-century Britain include Neil McKendrick, John Brewer, and J. H. Plumb, *The Birth of a Consumer Society: The Commercialization of Eighteenth-Century England* (Bloomington: Indiana University Press, 1982) and John Brewer and Roy Porter, eds., *Consumption and the World of Goods* (London: Routledge, 1993). Feminist studies of consumerism in this era include Marcia Pointon, *Strategies for Showing: Women, Possession, and Representation in English Visual Culture, 1665–1800* (Oxford: Oxford University Press, 1997); Elizabeth Kowaleski-Wallace, *Consuming Subjects: Shopping, and Business in the Eighteenth Century* (New York: Columbia University Press, 1997); Margot Finn, "Women, Consumption, and Coverture in England ca. 1760–1860," *The Historical Journal* 39:3, 1996, 703–722; Erika Rappaport, *Shopping for Pleasure: Women in the Making of London's West End* (Princeton: Princeton University Press, 2000) and Deidre Shauna Lynch, "Shopping and Women's Sociability," in Gillian Russell and Clara Tuite, eds., *Romantic Sociability: Social Networks and Literary Culture in Britain, 1770–1840* (Cambridge: Cambridge University Press, 2002). Lynch quotes "Don Manuel Alvarez Espriella"'s remark about English ladies going "a-shopping," from Robert

Southey [1807], *Letters from England by Don Manuel Alvarez Espriella; Translated from the Spanish*, ed. Jack Simmons (London: Cresset Press, 1951), p. 69. On gender and shopping in Regency England, see also Jane Rendell, *The Pursuit of Pleasure: Gender, Space, and Architecture in Regency London* (New Brunswick: Rutgers University Press, 2002.)

3. Feminist research on women shoplifters and the concept of kleptomania includes Elaine Abelson, *When Ladies Go A-Thieving: Middle-Class Shoplifters in the Victorian Department Store* (New York: Oxford University Press, 1989); Patricia O'Brien, "The Kleptomania Diagnosis: Bourgeois Women and Theft in Late Nineteenth-Century France," *Journal of Social History* 17 (1983), 65–77; Leslie Camhi, "Stealing Femininity: Department Store Kleptomania as Sexual Disorder," *differences* 5 (1993), 38–39; and Beverly Lemire, "The Theft of Clothes and Popular Consumerism in Early Modern England," *Journal of Social History* 24 (1990), 255–76. Psychoanalysts traditionally viewed female "kleptomania" as a form of fetishism; see Karl Abraham, "The Female Castration Complex," in *Selected Papers* (London: Hogarth Press [1920], 1949); George Zavitzianos, "Fetishism and Exhibitionism in the Female and their Relationship to Psychotherapy and Kleptomania," *International Journal of Psycho-Analysis* 52 (1971), 297–330; and Gregorio Kohon, "Fetishism Revisited," *International Journal of Psychoanalysis* 68 (1987), 213–28; for a feminist psychoanalytic approach, see Louise Kaplan, *Female Perversions* (New York: Doubleday, 1991) 284–320.

4. Camhi, "Stealing Femininity," 38–39.

5. Abelson, *When Ladies Go A-Thieving*; O'Brien, "The Kleptomania Diagnosis"; quotation is from James Cowles Prichard, *On the Different Forms of Insanity, in Relation to Jurisprudence* (London: Balliere [1842], 1847), 155–56; see also his *Treatise on Insanity and of the Disorders Affecting the Mind* (London: Sherwood, Gilbert, and Piper, 1835), 28–53.

6. Quoted in John Bucknill, "Kleptomania," *Journal of Mental Science* 1863, 8, 24: 264.

7. See, for example, the *Newgate Calendar's* account of the conviction in 1810 of Mary Jones and Elizabeth Paine, who appeared to be career shoplifters, of stealing twelve pairs of stockings worth four pounds, eight shillings, which concludes by reporting the officer's comment that "it was a great stretch of the jury's humanity that they were not capitally convicted." They were transported (Anon., *The Newgate Calendar, Comprising Interesting Memoirs of the Most Notorious Characters Who Have Been Convicted of Outrages on the Laws of England . . .*, vol. 5 (London: J. Robins, 1824–28), 5: 71–72. On shoplifting law, see Leon Radzinowicz, *A History of English Criminal Law and Its Administration from 1750*, vol. 1 (New York: Macmillan, 1948); Frank Douglas MacKinnon, *Grand Larceny, Being the Trial of Jane Leigh Perrot, Aunt of Jane Austen* (Oxford: Oxford University Press, 1937), 32–50; Samuel Romilly, *Observations on the Criminal Laws of England* (London: Cadell and Davies, 1810); *Memoirs of the Life of Sir Samuel Romilly*, 3 vols., (London: J Murray, 1840).

8. Harriet Martineau, *A History of the Thirty Years' Peace* (London: G. Bell and Sons [1849–50], 1877–78), 2:84.

9. Ibid., 3:136, 137.

10. Bucknill, "Kleptomania," 264.

11. See Abelson, *When Ladies Go A-Thieving*, and Camhi, "Stealing Femininity."

12. On women shopkeepers in early nineteenth-century England, see Alice Adburgham, *Shops and Shopping, 1800–1914* (London: Allen and Unwin, 1964), 25–32;

for the tricks of the professional shoplifter, see James Hardy Vaux, *The Memoirs of James Hardy Vaux Written by Himself* (London: W. Clowes, 1819). The nature of shops and shopkeeping in England during the period covered by this essay is subject to some historical debate. While some historians of consumption have argued that modern innovations in retail—window display, advertising, fixed prices on merchandise tickets, a preference for "ready money" over credit—were not significantly put into place until the mid-nineteenth century (or at least after 1815), others have argued that many if not most of these changes had already begun in metropolitan, high-class shops in the eighteenth century. See, in addition to Adburgham, *Shops and Shopping*, Dorothy Davis, *A History of Shopping* (London: Routledge and Kegan Paul, 1966); McKendrick et al., *The Birth of a Consumer* Society; Hoh Cheung and Lorna H. Mui, *Shops and Shopkeeping in Eighteenth-Century England* (London: Routledge, 1989); David Alexander, *Retailing in England During the Industrial Revolution* (London: Athlone, 1970); and Michael J. Winstanley, *The Shopkeeper's World 1830–1914* (Manchester: Manchester University Press, 1983).

13. W. Hamish Fraser, *The Coming of the Mass Market, 1850–1914* (Hamden, CT: Archon, 1981), 92.

14. On the "system of credit" and its susceptibility to corruption, see John Wade, *Treatise on the Police and Crimes of the Metropolis* (London: Longman, Rees, Orme, Brown, and Green, 29), 125–27. On De Quincey and debt, see Grevel Lindop, *The Opium Eater: A Life of Thomas De Quincey* (New York: Taplinger, 1981), 380. On the cultural politics of Regency Dandyism, see Ellen Moers, *The Dandy: Brummell to Beerbohm* (New York: Viking Press, 1960), and Donald A. Low, *That Sunny Dome: A Portrait of Regency Britain* (London, Dent, 1977). Running up debt could be a woman's weapon in her intimate war with a cheap husband, because until the Married Women's Property Act of 1870, married women could not be sued for delinquent debts.

15. Hariette Wilson, *The Memoirs of Harriette Wilson, Written by Herself* [1825] (London: Eveleigh Nash, 1909), 1:142.

16. Flora Tristan, *The London Journal of Flora Tristan* [1840], trans. Jean Hawkes (London: Virago Press, 1982), 174–77.

17. Thomas De Quincey, "On the Progress of Social Disorganization," *Blackwood's Edinburgh Magazine* 1834, 35:339.

18. Thomas De Quincey, "On the Approaching Revolution in Great Britain, and Its Proximate Causes," *Blackwood's Edinburgh Magazine* 1831, 30:323. On the political influence and interests of urban shopkeepers, see Winstanley, *The Shopkeeper's World*. My argument about shopkeepers is indebted to Don Herzog's study of the politics of contempt in England, 1789–1832, *Poisoning the Minds of the Lower Orders* (Princeton: Princeton University Press, 1998).

19. Several outstanding feminist historians have recently demonstrated persuasively that middle-type and upper-class British women of this era could and did participate in the public sphere, in often surprising ways; see Amanda Vickery, *The Gentleman's Daughter: Women's Lives in Georgian England* (New Haven: Yale University Press, 1998); Harriet Guest, *Small Change: Women, Learning, and Patriotism, 1750–1810* (Chicago: University of Chicago Press, 2000); and Anna Clark, *Scandal: The Sexual Politics of the British Constitution* (Princeton: Princeton University Press, 2004).

20. An extensive modern account of Jane Leigh Perrot's trial can be found in MacKinnon, *Grand Larceny*, which reprints one of several contemporary accounts, *The Trial of Jane Leigh Perrot . . . Charged With Stealing a Card of Lace* (Taunton, 1800). Edward

Copeland, *Women Writing about Money: Women's Fiction in England, 1780–1820* (Cambridge: Cambridge University Press, 1995) discusses the case briefly. Armed with the most revelatory investigation of the episode to date, William Galperin, *The Historical Austen* (Philadelphia: University of Pennsylvania Press, 2003) uses Jane Austen's non-response to her aunt's trial as a starting point for an analysis of the politics of Austen's representational practices.

21. Jane Leigh Perrot to Montague Cholmeley, September 11, 1799, in R. A. Austen-Leigh, ed., *Austen Papers 1704–1856* (London: Spottiswoode, Ballantyne, 1942), 183–85.

22. Perrot to Cholmeley, April 1, 8, 14, 1800, in Austen-Leigh, *Austen Papers*, 207, 208, 214, 218–19. Mrs. Perrot's counsel, Joseph Jekyll, confided later that he suspected that she was like other genteel women "who frequent bazaars and mistake other people's property for their own." For this and other evidence that Perrot may have been guilty, see Galperin, *The Historical Austen*, 36–43.

23. Adburgham, *Shops and Shopping*, 1–11.

24. Perrot to Cholmeley, September 11, 1799, in Austen-Leigh, *Austen Papers*, 183. Contemporary accounts of her trial, however, do suggest that she was a woman who cared about dress, describing in approving detail her elegant attire in the courtroom, including (of course) the "black lace veil, which was thrown up over her head" ("Account of the Trial of Mrs. Leigh Perrot," *The Lady's Magazine*, 31 (1800), 171–76).

25. The literature on the politics of "luxury" in the eighteenth and nineteenth centuries is extensive; see John Sekora, *Luxury: The Concept in Western Thought, Eden to Smollet* (Baltimore: Johns Hopkins University Press, 1977). On women's manipulation of the highly elastic "law of necessaries" in the eighteenth and nineteenth centuries, see Margot Finn, "Women, Consumption, and Coverture," *The Historical* Journal 39 (1996), 709–10.

26. Thomas De Quincey, "The Household Wreck" [1838], in *The Collected Writings of Thomas De Quincy*, ed. David Masson (Edinburgh: A. and C. Black, 1890) 12:13. In subsequent references, this text will be indicated by the abbreviation HW and page number.

27. HW, 168.

28. The passage De Quincey quotes is from Shakespeare's Sonnet 64: "Ruin hath taught me thus to ruminate / That Time will come and take my love away. / This thought is as a death, which cannot choose / But weep to have that which it fears to lose." On De Quincey and debt, see Lindop, *The Opium Eater*; Stacy Carson Hubbard, "Telling Accounts: De Quincey at the Bookseller's," in *Postmodernism Across the Ages*, Bill Readings and Bennet Schaber, eds. (Syracuse: Syracuse University Press, 1993); Josephine McDonagh, *De Quincey's Disciplines* (New York: Oxford University Press, 1994), 42–65. On De Quincey as a kind of literary pickpocket, see Alina Clej, *A Genealogy of the Modern Self: Thomas De Quincey and the Intoxication of Writing* (Stanford: Stanford University Press, 1995), 233.

29. W. J. B. Owen, "De Quincey and Shoplifting," in *The Wordsworth Circle* 21 (1990), 72–76.

30. HW, 210.

31. HW, 210, 188.

32. While "The Household Wreck" has received some passing attention from De Quincey's excellent recent critics, none have treated it as a story about what it is about: an accusation of shoplifting. Eve Sedgwick, *The Coherence of Gothic Fiction*

(New York: Arno Press, 1980) treats the shopping episode merely as a way to get to the story's final scenes of imprisonment and violence. McDonagh, *De Quincy's Disciplines*, focuses on the story's exposition of the structural vulnerability of the domestic sphere and the anxieties that attend woman's entry into the marketplace, as does Angela Leighton, "De Quincey and Women," in Stephen Copley and John Whale, eds., *Beyond Romanticism* (London: Routledge, 1992). Lindop, *The Opium Eater*, attributes the affects of the story to De Quincey's feelings of guilt after the death of his wife, Margaret, in 1837. A number of readings, most brilliantly and complexly John Barrell, *The Infection of Thomas De Quincey: A Psychopathology of Imperialism* (New Haven: Yale University Press, 1991), have linked some motifs from the story to the scene of De Quincey's sister Elizabeth's childhood death, which reverberates throughout his writing.

33. "Low plane reality": Norman Bryson, *Looking at the Overlooked: Four Essays on Still Life Painting* (Cambridge, MA: Harvard University Press, 1990), 14 and ff. I am indebted to Bryson's use of this phrase by which he designates the material, "authentically self-determining" (13) nature and slowness of the forms of everyday life and in particular the pressures these things put on modes of representation.

34. HW, 159, 160.

35. J. Hillis Miller, *The Disappearance of God: Five Nineteenth-Century Writers* (Cambridge, MA: Harvard University Press, 1963), 38–39.

36. See Bryson, *Looking at the Overlooked*, 52. My point in this paragraph could be confirmed by studying the place of De Quincey's favorite object of luxury consumption: the supplemental relation, that is, between language and opium. On lace as a figure for language and on both as luxuries that can be hoarded or amassed, compare Samuel Johnson: "Greek, Sir . . . is like lace; every man gets as much of it as he can" in James Boswell, *Life of Johnson* [1791], (Oxford: Oxford University Press: 1980), 1081.

37. HW, 214, 165–67, 173–74, 176–78.

38. Thomas De Quincey, "Toilette of the Hebrew Lady" [1828], in *The Collected Writings*, 6:164.

39. HW, 232–33.

40. HW, 173, 162–179, 190, 185.

41. HW, 164, 200, 232, 228.

42. On modern fears of attributing life to objects, see Miguel Tamen, *Friends of Interpretable Objects* (Cambridge, MA: Harvard University Press, 2001).

43. On the formation of the academic disciplines in the late nineteenth century, see Amanda Anderson and Joe Valente, ed., *Disciplinarity at the Fin de Siècle* (Princeton: Princeton University Press, 2002). For an interesting study of the interdisciplinary nature of Women's Studies research, see Lynn Westbrook, *Interdisciplinary Information Seeking in Women's Studies* (Jefferson, NC: McFarland Press, 1999).

Suggestions for Further Reading

Abelson, Elaine. *When Ladies Go A-Thieving: Middle-Class Shoplifters in the Victorian Department Store*. New York: Oxford University Press, 1989.

Adburgham, Alice. *Shops and Shopping, 1800–1914*. London: Allen and Unwin, 1964.

Alexander, David. *Retailing in England during the Industrial Revolution*. London: Athlone, 1970.

Brewer, John, and Roy Porter, eds. *Consumption and the World of Goods*. London: Routledge, 1993.

Cheung, Hoh, and Lorna H. Mui. *Shops and Shopkeeping in Eighteenth-Century England*. London: Routledge, 1989.

Copeland, Edward. *Women Writing about Money: Women's Fiction in England, 1780–1820*. Cambridge: Cambridge University Press, 1995.

Davis, Dorothy. *A History of Shopping*. London: Routledge and Kegan Paul, 1966.

De Grazia, Victoria, ed. *The Sex of Things: Gender and Consumption in Historical Perspective*. Berkeley: University of California Press, 1996.

Fraser, W. Hamish. *The Coming of the Mass Market, 1850–1914*. Hamden, CT: Archon, 1981.

Friedberg, Anne. *Window Shopping*. Berkeley: University of California Press, 1993.

Guest, Harriet. *Small Change: Women, Learning, and Patriotism, 1750–1810*. Chicago: University of Chicago Press, 2000.

Kowaleski-Wallace, Elizabeth. *Consuming Subjects: Women, Shopping, and Business in the Eighteenth Century*. New York: Columbia University Press, 1997.

McKendrick, Neil, John Brewer, and J. H. Plumb. *The Birth of a Consumer Society: The Commercialization of Eighteenth-Century England*. Bloomington: Indiana University Press, 1982.

Miller, Daniel, ed. *Acknowledging Consumption: A Review of New Studies*. London: Routledge, 1995.

———, ed. *Consumption: Critical Concepts in the Social Sciences*. 4 vols. London: Routledge, 2001.

Morris, Meaghan. *How to Do Things with Shopping Centers*. Milwaukee: University of Wisconsin Center for Twentieth-Century Studies, 1988.

Pointon, Marcia. *Strategies for Showing: Women, Possession, and Representation in English Visual Culture, 1665–1800*. Oxford: Oxford University Press, 1997.

Rappaport, Erika. *Shopping For Pleasure: Women in the Making of London's West End*. Princeton: Princeton University Press, 2002.

Rendell, Jane. *The Pursuit of Pleasure: Gender, Space, and Architecture in Regency London*. New Brunswick: Rutgers University Press, 2002.

Vickery, Amanda. *The Gentleman's Daughter: Women's Lives in Georgian England*. New Haven: Yale University Press, 1998.

Gender Sharing of Labor:
An Anthropological Perspective

Shanshan Du

Shanshan Du (1997) is Assistant Professor of Anthropology at Tulane University. Her current work focuses on a comparative study of gender egalitarian societies. Among her publications is *"Chopsticks Only Work in Pairs": Gender Unity and Gender Equality among the Lahu of Southwest China (2002).*

Shanshan Du's academic interest in the status of women derives from her own conflicting experiences as a Han Chinese female whose childhood was within the complex socio-historical context of the Mao era. "On the one hand, I was raised with a strong belief in sexual equality, not simply because of the political rhetoric of a socialist state, but also because of the attitudes of my parents and the vast majority of my school teachers. On the other hand, however, the gender-hierarchical tradition of Han culture was not only imprinted on me through the traumatic life histories of my grandmothers, but also experienced personally during the several years I spent with my brother under the supervision of my foot-bound paternal grandmother." She considers that "how and why gender is constructed differently and similarly across cultures are the central questions of feminist anthropology, or the anthropology of gender." Despite the insufficiency of existing theories to conceptualize the gender systems of many non-Western societies, she sees a promising increase in cultural inclusiveness in feminist scholarship in recent years.

In the first decade of a new century, both the diversity and the inclusiveness of feminist scholarship have continued to accelerate. As well as producing increasingly sophisticated and in-depth studies on women, scholars have paid growing attention to the complex overlapping of gender roles and interests in the contexts of culture, class, and race. In this chapter, I explore some of the intersections between gender and culture that occur in the relatively rare cases where gender overlapping is extreme. These cases challenge the presumed necessary link between feminist concerns and an exclusive focus on women.

Specifically, by examining the gender sharing of labor among four indigenous peoples who are socio-culturally unrelated to each other, I demonstrate the analytical limits of the approach that takes women as a separate social category in the study of gender relations, particularly as found in the concept of the "sexual division of labor."[1]

"Sexual division of labor" is perhaps one of the most widely used concepts in the past century and a half. Unfortunately, this concept is often erroneously associated with biological determinism, which assumes a natural and exclusive link between women and childrearing. Many earlier scholars—including Frederick Engels, Emile Durkheim, and Sigmund Freud—developed their theories on a biological determinist assumption of sexual division of labor. Ironically, similar misconceptions of sexual division of labor also serve as the premise for an array of contemporary feminist arguments, including those maintaining that "motherhood" oppresses women[2] or empowers women.[3]

Different perceptions of "the division of labor by sex" have provided, explicitly or implicitly, conflicting premises for the major debates in the feminist scholarship and social movement since the 1970s. The controversies revolving around this concept include the validity of the universality of female subordination, the causes of male dominance, gender-blind versus gender-differentiated strategies to enhance women's status, and the importance of sex roles in the acquisition of gender identity.[4] Various connotations of "the division of labor by sex" also extend themselves to many important concerns developed in more current feminist scholarship, including the concepts of boundaries, separate spheres, womanhood and the mother-child bond, father's roles, paternal care, and the division of labor in the household.[5]

Rather than perceiving the division of labor by sex as naturally given, contemporary research increasingly examines the interplay of biological, socio-cultural, and ecological variables.[6] Particularly, while revealing the near-universal division between men and women over a few tasks, such as hunting, cross-cultural studies also demonstrate the great mutability of sex roles in different societies.[7] As an extreme example, some Agta women of the Philippines regularly hunt the full range of prey animals with bow-and-arrow except during late pregnancy and the first few months of nursing, challenging the posited physiological incompatibility between mothering and hunting.[8]

Despite the enormous development in cross-cultural studies of sexual division of labor, an exclusive attention to the *division* of tasks between men and women has seriously hindered enhanced understanding of the relationship between sex difference and labor organization. I proposed the alternate term "sex/gender allocation of labor" as a check against a priori assumptions intrinsic to the concept of "sexual division of labor" that stem from a position of biological determinism.[9] While recognizing the correlation between sex difference and the near-universal division of a few tasks between men and women, this concept can also encapsulate the enormous diversity and flexibility of task assignment to the sexes resulting from biosocial interactions in different ecological contexts.

By presenting my own fieldwork research among the Lahu people of southwest China and some comparative ethnographic evidence, I will demonstrate the existence of gender sharing of labor and some of its features. In other words, I will show an extreme end of the spectrum of cultural patterns of gender allocation of labor. In so doing, I pay special attention to joint gender roles in childrearing, which even certain cross-cultural studies that intended to challenge the biological determinist perception of sexual division of labor still presumed to be exclusively associated with women.[10]

THE LAHU OF SOUTHWEST CHINA: MY OWN FIELDWORK RESEARCH

The Lahu are a Tibeto-Burman-speaking people living in the mountainous border regions of China, Burma, Laos, Thailand, and Vietnam.[11] According to the 2000 census, the Lahu population in China was 453,705, which was about two-thirds of the total Lahu population.[12] The subsistence pattern is typically a mixture of farming, raising domestic animals, hunting and gathering, and fishing. Monogamous couples jointly own and manage their households, which constitute the center of village life and serve as basic units for production and consumption.[13] Contrary to the widely held perceptions of sexual division of labor, Lahu men and women are unified in marital teams to share both reproductive and productive tasks, as expressed by the common saying "Husband and wife do it together" (*phawd mawd nud ma ted gie te*).

During a total of eighteen months of ethnographic fieldwork in both China and Thailand, I collected data by such methods as participant observation, formal and informal interviews, and household surveys. The main site of my fieldwork is what I call the Qhawqhat village cluster (approx. pop. 2,300 in 1995) in Lancang Lahu Autonomous County of Southwest China, where Lahu traditions or principles are maintained most systematically.[14] An important part of my observations is derived from my daily interactions with several Lahu Na families of Qhawqhat. One of my many long-standing Lahu friendships was with my Qhawqhat host family, who adopted me as one of their relatives for more than a decade. During fieldwork, I participated on a daily basis in their domestic work, and on a more occasional basis in their work in the fields. The couple also actively engaged in intense reciprocity with their relatives, and this led me to interactions with many other households in the village. Nevertheless, I had no opportunity to observe childbirth and postpartum practice because none of the Lahu households I was close to experienced childbirth during my stay, and villagers tended to share the local belief that prohibited outsiders from visiting the newborn.

CHILDREARING

Corresponding to the perception that the offspring of a couple are the "bone and marrow-blood and flesh" of both parties to a union, Lahu principle expects the husband and wife to share all child-related tasks, described by a gender-neutral term (*yad hu*) that means both "childbearing" and "childrearing."

According to some villagers I interviewed, the rationale for such social expectation is that "it took the two of them, not one, to conceive the child from the beginning, and they both will eat [depend on] the child's strength in the future."

Whereas biology assigns pregnancy and childbirth exclusively to women, Lahu origin myths trivialize such a division by depicting how women took over these tasks, which were originally performed by men, either by accident or through compassion.[15] Congruent with such epistemological explanations, traditional norms emphasize the joint effort of a married couple in pregnancy and childbirth. While a husband is expected to carry out a larger proportion of the work that the couple had previously shared and to track his wife's bodily changes during her pregnancy, he also serves as the midwife at childbirth. At the early stage of the contractions, the expectant father massages his wife's abdomen to examine the position of the fetus and to perform external manipulation if the fetus is in a transverse or breech position. Other tasks assigned to the husband include supporting his wife's back during childbirth, cutting the umbilical cord, picking up and washing the newborn, burying the placenta, and washing the bloodstained pajamas, cloths, and bed sheets. Among the personal stories I collected from Qhawqhat men and women of different ages, the following, told by a man I'll call Cal Lad, about seventy years old, was the most compelling:

I was afraid and did not do well in the birth of Cal Var [his first child], but all the rest of our five children I delivered by my own hands. In her first childbirth, Na Yawl [his wife] suffered a lot from the contractions. I was very afraid, and was constantly worried that there was a severe problem. . . . When I was little, I had seen my mother delivering my younger siblings. She was not in that much pain; she even chatted with me. When I saw Na Yawl in that pain, I was terrified by the thought that she may have difficulty in labor. I was also worried whether she could endure it, if it took too long, and if it was too painful. My mother told me not to worry, because Na Yawl would deliver when the time came. My father had passed away by that time. Only my mother and my wife's parents were present.

My mother asked Na Yawl to lie down on the bed, and then she taught me how to touch my wife's abdomen to see if the position of the baby was right. She showed me where the head and feet were. Yes, the position was right. She also showed me what it would feel like if the baby were not in the proper position. . . . My mother taught me how to support Na Yawl's back while she was delivering.

When Cal Var was born, my mother instructed me how to cut the cord and pick the baby up, but I was too nervous to do so. My mother kept telling me, "This is your child, you must pick him up by yourself. We [the grandparents] are here today, but what if we were not here? Don't be afraid, touch gently. . . . You won't hurt him."

I was still afraid, but I reached out my hand to the baby. He was so tender, so tiny, and only a little bigger than the size of my palm! My hands were so rough, and I was afraid of hurting him. My mother finally gave up [Cal Lad smiles]. She picked up the child herself and asked me to watch carefully so that I could learn. She taught me where and how to cut the cord. She also taught me how to bathe the baby slowly, gently, and softly while she was doing it.

That was my first time. I was just too nervous, and was very afraid that I could have hurt the baby. . . . The next day, my mother let me bathe the baby. Then, I learned to touch babies.

The second time, I made it; I had learned from the firstborn. This time only my mother and my wife's father were present. My wife's parents lived too far away. If they both left even for a couple of days, their home, young children, and animals would have to be left behind, requiring other people to take care of them, so her mother remained behind. My father-in-law came three or four days before my wife delivered. They counted the date, and we did not need to inform them. My older child was there too. My mother showed me again how to touch Na Yawl's abdomen and see the child's position, which I had already learned last time. I knew it was the right position as soon as I touched [my wife's abdomen]. This time, I was not worried and was not afraid. When the child was born, my mother told me to use my right hand first to reach for the child, then pick up with both hands. I picked him up, held him in my own hands. I was very glad. . . . Well, I was still afraid of hurting him and thus very worried and nervous. I was afraid to move my hand, and just let him lie on my palm for quite a while. My mother taught me how to cut and tie the cord. . . .

I was not nervous at all for the other childbirths, Cal Pheud, Cal Xat [who died after eight months], Na Shi, Cal Siq, Na Lawd. I delivered them *all* [Cal Lad smiles, brightly and proudly].

The joint role of a Lahu couple in childcare starts from the moment the child is born. During the period of postpartum rest, the husband typically stays to take care of both his wife and the newborn. While the mother breast-feeds the baby and serves as the primary caretaker, the father also plays a significant role in taking care of the newborn, including bathing the baby, cleaning the newborn after urination and defecation, and taking turns with his wife to hold the baby. When a couple returned to their normal work routine, they continued to play a unified role in childcare. Except for nursing, a Lahu couple was expected to take joint responsibility in all major tasks of childcare, including carrying, bathing, feeding solid foods, playing with, and comforting their child.

A typical Lahu strategy to cope with the commonly perceived incompatibility between childcare and many subsistence tasks is for the parents to alternate carrying the child on the way to work and sometimes while they work. Carrying a child to the fields and while working becomes a major task in Lahu childcare. During the first two to three months, an infant is carried in a basket that is very tightly woven with fine bamboo pieces and padded and covered with cloth. The couple often takes turns carrying (on their backs or sides) the infant in the basket on their way to work. Typically, while the couple is working, they place the basket on the ground in the fields in a spot where there is shade in the summer or sun in the winter. Both parents tend to the infant when he or she cries, and the mother nurses the baby when needed.

From the age of about four months, when the child's neck muscles are strong enough to support its head, the infant is carried in a cloth baby carrier, which is more flexible than a basket. Children up to five years old are occasionally carried in the cloth baby carrier, especially when they are sick or when a trip is made to more distant fields. While the parents are working, young children usually entertain themselves nearby or play with their older siblings. When a child is sleepy or clingy, whichever parent the child goes to will carry the child until he or she falls asleep. Once asleep, the child is often placed in bed while the parents do domestic work or on a wooden board in a nearby field shelter when they are working outside. If the weather is cold and there is no shelter near the work site, the child is often carried in the carrier in turn by both parents for the duration of the nap.

In addition to physical care of children, the husband and wife also share similar responsibilities in discipline, education, affection, and time spent with children. While the husband-wife team in childrearing is highly emphasized in society, many couples also receive supplementary childcare on a regular basis from their parents and older children, other relatives, and neighbors. Interestingly, the non-parental caretakers are of both sexes rather than being predominantly female.

"WORK HARD TO EAT"

In accordance with the gender sharing of tasks in childrearing, which creates a dual parent-child bond, the ideal of "husband and wife do it together" also includes the concept "work hard to eat." This phrase connotes all the tasks involved in feeding a household, from planting to weeding, harvesting, storing, pounding (rice), cooking, fetching water and firewood, raising pigs and chickens, and gardening. These tasks apparently blur the boundaries between food production and food preparation, commonly linked to males and females respectively.

The dyadic sociocultural ideal that unites a husband and a wife as a single labor team to jointly perform both productive and reproductive tasks is wide-ly realized in practice. According to the household surveys I conducted in the Abo village (sixty-three households in 1996) of Qhawqhat, fifty-one out of the sixty-three head couples of these households (81 percent) had an equal share of labor, both inside and outside the house. The remaining twelve pairs of household head couples were considered as exceptions because of one spouse's idiosyncratic conditions, which included eight excusable causes such as chronic diseases and non-traditional occupations as well as four "inexcus-able" cases of laziness and alcohol addiction.

Along with the ideal of gender unity, the practical necessity for making the maximum use of available labor also contributes to the overlapping of gender roles in Lahu village life. To achieve the optimal use of a household's labor pool, Lahu villagers generally focus on the availability of and demands for labor in-stead of emphasizing fixed criteria such as sex and age. Accordingly, rather than being constrained by a strict sexual division, the division of labor in a Lahu household tends to be flexible, varying according to daily circumstances as well as to the developmental cycle of the household. Such contingent logistics for managing the entire pool of household labor can enhance the efficiency of production—although at the cost of having to repeatedly recalculate solutions.

The arrangement of herding in a Qhawqhat household related to my host family exemplifies how optimal use of household laborers defies sex or age differences in task assignment. In 1996, the household consisted of the head couple, Cal Thid and his wife Na Var (both about seventy years old), their youngest daughter, Na Meiq, and a son-in-law, Cal Lawd (their early twenties), and a baby granddaughter, Na Xeul (ten months old). During the last few months before I left the village, the task of herding had shifted among all the adults of the household. Since herding was a relatively light task, Cal Thid and Na Var, the eldest members of the household, often took turns at the job. During a couple of days in the rainy season, the baby Na Xeul was not feeling well. Therefore, the young mother, Na Meiq, took over herding so that she could spend more time with the baby, staying in a shelter longer and going home earlier to keep the baby out of the cold. The son-in-law, Cal Lawd, also took the cattle to a remote field shelter, where he was plowing. A neighboring teenage relative also helped tend the cattle during the harvest season. According to Cal Thid, their household's arrangement of labor in herding, which was then basically an adult's task, was different from what it had been fifteen years earlier, when the household had three six- to ten-year-old children. At that time, the ten-year-old boy—who did not attend school so he could stay home and herd—often took the six-year-old and the family's cattle to the mountains. During school vacations, however, the eight-year-old girl, who attended school, took over herding, allowing her brother to be shifted to other agricultural tasks.

Despite the seamless gender unity suggested by the ideal that "husband and wife do it together," not all tasks performed by Qhawqhat men and women are identical in practice. In fact, clear division of labor by sex in Qhawqhat is observable in a few tasks, conforming to predominant patterns of the sex-based division of labor across almost all cultures. For instance, hunting, blacksmithing, and tasks in the fields that require intense strength (such as plowing and cutting trees) are typically men's work. In addition, weaving cloth is typically a woman's task. Similar patterns in the division of labor have also been reported among Lahu elsewhere.[16] Therefore, while the focus of Lahu villagers on optimal use of labor fosters greatly overlapping of gender roles in task assignments, it only minimizes, rather than completely eliminates, the impact of sex difference.

Nevertheless, the dominant Lahu ideology of gender unity largely ignores, or even denies, the existence of any sex-based division of labor. In Lahu mythology and ritual songs, men and women are often depicted playing joint roles in hunting large game, cutting bamboo and trees, reaching the honeycomb, blacksmithing, and hunting.[17] Furthermore, the emphasis on the teamwork of men and women as idealized by "husband and wife do it together" can transform some of the scholarly conceptualization of the sexual division of labor into the ideal of gender unity. For instance, all of the Lahu villagers I talked to considered it to be a perfect example of, rather than counter-evidence for, "husband and wife do it together" if a husband was plowing while his wife was seeding. In contrast, a couple was considered to be divided by their tasks if they had to work in separate fields—which frequently occurs due to the intensive labor exchange among relative households—even if they were performing the same task (such as harvesting). Most important, none of the tasks marked by sex division was accorded differential value, and many of them were not even gender-exclusive in everyday life.

While Lahu mythology and symbolism tend to portray the perfect unity of men and women in task performance, individual villagers do recognize the impact of sex difference in labor organization. For instance, the general advantage of men in physical strength was the common answer to my persistent inquiries concerning the reasons for the clear gender-based division of a few tasks. However, the villagers also acknowledged individual diversity in strength among members of the same sex. Many people gave me examples of some women in the village who were physically stronger than their husbands and performed heavy tasks such as plowing and woodcutting. Na Lad, a woman in her forties, proudly told me (in her husband's presence) that she was stronger than her husband and therefore performed all the heavy work in the household that was usually done by men. Other ethnographic studies have also recorded that some Lahu wives plow and hunt together with their husbands, although males typically perform tasks that require more strength. In this sense, while most Lahu villagers recognized the general sex difference in strength as being responsible for some task allocation, neither individual strength nor related productive tasks were strictly coded by sex.

SOCIALIZATION

The ideal of gender-blind sharing of labor in both domestic and outdoor work is socialized in childhood and often starts with playing and then gradually involves auxiliary responsibilities. Playing piggyback or "baby-holding," which is one of the most popular games for boys and girls between the ages of one and four, is perhaps the earliest and more effective socialization in gender sharing of labor in childcare. Upon the request of a child, an adult makes a "baby doll" out of cloth and ties it around the child's back with a scarf. The child usually pats the baby doll and pretends to hum the "baby" to sleep while rocking and walking. When tired of the game, the child may try to untie the scarf and often screams for help when unsuccessful. I observed a one-year-old boy making loud noises and eventually crying to get the attention of his parents, then pointing to his back to indicate that he wanted to play "baby-holding." Older toddlers sometimes find their own cloths and wrap them up as a doll in a scarf, asking their parents to tie the dolls to their backs and untie them when they finish the game. When children are between five and six years old, childcare is gradually transformed from a game to the responsibility of babysitting for younger siblings.

Besides childcare, another significant domestic role—cooking—is also intensively socialized in a gender-neutral manner through games. The game is called "playing cooking" and is most popular among young children between three and six years old. Lacking commercially made toys, Lahu children find leaves to roll into "bowls" and "woks," taking some ashes to use as "rice," breaking some leaves as "vegetables" or "dishes," and using some small sticks as "chopsticks." Cooking is typically played in a collective context. Two or three children, sometimes as many as eight, usually play cooking games together. They often "cook" their own food and then carry it to the "table" on the ground in the front yard to share. Sometimes they hold their own "dishes" to offer others a taste of their delicious "food." As explained by adults, a child will not play at cooking alone, because that makes it boring. The cooperative aspects of cooking games prepare boys and girls alike for entrance into the Lahu social reality that defines cooking as a cooperative effort by all household members, especially by a couple. There are sometimes so many children in a play group that parents may halfheartedly complain that "when a bunch of children are into 'playing cooking' in your front yard, you can never keep your yard clean because you are always sweeping off the broken leaves and sticks everywhere."

Both boys and girls between three and five also like to imitate work in the fields. "Hoeing" is most commonly played at because of children's access to real tools that they can carry. Boys and girls both like to play at digging using the small-size hoes that their parents use for weeding. Nevertheless, digging games are often discouraged by parents (who may hide the small hoes) to prevent the mud-padded ground of their front yards from being destroyed.

Typically from age six to age eight, children begin to apply their games to real-life situations or to play at enacting joint gender roles in work. More specifically, boys and girls start to assist their parents in performing domestic work such as babysitting, carrying water, and washing their own clothes. Encouraged by their parents, children at this stage are usually eager to try out their imitation of working games in real life. For instance, the parents may encourage children when they are willing to wash their own clothes—although the parents may later rewash the laundry if it is not clean. At this stage, little children's imitative activities, often supervised by adults, mainly serve as a transition between play and work.

From the ages of about eight to twelve, children start to take supplementary responsibilities in domestic and outdoor work, especially in childcare and cooking. In fact, these children provide one of the major sources for assistance in childcare, especially when the parents are busy working in the fields. The older children may stay at home taking care of their younger siblings, feeding chickens and pigs, carrying water, and cooking rice while waiting for their parents to come home from the fields. However, they are often discouraged from cooking complicated dishes because many Lahu parents feel that these children cannot wash the vegetables carefully enough and because the dishes will not remain fresh until the parents come back from the fields. Children may also go to the field in which their parents are working to take care of their younger siblings, collect firewood, and cut grass to feed the pigs. Boys and girls of this age are also starting to herd cattle in the fields without the presence of adults. Nowadays, however, more children attend public school, so such work is performed after school.

In brief, Lahu allocation of labor revolves around the principle of gender unity, which defines a married couple as a single labor team in which the husband and the wife share a variety of tasks, ideally functioning together "as smoothly as a pair of chopsticks." According to this principle, both productive and reproductive tasks are oriented toward the couple's common goal of sustaining their household, submerging the productivity of the husband and wife within the duty of the couple as a whole.

OTHER ETHNOGRAPHIC CASES

The extraordinary coherence of the Lahu cultural expectation and the social practice of joint gender roles in labor organization is indeed rare, but gender sharing of labor is by no means unique from a cross-cultural perspective. By examining three peoples, who live in Southeast Asia, Central Africa, and Melanesia respectively, I turn here to a consideration of additional ethnographic instances of gender sharing of labor across different ecological and social contexts. While all are characterized by the overlapping of gender roles in both productive and reproductive tasks, these three cases differ in the degrees of gender sharing of labor.

The Orang Suku Laut of Indonesia

The Orang Suku Laut ("Sea Tribe People"), or Orang Laut ("Sea People"), are a boat-dwelling fishing and foraging people in the Indonesian Riau Archipelago. Lioba Lenhart's work on the Orang Suku Laut gives an example of an extremely high degree of convergence in labor by men and women within a single undifferentiated sphere, focusing on married couples who live and work together in the same boat.[18] Orang Suku Laut have gradually shifted from living entirely as sea nomads to becoming semi-nomadic, especially since the implementation of large-scale development projects in the late 1980s.[19] The basic social units of Orang Suku Laut are the nuclear family and the groupings of a few nuclear families related to each other both through male and female lines.

Along with their equally shared responsibilities in most domestic tasks such as cooking, gathering firewood, and repairing boats or pile dwellings, Orang Suku Laut men and women are extremely committed to their joint effort in childrearing. Like those of the Lahu, Orang Suku Laut myths do not essentialize the reproductive difference between the two sexes, but claim that in ancient times, the biological tasks of becoming pregnant and giving birth were associated with men until women took over. In practice, the husband and wife play joint roles in childrearing, starting from childbirth. The husband is expected to be present at his wife's delivery, together with the midwife and other close relatives of the couple. In addition to offering moral support, the expectant father also offers important assistance in childbirth, including holding his wife's head when she is pushing, or, if needed, helping the midwife massage the wife's abdomen. After the child is born, the couple shares childcare activities, especially in rearing and educating a child. While assisted by family members and relatives of both sexes, father and mother are equally responsible for the bringing up their male and female children. It is important to note that no systematic distinctions are observed between the male and female caretakers concerning the time they spend with children and the amount of physical care, affection, and discipline they offer.

Not only do Orang Suku Laut men and women participate equally in production, they also perform similar economic tasks, especially going to sea to fish, collecting strand products, and trading the surplus with members of other ethnic groups. The husband and the wife typically work as a labor team at sea. For example, while one spears fish, the other rows. As sea nomads who are seldom separated from each other, husband and wife "do nearly everything together—eating, sleeping, working, making decisions and spending their leisure time."[20] Despite the great overlapping of gender roles, especially between the husband and the wife, a few tasks are indeed marked by gender division. For example, hunting sea mammals and coastal animals is largely a male task, whereas collecting crustaceans and shellfish tends to be the work of women and children. However, such gender-based tasks by no means exclude occasional reversals of roles based on individual abilities and preferences.

Orang Suku Laut socialization focuses on making boys and girls good fishermen and fisherwomen able to establish a family with many offspring. While learning how to handle boats and to fish, children of both sexes also perform many domestic tasks, including fetching water, collecting firewood, and cooking. Amazingly, by the age of about five, boys and girls can catch enough fish or other marine products for their own nourishment. By the time they are adolescents, both males and females are fully integrated in both domestic and economic activities.

The Aka of Western Congo

While the Lahu and the Orang Suku Laut share an extreme emphasis on the labor team of a husband and wife, the Aka people allocate their labor based both on marital unity and individual autonomy, as documented by Barry S. Hewlett's ethnography.[21] Living in the tropical rain forest of western Congo, the Aka Pygmies are a hunting-gathering people who are "fiercely egalitarian and independent."[22] The fundamental social units are the family, the camp, the clan, the band, and the regional community. Although Aka kinship is based on patrilineal descent, the remarkable shallowness of its patrilineages and weakness of patrilineage identity greatly undermines the male-bias embedded in a typical patrilineal society. Strikingly, few adults can trace their patrilineal links back to more than two generations. Meanwhile, the close relations between a married couple and their relatives from both sides provide significant social networks that unite, rather than divide, the two sexes. The core values of the Aka include individual equality, independence, and autonomy, as well as sharing and cooperation.

Aka men and women are actively involved in childrearing, a phenomenon best reflected by the culturally constructed image of what Hewlett has called "the intimate father." The joint roles of both sexes in childcare are manifested in the similar perceptions of the qualities of the good mother and good father, who are constantly "providing food for the child, staying near and protecting the child, and loving the child."[23] Although fathers typically do not participate in childbirth, some deliver their infants in special circumstances, such as when a wife goes into labor and gives birth while the couple are walking alone in the forest. When a child is born, the father becomes very active in infant care, complementing the primary role the mother plays. In fact, while other female and male members of a camp offer great assistance to the parents, especially in holding the infant, the father serves as the secondary caretaker of a couple's child. A couple often takes their infant to work, including net hunting. Occasionally, when the mother chases a game animal into the net, she may place the infant on the ground to run after and kill the game, leaving the infant crying until she returns.

Corresponding to the joint gender roles in childcare, gender sharing of labor also extends to subsistence activities. Both men and women hunt with nets or small traps and they jointly butcher and distribute game captured. The members of both sexes also engage in a wide variety of tasks in food collection, such as gathering leaves, fruits, nuts, mushrooms, and termites. While adults enjoy individual labor activities as well as working with same-sex groups, husbands and wives spend a remarkable amount of time together throughout the year to work as a team in a wide variety of subsistence tasks, including net hunting and collecting caterpillars, termites, honey, fruit, and sometimes fish. According to Hewlett, "on net hunting days husband and wife are within view of each other 47 percent of the time. They are not only in association with each other but actively cooperating in subsistence activity."[24] Although husbands typically go into the center of the nets and chase the game into the nets while wives stand nearby to jump on and kill the captured game, these roles are reversible. On days when there is no net hunt, it is not unusual to see a husband and wife going out together to collect plants or honey.

While gender sharing of labor characterizes the vast majority of the tasks of Aka economic life, there are a few divisions based on sex difference. Most significantly, women never hunt with spears for wild pig and elephants and they rarely participate in crossbow hunting for monkeys or trapline hunting for medium size game. Nevertheless, such divisions are not associated with different values, nor is individual flexibility being ridiculed. Accordingly, it is not uncommon to see women carry the nets, spears, and crossbows of the men and men carry the baskets and digging sticks of women.

Gender sharing of labor marks Aka socialization. Boys and girls of three or four can cook themselves a meal on the fire. By seven or eight, when they can keep up with the net hunting, they follow their parents on the hunt. At the age of about ten, Aka children tend to know enough skills to live in the forest alone when it is necessary. During adolescence, however, same-sex age peers of a camp sometimes gather and conduct separate tasks. For example, while adolescent girls often collect water, nuts, or fruit together, the boys tend to hunt together.

The Vanatinai Islanders of New Guinea

In contrast to all the preceding examples, the overlapping of gender roles among the Vanatinai islanders is based mainly on a strong cultural emphasis on individual autonomy, as recorded by Maria Lepowsky.[25] The islanders of Vanatinai, which is the largest among the chain of islands that separate the Solomon Sea from the Coral Sea, live in small coastal villages and practice shifting cultivation. Organized around the rules of matrilineal descendant, the basic social units of Vanatinai society are the household, the lineage, and the clan. The structured gender division embedded in the matrilineal kinship system is buffered by other gender-blind institutions such as the bilocal pattern of postmarital residence, which obligates a married couple to live alternately with their two natal families for many years. Core Vanatinai ethics promote both individual autonomy and communal solidarity.

Overlapping of gender roles in childcare and domestic work is remarkable among the Vanatinai, although many tasks are less evenly shared by the two sexes than those in the preceding cases. While childbirth is predominantly a female domain, men are included in the event and some of them are as knowledgeable of birth magic as some women. The father typically plays the role of putting the placenta and cord in a basket and placing it secretly in the crotch of a nearby tree. As tender and indulgent parents, siblings, and relatives, Vanatinai men and women actively engage in nurturing the children. For example, a crying infant receives immediate attention, either by being picked up and consoled with its mother's breast or nuzzled and talked to by its father or someone else nearby. However, whereas the Vanatinai sociocultural ideal encourages the father to actively engage in childrearing, his nurturing and giving are considered a gift rather than an obligation because he belongs to another lineage. The overlapping of gender roles is also observed in a wide range of other domestic tasks. Nevertheless, except for caring for domestic pigs, which is rather equally shared by men and women, most daily chores such as cooking and fetching water and firewood are shouldered predominantly by women. The most remarkable gendered division is manifested by the norms that exclusively require women to sweep the house and the hamlet ground and to pick up pig excrement.

A high degree of equal sharing of labor by Vanatinai men and women characterizes the vast majority of subsistence tasks, including those in agriculture, gathering, and hunting. In addition to playing joint roles in cutting forest trees and preparing land for cultivation, members of both sexes also plant, tend, and harvest a wide range of garden crops, such as yam, sweet potato, taro, manioc, and banana. Ambitious individuals can attain prestige as "big men" or "big women" through their extraordinary acts of public generosity. Accordingly, they have to work extremely hard to produce extra yams to feed the guests and collect large amounts of ceremonial valuables to give away. Beyond the agricultural arena, both men and women gather a wide range of food in the rain forests, including wild nuts, legumes, tubers, fruits, and leaves. They also dive in the lagoon for giant Tridacna clams and collect shellfish from the streams and among the fringe reefs. Men and women also share a variety of tasks in fishing and hunting rather equally, despite the fact that sexual division is observable in the objects and the methods of hunting. For example, based on the ideology that women should only give life while men may take it, women are not allowed to throw spears to kill animals.

Overlapping gender roles constitute part of Vanatinai socialization processes. Both boys and girls frequently care for younger children, although they often play on their own rather than work on the tasks assigned by adults. By around the age of six, children of both sexes learn to "build a fire, using an ember obtained from a neighbor, and peel and boil tubers or roast sago pancakes."[26] They also collect firewood and help their parents in the garden. However, gender difference exists in the slightly delayed age of boys compared to that of girls in performing these tasks and the rarity of boys being told to wash dishes.

THE IMPLICATIONS OF GENDER SHARING OF LABOR

Gender sharing of labor, as opposed to the sexual division of labor, characterizes the dominant patterns of labor organization among the Lahu, the Orang Suku Laut, the Aka, and the Vanatinai. Such extreme forms of the gender allocation of labor minimize the impact of sex difference, resulting in substantial overlapping of gender roles in both reproductive and productive activities. These ethnographic cases greatly challenge some misconceptions that are deeply rooted in the cultural traditions of the dominant societies of Europe and North America. In particular, they contradict the interrelated conceptual fallacies embedded in many problematic usages of the term "sexual division of labor."

Joint gender roles in the childrearing of these societies shatter the widespread myth of the "naturalness" and "exclusiveness" of the mother-child bond. With a subtle twist of biological determinism, the fact of the long-term dependency of human infants and women's exclusive roles in pregnancy, childbirth, and lactation is often translated into the belief that childrearing is also a role naturally and exclusively assigned to women in all societies. Contrary to this erroneous assumption found in both popular opinion and academia, the Lahu, the Orang Suku Laut, the Aka, and the Vanatinai have established a dual-sex, parent-child bond, in which men and women share the responsibility of nurturing and taking care of the children. Although their cultural practices are uncommon from a cross-cultural perspective, they do demonstrate that childrearing patterns are biologically based solutions to long-term infant dependency, in which the exclusive assignment of mothers to this role may merely be the logistically simplest form.

The presumed association of domestic work with women and subsistence work with men is another fallacy that often goes hand in hand with its twin assumption of the "naturalness" and "exclusiveness" of mother-child bond. The practice of the Lahu, the Orang Suku Laut, the Aka, and the Vanatinai show that when the child-related role is shifted from "motherhood" to "parenthood," the presumed universal link between women and domestic work tends to be expanded to include men. Meanwhile, being perceived as equally significant contributors to the economy, women and men can be fully integrated into the productive labor force of both household and society.

Finally, this comparative study reveals the insufficiency of the theoretical and methodological foci on sexual divisions in understanding cultural diversity and complexity concerning both gender allocation of labor and male-female relations in general. I argue that while the blending of women's orientation with other social categories may appear to undermine the foundations of feminism on the surface, it expands the boundaries of feminist scholarship by transcending the limits of dichotomous approaches to male-female relationships.

Notes

1. I am grateful to the American Council of Learned Societies for supporting this comparative research with a Charles A. Ryskamp Research Fellowship and to the Woodrow Wilson National Fellowship Foundation for supporting my earlier studies on Lahu gender equality with a Charlotte W. Newcombe Doctoral Dissertation Fellowship and a Doctoral Dissertation Grant in Women's Studies. I would also like to thank Du Yuting and James Wilkerson for their comments on the earlier versions of this essay.

2. Dorothy Dinnerstein, *The Mermaid and the Minotaur: Sexual Arrangements and Human Malaise* (New York: Harper Colophon Books, 1977); Shulamith Firestone, *The Dialectic of Sex: The Case for Feminist Revolution* (New York: William Morrow, 1970); Evelyn N. Glen, "Social Constructions of Mothering: A Thematic Overview," in *Mothering: Ideology, Experience, and Agency*, Evelyn N. Glen, Grace Chang, and Linda R. Forcey, eds. (New York: Routledge, 1994), 1–32.

3. Mary O'Brien, *The Politics of Reproduction* (New York: Routledge, 1981); Adrienne Rich, *Of Woman Born: Motherhood as Experience and Institution* (New York: W. W. Norton, 1976).

4. Reviewed in Rachel Alsop, Annette Fitzsimons, and Kathleen Lennon, *Theorizing Gender*, Chapters 1, 3, and 8 (Cambridge: Polity Press, 2002), and Michael S. Kimmel, *The Gendered Society*, Chapters 3, 4, and 5 (New York: Oxford University Press, 2004). Also see Gayle Rubin, "The Traffic in Women: Notes on the 'Political Economy' of Sex," *Toward an Anthropology of Women*, R. Reiter, ed. (New York: Monthly Review Press, 1975), 158, and Sylviane Agacinski, *Parity of the Sexes*, Lisa Walsh, trans. (New York: Columbia University Press, 2002 [1998]), 67.

5. Reviewed in Shanshan Du, "'Husband and Wife Do It Together': Sex/Gender Allocation of Labor among the Qhawqhat Lahu of Lancang, Southwest China," *American Anthropologist* (102) (3) 2000, 520–37. Also see Brian H. Harrison, *Separate Spheres: The Opposition to Woman Suffrage in Britain* (New York: Holmes & Meier,

1978), and Monika M. Elbert, ed., *Separate Spheres No More: Gender Convergence in American Literature, 1830–1930*, (Tuscaloosa: University of Alabama Press, 2000).

6. Reviewed in Shanshan Du, "'Husband and Wife Do It Together.'"

7. George P. Murdock and Caterina Provost, "Factors in the Division of Labor by Sex: A Cross-Cultural Analysis," *Ethnology*, 12 (1973), 203–225.

8. Agnes Estioko-Griffin, "Daughters of the Forest: Agta Women of the Philippines Hunt Large Animals and Still Raise Their Children," *Natural History* 5, (1986), 37–43; Madeleine J. Goodman, P. Bion Griffin, Agnes A. Estioko-Griffin, and John S. Grove, "The Compatibility of Hunting and Mothering among the Agta Hunter-Gatherers of the Philippines," *Sex Roles* 12, vol. 11/12 (1985), 1199–1209.

9. Du, "'Husband and Wife Do It Together.'"

10. Murdock, and Provost, "Factors in the Division of Labor by Sex," 207.

11. Chang Hong-En, ed., *Lahu Yu Jian Zhi* [*The Concise Annals of the Lahu Language*] (Beijing: Nationalities Publishing House, 1986); James A. Matisoff, *The Dictionary of Lahu* (Berkeley: University of California Press, 1988).

12. NBSC (National Bureau of Statistics of China), *Zhongguo 2000 Nian Renkoupucha Ziliao* [*Tabulation on the 2000 Population Census of the People's Republic of China*] (Beijing: China Statistics Press, 2002), 251.

13. Shanshan Du, "*Chopsticks Only Work in Pairs*": Gender Unity and Gender Equality among the Lahu of Southwest China (New York: Columbia University Press, 2002); Jacquetta Hill, "The Household as the Center of Life among the Lahu Shehleh of Northern Thailand," in K. Aoi, K. Morioka, and J. Suginohara, eds., *Family and Community Changes in East Asia* (Tokyo: Japan Sociological Society, 1985), 504–525.

14. To protect the privacy of my interviewees, the individual names and names for places below the county level are fictitious.

15. Du, "*Chopsticks Only Work in Pairs*," 43.

16. Zhang Dongfeng and Peng Yuancan, "Lancangxian Mugaqu Dabanlizhai Lahuzu Shehui Lishi Diaocha" [An Investigation of Lahu Society and History in Dabanli Village, Muga, Lancang], in *Lahuzu Shehui Lishi Diaocha* [*An Investigation of Lahu Society and History*] (Kunming: Yunnan People's Publishing House, 1982), 39–54; Zhang Qilong, Yue Faxing, and Zhang Xiaoga, eds., *Lancang Lahuzu Zizhixian Zhi* [*The Annals of the Lancang Lahu Autonomous County*] (Kunming: Yunnan People's Publishing House, 1996).

17. Hu Calkheu Hu, "*Xeu Sha de Zhangzi Zhang Nu* [The Senior Daughter and Son of Xeul Sha]," *Minzu Diaocha Yenjiu* [*The Journal of Ethnographic Researches*, 1996, vol. 12), 64–68; Lei Bo and Liu Junyong, *Lahu Wenhua Daguan* [*Perspectives on Lahu Culture*], (Kunming: Yunnan Nationalities Publishing House, 1999); Wang Zhenghua and He Shaoying, *Lahuzu Wenhua Shi* [*The History of Lahu Culture*] (Kunming: Yunnan Nationalities Publishing House, 1999), 68–69.

18. Lioba Lenhart, "Orang Suku Laut," in *The Encyclopedia of Sex and Gender: Men and Women in the World's Cultures*, Melvin Ember and Carol Ember, eds. The Human Relations Area Files Encyclopedia Series (Hingham, MA: Kluwer/Plenum, 2003).

19. Cynthia Chou and Vivienne Wee, "Tribality and Globalization: The Orang Suku Laut and the 'Growth Triangle' in a Contested Environment," *Tribal Communities in the Malay World: Historical, Cultural and Social Perspectives* (Singapore: Institute of Southeast Asian Studies, 2002), 319.

20. Lenhart, "Orang Luku Laut," 908.

21. Barry S. Hewlett, *Intimate Fathers: The Nature and Context of Aka Pygmy Paternal Infant Care* (Ann Arbor: University of Michigan Press, 1991).

22. Ibid., 27.

23. Ibid., 107.

24. Ibid., 38.

25. Maria Lepowsky, *Fruit of the Motherland: Gender in an Egalitarian Society* (New York: Columbia University Press, 1993).

26. Ibid., 92.

Suggestions for Further Reading

Du, Shanshan. "'Husband and Wife Do It Together': Sex/Gender Allocation of Labor among the Qhawqhat Lahu of Lancang, Southwest China." *American Anthropologist* 102, vol. 3 (2000), 520–37.

———. "*Chopsticks Only Work in Pairs*": *Gender Unity and Gender Equality among the Lahu of Southwest China.* New York: Columbia University Press, 2002.

Estioko-Griffin, Agnes. "Daughters of the Forest: Agta Women of the Philippines Hunt Large Animals and Still Raise Their Children." *Natural History*, vol. 5 (1986), 37–43.

Glen, Evelyn N. "Social Constructions of Mothering: A Thematic Overview." *Mothering: Ideology, Experience, and Agency*, Evelyn N. Glen, Crace Chang, and Linda R. Forcey, eds. New York: Routledge, 1994, 1–32.

Hewlett, Barry S. *Intimate Fathers: The Nature and Context of Aka Pygmy Paternal Infant Care.* Ann Arbor: University of Michigan Press, 1991.

Lenhart, Lioba. "Orang Suku Laut." *The Encyclopedia of Sex and Gender: Men and Women in the World's Cultures*, Melvin Ember and Carol Ember, eds. The Human Relations Area Files Encyclopedia Series. Hingham, MA: Kluwer/Plenum, 2003.

Lepowsky, Maria. *Fruit of the Motherland: Gender in an Egalitarian Society.* New York: Columbia University Press, 1993.

Murdock, George P., and Caterina Provost. "Factors in the Division of Labor by Sex: A Cross-Cultural Analysis." *Ethnology*, vol. 12 (1973), 203–25.

O'Brien, Mary. *The Politics of Reproduction.* New York: Routledge and Kegan Paul, 1981.

Rich, Adrienne. *Of Woman Born: Motherhood as Experience and Institution.* New York: W. W. Norton, 1976.

Understanding Agoraphobia: Women, Men, and the Historical Geography of Urban Anxiety

Felicity Callard

Felicity Callard (2000) is Lecturer in Human Geography at Queen Mary, University of London. Most recently, she has been researching historical and current understandings of "affect" and the emotions (particularly agoraphobia and depression). She is developing a new project on industrial psychology in the first half of the twentieth century. She has published in *Environment and Planning D: Society and Space, Social and Cultural Geography* and the *Journal of Mental Health Promotion*.

> *Felicity Callard writes that "Feminist scholarship on the body and psycho-analytic scholarship on subjectivity have deeply influenced my own research. Over the course of the last few years, I, along with many other scholars, have been preoccupied with formulating the relations between the social order and 'the psyche'—in other words, in understanding the articulation between internal and external worlds. I am particularly fascinated with understanding how psychic processes and phenomena such as anxiety, trauma, depression, and resistance intervene in, and often thwart, social, cultural, and political endeavors. In a course I teach on technology, I use a wide range of feminist scholarship on science and technology studies from the last three decades. It is a constant struggle for me to move debates away from the assumption that there is one feminist view on technology!"*

INTRODUCTION

"My way home lay through Chalmers-street, a short, broad, lonely street ending in a *cul-de-sac* with a gate into the 'Meadows,' lined with grey, un-compromising-looking stone houses, the road so unused to traffic that the grass grew up between the stones." This account of a walk home was published in 1898. We can, perhaps, see the "broad, lonely street" in our own minds, imagining that line of forbidding houses and the desolate, weed-filled road. The first-person narrative is, perhaps, an eerie start to a novel or short story: it draws on familiar figures of urban anxiety in which bleak spaces might always harbor crouching, potential dangers. But the narrative moves in a different direction—or, rather, the danger is located not quite where we might have thought it to be:

> Walking briskly one evening down the slope I have my first attack; and it is the suddenness and unexpectedness . . . that is so alarming. . . . I stop; the heart seems seized in an iron grip. . . . There is no semblance of giddiness or faintness in these attacks, it is more a feeling of collapse as though one were being shut up like a crush hat or a Chinese lantern. I have a strong inclination to cry out and I feel that I must fall, so I lay hold of, and steady myself by, the palings. A deep heaving sigh, the breaking out of a cold sweat upon the forehead, and in less time than it takes to describe . . . the attack has passed. Then quick as lightning comes the introspection and deception of the "agoraphobic." "Anyone looking out of his window will think I'm drunk," flashes through my mind, so I drop a book or stoop to tie a shoe-lace and then hurry homeward, restored by the con-sciousness that I am not dead."[1]

The danger comes not from a lurking figure or a ghostly apparition. The cli-max of the tale comes in the form of a painful, paroxysmal agoraphobic anx-iety attack. The term agoraphobia—literally fear of the "agora," the Greek place of assembly or marketplace—was coined in 1871 by the German physi-cian Carl Westphal to describe "Platzfurcht," a morbid fear of public places or squares.[2] The account from which I have just quoted is, in fact, in many ways typical of late nineteenth-century descriptions of this disorder: Clinicians at that time frequently reported that their patients felt as though they were about to die, were desperate to grab hold of something, and felt acutely ashamed.

But if that account is not unique in its enumeration of certain symptoms, this does not assuage my curiosity about the character experiencing such in-tense anxiety at that historical moment. Who was the figure negotiating a path along Chalmers Street at the very end of the nineteenth century? What did that figure think about those moments of intense, emotional distress? The narrator was a man, J. Headley Neale, a British physician attached to the Leicester Infirmary and Fever House, and he was describing his onset of agoraphobia as a medical student in Edinburgh. (Chalmers Street still exists, abutting the Edinburgh Royal Infirmary and opening on to "The Meadows.") Neale's tale was an autobiographical case history that appeared in the august pages of the British medical journal *The Lancet*.

What questions are raised in women's and gender studies by a middle-class professional man experiencing psychological near-collapse in public in a British city during the nineteenth-century *fin-de-siècle*? I will use Neale's autobiographical case history of agoraphobia to open up certain questions about gender, about the city, and about the emotions. More particularly, I want to consider why it is interesting that this particular agoraphobic individual was a professional man, and, second, how the fact that his complaint was *affective* (connected with feelings rather than with cognition) raises certain difficulties when one attempts to interpret the phenomenon of agoraphobia.

I hope to tell a story about some of the debates in which women's studies and gender studies have participated over the course of the last decade or so of the twentieth century.

My research on agoraphobia began in the mid 1990s when I was a doctoral student in geography at The Johns Hopkins University, specializing in feminist, cultural, and urban geography. I was committed to interdisciplinary scholarship and was working with scholars in cultural history and the history of psychiatry and psychoanalysis as well as with geographers. I had long harbored an interest in how urban anxiety has been described and conceptualized: There is a fascinating literature detailing the intimate ties between the rise of the metropolis in the nineteenth century and sensations of alienation, anxiety, desire, shock, and fear. Canonical texts include Edgar Allan Poe's short story "The Man of the Crowd," Charles Baudelaire's writings on the poetics of modernity, Walter Benjamin's magical commentaries on Baudelaire and Poe, and Georg Simmel's sociological essay "The Metropolis and Mental Life."[3] In much of that literature, as feminist scholars such as Janet Wolff, Elizabeth Wilson, and Rita Felski have variously pointed out, desire, anxiety, or alienation has been figured through a man.[4] I was therefore preoccupied with using feminist critical literature to think through the consequences of those gendered formulations: How did those canonical texts establish particular stories about the reasons for anxiety, about the socio-spatial configurations of metropolitan modernity, and about the relations between the internal and the external world? I was, in addition, compelled by psychoanalysis, and in particular by Freud's own contradictory and elliptical writings on trauma and anxiety. But those two interests—in urban anxiety and in psychoanalytic accounts of anxiety and trauma—remained separate until it became clear that it might be possible to begin to find the convergences between them—to locate psychoanalytic accounts of anxiety within a historically extensive body of literature that was preoccupied with the permeability and vulnerability of the individual to the spaces surrounding him or her. To find and illuminate those convergences would necessitate tackling head on how gender has been put to work in understandings of anxiety, the individual, and the milieu he or she inhabits.

My interest was piqued early on by an article by the architectural historian Anthony Vidler in which he asked how "modernist space" was produced largely by and for men. Underlying "the apparently serene transparency and all-dominating positivism of modernist urban space," Vidler averred, sat a morass of "rejection, suppression, anxiety, and phobic fear that its authors were attempting to cure."[5] On Vidler's account, master figures of modernist architecture such as Le Corbusier were far from being serene. Vidler specifically mentioned agoraphobia as one of the late nineteenth-century urban pathologies against which the modernist ideal of urban transparency was directed: if the city and its dwellers could be rendered open, "clean" and accessible to inspection, then perhaps the city's cobwebs—its dark fears and decrepit corners—might be blown away too. My study of the historical geography of agoraphobia began to take form: agoraphobia seemed to be a powerful lens through which one might bring together psychoanalysis, urban studies, questions of gender, and conceptualizations of space.

It was clear from the start that gender was to be a critical axis in my study, but not how exactly gender would feature in my arguments. On the one hand, many current references to agoraphobia in both clinical and nonclinical litera-ture assert that it is undoubtedly a "feminine" or "feminized" condition. On the other hand, Vidler's argument about the rise of late nineteenth-century urban pathologies such as agoraphobia did not seem *necessarily* to imply that those diagnosed with agoraphobia would be female or feminized. Indeed, one of the most interesting features of Vidler's argument was the way in which it presented a fascinating tale about male unease and anxiety.[6] But Vidler argued that although men predominated in the group of agoraphobic and claustro-phobic patients that were studied in the late nineteenth century, both agora-phobia and claustrophobia "were thought of as fundamentally 'female' in character"—so that it is "no accident" that agoraphobia today is sometimes known through the shorthand "housewives' disease."[7] Other scholarship on agoraphobia endorsed the intimate and long tie between agoraphobia and women. Another historian of architecture, Esther da Costa Meyer, announced that her essay on agoraphobia would "focus on the appearance of agorapho-bia and the imbrication of women, urban space, and pathology," pointing out that "this neurosis straddles the fault line between public and private, and af-fects women in particular."[8] Abram de Swaan, in his sociological theorization of agoraphobia, tied the emergence of agoraphobia in the late nineteenth cen-tury to the precise moment when women in West European cities faced fewer restrictions on moving around in public. Asserting that women patients con-stituted "a large majority of agoraphobic patients" at that time, he argued that the psychiatric category of agoraphobia expressed and replaced what had pre-viously been a lack of movement resulting from explicit social prohibitions.[9]

Armed with theoretical formulations such as these, I began to make my way through countless clinical (and some nonclinical) accounts of agorapho-bia that spanned the period from the 1870s to the 1990s. I began to bump into cases such as that of J. Headley Neale. Neale, in his contribution to the *Lancet*, provided his own characterization of "the agoraphobe." He asserted that "professional men" suffered most from agoraphobia, "clergymen in par-ticular," but he noted that he had also known "merchant princes, commercial travellers, middle-aged spinsters and even young married women caught in its toils."[10] For Neale, agoraphobia clearly predominantly affected men rather than women. His comments did not sit easily with scholars' assump-tions about women and agoraphobia. And when I read Neale's account with greater care, I still did not feel at ease with interpreting his references to pro-fessional men as straightforward accounts of "feminized" men. Nor did it seem easy to read Neale's account of *his own* agoraphobia as presenting a "feminized" masculinity.

At stake in my unease when faced with Neale's claims in his paper is the enormously important question of how scholars read and interpret textual ac-counts. A whole range of scholarship in women's studies and queer theory has, of course, done much to alert us to the difficulties and subtleties of how to read—of how to read rhetorically, to work against the grain, to spot what might otherwise remain hidden.[11] I asked myself what it would mean to do justice to Neale's account. Was I missing something in telling myself that Neale's account could not be read as presenting agoraphobic individuals as "feminized"? How ought I to work with, interpret, elaborate on, or even discount, Neale's statements in my own arguments concerning gender and agoraphobia? What follows is a consideration of some of the questions raised by my quandary over how to interpret Neale's account.

GENDER AND PUBLIC SPACE

The "good city" is measured, as a large literature in geography and other disciplines avers, at least in part by the quality of and access to its public spaces.[12] Mobility continues to be one of the most favored terms in current cultural-urban debates. Michael Sorkin, in his introduction to an important collection on the challenges facing urban sociability, notes that, "public spaces of the city are pre-eminently the spaces of circulation and exchange, overwhelmingly streets and sidewalks. We judge the good city by the quality of its public life and hence of its public space, yet the very idea of public space is now under siege."[13] Agoraphobia is one of many phenomena that rupture the ideal of public space. The agoraphobic individual's panicked response to squares, streets, highways, and trains—to all those most characteristic spaces of circulation and exchange—punctures the vision of the *agora* as a space of free intercourse. Agoraphobia marks a hiatus in industrialized, metropolitan life: It seems at once an archetypically metropolitan disorder and one that often pushes its sufferer to turn his or her back on metropolitan modernity, reducing the city to the size of a house, a room, or even a bed.

   Given that agoraphobia is regarded as an overwhelmingly female disorder in current clinical and sociological literature and in lay understandings, might, therefore, the legacy of women's restricted access to public space be coupled with a legacy of fear that has been generated around public space? There is clearly some relation between agoraphobia and the capacity to be mobile in public: Psychiatrists have suggested that at historical moments and in particular cultures in which women are expected to remain within the home and not venture outside, it would be difficult to know how and whether agoraphobia in women would appear. A woman's fear of the agora would not be read as requiring sympathy or explanation, and a phobia would not necessarily have a chance to manifest itself. Might we read Neale's comments about agoraphobic individuals being typically male, then, as a quirky commentary by a lone British physician? But let us not move too quickly. The agoraphobic individual's response to public spaces is difficult to understand because it is not *obviously* caused by direct public threats. Because it is unclear what precipitates the agoraphobic attack, it is equally unclear whether the "problem" lies with the individual, the society in which she or he cannot fully participate, or the built environment that would seem to be the immediate provocation of the terror. Agoraphobia immediately poses the difficult question: What, exactly, is the agoraphobic response a response *to*? There is, I believe, no neat, one-way line between, say, a history of restricted access to public space and anxieties regarding it. We cannot make a straightforward causal link between *material* inequities in men's and women's access to public space and the phenomenon of agoraphobia.

Let us look again at J. Headley Neale's account of his own agoraphobic anxiety attack in the environs of Chalmers Street. One of the reasons that his case jumped out at me is that Neale himself did not seem to fit my imagined agoraphobic "type." And this was doubtless because my thoughts about the obstacles and challenges to urban mobility have tended to center on the axis of femininity not masculinity. If the agoraphobic individual does populate our imaginary late-Victorian urban landscape, it is, I wager, through the figuring of feminine sequestration from the public sphere. Charlotte Perkins Gilman's famous short story "The Yellow Wallpaper" (1899) might serve here as a model of domestic confinement. Within such a framework, a figure such as Neale (a privileged young, male medical student) would ordinarily be regarded not as a figure of crippling anxiety, but as the epitome of the mobile, professional, male metropolitan dweller—the standard against which those less mobile might be measured.

Thus one of the central problems that surfaced in my historical research on agoraphobia was that the elegant narrative of agoraphobia *qua* femininity or domesticity either overlooked the agoraphobic man entirely, or too quickly feminized him. As I explored the late nineteenth-century psychiatric and neurological literature, it became clear that Neale was far from being the only agoraphobic man leading an awkward and anxious life when moving through public space. Descriptions of those numerous men cannot, I believe, be easily converted into stories of sequestered femininity. Clifford Allbutt, a prominent British physician, described in one of his essays on neurasthenia a "young and athletic" schoolmaster who found, to his great shame, that he could not, despite summoning all his self-command, cross the marketplace of his home town."[14] Charles Mercier described "a tall spare man" who, when going to and from his office "would sneak through all the alleys, courts, lanes, and narrow streets he could make use of" because he was seized with panic in a wide street.[15] George Beard described walking arm in arm with a physician who "could not go more than half a mile in a straight line," and so "continually turned off to the side streets, so as to keep a little distance from the hotel where he was stopping for the day."[16]

How might accounts such as these reconfigure how we, as feminist scholars, approach the figure of the agoraphobic individual? First, I have come to believe that it is too easy to read agoraphobia through the lens of representations of femininity as immobilized and domesticated. Not only does this jar with many of the accounts of agoraphobic men; in addition, it renders invisible too much of what is interesting about depictions of agoraphobic women— many of whom were and are *not* wholly sequestered in domestic space. Second, my fascination with descriptions of agoraphobic men scurrying down alleys, and going round in circles in order to keep close to particular buildings, has allowed me to perceive what I would describe as the viscosity of movement through the city. This is a viscosity that cannot be accounted for via prohibitions—real or imagined—on movement. Rather, it shows that there is no necessary equivalence between "real," material reasons for fear and objects or locales of phobia. No purely "material" reasons could explain the zigzagging paths taken by some of the men described above. Understanding this viscosity demands attending to the *unpredictable* ways in which the psychic shocks from the public world impacted, or did not impact, upon individuals' interior worlds. To explain Neale's feeling of being "shut up like a crush hat" or the "tall spare man['s]" haphazard route through alleys and narrow streets demands the formulation of a model of *psychic* as well as material constraints that affect individuals' passage through the city. This is not to discount the very significant material inequalities that operate through the axes of race, class, disability, and sexuality as well as gender that characterize individuals' ability to negotiate their way in the world. There is no easy jump that can be made between an individual's apparent "standing" in the public world and his or her experience of moving through or confronting elements of that world. The terms male and female, or "masculinity" and "femininity," cannot by themselves explain the operation or distribution of agoraphobic symptoms.

I hope that my arguments concerning agoraphobia, gender, and public space contribute to the debates over how to think about modernity, gender, and the city in relation to one another. Those debates have been enriched for many years by the scholarship of feminists in a wide variety of disciplines—including social and cultural history and geography, literature, architecture, sociology, and political theory. Much of that scholarship has focused particular attention on the multiple obstacles to women's mobility in public spaces—obstacles that range from prohibitions imposed on middle-class women for fear that they would have contact with the "lower classes," to the Victorian ideology of "separate spheres," to the real and pressing dangers that the metropolis posed and continues to pose.[17] This work has been groundbreaking and indispensable in terms of understanding differential access to public space and refining the analysis of relative mobility that contributes to a gendered experience of space. This work has also produced some unintended consequences. As the feminist cultural theorist Sharon Marcus (one of the contributors to this volume) has argued, the careful analysis of the separation between the home (commonly understood to be private and feminized space) and the street (commonly understood to be public and masculinized territory) has tended to make this opposition overly rigid—thereby endowing it with more analytical power than it perhaps warrants. Men and women have, in the process, been too easily spatially partitioned. This has obscured the frequent *failure* of correspondence between an ideology of separate spheres—of the separate operations of public and private—and the actual practices and phenomena occurring in those spaces. Marcus urges us, in this regard, to "question totalizing claims . . . that create oppositions between men and women, public and private realms, and exterior and interior spaces, then conflate the opposing terms of each pair."[18]

We would do well to heed her, for a commitment to an overly rigid and hierarchical opposition between street and home marks some of the critical scholarship on agoraphobia. While this literature has cogently articulated the connections between certain models of femininity and the dominant understandings of agoraphobia, it has had the tendency of assuming, rather than accounting for, an alliance between agoraphobia, confinement within a "feminine" role, and sequestration within the private realm. In the course of many years of reading case histories and autobiographical descriptions of agoraphobia and agoraphobic attacks, I have become as interested in descriptions of actual attacks of agoraphobic anxiety as in descriptions of agoraphobic avoidance. Those attacks are often experienced in what would commonly be regarded as that most "private" of spaces—the home—and by those commonly regarded as the most mobile and confident inhabitants of the public sphere—professional men. By refusing to align the categories of home–street, private–public, feminine–masculine, and immobile–mobile neatly one on the other, I have come to see a wider and more confusing conceptual terrain through which agoraphobic experiences might be understood. If, then, the usual understanding of the divide between home and world, between immobile women and mobile men, is not adequate as a structuring framework for a historical geography of agoraphobia, where might we turn? If I am right in emphasizing the unpredictable ways in which the psychic "shocks" from the external world impact, or do not impact, upon individuals' interior worlds, then it seems important to dwell further on how to conceptualize the emotionally charged psychic mediation between external and internal world.

GENDER AND AFFECT

Agoraphobia is regarded in the clinic as a pathology of affect. *Affect* has traditionally been separated within philosophy from the categories of intellect, cognition and representation. The term affect is usually used to signify phenomena that escape the operation of the will—passions, feelings, motivations—and is therefore a more capacious category than the emotions. (One could say that emotions occur as the recognizable "end product" of affective responses.) The affect underlying agoraphobia is anxiety. The concepts of pathology and affect are vexed and freighted terms in the social sciences and humanities today: for some time, feminist scholars and cultural theorists (particularly those working under the signature of Michel Foucault) have wisely cautioned us not to turn too quickly, if at all, to a diagnosis of pathology, but rather to investigate how societal conditions and medical and cultural assumptions both deem certain behaviors "pathological" and produce certain subjects as "pathological."[19] *Affect*, too, has been historicized: manifestations of emotion—love, anger, woe—are understood to be in some way shaped by, and therefore subject to, cultural narratives and framings. Emotions can be explained, it is argued, through recourse to various aspects of cultural and social organization. As Joel Pfister and Nancy Schnog put it, in their book subtitled *Toward a Cultural History of Emotional Life in America*, "we [want] to extend the possibilities of a history that would investigate emotions . . . as culturally structured experiences, interpretations, and performances of the self."[20]

What brings together many recent accounts of affective distress, then, is their shared investment in that heterogeneous school of thought termed *social constructionism*.[21] While this awkward term points to a great diversity of methodological frameworks and modes of argumentation, the main focus of inquiry would be the naming and interpretation of the various discourses surrounding the "suffering" individual. Discourses are series of practices, representations, and social processes through which meanings and categories are produced and legitimized. If one might account for those practices, representations, and social processes, one might better approach the reasons for the individual's suffering. Even if one acknowledges that the individual might "resist," "distort," or "recode" these messages and frameworks, the assumption still exists that the individual is always in some way responding to forces that construct her as subject.

Let me work with another account of agoraphobia from the nineteenth-century *fin-de-siècle* to provide a hypothetical illustration of this kind of interpretative procedure. Pierre Janet, the famous French physician and psychologist, reported the case of a thirty-three-year-old woman who was overcome with anxiety attacks whenever she was alone in the street. "[W]hat she really dreads," Janet claimed, "is an attack of madness 'which would make her run like a madwoman and would cause a scandal in public.'" He also noted that she "prefers streets lined with shops where she can seek refuge."[22] It would be easy to argue, using the social constructionist framework I have just sketched out, that the woman's behavior—her despair when walking alone—is indicative of nineteenth-century discourses of public and private (and of the lining up of the woman with the private); of her acquiescence to an ideology that construes lone female walkers as prostitutes and hence keeps most women at home; and of material social processes that render the city unsafe for women. One could also address her fears of being read as mad by pointing to the proliferation of discourses at this time that represented women *as* mad, and explain her taking refuge in shop-lined streets through the connection in this period between women and consumption. There are of course many compelling and important historical arguments that would bolster such claims.

This mode of interpretation provides us with a rich and nuanced explication of the various kinds and levels of context surrounding the agoraphobic individual. But I am concerned that, ultimately, it skirts the question of affect. For while, in this kind of reading, we are given several convincing arguments about why Janet's young female patient might be pushed toward the private sphere, there is no elaboration of why she actually has a particular affective response—overwhelming feelings of panic—when facing certain circumstances. But then one could argue that for this mode of interpretation, the particularity of the patient's anxiety is not actually that important. Such a reading may well stress how discourses produce certain psychological states and conditions, but it is not particularly concerned with adjudicating how discourses become embedded, or not, in the mental worlds of their subjects. It is simply assumed that individuals will suffer anxiety in the face of oppressive or problematic institutions and practices. Anxiety is assumed to be a straightforward response to something untoward, and, furthermore, "social anxieties" are assumed to be in some way inscribed on the body of the individual. While I have been providing a hypothetical reading of a case history of agoraphobia, readings that follow such a logic do occur in the critical literature on agoraphobia. The sociologist Bryan Turner, for example, has argued that "the disorders of women—hysteria, anorexia and agoraphobia—are . . . disorders of society."[23] For Turner, agoraphobia represents the successful conversion of a generalized fear of (or social anxiety about) the marketplace into a medical condition that furthermore serves to consolidate patriarchal domestic relations by ensuring the woman's fragility and immobility in relation to her husband. In his mapping of social anxieties on to the individual, the complexity of the psychic processes that mediate between the "external" and the "internal" world is, I suggest, ignored.

In my own research on agoraphobia I have been helped, compelled, and impressed by the vigor with which both feminist and less explicitly feminist scholarship have provided powerful resources for understanding the various institutions, practices, structures, and cultural processes that surround the emergence and consolidation of agoraphobia as a medical category. Nonetheless, I want to suggest that there are some pitfalls attached to this mode of interpretation. Let me summarize, therefore, what I have come to see as some of the costs of this kind of approach when thinking through the phenomenon of agoraphobia.

First, we find, once again, that the agoraphobic individual tends to be imagined as paradigmatically female. This assumption derives in part from a presentist logic: Because agoraphobia is installed in current discussions so firmly as a female disorder, most work on agoraphobia has used such characterizations as the enabling framework through which to study late nineteenth-century incidences of agoraphobia. It has also been taken as self-evident that a disorder that seems to be about avoiding public space would particularly afflict women. Furthermore, within an account that describes how social anxieties are played out on the bodies of particular individuals, it seems eminently plausible that it would be *female* bodies that would be most vulnerable to such inscriptions—particularly because an argument about the production of "pathological" individuals most commonly sees women and other subjects deemed marginal as most likely to be produced as pathological. This kind of account in turn leads to two further problems: It obscures certain lines of evidence in the historical record, and makes it very difficult to understand agoraphobia outside of a narrative of feminization. I have already emphasized that many late nineteenth-century descriptions of agoraphobia feature men rather than women: this point is so routinely ignored, downplayed, or disavowed in the critical literature on agoraphobia, that it is as though it is rendered literally invisible.

Second, much is made of the role that public and private space have in shaping discourses of agoraphobia. Gillian Brown, for example, in her fascinating analysis of nineteenth-century agoraphobia, describes how her own argument develops "from the imagery of public and private space" that recurs in representations of agoraphobia.[24] But such invocations of public and private space can end up presuming how "the public" and "the private" are subjectively experienced. There is no guarantee that public space and private space are experienced as "public" or as "private" by the agoraphobic individual. Indeed, cases in which an individual's agoraphobia ends up rendering everywhere but his or her bed off-limits show the inadequacy of the usual mapping of street versus home, public versus private, and unsafe versus safe. Furthermore, because the divide between the public and the private often has such an important role in conceptualizations of agoraphobia, the use of such a model makes it difficult to acknowledge that agoraphobic behavior—in both the late-nineteenth and twentieth century—cannot be characterized as a straightforward rejection of the public sphere and a turn toward the private. As I have mentioned, I have found several accounts describing agoraphobic individuals' horror at having to spend time in their own home, the quintessential private space, just as there are several accounts that make it clear that it is not public space *tout court* that those with agoraphobia fear.

Third, this kind of interpretative procedure is directed toward delineating details of the social sphere, such that we may discern the ideologies, discourses, and categories of thought and social organization that construct the agoraphobic individual's fears, desires, and behavior. Such accounts therefore end up being remarkably uninterested in the "subjectively" felt conditions of agoraphobia. For, since the "objective" world is assumed to construct both the fears and desires of the agoraphobic individual, all interpretative weight falls away from thinking about how to conceptualize the agoraphobic individual's subjective, mental world. Indeed, we need not be overly concerned with this mental world since on this account the "subjective" psychic register is assumed to be bound to the social in a predictable way. The psychoanalytic feminist Joan Copjec takes up this problem in her critique of claims that hysteria was "invented" via *fin-de-siècle* medical practices, confessional practices, and psychoanalytic discourses. Copjec shows that the construction of the subject in such an argument depends "on the subject's taking social representations as images of its own ideal being, on the subject's deriving a 'narcissistic pleasure' from these representations. This notion of pleasure, however vaguely invoked, is what makes the argument stick; it 'cements' or 'glues' the realm of the psychic to that of the social."[25] Copjec shows how arguments that take such an approach too neatly install the individual within the social order by virtue of her assumed identification with the discourses and representations surrounding her.

CONCLUSIONS AND REMAINING QUESTIONS

This essay has explored my quandary over how to interpret Neale's account of agoraphobia by scrutinizing several of the concepts (public–private, mobility–immobility, gender, affect, discourse, and so forth) that have framed discussions of agoraphobia. I have shied away from producing any straightforward explanation of Neale's agoraphobic anxiety attack in late nineteenth-century Edinburgh, and instead have attempted to outline some of the interpretative dilemmas that his case raises in relation to my historical geography of agoraphobia. In this final section, I shall first outline more explicitly the kinds of methodological decisions I have taken when developing my historical geography of agoraphobia; and second, recapitulate my major points about agoraphobia, gender, and affect and indicate how they bear on current questions in the field of women's studies.

For a long time, I have been compelled by psychoanalysis, and in particular by Freud's own contradictory and elliptical writings on trauma and anxiety, which fundamentally transformed the way in which affect and phobias were conceptualized. It was not, indeed, until Freud's detachment of "anxiety neurosis" from the hold-all condition of neurasthenia in 1895 that the category of anxiety emerged into medical discourse.[26] In Freud's formulations concerning phobia, the bond between the subjective world of the phobic individual and the objective world of the social order is accounted for in several, sometimes contradictory, ways. His formulations are fascinating not because he, as opposed to everyone else, got the theory of agoraphobia "right"—far from it—but because his writings on anxiety and phobia do not gloss over the difficulty of deciding upon the reasons for, and origins of, fear and anxiety. Whether Freud was pointing to the individual's recourse to certain psychic processes that would help shield her from pain, or whether he was addressing how anxiety "slipped" from object to object such that a dog phobia could never simply be about a dog *per se*, what he never took for granted was the work demanded in the translation from subjective internal world to objective external world, and from external world to internal world. I have, therefore, used Freud in my work not to provide me with a neat set of tools with which to read historically and geographically varied material, but rather to help me understand the variety of psychic responses to "objective," material conditions. I use Freud, in other words, not to discount history or geography, but to think further about the missing story of anxiety that ties and unties the agoraphobic city dweller to and from the world surrounding her. How the category of gender inflects the operation of anxiety in Freud's writings is enormously difficult to untangle and, therefore, exciting.

My engagement with psychoanalytic writings has allowed me to think about agoraphobia as a manifestation of phobic anxiety and not of fear. The distinction is important: anxiety, unlike fear, is not precipitated by a particular thing, object, person, or event. Anxiety therefore operates far more unpredictably than fear: It does not "behave" itself in terms of attaching itself to particular, predictable individuals, and occurring in certain, predictable spaces. Agoraphobia can be addressed only by taking seriously the difficulty of understanding the articulation between the sphere of the psychic and that of the social. Doing justice to the sphere of the psychic entails acknowledging that it might not be smoothly derived from the sphere of the social—in other words, that interior, mental states might not be wholly accounted for by delineating the institutions, social arrangements, and practices that surround social individuals. (I have found inspiring in this regard the work of scholars such as Ruth Leys, Jacqueline Rose, and Lyndsey Stonebridge—all of whom are deeply committed to understanding the incommensurability between the psychic and the social.)[27] As Carolyn Steedman so beautifully demonstrated in her autobiographical book *Landscape for a Good Woman*, attending to the complex mediation between the external world and mental life is vital if one is to understand the ambivalence that structures the social relations of women and men.[28] One of the challenges that feminist scholars in both the humanities and the social sciences continue to face is to formulate how the unpredictable operation of psychic, affective processes intervenes in and reconfigures social relations.

One cannot approach agoraphobia without thinking about gender. That statement sounds today flat-footed—and of course its very flat-footedness is a measure of the success that women's studies and gender studies have had in demonstrating the indispensability of the category of gender to any investigation of the social and cultural world. Here too, the centrality that the terms "femininity" and "masculinity" have in my argument bears witness to much scholarship in women's studies that has demonstrated that the work of gender as a structuring framework does not neatly map masculinity on to men and femininity on to women.[29] It is unsurprising, then, given the vigor of gender studies and "masculinity" studies today, that my account of agoraphobia features discussions of men and "masculinity" as much as women and "femininity." One indication of this is the fact that at the center of this essay lies an arguably insignificant account written by an unknown British male physician.

J. Headley Neale is important in my account because he exemplifies my attempt to attend to the particularities of the historical record without being absolutely clear about which conceptual axes I ought to privilege. I do believe that Neale challenges narratives of agoraphobia that read it as a kind of femininity, but I also want to leave open the question of his exact place in the medical history of agoraphobia. (To what extent, for example, should his gender, class, and profession operate as critical variables in formulating arguments about agoraphobia in the late nineteenth century?) I have come to be convinced of the necessity of not approaching the phenomenon one is studying with "grids" or "matrices" already set up. If I had persisted in using a series of neat oppositional pairs that overlapped perfectly with one another—home and street, feminine and masculine, safe and unsafe, private and public—I would have missed not only the particularities of J. Headley Neale's account, but much else that is of great importance in the history of agoraphobia. For just as agoraphobia is not simply a story about women, it is also not simply a story about wholesale retreat into the private sphere. Both the material effects of gender (for example, men's and women's differential mobility in spaces), and the imagined characteristics of men and women (and of masculinity and femininity) have undoubtedly played a crucial role in shaping models of and experiences of agoraphobia. So too have the variable ways in which the divides between public and private have been both actively patrolled and subjectively imagined. But the oppositional pairs of male and female, of public and private cannot be used wholly *to explain* the affective phenomenon of agoraphobia. The gendering of agoraphobia shifted, I believe, at some point in the early twentieth century—moving from a disorder that was largely associated with men, to one that was predominantly associated with women. If this historical argument is correct, it raises numerous questions about how and why such a change occurred. Before those questions can be answered, one would, I contend, have to consider whether, how, and in what relation to one another, the terrains of the discursive, the material, and the psychic experienced transformation.

Notes

This chapter is dedicated to David Harvey, Ruth Leys, Erica Schoenberger, and Judith R. Walkowitz.

1. J. Headley Neale, "Agoraphobia," *Lancet* 2 (Nov. 19, 1898), 1322–23.
2. Carl Westphal, "Die Agoraphobie: eine neuropathische Erscheinung," *Archiv für Psychiatrie und Nervenkrankheiten* 3 (1871): 138–61.
3. Edgar Allan Poe, "The Man of the Crowd," *Poetry and Tales* (New York: Library Classics of the United States, 1984 [first published in 1840]); Charles Baudelaire, *The Painter of Modern Life and Other Essays*, trans. Jonathan Mayne (London: Phaidon Press, 1964); Walter Benjamin, "On Some Motifs in Baudelaire," in *Illuminations*, ed. and intro. Hannah Arendt, trans. Harry Zohn (London: Fontana, 1992 [first published in German in 1939]); Georg Simmel, " The Metropolis and Mental Life," in *On Individuality and Social Forms: Selected Writings*, ed. and intro. Donald Levine (Chicago: University of Chicago Press, 1971 [first published in German in 1903]).
4. Janet Wolff, "The Invisible *Flâneuse*: Women and the Literature of Modernity," *Theory, Culture, and Society* 2(3) (1985), 37–45; Elizabeth Wilson, "The Invisible *Flâneur*," *New Left Review* 191 (January–February 1992): 90–110; Rita Felski, *The Gender of Modernity* (Cambridge, MA: Harvard University Press, 1995).
5. Anthony Vidler, "Bodies in Space/Subjects in the City: Psychopathologies of Modern Urbanism," *differences: A Journal of Feminist Cultural Studies* 5 (1993), 37.
6. Vidler's essay provides striking vignettes of anxious men (Vidler, "Bodies in Space/Subjects in the City").
7. Vidler, "Bodies in Space/Subjects in the City," 35.
8. Esther da Costa Meyer, "La donna è mobile," *Assemblage* 28 (1996), 7.
9. Abram de Swaan, "The Politics of Agoraphobia: On Changes in Emotional and Relational Management," *Theory and Society* 10 (1981), 365.
10. Neale, "Agoraphobia," 1323.
11. Exemplary texts include Shoshana Felman, *The Literary Speech Act: Don Juan with J. L. Austin, or Seduction in Two Languages*, trans. Catherine Porter (Ithaca: Cornell University Press, 1983); Barbara Johnson, *The Critical Difference: Essays in the Contemporary Rhetoric of Reading* (Baltimore: Johns Hopkins University Press, 1980); Eve Kosofsky Sedgwick, *Between Men: English Literature and Male Homosocial Desire* (New York: Columbia University Press, 1985); and Gayatri Chakravorty Spivak, *In Other Worlds: Essays in Cultural Politics* (New York: Routledge, 1988).
12. Classic formulations of this view include Jane Jacobs, *The Death and Life of Great American Cities: The Failure of Town Planning* (New York: Random House, 1961) and Iris Marion Young, *Justice and the Politics of Difference* (Princeton: Princeton University Press, 1990).
13. Michael Sorkin, "Introduction: Traffic in Democracy," in *Giving Ground: The Politics of Propinquity*, Joan Copjec and Michael Sorkin, eds. (London: Verso, 1998), 4.
14. Thomas Clifford Allbutt, "Neurasthenia," in *A System of Medicine: By Many Writers*, Allbutt, ed., vol. 8 (London: Macmillan, 1899), 142.

15. Charles Mercier, "Agoraphobia—A Remedy," *Lancet* 2 (Oct. 13, 1906), 991.

16. George Beard, *A Practical Treatise on Nervous Exhaustion (Neurasthenia), Its Symptoms, Nature, Sequences, Treatment*, 5th ed. (New York: E. B. Treat, 1905), 56.

17. That extensive body of work includes Leonore Davidoff and Catherine Hall, *Family Fortunes: Men and Women of the English Middle Class, 1780–1850* (Chicago: University of Chicago Press, 1987); Doreen Massey, *Space, Place, and Gender* (Minneapolis: University of Minnesota Press, 1994); Deborah Epstein Nord, *Walking the Victorian Streets: Women, Representation, and the City* (Ithaca: Cornell University Press, 1995); Mary Ryan, "Gender and Public Access: Women's Politics in Nineteenth-Century America," in *Habermas and the Public Sphere*, Craig Calhoun, ed. (Cambridge: MIT Press, 1992); Judith Walkowitz, *Prostitution and Victorian Society: Women, Class, and the State* (Cambridge: Cambridge University Press, 1980); *City of Dreadful Delight: Narratives of Sexual Danger in Late-Victorian London* (Chicago: University of Chicago Press, 1992).

18. Sharon Marcus, *Apartment Stories: City and Home in Nineteenth-Century Paris and London* (Berkeley: University of California Press, 1999), 5–8.

19. See Michel Foucault, *Madness and Civilization: A History of Insanity in the Age of Reason*, trans. Richard Howard (New York: Pantheon Books, 1965). Important feminist accounts of madness include Elaine Showalter, *The Female Malady: Women, Madness and English Culture 1830–1980* (London: Virago, 1987); Carroll Smith-Rosenberg, "The Hysterical Woman: Sex Roles and Role Conflicts in Nineteenth-Century America," *Social Research* 39 (Winter 1972): 652–78.

20. Joel Pfister and Nancy Schnog, "On Conceptualizing the Cultural History of Emotional and Psychological Life in America," in *Inventing the Psychological: Toward a History of Emotional Life in America*, Pfister and Schnog, eds. (New Haven: Yale University Press, 1997), 17.

21. Social constructionism is indebted to many philosophical and critical traditions, and I certainly do not intend social constructionism to be read as an equivalent term to Foucauldianism. Nonetheless, the two terms are often understood in critical literature to be more or less the same as one another.

22. Pierre Janet, *Les obsessions et la psychasthénie* (Paris: Félix Alcan, 1908), 211–12.

23. Bryan Turner, *The Body and Society: Explorations in Social Theory* (Oxford: Blackwell, 1984).

24. Gillian Brown, "The Empire of Agoraphobia," *Representations* no. 20 (1987), 155.

25. Joan Copjec, *Read My Desire: Lacan against the Historicists* (Cambridge, MA: MIT Press, 1995), 41–42.

26. Sigmund Freud, "On the Grounds for Detaching a Particular Syndrome from Neurasthenia under the Description 'Anxiety Neurosis'" (1895), *The Standard Edition of the Complete Psychological Works of Sigmund Freud*, trans. and ed. James Strachey (London: Hogarth Press, 1953–1974), vol. 3: 90–115.

27. Ruth Leys, "The Real Miss Beauchamp: Imitation and the Subject of Gender," in *Feminists Theorize the Political*, Judith Butler and Joan Scott, eds. (London: Routledge, 1992), 167–214; Leys, *Trauma: A Genealogy* (Chicago: University of Chicago Press, 2000); Jacqueline Rose, *Why War?—Psychoanalysis, Politics, and the Return to Melanie Klein* (Oxford: Blackwell, 1993); and *States of Fantasy* (Oxford: Oxford University Press, 1996); Lyndsey Stonebridge, "Anxiety at a Time of Crisis," *History Workshop Journal* 45 (1998): 171–82.

28. Carolyn Steedman, *Landscape for a Good Woman* (London: Virago, 1986).

29. See, for example, Judith Halberstam, *Female Masculinity* (Durham: Duke University Press, 1998).

Suggestions for Further Reading

On Agoraphobia

Bankey, Ruth. "La donna é [sic] mobile: Constructing the Irrational Woman." *Gender, Place and Culture* 8 (2001), 37–54.

Brown, Gillian. "The Empire of Agoraphobia." *Representations* no. 20 (Fall 1987), 134–57.

Callard, Felicity. "Conceptualisations of Agoraphobia: Implications for Mental Health Promotion." *Journal of Mental Health Promotion* 2(4) (2003), 37–45.

Carter, Paul. *Repressed Spaces: The Poetics of Agoraphobia*. London: Reaktion, 2002.

Costa Meyer, Esther da. "La donna è mobile." *Assemblage* 28 (1996), 6–15.

Davidson, Joyce. "'. . . The World Was Getting Smaller': Women, Agoraphobia and Bodily Boundaries." *Area* 32 (2000), 31–40.

———. *Phobic Geographies: The Phenomenology and Spatiality of Identity*. Burlington, VT: Ashgate, 2003.

De Swaan, Abram. "The Politics of Agoraphobia: On Changes in Emotional and Relational Management." *Theory and Society* 10 (1981), 359–85.

Gardner, Carol Brooks. "Out of Place: Gender, Public Places, and Situational Disadvantage." In *NowHere: Space, Time and Modernity*, Roger Friedland and Deidre Boden, eds., 335–55. Berkeley: University of California Press, 1994.

Reuter, Shelley Z. "Doing Agoraphobia(s): A Material-Discursive Understanding of Diseased Bodies." *Sociology of Health and Illness* 24 (2002), 750–70.

Vidler, Anthony. "Bodies in Space/Subjects in the City: Psychopathologies of Modern Urbanism." *differences* 5 (fall 1993), 31–51.

———. "Psychopathologies of Modern Space: Metropolitan Fear from Agoraphobia to Estrangement." In *Rediscovering History: Culture, Politics, and the Psyche*, Michael S. Roth, ed. 11–29. Stanford, CA: Stanford University Press, 1994.

Westphal, Carl Friedrich Otto. *Westphal's "Die Agoraphobie."* Trans. Michael T. Schumacher and ed. Terry J. Knapp. Lanham, MD: University Press of America, 1988.

On Modernity, the City, and the Body

Benjamin, Walter. "On Some Motifs in Baudelaire." In *Illuminations*, ed. and intro. Hannah Arendt; trans. Harry Zohn, 152–96. London: Fontana, 1992. Originally published 1939.

Bordo, Susan. *Unbearable Weight: Feminism, Western Culture and the Body*. Berkeley: University of California Press, 1993.

Felski, Rita. *The Gender of Modernity*. Cambridge, MA: Harvard University Press, 1995.

Marcus, Sharon. *Apartment Stories: City and Home in Nineteenth-Century Paris and London*. Berkeley: University of California Press, 1999.

Pile, Steve. *The Body and the City: Psychoanalysis, Space and Subjectivity*. London: Routledge, 1996.

Schorske, Carl E. "The Ringstrasse, Its Critics, and the Birth of Urban Modernism." In *Fin-de-Siècle Vienna: Politics and Culture*. New York: Vintage Books, 1981.

Simmel, Georg. "The Metropolis and Mental Life." In *On Individuality and Social Forms: Selected Writings*. ed. and intro. Donald N. Levine, 324–39. Chicago: University of Chicago Press, 1971 [first German edition published in 1903].

Turner, Bryan S. *The Body and Society: Explorations in Social Theory*. Oxford: Blackwell, 1984.

Walkowitz, Judith R. *The City of Dreadful Delight: Narratives of Sexual Danger in Late-Victorian London*. Chicago: University of Chicago Press, 1992.

Wilson, Elizabeth. "The Invisible *Flâneur*." *New Left Review* 191 (January–February 1992), 90–110.

Wolff, Janet. "The Invisible Flaneuse: Women and the Literature of Modernity." *Theory, Culture, and Society* 2(3) (1985), 37–45.

On Psychiatry, the Emotions and Mental Life

Berrios, German E., and Roy Porter, eds., *A History of Clinical Psychiatry: The Origin and History of Psychiatric Disorders*. London: Athlone, 1995.

Borch-Jacobsen, Mikkel. *The Emotional Tie: Psychoanalysis, Mimesis, and Affect*. Stanford, CA: Stanford University Press, 1992.

Foucault, Michel. *Madness and Civilization: A History of Insanity in the Age of Reason*. Trans. Richard Howard. New York: Random House, 1965.

Freud, Sigmund. "On the Grounds for Detaching a Particular Syndrome from Neurasthenia under the Description 'Anxiety Neurosis'." *The Standard Edition of the Complete Psychological Works of Sigmund Freud*, trans. and ed. James Strachey (London: Hogarth Press, 1953–74), vol. 3, 90–115.

———. *Inhibitions, Symptoms and Anxiety* (1926). *SE* 20: 87–172.

Leys, Ruth. *Trauma: A Genealogy*. Chicago: University of Chicago Press, 2000.

———. "The Real Miss Beauchamp: Imitation and the Subject of Gender." In *Feminists Theorize the Political*, Judith Butler and Joan Scott, eds. 167–214. London: Routledge, 1992.

Pfister, Joel, and Nancy Schnog, eds. *Inventing the Psychological: Toward a Cultural History of Emotional Life in America*. New Haven: Yale University Press, 1997.

Showalter, Elaine. *The Female Malady: Women, Madness and English Culture 1830–1980*. London: Virago, 1987.

Smith-Rosenberg, Carroll. "The Hysterical Woman: Sex Roles and Role Conflicts in Nineteenth-Century America." *Social Research* 39 (Winter 1972), 652–78.

Stonebridge, Lyndsey. "Anxiety at a Time of Crisis." *History Workshop Journal* 45 (1998), 171–82.

Study Questions

1. Compare the ways in which Freedman, Guy-Sheftall, and Jones use the word "feminist" and "feminism." How do their usages compare with your own?

2. In her essay, Laurel Thatcher Ulrich uses scraps of linen found in a museum as well as store accounts to paint a picture of the independence early New England women achieved through spinning yarn and making cloth. What old artifacts in your own home or neighborhood might be used to reconstruct the lives of earlier local women? What are the advantages and disadvantages of using objects found in a museum or an attic rather than documents preserved in the archives of a city hall or town library in telling these women's stories?

3. As you read the chapters in this section by writers from a variety of fields, you will notice that most disciplines have a distinctive or specialized vocabulary. Consider what role these specialized vocabularies play in helping scholars to explore their chosen subjects.

4. Caroline Brettell in Part II suggests that feminist anthropologists have returned to the methods of life histories and narratives. In what ways does Shanshan Du's approach fit this trend?

5. Both Felicity Callard, writing about agoraphobia, and Antoinette Burton, writing about Victorian Britain in Part I, refer to Michel Foucault. Who is Foucault and why do you think he had an influence on feminist scholars?

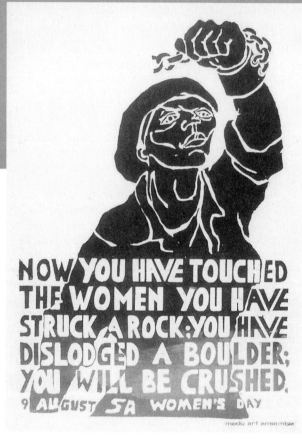

South African Women's Day, August 9, commemorates a 1956 march in Pretoria by thousands of women of all backgrounds who protested the apartheid racial "pass laws," chanting "You have touched the women, you have dislodged a boulder; you will be crushed."

(This poster was produced in 1981 by the Medu Art Ensemble of Botswana—Courtesy of South African History Archive. Copyright SAHA. All rights reserved.)

part 4

Rights, Reforms, and Welfare

In this section, four scholars examine welfare and welfare reform movements to discover the gendered aspects of public policy decisions. Yet here, as in other sections, the contributors do not frame their stories entirely around issues of gender; they take care to factor in class and race as well, sometimes as real components and sometimes as metaphors for gender.

Miriam Cohen's essay, "The Politics of Gender and Schooling in the Progressive Era," is set in a period when laissez-faire approaches to social welfare were being challenged by a new belief that the quality of American family life must be a matter of public concern. Cohen examines the reforms that white, middle- and upper-class women activists proposed in an effort to improve the family lives of the poor. Those reforms that focused on women were couched in the traditional middle-class language of "proper" gender roles, especially motherhood. This was true, in part, because the reformers embraced the middle-class values embodied in them. But linking the reforms they sought to traditional gender roles was also a conscious strategy to ensure their success. In a country dominated by business interests, with little history of state spending for social welfare, reformers had to rely on arguments about the special needs of women and children and to appeal to the popular commitment to motherhood. In their campaigns to see child labor laws enacted, however, they could also rely upon America's strong tradition of public expenditure for education. Finally, Cohen astutely observes that, in advocating a middle-class model of motherhood for poor women, the reformers were able to carve out a new role for themselves outside the home in the public, or civic, realm. In her historiographical essay, "Women's History with the Politics Left *In:* Feminist Studies of the United States Welfare State," Felicia Kornbluh also focuses on the role of women as creators and clients of the modern welfare state. Kornbluh reviews the literature that analyzes and reconstructs these roles, not only in history but also in sociology and political science. She argues that the gendered study of welfare states arose at a particular moment in time, in a specific historical context: as a response to the anti-welfare politics of the Reagan, Bush, and Clinton administrations and as a result of scholarly efforts to create feminist political theory. Kornbluh criticizes this scholarship for what she considers its attempt to defend or recreate the very motherhood-based politics it discovered in the past. She urges scholars of gender and the welfare state to consider the links between this scholarship and domestic racial conflicts, colonialism, and the differences of power among women.

Ellen Reese's essay, "Patriarchy, Racism and Business Interests: Cross-Class Support for Welfare Retrenchment in the United States," returns us to the topic addressed by Miriam Cohen and Felicia Kornbluh. Reese examines the backlashes against welfare programs and female welfare recipients in the 1950s and today. She finds that the anti-welfare campaigns in both instances have been led by business organizations seeking to ensure a ready supply of low wage casual labor and to minimize their taxes. These business interests have found allies in those concerned with the changes in the racial status quo and the traditional family. She also finds that the racist stereotype of black welfare mothers has intensified since the 1980s and that nativist opposition to Latinos and Asians has added a new dimension to the welfare backlash.

In "Metaphors of Class and Race: Comparing German and American Feminisms," Myra Marx Ferree analyzes the differences in the cultural vocabulary of German and American feminists as they search for metaphors for their oppression. In Germany, Ferree argues, the metaphor is class; in America, it is race. The choice is related to the national histories of each society. In America, for example, the first women's rights appeal, the Declaration of Sentiments, appears as the debate over slavery begins to reach crisis proportions. In Germany, class struggle is the central theme of the nineteenth and early twentieth centuries. In modern times, a similar distinction can be seen, as American feminism builds on the anti-war and anti-imperialist movements that see racism in America's foreign policies and as German feminism builds on the debates over the merits of socialism and capitalism.

The Politics of Gender and Schooling in the Progressive Era

Miriam Cohen

Miriam Cohen (1975) is Evalyn Clark Professor of History at Vassar College. She is working on a comparative historical study of the welfare state in England, France, and the United States. She and her co-author, Michael Hanagan, have published numerous articles on their work, including, "Politics, Unemployment and Citizenship: Unemployment Policy in England, France and the United States," in *Citizenship, Identity and Social History*, Charles Tilly, ed. (1996), and "The Politics of Gender in the Making of the Welfare State: A Comparative Perspective," in the *Journal of Social History* 24 (1991). She is also the author of *Workshop to Office: Two Generations of Italian Women in New York, 1900–1950* (1993).

> *Miriam Cohen chose to do a thesis on the work, leisure, and educational life of immigrant women in 1974 because, "like so many young scholars of the time, I consciously turned away from the study of elite social and political structures that had so dominated the historical scholarship of the recent past. I was particularly fortunate to have as my dissertation director Louise Tilly, then working with Joan Scott on their soon-to-be famous history of women and work. In the course of my research, it became clear to me that one had to pay attention to government rules and regulations, both on the local and national level, regarding work and school. This marked the beginning of my interest in understanding how the changes in state regulations affected changes in the everyday lives of ordinary Americans. Moreover, as the welfare state was being dismantled at the end of the twentieth century, a reawakened interest in its history, why it was enacted and why it had become unpopular, seemed urgent."*

Writing about the activities of their Propaganda Committee, Sophie Loeb of the Allegheny County Mothers' Pension League focused on a new initiative for their campaign in Greater Pittsburgh on behalf of state funding for poor, widowed mothers:

> At Soldiers' and Sailors' Memorial Hall, on Sunday, May 19, 1914, the [Allegheny County Mothers' Pension] League held its first public celebration of Mother's Day ever observed in the United States. It is to the credit of the League to say that 1,100

people attended. This gathering was unique in the fact that not only was tribute paid to Motherhood in speech and flower, but Mother was honored in a more practical way by trying to assist the mothers less fortunate, in their struggle to rear her children under her [sic] own roof.[1]

The Mother's Day gathering exemplified the kinds of initiatives organized by women social reformers across the country in the early decades of the twentieth century. Sophie Loeb and women like her, from middle- and upper-class backgrounds, sought to improve the lives of poor families by concentrating on the plight of women and children. Focusing on issues that appealed to women as wives and mothers, and promoting the notion that women were particularly good at addressing such concerns, they practiced what women's historians call "maternalist politics." Though all maternalists concentrated on the problems of mothers and children, they didn't necessarily share the same political vision. Borrowing from Molly Ladd-Taylor, I use the term "progressive maternalists" to refer to women like Sophie Loeb, who used the politics of maternalism to expand the welfare state.[2]

In Europe as well as the United States, in the late nineteenth and the first half of the twentieth century, coalitions of labor union activists, liberals and leftists, worked to improve social welfare by building government expenditure programs and expanding government regulations. The collection of these programs, which are now termed the welfare state, might encompass any public expenditures, regulations and enactments that protect people from the full force of market competition, including unemployment, old age, and health insurance, income guarantees, or labor legislation regulating wages and working conditions. This chapter, part of a comparative project on the history of the welfare state in England, France and the United States, focuses on two areas of interest to American women reformers: government relief for poor, widowed mothers and child labor legislation. While looking at national and regional trends, I concentrate on reform activities between the 1890s and World War I in two cities that were hotbeds of social reform in the Progressive era, New York and Pittsburgh.[3] During those years, progressive maternalists concentrated on state-level legislation; national legislation regarding poor relief or the regulation of child labor would have to await the crisis of the Great Depression.

Throughout the Progressive era and beyond, social reformers worked for programs that would help poor families conform to dominant gender norms, with men as successful breadwinners and women proper domestic caretakers. Campaigning on behalf of poor relief and for protective labor legislation, maternalists stressed that both programs would help women become better mothers. Progressive maternalists advocated specific programs because of traditional convictions regarding gender roles and family life, but they were also strategic politicians. In Europe and the U.S., women knew that their participation in the political arena flew in the face of conventional norms. On both sides of the Atlantic, concentrating on issues already associated with women's traditional roles lessened the impact of that challenge. The politics of maternalism, however, figured more prominently in America because social and political circumstances made it particularly hard to build a welfare state. Especially before the Great Depression, reformers faced several formidable obstacles, including a weak tradition of state spending for social welfare, hostile courts that unlike Europe had enormous power to stymie the growth of the regulatory state, and a business community that wielded power almost unopposed. Nor could American reformers count on joining forces with organized labor; wary of government regulations, the labor movement preferred to rely on the power of unions, not the state, to limit corporate power. These circumstances encouraged American reformers to rely on arguments about the special needs of both women and children in campaigning for government guarantees to the poor.[4]

By naming these activists feminists, I take my place alongside scholars who argue that feminism embraces not only those women who worked for equal rights. It includes women who worked to increase women's social and political rights even as they used arguments about women's special needs and attributes to achieve their goals. In looking at how women's particular circumstances influenced both their approach to activism and their political agenda, this study also builds on a large body of feminist scholarship on the history of women and the welfare state.[5] But my analysis also suggests, along with other recent work on women and politics, that an emphasis on women's difference ought not to obscure the extent to which women behaved like their male counterparts. As pragmatic politicians, women adapted more than one strategy in order to achieve reforms.[6] Moreover, like men, their politics were multifaceted; gender issues were intertwined with and often shaped by other concerns. Progressive maternalists put a high priority on class issues and most especially were interested in social provisions for the poor; toward that end, they worked with various reform organizations, often tailoring their rhetoric to strengthen coalitions.[7]

Like politicians everywhere, American women reformers framed their arguments in order to tap into the cultural understandings of the audiences they were trying to influence.[8] Mobilizing support for public poor relief and child labor legislation, women in the first half of the twentieth century not only appealed to the popularity of motherhood, they also exploited America's unique commitment to universal education. While the United States had a weak tradition of state spending for social welfare, it had the strongest tradition of public expenditure for education. In the United States, access to education is considered a fundamental right of citizenship, but we have never agreed that citizens have the right to jobs, to health care, or to homes. Even our courts have acted to enforce children's right to schooling.[9]

Of course, the right of all Americans to an equal education has never been assured, but as far back as the early nineteenth century, Americans, especially in urban middle-class and elite circles, were convinced that widespread access to education was central to the nation's success. An educated public would act as a bulwark against tyranny. Universal public education would also be a vehicle for nation building, disseminating national values in a country continually faced with the absorption of newcomers, a country of ethnic and deep racial divisions. Finally, educational access ensured economic opportunity.

Scholars of the American welfare state emphasize the orientation toward schooling as an individualist alternative to European state spending, with its focus on communal guarantees. In America, we have little inclination to provide "floors"—that is, social guarantees for a minimum standard of living, but most Americans are willing to open "doors" of opportunity by providing education.[10] I argue that attitudes about schooling and social entitlement cannot be understood adequately in dichotomous terms, the commitment to schooling versus state spending for social programs. In the early part of the twentieth century, many American social activists, particularly the progressive maternalists, successfully appealed to widespread norms about the right to schooling in order to foster support for government expansion. Whether they were promoting relief funds for poor mothers or fighting against child labor, reformers tried to show that these government programs were logical outcomes of the entitlement to schooling.

Studying how women campaigned for increased government responsibility in the Progressive era reminds us that although political and cultural values are deeply rooted and can affect political developments, their meanings are not fixed and, as Sidney Tarrow argues, cannot be divorced from agency and strategy. Social movements are not "merely cognitive message centers" about the culture. Their meanings are constructed in the context of specific social and political interactions as activists try to make use of, but also adapt their political rhetoric in light of the power structure, the forces of opposition, and the values of their supporters.[11]

During three decades before World War I, maternalists made use of the politics of gender and schooling in order to move their country away from laissez faire to a new era of social responsibility. The campaign for government payments to poor mothers, known as mothers' or widows' pensions, was part of the mobilization among many middle-class and elite Americans in the 1890s. The economic panic of 1893 was a striking wake-up call to the dangers of relying solely on the free market to ensure prosperity. The specific crisis contributed to a sense of urgency about long-term social trends, including corporate abuse of power, the spread of urban slums, the influx of new immigrants from Southern and Eastern Europe, and increasing labor strife.

Within a decade, vast networks of middle-class women were energetically addressing how these social problems affected women and children. Their work on behalf of family welfare ranged widely and included campaigns to eliminate sweated labor along with projects to teach immigrant mothers "modern" child rearing practices; many of the women staffed urban settlement houses. Reform women also expressed concern about the inadequate sources of relief available to poor families. To aid one important group of poor families—single mothers forced to raise children without male incomes—they endorsed the idea of extending state aid to widowed mothers.

The campaign to aid widowed mothers was related to the growing disenchantment with institutionalization of poor children. By the end of the nineteenth century, efforts to provide adoptive homes for orphan children who had lost both parents were well established but there were also large numbers of children at risk for institutionalization who were not parentless, but fatherless. Given the high mortality of men due to work accidents and poor job conditions, the growing numbers of young, very poor, widowed mothers was a major social problem. By the turn of the twentieth century, many family welfare experts were convinced that, if at all possible, children of widowed mothers should be kept at home, rather than placed in orphanages. This view reflected the growing assumption that working-class mothers were just as vital for proper child rearing as their middle-class counterparts.

The call for state funding to poor mothers centered on coalitions of reformers, including many active in various women's clubs. In states such as Pennsylvania and Illinois, reformers founded mothers' pension leagues to lobby for the initial legislation and then to agitate for increased funding. Organizations were not exclusively female; the pension leagues had men in many supervisory roles, but they all relied heavily on large numbers of activist women, who often belonged to more than one reform group.

Illinois enacted the first mothers' pension law in 1911; two years later, eighteen states had followed suit. By 1920, the vast majority of American states had enacted some sort of mothers' pensions program.[12] In most cases, the laws provided assistance to poor widows, determined to be of "good character" with children of school-age or younger; in some cases, they included mothers whose husbands were physically or mentally incapacitated or imprisoned.[13]

Much has been written about the quick successes of the mothers' pension campaigns in the U.S., a country that at the same time had no health insurance, unemployment insurance, or old age pensions, a nation where many cities actually banned the provision of public money for direct relief to the poor. By the end of the second decade of the twentieth century, the U.S. had in place state-level, publicly financed programs of outdoor relief, that is relief provided outside of institutions such as orphanages, poorhouses, and charity hospitals, to poor families in all parts of the country. Mothers' pensions, were, in fact, the precursors of the Aid to Dependent Children Program, which became federal law during the New Deal, as part of the Social Security Act.

In putting mothers' pensions into place, the women behind the programs not only showed the political power of mobilized women's groups even before suffrage; they also succeeded in broadening women's place in the civic arena. The pension programs depended on the certification of a mother's fitness, so the enhanced need for caseworkers to conduct investigations created vast opportunities for women who went into the burgeoning field of social work. Moreover, in many states, like New York, the law stipulated the appointment of at least some women to the county boards that ruled on the distribution of the pensions. In Pennsylvania, the law required that the Governor appoint a woman in a salaried position as state Supervisor of the county boards.[14]

The quick success of the widows' pensions campaigns can be viewed as a triumph of mobilization that made effective use of popular norms about women's roles and the innocence of children. Such rhetoric, which appealed to traditional ideals of motherhood in order to promote something much less traditional, state-funded aid to poor families, typified middle-class women's effort to build the early American welfare state. The organizations spearheading the fight against women and children's sweated labor, the National

Consumers League (NCL) and the National Child Labor Committee (NCLC), were also dominated by women and made use of similar appeals.

In the early twentieth century, the NCLC and their allies in the NCL campaigned tirelessly against the use of child labor in factories and tenement labor at home. In arguing the case against child labor, progressive women tapped into a growing consensus among prosperous whites, especially in urban America, that all children ought to be protected from working at paid labor.[15] From the 1870s to the 1920s, the proportion of young children in factory work steadily declined. There were certainly some violations of the law, but the widespread use of sophisticated machinery made child labor problematic for manufacturers as well as reformers. In the highly mechanized large steel plants of Pittsburgh, for example, factory work required too much skill and attention for very young workers.

Ending the labor of young adolescents was more difficult. In Pittsburgh glass factories, young adolescent boys could clean blow pieces, close molds, and reheat bottles; they could also do a few unskilled jobs in the metal trades. Girls worked in pickle or cork factories, in laundries, or in retail. New York City provided lots of work for youth in the garment industry and in other consumer goods, which still made use of fairly simple machinery. Girls worked as clothing finishers, box packers and folders, and candy wrappers; boys as machine helpers, carriers, and runners.[16]

Beyond young adolescent labor, reformers faced a massive task eliminating child labor in homework. Immigrant women and their children, working at home on clothing, jewelry, candy, and artificial flowers, played vital roles in important New York City industries. Child labor was a major component of homework enterprises precisely because it was so hard to regulate. In 1908, Mary Van Kleeck noted, despairingly, that "No maker of artificial flowers can employ in his factory any child under fourteen years of age, but he may give out work to an Italian family, in whose tenement rooms flowers are made by six children, aged two and one-half, five, eight, ten, fourteen and sixteen years."[17]

To generate public support for stiffer child labor laws, progressive maternalists, enlisting the aid of important social photographers like Lewis Hine, used powerful images to show how damaging industrial work, both in the factory and at home, could be to children's health. In publicizing the evils of homework to middle-class audiences, the NCL also pointed out that many of the goods sold in stores carried the germs of sweated homeworkers. Since the mid-nineteenth century, both state and federal courts, hostile to labor legislation, had struck down a number of statutes regarding working conditions, but they had made exceptions when it came to issues of public health. Reformers thus not only invoked public health dangers to grab the attention of America's middle class; stressing public health was part of the ongoing legal battle to obtain court approval for the constitutionality of laws at least regulating, if not prohibiting, homework.[18]

Because child labor was inextricably connected to the struggles for economic survival in immigrant communities, women in the anti-sweating campaign also tapped into the growing concern about gender, class, and the immigrant problem. For example, they argued that eliminating homework would help immigrant women become good mothers. When anti-sweating activists could connect the issue of good mothering with fears about disease, the effect was particularly dramatic. Thus, when the public health expert Dr. Annie Daniels testified about diseased conditions among New York City homeworkers to state officials in 1912, she reported on her visit to one tenement where a child was gravely ill with tuberculosis. The mother "hardly stopped her work while the child was dying. She was finishing trousers. Q[uestion]. And the child was dying? A[nswer]. The child was dying. Q. And the woman did not stop work? A. She could not."[19]

Along with appeals to motherhood and the innocence of children, women reformers generated support for government relief and anti-sweating laws by focusing on the American appreciation for widespread education. In her excellent analysis of the mothers' pensions movement, Gwendolyn Mink rightly emphasizes the value that American maternalists, in contrast to their European counterparts, placed on schooling. She argues that in addition to reflecting the American preference for education rather than social entitlements, the focus on schooling reinforced the cultural strategy that lay behind the various social service programs. Just as maternalists designed mothers' pensions programs to encourage good mothering, they also tried to get immigrant girls into the public school classrooms so they could learn could learn white, elite values regarding mothering.[20]

A broad coalition of maternalist reformers and organizations certainly supported expanding education; however, their priorities often differed. For educators such as Frances Kellor, ensuring that children attend school was critical to the assimilation process. But the emphasis on immigrant education in the case of Florence Kelley, Executive Director of the National Consumer's League, whose lifelong priority was the eradication of sweated labor, was part of a different social and political project. While all maternalists sought to help the poor by spreading dominant norms about family life, progressive maternalists interested in building a welfare state were also challenging some important elite ideals, in particular, a hostility to government responsibility for social welfare. To legitimize government relief programs and state regulation of the workplace, progressive maternalists appealed to another widely shared value, already codified in state laws; that is, government's responsibility for ensuring educational opportunity.

How the campaign on behalf of mothers' pensions was couched as a vehicle for advancing education is one excellent example of this strategy. At the Third New York City Conference on Charities and Corrections in 1912, the majority report of the Committee on Governmental Aid to Widows came out in favor of state-funded mothers' pensions. They reasoned that children should be kept with the mothers, that private charities were no longer able to administer enough relief to ensure that this was possible, and that "through the enforcement of the compulsory education act, the State or the political divisions of the State are rendered responsible for the proper support of dependent families in which children of school age are found."[21]

The New York State Commission on Relief for Widowed Mothers took up the same argument in 1914, when it proposed the state law, declaring that pensions for widows were not outright gifts to poor adults, something they knew was controversial, but, rather, extensions of the American commitment to educate children:

> The duty of the State of New York to alleviate the condition of the adult poor is a debatable question, but that it is morally obligated to care for the dependent child cannot be doubted. This principle has always been recognized by our government; indeed, it is but the counterpart of its right to compel all children to be educated in the public schools. Therefore, the purpose [of widows' pensions] is not to impose any new duty upon the State, but rather, to bring the performance of an established and inherent standard of efficiency and adequacy that will conform with our wisest conceptions of the proper method of rearing the best citizens of the future.[22]

Maternalists often used educational discourse in characterizing mothers' pension programs, referring to them as home scholarships or school pensions. Whether they emphasized motherhood, deserving widowhood, the innocence of children, or the importance of schooling, depended on time and context. In a 1913 lecture at Columbia Teacher's College, Florence Kelley noted that the movement for mothers' pensions or parents' aid was so widespread, nationally, that states, cities, and charitable organizations were vying with one another "in assuring us that no child be undernourished or unfitted for school life by reason of destitution." One year earlier, when Kelley encountered strong opposition to mothers' pensions at the New York City Conference on Charities she referred to them as "school pensions," which she went on to say "is no new sudden demand. It is an integral part of the effort to deal effectively with the interlocking evils of child labor, irregular school attendance and dependence."[23]

Women also faced formidable resistance in the fight for labor laws. Judges reluctant to sanction state regulations were backed by business interests and their allies. All thought such statutes interfered with the property rights of owners to hire whom they pleased. Furthermore, many ordinary Americans, including immigrants, believed that eliminating child labor interfered with the right of parents to put their children to work. To counter these arguments, progressive maternalists often pointed out that large numbers of children doing work at home and the widespread employment of young adolescents in factories were threats to another of the most fundamental of American rights, that of education for all children. When New York took an early lead in introducing factory inspectors to enforce child labor laws, state officials explained this new interference with both the rights of property owners and the privacy rights of parents by appealing to the larger community's interest in education, which had already been legally established. As the inspectors noted in their Second Annual Report of 1887, "The Compulsory Education Law practically makes it everybody's business to see that it [the Penal Code that protects children from doing machine labor] is enforced."[24]

In arguing their case for greater government intervention with both the rights of employers and parents, activists in the anti-child labor campaign did not hesitate in reaching out to those who looked to the schools to Americanize immigrants. Settlement house leader Lillian Wald certainly used this approach when testifying to a New York legislative committee set up to investigate sweated labor conditions following the deadly Triangle Shirtwaist Fire in 1911. During public hearings, Wald called upon the Commission to look into homework because "If, as I hope you will, recommend a thorough investigation of this [homework] problem, you will find that our desire to have the children educated for citizenship is nullified to a great extent among the [very] children whom we greatly desire to have all the advantages of their few years of schooling."[25] In justifying their recommendations for new laws, the Commission pointed both to government's responsibility to provide schooling as well as to ensure public health. "The Commission does not believe that the sacred right of parents to order the conduct of their offspring is such that it permits them to require of their very young children incessant toil for long hours to the injury of their health and the prevention of their receiving sufficient education."[26]

The appeal to dominant values regarding education was not only important as a political strategy. In expanding, bit by bit, the welfare state, Americans began with the education bureaucracy. Some states, as part of their compulsory education laws, had already been providing outdoor relief in the form of clothing and books for needy children so that they could attend school. In Oklahoma, Michigan, and New Hampshire, expanded funds for widows' pensions passed as part of the state education programs and were designed to pay scholarships so that children under sixteen would not have to work to assist their widowed mothers. Many states administered their mothers' pension programs through the juvenile courts in coordination with public school bureaucracies. Pennsylvania's law charged the state Department of Public Instruction with supervising the local boards and their staffs. Pennsylvania was also one of several states whose mothers' pension laws stipulated that in order for the mother to receive aid, school-age children must be certified as attending school. So too, in Delaware, in order to qualify for aid, a mother needed to show that she could not "support, maintain or educate her children."[27]

Reformers struggling to improve the enforcement of child labor laws and to broaden their reach also relied on the school system, which, unlike in England or France, was the only reasonably well-funded bureaucracy available to them. As Florence Kelley put it so well in 1905, "The best child-labor law is a compulsory education law covering forty weeks of the year and requiring consecutive attendance of all the children to the age of fourteen years."[28] How much the maternalists relied on school officials is illustrated by the state of Pennsylvania. At the second annual meeting of the NCLC, Laura Platt, member of the Pennsylvania branch of the organization, reported that in mobilizing support for a new anti-child labor bill, the group solicited help from school superintendents across the state, and a number of teachers, as well as other organizations, including Pittsburgh women's clubs. After the new law, which raised the legal age for work from thirteen to fourteen, was enacted in 1905, the state Bureau of Compulsory Education was charged with issuing employment certificates verifying the legality of teenage workers. The Child Labor Committee, which was "primarily responsible for the certificate features of the new law," and more so than any officials, "had more clearly in mind as to the details," met with local school superintendents, who were now in charge of issuing the employment certificates, to advise and interpret the law for them.[29] By the 1920s, most states had set a minimum age of fourteen for industrial employment, with state or local school officials in charge of issuing employment certificates to working youth.

Neither the popularity of mothers, the innocence of children, or the commitment to universal education led to an adequate program of relief to poor widows and their families, nor did it end sweated labor. Focusing on women's needs, rather than their rights, maternalist discourse, as Linda Gordon has so well argued, was part of a complex effort on the part of activist women to foster a new American commitment to social rights, but relying on this approach "weakened the claim of entitlement." Because the mothers' pensions campaign tended to rely on pity and compassion for women and children, they helped create support for "an allowable state function, but not an obligatory one."[30] The aversion to any large-scale relief remained, and along with widespread fears that generous programs would encourage dependency, kept the programs restrictive and very poorly funded.

Mothers' pensions discriminated by race and ethnicity. Sometimes, southern European immigrants received less funding than immigrants from northern Europe, and Mexicans often received none. In 1916, the Allegheny Mothers' Pension League proudly announced that in reviewing applications, "absolute fairness has been the rule. The first and last mothers recommended were colored women." In truth, maternalist ideology was deeply racialized, to borrow Eileen Boris's term, and affected mothers' pension programs.[31] In some states African-American women received no aid; in others, they received less money than whites on the grounds that blacks were accustomed to a lower standard of living. White Americans expected that black mothers would work, and maternalists felt little urgency about providing the resources to allow black women to stay at home.[32]

Regardless of ethnicity or race, while the pension programs may have kept children out of the orphanages, they did not eliminate the need for mothers to do wage work. This failure left their most ardent proponents deeply disappointed. Most believed that a successful program would have at least provided the possibility for widows to work part-time at home, as laundresses, perhaps, or janitors, rather than do outside labor. But most pension recipients were forced to do domestic service, or sweated garment work at home, often doing more than one job.[33] Despite the rhetoric about mothers' pensions and educational opportunity, the lack of adequate financing thus undermined its purpose as a scholarship program. Not only were mothers forced to put their young children to work at home, they were also under pressure to put their adolescent children into factories as soon as possible.

Maternalist efforts notwithstanding, poor mothers in many parts of the country could put their children to work with relative ease; depending on the schools to regulate child labor meant relying on state bureaucracies and the local school boards, whose policies varied a great deal. Moreover, even in states that had led the nation in passing new laws, there were other interests more powerful than the ability of reformers to appeal to norms regarding motherhood or schooling. Because of its importance to the men's garment industry in New York, for example, child labor in homework flourished until the New Deal.

In the 1920s, most states mandated school attendance to age fourteen, yet lots of underage children still did paid labor, because many states did not enforce either the school or work laws. Furthermore, employment certification and factory inspection applied only to industry and mining. Vast numbers of children, particularly African-American youngsters in the South, worked unprotected by labor laws in agriculture and domestic service.

The powerful resurgence of conservative forces in the 1920s put maternalists, along with others interested in building the welfare state, on the defensive. Unable to extend income support programs or workplace regulation, social activists would have to wait until the Great Depression made the more expansive views of government that characterized the New Deal possible.

In the new historical context of the Depression, business interests, unable to deliver on their promise of prosperity, were weakened. Maternalists and other social reformers entered into powerful coalitions, which included a strong labor movement, now willing to embrace more government guarantees of income as well as workplace regulations, and well-placed officials in the New Deal government. During the New Deal, the United States enacted for the first time national level income support programs in the form of old age pensions and unemployment insurance. The country also established national protective labor legislation that, among other things, banned child labor in industries across the country. The New Deal legislation did not cover all who needed benefits, but the national programs were better enforced and more effective than the state-level initiatives that characterized the Progressive period.

During the Depression, campaigns promoting government intervention in the market relied less on the appeals about safeguarding motherhood, or expanding educational opportunities for children. Government had a right and a responsibility, activists now argued, to regulate the economy in order to diminish the current crisis and prevent a new one. Not only was this argument effective with much of the voting public; by the end of the 1930s, American courts also embraced the new view of government's role in the economy, reversing their long-held hostility to regulations. Under these circumstances, the politics of maternalism and schooling were not as crucial to building the welfare state as they had been a generation earlier.

Yet traditional notions regarding gender and schooling continued to shape the American welfare state. Both female and male activists still assumed that most women would, and should, spend most of their adult lives as domestic caretakers. Government officials and many of their liberal allies thus defined the economic crisis first and foremost as a crisis of the male breadwinner. The national welfare policies put into place focused on sustaining family welfare by offering programs that would directly benefit male household heads. Maternalists, who had so long been concerned about poor single mothers, achieved an important victory when the Social Security Act of 1935 included the Aid to Dependent Children statute, a national program to help states with their mothers' pension initiatives. But with most resources going elsewhere, ADC was plagued from the beginning with problems of underfunding and states continued to exercise tremendous discretion in setting payment levels and eligibility rules.

If the commitment to traditional gender roles remained during the Depression, so too, did the American commitment to schooling. When the economic crisis itself, and then New Deal protective labor legislation, made it increasingly difficult for teenagers to find work, American youth surged into high schools. Even during this financial crisis, public spending on school expansion exploded. American increases in school attendance during the 1930s far outstripped those in England and France, even though all three countries were experiencing a crisis of youth unemployment.[34] During the post–World War II years, when the conservative political climate turned against direct income support programs in the U.S., liberals relied heavily on the Americans' faith in and commitment to schooling, just as they had before the Depression, to expand government. In post-war Europe, while governments enacted numerous new social entitlement programs, they placed little priority on expanding access to education. By contrast, here at home, liberals extended educational opportunities for millions of ordinary Americans to attend college and graduate school by arguing that massive federal funding for education was necessary in order to have the technical expertise to fight communism.

Looking back from the vantage point of the early twenty-first century, we can easily conclude that the politics of maternalism and schooling were only partially successful in establishing greater government responsibility for social welfare. In reinforcing traditional gender roles, the politics of maternalism was not only detrimental to enhancing meaningful opportunities for women; in the last decades of the twentieth century, it seemed increasingly out of step with the realities of American life. While American school systems continued their expansion in the second half of the twentieth century, they remained hampered by tremendously unequal funding. To note that our schools have been unable to guarantee equal opportunity to jobs and a decent standard of living is to state the obvious. In today's America, however, when the celebration of market values seems limitless, even encroaching on our traditional commitment to public schooling, we can appreciate the efforts of progressive women who, one hundred years ago, used the political and cultural values of the society—middle-class ideals surrounding maternalism and the American commitment to schooling—in order to chip away at a most formidable American institution, laissez-faire government.

Notes

1. "Report of the Propaganda Committee," *Report of the Mothers' Pension League of Allegheny County*, 1915–16 (Pittsburgh, PA.), n.p.
2. Molly Ladd-Taylor, *Mother-Work: Women, Child Welfare, and the State, 1890–1933* (Urbana: University of Illinois Press, 1994), Chapters 1, 3.
3. The larger study, co-authored with Michael Hanagan, "Families, Reformers and the State: A Comparative History of the Welfare State in England, France, and the United States," involves a comparison of national policies in England, France and

the United States and a detailed look at the politics and policies enacted in two cities for each country. In addition to Pittsburgh and New York City, we look at Birmingham and London in England, Paris and St. Etienne in France.

4. For an elaboration of this comparison, see Miriam Cohen and Michael Hanagan, "The Politics of Gender in the Making of the Welfare State in England, France and the United States," *Journal of Social History* 24 (Spring, 1991), 469–84. See also Kathryn Sklar, "Historical Foundations of Women's Power in the Creation of the Welfare State," in *Mothers of a New World: Maternalist Politics and the Origins of Welfare States*, Seth Koven and Sonya Michel, eds. (New York: Routledge, 1993), 43–93.

5. An excellent discussion of progressive maternalists as feminists can be found in Linda Gordon, *Pitied But Not Entitled: Single Mothers and the History of Welfare* (New York: The Free Press, 1994), Chapters 1, 2. In her recent history of women in the American labor movement, Dorothy Sue Cobble makes a powerful case for understanding the multiple forms of feminism. See *The Other Women's Movement: Workplace Justice and Social Rights in Modern America* (Princeton: Princeton University Press, 2004). On the history of women's special role in the politics of the welfare state and women's particular perspective, see, for example, Robyn Muncy, *Creating a Female Dominion in American Reform, 1890–1935* (New York: Oxford University Press, 1991), along with Ladd-Taylor, *Mother-Work*; Sklar, "Historical Foundations."

6. Rebecca Edwards, *Angels in the Machinery: Gender in American Party Politics from the Civil War to the Progressive Era* (New York: Oxford University Press, 1997), 8, 172, 173. On the pragmatism of women activists, see Cobble, *The Other Woman's Movement*; Robyn Rosen, "Federal Expansion, Fertility Control and Physicians in the United States: the Politics of Maternal Welfare in the Interwar Years," *Journal of Women's History* 10:3 (Autumn, 1998), 53–73.

7. The importance of understanding the multifaceted nature of women's politics is explored in Nancy Cott, "What's In A Name?: The Limits of 'Social Feminism' or Expanding the Vocabulary of Women's History," *Journal of American History* 76:3 (December, 1989), 809–829. On how the priority that progressive maternalists placed on building social programs for the poor influenced their approach to various reforms see Sklar, "The Historical Foundations." See also Landon Storrs, *Civilizing Capitalism: The National Consumer's League, Women's Activism and Labor Standards in the New Deal Era* (Chapel Hill: University of North Carolina Press, 2000).

8. My analysis of the strategic ways that social and political activists name injustices and propose solutions, by "finding symbols that are familiar enough to mobilize people" (119), is most heavily influenced by Sidney Tarrow, *Power in Movement: Social Movements, Collective Action and Politics* (New York: Cambridge University Press, 1994), Chapter 7.

9. Lizabeth Cohen, *A Consumer's Republic: The Politics of Mass Consumption in Postwar America* (Cambridge: Harvard University Press, 2003), 244; Ira Katznelson and Margaret Weir, *Schooling for All: Class, Race, and the Decline of the Democratic Ideal* (New York: Basic Books, 1985).

10. James Patterson, "Floors and Doors," Chap. 12 in *America's Struggle Against Poverty, 1900–1994* (Cambridge: Harvard University Press, 1994); Arnold J. Heidenhammer, "Education and Social Security Entitlements in Europe and America," in *The Development of Welfare States in Europe and America*, Peter Flora and Arnold Heidenhammer, eds., 269–304 (New Brunswick, NJ: Transaction Books, 1981).

11. Tarrow, *Power in Movement*, 119, 121–23.

12. Theda Skocpol, *Protecting Soldiers and Mothers: The Political Origins of Social Policy in the United States* (Cambridge: Harvard University Press, 1992), 466, 426.

13. U.S. Children's Bureau, *Laws Relating to "Mothers' Pensions" in the United States, Canada, Denmark, and New Zealand* Legal Series No. 4, Bureau Publication No. 63, Compiled by Laura A. Thompson (Washington D.C.: U.S. Government Printing Office, 1919), 12.

14. State of New York, State Board of Charities, *The Hill-McCue Bill for the Relief of Children of Widowed Mothers* (Albany, NY: J. B. Lyon, 1915), 2; Mothers Pension Act–No. 439–An Act approved, April 29, 1913; *Allegheny County Mothers' Pension League Report*, 1915/1916, n.p.

15. Viviana A. Zelizer, *Pricing the Priceless Child: The Changing Social Value of Children*, 2nd ed. (Princeton: Princeton University Press, 1994).

16. Miriam Cohen, *Workshop to Office: Two Generations of Italian Women in New York, 1900–1950* (Ithaca, NY: Cornell University Press, 1992), Chapters 2, 4; Miriam Cohen and Michael Hanagan, "Work, School and Reform: A Comparison of Birmingham, England and Pittsburgh, USA, 1900–1950," *International Labor and Working Class History* 40 (Fall, 1991), 67–80.

17. M. Van Kleeck, "Child Labor in New York City Tenements," *Charities and the Common*, 19 (January 18, 1908), 1405.

18. On the efforts of reformers to establish that poor working conditions were a matter of public health, see Eileen Boris, *Home to Work: Motherhood and the Politics of Homework in the United States* (New York: Cambridge University Press, 1994).

19. New York State Factory Investigating Commission, *Second Report of the Factory Investigating Commission*, 3 (Albany, NY: J.B. Lyon, 1913), 98.

20. Gwendolyn Mink, *The Wages of Motherhood: Inequality in the Welfare State, 1917–1942* (Ithaca, NY: Cornell University Press, 1995), 78.

21. Third New York City Conference of Charities and Corrections, *Proceedings* (Albany, NY: J. B. Lyon, 1912), 95.

22. State of New York, *Report of the New York State Commission on Relief for Widowed Mothers*, transmitted to the legislature, March 27, 1914 (New York: Arno Press, 1974, c.1914), 19.

23. Florence Kelley, *Modern Industry, in Relation to the Family, Health, Education and Morality* (New York: Longmans, Green, 1914), 9; Third New York City Conference of Charities and Corrections, *Proceedings*, 79.

24. "Second Annual Report of the Factory Inspectors of the State of New York, for the Year Ending December 1, 1887," *The Child and the State*, Vol. 1, *Legal Status in the Family, Apprenticeship and Child Labor, Select Documents and Introductory Notes*, Grace Abbott, ed. (Chicago: University of Chicago Press, 1938), 416.

25. New York State, Factory Investigating Commission, *Public Hearings in New York City, Second Series*, reprint from the *Preliminary Report of the New York State Factory Investigating Commission* (Albany, NY: J. B. Lyon, October 1912), 1740.

26. New York State, *Preliminary Report of the New York State Factory Investigating Commission*, Vol. 1. (Albany, NY: J. B. Lyon, 1912), 89.

27. State of New York, *Report of the New York State Commission*, 165–66; Third New York City Conference of Charities and Corrections, *Proceedings*, 1912, 79; *Allegheny County Mothers' Pension League Report*, 1915/1916; State of New York, State Board of Charities, "Senator William Hill's Letter to Governor Whitman, Memoranda of Conditions Upon Which Relief is Granted in Other States" (Albany, NY, April 1, 1915), 14–16; U.S. Children's Bureau, *Laws Relating to "Mothers' Pensions" in the United States, Canada, Denmark, and New Zealand*, 13; Commonwealth of Pennsylvania, Department of Public Welfare, *Public Welfare in Pennsylvania, 1696–1966: A Chronology* (Harrisburg, 1969), 19; Skocpol, *Protecting Soldiers and Mothers*, 428.

28. Florence Kelley, *Some Ethical Gains Through Legislation* (New York: Macmillan Company, 1905), 96.

29. National Child Labor Committee, "Reports from State Committees," *Child Labor* (American Academy of Political and Social Science, 1906), 130, 131.

30. Linda Gordon, *Pitied But Not Entitled,* 66.

31. *Allegheny County Mothers Pension League Report, 1916/1916,* n.p. "'You Wouldn't Want One of 'Em Dancing with your Wife': Racialized Bodies on the Job in World War II," *American Quarterly* 50, 1 (1998), 77–108.

32. Gordon, *Pitied But Not Entitled,* 47, 48; Joanne Goodwin, *Gender and the Politics of Welfare Reform, Mothers' Pensions in Chicago* (Chicago: University of Chicago Press, 1997), 162–164; Mink, *The Wages of Motherhood,* 50.

33. Goodwin, *Gender and the Politics,* 170–71.

34. For an extensive discussion of the role of schooling during the Great Depression in England, France, and the United States see Cohen and Hanagan, "Families, Reformers and the State," not yet published.

Suggestions for Further Reading

Boris, Eileen. *Home to Work: Motherhood and the Politics of Homework in the United States.* New York: Cambridge University Press, 1994.

Cohen, Miriam, and Michael Hanagan. "The Politics of Gender in the Making of the Welfare State in England, France and the United States." *Journal of Social History* 24 (Spring, 1991), 469–84.

———. "Work, School and Reform: A Comparison of Birmingham, England and Pittsburgh, USA, 1900–1950." *International Labor and Working Class History* 40 (Fall, 1991), 67–80.

Felt, Jeremy P. *Hostages of Fortune: Child Labor in New York State.* Syracuse, NY: Syracuse University Press, 1965.

Goodwin, Joanne L. *Gender and the Politics of Welfare Reform: Mothers' Pensions in Chicago.* Chicago: University of Chicago Press, 1997.

Gordon, Linda. *Pitied But Not Entitled: Single Mothers and the History of Welfare.* New York: The Free Press, 1994.

Katznelson, Ira, and Margaret Weir, *Schooling for All: Class, Race, and the Decline of the Democratic Ideal.* New York: Basic Books, 1985.

Kessler-Harris, Alice. *In Pursuit of Equity: Women, Men and the Quest for Economic Citizenship in 20th Century America.* New York: Oxford University Press, 2001

Ladd-Taylor, Molly. *Mother–Work: Women, Child Welfare and the State.* Urbana: University of Illinois Press, 1994.

Michel, Sonya, and Seth Koven, eds., *Mothers of a New World: Maternalist Politics and the Origins of Welfare States.* New York: Routledge, 1993.

Mink, Gwendolyn. *The Wages of Motherhood: Inequality and the Welfare State.* Ithaca, NY: Cornell University Press, 1995.

Sklar, Kathryn Kish. *Florence Kelley and the Nation's Work: The Rise of Women's Political Culture, 1830–1900.* New Haven: Yale University Press, 1995.

Trattner, Walter I. *Crusade for the Children: A History of the National Child Labor Committee.* Chicago: Quadrangle Books, 1970.

Zelizer, Viviana A. *Pricing the Priceless Child: The Changing Social Value of Children.* 2nd ed. Princeton: Princeton University Press, 1994.

Women's History with the Politics Left IN: Feminist Studies of the U.S. Welfare State

Felicia A. Kornbluh

Felicia A. Kornbluh (1996) is Assistant Professor of History at Duke University. Her book *The Rise and Fall of Welfare Rights: Gender, Law, and Poverty in Postwar America* is forthcoming. She has published in a range of academic and nonacademic journals, including the *Women's Review of Books*, the *Nation, Feminist Studies*, the *Los Angeles Times Op-Ed Page*, and the *Journal of the History of Sexuality*. Kornbluh is an active member of the Women's Committee of 100, a welfare advocacy group, and is the Secretary of the Board of Directors of Genesis Home, a family shelter and child care center in Durham, North Carolina.

> *In the decade or so that she has been a professional historian, Felicia Korn-bluh has seen questions about women and state policy become absolutely central. "The left feminists who once wrote about women and work have largely moved to considering women's (and men's) relationships with state policy and judge-made law. Many have moved from studying women as waged workers to studying women as mothers whose lives shape and are shaped by labor-market policies. And many of us have studied state policy toward women who work as mothers, who receive little income from the labor market or from male partners, and who rely for help on government transfer programs."*

In 1967, a poor woman from Mount Vernon, New York, took the welfare department to court. With help from an activist lawyer, Joyce Johnson brought a "fair hearing" to get an increase in her grant and to spur changes in the way women and men in the bureaucracy routinely treated their clients. Johnson stepped onto a historical stage that had been set by a mass movement of women like herself who demanded what they called welfare rights. The record of her hearing offers a rare glimpse of public policy as seen by an African-American recipient of government aid in the years after women reformers helped write the Social Security Act of 1935. Johnson remembered the home visit her case worker, Miss Demo, made to decide how to answer some of Johnson's requests. Demo, she said, "arrived at my home approximately eleven o'clock and she left at approximately ten after two in the afternoon":

> Well, at my kitchen table we sat down and we talked about, of course, my children, the health of my children, the things that I needed in the apartment. She took a tour, accompanied by me of my apartment. She went into every closet, she ripped the sheets off every bed. . . . Of course, I let her do this. I had to open up the castro-convertible couch which was in my living room to show her what was on that. She asked me who was using it; I told her I was sleeping on it. We went back to the table after the tour of my home. We sat down. She asked me, "What are your dire needs? I told her I needed a dresser for my girls' room, my room and my son's room, which is the baby. She said, "Okay." She wrote it down. I said, "I need sheets." I said, "I really need a bed for myself." . . . She said, "You can't buy a bed. Buy kingsize sheets instead; it's cheaper for the Department of Welfare. Buy king-size sheets instead of the bed." I agreed with that. What could I do?[1]

Johnson may have exaggerated Miss Demo's heartlessness. But even if it only reveals her own impressions (as shaped by welfare rights rhetoric and legal conventions), her story tells something of the distance social welfare had traveled from its optimistic origins in the first third of the twentieth century to a period only a generation later.

Like other dissatisfied welfare clients in the 1960s, Joyce Johnson was caught in the gap between what the welfare system promised and what it actually delivered. She was a recipient of the federal program Aid to Dependent Children (ADC), created in 1935 with the mandate to help mothers when they did not have husbands or boyfriends to help them economically. ADC grew from decades of activism by women who claimed that the capacity to raise children made mothers valuable as citizens and worthy of financial aid. But Johnson and other welfare mothers spoke eloquently about the ways they believed the system blocked their efforts to be good parents. Woven into the ideal of family aid were power relations between budget-conscious and moralistic governments (represented by social workers) and their citizens.[2] (For further discussion, see Miriam Cohen's essay on the pre–New Deal period and Ellen Reese's on the post–New Deal period, in this volume.)

Welfare changed dramatically in the generation after Joyce Johnson's lament. In 1996, President Clinton signed legislation that undid many of the admittedly partial achievements of the early-twentieth-century activists. President and Congress together expunged Aid to Families with Dependent Children (AFDC) from the statute books, and with it the statutory commitment to mothers raising their own children in their own homes. The replacement was Temporary Assistance to Needy Families, a limited grant program whose stated objectives were to place poor people in the waged labor market and to make them marry one another.[3]

Post-1996, pro-welfare activists could hardly help looking nostalgically at the very circumstances that drove Joyce Johnson 'round the bend. The 1960s appear in hindsight as a golden age of public generosity and deep pockets, a time when "welfare reform" at least sometimes meant pushing for more social provisions rather than less. Incidents like Johnson's day in court, and the large-scale welfare rights effort that informed it, may inspire not only nostalgia but incredulity. From where we sit today it is literally hard to believe that women of color without any money could ever have made much space for themselves in the public arena, or that powerful wealthy white people would ever have ceded it to them.

Feminist students of modern politics inevitably wrestle with the ambiguous legacy of twentieth-century social welfare. How do we explain the good and the bad of public policy toward women? What was it about the political mix at the very beginning of the century that made every succeeding moment— from the proto-welfare programs of the Progressive 1910s, to the New Deal's Social Security Act, to the post–New Deal world of welfare administration that Joyce Johnson encountered—so tangled? How did these tangles produce both a robust movement for welfare rights and, a blink of an eye later, the end of welfare as Bill Clinton knew it? Finally, how do we assess this history, with its leitmotif of big promises and big disappointments?

In the 1970s and 1980s, most feminist scholars in the United States understood welfare as an instrument of "public patriarchy," social control, and sexual regulation.[4] Beginning in the Reagan years, thinkers such as Barbara Ehrenreich, Zillah Eisenstein, and Diana Pearce broadcast their sense that cutbacks in social welfare programs represented a form of anti-feminist attack.[5] The most recent wave of scholarly writing, which began with Linda Gordon's family violence study, *Heroes of Their Own Lives*,[6] turned this negative conclusion into a positive and thus stood the old normative reading of welfare on its head: If anti-welfare policy is a form of antifeminism, then maybe welfare is something for which feminists should be willing to fight.

This most recent generation of scholarship is rich with paradoxes. Rather than looking through the progressive rhetoric of welfare to find the repressive apparatus hidden beneath, many feminist scholars have learned to emphasize the simultaneity of progressive and repressive strands in welfare systems. We downplay a determinist or functionalist understanding of the purpose of the welfare state, emphasizing instead the historical contingency and fluidity that have characterized all welfare systems. Our understandings of the relationship between middle-class welfare workers and working-class clients have evolved as well. From a fairly simple one-way street of domination, many have come to see a complex field that includes the inchoate resistance of clients and the gender-based pressures on the vast majority of caseworkers—no doubt including Mount Vernon's Miss Demo—who have been women with tenuous claims to professional status. Adding to these complications, feminist historians have rediscovered generations of women activists and bureaucrats who helped create the "patriarchal" welfare state and may have been responsible for its most blatant sex-specific policies.

INTELLECTUAL BACKGROUND
TO THE NEW WELFARE LITERATURE

In addition to its immediate political precipitant in benefit cutbacks, this new wave of writing on welfare states results from diverse currents of change in historical scholarship, feminist theory, and state theory. The first of these currents is an emergent effort on the part of many scholars to practice women's history with the politics left in.[7] The political women's history of today offers new readings of "high," electoral or bureaucratic, politics and redefines the political to include women's unpaid activities in civil society.[8] The second is the slow process of freeing U.S. history from its American Exceptionalist moorings.[9] The post–World War II scholarly generation often overemphasized differences between the U.S. and European industrial states, on the one hand, and the impoverished "Third World," on the other. In recent years, those of us who study the U.S. past have learned to recognize the similarities among national histories, rather than fetishizing differences. As we have rediscovered ideological formations in the United States that resemble European fascism, and foreign policies that resemble European imperialism, scholars on this side of the Atlantic have belatedly come to see our social benefits as a welfare state that can stand comparison with the British, Swedish, or French.

Although the center of this new work is the relationship between gender and state politics, it is not beholden to any one school of contemporary feminist theory. Interestingly, post-structuralist theoretical innovations have had only a limited influence on feminist welfare scholars. To be sure, these scholars are cautious in treating working-class women's "experience" and resist totalizing statements about the ultimate foundations of the welfare state. However, they dwell relatively little on the autonomous power of language to shape social life or presage historical outcomes.[10] Unlike such theorists as Wendy Brown, whose 1992 *Feminist Studies* article warned that state-based political strategies were likely to enhance disciplinary surveillance of women while drawing us into an (almost) ineffably "masculinist state,"[11] the new welfare scholars see little danger in women's engagement with state policy *per se*. In other words, while recognizing that women like Joyce Johnson were often treated unkindly by government officials and social workers, we still value the work it took to create AFDC, as well as Johnson's work both to get public aid and to complain about its worst features.

The pragmatic focus of this literature owes much to recent developments in state theory. The relevant conversation began in the early 1970s, with the first neo-Marxist suggestions that a national government might be more (or less) than a simple tool of the capitalist ruling class. Theorists discovered that, at least in the short run, government activities could depart dramatically from the material interests of the wealthy and that bureaucrats and politicians could pursue distinct interests of their own.[12] Critics and historians of Western social policies initially identified welfare benefits as means of stabilizing the labor market and obscuring more venal state practices. By the late 1970s, however, some New Left and neo-Marxian scholars, such as James O'Connor, saw welfare instead as a disruptive force, the source of a "fiscal crisis of the state" that could erode the legitimacy of the capitalist/democratic *status quo*. In the early 1980s, the leading welfare scholars in this left tradition, Frances Fox Piven and Richard Cloward, rewrote welfare history to emphasize the role of state transfer payments in increasing wages and enhancing the bargaining power of working people.[13]

To this already weakened edifice of Marxian theory, the historical sociologist Theda Skocpol delivered a series of blows that threatened to bring it tumbling down. "[C]apitalism in general has no politics," she argued in 1980, "only (extremely flexible) outer limits. . . . State structures and party organizations have (to a very significant degree) independent histories."[14] This insight redirected the focus of study, from whether and how economic elites could determine political outcomes, to the emergence of particular government policies from particular governments.[15] In Skocpol's vision, the shape of a government in itself—which she takes as mostly invariant over time, that is, the United States possesses a decentralized, weakly bureaucratic "Tudor polity," whereas historic monarchies like Sweden and France have strong central states—has enormous weight in shaping public policy. State structure plus conventional politics (negotiations and conflicts among politicians, bureaucrats, and elite interest groups) explain most policy outcomes. In her major work on welfare history, *Protecting Soldiers and Mothers*, Skocpol introduced the term "structured polity" to describe the mix of political autonomy and social and economic forces that produce policy.[16] However, just as the neo-Marxists admitted the "relative autonomy" of politics while arguing for "determination in the last instance" by economic power, Skocpol cries "structured polity" while clearly privileging "polity" over "structure."[17]

Neither neo-Marxists nor Skocpolians offered a model that entirely works for feminist students of welfare. However, the emphasis of both on determination and autonomy, in combination with the postmodern suspicion of theories that make social life sum up into a neat coherent whole, has helped in describing the complex historical relationships between masculine power and government policy.

MATERNALISM AND MATERNALISTS

In line with their reappraisals of welfare policies, many scholars have reassessed the reform work of white bourgeois women in the late nineteenth and early twentieth centuries. These were the women who ultimately made AFDC, and would have been distressed by the way it was implemented in 1960s Mount Vernon. Joanne Goodwin, Sonya Michel, Gwendolyn Mink, Molly Ladd-Taylor, Linda Gordon, Kathryn Kish Sklar, and Skocpol all recognize the work of such women, whom they term "maternalists," as a remarkable historical occurrence.[18] On the other hand, the historian and civil rights lawyer Mary Frances Berry argues that such reformers did not differ appreciably from their nineteenth-century white bourgeois predecessors.[19]

Chroniclers of maternalism have devised various definitions of the term. While some historians have tried to find the common philosophical or strategic thread that united all these reformers, Ladd-Taylor distinguishes among three types of maternalists: *sentimental, progressive,* and *feminist.* Skocpol helps clarify the term by comparing maternalism to "paternalism." "Pioneering European and Australasian welfare states," she writes in *Protecting Soldiers and Mothers,* "were doubly paternalist."[20] As they were paternalist in two ways—in their content, which treated men as fathers and heads of families, and in their processes of creation, which were largely closed to their putative working-class beneficiaries—so were maternalist policies maternalist in two ways. In content, they treated women as mothers who made claims on the state thereby; in their processes of creation, they were designed by ambitious middle-class women for working-class women, with the latter's perceived best interests in mind.

Maternalist reformers may be familiar to some readers, who know them as "social feminists,"[21] or as the fractious, exhausted, post-suffrage women's movement. Readers may also hear in maternalism, which simultaneously justified a public role for women and affirmed women's primary responsibility for children, echoes of what historians of the early national United States have termed "republican motherhood." However, we may distinguish maternalism from social feminism, republican motherhood, and other reform ideologies by emphasizing its special, time-bound contribution to political thought. The great political struggles of the late eighteenth and early nineteenth centuries were republican and democratic; republican motherhood answered the question of women's role in the American Revolution and the expansions of democratic participation that followed.[22] The struggles of the turn of the twentieth century concerned the parameters of national citizenship in an industrial republic; maternalism answered the question of women's place in that polity although most did not participate continuously in the waged labor market and virtually none served the nation as soldiers.

WOMEN REFORMERS AND THE GENDERED STATE

The women who participated in maternalist politics were a relatively homogeneous lot. They were settlement house residents, authors of children's welfare bills in the states, professors at the School of Social Service Administration (social work) at the University of Chicago, and officials of the federal Children's Bureau. Nearly all were from wealthy, Northern European, Protestant backgrounds, and the parents of many had been abolitionists and/or charitable reformers. Gordon notes that the few Jews and Catholics among them were likely to have been born in the United States and well-off financially.[23] These women valued education and expertise and possessed a remarkable share of each. They formed a "women's network" shaped by common characteristics and interpersonal bonds,[24] which helped members find employment and coached them on the distinctly nonmaternal mores of bureaucracies and political parties.

The network relied on the fact that its members were relatively free of commitments to husbands and children. Many never married, and among those who had, many were divorced or widowed. The roughly one-quarter who had children were also, in the main, able to delegate daily childcare responsibilities to someone else.[25] A large portion either lived long-term with other unmarried women in social settlements or shared apartments with their friends and colleagues from the world of reform. Gordon found that at least 28 percent shared their lives with other women in what the late nineteenth century would have termed "Boston marriages" and the late twentieth would (probably) call monogamous lesbian unions.[26]

What strikes historians of the United States as remarkable is not only the presence of these women in politics but also the degree to which, between about 1880 and the middle 1920s, government policies took women as their objects. The turn-of-the-century labor movement failed decisively to use the government to protect working people.[27] An aggressively pro-corporate judiciary defeated modest wages and hours regulations for workers; labor leaders had so little faith in legislative reform that they barely participated in campaigns for health insurance and old-age pensions.[28] In contrast, and apparently in consequence, many social policies of the period focused on women and children. The shift from the Supreme Court decision in *Lochner v. New York* of 1905, which rejected a work maximum for all bakers, to *Muller v. Oregon* of 1908, which sustained a maximum exclusively for women, encapsulates the trend. Following the arguments of the Brandeis brief (largely prepared by Brandeis's sister-in-law, Josephine Goldmark of the National Consumers' League) the majority decision in *Muller v. Oregon* read, in part:

> Women's physical structure and the performance of maternal functions place her at a disadvantage. This is especially true when the burdens of motherhood are upon her. . . . As healthy mothers are essential to vigorous offspring, the physical well-being of woman becomes an object of public interest and care in order to preserve the strength and vigor of the race.[29]

As judges accepted hours regulations for women that they rejected for men, so did legislators prefer "widows'" or "mothers' pensions" to public payments for unemployed or aged working-class men. The widows' pension came into being in Illinois in 1911; by the 1930s, nearly all states made small amounts of income available to destitute women through pensions.[30] Similarly, although expansions of the national bureaucracy were few and far between in the early twentieth century, the United States added a Children's Bureau in 1912 and a Women's Bureau after World War I. The maternalist imperium expanded dramatically in 1922, with passage of the Sheppard-Towner law, the first national health legislation in U.S. history. Sheppard-Towner gave funding and authority to the Children's Bureau to educate mothers about the virtues of hospital births and allopathic medical attention (as opposed to home births with midwives), to push states to register births and keep other vital statistics, and to answer thousands of letters from mothers about everything from proper nutrition to local sources of government aid. Until its final defeat in 1929, Sheppard-Towner made it possible for the quintessentially Progressive Children's Bureau to continue expanding under the administrations of Harding, Coolidge, and Hoover. The sex-specific pattern of public policy in this period convince Skocpol of a "possible" or even a "nascent maternal welfare state" in the United States.[31]

A POSSIBLE MATERNAL WELFARE STATE?

The scholars who have recognized a maternalist strand in reform work and public policy all see some combination of liberatory and limiting elements in it. They divide over which to emphasize, depending in part on whether they judge maternalist policy by its architects' intentions or its effects on people like Joyce Johnson. They agree that maternalists were effective, especially relative to the U.S. labor movement, but disagree about such apparent policy successes as mothers' pensions and AFDC. Skocpol is perhaps the most enthusiastic, chastising historians for having failed to notice the fundaments of "a generous and caring American welfare state inherent in the maternalist policy breakthroughs."[32]

Ladd-Taylor and Mink find a more mixed record. "Maternalist politics were necessarily racial politics," Ladd-Taylor argues. "They celebrated healthy and virtuous (white) women as mothers of the nation's citizen-soldiers and censured those whose heredity, homes, and family lives did not fit the ideal."[33] Mink understands maternalists as racial progressives who "eschewed the dominant racial discourse and substituted the promise of assimilation for the ideology of subordination and exclusion."[34] She sees their views about race and gender as equally double-edged; maternalists helped justify women's public roles while naturalizing the typical sexual division of labor, and they offered new immigrants incorporation if they would let native-born women tell them what to do. Ladd-Taylor is particularly critical of pension programs, which denied benefits to most African-American women, divorcees and unmarried women, and many deserted women. However, she is enthusiastic about Sheppard-Towner.[35]

Sonya Michel and Linda Gordon take up the critique of maternalists from the perspective of women's needs for economic autonomy. Michel compares mothers' pensions to a contemporary alternative, the provision of child care services to the minor dependents of working women. Maternalists, she argues, expected pensions to keep mothers out of the waged labor market— even though, like cash welfare today, low benefit levels hardly made this possible for many mothers.[36] In her comprehensive study of child care policy, Michel attributes the near absence of such policy in the U.S. in part to "a politics of maternalism" fashioned by activist women.[37] Gordon follows the state pension campaigns from their beginnings through their apotheosis in congressional inclusion of ADC in the 1935 Social Security Act. "By the time of the Social Security Act," Gordon argues, "it was clear that these programs had been outmoded from the beginning" in their understanding of women's economic dependence on men and of women's ability to survive on state stipends when men were not around.[38]

Mary Frances Berry is so critical of the maternalists that she barely marks their emergence as a meaningful historical event. From the rise of gender-based "separate spheres" in the early nineteenth century until the feminist and welfare rights critiques of the 1960s, Berry perceives a virtually unbroken pattern of endorsements of woman's role as wife and mother. White women's organizational work in the late nineteenth and early twentieth centuries does not impress Berry as a covert critique of the male-dominated *status quo* but as another example of "[b]ourgeois and upper-class women involving themselves in a number of activities for self-development that were consistent with the true womanhood ideal."[39]

Berry's book is strongest in drawing parallels between reformist errors in the 1920s and in the very recent past. (Full disclosure: in 1985–86 and 1989–90, I worked for one of the protagonists of Berry's story, the U.S. House Select Committee on Children, Youth, and Families.) Decades after the maternalist heyday, Congress passed a national child care law, but it did not create the broad-based entitlement for which advocates had dreamed. Berry concludes that at least part of the problem lay in the child care advocates' squeamishness about representing the policy as women's need or appealing to wage-working women to support the measure. "Much like the 'feminist' social reformers" earlier in the century, according to Berry, "their message became increasingly mother and child centered, not woman centered."[40]

PROFESSIONALISM, RESISTANCE, AND ORGANIZING

Behind the appreciation of maternalism by scholars like Skocpol, Mink, and Michel lies a renewed interest in the women's profession (or semi-profession) of social work.[41] The U.S. Children's and Women's Bureaus rose in tandem with the practice and academic discipline of social work. The School of Social Service Administration at the University of Chicago was both a laboratory for new social policies and a school of social work.[42] Still, only recently have historians learned to problematize both parties to the social work relationship, to look for Miss Demo's side of the story as well as Joyce Johnson's. In part, this shift of emphasis occurred because the social control paradigm eroded. As we ceased thinking of welfare clients as social workers' victims, we have increasingly come to see the Miss Demoses of the world as themselves experiencing constraint as well as power.

The historian Regina Kunzel, in *Fallen Women, Problem Girls: Unmarried Mothers and the Professionalization of Social Work, 1890–1945*, documents the limitations on social workers' power in her study of homes for unwed mothers. For at least half of the period she covers, evangelical Protestant volunteers and trained social workers actively fought one another for control over the homes. Even after the social workers won, they had to contend with male professionals who maintained that social work was not a true profession.[43] Social workers attempted to downplay their similarities to their religiously motivated predecessors while emphasizing their differences from male competitors.[44]

Kunzel is in line with other recent scholarship in finding that the managers of late-nineteenth- and twentieth-century maternity homes never had total control over their clients.[45] She found maternity home residents fighting with staff, complaining about work assignments, and destroying the institutions' property. Although staff of the homes insisted that residents stay for long, rehabilitative periods before and after giving birth, many departed at their first opportunity. The homosocial maternity home was to distract residents from heterosocial city streets and dance halls; instead, residents formed a "shared sisterhood" that centered on "the common experience of out-of-wedlock pregnancy, and shared information about sex," including birth control and abortion.[46]

Beyond the unorganized, and often covert, resistance to the authority of social welfare institutions, recent writing on the welfare rights movement offers models of overt, organized resistance. My own work has emphasized the strategic ideas and political theories that informed welfare rights struggles in the 1960s. I find that welfare rights discourse created new opportunities in U.S. legal and political culture; for every card-carrying member of the National Welfare Rights Organization there were at least two Joyce Johnsons demanding to be heard.[47]

One of the most interesting contributions to this literature is Theresa Funiciello's *Tyranny of Kindness*,[48] a memoir by a former welfare recipient who headed a welfare rights group called the Downtown Welfare Advocate Center (DWAC) in New York City during the 1980s. Funiciello is harshly critical of social work and welfare management as they had evolved in the sixty years since the maternalist high point. However, she also draws on a version of maternalism and shows how it worked as a mobilizing rhetoric for women welfare recipients. She believes that social workers were completely complicit in the stinginess and judgmental nature of AFDC.[49] However, far from resisting maternalism's opposition to waged work, she wants nothing more for low-income women than a release from working for money. Funiciello remembers that, in the 1980s, "[p]oor women kept saying, We need more money and a better way to make rational choices about the care of our children. We did not say we needed more work. Everyone else said that."[50]

RACE, DEMOGRAPHY, AND EMPIRE

Why did it seem so radical for Funiciello's group to demand in the 1980s what had been the basis of AFDC and mothers' pensions at their creation? Part of the answer lies in changing patterns of labor-force participation by white married women, such that the cultural presumption largely switched from mothers' removal from the labor force to their continued participation in it. But perhaps a larger part lies in the changing racial and ethnic characteristics of the mothers receiving aid. Maternalism seems to have ceased to attract white bourgeois adherents at least partly because nonwhite women tried to make the doctrine work for them.

Feminist scholars have begun to appreciate the effects of racial thinking and race-based power relations on theories of political entitlement, the structure of state programs, and the dynamics between social workers and clients.[51] Some scholars, like Gordon and Eileen Boris, and Berry, have compared white and African-American women reformers in the years before the New Deal. Building upon scholarship on the black reformers by Paula Giddings, Elsa Barkley Brown, Evelyn Brooks Higginbotham, and Deborah Gray White,[52] they have found a range of differences between these two groups.

Berry, Boris, and Gordon all argue that African-American reformers accepted the necessity, if not the desirability, of women's wage earning. They were therefore relatively supportive of out-of-home care for children. Gordon concludes that, if the African-American reformers had had as much political influence as the whites on the eve of the New Deal, "the working mothers of the past few decades would have been much better supplied with child care and other measures to lighten the double day."[53]

While white women reformers devoted most of their energies to programs for mothers and children, African-American women combined such efforts with opposition to Jim Crow and to lynching. Boris and Gordon point out that white women could expect their innovative voluntary programs to serve as models for municipal or, in the case of Sheppard-Towner, national policy. African-American women had no such expectations. "[B]lack women," Boris writes, "usually were fighting the state"—for its complicity in segregation, violence, and the extreme poverty of black communities— "rather than courting it."[54]

The racial specificity of maternalist arguments, and the implicit exchange they describe between women and governments, points to an especially promising area for research: the relationships among maternalist politics, militarism, and imperialism. Scholars accept that the ubiquitous pro-motherhood, pro-childbearing discourse in France at the turn of the twentieth century, which supported welfare expansion, was connected to fears about rising German power.[55] It seems clear that German social and family policies in the late nineteenth and early twentieth centuries were tied to the expansionist ambitions of rulers from Bismarck to Hitler.[56] And Antoinette Burton has taught us to understand English women's domestic reform agenda (including all kinds of poor relief *and* feminism) as inextricable from the nation's imperial projects.[57]

Feminist scholars who write about the U.S. have given fairly short shrift to imperial and colonial concerns.[58] No doubt, this is a manifestation of the difficulty we have in seeing this country's military adventures, cultural manipulations, and ready use of economic thumbscrews when things don't go our way, as comparable to the hardware of European empire.[59] However, the idea of empire may explain a lot about what happened in the formation of the U.S. welfare state. Obviously, turn-of-the-century reformers were not preoccupied with fear of a European land war. However, after 1898, many believed their country would need soldiers to maintain a hemispheric pax Americana.[60]

Imperial concerns quite likely gave claims for women's citizenship, rooted in the service they performed by raising a next generation of soldiers and workers, political force they would not otherwise have had.

Placing empire and gender at the center of the historical frame may also help explain some peculiarities of the U.S. welfare state. Perhaps because, unlike France, the United States did not suffer a major military defeat in the last third of the nineteenth century, or lose a large portion of its population in World War I, the turn-of-the-century discourse did not simply support childbearing by all women. U.S. political elites favored childbearing by native-born whites and those immigrants who were thought capable of Americanizing (and the line between those who could and couldn't be assimilated shifted over time). But they discouraged childbearing by many immigrants and African-Americans. There are suggestive parallels between this two-track approach to demographic thinking and the ambiguous trajectory of maternalist policies. On the one hand, such policies enjoyed remarkable success relative to the work-based policies advocated by the labor movement; on the other hand, the policies were underfunded, with stiff eligibility criteria and elaborate surveillance. For decades, the people whose moral or biological endowments the reformers did not care to have passed on to future generations were ineligible for benefits altogether.

SEXUALITY AND THE POLITICS OF MATERNITY

One urgent priority is to make empire integral to our analyses, while keeping domestic race relations in view. A second is to treat the sexuality of early welfare reformers more seriously. Without imposing anachronistic labels on them, it is fair to observe the number of prominent maternalists who lived unconventionally. In addition to the 28 percent of reformers Gordon studied who lived in dyadic unions with other women, there are numerous others: Charlotte Perkins Gilman, the socialist feminist whose writings supported maternalism, was passionately attached to a woman while in her twenties and married only after the friend had married and withdrawn from the relationship. Perkins Gilman responded to the birth of her daughter with a nervous breakdown; after psychological treatment, she separated from her husband and relinquished her child to a woman friend.[61] Reformer and First Lady Eleanor Roosevelt's closest friends were lesbian couples, and she was for a time passionately attached to the journalist Lorena Hickok.[62] In England, Eleanor Rathbone, the leader of the movement for family allowances and key spokeswoman for maternalist feminism, shared her life with a Scottish social worker named Elizabeth Macadam.[63]

It is less important to sort out these women's sexual identities than to appreciate the distance between what they preached for women like Joyce Johnson and what they did themselves. Perhaps they saw no contradiction between their prescriptions for others and their life choices. After all, women reformers were separated from the objects of their reform by high walls of class, education level, and, generally, religion and ethnicity. Nineteenth-century social norms did not forbid close friendships between women—even when the women spoke passionately to one another—or associate such friendships with homosexuality. However, it is difficult to suppose that the post–World War I emergence of lesbianism as a visible social practice did not produce anxiety for women who spent their adult lives in quiet romantic (or even nonromantic) friendships with other women. Howsoever innocent they appeared in the 1890s, these women's relationships may have looked different even to them by the 1920s and 1930s.[64]

Considering maternalists' sexuality opens up the possibility that maternalist philosophy, especially at its fuzziest, most roseate edge, was a kind of cover for the reformers' own life choices. Rather than as an extension of women's routine duties, advocacy of public motherhood emerges in many reformers' lives as a substitute for them. The same-sex dimension of maternalists' lives may also help explain the ambiguous quality of modern welfare. Although paying respect to conventional gender roles and family structures, policies also promoted limited economic (and sexual) independence for women.

The relationship between the personal and political was not a simple one in the lives of these reformers. Maternalist politics did not emanate from the experience of motherhood or from women's biologically (or even socially) derived maternal perspective. Although women may have extrapolated their vision of a caring, "maternal" welfare state from an idealized vision of domestic motherhood, they were not reading from their own experiences of motherhood or domesticity. Again, it is helpful to think of maternalism as a political philosophy that described a particular relationship between mothers and governments, to which anyone could adhere for her or his own reasons.

Studies of welfare in the United States have come a long way in a short period of time. Feminist scholars, who only recently began insisting on the significance of gender in social policy, have come to an increasingly nuanced understanding of how gender-based power helps create state policies and determine their effects. From a fairly confident critique of welfare as "public patriarchy," closer attention to the historical record—and years of antiwelfare sentiment in mainstream politics—has driven scholars to a sound appreciation of ambiguity. The public patriarchs turned out to be middle-class women, some of whom the early twenty-first century would certainly call lesbians. "Social control" turned out to be a myth, or, at best, a rarely realized ambition of social workers, philanthropists, and administrators; they could tear the sheets off Joyce Johnson's Castro convertible, but they could not make her think it was right to do so. Welfare policies like widows' pensions and ADC contained sexist assumptions about women's primary responsibility for childrearing, but they also offered (and were designed to offer) recipients some degree of economic and personal autonomy. At the same time, they often excluded African-Americans, immigrants, and women with non-conforming standards of sexual morality. Future studies of the intersections among gender, race, empire, and sexuality in welfare states only promise to make the picture more complicated. And that is probably all for the best.

Notes

1. Joyce Johnson fair hearing transcript, March 30, 1967, 70–71, in case of Joyce Johnson, Box 48, Folder 22, papers of the Scholarship, Education, and Defense Fund for Racial Equality, State Historical Society of Wisconsin, Madison, WI.

2. Johnson's hearing also included a discussion of her sexual behavior. Johnson hearing, 49–50, 57, 64.

3. Gwendolyn Mink, *Welfare's End* (Ithaca: Cornell University Press, 1998). For important discussions that do not place gender at the center of their analyses, see Michael B. Katz, *The Price of Citizenship: Redefining the American Welfare State* (New York: Metropolitan Books, 2001); and Alice O'Connor, *Poverty Knowledge: Social Science, Social Policy, and the Poor in Twentieth-Century History* (Princeton, NJ: Princeton University Press, 2001), 284–95. For Clinton's health care proposals, see Theda Skocpol, *Boomerang: Health Care Reform and the Turn against Government* (New York: W. W. Norton, 1997).

4. See Carol Brown, "Mothers, Fathers, and Children: From Private to Public Patriarchy," in *Women and Revolution*, Lydia Sargent, ed. (Boston: South End Press, 1981), 239–67; Sylvia Law, "Women, Work, Welfare, and the Preservation of Patriarchy," *University of Pennsylvania Law Review* 131 (May 1983), 1251–1331; Barbara Brenzel, *Daughters of the State: A Social Portrait of the First Reform School for Girls in North America, 1856–1905* (Cambridge: MIT Press, 1983); Mimi Abramovitz, *Regulating Lives of Women* (Boston: South End Press, 1988); and Dorothy C. Miller, *Women and Social Welfare: A Feminist Analysis* (New York: Praeger, 1990).

5. Karin Stallard, Barbara Ehrenreich, and Holly Sklar, *Poverty in the American Dream: Women and Children First* (Boston: South End Press 1983); Zillah Eisenstein, *Feminism and Sexual Equality: Crisis in Liberal America* (New York: Monthly Review Press, 1984), and "The Patriarchal Relations of the Reagan State," in *Women and Poverty*, ed. Barbara C. Gelpi, et al. (Chicago: University of Chicago Press, 1984), 181–89; Diana Pearce, "The Feminization of Poverty: Women, Work, and Welfare," *Urban and Social Change Review* (Winter/Spring 1978), 28–36, and "Toil and Trouble: Women Workers and Unemployment Compensation," in *Women and Poverty*, 141–61.

6. Linda Gordon, *Heroes of Their Own Lives: The Politics and History of Family Violence, Boston, 1880–1960* (New York: Penguin Books, 1988).

7. This is a play on the title of Gertrude Himmelfarb's article, "History with the Politics Left Out," most accessible in her *The New History and the Old* (Cambridge: Harvard/Belknap, 1987), 13–32.

8. See Sara Evans, "Women's History and Political Theory: Toward a Feminist Approach to Public Life," in *Visible Women: New Essays on American Activism*, Nancy Hewitt and Suzanne Lebsock, eds. (Urbana: University of Illinois Press, 1993), 119–39, and Paula Baker, "The Domestication of Politics: Women and American Political Society, 1780–1920," in *Unequal Sisters: A Multicultural Reader in U.S. Women's History*, Ellen Carol DuBois and Vicki L. Ruiz, eds. (New York: Routledge, 1990), 66–91.

9. Among the fullest efforts at cross-national history is Daniel T. Rodgers, *Atlantic Crossings: Social Politics in a Progressive Age* (Cambridge: Harvard/Belknap, 1998). Also see Nancy J. Hirschmann and Ulrike Liebert, "Engendering Welfare, Degendering Care: Theoretical and Comparative Perspectives on the United States and Europe," in their

edited volume, *Women and Welfare: Theory and Practice in the United States and Europe* (New Brunswick, NJ: Rutgers University Press, 2001), 1–19; Seth Koven and Sonya Michel, eds., *Mothers of a New World: Maternalist Politics and the Origins of Welfare States* (New York: Routledge Press, 1993); and Kathryn Kish Sklar, "A Call for Comparisons," *American Historical Review* 95 (October 1990), 1109–14.

10. Joan Scott, "Experience," in *Feminists Theorize the Political*, Judith Butler and Joan Scott, eds. (New York: Routledge, 1992), 22. One exception to the general trend of neglecting the role of language in shaping social policy is Regina Kunzel's *Fallen Women, Problem Girls: Unmarried Mothers and the Professionalization of Social Work, 1890–1945* (New Haven: Yale University Press, 1993).

11. Wendy Brown, "Finding the Man in the State," *Feminist Studies* 18 (Spring 1992), 7–34.

12. Classic statements of this position are Louis Althusser, "Ideology and Ideological State Systems," in his *Lenin and Philosophy* (New York: Monthly Review Press, 1971), 127–86, and Fred Block, "The Ruling Class Does Not Rule," *Socialist Revolution* 33 (August 1973), 6–28.

13. James O'Connor, *The Fiscal Crisis of the State* (New York: St. Martin's Press, 1973) and Frances Fox Piven and Richard Cloward, *The New Class War: Reagan's Attack on the Welfare State and Its Consequences* (New York: Pantheon Press, 1982).

14. Theda Skocpol, "Political Response to Capitalist Crisis: Neo-Marxist Theories of the State and the Case of the New Deal," *Politics and Society* 10/2 (1980), 200.

15. Peter Evans, Dietrich Rueschemeyer, and Theda Skocpol, eds., *Bringing the State Back In* (Cambridge: Cambridge University Press, 1985).

16. Theda Skocpol, *Protecting Soldiers and Mothers: The Political Origins of Social Policy in the United States* (Cambridge: Harvard University Press, 1992).

17. See discussion in Bob Jessop, *State Theory: Putting Capitalist States in Their Place* (University Park: Pennsylvania State Press, 1990), 79–104.

18. Sonya Michel, *Children's Interests/Mothers' Rights: The Shaping of America's Child Care Policy* (New Haven: Yale University Press, 1999); Joanne Goodwin, *Gender and the Politics of Welfare Reform: Mothers' Pensions in Chicago, 1911–1929* (Chicago: University of Chicago Press, 1997); Gwendolyn Mink, *The Wages of Motherhood: Inequality in the Welfare State, 1917–1942* (Ithaca: Cornell University Press, 1995); Molly Ladd-Taylor, *Mother-Work: Women, Child Welfare, and the State, 1890–1930* (Urbana: University of Illinois Press, 1994); Linda Gordon, *Pitied But Not Entitled: Single Mothers and the History of Welfare* (New York: Free Press, 1994); Sklar, "The Historical Foundations of Women's Power in the Creation of the American Welfare State, 1830–1930," from *Mothers of a New World*, ed. Koven and Michel; and Skocpol, *Protecting Soldiers and Mothers*.

19. Mary Frances Berry, *The Politics of Parenthood: Child Care, Women's Rights, and the Myth of the Good Mother* (New York: Vintage Press, 1993).

20. Skocpol, *Protecting Soldiers and Mothers*, 317.

21. On social feminists, see J. Stanley Lemons, *The Woman Citizen: Social Feminism in the 1920s* (Charlottesville: University Press of Virginia, 1973). For another view before the current wave of interest in these women, see Lela Costin, *Two Sisters for Social Justice: A Biography of Grace and Edith Abbott* (Urbana: University of Illinois Press, 1983).

22. See discussions of republican motherhood in Linda Kerber, *Women of the Republic: Intellect and Ideology in Revolutionary America* (Chapel Hill: University of North

Carolina Press, 1980); and Christine Stansell, *City of Women: Sex and Class in New York, 1789–1860* (New York: Alfred Knopf, 1982).

23. Gordon, *Pitied But Not Entitled* 308–309, 72–76. Goodwin, *Gender and the Politics of Welfare Reform*, includes much biographical information on leading maternalists, esp. in Chapter Three. The homogeneity of the women reformers, which both helped them be effective politically and limited their vision, resembles the homogeneity Leila Rupp noted in the international women's movement of roughly the same historical moment. See Rupp, *Worlds of Women: The Making of an International Women's Movement* (Princeton: Princeton University Press, 1997).

24. In addition to Gordon, see Robyn Muncy, *Creating a Female Dominion in American Reform, 1890–1935* (New York: Oxford University Press, 1991); and Kathryn Kish Sklar, "Hull House in the 1890s: A Community of Female Reformers," in *Unequal Sisters*, 109–122. For the idea of "women's network" in a slightly later period, see Susan Ware, *Beyond Suffrage: Women in the New Deal* (Cambridge, MA: Harvard University Press, 1981).

25. Among the leading U.S. maternalists, Florence Kelley was one of the few who had children, and for whom child care was a serious practical as well as political issue. See Kathryn Kish Sklar, *Florence Kelley and the Nation's Work: The Rise of Women's Political Culture, 1830–1900* (New Haven: Yale University Press, 1995), esp. 171, 178–80.

26. Gordon, *Pitied But Not Entitled*, 78–79.

27. For the gendered (in this case, masculinist or patriarchal in the literal sense) dimensions of labor leaders' resistance to government social provision, see Alice Kessler-Harris, *In Pursuit of Equity: Women, Men and the Quest for Economic Citizenship in 20th-Century America* (New York: Oxford University Press, 2001), 67–70, 109–111. Kessler-Harris details the debates within the American Federation of Labor both before and during the New Deal over government's role in shaping economic labor relations; her book reveals both that labor's "voluntarism" was contested, and that it remained a powerful force well into the 1930s.

28. On *Lochner v. New York*, *Muller v. Oregon*, and relations between labor and the courts in this period, see Nancy Woloch, *Muller v. Oregon: A Brief History with Documents* (Boston: Bedford Books, 1996); Eileen Boris, *Home to Work: Motherhood and the Politics of Industrial Homework in the United States* (Cambridge: Cambridge University Press, 1994), 21–47; and William Forbath, *Law and the Shaping of the American Labor Movement* (Cambridge: Harvard University Press, 1991). Rodgers, *Atlantic Crossings*, argues in general for similarities between the U.S. and Europe. However, insofar as Rodgers sees cross-national differences in social policies, he attributes these in part to distinctive legal norms and a special role for the courts in revising statutory regulations. See 153, 201, 443, 476.

29. Quoted in Ladd-Taylor, *Mother-Work*, 123.

30. For detail on the creation and administration of the pioneering Illinois pension, see Goodwin, *Gender and the Politics of Welfare Reform*. For comparison with another locality, see Susan Traverso, *Welfare Politics in Boston, 1910–1940* (Amherst: University of Massachusetts Press, 2003), 27–51.

31. Skocpol, *Protecting Soldiers and Mothers*, 2, 522–23.

32. Ibid., 524.

33. Ladd-Taylor, *Mother-Work*, 49.

34. Mink, *Wages of Motherhood*, 12.

35. In her essay, "My Work Came Out of Agony and Grief: Mothers and the Making of the Sheppard-Towner Act," Ladd-Taylor recognizes the drawbacks to Sheppard-Towner: its programs "provided no hospital or medical care, forbade outright financial aid" for health services, were funded on a shoestring, and so privileged allopathic medical techniques over others that they precipitated a drop of thousands in the number of rural midwives in the United States. Ladd-Taylor in Koven and Michel, *Mothers of a New World*, 330, 333. But see *Mother-Work*, 169.

36. Michel, "The Limits of Maternalism: Policies toward American Wage-Earning Mothers during the Progressive Era," in Koven and Michel, *Mothers of a New World*, 307–308.

37. Michel, *Children's Interests/Mothers' Rights*, 3.

38. Gordon, *Pitied But Not Entitled*, 38.

39. Berry, *Politics of Parenthood*, 74.

40. Ibid., 172.

41. Landmarks in the new history of social work include Daniel J. Walkowitz, *Working with Class: Social Workers and the Politics of Middle-Class Identity* (Chapel Hill: University of North Carolina Press, 1999); Elizabeth Lunbeck, *The Psychiatric Persuasion: Knowledge, Gender, and Power in Modern America* (Princeton, NJ: Princeton University Press, 1994); and Kunzel, *Fallen Women, Problem Girls*. On the ambiguous status of women's professions outside of social work, see Barbara Melosh, *The Physician's Hand: Work Culture and Conflict in American Nursing* (Philadelphia: Temple University Press, 1982).

42. See especially Goodwin, *Gender and the Politics*, 91, 97–101.

43. Kunzel, *Fallen Women*, 44. Lunbeck, *Psychiatric Persuasion*, describes similar border skirmishes between social workers and all the other aspiring professionals in turn-of-the-century mental hospitals. For a general statement of these processes, see Andrew Abbott, *The System of Professions: An Essay on the Division of Expert Labor* (Chicago: University of Chicago Press, 1988).

44. For these dynamics, also see Gordon, *Pitied But Not Entitled*, and Felicia Kornbluh, "Class, Gender, and Social Control: The Charity Organization Society of New York, 1883–1917" (Senior Thesis, Harvard-Radcliffe College, May 1989).

45. Kunzel, *Fallen Women*, 102.

46. Ibid., 83.

47. See Felicia Kornbluh, *The Rise and Fall of Welfare Rights: Gender, Law, and Poverty in Postwar America* (forthcoming), "A Human Right to Welfare? Social Protest among Women Welfare Recipients after World War II," *Women's America*, 6th ed., Linda K. Kerber and Jane DeHart, eds. (New York: Oxford University Press, 2004), and "The Goals of the Welfare Rights Movement: Why We Need Them Thirty Years Later," *Feminist Studies*, 24/1 (Spring 1998), 65–78. Also see Jennifer Frost, *'An Interracial Movement of the Poor': Community Organizing and the New Left in the 1960s* (New York: New York University Press, 2001); Eileen Boris, "When Work Is Slavery," in *Whose Welfare?*, Gwendolyn Mink, ed. (Ithaca: Cornell University Press, 1999), 36–55; Nancy Naples, *Grassroots Warriors: Activist Mothering, Community Work, and the War on Poverty* (New York: Routledge, 1998); Mimi Abramovitz, *Under Attack, Fighting Back: Women and Welfare in the United States* (New York: Monthly Review Press, 1996); and, on the most important welfare rights organizing of the 1990s,

David Zucchino, *Myth of the Welfare Queen* (New York: Touchstone/Simon and Schuster, 1997).

48. Theresa Funiciello, *Tyranny of Kindness: Dismantling the Welfare System to End Poverty in America* (New York: Atlantic Monthly Press, 1993).

49. Ibid., xvii.

50. Ibid., 71, 73–74, 262.

51. In addition to Ladd-Taylor, *Mother-Work*, and Mink, *Wages of Motherhood*, see the following cultural studies: Holloway Sparks, "Queens, Teens, and Model Mothers: Race, Gender, and the Discourse of Welfare Reform," in *Race and the Politics of Welfare Reform*, Sanford Schram, ed. (Ann Arbor: University of Michigan Press, 2003), 171–95; Ruth Feldstein, *Motherhood in Black and White: Race and Sex in American Liberalism* (Ithaca: Cornell University Press, 2000); and Wahneema Lubiano, "Black Ladies, Welfare Queens, and State Minstrels: Ideological War by Narrative Means," from *Race-ing Justice, En-gendering Power*, Toni Morrison, ed. (New York: Pantheon Press, 1992), 323–63. Among the important treatments of race and welfare that pay relatively little attention to gender are Michael Brown, *Race, Money and the American Welfare State* (Ithaca: Cornell University Press, 1999); Daryl Scott, *Contempt and Pity: Social Policy and the Image of the Damaged Black Psyche, 1880–1996* (Chapel Hill: University of North Carolina Press, 1997); and Jill Quadagno, *The Color of Welfare: How Racism Undermined the War on Poverty* (New York: Oxford University Press, 1994).

52. Paula Giddings, *When and Where I Enter: The Impact of Black Women on Race and Sex in America* (New York: Bantam, 1984); Elsa Barkley Brown, "Womanist Consciousness: Maggie Lena Walker and the Independent Order of Saint Luke," in *Unequal Sisters*, 208–23; Evelyn Brooks Higginbotham, *Righteous Discontent: The Women's Movement in the Black Baptist Church, 1880–1920* (Cambridge: Harvard University Press 1993); and Deborah Gray White, "The Cost of Club Work, the Price of Black Feminism," in *Visible Women*, 247–69. Important additions to this literature, which appeared after Boris's and Gordon's reflections, include Patricia Schechter, *Ida B. Wells-Barnett and American Reform, 1880–1930* (Chapel Hill: University of North Carolina Press, 2001); Kevin Gaines, *Uplifting the Race: Black Leadership, Politics, and Culture in the Twentieth Century* (Chapel Hill: University of North Carolina Press, 1996); and Glenda Gilmore, *Gender and Jim Crow: Women and the Politics of White Supremacy in North Carolina* (Chapel Hill: University of North Carolina Press, 1996).

53. Gordon, *Pitied But Not Entitled*, 142.

54. Boris, "Power of Motherhood," 229.

55. For an overview on the French case, see Philip Nord, "The Welfare State in France, 1870–1914," *French Historical Studies* 18 (Spring 1994), 821–38; on ubiquitous French pronatalism, see Karen Offen, "Depopulation, Nationalism, and Feminism in Fin-de-Siècle France," *American Historical Review* 89 (June 1984), 648–76.

56. Rodgers, *Atlantic Crossings*, includes several adept discussions of Bismarckian social provision. See especially 222–25. For Nazi policies, see Christoph Sachsse, "A Nazi Welfare State? Structures and Features of National-Socialist Social Policy, 1933–1945" (History Department Colloquium, Princeton University, 14 Oct. 1992); Gisela Bock, "Antinatalism, Maternity, and Paternity in National Socialist Racism," in *Maternity and Gender Politics. Women and the Rise of European Welfare States,*

1880s–1950s, Gisela Bock and Pat Thane, eds. (New York: Routledge, 1991), 233–55; and Claudia Koonz, *Mothers in the Fatherland: Women, the Family, and Nazi Politics* (New York: St. Martin's Press, 1987).

57. Burton, *Burdens of History: British Feminists, Indian Women, and Imperial Culture, 1865–1915* (Chapel Hill: University of North Carolina Press, 1994), 12, finds "a slippage between the redeemable at home and in the empire that was not exclusive to British feminists." For more general treatments of the implications for historical study of making empire central, see *After the Imperial Turn: Thinking With and Through the Nation*, Burton, ed. (Durham, NC: Duke University Press, 2003).

58. Without negating the point, it is fair to point out that Burton singles out scholarship on the U.S. for making "racialist attitudes . . . a fairly conventional aspect of narratives of American feminism" (*Burdens of History*, 22). However, recognizing the domestic racial dimension of women's politics has not been the same as recognizing the ties between the domestic and international scenes.

59. For one influential treatment of U.S. economic and cultural activity around the world as imperial, see Michael Hardt and Antonio Negri, *Empire* (Cambridge: Harvard University Press, 2000).

60. There is an excellent emerging literature on the gendered dimensions of U.S. power around the world. See especially Laura Briggs, *Reproducing Empire: Race, Sex, Science, and U.S. Imperialism in Puerto Rico* (Berkeley: University of California Press, 2002); Sally Engle Merry, *Colonizing Hawaii: The Cultural Power of Law* (Princeton: Princeton University Press, 2000), 3–32, 221–57; and Eileen Scully, "Prostitution as Privilege: The 'American Girl' of Treaty Port Shanghai," *International History Review* 20 (December 1998), 855–83. The classic statement of the relationship between domestic U.S. reform and turn-of-the-twentieth-century expansion is William Leuchtenberg, "Progressivism and Imperialism: The Progressive Movement and American Foreign Policy," *Mississippi Valley Historical Review* 39 (December 1952), 483–504. Thanks to Anore Horton for informing me about this literature and reminding me of its importance.

61. Ann J. Lane, *To 'Herland' and Beyond: The Life and Work of Charlotte Perkins Gilman* (New York: Pantheon Press, 1990), 66–79, 133–57.

62. Blanche Wiesen Cook, *Eleanor Roosevelt, vol. 1, 1884–1933* (New York: Vintage, 1992). For discussion of Roosevelt and the problem of how to label women reformers' relationships generally, see Leila J. Rupp, "'Imagine My Surprise': Women's Relationships in Mid-Twentieth Century America," in *Hidden from History: Reclaiming the Gay and Lesbian Past*, Martin Duberman, Martha Vicinus and George Chauncey, Jr., eds. (New York: Penguin, 1990), 395–410.

63. Susan Pedersen, *Family, Dependence, and the Origins of the Welfare State—Britain and France, 1914–1945* (Cambridge: Cambridge University Press, 1993), 140–41.

64. For one suggestion of how outsiders viewed the reformers' sexuality see Gordon, *Pitied But Not Entitled*, 81. On the emergence of lesbianism, see Lillian Faderman, *Odd Girls and Twilight Lovers: A History of Lesbian Life in Twentieth-Century America* (New York: Penguin, 1991), 63–92. Although it concerns working-class (rather than bourgeois) women, a model for studying women's activism and sexuality is Annelise Orleck, *Common Sense and a Little Fire: Women and Working-Class Politics in the United States, 1900–1965* (Chapel Hill: University of North Carolina Press, 1995).

Suggestions for Further Reading

Berry, Mary Frances. *The Politics of Parenthood: Child Care, Women's Rights, and the Myth of the Good Mother*. New York: Vintage Press, 1993.

Goodwin, Joanne. *Gender and the Politics of Welfare Reform: Mothers' Pensions in Chicago, 1911–1929*. Chicago: University of Chicago Press, 1997.

Gordon, Linda, ed. *Women, the State, and Welfare*. Madison, WI: University of Wisconsin Press, 1990.

———. *Pitied But Not Entitled: Single Mothers and the History of Welfare*. New York: The Free Press, 1994.

Kornbluh, Felicia. *The Rise and Fall of Welfare Rights: Gender, Law, and Poverty in Postwar America*. Philadelphia: University of Pennsylvania Press, forthcoming 2006.

Ladd-Taylor, Molly. *Mother-Work: Women, Child Welfare, and the State, 1890–1930* (Urbana: University of Illinois Press, 1994).

Mink, Gwendolyn, and Rickie Solinger, eds. *Welfare: A Documentary History of U.S. Policy and Politics*. New York: New York University Press, 2003.

Mink, Gwendolyn. *Welfare's End*. Ithaca: Cornell University Press, 1998.

Michel, Sonya. *Children's Interests/Mothers' Rights: The Shaping of America's Child Care Policy*. New Haven: Yale University Press, 1999.

Rodgers, Daniel T. *Atlantic Crossings: Social Politics in a Progressive Age*. Cambridge, MA: Harvard/Belknap, 1998.

Patriarchy, Racism, and Business Interests: Cross-Class Support for Welfare Retrenchment in the United States

Ellen Reese

Ellen Reese (1997) is Assistant Professor of Sociology at the University of California, Riverside. Her research focuses on political struggles over poor mothers' welfare rights in the United States, past and present. Her work has been published in such journals as *Gender & Society; Social Politics;* and *Race, Gender, and Class*. She is author of *Blacklash Against Welfare Mothers: Past and Present* (2005).

> *As Ellen Reese was studying the creation of mothers' pensions and Aid to Dependent Children as a graduate student in the mid-1990s, she "was struck by how dramatically discourses about women and welfare had shifted in the United States. At the beginning of the century, maternalist reformers and politicians argued that poor women should receive welfare so that they could stay at home and take care of their children. By the end of the century, there was bipartisan support for 'ending welfare' and putting poor mothers to work. How did a welfare program designed to prevent poor mothers' labor force participation grow into a 'workfare state'? Why did poor mothers' rights become so controversial? I sought to answer these questions."*

Feminist scholars have traditionally paid more attention to the creation and consolidation of welfare programs for poor mothers than to welfare state retrenchment. As they have shown, gender, race, and class inequalities shaped the development of these programs from the start. At the beginning of the century, female reformers, mainly white upper- and middle-class women, pushed for the creation of state and local mothers' pensions to allow poor mothers to stay at home with their children. These programs thus reinforced the traditional gender division of labor within families even as they redistributed income across classes.[1] Mothers' pensions were meagerly funded in comparison to veterans' benefits and workmen's compensation programs that largely served men, reinforcing gender inequalities in the welfare state.[2] Limited funding and employers' demands for women's labor minimized the reach of mothers' pensions. Although most states had authorized mothers' pensions by 1920, many counties, especially in rural areas, did not implement them and grants were so low that many recipients were forced to work in order to make ends meet. These pensions were also granted very sparingly and given almost exclusively to white widows, reinforcing the racial hierarchy and patriarchal "family values."[3]

With Congressional passage of the 1935 Social Security Act, Aid to Dependent Children (ADC) replaced mothers' pensions. This act was passed in the midst of the Great Depression in response to agitation by social reformers and popular movements that demanded that Congress provide relief to the poor, unemployed, and elderly.[4] As feminist historians have shown, maternalist reformers in the Children's Bureau designed the basic contours of the ADC program. Assuming that most mothers would be married and eventually covered by social insurance through their husbands, they sought only limited funds for the program. Contrary to their wishes, Congress refused to create national standards for ADC, largely in response to southern politicians' fears that they would undermine racial segregation and farmers' supply of cheap labor.[5] As a result, ADC coverage was highly uneven across states and discrimination was rampant in the program. Welfare offices also continued to push poor mothers, especially blacks, into low wage employment.[6] Because it mainly served "worthy" white widows, ADC remained one of the least controversial welfare programs in these early years.[7]

In this chapter, I explore how race, class, and gender have shaped, and continue to shape, past and present efforts to roll back poor mothers' rights to welfare. I do so by comparing the political forces behind the first major backlash against welfare, which took place in the late 1940s and 1950s, with the contemporary one, on the rise since the 1980s. In both periods, race, class, and gender interests interacted to produce strong, cross-class support for welfare cutbacks. In both cases, business leaders—especially conservative and low-wage employers—interested in minimizing their tax burdens and protecting their supply of cheap labor, attacked welfare mothers. They and their ideologues also spread a moral panic about rising welfare caseloads, blaming welfare and its clients for all kinds of social problems, ranging from intergenerational poverty to the decline of "family values." In this way, they channeled public resentments against, and anxieties about, single mothers, "deadbeat dads," and racial and ethnic minorities into opposition to welfare, much as they did in the 1950s. Despite these continuities, today's welfare backlash is far more intense and widespread than it was in the 1950s as both business leaders and the public grew more hostile to welfare. The Christian right, increasingly powerful after 1980, also emerged as a new political force behind welfare cutbacks.

THE FIRST MAJOR BACKLASH

The 1950s welfare backlash was a response to the dramatic expansion of ADC. After the wartime economy demobilized, the number of recipients in the nation more than doubled, from under a million to over two million between 1945 and 1950 and more than tripled between 1945 and 1960.[8] The characteristics of welfare mothers also changed, in part because federal officials stepped up their pressure on states to stop discriminating against non-white and unwed mothers. By 1961, the percent of widowed families comprised less than 8 percent of welfare cases, compared to 43 percent in 1937. Meanwhile, the share of national welfare cases made up of blacks rose from 31 percent in 1950 to 48 percent in 1961, while black families made up more than half of all cases in the Northeast and South.[9] As ADC became more inclusive of unwed mothers and minorities, it became more controversial. By 1960, researchers who studied the program proclaimed that it "had become one of the most controversial and misunderstood programs in the United States. . . ."[10]

In response to growing hostility toward welfare, states adopted all sorts of restrictive rules to limit access to it. Among the most common types of eligibility policies adopted in this period were "employable mother" rules and stricter "suitable home" policies. Between 1949 and 1960, almost half of U.S. states, mainly in the South and West, restricted welfare through one or both of these policies. Eighteen states adopted work requirements that, contrary to the original intent of ADC, made it mandatory that poor women accept available employment if suitable care could be found for their children. Nine states (eight of them southern) adopted new or tougher "suitable home" policies that were used to regulate poor mothers' sexual lives by denying aid to women considered promiscuous on the grounds that their homes were unfit for children.[11] By 1962, twenty-four states had adopted a "substitute father" or "man in the house" policy that denied welfare to women if they had a live-in boyfriend based on the (often wrong) assumption that he would provide financial support for their children. In some states, even mothers who had a casual affair with a man were considered to have a "substitute father." Four southern states—Georgia, Mississippi, Louisiana, and Tennessee—also passed laws to exclude children born out of wedlock.[12] Because unwed motherhood was far more common among blacks than whites, these policies served as proxies for race-based exclusions.[13] Blacks were also about twice as likely as whites to be denied welfare on the grounds that their homes were "unsuitable."[14]

States adopted other kinds of welfare regulations as well, including limits on property ownership, restrictions on aid to pregnant women, grant ceilings that denied additional aid to large families, and requirements for accepting medical rehabilitation. To reinforce the male breadwinner role in poor families, nineteen states required ADC applicants to take legal action against the father for child support while fourteen states made a continuation of aid contingent on this. After receiving federal authorization in 1951, about half of U.S. states also passed laws to open their welfare rolls to public inspection.[15]

The most active support for this welfare backlash came from two, partly overlapping, social groups: large farmers and white racists. Large farmers, occasionally joined by other business leaders, were interested in limiting poor mothers' welfare rights in order to minimize their taxes and ensure their supply of cheap labor. As the Secretary of New York's Conference Board of Farm Organizations noted, "Farmers felt particularly 'touchy' about rising welfare costs because of continued difficulties in recruiting farm manpower among rural residents who, they said, are on relief and content to remain there."[16] Historical records provide ample evidence of farmers' participation in antiwelfare campaigns. Newsletters from California and Illinois, for example, reveal that farm bureaus lobbied for work requirements in states.[17] Once these rules were adopted, rural county welfare departments across the nation used seasonal employment requirements to regulate the supply of agricultural labor. Indeed, as North Carolina's state welfare board members noted, its new work requirement for ADC "[was] expected to be of particular value in counties where there is considerable amount of seasonal work in agriculture."[18] Restricting these programs during the harvest season provided farmers an ample supply of cheap labor, while expanding them in the off-season prevented the out-migration of workers.[19] Farmers also benefited from, and lobbied for, other kinds of restrictive welfare rules to reduce welfare use and expenditures besides work requirements.[20] For example, the Illinois Farm Bureau Federation urged the state to deny aid to mothers who had more than one child out of wedlock,[21] while New York's farm organizations urged their state to open up the welfare rolls to public inspection.[22]

The political influence of agribusiness should not be underestimated. It was, by the postwar period, a highly organized political group. The biggest and most powerful farm organization was the American Farm Bureau Federation, but farm leaders also belonged to other organizations representing particular kinds of agricultural commodities, which amplified their political voice.[23] More important, agribusiness benefited from unequal state legislative apportionment. By 1955, "inequality of legislative representation was solidly entrenched in all but a handful of the forty-eight states." Rural areas were overrepresented in at least one house in most states, and both houses in many. As a result, "organized agricultural interests [were] usually in a favorable position to influence state legislation."[24]

Racist organizations and politicians were the other major group pushing for welfare cutbacks. As black families gained access to welfare, anti-welfare campaigns merged with a broader backlash against blacks' civil rights gains in the 1940s and 1950s. Such gains included the presidential appointment of a civil rights commission and executive orders prohibiting racial discrimination in the military and the federal civil service. The Supreme Court also declared that segregation in public schools and public transportation was unconstitutional in 1954 and 1955.[25] "Massive resistance"[26] rose in response, especially in the South, where the legacy of slavery left its mark, and where most blacks continued to live.[27] In the 1948 "Dixiecrat Revolt," J. Strom Thurmond, a white supremacist presidential candidate, won the Democratic nomination in four southern states. In the 1950s, southern states passed bills to obstruct the de-segregation of public schools and outlaw the National Association for the Advancement of Colored People, while state registrars barred blacks from voting. White anger over civil rights gains also took the form of racial violence, which rose significantly in the postwar period and in the wake of the 1954 Supreme Court decision. Hundreds of thousands of southern whites also joined pro-segregationist organizations in the 1950s, such as Citizens' Councils and the Klu Klux Klan (KKK).[28]

White supremacist organizations were strongly opposed to the postwar expansion of welfare. As William J. Simmons, a Citizens' Council leader, reported to the press in 1955, "Many of our membership is concerned [sic] . . . about the trend toward the welfare state."[29] Pro-segregationist politicians and Klu Klux Klan leaders also criticized the "communistic welfare state" in the postwar period.[30]

Racism pervaded the anti-welfare discourse of the 1950s. One of the most enduring stereotypes created then was that of the black welfare queen, which portrayed black welfare mothers as purposefully having children so that they could avoid work and receive welfare.[31] This stereotype figured prominently in politicians' and welfare officials' justifications of "suitable home" policies. For example, the Florida Department of Public Welfare claimed this policy was needed because many recipients, especially blacks, misunderstood the purpose of ADC, and "even believe[d] that the State pays them for the illegitimate child."[32] Not surprisingly, about 90 percent of the cases denied under Florida's new "suitable home policy" were black.[33] Politicians in Arkansas also appealed to similar kinds of racist stereotypes. Describing Governor Faubus's address to a convention in Hot Springs, Arkansas in 1959, a newspaper reporter wrote:

> Governor Faubus mounted the well-worn hobby horse of criticizing welfare pay-ments to mothers of illegitimate children: "By taxing the good people to pay for these programs, we are putting a premium on illegitimacy never before known in the world." . . . There was little doubt that Mr. Faubus was referring primarily to Negro unwed mothers and not to any 'good, honest, hard-working' white folks who have been remiss in getting down to the licensing bureau. . . .[34]

The black welfare queen stereotype was even used to justify the sterilization of unwed mothers by a Mississippi politician who argued that, "The Negro woman because of child welfare assistance [is] making it a business, in some cases, of giving birth to illegitimate children."[35] Limiting unwed mothers' access to welfare simultaneously purged black families from the welfare rolls, reduced welfare expenditures, and maintained a ready supply of cheap labor. Punishing unwed mothers for having children out of wedlock also reinforced the sexual double standard and the patriarchal expectation that women should get and stay married, which experienced a resurgence after World War II.

Campaigns for "employable mother" rules, on the other hand, challenged the patriarchal expectation that mothers should stay at home with their children. To justify such rules, welfare critics frequently appealed to the racist view of black women as more employable than white women. As a social worker employed in the 1950s explained, black welfare mothers were attacked because "the Negro mother has always worked in the past."[36] While white middle-class women were urged to stay at home with their children in the postwar period, poor black mothers were chastised for doing so.[37] As a social worker remarked in 1950, "what these people [welfare critics] . . . are chiefly interested in is cheaper servants."[38] In response to such pressures, southern social workers routinely used employment requirements to deny aid to black women when domestic service jobs became available.[39]

Racial opposition to welfare was not confined to the South, nor was it solely directed at black women. In the North and West, anti-welfare campaigns provided a vehicle for expressing racial resentment against the in-migration of Puerto Ricans, Mexicans, and southern blacks. In California, welfare critics quickly resorted to negative stereotypes of Mexicans as well as blacks. As one state welfare official recounted in 1949, he had received complaints from a rural official who was "afraid that the Negroes and Mexicans and Okies in his area will take advantage of a program like this. He claims that they are very ignorant people and that they make a profession almost of getting as much assistance as possible."[40] In New York, welfare critics mainly picked on Puerto Ricans and blacks, claiming that they had purposefully migrated to the state to obtain welfare and avoid work. For example, one New York City politician claimed that, "many persons, particularly Puerto Ricans, came to this city simply to get on relief."[41] Such views increased support for a residency requirement for welfare, which required poor people to live in the state for one to two years before they could receive welfare. In response to a six-year campaign, legislators finally passed a one-year residency requirement for welfare in 1960, after a "stormy three-hour debate."[42] Criticizing the bill's proponents, a legislator pointed out that, "You're not concerned about poor whites. You're concerned about Negroes and Puerto Ricans coming into the state. They are all American citizens and you're trying to keep them out."[43] Indeed, Puerto Ricans and southern blacks were the main groups affected by the bill, which remained in effect until 1969.[44]

Perhaps because they disproportionately affected racial minorities, many of the new eligibility policies created for welfare in the 1950s enjoyed considerable public support. A 1961 Gallup poll found that 90 percent of respondents said that the amount of aid to unwed welfare mothers should not be increased each time they had a child.[45] Similarly, a 1961 Gallup poll found that 85 percent of those surveyed supported employment requirements for relief recipients, and 74 percent agreed with a plan to make ADC applicants prove they were looking for a job.[46]

On the other hand, one should not overstate political opposition to welfare in the 1950s. The welfare backlash was mainly concentrated in the South and West, where states had a significant agribusiness sector, were fiscally constrained by a small tax base, and/or had a relatively large black welfare population.[47] In those states, large farmers were more powerful, racist opposition to welfare was more salient, and fiscal pressures were stronger. Elsewhere, the ADC program, still a relatively small program, remained fairly uncontroversial.

THE CONTEMPORARY WELFARE BACKLASH

Half a century later, we are in the midst of a national welfare backlash that is even stronger than the first one. Attacks on welfare mothers, on the rise since the 1980s, culminated in Congressional passage of the 1996 Personal Responsibility and Work Opportunity Reconciliation Act (PRWORA). PRWORA replaced Aid to Families with Dependent Children (AFDC) with a more restrictive and decentralized welfare program known as Temporary Aid to Needy Families (TANF). Along with other new rules and regulations, PRWORA greatly expanded welfare-to-work programs, created new time limits on welfare receipt, and restricted legal immigrants' access to public assistance. Congress also sought to reduce unwed motherhood by allocating funds for marriage and abstinence promotion.

By 2001, the prevailing consensus in Washington was that liberal Democrats who defended welfare entitlements in 1996 had lost all credibility as welfare rolls plummeted and poor mothers' labor force participation rose in the booming economy of the late 1990s.[48] Confidence in welfare reform was so strong that it was not even shaken when, after the economic recession that began in 2001, welfare caseloads rose. Even then, politicians of both parties insisted that work requirements and time limits were essential to the success of welfare reform.[49] Declaring welfare reform a success, the Bush administration pushed for an expansion of the reforms created under PRWORA, calling for even more stringent work requirements for welfare mothers, additional funds for marriage and abstinence promotion, and an expansion of "charitable choice" policies authorizing states to contract out their welfare services to religious institutions. Despite partisan differences over the details of the legislation, Congress appeared poised to carry out these directives as of 2005.[50]

Welfare is vulnerable to attack because it serves groups perceived to be the "undeserving poor." The vast majority of adult recipients are single mothers. By 1995, when PRWORA was considered, 57 percent of children receiving welfare had an unwed mothers, while another 25 percent had divorced or separated mother. Most, or 58 percent, of adult recipients were also black or Latino, racial groups most likely to be perceived by the public as lazy.[51] While the median length of time that welfare mothers received welfare was less than two years, about one-fifth received it for more than five years, which contributed to concerns about long-term dependency.[52]

Just as in the 1950s, business leaders continue to be at the forefront of the attack on welfare. Unlike the 1950s, however, business opposition to welfare has become national in scope. In response to economic restructuring, the rise of neoliberal ideas, and increased international competition, the demand for welfare cutbacks broadened within the corporate community, but still remains most highly concentrated among low-wage and conservative employers.[53] Their support for welfare reform is not hard to understand as it reduces social expenditures, expands the pool of cheap labor, and symbolically reaffirms the importance of self-sufficiency through work.

Business leaders promote welfare cutbacks in at least two ways: direct lobbying and sponsoring the production and distribution of anti-welfare propa-

ganda. By the 1990s, members of the broadest American business association—
the U.S. Chamber of Commerce—gave the issue of welfare reform high priority.
As its lobbyist explained to Congress:

> In a recent survey to construct the Chamber's 1995-1996 National Business Agen-
> da, welfare reform was second (behind unfunded mandates) on a list of 64 issues
> ranked by importance to Chamber members. . . . Ninety-eight percent [of mem-
> bers surveyed] believed that those who receive such services should be required to
> work. An overwhelming percentage—94 percent—supported placing a limit on
> the amount of time that one can receive welfare benefits.[54]

In addition to directly lobbying Congress, conservative business leaders and
wealthy families also sponsor a highly developed network of conservative
think tanks, which lobby for "welfare cutbacks" and disseminate vast quanti-
ties of anti-welfare propaganda through the media. While moderate think
tanks, such as Brookings Institution, are mainly interested in putting more
poor people to work, conservative think tanks—including the Heritage
Foundation, the American Enterprise Institute, Manhattan Institute, and Cato
Institute—ultimately seek to replace federal welfare with private religious
and secular charities. In the short term, however, they push for various
restrictions on welfare eligibility.

One of the most influential scholars supported by conservative think
tanks was Charles Murray, best known for his 1984 book, *Losing Ground: American Social Policy, 1950–1980*. According to Murray, contemporary poverty is
mainly due to the twin evils of "dependency" and "illegitimacy," encouraged
by the expansion of welfare. Playing the race card, Murray blamed white
liberals for the "welfare mess":

> Race is central to the problem of reforming social policy . . . because the debate has
> been perverted by the underlying consciousness among whites that "they"—the
> people to be helped by social policy—are predominantly black and black people
> are owed a debt. . . . Whites began to tolerate and make excuses for behavior
> among blacks that whites would disdain in themselves or their children.[55]

As this quote illustrates, Murray blamed poor blacks' behavior, encouraged by
liberal social policies, for poverty. His indictment revived "culture of poverty"
arguments and long-standing racist stereotypes of poor black women as lazy,
promiscuous, and irresponsible in their childbearing. To solve the problem of
black poverty, Murray argued that the government must abolish federal
welfare for working-age adults. The Manhattan Institute paid Murray $35,000
to write *Losing Ground*, originally based on a pamphlet he produced for the
Heritage Foundation, and then promoted it through a $125,000 advertising
campaign, funded mainly with grants from the Scaife and Olin Foundations.[56]
Murray later became the leading spokesman on welfare for the American
Enterprise Institute. Realizing that Congress would never end welfare, he
advocated a "realistic" welfare plan in 1994, that included abolishing AFDC's
"entitlement" status and states' adoption of strict time limits, work requirements, family caps, and rules banning welfare to teen mothers. He hoped such
draconian measures would reinforce the traditional family by scaring young
women into using contraceptives, abstaining from sex, and/or marrying their

partners.[57] Murray's "pragmatism" did not last long however. By 1998, he was calling, once again, for the complete elimination of welfare.[58]

Murray's views are echoed in the books, articles, and Congressional testimonies of other fellows of conservative, corporate-sponsored think tanks. For example, in 1996, AEI fellow Doug Besharov urged Congress to adopt strict time limits and work requirements, claiming that they would increase the "inconvenience level of being on welfare."[59] Similarly, the Heritage Foundation urged Congress in 1995 to adopt stricter work requirements, claiming that they would reduce recipients' "addiction" to welfare.[60] Congressional testimonies by representatives from Empower America, the Hudson Institute, and the Cato Institute also claimed that welfare encouraged dependency and out-of-wedlock childbearing and urged Congress to adopt major cutbacks in welfare spending.[61] After PRWORA's passage, conservative think tanks continued to urge Congress to expand workfare programs.[62] They also pushed for additional money to promote traditional "family values" among the poor through abstinence education, marriage counseling, and "responsible fatherhood" programs.[63]

Often working hand in hand with conservative corporate-sponsored think tanks, Christian right groups called for restrictions on aid to unwed and teenage mothers in the mid-1990s. These groups, especially powerful in the South, represented the views of socially conservative white voters. The Christian Coalition, claiming 1.7 million members, and having distributed 45 million voter guides in 1994, held considerable sway over Congressional Republicans.[64] Christian Coalition's founder, Pat Robertson, framed his hostility towards welfare in populist terms, claiming that, "It doesn't take a rocket scientist to deduce that this [welfare] system promotes illegitimacy, discourages stable families, and promotes dependency."[65] Between 1994 and 1996, the Christian Coalition stepped up its efforts to influence welfare policies. Along with other groups, it "visited and telephoned senators and their staffs" and even "stake[d] out hallways outside the Senate Chamber during the floor debate" on welfare reform.[66] Along with conservative think tanks, the Christian Coalition called for "tough illegitimacy provisions."[67] These views were echoed by other grassroots Christian right groups, including the Eagle Forum, the Traditional Values Coalition, and Concerned Women of America, who also lobbied Congress to adopt punitive policies towards unwed and teen welfare mothers. After PRWORA's passage, the Christian Coalition, Concerned Women of America, Eagle Forum, Traditional Values Coalition, and Focus on the Family have pushed for additional funds for "abstinence-only" and "marriage promotion" programs and faith-based welfare initiatives.[68]

While conservative institutions such as the Heritage Foundation provided well-funded experts to legitimate the views of the Christian right, the Christian right provided electoral power to the demands of conservative think tanks. By the mid-1990s, the Christian right had become a powerful interest group inside the Republican Party. A 1994 study found that the Christian right played a dominant or substantial role in the state Republican Party in thirty-one states. Its influence was especially strong in the South. It played a dominant role in the state Republican Party in eight out of the eleven former Confederate states and a substantial role in two others.[69] In the 2000 election, more than half of Bush's supporters were white Christians who regularly attended church, while two-fifths were evangelicals.[70]

To social conservatives' dismay, Congress failed to deny aid to all unwed and teen mothers. Nevertheless, this cross-class coalition of conservative think tanks and the Christian right profoundly influenced PRWORA. As the act's preamble made clear, one of the main goals of PRWORA was to reduce the rate of single motherhood and reinforce the traditional patriarchal family. For this purpose, Congress allocated funds for abstinence education, marriage promotion, and "responsible fatherhood" programs, created financial incentives for states to reduce their rate of out-of-wedlock childbearing, and authorized states to deny additional aid to poor mothers who had a child while receiving welfare. The Christian right and conservative think tanks were also the main advocates for PRWORA's "charitable choice" provisions that allowed faith-based organizations to compete for government social service contracts. After 1996, these groups' influence over welfare reform debates increased with the election of George W. Bush as President and more southern Republicans in Congress.

While the Christian Right attacked unwed and teen welfare mothers, anti-immigrant groups urged Congress to end welfare to legal immigrants, who are mostly Latino or Asian. Just as welfare critics in the 1950s claimed that welfare was attracting poor black and brown migrants to their states, Federation for American Immigration Reform argued that, "Welfare programs are an incentive to attract immigrants without education, skills, or literacy to move to the United States."[71] In response to the recent immigration wave, such sentiments were not isolated to particular states as they were in the 1950s, but shaped national welfare debates. House Republicans lobbied for the harshest measures, promising to cut off virtually all welfare benefits for legal immigrants under 75 years of age in 1994.[72] Defending the proposal, Representative Clay Shaw (R-Florida), argued that, "Our welfare benefits are an attraction to people to come to this country, and they should be cut off."[73] Politicians also claimed that immigrants were overly dependent on welfare, despite research showing that working-age legal immigrants (excluding refugees) were 27 percent less likely to use welfare than native-born residents.[74] Moderate and conservative Democrats known as the "Mainstream Forum" also supported cutting legal immigrants' rights to the four main federal public assistance programs to finance welfare reform without raising taxes. The cutbacks were expected to generate $21 billion over five years.[75]

PRWORA's anti-immigrant provisions proved to be highly controversial. After signing the law, Clinton quickly vowed to restore aid to legal immigrants and a loose coalition of ethnic, immigrant, and welfare organizations mobilized grassroots support for these restorations. In response to this pressure and the growing Latino and Asian vote, Congress partially restored food stamps and disability benefits to legal immigrants under the Clinton administration, while most states restored legal immigrants' rights to at least one public assistance program.[76] Courting the Latino vote, Bush actively supported provisions of a farm bill restoring most legal immigrants' right to receive food stamps and signed it into law in 2002.[77] He did not support other, more expensive, benefit restorations however.

As think tanks, politicians, and other welfare critics stepped up their attacks on welfare mothers, public opposition to welfare increased. By 1994, 60 percent of Americans surveyed said that government was spending "too much" on welfare, compared to 40 percent who felt this way in 1984.[78] This sentiment was strongest among conservatives, whites, and those with middle or high incomes.[79] By 1995, about 69 percent of respondents agreed with the statement that the "welfare system does more harm than good because it encourages the breakup of the family and discourages the work ethic."[80] Although most beneficiaries receive welfare for less than two years, a 1995 survey found that 79 percent of respondents said that most recipients were "so dependent on welfare that they will never get off of it."[81] Many of PRWORA's provisions, including work requirements and time limits for welfare receipt, enjoyed strong public support when it was passed.[82] The act continued to be highly popular, with most survey respondents crediting the law, rather than the booming economy, for caseload declines.[83]

Based on his analysis of public opinion data, Martin Gilens concludes that negative perceptions of blacks as lazy, and the false belief that most welfare recipients are black, are the most important source of opposition to welfare spending in the United States.[84] In fact, in 2000 only about 39 percent of families receiving welfare were black.[85] Americans' strong work ethic, along with the increasing commonality of maternal labor force participation, also contributed broad public support for welfare reform.[86] After 1960, labor force participation rates rose for all groups of women, even white, middle class women, previously expected to become full-time housewives. Increases in women's labor force participation were particularly pronounced among married mothers of young children, who traditionally had the lowest labor force participation rates. For all married mothers with children under six, this rate more than doubled between 1960 and 1980, from 19 to 45 percent and continued to rise after 1980. By 1996, nearly 63 percent of married mothers with children under six were employed, although not all of them worked full-time.[87]

Given such high levels of public hostility to welfare, politicians of both parties viewed welfare cutbacks as a way to gain political credit rather than incur blame.[88] Republicans, who dominated Congress after 1994, pushed for the most punitive measures. Yet, even before this, the Clinton administration and other moderate Democrats advocated many of the key features of PRWORA, including time limits for welfare receipt, stricter employment requirements, and looser federal control over the program. These "new Democrats" championed welfare reform, and other conservative social policies, in an effort to revive support for their party among traditional white working class voters, especially in the South, and corporate campaign contributors, many of whom defected to the Republicans in the 1980s and 1990s.[89]

Quantitative research on PRWORA's implementation suggests that the demand for cheap labor, racism, and opposition to unwed motherhood, continue to shape efforts to restrict welfare. States were more likely to adopt a short time limit where their unemployment rate was lower, which suggests that they were more willing to push poor mothers into the labor force when there was a higher demand for labor. It also shows that states were more likely to adopt stricter time limits, tougher sanction policies, and family caps when a higher percentage of the state's TANF caseload was black or Latino. States were also more likely to adopt tougher sanctions against noncompliant recipients if the state's rate of unmarried births was high.[90] Together, these findings suggest that the politics of race, class, and gender continue to drive welfare cutbacks, just as they did in the 1950s.

CONCLUSION

The underlying politics behind welfare cutbacks is not so different at the end of the century than it was at mid-century. Support for welfare cutbacks continues to be based on a combination of business interests in cutting wages and taxes, and a reactionary politics of race and gender. As such, it continues to draw its greatest strength from a cross-class political alliance composed of low-wage employers, ideologically conservative corporations, and conservative whites. In both periods, business-led anti-welfare campaigns were shaped by and drew strength from the resurgence of patriarchal "family values" and white racism.

On the other hand, the scope and severity of the current welfare backlash is novel, as is the influence of the Christian right on welfare policies. The welfare backlash in the early 2000s was far more intense and widespread than it was in the 1950s. In response to the rise of neo-liberalism, economic globalization, and economic restructuring, American corporations, especially conservative and low-wage employers, became more committed to reducing welfare entitlements, expanding workfare, and privatizing social services. They poured money into right-wing think tanks that disseminated anti-welfare propaganda and helped to arouse a moral panic about rising welfare caseloads. These well-orchestrated attacks on welfare, along with the anti-welfare campaigns of the Christian right and anti-immigrant groups, struck a chord among the broader public for several reasons. First, the rise in maternal labor force participation, evident even among white, middle-class women, increased popular support for work requirements for mothers receiving welfare. By the 1990s, most welfare mothers were also women of color, traditionally expected to work. Second, welfare critics attacked unwed mothers and "deadbeat dads," exploiting popular concerns about the rise of single motherhood and shifts away from the patriarchal, heterosexual family form, and catering to the demands of the Christian right. Finally, racial stereotypes of black welfare mothers that had only begun to emerge in the 1950s have since become pervasive. This, the rise in nativism, and the fact that most mothers receiving welfare were now black or Latina, made it easy for politicians and other welfare critics to demonize poor mothers in their assault on welfare.

Although proponents of neo-liberalism portray welfare cutbacks as an inevitable part of a competitive global economy, they really are the work of a resurgent, cross-class conservative coalition of business groups and white voters. To expand poor mothers' rights to welfare, a new kind of progressive movement is needed to effectively counter the racist, sexist, and classist rhetoric of the right and mobilize political support for a new kind of welfare rights agenda that would meet the needs of all working parents, especially working mothers and those struggling to make ends meet in the new economy. Such an agenda might include living wages, paid parental leave, publicly guaranteed jobs, and publicly subsidized childcare and health insurance. This agenda may seem far-fetched, but so too did mothers' pensions at one time.

Notes

1. Linda Gordon, *Pitied But Not Entitled: Single Mothers and the History of Welfare* (New York: The Free Press, 1994); Theda Skocpol, *Protecting Soldiers and Wives: The Political Origins of Social Policy in the United States* (Cambridge: The Belknap Press of Harvard University Press, 1992), 424–78.

2. Gwendolyn Mink, *The Wages of Motherhood: Inequality in the Welfare State, 1917–1942* (Ithaca: Cornell University Press, 1995); Gordon, *Pitied But Not Entitled*; Barbara J. Nelson. "The Origins of the Two-Channel Welfare State: Workmen's Compensation and Mothers' Aid," in *Women, the State, and Welfare*, Linda Gordon, ed. (Madison: University of Wisconsin Press, 1990), 123–51.

3. Barbara J. Nelson, "The Origins of the Two-Channel Welfare State: Workmen's Compensation and Mothers' Aid," 123–51; Ann Shola Orloff, "Gender in Early U.S. Social Policy," *Journal of Policy History* 3 (1991), 249–81; Theda Skocpol, *Protecting Soldiers and Wives*, 471–77; Mimi Abramovitz, *Regulating the Lives of Women: Social Policy from Colonial Times to the Present* (Boston: South End Press, 1989), 201; Mink, *Wages of Motherhood*, 49–50.

4. Abramovitz, *Regulating the Lives of Women*, 315; Gordon, *Pitied But Not Entitled*; Frances Fox Piven and Richard A. Cloward, *Regulating the Poor: The Functions of Public Welfare*, updated version (New York: Vintage Books, 1993 (1971), 45–119.

5. Gordon, *Pitied But Not Entitled*, 266–75; Jill Quadagno, "From Old-Age Assistance to Supplemental Security Income: The Political Economy of Relief in the South, 1935–1972," in *The Politics of Social Policy in the United States*, Margaret Weir, Ann Shola Orloff, and Theda Skocpol, eds. (Princeton: Princeton University Press, 1988), 235–63; Jill Quadagno, "Two Developments of Welfare State Development: Reply to Skocpol and Amenta," *American Sociological Review* 50 (1985), 575–78.

6. Abramovitz, *Regulating the Lives of Women*, 329; Winifred Bell, *Aid to Dependent Children* (New York: Columbia University Press, 1965), 35; Lucy Komisar, *Down and Out in the USA: A History of Public Welfare*, revised edition (New York: Franklin Watts, 1977), 84; Joyce Louise Rowe, *The 'Working Poor': Single Mothers and the State, 1911–1950*, Ph.D. dissertation (Columbus: Ohio State University, 1993), 446–55; Joanne L. Goodwin, "'Employable Mothers' and 'Suitable Work': A Re-evaluation of Welfare and Wage-Earning for Women in Twentieth Century United States." *Journal of Social History* 29 (1995), 253–74.

7. Gordon, *Pitied But Not Entitled*.

8. United States Department of Health, Education, and Welfare, *Public Assistance Under the Social Security Act*, Public Assistance Report 47 (Washington, D.C.: U.S. Government Printing Office, 1961), 20.

9. Abramovitz, *Regulating the Lives of Women*, 321; Michael K. Brown, *Race, Money, and the American Welfare State* (Ithaca: Cornell University Press, 1999), 184.

10. Greenleigh Associates 1960: 1-2, cited in Bell, *Aid to Dependent Children*, 75.

11. Abramovitz, *Regulating the Lives of Women*; Linda Gordon, "Who Deserves Help? Who Must Provide?" *Annals of the American Academy of Political and Social Science* 577 (2001), 13–23, 16, 19; Gwendolyn Mink, "The Lady and the Tramp (II): Feminist Welfare Politics, Poor Single Mothers, and the Challenge of Welfare Justice," *Feminist Studies* 24: 1 (1998), 55–64.

12. Cited in Bell, *Aid to Dependent Children*.

13. The race gap in the percentages of welfare mothers who were unwed declined in the 1950s, but remained substantial. By 1960, 19 percent of non-white welfare mothers were unwed, compared to 6 percent for white welfare mothers. See Rickie Solinger, *Wake Up Little Susie: Single Pregnancy and Race Before Roe v. Wade* (New York: Routledge, 1992).

14. Komisar, *Down and Out in the USA*, 76.

15. Bell, *Aid to Dependent Children*, 66–67; Brown, *Race, Money*, 175; Komisar, *Down and Out in the USA*, 89.

16. "Farmers Ask Dewey for Welfare Study," *New York Times*, 10 Dec. 1952, 39, col. 3.

17. California Farm Bureau Federation, "Supplement X: Adopted Resolutions" in *Minutes of the Thirty-second Annual Meeting, California Farm Bureau Federation* (Berkeley, November 12–16, 1950); California Senate Interim Committee on State and Local Taxation, *Report on Aid to Needy Children Program of the State of California*, in *Journal of the Senate, Regular Session, 1951 Volume 2, Appendix* (Sacramento: California Legislature, January 23 1951), 10; Illinois Agricultural Association, "I.A.A. Resolutions," *I.A.A. Record* 34:12 (1956), 30–32.

18. North Carolina State Board of Public Welfare, "Minutes for August 8, 1952," *Minute Books, 1920–1961* (North Carolina State Archive, 1952).

19. Joanne L. Goodwin, "'Employable Mothers' and 'Suitable Work'", 253–74; Michael S. Holmes, *The New Deal in Georgia: An Administrative History* (Westport, CT: Greenwood Press, 1975); Paul E. Mertz, *New Deal Policy and Southern Rural Poverty* (Baton Rouge: Louisiana State University Press, 1978), 54–56; Gwendolyn Mink, *Welfare's End* (Ithaca: Cornell University Press, 1998), 37–38; Piven and Cloward, *Regulating the Poor*, 125; Jill Quadagno, "From Old-Age Assistance to Supplemental Security Income," 235–63; Jill Quadagno, "Welfare Capitalism and the Social Security Act of 1935," *American Sociological Review* 49 (1984), 632–47.

20. California Farm Bureau Federation, "Supplement X: Adopted Resolutions"; California Senate Interim Committee on State and Local Taxation, *Report on Aid to Needy Children Program*, 10.

21. Illinois Agricultural Association, "I.A.A. Resolutions," 30–32.

22. Warren Weaver, "New Battle Looms Over Colored Oleo," *New York Times*, 28 December 1951, 11, col. 6; "Would Bare Relief Rolls," *New York Times*, 31 December 1951, 14, col. 8.

23. Lowell K. Dyson, *Farmers' Organizations: The Greenwood Encyclopedia of American Institutions* (New York: Greenwood Press, 1986), 14; Grant McConnell, *The Decline of Agrarian Democracy* (Berkeley: University of California Press, 1953).

24. Gordon E. Baker, *Rural Versus Urban Political Power: The Nature and Consequences of Unbalanced Representation* (Garden City, NY: Doubleday, 1955), 24.

25. Harry S. Ashmore, *Civil Rights and Wrongs: A Memoir of Race and Politics, 1944–1994* (New York: Pantheon Books, 1994), 31–86; V. O. Key, *Southern Politics in State and Nation* (New York: Alfred A. Knopf, 1949), 334–42; John Frederick Martin, *Civil Rights and the Crisis of Liberalism: The Democratic Party 1945–1976* (Boulder: Westview Press, 1979), 68–72; Frances Fox Piven and Richard A. Cloward, *Poor People's Movements: Why They Succeed, How They Fail* (New York: Vintage Books, 1979), 198–211.

26. Numan V. Bartley, *The Rise of Massive Resistance: Race and Politics in the South in the 1950s* (Baton Rouge: Louisiana State University Press, 1969).

27. By 1960, 60 percent of blacks still lived in the South. See Joseph Himes, "Some Characteristics of the Migration of Blacks in the United States," *Social Biology* 18:4 (1971), 361.

28. Bartley, *The Rise of Massive Resistance*, 82–122; David M. Chalmers, *Hooded Americans: The First Century of the Klu Klux Klan, 1865–1965* (Garden City, NY: Doubleday, 1965), 354; Civil Rights Congress, *We Charge Genocide: The Historic Petition to the United Nations for Relief from a Crime of the United States Government against the Negro People*, William L. Patterson, ed. (New York: International Publishers, 1970 [1951]); Key, *Southern Politics*, 334–42; Martin, *Civil Rights and the Crisis of Liberalism*, 28, 133–34.

29. Cited in Bartley, *The Rise of Massive Resistance*, 241.

30. Chalmers, *Hooded Americans*, 340.

31. Patricia Hill Collins, *Black Feminist Thought: Knowledge, Consciousness, and the Politics of Empowerment* (New York: Routledge, 1990), 77; Solinger, *Wake Up Little Susie*, 187.

32. Cited in Kentucky Legislative Research Commission, *Illegitimacy in Kentucky, Research Report 4* (Frankfort: Kentucky Department of Archives and History, 1961), 41–42.

33. Michael K. Brown, *Race, Money*, 198.

34. Cited in Bell, *Aid to Dependent Children*, 68.

35. Cited in Solinger, *Wake Up Little Susie*, 41.

36. Cited in Bell, *Aid to Dependent Children*, 64.

37. Grace Chang, "Undocumented Latinas: The New 'Employable Mothers,'" in *Mothering, Ideology, Experience, Agency* (New York: Routledge, 1994), 259–85; Mink, *Welfare's End*.

38. Cited in Bell, *Aid to Dependent Children*, 64.

39. Sara J. Hill, "Deposition, 1968," 8–19, 53; Mary Louise Maxwell, "Deposition, 1966," 55–56; and Josephine Boulinean Craig, "Deposition, 1967," 24–25, Records of Civil Action Number 10443.

40. California State Social Welfare Board, "Minutes of Executive Session, August 26, 1949," Earl Warren Papers 423, Proposed Legislation, General Social Welfare (Sacramento: California State Archive).

41. Douglas Dales, "Relief Cost Study Urged at Albany," *New York Times*, December 29, 1949, 27.

42. Layhmond Robinson, "Curb on Welfare Passed in Albany," *New York Times*, March 18, 1960, 1, col. 2.

43. Douglas Dales, "State Relief Bill Voted by Senate," *New York Times*, March 8, 1960, 1, col. 4.

44. According to a 1957 report, 52 percent of non-resident relief recipients in New York City were Puerto Rican, while 24 percent were from the South, many of them black. In the upstate area, 44 percent of non-resident relief recipients were from the South,

while only 4 percent were from Puerto Rico (Warren Weaver Jr., "Non-resident Aid Heaviest in the City," *New York Times*, 18 February 1957, 16, col. 1). In 1969, the Supreme Court ruled that such laws were illegal because they violated the Fourteenth Amendment's equal protection clause and individuals' right to travel. See Scott W. Allard and Sheldon Danziger, "Welfare Magnets: Myth or Reality?" *Journal of Politics* 62:2 (2000), 350–68; Martha F. Davis, *Brutal Need: Lawyers and the Welfare Rights Movement, 1960–1973* (New Haven: Yale University Press, 1993), 80.

45. George H. Gallup, *The Gallup Poll, Public Opinion 1935–1971* (New York: Random House, 1972), 1731.

46. Lisa Levenstein, "From Innocent Children to Unwanted Migrants and Unwed Moms: The Public Discourse on Welfare 1960–1961," *Journal of Women's History* 11:4 (2000), 10–33.

47. Ellen Reese, "The Politics of Motherhood: The Restriction of Poor Mothers' Welfare Rights in the United States, 1949–1960," *Social Politics: International Studies in Gender, State, and Society* 8:1 (2001), 65–112.

48. Robert Pear, "G.O.P. Dispute Delays Vote on Welfare Bill," *New York Times*, 16 May 2002, A20.

49. *Star Tribune*, "Welfare Reform II: A Congress Detached from Reality" 13 September 2003, 24A.

50. Robin Toner and Robert Pear, "Bush's Plan on Welfare Law Increases Work Requirement," *New York Times*, February 26, 2002, A23; Robin Toner and Robert Pear, "Bush Urges Work and Marriage Programs in Welfare Plan," *New York Times*, February 27, 2002, A18; Jonathan Peterson, "The Nation: Welfare Plan Would Count Family Time," *Los Angeles Times*, March 28, 2002, A1; Robert Pear, "G.O.P. Dispute Delays Vote on Welfare Bill," *New York Times*, May 16, 2002, A20; Sheila R. Zedlewski, and Pamela Loprest, "Welfare Reform: One Size Doesn't Fit All," *Christian Science Monitor*, August 25, 2003, 9; Jacqueline Marino, "How Marriage Has Gone from a Private Matter to Public Policy," *Plain Dealer*, September 14, 2003, 17.

51. Martin Gilens, *Why Americans Hate Welfare: Race, Media, and the Politics of Antipoverty Policy* (Chicago: University of Chicago Press, 1999).

52. Committee on Ways and Means, United States House of Representatives, *1998 Green Book* (Washington, D.C.: U.S. Government Printing Office, 1998), Table 7-19.

53. Charles Post, "The Capitalist Policy Planning Network and the Welfare Reform Act of 1996," unpublished paper (Department of Social Science, Borough of Manhattan Community College—City University of New York, 1997).

54. Jeffrey H. Joseph, "Statement for the Record on Welfare Reform Before the Subcommittee on Human Resources of the House Committee on Ways and Means for the U.S. Chamber Commerce," *Hearing Before the Subcommittee on Human Resources of the Committee on Ways and Means, House of Representatives, 104th Congress, First Session, Part 2, 2/10/95, Serial 104-44* (Washington D.C.: U.S. Government Printing Office, 1995), 1706–7.

55. Cited in Sylvia Weinberg, "Mexican American Mothers and the Welfare Debate: A History of Exclusion," *Journal of Poverty* 2:3 (1998), 53–75.

56. Alice O'Connor, *Poverty Knowledge: Social Science, Social Policy, and the Poor in Twentieth Century U.S. History* (Princeton: Princeton University Press, 2001), 250; Jean Stefancic and Richard Delgado, "The Attack on Welfare," in *No Mercy: How Conservative Think Tanks and Foundations Changed America's Social Agenda* (Philadelphia: Temple University Press, 1996), 58, 82, 95.

57. Post, "The Capitalist Policy Planning Network and the Welfare Reform Act of 1996," 11–12.

58. Charles Murray, "The Underclass Revisited," *American Enterprise Institute Papers and Studies*, 1998, *http://www.aei.org/ps/psmurray.htm* (accessed February 12, 1999).

59. Doug Besharov, "Working to Make Welfare a Chore," *Wall Street Journal*, 9 February 1994; see also "Testimony of Doug Besharov, American Enterprise Institute," in *Teen Parents and Welfare Reform, Hearing Before the Committee on Finance, United States Senate*, 104 Congress, First Session (Washington, D.C.: U.S. Government Printing Office, 1995).

60. Robert Rector, "Why Congress Must Reform Welfare," *The Heritage Foundation*, Backgrounder No. 1063 (1995), 6.

61. William Bennett, "Testimony for Empower America," *Contract with America—Welfare Reform, Hearing before the Subcommittee on Human Resources of the Committee on Ways and Means, House of Representatives*, 104 Congress, First Session. (Washington, D.C.: U.S. Government Printing Office, 1995), 165; Stefancic and Delgado, "The Attack on Welfare," 92–93; CATO Institute, "Welfare Reform," *Congressional Testimony before the Finance, Committee United States Senate of Michael Tanner Director Health and Welfare Studies*, CATO Institute, March 9, 1995, *http://www.cato.org/testimony/ct-ta3-9.html*

62. Douglas Besharov, "Testimony before the Subcommittee on Human Resources Hearing on Welfare and Marriage Issues," Committee on Ways and Means, March 7, 2002, *www.house.gov/ways_means/humres* (accessed July 15, 2003).

63. Wade Horn and Andrew Bush, "Fathers, Marriage, and Welfare Reform," *Welfare Policy Center of the Hudson Institute*, *http://www.hudson.org*, 1997; Robert Rector, "The Effects of Welfare Reform," *Testimony before the Subcommittee on Human Resources, The Committee on Ways and Means*, March 15, 2001, *http://www.heritage.org/library/testimony/test031501b.html*; Patrick F. Fagan, "Encouraging Marriage and Discouraging Divorce," *The Heritage Foundation*, No. 1421, 2001.

64. Kent Weaver, *Ending Welfare As We Know It* (Washington, D.C.: Brookings Institution, 2000), 211–15.

65. Cited in Justin Watson, *The Christian Coalition: Dreams of Restoration, Demands for Recognition* (New York: St. Martin's Press, 1997), 146.

66. Weaver, *Ending Welfare As We Know It*, 211–15.

67. Elizabeth Shogren, "Senate, House on Own Paths in Welfare Debate; Congress: Upper Chamber's Provision Suggest it is Not as Attuned to the Conservative Groups Seeking Support for 'Family Values' Legislation," *Los Angeles Times*, 16 September 1995b, A4.

68. Elizabeth Bossom, "President Bush Endorses Abstinence and Marriage: Both Programs Vital to Reform of Welfare System," *Concerned Women For America*, 2002, *http://cwfa.org/library/family/2002-02-27_welfare-reform.shtml*; Sara Diamond. *Not By Politics Alone: The Enduring Influence of the Christian Right* (New York: Guilford Press, 1998), 111; Phyllis Schlafly, "Sex Education Has Become X-Rated," *Education Reporter*, September 20, 2000, *www.eagleforum.org/column/2002/sept 00/00-09-20.shtml* (accessed June 5, 2002); Traditional Values Coalition, "Welfare Reform Legislation Passes," May 24, 2002, *http://traditionalvalues.org/article.php?sid=304*; Traditional Values Coalition, 2002, "White House Faith-Based Initiative Leader Outlines Future," May 24, 2002, *http://traditionalvalues.org/article.php?sid=303*; Charles R. Miville, 2001, "Faith-Based Push Changes Course," Focus on the Family, December 11, 2001, *http://www.family.org*; Charles R. Miville, 2001, "State Leaders Back Welfare Funds for Marriage," Focus on the Family, December 13, 2001, *http://www.family.org*;

Bob Ditmer, "Study of American Fatherhood Revealing," Focus on the Family, April 12, 2002, *http://www.family.org*; Pete Winn, "Abstinence Funding Battle Heats Up," Focus on the Family, April 24, 2002, *http://www.family.org*.

69. The study was based on interviews with GOP officials, campaign activists, political consultants, news reporters, and university professors from all 50 states (John F. Persinos, "Has the Christian Right Taken Over the Republican Party," *Campaigns & Elections*, September [1994], 21–24).

70. John C. Green, James L. Guth, Lyman A. Kellstedt, and Corwin E. Smidt, "Faith in the Vote: Religiosity and the Presidential Election," *Public Perspective: A Roper Center Review of Public Opinion and Polling* 12:2 (2001), 33–35.

71. Dan Stein, "Testimony of Dan Stein, Federation for American Immigration Reform," *Contract with America–Welfare Reform, Hearing Before the Subcommittee on Human Resources of the Committee on Ways and Means, House of Representatives*, 104 Congress, First Session, Part 1 (Washington, D.C.: U.S. Government Printing Office, 1995), 446–457.

72. Michael J. Shapiro, "Narrating the Nation, Unwelcoming the Stranger: Anti-Immigration Policy in Contemporary 'America,'" *Alternatives* 22:1(1997), 1–34.

73. Elizabeth Shogren, "Plans to Cut Safety Net Leave Legal Immigrants Dangling," *Los Angeles Times*, November 21, 1994, A1.

74. Michael E. Fix and Jeffrey S. Passel (1994), "Immigration and Immigrants: Setting the Record Straight," Research Report, The Urban Institute. *http://www.urban.org* (accessed February 12, 1998).

75. Elizabeth Shogren, "Bill Ties Welfare Reform to Cut in Immigrant Aid," *Los Angeles Times*, May 11, 1994, A4.

76. Ellen Reese and Elvia Ramirez, "The Politics of Welfare Inclusion: Explaining State-Level Restorations of Legal Immigrants' Welfare Rights," paper presented at the 2002 Society for the Study of Social Problems Conference in Chicago.

77. Elizabeth Becker, "Politics; Farm Compromise," *New York Times*, April 28, 2002, 2:2.

78. Gilens, *Why Americans Hate Welfare*, 45–50; Paul Pierson, *Dismantling the Welfare State? Reagan, Thatcher, and the Politics of Retrenchment* (New York: Cambridge University Press, 1994); Steven M. Teles, *Whose Welfare? AFDC and Elite Politics* (Lawrence: University of Kansas Press, 1996), 43–45; R. Kent Weaver, Robert Y. Shapiro, and Lawrence R. Jacobs, "The Polls—Trends: Welfare," *Public Opinion Quarterly* 59 (1995), 618.

79. Tammy Draut, "New Opportunities? Public Opinion on Poverty, Income Inequality, and Public Policy: 1996–2001," New York: Demos: A Network for Ideas & Action, *www.demos-usa.org*, 5 (acccessed March 14, 2002); Geoffrey Garin, Guy Molyneux, and Linda DiVall, "Public Attitudes toward Welfare Reform," *Social Policy* 25:2(1994), 44–49; Gilens, *Why Americans Hate Welfare*, 51–58, 72, 95. High-income people who have had personal or familial experiences with being on welfare are less likely than other high-income people to want to cut welfare spending, which suggests that perceptions of poverty and welfare, not self-interest, drives their animosity to welfare (Gilens, *Why Americans Hate Welfare*, 54).

80. American Broadcast Company/Washington Post surveys, cited in Weaver, Shapiro, and Jacobs, "The Polls—Trends: Welfare," 606–27.

81. Gilens, *Why Americans Hate Welfare*, 37.

82. The public supported softer time limits and work requirements than those enacted by Congress however. See Garin, Molyneux, and DiVall, "Public Attitudes toward Welfare Reform," 44–49; Weaver, *Ending Welfare As We Know It*, 181–84.

83. National Public Radio/Kaiser Family Foundation/Kennedy School of Government. *National Survey on Poverty in America* (Menlo Park: Henry J. Kaiser Family Foundation, *http://www.kff.org*, 2001); Greg M. Shaw and Robert Y. Shapiro, "The Polls—Trends: Poverty and Public Assistance," *Public Opinion Quarterly* 66 (2002), 105–128.

84. Gilens, *Why Americans Hate Welfare.*

85. While blacks make up the largest share of recipients, this is a recent development. As late as 1994, 37.4 percent of recipients were white, while 36.4 percent were African-American (U.S. Department of Health and Human Services 2002: 110).

86. Ann Shola Orloff, "Explaining U.S. Welfare Reform: Power, Gender, Race and U.S. Policy Legacy," *Critical Social Policy* 22:1 (2002), 96–118.

87. U.S. Bureau of the Census 2001b, Tables 576, 577, p. 373; Mink, *Welfare's End*, 118; Janet C. Gornick and Marcia K. Meyers, *Families that Work: Policies for Reconciling Parenthood and Employment* (New York: Russell Sage Foundation, 2003) 46.

88. Weaver, *Ending Welfare As We Know It.*

89. Michael Schwartz, "Introduction: What Went Right? Why the Clinton Administration Did Not Alter the Conservative Trajectory in Federal Policy," in *Social Policy and the Conservative Agenda*, Clarence Y. H. Lo and Michael Schwartz, eds. (Malden, MA: Blackwell, 1998), 10; Frances Fox Piven, "Welfare and the Transformation of Electoral Politics," *Social Policy and the Conservative Agenda*, 21; Ronald Walters, "The Democratic Party and the Politics of Welfare Reform," *Social Policy and the Conservative Agenda*, 44–46; Dan Clawson, Alan Neustadtl, and Mark Weller, *Dollars and Votes: How Business Campaign Contributions Subvert Democracy* (Philadelphia: Temple University Press, 1998).

90. Joe Soss, Sanford P. Schram, Thomas P. Vartanian, and Erin O'Brien, "Setting the Terms of Relief: Explaining State Policy Choices in the Devolution Revolution," *American Journal of Political Science* 45:2 (2001), 378–95.

Suggestions for Further Reading

Albelda, Randy, and Ann Withorn, eds. *Lost Ground: Welfare Reform, Poverty, and Beyond.* Cambridge, MA: South End Press, 2002.

Abramovitz, Mimi. *Regulating the Lives of Women: Social Policy from Colonial Times to the Present.* Boston: South End Press, 1989.

Bergmann, Barbara. *Saving Our Children From Poverty: What the United States Can Learn from France.* New York: Russell Sage Foundation, 1996.

Brown, Michael K. *Race, Money, and the American Welfare State.* Ithaca: Cornell University Press, 1999.

Dujon, Dianne, and Ann Withorn, eds. *For Crying Out Loud: Women's Poverty in the United States.* Boston: South End Press, 1996.

Edin, Kathryn, and Laura Lein. *Making Ends Meet: How Single Mothers Survive Welfare and Low-Wage Work.* New York: Russell Sage Foundation, 1997.

Gilens, Martin. *Why Americans Hate Welfare: Race, Media, and the Politics of Antipoverty Policy.* Chicago: University of Chicago Press, 1999.

Goodwin, Joanne L. *Gender and the Politics of Welfare Reform: Mothers' Pensions in Chicago, 1911–1929.* Chicago: University of Chicago Press, 1997.

Gordon, Linda. *Pitied But Not Entitled: Single Mothers and the History of Welfare.* New York: The Free Press, 1994.

————, ed. *Women, the State, and Welfare*. Madison: University of Wisconsin Press, 1990.

Hays, Sharon. *Flat Broke with Children: Women in the Age of Welfare Reform*. New York: Oxford University Press, 2003.

Levenstein, Lisa. "From Innocent Children to Unwanted Migrants and Unwed Moms: The Public Discourse on Welfare 1960–1961." *Journal of Women's History* 11–4 (2000), 10–33.

Lo, Clarence Y. H., and Michael Schwartz, eds. *Social Policy and the Conservative Agenda*. Malden, MA: Blackwell Publishers, Inc, 1998.

Mink, Gwendolyn. *Welfare's End*. Ithaca: Cornell University Press, 1998.

————. *Wages of Motherhood: Inequality in the Welfare State, 1917–1924*. Ithaca: Cornell University Press, 1995.

Misra, Joya, and Frances Akins. "The Welfare State and Women: Structure, Agency, and Diversity." *Social Politics* Fall (1998), 259–85.

Neubeck, Kenneth J., and Noel A. Cazenave. *Welfare Racism: Playing the Race Card against America's Poor*. New York: Routledge, 2001.

Noble, Charles. *Welfare As We Knew It: A Political History of the American Welfare State*. New York: Oxford University Press, 1997.

O'Connor, Alice. *Poverty Knowledge: Social Science, Social Policy, and the Poor in Twentieth-Century U.S. History*. Princeton: Princeton University Press, 2001.

Peck, Jamie. *Workfare States*. New York: Guilford Press, 2001.

Pierson, Paul. *Dismantling the Welfare State? Reagan, Thatcher, and the Politics of Retrenchment*. New York: Cambridge University Press, 1994.

Piven, Frances Fox, and Richard Cloward. *Regulating the Poor: The Functions of Public Welfare*, Updated Version. New York: Vintage Books, 1993 [1971].

————. *Poor People's Movements: Why They Succeed, How They Fail*. New York: Vintage Books, 1979.

Quadagno, Jill. *The Color of Welfare: How Racism Undermined the War on Poverty*. New York: Oxford University Press, 1994.

Reese, Ellen. *Backlash Against Welfare Mothers: Past and Present*. Berkeley: University of California Press, 2005.

Rose, Nancy E. *Workfare or Fair Work: Women, Welfare, and Government Work Programs*. New Brunswick, NJ: Rutgers University Press, 1995.

Schram, Sanford. *After Welfare: The Culture of Postindustrial Social Policy*. New York: New York University Press, 2000.

Schram, Sanford, Joe Soss, and Richard C. Fording, eds. *Race and the Politics of Welfare Reform*. Ann Arbor: University of Michigan Press, 2003.

Seccombe, Karen. *"So You Think I Drive a Cadillac?": Welfare Recipients' Perspectives on the System and Its Reform*. Boston: Allyn & Bacon, 1999.

Sidel, Ruth. *Keeping Women and Children Last: America's War on the Poor*, Revised Edition. New York: Penguin Books, 1998 [1996].

Solinger, Rickie. *Wake Up Little Susie: Single Pregnancy and Race Before Roe v. Wade*. New York: Routledge, 1992.

Stefancic, Jean, and Richard Delgado. *No Mercy: How Conservative Think Tanks and Foundations Changed America's Social Agenda*. Philadelphia: Temple University Press, 1996.

Weaver, Kent. *Ending Welfare As We Know It*. Washington, D.C.: Brookings Institution, 2000.

Weinberg, Sylvia. "Mexican American Mothers and the Welfare Debate: A History of Exclusion." *Journal of Poverty* 2–3 (1998), 53–75.

Metaphors of Class and Race: Comparing German and American Feminisms

Myra Marx Ferree

Myra Marx Ferree (1974) is Professor of Sociology at the University of Wisconsin at Madison. She began her career with a study of working-class women's jobs and orientations to feminism, and has increasingly focused on varieties of women's movements. Among her publications are *Feminist Organizations: Harvest of the New Women's Movement* (1995), *Controversy and Coalition: The New Women's Movement through Three Decades of Change* (3rd edition, 2000), and *Shaping Abortion Discourse: Democracy and the Public Sphere in Germany and the U.S.* (2002). Her current work includes a project on transnational feminist networks on the Web and a book on transformations of German feminism.

> *For Myra Marx Ferree, social class was the dirty little secret in feminist theory. The more feminist scholarship she read about working-class women, the more irritated she was with the patronizing attitude it displayed. She became "committed to trying to correct the picture to better fit my mother and other working-class women I knew. Even though they hated their bosses and much about their jobs, they valued the power at home created by going out to work and making such sacrifices for their families. Now there is a general acceptance of this and of many other ideas that were controversial (the significance of housework as work, that family relations are power relations, that violence is still being used as a political tool to subordinate women), but still too little attention to gender as a social institution (social relations that extend over time and place) in relation to other institutions like class. Gender inequality is not about women's economic opportunities alone or about changing women's individual job choices but about the structures in which these choices get made."*

Feminism is a global movement toward bringing women in as full citizens of their societies while also rethinking the narrow standards of individualism, independence, productive work, and achievement that were based only on men's lives. Yet every feminist mobilization is local and particular, tied to specific histories of struggle and opportunities for change. Although expressing some common concerns about exclusion, subordination, and devaluation, feminist claims take shape though discursively framing the issue of gender, that is, by naming the problems women face in ways that have a local form and focus. Thus women's movements in different countries are singular and distinctive, not merely manifestations of one universally defined common agenda. Thinking about feminism as an issue of comparative politics brings out these particularities.

For comparative analysts, one of the enduring issues in understanding U.S. politics is its obvious "exceptionalism" with regard to social perspectives. In most of the world, class analysis is taken as a legitimate, though not exclusive, way of understanding inequality. For most Americans, including many social scientists here, thinking about economic relations as exploitation rather than opportunity is foreign and uncomfortable. To a degree, the opening to the left in American politics in the 1960s allowed for more consideration of class, race, and gender in the academy as well, and these were thus boon years for critical social inquiry.

But even for sociologists, for whom class is an important category of analysis, class was separated from gender. In the 1970s, the sociologists working on class analysis still often ignored women, while the issues of gender that initially engaged most American feminists often ignored class, assuming "women" in the abstract to be both white and middle class. In the 1980s, women of color successfully challenged their invisibility in this model, but sociologists (such as myself) who studied white working-class women or who wanted to rethink class analysis from a woman-centered perspective were left without many tools for this further expansion.[1] Indeed, my research initially turned toward Germany in pursuit of a usable, class-aware model for analyzing working-class women's struggles with work and family demands.[2]

The comparative turn that I took in the early 1980s was then relatively uncommon among sociologists, most of whom still focused on the U.S. alone. Indeed, into the late 1980s, American sociology textbooks separated gender, race, and class into different levels of analysis (micro, meso, and macro respectively) and for gender used macro-comparative data about cultures and political systems in very rote and stereotypical ways, as an analysis I did with Elaine J. Hall at that time showed.[3] As gender has come to be seen more as an institutional and thus also macro-social factor, comparative analysis has become more prevalent.

In this chapter, I compare the specific experiences of the German and American women's movements. I argue that each movement uses a symbolic repertoire for conceptualizing oppression that is inflected with nationally specific understandings, particularly in how this cultural vocabulary draws upon race or class as the main metaphor for thinking about gender. In calling race and class "metaphors" for thinking about gender, I suggest that they are invisible images of what the concept gender means in a particular political culture. Seeing gender "as if" it were like race (or class) in some fundamental way that is left unarticulated hides the operation of this imagery in framing our feminism. By offering a theoretical sketch of how the metaphors of race and class have been used to think about gender differently in each country, I try to demonstrate the way discursive politics matters to movements generally, and also to provoke thought about the specific illuminations and blind spots that each dominant frame produces. The attractions and implications of using either or both of the metaphors of class and race are not limited, I suggest, to Germany and the U.S., but have resonance in other parts of the world as well. To develop this argument, I first present some general points about the uses of discourse in social movements. I then apply this analysis to German and American feminists in their different historical struggles with race and class relations, and with the other social movements mobilized around social inequality in each country. Finally, I take up the question of what these metaphors of class and race mean for thinking about specific issues and alliances today, emphasizing what each analogy obscures as well as illuminates in global gender politics.

DISCOURSES AND MOBILIZATION

All social movements offer a way of defining an issue as social problem and a sense that something can be done to change this problematic state of affairs, or what is called both diagnostic and prognostic framing.[4] Framing is an important part of the work that social movement organizations do, and the *interpretative packages* or frames that are chosen in any particular context reflect the specific histories, needs and intentions of those who are doing this work. As a socially constructed meaning given to events and issues, each frame presented by a social movement is simultaneously a *scaffold* on which other ideas are hung and a *limit*, like a picture frame, around what can be seen from that perspective.

Frames are constructed by movements doing active work. Frames take their particular shape from the conceptual materials available to the social movement actors who are putting them together and the purposes movements bring to their work. Social movement organizations use frames strategically to appeal to their potential constituents and to make opposition to their goals difficult; thus, frames often invoke generally supported values such as fairness and freedom. But social movements also use frames as ways of creating new ways of thinking, challenging the verities and invisibilities built in to the status quo. Thus, movement language also tries to expand the vocabulary available for talking about injustice, and analogies with existing models can be points to build upon. The framing that movements do is also not only an attempt to gain strategic advantage but expresses a general self-concept and self-location in relation to various other groups and struggles. By saying what is worth fighting about (and what is not), a movement identifies its allies and opponents as well as naming what is at stake in the conflict. Thus, to name an act "discrimination" highlights it as unfair, locates it in relation to legally recognized forms of unjust treatment, whether based on race, gender, age, or disability, and suggests that these other groups should join in fighting against the common injustice it represents.

An important part of the way that movements do their framing work is by invoking metaphors and similes, that is, by using some more or less explicit analogy to other problems, issues, and groups to highlight what is to be seen as important in this case. In the case of feminism, the gender relations that subordinate women are often framed as socially unjust by relating them metaphorically to relationships of race and class oppression (the diagnostic framing) and situating feminist mobilization in relation to other movements for social justice (the prognostic framing). I argue that these dominant images are very different in the United States and in Germany. For American feminists, framing gender in relation to race makes social and political sense; in an American context it seems self-evident that there is a relationship between the kinds of exclusions and oppressions that are organized by the concept of *race* and those of gender. German feminists talk about gender in relation to *class*, and their historical struggles and current mobilizations are shaped by the way that class issues have mattered there.

RACE AND RIGHTS

Consider, first, the American case. For American feminists, organizing a movement has always meant dealing in some way with the dominant political struggle over who counts as an American. Literally from the moment that the Constitution was drawn up to count slaves as less than full people and to exclude Native Americans from the newly forming state, the political question has been who has the rights of citizenship. What do "equal rights" mean in a context that is both a democracy and a compact to exclude some people from participation in its promises?

Because the Declaration of Independence claims that it is "self-evident" and "natural" in how people are "endowed by their Creator" that they should have rights, American movements claiming political and social rights engage in a framing struggle with the idea of "nature" and "natural difference" as warrants for inequality. The centrality of political liberalism, the legitimacy of claiming rights, and the experience of being excluded from rights on the basis of "natural difference" combine to give resonance to the idea that "race" is like gender in such fundamental ways. Race and racial oppression are therefore available to be used an explicit analogy for gender and gender subordination.

When American feminists began to mobilize in 1848 in Seneca Falls, they used the institutionalized discourse of the Declaration of Independence to frame to their aspirations, modeling the structure of their Declaration of Sentiments upon it. But the specific meaning they gave to these words was also shaped by the looming struggle over slavery and their own experiences of exclusion as women from an international antislavery meeting in London. The claims of classical political liberalism—individualism, self-determination, independence—were successfully institutionalized in the U.S. as the world's first democratic state and made highly charged points of debate as African-Americans and white women challenged the limits and exclusions that were also institutionalized in American laws. Because the issues of rights and exclusion from the status of a rights-bearing citizen resonated deeply with the principles and process of American nation-building, rights have been called the *master frame* for all American social movements.[5]

The metaphor of the master frame of race for gender inequality can cut both ways. On the one hand, by providing a common point of reference it can be used to "compare oppressions" and so to naturalize and legitimate the rights of one group as more important than others. This use of race frames the issue as a matter of relative rights and exclusions. On the other hand, the race frame can provide a space from which to critique and undermine the idea of "natural difference" as a justification for inequality, offering a basis for an absolute critique of exclusionary politics. Because the United States is a country that claims to be committed to a principle of equal rights and opportunities for all, these absolute and relative exclusions matter deeply.[6]

It is therefore hardly surprising that American history is studded with specific framing struggles over the relative significance of race and gender in providing access to the rights associated with citizenship, including uses of the comparison to legitimate white women's claims to racial superiority. White feminists who saw racial exclusions as more "natural" and thus more legitimate than those of gender, for example, were horrified that black men should receive the right to vote after the Civil War while this was denied to white women; other feminists saw the struggle for racial equality as taking priority over gender and accepted a definition of the era of reconstruction as the "Negro's hour." The tides of immigration in the later nineteenth and early twentieth century were interpreted in racial terms: Jews, Irish, Greeks, and Italians were all seen as inferior "races" until processes of assimilation and anti-black mobilization made them "white." For many white suffragists, the idea that gender should produce disenfranchisement when race did not was especially galling.[7] As Glenn shows, white women often gave defending racial privilege a higher priority than creating gender solidarity in struggles for women's rights.[8]

In all of these struggles, ethnic nationalism, in the form of a belief in white superiority and the equation of "American" interests with those of white Americans, was the frame within which the struggle for gender equity was waged, both when it was taking the exclusions of racism for granted and when it was mobilizing to challenge these limits. This diagnostic framing of the problem of gender, by comparing the treatment of white women to the way "racially inferior" groups of men were treated, assumed an analogy between gender and race, focused attention on the issue of exclusion from full citizenship, and made "gaining equal rights" the prognostic framing that made sense for addressing both race and gender subordination. This prognostic frame created a particular blind spot about the position of women of color, by eliding the question of "equal to whom?"

Women's movements in the U.S., which were committed to a liberal definition of women's rights as equality and individualism, were constantly confronted with the question of whether or not their demands for inclusion, citizenship, and self-determination were really being made on behalf of *all* women or only represented the empowerment of racially dominant white women. Some feminist activists—Chicana and African-American even more than whites—were actively engaged in struggles against racism and, as Benita Roth shows, this experience was formative of their consciousness as women and as feminists.[9] Women of color needed to struggle both with men of their own racial/ethnic group and with white women in defining the significance of gender oppression in their lives. While white women were often racist, they were indebted to the analogy with race to criticize their own oppression; for some white feminists, this enhanced their ability to challenge myths of racial superiority and actively engage in supporting African-American struggles for freedom. Feminist politics has thus also always included efforts to define all exclusions from citizenship rights on the basis of group difference as absolutely unacceptable. But for Americans of all racial/ethnic backgrounds, the issues of legal rights, inclusion, and natural differences loomed large in the framing of injustice. Gender is like race in this regard, and makes claims of group differences and group entitlements both deeply suspect.

In the 1980s, when women of color successfully challenged feminist social scientists to rethink their assumption that "all the women were white and all the blacks were men," the new incorporation of intersections of race and gender often paid little more than lip service to class. The newly included women were, more often than not, characterized as simultaneously "low income" and "minority." For many sociologists, all the blacks are poor, and all the poor are black, and poor black women are characteristically analyzed in terms of individualized gender and race "disadvantages" rather than in terms of the systematic class relations that affect poor and working-class families in gendered ways. In this regard, American feminist sociologists in general are still not very different from other sociologists or other feminists in marginalizing the issue of class inequality.

CLASS AND VOICE

German political discourse was, by contrast, shaped by class struggle rather than racial privilege. A liberal revolution, enshrining notions of individual rights and liberty along with notions of democracy, property rights, and personal self-development, succeeded in the United States in 1776 but failed in Germany in 1848. The bourgeois individual as a politically empowered citizen became an important element of the American self-understanding, but was not central to German political thought.[10] Instead, the conflict between capital and labor in Germany gave rise to the largest socialist party in Europe in the nineteenth century and made Germany the center of an emerging socialist internationalism. The welfare state that began to be constructed at the turn of the century under Chancellor Otto von Bismarck tried to co-opt this class discontent with relatively generous health and welfare measures. But the German state also actively tried to repress class and gender mobilization: Both socialist groups and gatherings of women to discuss politics were specifically prohibited into the early twentieth century. The struggle against social injustice was thus joined with a struggle against political authoritarianism, and gender was framed as "like class" in demanding a voice for the disenfranchised.

Because Germany was neither democratic nor liberal, to merely articulate political demands as such was not as self-evident or simple as in the United States; the demands that were made took struggle, and the socialists were the loudest and leading voice. In the classic socialist analysis, however, the single most determinative form of oppression is that of class, and all other types of subordination are secondary by-products. Socialist leadership was institutionalized in the form of a political party that should have the right to speak on behalf of all oppressed people. Its challenge to state authoritarianism did not open a space for multiple, independent critiques but defined a single dimension of opposition. The unity of the working class as a frame made this a political demand rather than an appeal to biological similarity. That a group defined collectively as a unitary political actor, as the working class was, could be entitled to have the state respond to the needs expressed by a political party on its behalf was the central issue.

The master frame for understanding inequality was thus class conflict. This diagnostic framing put class at the forefront even when other issues such as gender or race were addressed. Group needs were legitimate political demands, and class was the most important grouping. For socialists, the prognostic frame further deferred all other struggles to wait for the success of "the revolution." The party defined itself as able to speak and act for women. When the socialist revolution actually came about after World War I, the short-lived Weimar Republic under Socialist Party leadership gave women the vote, but then the ascendancy of the Nazi dictatorship made this right moot. Even when German racism, in the form of anti-Semitism, was taken to the furthest extreme in the Holocaust, the explicit focus of political struggle was still framed as a class-based conflict between communism and National Socialism. Many German Jews found the threat hard to take seriously until too late because they didn't believe that most Germans were racist. The Nazis created the notion that there was an Aryan race, a master race, and too many Jews didn't realize soon enough that they would be killed because they weren't part of it. Politics was carried out in a discourse centered on class, which was the master frame organizing all conflict on a single left-right dimension.

Because the class dimension dominated so strongly from the late nineteenth century onward in Germany, conflicts in diagnostic and prognostic framing between feminists and socialists led to fragmentation into specifically upper-middle-class feminism and a working-class feminism. Working-class feminism was subsumed within the Socialist Party and saw its claims for women's full citizenship and empowerment as being achieved only after and through a socialist revolution. Upper-middle-class feminists demanded access to education, imagined women as economically self-sufficient professionals who would be free not to marry, and contested the stigmatization of unmarried motherhood. These movement activists sought the vote for women, but on the same basis as men. In Germany, this meant limitation to property owners. Upper-middle-class feminists argued that women could and should be economically free to compete for jobs, but working-class feminists accepted the Socialist Party's contention that women would be better off by supporting the demand for a family wage for men sufficient to support wives as dependents at home rather than seeking their own access to "male" jobs. This class-based division in women's movements was not only typical of Germany, but spread around the world along with international socialism to typify many of the world's women, with the notable exception of the United States.[11]

In sum, demands for gender equity in both Germany and the U.S. took distinctive shape within and through these race and class cleavages. Although it is often argued that the women's movement that remobilized in the late 1960s and early 1970s was a single worldwide phenomenon, it is also the case that feminism in each individual country took a distinctive route guided by the master frames that provided the particular "scaffolding" for ideas about injustice. The way each movement confronted gender issues took shape in relation to the dominant framing of race and class in each political culture. These different master frames privileged certain specific understandings of injustice, put limits around the diagnoses and prognoses that feminists even considered, and shaped the most enduring and acrimonious conflicts among feminists in each country.

Ideas of difference as warrants for exclusion and subordination as in the case of race guided the U.S. framing of gender into debates about natural differences and entitlements to rights. In Germany, the problem was more one of political priorities and voice, as struggles over which socially structured relations of group conflict took theoretical priority meant deciding what organized group's political leadership would decide how to go about ending injustice. Each framing, in telling a different story about what gender was like, provided a different set of materials for building a women's movement: naming different constituencies, preferring different organizational styles, disposing toward certain conflicts.

FEMINIST REMOBILIZATIONS IN GERMANY AND THE UNITED STATES

The Cold War provides an important shared context for understanding the renewal of the women's movement internationally in the late 1960s. The remobilization of feminism in both West Germany and the U.S. sprang from social movements that questioned the attacks on Communists (and so-called Communist sympathizers) that were widely used to suppress criticism of both governments and their policies in the 1950s. Both Germany and the United States were deeply affected by the Cold War in their self-conceptions. The U.S. was positioned as the opposite pole from the Soviet Union in this conflict and Germany was divided in two at the very fracture point dividing East and West blocs.

Both East Germany (the German Democratic Republic, or GDR) and West Germany (the Federal Republic of Germany, or FRG) were shaped by the global battle between socialism and capitalism as systems. Each formed its self-image and shaped its politics through processes of "system-competition" in which the other side became an important negative reference point, but also, therefore, a primary locus of self-criticism.[12] Both the GDR's "baby-year" (the full year of paid maternity leave offered from the 1970s onward) and the FRG's active peace movement (particularly mobilized in opposition to the Vietnam War, but also opposing German re-militarization and the country's weak de-Nazification efforts) were used by dissidents on the other side to pressure their own governments. Each dissident group—among whom feminists came to be increasingly prominent—saw the other Germany as offering something important that their own country lacked.

The anti-communist politics of both the Federal Republic and the U.S., however, included an emphasis on conservative gender values. Thus, for both countries, the state socialism of the East bloc could be construed as threatening in part because it challenged the organization of gender along explicitly patriarchal lines in the family. The Communist party did not achieve the emancipation of women it proclaimed in the GDR or anywhere else in the East bloc, but as an "other" it served as a reference point in politically justifying women's subordination in both the Federal Republic and the United States. The defense of the nuclear, male-dominated family was equated with the defense of capitalism, of religion, and of Western civilization.[13]

Challenges to this conservative view of states and families as engaged in a struggle with an international enemy arose in the 1960s. This international context changed through the remobilization of student movements, with their concern with issues of peace and environmental protection and anti-authoritarian politics. This general "thaw" in Cold War politics helped to support the new women's movement. Despite the common, transnational impetus of the period, the way the women's movement developed in Germany and the United States shows marked differences as well as similarities. The race and class analogies embedded in each national context for framing social politics particularly influenced where and how women began to name gender injustice.

THE GERMAN REVIVAL OF FEMINISM

In the Federal Republic, the context of feminist mobilization was the student movement that arose, as in most of Europe, out of dissatisfaction with the conservatism and environmental insensitivity of the trade unions and the militarism of Cold War geo-politics.[14] The theoretical argument central to their self-understanding was that students, youth, and certain types of white collar workers were the new proletarians and the intellectual vanguard of the revolution; the explicit analogy was to a "new class," redrawing of the lines of social conflict away from the "old left" of labor unions and social democracy to "new left" concerns with anti-authoritarianism. While the New Left, and its arguments with both capitalism and the conventional organizations of classic socialism, was a significant part of feminist mobilization in the U.S. as well, it did not have the overall political resonance in the wider culture that socialist ways of framing the gender question had in Germany.

In the Federal Republic, feminism developed through three distinct phases. The first phase was marked particularly by the historical confrontation between feminism and socialism, and was distinguished by a rejection of the once-dominant division between working-class socialist feminism and bourgeois equal rights feminism. This rejection took the form of a claim for *autonomy* for women, which carried multiple meanings in this historical context. One central meaning was a rejection of the classic socialist position that subordinated women's claims to the success of the party as a whole, and thus a refusal to see the party-based women's organizations of the GDR as authentic carriers of women's demands for liberation. This also meant the repudiation of male-dominated leftist student groups and male-dominated socialist revolutionaries in the rest of the world as being appropriate representatives of women. Instead, women committed to autonomy formed new, non-hierarchical local groups that began from the position of women's interests as women taking priority, and rejecting cooperation with men as necessarily leading to subordination.[15] Thus autonomy also came to mean a commitment to a certain type of organizational style and to the principle of women speaking directly for themselves, defining their own needs.

Rethinking socialist orthodoxies about whether the overthrow of capitalism would really usher in a new age of equality for women did not mean accepting that capitalism was or could be good for women. In that sense, the new feminism developing in the FRG remained far more influenced by socialism than American feminism ever was. But the question of whether socialism was good for women became a central one, and the countries of Eastern Europe became a central point of comparison and critique. In another sense, the demand for autonomy was also an appeal for individual rights and self-determination that were central to classical liberalism. This was a weak political position in Germany. Neither conservative Catholic nor Social Democratic parties in West Germany after World War II were particularly interested in issues of individual rights, and both saw meeting women's needs indirectly though the improvement of the position of the male head of household as taking priority over increasing women's ability to act freely as individuals.[16]

The defining developments during this first period of feminist remobilization in West Germany can thus be seen as both the call for personal autonomy in the context of new and equally autonomous women's organizations and an intensified questioning of what, if anything, socialism had to offer women. The generally negative view of the party-dominated women's organizations in East-Central Europe and of the GDR in particular was in tension with the recognition that women in the West continued to be denied substantive benefits, such as abortion rights and state-supported childcare, that GDR women enjoyed under state socialism. Nonetheless, the commitment to improving women's status took first priority for feminists in the FRG, and changing gender relations was seen as uniting women in a common struggle for autonomy. All women were assumed to share common experiences, a claim that in the German context seemed to echo the socialist claims of class unity more than any implication of biological essentialism.

By the early 1980s, this stance was already beginning to change. The idea that women were oppressed primarily by male power in the family, which both rested upon male advantages in the labor market and reproduced this inequality by making wives and mothers into inherently unequal competitors, was becoming complicated by a greater awareness of the role of the state and political regimes on gender relations. Women in the GDR, who only began to be able to mobilize, even in a small way and with constant repression, in the mid-1980s, made peace politics a more salient element of what it appeared that women wanted. Their focus on the macro-level dynamics of war and peace as gendered state politics challenged the single-minded focus on gender relations in the family that had largely characterized the earliest West German feminists. Moreover, feminists in the FRG who had experience in autonomous women's groups and local projects began to question their separation from party politics and the lack of control over mainstream political decision-making that this entailed. Two additional, related developments began to bring feminists in the Federal Republic out of their original separatist stance.[17]

On the one hand, the Green Party offered a political alternative that was not easily classifiable in the left-right terms of conventional class politics. The anti-hierarchical, counter-cultural political style of organizing that initially characterized the party was compatible with the loose local network structure of the autonomous women's movement, and many of the environmental and anti-war positions of the party were also consistent with feminists' substantive political preferences. Thus some autonomous feminists became Green Party loyalists without necessarily feeling that they had given up their commitment to women as a political priority. This feeling was not necessarily shared by other autonomous feminists. Conflicts and compromises within the Green Party also raised questions for the feminists who did join them.

On the other hand, the 1980s also saw the emergence and spread of "Frauenbeauftragten" or women's affairs officers, from the local to the state level. There was a clear tendency for Green and SPD governments to take the lead in bringing women's concerns into government in this way and to give greater resources, authority, and status to such offices as were established. These women's affairs officers provided a new source of networking among autonomous feminist activists and their projects but also linked them increasingly with women in the parties and in professional and civic organizations.

Interestingly, in the 1980s, as feminists in the Federal Republic began to turn increasingly to the state and make demands on state resources, feminists in the GDR began to find more autonomous venues in which to organize, particularly in the shelter of the churches, and began to make more critical demands on the state, starting with a critique of militarism and widening into a general perception of the state as not nearly as helpful to women as it had long claimed to be.

Thus, if phase one of the reemergence of feminism in Germany was marked by a tension between autonomy and socialism and colored by the Cold War, phase two was characterized by a tension between autonomy and integration within the political structure that moved in different directions in each of the two German states. Because the articulation of collective needs is not seen as an expression of some biological essentialism when it is a class-based voice, it was also not especially problematic for German feminists to claim to speak for women as if this were a unified group or to define certain experiences, such as motherhood or housework, as fundamental expressions of gender subordination that all women shared. This became problematic in the next period, when unification made differences in experience among women harder to ignore.

Phase three, the 1990s, is the period of German unification, ushered in by the fall of the Berlin Wall in 1989. The predominant theme here is the tension between East and West. The very different organization of women's lives in each country led to quite different understandings of women's oppression and freedom in each. In the GDR, full employment, state-run child care, and legal abortion gave women more freedom from the family and private forms of patriarchal control without weakening male dominance in the public sphere of the state power or challenging the political control of the state over both men and women.[18] East German women experienced full time employment and access to many conventionally "male" jobs without being able to challenge politically the disparaging attitudes and exclusion from positions of power that they still faced. By contrast, in the FRG, women's public citizenship had grown both through autonomous feminist organizing and women's integration into the political parties and administrative system of government without being able to dislodge the private patriarchy of the nuclear family dependent on a male breadwinner.[19]

Because the German feminist revival was initially complicated by "system competition" between East and West, with the GDR's version of socialist liberation for women providing both a negative referent and an enticing alternative for thinking about gender, unification provided a new lens on these differences. Neither form of gender relations, though markedly different in how each was carried out, was experienced as "emancipation" by women in that country, even though much of what their system offered (social benefits in the East, political freedoms and consumer goods in the West) was envied by women in the other Germany. The frame of class conflict and Socialist Party dominance had implications in both halves of the newly unified German state, as the question of just what socialism could and could not offer women was debated with specific examples drawn from women's previous experiences on both sides of the wall. Working out issues of autonomy, voice, and relationships to the state that were given by framing gender in class terms were thus central to women's thinking about oppression in both parts of Germany. Even when the specifics of the problems posed for women differed in each Germany, the master frame of class and the politics of socialism gave a distinctive shape to the German feminist movement.

FEMINIST REMOBILIZATION IN THE UNITED STATES

The phases of feminist development in the United States were quite different from those in Germany, despite some superficial similarities.[20] The American experience with socialism at the height of the Cold War was as a distant and opposite other; political liberalism and free market capitalism defined American values, and socialist views of welfare and of liberation were not potential rivals next door, as they were in Germany. In the U.S., the context for recognizing gender subordination as a problem was the Southern civil rights movement initially and then the wider anti-war mobilization and New Left politics of students in the North.[21] Race was an important, explicit metaphor for thinking about gender in the United States; both academics and activists talked about parallels between the status of women and African-Americans and coined the word *sexism* as a direct analogy with racism. The anti-war movement of the 1960s simultaneously questioned the racism of the war in Vietnam and the racism of American apartheid in the South. The ties between the civil rights movement and feminism were explicit and personal, as Sara Evans has documented.[22]

Lacking the historical confrontation with socialism as a defining feature of the first phase, American feminists experienced the 1970s as a period of uncontested success and growth. The women's movement in Washington built directly on the civil rights movement for African-Americans; the National Organization for Women (NOW) was explicitly modeled on the National Association for the Advancement of Colored People, and was open to male members from the start, just as the NAACP had long welcomed white anti-racists as members. The analogy between gender and race was used to extend federal guarantees of equal citizenship to both of these previously excluded groups in the Civil Rights Act and subsequent laws and executive orders. With race as their central analogy, the issue of rights (rather than autonomy, as in Germany) became American feminists' central claim. The language of rights was deeply entwined with a commitment to liberalism in the American system as a whole. This commitment to liberal ideology could be rhetorically used to claim, "equal rights" and make feminist claims legitimate, but only by making "difference" suspect.

This tactic of connecting gender and race as issues of equal rights provided a supportive background for a wave of early legislation that mandated equal treatment of women and men in education and on the job. Anti-discrimination laws with regard to employment, education, housing, and credit were written to apply to women in explicit parallel to race. The *Roe v. Wade* decision in 1973 secured an individual right to abortion without a massive feminist mobilization on this issue by also extending a gender-free idea of privacy to include women as citizens who had a right to control their own bodies as their own property. The mainstream American view of individual achievement and meritocracy could be stretched to accommodate equal rights for women, but only (as with the discourse about race on which it built) by claiming that no natural differences existed to warrant unequal treatment.[23]

Because liberalism was the defining discursive framework for talking about individuals and their rights, both radical feminism and socialist feminism were discursive challengers and fringe organizations. The radical feminists emphasized cultural differences between women and men, the underlying androcentrism of the liberal system as a whole, and the exclusion of women's distinctive role as mothers from an equal rights model of feminism. Socialist feminists spoke, as in Germany, about structural differences that produced gender conflict and that needed to be institutionally reorganized at a group level, but in thinking about group positions (in a way that invoked a class frame) rather than individual chances (more congenial to the way American liberalism framed race) failed to find resonance with the American master frame. It was not true that Americans could not or did not speak about class or about group differences in experience by class, but that such concerns, when uttered, seemed to run at cross purposes to the dominant understanding of inequality as exclusion from the American promise of "equal rights" that the race metaphor framed as central. When class issues were addressed, the tendency was to assume that women of color represented working class and poor women; white women were typically addressed as if they all were middle class.[24]

In the 1970s, feminist awareness of race still typically took the form of a positive analogy between gender and race as systematic forms of exclusion and a confidence that both could be addressed by comparable programs and policies. The critique that in this model "all the women are white and all the blacks are men" raised by women of color in the late 1970s shook this confidence. The invisibility and exclusion of women of color highlighted the dominance of white feminists and their ways of thinking in what was defined as the feminist movement, leading black feminists to seek other ways (such as "womanist") to characterize their struggles. Both legally and organizationally, however, race and gender were conceptualized as parallel, be it in the joint mandate to provide equal employment opportunities through a single "affirmative action office" or in the separate but similar organizations such as NOW and the NAACP that were the liberal backbone of each movement.

The 1980s in the U.S. was a period of reaction and resistance, marked by the mobilization of active anti-feminist organizations. Campaigns against abortion rights gained an important victory when the Supreme Court upheld the Hyde Amendment's definition of choice as something that could legitimately be limited by a woman's ability to pay. The classically liberal Equal Rights Amendment was stopped dead in the state legislatures by the campaign mounted by Phyllis Schlafly and her allies.[25] The once-Democratic southern states turned Republican in reaction to the Democratic Party's support of civil rights, and the Reagan revolution shifted the political landscape such that support for social spending on domestic issues of poverty and social justice became a political liability. Both parties began to move to the right. Feminist groups increasingly became explicitly allied with the Democratic Party, which became cast (for better and for worse) as the one party that represented African-Americans. Within feminist organizations, conflict over the dominance of an agenda shaped only by privileged white women took place throughout the decade. In this second phase, women of color pushed with increasing success for all feminists to acknowledge the intersections of gender, race, and class and to campaign for social justice across the board. Feminists emerged as an important Democratic Party constituency for the first time, as differences between women's and men's voting patterns took shape over issues of social justice.[26]

The 1990s in the U.S. were the Clinton years, and in this third phase offered many American feminists the problematic choice of supporting a Democratic Party that was moving to the right on some issues, abandoning its commitment of support to poor mothers and their children in the name of welfare reform, or looking for an alternative despite a winner-take-all electoral system in which third parties are ineffective. The opposition to race and gender equality that mobilized in the 1980s coalesced into a New Right agenda of so-called "family values" that were explicitly anti-abortion and anti-gay rights and favored male authority in the family, a radical repeal of progressive taxation, and sharp limits on all forms of social redistribution to the poor. To the extent that the Republican Party renounced classic liberal individualism and embraced the New Right, it also demonized feminists as its political opposition. Race and gender politics were used to appeal to white men, who increasingly were the modal Republican voters, while self-identified feminists and African-Americans emerged as the two most reliably Democratic constituencies in the 2000 presidential election. Disappointment with Democrats' commitment to social justice fueled the third party candidacy of Ralph Nader that may have led to the selection of George W. Bush as president that year.

By the end of the 1990s, the issue of when and how political alliances connect gender and race emerged as a critical question in American party politics, as it had been at the height of the suffrage campaign in the 1910s (also a period of aggressive American foreign policy and resurgent domestic racism).[27] As the defense of white American dominance at home and abroad became more politically salient, the race analogy was no longer a tool to support claims for gender equality, but a weapon to discredit calls for addressing race and gender oppression. Both feminists and racial-ethnic minorities can be attacked as insufficiently loyal to the "American" cause, construed as the interests of the hegemonic white male. Ethnic nationalism, in the form of claims to the right of "Americans" to wield global power, is also used to define masculinity as part of "American" national character in the post–Cold War era, as in Robert Kagan's much quoted claim that "Americans are from Mars and Europeans are from Venus."[28]

COMPARING THESE TWO "WESTERN" FEMINISMS

Although the feminist movements of the United States and of Germany drew their initial impetus from challenges to the Cold War frame that in the 1950s had suppressed a wide range of critiques of injustice in the West, the course of those respective remobilizations in the late 1960s and movement developments from then to the 2000s were not as similar as the idea of a global second-wave feminism would suggest. Instead, each movement had a distinctive flavor and terms of argument drawn from its own dominant framing and historical conflict.

For Germany, this frame was class, evidenced not only in the system-competition between East and West but also in the central value feminists gave to autonomy and the ability to make group-based political claims. Both as a rejection of the claims of a socialist orthodoxy to define women's needs for them and as a positive valuation of a liberal idea of personhood that had not been institutionalized in Germany, the concept of autonomy shaped feminism. It made forming any one central organization to press women's claims anathema, being too similar to socialist centralism and theory-driven demands, and instead encouraged defining non-hierarchical, local grassroots groups as the essence of feminist organization. These groups often developed structural arguments about women's subordination as wives and mothers and about men's violence that became hallmarks of what in the U.S. was called *radical feminism* and in Germany was simply called *autonomous feminism*.

But autonomy as a concept also provided a new way to begin to think about individuals and difference, and the systematic collapse of the GDR as a socialist state also suggested the need to transcend the old model provided by the frame of class and class conflict. Particularly in the wake of German unification, the definition of "women" as a unitary group that could make a single set of claims was thrown into question, since the experiences of GDR women were very different from those of women in the FRG. A focus on state-level rather than familial forms of patriarchal oppression was helpful in bringing feminists out of the political marginality that their small autonomous groups had experienced (in part by choice). Engaging more directly with party politics also implied rethinking what women (in their undeniable diversity) wanted from the state, and what means were best to express these demands. Class was a master frame for thinking about gender in Germany, but feminists in the late twentieth century were also challenging the limits of this frame and attaching new ideas to this scaffold of understanding gender. If state socialism was not the answer, neither was rejecting the state or the rights it might offer.

In contrast, U.S. feminist framing was already propelled by a discourse of individualism, rights, difference, and exclusion. This provided a ready language for making successful claims on the state by analogy to race but it also placed women of color in a marginalized position rather than at the center of thinking about social justice. The analogy between gender and race was partially imposed on the movement by the long history of racial exclusions that characterized U.S. movements, and partially chosen by feminist academics and activists to name sexism and claim equal rights for women in terms that were familiar, therefore resonant with American experience.

In the U.S., the master metaphor of race made equal rights, rather than autonomy, the core claim that feminists could make. Because the locus for doing political work was either the individual (who needed help) or the state (which could be lobbied to provide it), rather than a mobilized group (a social movement), rights-based thinking also helped to convert American feminist organizations into local service providers on the one hand (as with many rape crisis centers and shelters for battered women) and national lobbying groups on the other (not only NOW but a plethora of feminist groups have become staff-driven, Washington-based organizations supported by "checkbook activists" around the country). The focus on rights for persons in disempowered and excluded groups, which is the direction in which the race frame points American feminist attention, gives no reason to find either of these organizational developments troubling. In addition, the emphasis on *civil rights*, understood on the analogy with racial struggles for political inclusion, is a narrower and less economically meaningful demand than women's claim for both political freedom and economic security as *human rights*.

The equation of gender with race has produced both alliances and overlaps in political concerns on the left of the political spectrum, but also has made political space for a resurgent ethnic nationalism on the right, both at home and abroad. Struggling against the political ascendancy of the political right can mean either a common struggle against all exclusions or accepting the logic of comparing oppressions, choosing whether race or gender is "worse" and thus deciding it deserves political priority. Both tendencies can be seen in American feminism in this new millennium.

CONSEQUENCES OF CLASS AND RACE ANALOGIES

This comparative perspective reveals U.S. and German feminism to be not simply two pieces of a single global movement with a common agenda, but distinctive political challenges that have their own ways of framing what women are like and what gender equality demands. But they are also participants in a wider transnational feminist mobilization that has been growing ever since the first United Nations conference on women in Mexico City in 1976. Since the U.N.'s Beijing conference in 1995, the impact of transnational networks and mutual influences among feminists has been unmistakable. It is easy to mischaracterize this global mobilization as merely divided between "Western" and "non-Western" ways of defining gender issues and so miss the variety that obtains among both Western and non-Western women's movements. German feminism has a different way of seeing and relating to the rest of the world than American feminism does, for reasons that reflect the continuing significance of the class and race metaphors for their respective movements.

Both countries have a tradition of feminist internationalism that was interrupted mid-century by the atrophy of international cooperation in civil associations that went along with the polarization of the whole world in the Cold War.[29] Both socialism and liberalism have long histories of outreach into the "third world" or global South, deeply intertwined with the nationalism and colonialism that also characterized these international relations.[30] The transformation of global relations in the postcolonial, post-socialist era affects feminists in both countries, even though it is likely to be perceived differently through a lens of race than when using a lens of class.

The different master metaphors of class and race in Germany and in the U.S. influenced how feminists in each country framed the transformations of women's lives in the restructured global context that developed after World War II. Colonial empires came apart as movements of national resistance grew. The connections between socialism and nationalism in these movements and in the newly independent countries of Africa and Asia encouraged Europeans to see postcolonial developments most readily through the lens of class. While some saw the new nations emerging in the global South as an expanded arena of class conflict and exploitation, others viewed the situation as the extension of the benefits of capitalist development to the so-called "underdeveloped" world. But Europeans, including European feminists, were slow to see gender relations as important or relevant to racial and national identities, including their own, and more apt to label gender oppression an indicator of cultural "backwardness" in other countries.

In contrast, American women were predisposed to understand the position of women in postcolonial societies though their already well-developed lens of race. This meant that American feminists, both white and black, tended to place all so-called "women of color" into the same conceptual category. As a consequence, American feminists were often slow to acknowledge the significance of the great gulf in economic resources between women of color in the U.S. and women struggling for survival in Africa, Asia, and Latin America or to examine the consequences of American economic policy abroad. But they were more inclined to question the assumption that women's experiences could be organized around a single dimension of economic oppression, tended to see family structures as only one of many social institutions that women could find sometimes supportive as well as oppressive, and were eager to work with states and nongovernmental organizations in expanding the reach of policy to address gender relations.[31]

The collapse of the Cold War standoff between capitalist and socialist blocs has weakened the usefulness of classic left-right terminology without at all reducing global problems of social and economic inequality. The class-conflict framing of politics and leading role of the socialist party is still a major mode of political discussion about social justice in much of the world today, as it has been in Germany. The ethnic nationalism that has complicated American claims to stand for democracy and equality also has global resonance. Race as a line of division and domination, among women no less than among men, is a point of conflict around the world, and claims of ethnic superiority split and segregate many movements for social justice.

In the global North and South, a neo-liberal economic order of free trade and global exploitation of human and environmental resources has brought the world back to conditions of dominance more reminiscent of the colonial empires of the early twentieth century than those of their dissolution in the aftermath of World War II. Not only the internationalism but also the inequalities of the early twentieth century have returned, most obviously in the United States where the rollback of rights and protections for the poor is a dominant political theme. Structural adjustment and European market integration are also neo-liberal policies with similar implications, even if on a less dramatic scale.

Most German feminists, for the historical reasons sketched out earlier, do not acknowledge political liberalism as a whole as having a value for women, even though German feminists' long-standing concern with autonomy fits well with the liberal discourse of women's rights, women as human resources, and women's individual empowerment that has diffused though the international system. By contrast, American feminism has deep resonances with this contemporary transnational liberal discourse.[32] Women in postcolonial societies, like women of color in the U.S., are not nearly as dismissive of rights language and personhood issues as the classic socialists, and a rethinking of rights and race in the post–Cold War era may be part of what feminist discourse contributes globally. In the new era of immigration facing Europe, the challenge of race relations with which American feminists have long struggled has also taken on increased significance for German feminists.

The old discursive standoff that placed the West as the defender of theism and family values against the so-called "godless communism" associated with women's emancipation in the East bloc has also shifted. Women's rights are now discursively placed in the West, along with secular and multi-ethnic, multi-national democratic states, and counterposed to theocratic authoritarian regimes of the Muslim world, which is orientalized as the new "East." Although opportunities are offered by this shift, most obviously to hold the West to the liberal standard of women's rights it now claims as its characteristic principle, there are also dangers. Most obviously, this global polarization offers a risk in succumbing to the racist discourse it offers about Islam and the backward, Eastern *other*. But there is also the danger of allowing the claim of emancipation under modern capitalism to replace the socialist claim of having liberated women, and with as little reality. In the newly realigned world, with the ever greater visibility and political significance accorded to Islam, it might be fruitful to ask what transnational opportunities exist for feminists who do not want to repeat the class and race mistakes of their early twentieth-century counterparts.

The Cold War polarization of East and West entrenched a conservative gender order organized around so-called Christian family values in the West, and failed to challenge the failures of communism to emancipate women in the East, despite its rhetorical claim to have done so. As today's rhetoric poses the Islamic world against the West, variously described as Christian or secular, it seems to run the real risk of both further entrenching a conservative version of Islamic gender relations in East and overlooking the failures of capitalist, social democratic, and liberal regimes to liberate women in the West. If the discourse of the West is to be helpful rather than hurtful to the mobilization of non-Western women around feminist goals, integrating lessons about the blind spots produced in framing gender in either class or race terms would seem to be necessary. Feminist successes in challenging gender relations will demand a thoughtful reevaluation of the legacies of both liberalism and socialism, and expanding the framing metaphors of class and race that have animated gender politics in different but equally limited ways in both Germany and the United States. Understanding the differences within the West is an important step in that direction.

Notes

1. My own dissertation work, published in such articles as "Working-Class Jobs: Paid Work and Housework as Sources of Satisfaction," *Social Problems* 23–4 (1976), 431–441 and "Working Class Feminism: a Consideration of the Consequences of Employment," *The Sociological Quarterly* 21:2 (1980), 173–184, made me dissatisfied with feminist theories based on middle-class women's lives.

2. The very fruitful models I did find in Germany are discussed in "Between Two Worlds: West German Research on Working Class Women and Work," *Signs: A Journal of Women in Culture and Society* 10–3 (1985), 517–36.

3. Myra Marx Ferree and Elaine J. Hall, "Rethinking Stratification from a Feminist Perspective: Gender, Race and Class in Mainstream Textbooks," *American Sociological Review* 61–6 (1996), 1–22.

4. See the review of this extensive literature in Robert D. Benford and David A. Snow, "Framing Processes and Social Movements: An Overview and Assessment,"

Annual Review of Sociology 26 (2000), 611–39 as well as the discussion of radicalism and resonance as conflicting tendencies in movement frames in Myra Marx Ferree "Resonance and Radicalism: Feminist Abortion Discourses in Germany and the United States," *American Journal of Sociology*, 109(2) (2003) 304–344.

5. David Snow and Robert Benford argue specifically for the concept of the "master frame" for all movements in "Master Frames and Cycles of Protest" in Aldon Morris and Carol McClurg Mueller, *Frontiers of Social Movement Theory* (New Haven: Yale University Press, 1992), 133–55.

6. This is the thrust of the classic comparison found in the gender-focused Appendix 5 to Gunnar Myrdal's indictment of racism in *The American Dilemma* (New York: Harper, 1944). See also Helen Hacker's influential use of this analogy in "Women as a Minority Group," *Social Forces* 30 (1951), 60–69 and Catharine Stimpson, "Thy Neighbor's Wife, Thy Neighbor's Servant: Women's Liberation and Black Civil Rights" in Vivian Gornick and Barbara K. Moran, *Woman in Sexist Society* (New York: Basic Books, 1971), 622–57.

7. The classic account is in Eleanor Flexner, *Century of Struggle* (New York: W. W. Norton, 1959).

8. Evelyn Nakano Glenn, *Unequal Freedom: How Race and Gender Shaped American Citizenship and Labor* (Cambridge: Harvard University Press, 2002).

9. Benita Roth, *Separate Roads to Feminism: Black, Chicana and White Feminist Movements in America's Second Wave* (New York: Cambridge University Press, 2004).

10. See, for example, Ute Gerhard, *Debating Women's Equality: Toward a Feminist Theory of Law from a European Perspective* (New Brunswick, NJ: Rutgers University Press, 2001).

11. Raka Ray, *Fields of Protest* (Minneapolis: University of Minnesota Press, 1999) provides a good illustration of the different forms feminist politics take in a socialist dominated city and a more politically diverse city in India in the late twentieth century that echo some of the agenda-setting effects of socialist predominance among social movements in late nineteenth- and early twentieth-century Germany.

12. Robert Moeller, *Protecting Motherhood: Women and the Family in the Politics of Postwar West Germany* (Berkeley: University of California Press, 1993) provides a detailed analysis of the entanglement of gender ideology and Cold War politics in the self-definition of Germany through the lens of family law revisions made in the immediate postwar period.

13. Ibid.

14. The U.S. origins story is told effectively in Sara Evans, *Personal Politics: the Roots of Women's Liberation in the Civil Rights Movement and the New Left* (New York: Knopf/Random House, 1979) as well as in Ruth Rosen, *The World Split Open: How the Modern Women's Movement Changed America* (New York: Viking, 2000). The German origins story is best captured in Herrad Schenk, *Die feministische Herausforderung: 150 Jahre Frauenbewegung in Deutschland* (München: Beck, 1980).

15. I offer a more detailed overview of this period in "Equality and Autonomy: Feminist Politics in the United States and West Germany" in *The Women's Movements of Western Europe and the United States*, Mary Katzenstein and Carol Mueller, eds. (Philadelphia: Temple University Press, 1987).

16. Moeller, *Protecting Motherhood*, is particularly enlightening on this point. Note that while this history highlights the West German experience, the East German Communist party, the SED, shared with the SPD in the West the classic socialist position of subordinating gender interests to class mobilization and class-based policy-making. However, SED policy did focus on freeing women for "productive labor"

by positive support for caretaking needs in the family. It trumpeted this instrumental use of women's labor power as the emancipation of women as a substantive accomplishment for which women should be grateful; increasingly women in the GDR criticized this approach, expressing this critique first in fiction and eventually in feminist mobilization. See Myra Marx Ferree, "The Rise and Fall of 'Mommy Politics': Feminism and German Unification," *Feminist Studies* 19–1 (1993), 89–115.

17. I discuss these developments in more detail in "Institutionalizing Gender Equality: Feminist Politics and Equality Offices," *German Politics and Society*, Issue 24 & 25 (Winter 1991–2), 53–66.

18. I describe this approach to gender politics in the GDR more fully in "The Rise and Fall of 'Mommy Politics.'"

19. I discuss this phase in more detail in "Patriarchies and Feminisms: The Two Women's Movements of Unified Germany," *Social Politics*, 2–1 (1995), 10–24.

20. The account here is an abridgment of an argument first offered in the historical overview of U.S. feminism in Myra Marx Ferree and Beth B. Hess, *Controversy and Coalition: The New Women's Movement through Three Decades of Change*, 3rd ed. (New York: Routledge, 2000).

21. See Benita Roth, *Separate Roads*, for a discussion of how these common dynamics were experienced differently by African-American, Chicana and white feminists.

22. Evans, *Personal Politics*.

23. Note that Germany had no antidiscrimination laws that applied to women until the 1990s, and the reach of such laws is still much more limited than those of the U.S. (for example, German employers are allowed to ask women their age, marital status, and childcare arrangements and use any of these considerations legally to exclude a potential employee).

24. Benita Roth, *Separate Roads*, provides some excellent examples of how class issues were raised using the rhetoric of race; the dissertation research I conducted on working-class women (predominantly white) in the Boston area in 1974 through 1976 was explicitly intended to challenge the widespread assumption that white-working class women had no interest in feminism.

25. There is a more extensive discussion of this chronological development and the specific forms that backlash took in the 1980s in Ferree and Hess, *Controversy and Coalition*.

26. Carol Mueller, *The Politics of the Gender Gap* (Newbury Park, CA: Sage Publications, 1988) explores this dynamic.

27. Compare Kristen Hoganson, *Fighting for American Manhood: How Gender Politics Provoked the Spanish-American and Philippine-American Wars* (New Haven: Yale University Press, 1998) on the race and gender implications of these earlier wars and the contemporary discussion of the first and second U.S.-Iraq wars to see the ubiquity of gender metaphors for power.

28. Robert Kagan, *Of Paradise and Power: America and Europe in the New World Order* (New York: Knopf/ Random House, 2003).

29. Actually the 1950s are the bottom of a curvilinear path taken by many diverse social indicators in the twentieth century: Women's age at marriage, likelihood of not marrying at all, higher education, formation of women's social organizations, and explicitly feminist activism are all higher in the 1920s and 1980s than in the 1950s. The rates of international trade, formation of international organizations, and immigration also hit bottom in the 1950s and are just now equaling or in some cases

surpassing the rates that were typical of the early twentieth century. Some of the current expansion of global consciousness and organizing among women's movements in many countries also needs to be understood historically in reference to the reemergence of internationalism that the Cold War had blocked.

30. See for example Margaret Keck and Kathryn Sikkink's discussion of the transnational feminist advocacy networks involved in ending footbinding in China and participating in the global campaign to end slavery in the nineteenth century as important precursors of modern transnational activists: *Activists beyond Borders: Advocacy Networks in International Politics* (Ithaca: Cornell University Press, 1998).

31. Nancy Fraser's discussion of recognition as well as redistribution is an influential version of this effort to think multidimensionally about oppression. See her essay in Barbara Hobson, ed., *Recognition Struggles and Social Movements* (Cambridge: Cambridge University Press, 2004).

32. See Nitza Berkovitch, *From Motherhood to Citizenship* (Baltimore: Johns Hopkins University Press, 1999) for an insightful analysis of the institutionalization of liberal concepts as norms applicable to women throughout the world polity.

Suggestions for Further Reading

Evans, Sara. *Personal Politics*. New York: Random House, 1979.

Ferree, Myra Marx, and Beth B. Hess. *Controversy and Coalitions: The New Women's Movement through Three Decades of Change*. New York: Routlege, 2000.

Flexner, Eleanor. *Century of Struggle*. New York: W. W. Norton, 1959.

Glenn, Evelyn Nakano. *Unequal Freedom: How Race and Gender Shaped American Citizenship and Labor*. Cambridge: Harvard University Press, 2002.

Keck, Margaret, and Kathryn Sikkink. *Activists beyond Borders: Advocacy Networks in International Politics*. Ithaca: Cornell University Press, 1998.

Moeller, Robert. *Protecting Motherhood: Women and the Family in the Politics of Postwar Germany*. Berkeley: University of California Press, 1993.

Roth, Benita. *Separate Roads to Feminism: Black, Chicana and White Feminist Movements in America's Second Wave*. New York: Cambridge University Press, 2004.

Study Questions

1. Miriam Cohen and Felicia Kornbluh are historians writing about the politics of welfare in America. Ellen Reese writes about welfare from a sociologist's perspective. Compare Reese's sources and approach to those of the two historians.

2. Ellen Reese focuses on race as a critical element in society. Which other authors in this volume take note of race and in what ways do they find it significant?

3. Myra Marx Ferree compares women's movements in the United States and Germany, arguing that race is the appropriate metaphor for women's oppression in America while class is a better metaphor in Germany. Do you agree? Can you suggest other types of struggles that could serve as models for describing women's inequality in African, Latin American, or Asian nations?

4. The essays in this section emphasize the importance of considering gender, race, and class as key variables when a historian or sociologist looks at a specific movement or era. How would the analysis of some of the major movements in American history—the Great Awakening, the American struggle for independence, the New Deal—be different if one or all of these variables were included?

Deborah Nord, Professor of English and Women's Studies at Princeton University, teaching "Men and Women," a seminar designed for first-year students. The course uses theory—from Darwin and Freud to Judith Butler—and literature—from Milton's *Paradise Lost* to Emily Bronte's *Wuthering Heights* and Jeffrey Eugenides' *Middlesex*—to encourage students to think critically about gender and to consider the variety and complexity of relations between men and women.

(Photo by Denise Applewhite)

part 5

Knowledge Production

In this final section, our contributors take a close look at the impact of a feminist perspective on literary criticism, film theory, art history, and the disciplines that comprise the humanities. They not only challenge their own disciplines to rethink traditional interpretations—they demonstrate how this can be done and how valuable it is, not simply for feminist scholarship but for *all* scholarship in these fields.

In "Taking the 'man' Out of the Humanities: How Feminism and Technology Are Transforming the Disciplines," Martha Nell Smith provides a unique demonstration of the connections between technology and feminism. Smith reminds us that one of the major contributions of feminist scholarship has been its willingness to ask crucial questions about the gendered nature of the organization, reproduction, and transmission of knowledge. These questions gain new urgency with the rise and spread of humanities computing, for its organization and reproduction of knowledge is no more "objective" than earlier, less technologically advanced mechanisms. Smith asks us to be aware of the gendering of this technology. She also urges us to recognize the liberating power of computing technology for women's studies. It can make possible the exchange of feminist information and ideas, give scholars ready access to archival materials, and increase the opportunities for women scholars to share their work with one another.

In "The Art of Darkness: Willa Cather's Aesthetics," Michèle Barale shows us how feminist inquiry can add new depth to a much examined subject. Although there are many biographies of Willa Cather, Barale offers new insights into the life and work of the novelist by focusing on Cather's personal and literary concerns with being a lesbian, a woman, and a professional writer. Barale uses the short story, "Coming, Aphrodite!" to examine the relationship of gender and sexuality that was central to Cather's identity. She shows us how the story's main characters represent the differences between the male and female artist and how these differences coexisted within Cather herself.

Sabrina Barton's essay, "Feminist Film Theory and the Problem of Liking Characters," looks at one of the negative results of the new feminist and poststructuralist approaches of recent years: the failure to consider if a viewer likes or dislikes a work of art. In her own research, Barton finds that women viewers like strong women characters in film. By focusing on two films, *Coma* and *Double Jeopardy*, Barton is able to illustrate women viewers' desire to identify with active, powerful female protagonists. She argues that feminist film scholars must consider the political as well as personal significance of this relationship between the viewer and the film character.

In "Feminism and Art History: Past Achievements and New Directions," Susan Casteras explores the challenge to traditional art history posed by feminist theory and other approaches, including Marxist theories, French literary criticism, and colonialist inquiries. This revolution in art history has been met with resistance, however, and Casteras analyzes the obstacles that remain formidable to feminist scholars.

Taking the "man" Out of the Humanities: How Feminism and Technology Are Transforming the Discipline

Martha Nell Smith

Martha Nell Smith (1984) is Professor of English and Director of the Maryland Institute for Technology in the Humanities at the University of Maryland (MITH). Her publications include *Open Me Carefully: Emily Dickinson's Intimate Letters to Susan Dickinson*, with Ellen Louise Hart (1998); *Comic Power in Emily Dickinson*, with Cristanne Miller and Suzanne Juhasz (1993); and *Rowing in Eden: Rereading Emily Dickinson* (1992). With Mary Loeffelholz, she edited the *Blackwell Companion to Emily Dickinson* (2005). She is also Coordinator and General Editor of the *Dickinson Electronic Archives* projects at the Institute for Advanced Technology in the Humanities at the University of Virginia (IATH). With Lara Vetter, she is a general editor of *Emily Dickinson's Correspondences*, forthcoming from the Mellon-sponsored University of Virginia Press Electronic Imprint.

> *Martha Nell Smith writes, "My digital humanities work is an extension of my work as a feminist literary theorist and scholar. Because my interest in the possibilities afforded by computers as powerful and empowering tools of humanities scholarly work became so keen as the World Wide Web was gaining precedence, my work in humanities computing has been powerfully influenced by cyberculture and new media studies. My commitment to feminist critical inquiry is stronger than ever, and as a digital humanities specialist, I have focused on the sociologies of knowledge production in our technology-saturated world—what data are reproduced and made accessible, and to whom."*

The editors of a special issue of *Signs: Journal of Women in Culture and Society*, a prominent scholarly feminist journal, wrote in 1990 that "the degree to which American society has embraced and absorbed computer technologies is astonishing. The degree to which the changes provoked by computers leave prevailing inequalities is troubling."[1] This observation preceded not only the development of the World Wide Web, but also my own work in humanities computing (or digital humanities), which began ten years ago when I proposed and became coordinator of the *Dickinson Electronic Archives (DEA)*, a project that was first imagined as producing electronic scholarly editions of the manuscripts of Emily Dickinson. Because of the feminist ethos that imbues my work and life, the DEA has become a resource of teaching materials, creative responses to Dickinson, and out-of-print or never-printed cultural artifacts crucial for establishing literary history that includes and values women's and other underrepresented groups' work. For the last five years, I have served as the founding director of the Maryland Institute for Technology, which is funded by the National Endowment of the Humanities because of our explicit promise to capitalize on the work of early adopters of computing tools and resources for humanities work in order to mainstream digital humanities throughout academe and reach underserved constituencies while doing so.

The questions that have informed my work as a feminist literary critic—how do our items of knowledge come into being, who made them, for what purposes, and how does gender play a role in knowledge making—inhere in my digital humanities work. That the two fields are or should be inextricably intertwined seems, therefore, an inevitable fact of life to me. But is this just a personal coincidence, a fact produced by the trajectory of my career and individual interests? What is humanities computing anyway, and why should it be important for feminist cultural, social, and intellectual work? Can feminism enhance and improve the world and work of computer science, of humanities computing, of digital humanities? After all, as the authors of a book on women in computing writes, "very early in life, computing is claimed as a male territory. At each step from early childhood through college, computing is both actively claimed as 'guy stuff' by boys and men and passively ceded by girls and women. The claiming is largely the work of a culture and society that links interest and success with computers to boys and men."[2] Men outnumber women anywhere from 2 to 1 to 10 to 1 in computer science programs and departments. According to a study released in 2004, for all of our progress in situating women in higher academe, "Women account for only a very small proportion of the scientists, mathematicians, and engineers working at the nation's top research universities."[3] The number of women in computer science has actually declined over the last two decades. Is computing not as useful for women as for men? Surely it is. So why are women not going into computing order to take advantage of what it may provide for knowledge production and distribution? I concur with other critics and theorists that it is not computing itself that puts women off, but the culture of computer science that discourages women from entering or staying in the field. To put it bluntly, at present a kind of "jockdom" in the culture of computer science also infects humanities computing. To participate more fully in the world of humanities computing, women need to be full participants in the paradigm and cultural climate shifts within the disciplines of computer science and humanities computing. As we have seen in the discipline of humanities at large, such a cultural change will benefit not only women but all participants and the computing disciplines themselves. As a humanist, I will focus for the rest of this chapter on humanities computing (not on computer science) and how it will benefit from reform imbued with a feminist ethic.

A culture that says that to use computing tools expertly one must know how machines work, or at least must be deft programmers, dominates much of the world of humanities computing. It is as if those who have fretted over literary and other humanities fields becoming feminized or soft have been rescued by a field that is hard science. Thus some people hope that through computing the humanities are being remasculinized. Many who are deeply involved in computing are fascinated with hardware: I am even more fascinated by the knowledge production enabled by the hardware: access, multimedia study objects, collaboration, self-consciousness, and audience. With the possible exception of multimedia study objects, these technologies are tools I came to see as essential in my work as a feminist scholar.

Humanities computing warrants some explaining. The phrase seems a contradiction in terms. The *OED* (*Oxford English Dictionary*) defines computing as "the action of calculating or counting," especially with a computer, specifically an "automatic electronic device for performing mathematical or logical operations." Such defining terms call to mind not poetry, novels, or plays—the stuff of literary history—but logarithms, algorithms, arithmetic processes, or sets of rules. Whatever philosophical rigor imbues our critical inquiry, no feminist literary critic or theorist, history scholar, art critic or practitioner, music critic or practitioner, or dramatist or drama critic I have heard argues that her work computes, performs the hard logic bound by sets of rules, processes via algebraic equation. By contrast, we find humanities defined as "learning or literature concerned with human culture" in all its messiness and imprecision. Humanists—professors of literature, art, history, music, theater—think of ourselves not as tribes of information technologists, but as tribes of knowledge producers.

In defining myself as a humanities computing specialist, I join a group of scholars who have been arguing for the profound advantages of employing computer resources in our literary work for the past generation or more, even before the advent of the World Wide Web in the early 1990s. In 1949, for example, Father Roberto Busa initiated the first electronic text project in the humanities, *Index Thomisticus*, a concordance to the works of Thomas Aquinas. I believe that digital resources are more than advantages for our work, especially our work as feminists—they are necessities. Twenty-first-century feminist scholars would be wise to continue and expand the work of these early adopter projects and seize the opportunities proffered by new media that many in the humanities still resist as they sentimentally worry whether things digital will displace and ruin things bibliographic.[4]

Indeed, the pioneering work of humanities computing projects demonstrates that rather than putting the "man" back in humanities, new media projects are extending and deepening feminist critical inquiry and intellectual exchange. Most obviously, new media publications can make available out-of-print or never-printed materials, many of which tend to have been produced by women or other underserved groups. In practice, one of the greatest joys of the ways that humanities computing has reshaped my day-to-day intellectual work life is that production of resources and tools for digital studies takes the feminist model of collaboration as a mode of knowledge production to new heights. Much can be learned from analysis of the happy and challenging effects of these new working models, particularly when that analysis is framed according to a feminist ethic that values the technologies previously invoked—especially access, collaboration, self-consciousness, and audience. Conscientiously building on these, feminist scholars can continue to help lead the way in harnessing new media opportunities for research, education, and outreach.

Working in humanities computing, one cannot help but ponder the basic questions about knowledge representation. Because feminism has asked crucial questions about the organization, reproduction, and transmission of knowledge, it might seem predictable or even inevitable that feminists would flock to and be welcomed by the discipline of humanities computing. As Jane Margolis and Alan Fisher said in 2002,

> At the turn of the century, women are surfing the web in equal proportion to men, and women make up a majority of Internet consumers. Yet few women are learning how to invent, create, and design computer technology. In the nation's research departments of computer science, fewer than 20 percent of the graduates are female. Fewer still enroll in high school programming or advanced computer science classes. Despite the relative youth of the computer industry, much of which has developed since the rise of the women's movement, women have lost ground in the world of computing. As featured in a thirty-year-old children's book titled *I'm Glad I'm a Girl!*, the gender distinction "boys invent things and girls use things that boys invent" remains uncomfortably true today.[5]

This paucity of women as inventors, as creators, in the world of computing seems curious when one considers the fact that the world's first computer programmer, the founder of scientific computing, is widely regarded to be Ada Byron, Countess of Lovelace, the famed poet Lord Byron's daughter, who lived in the early nineteenth century. Ada's image serves as Microsoft's watermark, and the United States Defense Department's computer language is "ADA." "She became the first person known to have crossed the intellectual threshold between conceptualizing computing as only for calculation on the one hand, and on the other hand, computing as we know it today: with wide applications made possible by symbolic substitution."[6]

Yet when I first started attending humanities computing conferences in the mid-1990s, I was struck by how few women were in attendance, either as presenters or audience members. Also, I was struck by how many of the presenters remarked, either explicitly or implicitly, that concerns that had taken over so much academic work in literature—of gender, race, class, sexuality—were irrelevant to humanities computing. Two plus two, so the reasoning goes, always equals four, whether you are black, female, queer, or straight. HTML (HyperText Markup Language), SGML (Standardized General Markup Language, of which HTML is a DTD, or Document Type Definition), XML (eXtensible Markup Language)—the codes that make words processable via Word or Word Perfect, that make images and text displayable through Internet Explorer or Netscape across the World Wide Web, or on CD-ROM or DVD—are gender-, race-, class-neutral. The codes always work, whatever one's personal identity or social group. Those interested are also folks who do not want to clutter sharp, disciplined, methodical philosophy with considerations of the gender-, race-, and class-determined facts of life. In the wake of the sixties, the humanities in general and their standings in particular had suffered, according to some, from being feminized by these things. Humanities computing seemed to offer a space free from all this messiness and a return to objective questions of representation.

Yet such dreams of a return to the "objective," uncluttered by messy identity questions, are nostalgic. That humanities disciplines were in fact foundationally changed by feminist scholarship of the twentieth century is obvious from project development within humanities computing itself, which is very good news indeed when mainstream magazines have so gleefully proclaimed that feminism is dead. But the quiet word from primary works developed within humanities computing itself is that many of feminist scholarship's goals are being accomplished and that we now have a medium to realize even more of those goals. Though there has been some inevitable recanonization (projects on Shakespeare, for example, easily obtained funding while projects on relatively unknown authors did not), several of the most sophisticated and widely admired early humanities computing projects witness that the changes dreamed by our feminist foremothers have occurred: the *Women Writers Project* (*www.wwp.brown.edu*) at Brown focuses on early modern women writers and text encoding; the *Orlando Project* (*www.ualberta.ca/ORLANDO/*) presents an online history of women's writing in the British Isles; the *Victorian Women Writers Project* (*www.indiana.edu/~letrs/vwwp/*); the *Women's Travel Writing 1830-1930* Project (*etrc.lib.umn.edu/womtrav.htm*); and my own *Dickinson Electronic Archives* Projects (*emilydickinson.org*). Each of these makes much more widely available women's studies resources long out of or never in print (such as the writings of Emily's sister-in-law Susan Dickinson), as well as making available in new forms texts that are more familiar (images of Emily Dickinson's manuscripts), giving access to histories and literatures long buried by the biases of traditional scholarship. That these projects are leaders in the field of humanities computing is a cause for feminist celebration, and feminists need now to seize the advantages of working in this field where out-of-print work can be reproduced and accessed from across the world, and where collaboration, a feminist ethic, is necessary to produce digital works.

Tech-Savvy: Educating Girls in the New Computer Age (2000), a publication of the American Association of University Women, describes focus groups with seventy middle school and high school girls and surveys of 892 teachers. The conclusions of these studies is that girls today have a "can do, but don't want to" attitude toward computing. The authors argue that while the small number of girls in computer science is often attributed to computer phobia, such behavior is instead "a choice that invites a critique of the computing culture." Instead of hearing a lot about computer anxiety, the Commission heard girls critiquing the culture of the field—the way computer science is conceived and taught and the violent way it is used in computer games.[7]

My work as a feminist makes me concur with Margolis and Fisher that "the goal is not to fit women into computer science as it is currently taught and conceived. Rather, a cultural and curricular revolution is required to change computer science so that the valuable contributions and perspectives of women are respected within the discipline."[8] In fact, that change needs to occur in all disciplines, and though it has begun and is more evident in some than in others (in my own, for example, compared with that of the sciences), the cultural and curricular structures of study all need to value and respect the contributions and perspectives of women and other minorities.

What I label technologies are the means by which we accomplish various ends—the tools and devices on which our critical suppositions rely. In what follows, I will focus on four areas in which I believe the humanities will significantly benefit from the tools afforded by the new technologies, thereby turning our "crises" to productive ends.

PRIMARY MATERIALS:
DEMOCRATIZING THE TECHNOLOGY OF ACCESS

Democratizing access to primary materials involves a more capacious range of objects to study and treasure and a much wider audience of readers able to examine these previously unavailable resources. In the digital environment, both terms of access—numbers of objects and numbers of audience members—are facilitated on an unprecedented scale. By access in the first instance I refer to BE-O objects—artifacts that have customarily been viewed *By Experts-Only*. Making available images that were previously locked away in library and museum archives for exclusive view by a very few is probably the technological boon with which scholars and readers are most familiar, for such access really is quite a big (and well-advertised) affair. That what primary materials get to be seen and who gets to see them are both changing at such a breathtaking pace informs the more *demotic* ethic characterizing new paradigms of scholarly editing in the digital realm. No longer is the image of a Dickinson or a Whitman manuscript available only to the eye of the specialist, who gets to view the original artifact or its photostat replica, while only its verbal description (represented in editions usually made by the access-privileged specialists) is available to the general reader.

Online, the common reader can now view images and painstakingly encoded (thus deeply searchable) transcriptions of Dickinson's poetic and epistolary manuscripts; of Whitman's drafts for "Song of Myself" and "Calamus," as well as all printed editions of *Leaves of Grass;*[9] and of hundreds of nineteenth-century American novels. These technologies make more visible the quantity and variety of work that has gone into the making of American literary history. Such access to primary and out-of-print materials was unimaginable as recently as the mid-nineties. In fact, most scholarly editorial projects are still produced as if this kind of access is not possible; thus, detailed notes, rather than digitized photographs with detailed notes, are the conventional surrogates for the objects under study.

An outstanding example of a contemporary variorum employing high standards but nevertheless relying on detailed description and print translation to serve as surrogate for manuscript text is R. W. Franklin's *The Poems of Emily Dickinson* (1998). Expected to set the standard for Dickinson study, this edition depends almost entirely on detailed linguistic description and print translation for helping readers to visualize Dickinson's poetry. Representing her lyric poems, in all their various versions, Franklin contextualizes them with the twin assumptions that Dickinson's highest writing goals incorporated the conventions of poems she saw published in the print medium and thus she held to conventional genre distinctions between prose and poetry. In Franklin's introduction are eight exemplary halftone photographs to demonstrate how he regards Dickinson's compositional practices and what he considers the key characteristics of her writing habits. Because there are only eight images to represent writing across 1,789 poems (by Franklin's count), many with multiple drafts or copies (so the number of documents represented by the eight easily exceeds 3,000), assessments of Franklin's generalizations rely on highly selective, subjective criteria. From the examples and the print translations, the new variorum's readers are asked to imagine the record of Dickinson's literary work, which is practically all in manuscript. Franklin is especially concerned with transporting lyrics from the messiness of Dickinson's written work, so he separates text that has or can be identified as a line or stanza of a poem from writing that may be poetic but has not been deemed poetic enough to count as a constitutive part of a lyric. In doing so, Franklin's judgments and subsequent representations, or print translations of Dickinson's poetry, are usually formed according to codes of hearing and metrical conventions, not codes of seeing.[10]

Franklin's position is certainly reasonable. After all, Dickinson's writings indicate her acute consciousness of and work within and without nineteenth-century conventions of poetry, which were driven by aurally oriented metrical designs, such as iambic tetrameter and ABAB rhyme schemes. However reasonable, such a position is nonetheless presumptive, as are all editorial projects in determining what scholarly and general readers alike get to or do not get to see of Dickinson's writing practices. Thus access to data that in turn is used to render critical judgments is mediated, the presumption being that there is a consensus around the meanings of the data to be found in Dickinson's manuscripts (how lines are arranged horizontally and vertically; where lines are physically broken; what marks of punctuation go up, down, or are curved in unconventional ways; and what her lower-, upper-, and middle-case letters might signify), especially with regard to their trajectory toward publication of her work.

Dickinson critics have characteristically imagined her poems as print objects, assuming that any variable in the handwriting that does not cohere with the regularizations of print is due to her personal writing implements and that such accidents need not be conveyed to readers. As it is transmitted into print, manuscript data is accordingly mediated. The *Dickinson Electronic Archives* has not solved the problem of data mediation, but the technology allows us to involve readers differently in the experience of Dickinson's manuscripts, especially with regard to their trajectory toward publication. The reader can actually trace for herself each document's journey from Dickinson's desk to a correspondent or to a manuscript book or to a sheet left unbound, then to an editor, to print, to the image on one's computer screen. With this focus on process, images of extant manuscripts are offered for readers' perusals, and readers can then test assertions that Dickinson's poetic embodiments clearly evolve, that for her the "iconic page, or the image of the poem, moved from the printed to the handwritten object."[11] By contrast, centering editorial judgments on the printed poem results in offering print translations for readers' perusals and appraisals. Thus decisions about the meanings of Dickinson's holographic marks and choreographies (angled marks, line breaks, letter cases, arrangements on the page, and juxtaposition of genres) are, as my examples show, necessarily made for readers of print editions.

What are the costs, then, to us as critics, interpreters, theorists if what is being argued about cannot be seen by the readers who must judge the validity of the arguments? In the case of Emily Dickinson, and more than a half century of authorized, purportedly definitive productions of her texts, debates about aspects of her written work have been launched in books and journals, and audiences have been asked to formulate opinions without access to evidence and without sufficient reflection on the ways in which knowledge and texts are produced and reproduced for our field. On what, then, would we base evaluations of her textual play and literary experimentation that depend only or primarily on those analytical descriptions? Extending that question to American literature in general, on what do we base our histories of authorship, textual play, and literary experimentation?

A medium that reproduces images as well as print translations of Dickinson's holographic and handmade literary works creates opportunities for far more members of her audience to take into account elements of writing practices not seen in print. Many more pairs of eyes have the opportunity to join in informed debate about Dickinson's manuscripts than has been previously possible. Humanities computing and the group work it requires can engender a critical ethos that is decidedly more demotic. It makes clear to readers what editors have long known: editing is interpretation, critical storytelling, writing.[12] Editing actually produces a narrative, a story or set of stories, about texts. Humanities computing allows "readers" both to witness the process and to participate in it. Thus I see the *Dickinson Electronic Archives* as an extension of the kind of project that Ellen Louise Hart and I undertook in *Open Me Carefully: Emily Dickinson's Intimate Letters to Susan Huntington Dickinson*. In that work, we sought to represent the context of Dickinson's writing literally as part of that process. That Dickinson "published" herself in her 99 or more correspondences, and that the bulk of the writing she shared with her contemporaries went to a single audience, Susan Dickinson, actually requires that we think differently about genre when we read Dickinson. The electronic archives allow us to make that case—to show how process is inextricably a part of product, how her manuscripts show that she was not bound by print-determined distinctions between poetry and prose. And best of all, the technology allows the readers to draw different conclusions based on their firsthand experiences not only of the materials but also of the editorial process; something closer to a critical, rather than a priestly, method can therefore drive definitions of and critical debates over what constitutes a Dickinson poem, a letter, a letter-poem. A decade ago such widespread access to her manuscript work and consequent ability for the scholarly community to take in a much wider range of opinion was unimaginable.

Although my example is from Dickinson studies, the technology has the potential to intervene positively in the canon debates, again providing access to material deemed not financially expedient to publish. Those involved in recovery projects have long been aware of how the publishing industry skews literary history. A "minor" woman writer as prolific as Catharine Sedgwick, for example, is known primarily by only one work (*Hope Leslie*) while every long-canonized novel that James Fenimore Cooper published is available in an affordable paperback. Via electronic publications, such as *Early American Fiction* at the University of Virginia's Electronic Text Center, a much broader scope of texts written by "minor" writers can be made available than what the print industry has been able to bear; can foster critical inquiry into a much wider range of African-American, Asian-American, Native American, and other "minority" writers and texts; and can offer a much more full sense of literary history.[13]

TECHNOLOGY OF MULTIMEDIA STUDY OBJECTS, DIGITAL SURROGATES, AND BORN-DIGITAL ARTIFACTS

If technology has given us new access to original manuscripts, the new media have also introduced new means and standards of organizing and structuring information. Initiatives calling for quality in encoding standards (such as the Text Encoding Initiative, or TEI), will require even the most scrupulous editors to be more responsible and accountable, as the details of editorial processes and practices become more widely visible. Moreover, because critical editions can be revised without incurring the expense of reprinting, the editorial process will be increasingly dynamic and collaborative. These changes will encourage editors to exploit theories and practices of structured information for creative ends.

Additionally, online editors must make decisions about how to transcribe textual material into, and preserve it in, digital form (in what are known as markup languages). Crucial components of any multimedia display, markup languages make a tremendous difference in determining what kind of electronic tool is at researchers' disposal. Markup languages can significantly enhance search and retrieval capacities, thereby transforming the way scholars conduct research.

For example, indexing and cataloging are tools for completing successful research that many take for granted. The Library of Congress catalog numbers point precisely to the spot in the stacks where a book should be. Yet book indexes are not so precise, for they point to the page and not the exact line that might be sought. Web searches are even less precise. Every researcher familiar with the Web knows its powerful ability to ferret out resources not so easily obtainable from conventional library finding aids, but

Google and other Web-based search engines will return thousands of hits for every item sought. In the descriptions that follow, I'll be using the common computer acronyms HTML, URL, SGML, and XML. These stand for, respectively, HyperText Markup Language, Uniform Resource Locater, Standard Generalized Markup Language, and eXtensible Markup Language. As with book indexes pointing to pages and not specific lines, search engines, depending on HTML markup, point to a URL on which information can be obtained but not to the exact place on the Web-based document. By contrast, SGML and XML markup provide for unparalleled textual search, navigation, and retrieval facilities. When documents are marked up with one of these, especially using the protocols of the TEI, search results point directly to the place in the text one wishes to find. Via the XML/TEI-encoded markup, a researcher can quickly arrive at the exact location of the information desired and does not have to depend on searching by name or title or place alone. In fact, because retrieving word strings is possible, the markup allows searches that no index could ever provide. The constraints of HTML tagging limit searches to literally exact matches solely on the displayed page unless one has access to a search engine which can search an entire site. An XML-encoded text or series of texts would not only retrieve a search term such as *greed*, but also an archaic synonym like *avarice*, as well as any other more remote references throughout a text, regardless of the number of pages involved.[14] Annotations in such a digital publication are likewise marked up and can be searched in ways no book provides or can be made to provide.

Thus, one advantage of digital surrogates for texts is the publication of highly structured information that will expand and deepen information retrieval with precision and scope heretofore impossible. A vast new potential for scholarship emerges as these new search tools not only enable but actually encourage us to unbind ourselves from exclusive reliance on the familiar subject-author-title catalogs. Yet none of these advances in markup, nor any of these guidelines, is robust enough to accommodate all facets of the actual textual experience of editors working with primary artifacts, and feminists, very experienced with such work, can bring keen insights to the world of the humanities computing markup community. Original documents, the raw materials with which editors must work, are by their very nature odd, and must be normalized to some degree in order to be put into an edition. In part, this is a result of the fact that "there are certain basic—irresolvable—philosophical tensions in language—most particularly between its capacity to represent knowledge systematically and its capacity to be knowledge experientially and perceptually—and this tension intensifies in an electronic environment as a tension between machine language and natural language—since it is a reductive hybrid version of the one which can be encoded/encrypted in order to serve as the basis of the other."[15] This characteristic of language itself is much more visible in an environment such as that of digital reproduction that reveals how "normalized" our relation to printed texts has become. In a case such as the *Dickinson Electronic Archives*, the editions are explicitly designed not to define and normalize texts, as has been the objective of most bibliographic scholarly editions, and has been the practice of many electronic scholarly editions. Many electronic editions are still framed by the good work of the book because the dream of shedding the inertia imported from the bibliographical realm is only gradually finding its modes of practice. The TEI was developed to represent already existing literary texts in electronic media, but in its years of development it has been confronted by strange texts and by editors whose commitment to integrity means that they cannot simply normalize those texts to fit a predetermined grid. This, in turn, demands that we grasp the real significance of the truism that editing is a kind of encoding and encoding is a kind of editing, and it also requires that we probe the politics of the encoding standards we are embracing. Readers too ". . . rarely think about the myriad of databases, standards, and instruction manuals subtending our reading lamps, much less about the politics of the electric grid that they tap into. And so on, as many layers of technology accrue and expand over space and time. Systems of classification (and of standardization) form a juncture of social organization, moral order, and layers of technical integration. Each subsystem inherits, increasingly as it scales up, the inertia of the installed bases of systems that have come before."[16] Besides asking who made our objects of study, we should pose generative questions about standards, who made them, and for what purposes. Feminists can make a profound contribution in this area of humanities computing, just as they have made similar profound contributions in other scholarly fields.

The advantages of technology are evident in a project such as *Titanic Operas, a Poets' Corner of Responses to Dickinson's Legacy*,[17] which features digitized readings by twentieth-century women poets. Listeners can hear and see poets like Gwendolyn Brooks, Maxine Kumin, Adrienne Rich, and Toi Derricotte reading not only Dickinson's but also their own poems as they honor the centennial of the New England poet's death by reflecting on her legacy in American poetry, specifically for women poets. This technology not only marks a return to emphasis on the aural, which for centuries was the poet's tradition, but also adds the dynamically visual to the experience of poetry. Dickinson herself surely had in mind the power of sensory input when she wrote: "a Pen has so many inflections and a Voice but one,[18] for tone binds linguistic elements into meanings, removing ambiguities produced when tone is not evident. Texts do not live simply on the printed page. The new media challenge us to consider what can be gained by amplifying our critical commentary into more media and how our critical-theoretical tools can be shaped to exploit multimedia most effectively.

NEW MODELS OF WORK:
THE TECHNOLOGY OF COLLABORATION

For the humanist tribe, at least in the Western world of the academy, the primary work model has been the singular author-scholar sitting at her desk laboring independently. Even after decades of critical understanding informed by insights about the corporate nature of the author and the author function, humanities scholars remain invested in individualistic notions of genius and authorship, which are in turn inscribed in the academy's promotion and reward systems. In contrast to our colleagues in the sciences, who value co-authorship, collaborative humanities work is often, perhaps even usually, seen as inferior to that produced alone. By its very nature, humanities computing demands new models of work, specifically those that exploit the technology of collaboration, for humanities computing projects cannot be realized without project managers, text encoders, scanners, visionaries, and others with a variety of responsibilities to produce effective multimedia projects. Although these models demand different kinds of formulas for evaluating and rewarding individual contributions and thus additional work for referees and for tenure and promotion committees, the necessity that work in humanities computing be self-consciously collaborative is all to the good (not least because recognizing collaborative contributions disrupts our conventional reward systems, which are increasingly recognized as outmoded and themselves insufficiently evaluated).

Collaboration not only increases the opportunities for critical exchange but also challenges individualistic contests over whose story of reading is the official, the authentic, the authorized one. The technologies I have been describing implicitly encourage collaboration. The dynamic interplay of the audience, the original writer who inscribes the marks, and the editors communicating those marks to posterity is thereby more likely to open what Emily Dickinson would call "doors and windows of possibility."[19] In turn, these myriad perspectives can enable a much more sustained reflection on how our critical findings are produced and then transmitted, on the mechanisms of authorization, and on the criteria for authenticity. These assessments can then begin to penetrate critical mystiques in ways likely to expand rather than restrict knowledge, and to focus attention more on the knowledge itself than on the individual responsible for bringing it to the fore. Access to such knowledge can in turn foster a variety of new co-editorial collaborations among authors, editors, and readers, for digital surrogates make definitive analytical descriptions neither possible nor desirable.

While print editions are containers for static objects, by definition unchangeble, the world of digital surrogates practically demands new models for editorial praxes in which editors and readers work together, models encouraged by the fact that in a world with access to photographic copies of texts and images, no one has to bear the burden of forging the perfect linguistic description of the artifact. After all, digital surrogates featuring high-quality full color images of Dickinson's manuscripts render a more ample sense of their textual conditions, including the conditions for the writing scene in which they were produced. Informed more fully about the textual conditions, readers can collaborate with the postulating editor in ways not possible when decisions have already been made to exclude or include data and seal the result into print.

To think of this model as a collaboration is already to make a case for how new technologies might change the idea of critical practice in the humanities. While that model may still be hard to recognize when we are talking about individual readers, it is more visible when we turn to the editorial practices already at play in the electronic archives. Ellen Louise Hart, Lara Vetter, Marta

Werner, the other general editors of the *Dickinson Electronic Archives*, agree neither with one another nor with me on every point to be made about Dickinson's handwritten work, but we do not need complete consensus to produce digital editions together. None of our opinions needs to override, supersede, act as more definitive than those of the others; rather, the various viewpoints, analytical interpretations, and disagreements can all be displayed and in fact become part of the critical work of the dynamic editions. After all, disagreements about the constitution and ontologies of Dickinson's texts (from determining their genre to what counts as a poetic line and what punctuation her marks represent) are legion, and the various constituencies can be represented in a digital edition in ways that are nearly impossible in print. When editors work to make as much about a text visible to as wide an audience as possible, rather than to silence opposing views or to establish one definitive text over all others, intellectual connections are more likely to be found than lost. A brief example from the editorial practices of the *Dickinson Electronic Archives* shows the importance of forging intellectual connections and of having as many pairs of eyes as possible looking at primary evidence. My example also demonstrates how vital are "recent moves to reframe objectivity from the epistemic stance necessary to achieve a definitive body of knowledge, to a contingent accomplishment of dynamic processes of knowing and acting" for enriching our intellectual commons, as Lucy Suchman has written.[20]

Editing *Writings by Susan Dickinson* began in the most conventional way, with a solitary editor (me) transcribing documents in the Houghton Library at Harvard University and the John Hay Library at Brown University. Susan Dickinson's handwriting is even more difficult to read than Emily Dickinson's, and no one had transcribed her corpus before, so I began developing a key to her alphabet, recording how various letters were shaped during different times of her life and noting variances between her private draft hand and her performance script for other readers. I transcribed a series of her poems housed at the Houghton and was very excited after determining that one began, "I'm waiting but the cow's not back." That might seem an odd first line for a poem, but I knew that one of Susan Dickinson's most beloved original art works was John F. Kensett's *Sunset with Cows* (1856), a work in the collection of Susan's husband Austin, first discussed by Barton Levi St. Armand, and then in a short biography for *An Emily Dickinson Encyclopedia*, I interpreted Susan's draft lyric as a poetic response to that painting.[21] Reviews of that short biography especially praised me for making the connection and remarking such an important textual "fact." Had editing of *Writings by Susan Dickinson* remained a conventional enterprise, the error of what I had deemed and what others had received as fact might have remained inscribed in literary history for years.

As coeditors working within conventional frameworks, Vetter and Lauth might have relied on my multiply checked transcriptions and photocopies of the originals and worked to coauthor critical notes from analytical description and lower-grade facsimile reproduction. Many assistants on "definitive" editions never see the primary sources that the editor sees, especially if they are graduate students working with a faculty advisor. Concomitantly, many editors view a primary document once or a very few times and then rely on their notes and perhaps photocopies. Yet to produce an online edition, we digitized high-quality color slides taken of the originals so that we could render surrogate images of Susan Dickinson's papers as part of the production. In doing so, we realized that our fact-checking would supersede even the most punctilious fact-checking used for print transcriptions. Working in concert with one another, we began to improve our respective keys to Susan Dickinson's alphabet, and Vetter and Lauth fastidiously began to check my transcriptions by repeatedly viewing the high-quality, luminous images of the originals. In February 2000, a little over a year into the process, I received an e-mail from Vetter: they had identified an error in my work. Vetter's e-mail read: "It's not 'I'm waiting but the cows not back' but rather 'I'm waiting but she comes not back.' Laura and I have been working on the dawn and cow poems all afternoon, and we're sure about this." Had we not been working in concert with one another, and had we not had the high quality reproductions of Susan Dickinson's manuscripts to revisit and thereby perpetually reevaluate our keys to her alphabet, my misreading might have been congealed in the technology of a critical print translation and what is very probably a poetic homage to Emily Dickinson would have lain lost in the annals of literary history.

TECHNOLOGY OF SELF-CONSCIOUSNESS

As it promotes a collaborative model of scholarship, new technology also demands that we rethink the basic premises of research and its rewards. Self-consciousness is a technology with which humanists are familiar: highly self-conscious literary works are usually highly valued. But I am interested in the ways that this technology unsettles us and in ways that unsettling can be effectively exploited.

Maintaining relentless self-consciousness about how critical "facts" have been produced, about how items of knowledge are part of the circumstances of their creation, is crucial and vital for providing democratizing access to materials while maintaining intellectual rigor. More than a decade ago, before Franklin had produced the variorum, before Hart and I made *Open Me Carefully*, and before I was aware that there could be anything called an electronic archive, I noted that "neither the reproductions of texts nor critical interpretations can be innocent of or superior to politics, since both require negotiations among authors, editors, publishers, and readers. Dickinson interpretation will be powerfully enhanced by cultivating constant awareness of the 'official' repatternings of the variorum, the three-volume letters, and the separate publication of the 'Master' documents." My work on the electronic archive has only reinforced these words for me (as it has provided tools to make such considerations possible beyond my earlier dreams), and the words apply to the reception of all editions, including any in which I have had a hand.

So how might these technologies and their potential begin to address crises in publishing and in humanities education? They implicitly argue for new publishing models and for reconfiguring humanities education. New models of publishing are already evolving, in which universities and libraries formulate paradigms of funding and exchange not driven by profit margin models. Readers' willingness to spend time with Susan Dickinson's work is undoubtedly encouraged by the fact that those resources are freely available. There is no charge for viewing them, for printing out transcriptions of them, for incorporating them into scholarly work. In developing models outside the profit-driven box, university presses and libraries also need to play key roles in restoring copyright laws to their original goals: to promote learning and distribute knowledge for the common good. I am persuaded that protecting information flow should trump protecting profit in academic publishing. Economic sustainability for such models needs to be achieved outside the reward system of the free market. The newness of this technology—its uncharted domain—offers us the opportunity to examine, refine, and reform our current procedures.

Besides these new models of publishing, new models of scholarly and pedagogical praxes are needed. What would it mean for critical inquiry if we really incorporated a wider range of user and multimedia responses into our critical review processes, for example?[22] What if we changed the ways in which we train our students, really incorporating group work throughout our humanities mentoring system? Rather than rewarding work done primarily in a solitary carrel using a single pair of eyes to then report results, serious work on collaborative projects requiring many pairs of eyes to look at and achieve consensus (or generative dissensus) on what is seen could be rewarded and its value recognized. In humanities computing, one cannot work otherwise. Indeed, humanities computing will continue to change the way humanities scholarship is practiced, expanding objects of study and lines of critical inquiry, thereby making more expansive, responsible critical histories. If practiced with a feminist ethos, such profound changes will be even more expansive, responsible, incisive, and generative. As these evolutions occur, we need to be relentless in the scrutiny of our tribe's practices. Central to the formulations and speculations of this critique is evaluating the effects of a technology already discussed at length, that of audience. If one considers a sense of audience a technology (with explanation and performance as kinds of knowledge application), then the technology of audience provides analytical perspectives that would not have been obtained and a more capacious sense of responsibility than when one writes with only one audience in mind. The new media, and the new critical technologies they produce, require that we scrutinize anew how our items of knowledge come into being, who makes them, and for what purposes. A feminist ethos will only deepen, widen, and enrich this field of new media scholarly production and study, and in ways that will help insure that it not be hobbled by the constraints that have characterized its young past.

Notes

1. Jean F. O'Barr, ed., "From Hard Drive to Software: Gender, Computers, and Difference," Special Issue of *Signs: Journal of Women in Culture and Society* 16:1 (Autumn 1990).

2. Jane Margolis and Allan Fisher. *Unlocking the Clubhouse: Women in Computing* (Cambridge: MIT Press, 2002), 4. Efforts to redress this gender imbalance include the

Center for Women and Information Technology (*http://umbc.edu/cwit/*) at the University of Maryland Baltimore County.

3. Robin Wilson, "Women Are Underrepresented in Sciences at Top Research Universities, Study Finds," *Chronicle of Higher Education* 50: 20 (Jan. 23, 2004): A9.

4. Sven Birkerts and Nicolson Baker have written extensively to warn of the cost of displacing books with digital resources. I and others argue that books will never be displaced but will only be enhanced by digital works.

5. Margolis and Fisher, *Unlocking the Clubhouse*, 2.

6. Mary Croarken, "Mary Edwards: Computing for a Living in 18th-Century England," 9; John Fuegi and Jo Francis, "Lovelace & Babbage and the Creation of the 1843 'Notes'," 16, in *Annals of the History of Computing* 23: 4 (Oct.-Dec. 2003).

7. Margolis and Fisher, *Unlocking the Clubhouse*, 73.

8. Ibid., 6.

9. Ed Folsom and Ken Price, eds., *The Walt Whitman Archive*, online, available: *http://jefferson.village.virginia.edu/whitman/* 1996 to the present.

10. R. W. Franklin, ed., T*he Poems of Emily Dickinson: Variorum Edition* (Cambridge: Belknap Press of Harvard University Press, 1998); *New Poems of Emily Dickinson*, William H. Shurr, ed., with Anna Dunlap and Emily Grey Shurr (Chapel Hill: University of North Carolina Press, 1993); see also Ellen Louise Hart and Martha Nell Smith, eds. *Open Me Carefully: Emily Dickinson's Intimate Letters to Susan Huntington Dickinson* (Ashfield, MA: Paris Press, 1998). To view images of these manuscripts, see "Morning / might come ... Show / me Eternity" (*http://jefferson.village.virginia.edu/dickinson/letter/hb90.htm*) in "The Letter-Poem, a Dickinson Genre," Dickinson Electronic Archives *DEA*, and "... Who loves you most" (*http://jefferson.village.virginia.edu/dickinson/working/zhl9d.htm*) in "Correspondence with Susan Dickinson," *Emily Dickinson's Correspondences, DEA*.

11. Martha Nell Smith, "Corporealizations of Dickinson and Interpretive Machines" in *The Iconic Page in Manuscript, Print, and Digital Culture*, George Bornstein and Theresa Lynn Tinkle, eds. (Ann Arbor: University of Michigan Press, 1998), 195.

12. Martha Nell Smith, *Rowing in Eden: Rereading Emily Dickinson* (Austin: University of Texas Press, 1992), 1, 18–19, 31, 44, 57.

13. See *Early American Fiction*, Electronic Text Center, University of Virginia, online, available: *http://etext.lib.virginia.edu/eaf/*, accessed Spring 2002.

14. I am indebted to Susan Schreibman, Assistant Director of MITH, for assistance with this description of heightened searchability with XML/TEI encoding. The example given here is part of her contribution to MITH grant and conference proposals. See "MITH's Mean, Lean Versioning Machine," *ALLC/ACH 2002 Conference. New Direction in Humanities Computing*, online, available: *http://www.uni-tuebingen.de/cgi-bin/abs/abs?propid=93*, accessed Spring 2002.

15. Johanna Drucker, *Figuring the Word: Essays on Books, Writing, and Visual Poetics* (New York: Granary Books, 1998), 219.

16. Geoffrey C. Bowker and Susan Leigh Star. *Sorting Things Out: Classification and its Consequences* (Cambridge: MIT Press, 2000), 33.

17. See Martha Nell Smith, with Laura Lauth, eds. *Titanic Operas, Folio One: a Poets' Corner of Responses to Dickinson's Legacy*, online, available: *http://jefferson.village.virginia.edu/dickinson/titanic*, 1998 to the present.

18. Thomas H. Johnson, ed. *The Letters of Emily Dickinson*, 3 vols. (Cambridge: Belknap Press of Harvard University Press, 1958).

19. "I dwell in Possibility."

20. Lucy Suchman, "Located Accountabilities in Technology Production," published by the Department of Sociology, Lancaster University, online, available: *http://www.comp.lancs.ac.uk/sociology/soc039ls.html*, accessed fall 2003.

21. St. Armand discusses Austin Dickinson's art collection, and mentions the works purchased or specially prized by Susan. Her name is penciled on the back of *Sunset with Cows* (see *Emily Dickinson and Her Culture: The Soul's Society* [Cambridge: Cambridge University Press, 1984], 251, 260, 282.) Also see my biographical sketch, "Dickinson, Susan Huntington Gilbert (1830–1913)," in *An Emily Dickinson Encyclopedia*, Jane Eberwein, ed. (Westport, CT: Greenwood Press, 1998), 78–82.

22. The humanities professions would surely benefit from establishing an e-Print archive such as those based upon activities supported by the U.S. National Science Foundation, Cornell University, and the Los Alamos National Laboratory. Papers are posted there for open critical review before they are published in peer-reviewed journals. This counts as a kind of publication, and also broadens the vetting process. See *e-Print Archive*, online, United States National Science Foundation with Cornell University, available: *http://arXiv.org/*; *e-Print Archive Mirror*, Los Alamos National Laboratory, online, available: *http://xxx.lanl.gov/*, accessed Spring 2002.

Suggestions for Further Reading

Abbate, Janet, guest ed. "Women and Gender in the History of Computing." *Annals of the History of Computing* 25: 4 (Oct.-Dec. 2003), *http://computer.org*.

Bowker, Geoffrey C., and Susan Leigh Star. *Sorting Things Out: Classification and its Consequences*. Cambridge: MIT Press, 1999.

Cassell, Justine, and Henry Jenkins, eds. *From Barbie to Mortal Kombat: Gender and Computer Games*. Cambridge: MIT Press, 1998.

Hockey, Susan. *Electronic Texts in the Humanities*. New York: Oxford University Press, 2000.

———, Allen Renear and Jerome McGann. "What Is Text? A Debate on the Philosophical Nature of Text in the Light of Humanities Computing Research. Available: *http://www.humanities.ualberta.ca/Susan_Hockey/achallc99.htm*. Accessed Spring 2003.

Lakoff, George. *Women, Fire, and Dangerous Things: What Categories Reveal about the Mind*. Chicago: University of Chicago Press, 1987.

Margolis, Jane, and Allen Fisher. *Unlocking the Clubhouse: Women in Computing*. Cambridge: MIT Press, 2002.

———, Allen Fisher, and F. Miller. "Caring about Connections: Gender and Computing." *Technology and Science* 18: 4 (Winter 2000), 13–20.

Smith, Martha Nell. "Computing: What's American Literary Study Got to Do with IT?" *American Literature* 74 (Fall 2002), 833–57. Online. *Project Muse*. Available: *http://muse.jhu.edu/journals/american_literature/v074/74.4smith.html*. Accessed Spring 2003.

———. "Electronic Scholarly Editing," in *A Companion to Digital Humanities*, Susan Schreibman, Ray Siemens, John Unsworth, eds. Oxford: Blackwell, 2005.

Suchman, Lucy. "Located Accountabilities in Technology Production." Published by the Department of Sociology, Lancaster University. Online. Available: *http://www.comp.lancs.ac.uk/sociology/soc039ls.html*. Accessed Spring 2003.

The Art of Darkness:
Willa Cather's Aesthetics

Michèle Aina Barale

Michèle Aina Barale (1981) is Professor of English and Women's and Gender Studies at Amherst College. She is a co-editor of *The Lesbian and Gay Studies Reader* (1993) and has written on Radclyffe Hall's *The Well of Loneliness* and Ann Bannon's *Beebo Brinker*, as well as other topics. She is currently working on Willa Cather's aesthetics.

> *Michèle Barale recalls that the critical questions in women's studies in the early 1980s were concerned with trying to establish a relationship between a woman writer and the story she tells. "Initially, gender resided in the author, though the text itself got gendered pretty quickly. And it was not very long before gender was handled as a symbolic system whose operation did not rely on the presence of a female or male body. It took longer for us to figure out that you couldn't fully explicate femininity without recourse to masculinity and vice versa: femininity was constructed in particular ways so as to be able to construct masculinity in particular ways." Today, she observes, "in very real ways, professional literary critical studies are attentive to gender. It is a respectable thing to do."*

IN THE CLOSET

Don: "I'm not fond of taking foolish risks."
Eden: "I shouldn't think sensible risks would be very much fun."

Willa Cather's aesthetics—the structure of values and apprehensions that shape and are in turn shaped by the stories she tells, tells us and tells herself, over the course of her writing life—are best considered in tandem with her own understanding of herself as an author having both gender and sexuality. Cather never lost her fascination with the process and meaning of artistic production. All her life she wrote novels and stories specifically about artists (*manqué*, failed, perfected, and past prime) as well as narratives in which the

318

creative life is a central theme. Willa Cather (1873–1947) began writing professionally as a drama and opera reviewer even before she graduated from the University of Nebraska as a classics major. Her first novel, *Alexander's Bridge,* was published in 1912 and her last, *Sapphira and the Slave Girl*, in 1940. In the course of her life, Cather wrote twelve novels and numerous short stories and essays; in addition, she ghost-wrote at least one biography, the life of Mary Baker Eddy, and one autobiography, that of S. S. McClure, her editor-in-chief at *McClure's Magazine*. Given both the quality of her work as well as her productivity, it is hard to name any single work as most representative. *O Pioneers!* (1913), *My Antonia* (1918), and *Death Comes for the Archbishop* (1927) have been her most consistently admired novels over the decades, not only because of the clean elegance of Cather's prose but also because their preoccupation with the American West and Southwest allowed them to be claimed as American Classics, as narratives of nation building. More recent critics have focused their attention on the homoerotic intensities of *The Professor's House* (1928) and the racial dynamics of *Sapphira and the Slave Girl*. Cather wrote and published for more than fifty years, and she wrote about creativity for just as long a time.

One particular story, "Coming, Aphrodite!"[1] (1920), in its tale of two young artists, Don Hedger, a painter, and soprano Eden Bower, depicts unusually well Cather's understanding of creativity's origins. The story is far from simple. It not only encloses a second narrative within itself, but it sets up aesthetic problems that it does not resolve. I am not going to fully explicate the story, nor am I going to spend time on the inner narrative. I want, instead, to pursue Cather's creation of a very distinct gender binary in her portrait of the artist, a gender distinction that makes us uncomfortable, at the very least, and confuses us at best. It is a dichotomy that is absolutely conscious, and one whose ironies were not, I think, lost on her. What makes a discussion of Cather's aesthetics so interesting is that Cather is a lesbian and a butch, a woman who identifies as masculine.[2] Thus in a story that not only presents us with a male and a female artist but also uses their gender opposition as the means by which two contradictory representations of the artist are delineated, Cather gets to play all the parts. Cather can be exactly what she seems most visibly not to be: Don Hedger, a heterosexual male artist. But she cannot be—and I do mean *cannot* rather than *will not*—Eden Bower, the muse and model for Don's art. Cather *cannot* be the heterosexual male artist's visual object and she cannot be his inspiration because she shares his pleasures. She too finds her creative energy in the female body. Cather could no more be the artistic object for (another) heterosexually desiring male than he could be his own. This is the case not because she is a lesbian but because she is a butch: not feminine but masculine.

Thus "Coming, Aphrodite!" allows Cather to separate into heterosexual male painter and female soprano what Cather herself experiences as unified: as a lesbian/butch writer whose source of inspiration is, and whose gaze is focused through narratively male eyes upon, the feminine. For the mannish female author,[3] just as for the heterosexual male artist, the female subject's creative inspiration is hardly far removed from her erotic stimulation.

It has taken me a long time to realize that the dark matter of Cather's art is not her lesbianism, however. I now would argue that at some point after her youth, Cather ceased to worry about what we today would call her sexual identity. Her butchhood, her mannish identity, muted that fear. She wasn't a lesbian; she was a serious, professional, experienced writer—and as such, she was not a *woman writer*, that thing she scorned. Authorship provided her not only with authority in the world, but with identity.[4] And that identity was not a woman's.

What demands concealment in "Coming, Aphrodite!" has to do with its association of art with filth. Cather needs to mask her knowledge of creativity's anal origins. Just as the story of young love encloses an inset tale of sexual behavior far crueler than anything either of the two lovers does to the other, so too the erotic excitement of their romance cannot be uncoupled from the fact that they first meet in front of a bathroom where they argue over the state of its cleanliness. Neither love nor art can be cloistered from sites more soiled than pure. Of course, as we will see with both artists, dirty origins give rise to glorious stuff. And Cather is clear that this is the way it is supposed to be. But despite Cather's clarity about the conjunction of the soiled and the sublime, "Coming, Aphrodite!" makes us have to work to learn it. And work hard. Nor does Cather assume that we will necessarily like what we learn.

Cather even goes so far as to allow us to evade this knowledge and instead find art's filthy origins humorous, offering us, if we prefer, descriptions of cleaning ladies even smirchier than the spaces they have been hired to clean. All we need do to preserve our innocence is assent to familiar gender stereotypes. If we will agree that men don't clean their rooms as they ought and that women are neat and tidy, we can slip into and then out of "Coming, Aphrodite!" undisturbed by the unpleasant knowledge that the story so artfully conceals.

And Don is, indeed, a messy guy while Eden is Ms. Clean. I argue, however, that we are not supposed to accept this simple binary, not supposed to share Don's assumptions about Eden. She is neither a marble statue nor the mythic and immortal. If she is anything, Eden is a very material girl; she wants all the filthy lucre she can come by. And she wants all the fame and adulation that comes the way of a beautiful woman with a beautiful talent. Moreover, Eden is aware of her own sexual desire, though she does not divulge her knowledge of it even, or especially, to us. Don is a great artist in the making, but he is a terrible gender analyst. And Eden will become a great diva, but we really can't like her very much.

PORTRAIT OF THE ARTIST AS NOT A GRECIAN URN

. . . the pull of that aperture was stronger than his will . . .

When the story begins, Don Hedger is a young painter at the start of what will be a long and fruitful, though never lucrative, career. Don is the aesthetic center of the story. His judgment is never wrong, never swayed by fashion or profit, and his art is never produced for any other reason than that it seems the right way to proceed. At 26, Don has "twice been on the verge of becoming a marketable product"—but the cost of success is too great since it demands repetition of mastery rather than experimentation and growth (67). Eden's arrival at the Washington Square rooming house this particular summer will offer Don an aesthetic revelation important at this moment in his life. She will catalyze his art. But it is her body that will bring this about and not her own art. She becomes Don's perfect object: incandescent beauty living just the other side of the door that divides their apartments in the grungy rooming house.

If Don is the aesthetic impulse in its most pristine form, he is not that in terms of hygiene. Don sleeps where he sits, paints where he sleeps. His only light is that preferred by the painter—north—but it leaves his room otherwise dark. Furthermore, Don himself is habitually and unblushingly unkempt. He bathes his dog Caesar more often than himself, we are to—and Eden certainly does—believe. And his studio is squalid: sour milk, long-forgotten dog bones, and even dog urine add their own special effulgence to the room's more expected odors of paint and turpentine. And there are, too, the steak and onion dinners Don cooks on occasional evenings, leaving dishes and frying pans to harden in the sink for days. It is no wonder that he fears that the presence of a woman in the house will cramp his style; anyone with a nose would. Thus Don's art is quite literally situated in the impure. There is nothing sanitary about its origins. Even his choice of medium is one of spatters and spills and drips. If art is to be made, then Don's hands will have to get dirty.

Caesar, Don's faithful canine companion, also serves as his metaphorical body. It seems fitting that the first face-to-face meeting between Don and Eden is brought about by Caesar's dirt, by the doggy odor and bathtub residue left in the communal bathroom after Don has given him his daily bath: "Before the door, lying in wait for him, as it were, stood a tall figure in a flowing blue silk dressing gown that fell away from her marble arms. In her hand she carried the various accessories of the bath" (70). Don attempts to defend himself and his dog by pointing out that Caesar is cleaner than most people. But to Eden's query of "Cleaner than me?" he can only lamely offer, "Cleaner than I am," which Eden easily caps: "That I don't doubt!" (70).

Although the well-laundered Caesar contrasts with his master's slovenliness, by spending his doggy days sniffing out the world in general and the gynecological world especially, he is Don's body double. Caesar represents his master's instinctual responses rather than his aesthetic perceptions and, like Don, is the perpetrator of dirt. Caesar's bones, his hair, his putative carpet-soaking urine (a charge Don loyally denies [66]) mark his presence in the rooming house, as does his growling complaint and confusion at the new odors that Eden brings. Caesar's nose admits the world as scent; he is the intimate apprehender of bodies as essence, even as he leaves behind evidence of his own animal life. Caesar is more than phallus, although he is certainly that: standing before Eden's door with his nose pressed to the crack, "his bony tail stuck out hard as a hickory withe . . ." (65). Dog-bodied, and making dirt as a way of achieving cleanliness, Don is the most maculate of men. But he is not without his virtues.

Don is an orphan and his education has been idiosyncratic. He has gained a great deal of experience, however, having "already lived a succession of convictions and revelations about his art" (67). Don looks to life for models: he is working on a study of fish when the story opens; he hires a young carnival performer, Molly Welch, as a model for nude figure work. As a painter, he is an experimentalist rather than realist and in time will become "one of the first men among the moderns . . . the very moderns" (100). A bachelor, Don prefers Caesar's company to that of women. Indeed, even Don's amorous relations with women have been merely friendly, casual but not serious (74). In general he shies away from social interaction. He wants to be left alone to do his work. As time goes by and as his work matures, Don becomes an artist's artist. His paintings please rarified tastes, offering satisfactions not for the naive. Furthermore, he lacks all identification with any single style or movement: "one can't definitely place a man who is original, erratic, and who is changing all the time" (101). In this, we might say that his preferences are protean, multifaceted, and perhaps even omnivorous.

For the young Don Hedger of the story's romantic tale, the presence of Eden's body catalyzes his art in some way essential for its development. Her naked body becomes the central—and illicit—fact of Don's creative growth that summer. Central also is the soiled locale—Don's cluttered closet, knee-deep in soiled laundry—in which his creative vision takes place. Cather makes filth and deception and not purity and not truth the precondition for aesthetic perception. Don becomes a voyeur. Through a peephole in his closet he can observe Eden as she exercises naked in the golden afternoon light. The vision stuns him. What he observes is both a beautiful woman's body and a muscular energy that seems to flow through her from her toes to her fingertips. "The soft flush of exercise and the gold of afternoon sun played over her flesh together, enveloped her in a luminous mist which, as she turned and twisted, made now an arm, now a shoulder, now a thigh, dissolve in pure light and instantly recover its outline with the next gesture" (72).

Flashing in and out of materiality, Eden appears—to Don and even to us—to be something other than mortal, although it will be nearly two decades before she becomes Aphrodite in New York. Cather has Don perceive Eden as substance and energy, as both flesh and "pure light." Her body is matter that can transcend itself and still return to itself. It is hardly surprising that this vision stimulates Don creatively and otherwise. Cather carefully poses Don. As he crouches "among his old shoes in the dark" of his closet (74), eye to the hole, Don's fingers take on a curve "as if he were holding a crayon; mentally he was doing the whole figure in a single running line, and the charcoal seemed to explode in his hand at the point where the energy of each gesture was discharged into the whirling disc of light, from a foot or shoulder, from the up-thrust chin or the lifted breasts" (72). There is no possible distinction at this moment between the erotic and the aesthetic. Furthermore what is illicitly obtained is also utterly pivotal. Forbidden knowledge of Eden's body provides a vision of the physical in which matter transcends itself but never ceases to be beautiful flesh. It is, however, flesh that reveals a stain.

At the conclusion of her exercise, Eden tucks up a lock of hair that has come loose and pauses to examine "with solicitude a little reddish mole that grew under her left armpit" (72). It would be a good thing if Don heeded that mole. If nothing else, it might suggest to him that he not expect that Eden to become the most faithful of lovers. It would certainly keep him from making her into something more than flesh and blood, someone radically different from the other models he has used for figure studies. Hers is not the first female body he has seen nude. Don *is* Eden's first lover, but far from her last. We know now both Don's dirt as well as Eden's stain.

Because Don cannot refrain from returning to his closet to spy upon Eden with regularity, he cannot be the story's moral center, although I would argue that moral centers are exactly what Cather does *not* think art is "about." Beauty and virtue do not occupy the same space since art and the illicit go hand in hand. And, we have to assume that Don's last name, Hedger, has some larger meaning. Though he works from life and has graduated from the school of hard knocks, there is something that Don dodges, something other than women that he skirts, circumvents, avoids—which is a slightly different thing from the poetic privacy and concealment, the secrecy implied by a bower.

Eden, too, is an artist in training, although she is younger than Don and lacks entirely the European education at the knee of a famous mentor, "C—" in "the south of France" that Don so easily effected (77). Eden, in fact, is awaiting her first trip to Europe. But already at twenty, she has real talent even if she does not, or at least not yet, have taste. Early in their relationship, when Don exhibits his work for her, she is unimpressed—though smart enough not to reveal her ignorance: her favorite pictures are Christ before Pilate and a red-haired Magdalen of Henner. In other words, she prefers narrative art—pictures that tell her stories she already knows—and art into which she can project herself. It is not surprising that she finds Don's landscapes "not at all beautiful," their lack of verisimilitude providing her with "no idea of any country whatsoever. She was careful not to commit herself, however. Her vocal teacher had already convinced her that she had a great deal to learn about a great many things" (78). What she does have plenty of, however, is real ambition, although whether we are to understand that her ambition and Don's unswerving allegiance to his art are the same thing is not so easy to answer. But then, Cather warns us early on that "people like Eden Bower are inexplicable" (79). Eden will complicate absolutely everything, including Don's life, from the first moment she moves in and leaves her trunk in the hallway. That trunk remains a closed case.

Just as Caesar represents Don's animal body, Eden's trunk represents hers, a massive piece she cannot maneuver without help from men. Not only does its size make it an obstruction in Don's way, but its locked and looming enormity suggests its capacity to contain, in secret, Eden's most personal detritus. Although her names suggest that she initially offers paradise, in the end she is the most private of spaces, a hidden, inner room for creativity. But not for reproduction; Eden's bower is no womb for another's creation.

Don's spying will reveal Eden's private body. His nightly airings on the roof and the semi-privacy offered by the locked double doors that separate his quarters from hers have given Don evidence of Eden's public, professional self since he can hear her singing. Caesar has discovered her odor and understood it as a threat. Mail left in the hall has divulged her name as well as some kind of postal connection to Chicago. And their bathroom altercation has revealed both her "blazing" beauty (69) and her outraged divinity. "She was the immortal conception, the perennial theme" (75).

But if Eden's beauty—like that of Keats's Grecian urn—is outside time and hence culture, her own art is not. Eden's career is utterly dependent upon capitalism or, at least initially, upon men with capital. Singers who would be divas require operas mounted on a grand scale, as well as salaries commensurate with such productions. Part of Eden's predicament in "Coming, Aphrodite!" is that she must make her way between conflicting demands: as the "perennial theme," she is object; as artist, and particularly as singer, she is subject—but she also must become the part she sings. Thus as woman and as artist she must find a way by which her status as the subject of another's art does not preclude her own subjectivity.

Don is not the story's moral center and Eden lacks all aesthetic purity of intent; she seems mainly interested in being wealthy and famous. Moreover, she is quite willing to use her sexuality—certainly its promise but probably its delivery as well—to get her what she wants.[5] Don has always easily gained precisely what Eden most craves: experience. Middle-class and baptized "Edna Bowers," Eden learns of possibilities other than those of wife and mother while reading books her mother has hidden in the attic. Thereafter, Edna/Eden spends her night imagining herself as mistress of the Czar of Russia. But we have to know that becoming Aphrodite, as she is by the story's conclusion, is her true destiny. Eden, therefore, is hardly going to be content as either Don's mistress or his subject matter—or anyone else's for that matter. She is impatient to get on with her own experience and her own art. And she will stop at nothing. Eden's callous treatment of Don, her cold-blooded appraisal of what she will have to do to get herself to Europe and what she will do to make her way in the opera world are all required of the female artist. Though she may be historically destined to be wife and mother, muse and model if not mistress, Eden's education in her art begins with her refusal to remain Edna. Maternity and wifehood—but not sexuality—are what Eden must abjure.

The quarrel that prefaces Eden's leaving is about "an abstraction" (93), but it is one that has a proper name: Burton Ives. Eden has just spent an afternoon at his studio—which Don refers to as "a very good department-store conception of a studio"—while Eden gushes over Ives's work (he paints "the kind of pictures people can understand") and his success ("he has a Japanese servant and a wine cellar, and keeps a riding horse"), and implies that Don has something to learn ("he said I could bring you to see him . . . you might get something out of it") (94). When Don accuses Eden of thinking of him as "a scrub painter, who needs a helping hand from some fashionable studio man," Eden feels ill-used: "I've been trying to pull strings for you all afternoon, and this is what it comes to" (95). Eden had been indulging in fantasies lacking any basis in reality, thinking how "she might gild Hedger's future, float him out of his dark hole . . . see his name in the papers and his pictures in the windows on Fifth Avenue" (95). But it will be Eden whose name will appear in bright lights and who will proceed down Fifth Avenue after years of "spectacular success in Paris" (99). And it is Eden whose face will become "hard and settled, like a plaster cast; so a sail, that has been filled by a strong breeze, behaves when the wind suddenly dies. Tomorrow night the wind would blow again, and this mask would be the golden face of Aphrodite. But a big career takes its toll, even with the best of luck" (101). But that is eighteen years away still.

At this heated moment, Don takes Caesar and heads for a bar. A few hours later he stows some clothes in a bag and leaves town to paint on the north end of Long Island. When he returns five days later—an unsettled mixture of wretchedness and contrition and playful tenderness—he knocks at Eden's door but gets no answer. Instead he is greeted by five days worth of milk bottles standing before his own door: "The milk-boy had taken spiteful pleasure in thus reminding him that he forgot to stop his order" (98). It is the ever besmirched janitress (98) who informs Don that Eden sailed for Europe the day before.

Back in his room, Don goes to hang his coat in the closet only to find that Eden has left there her "pale, flesh-tinted dressing gown" still bearing her perfume. In the gown's pocket is a hastily written note which Don reads beneath the gas light. Eden writes that she is sorry he is angry, but doesn't really understand why. She honestly thought that Burton Ives could be helpful. She wants to see Don but "Fate came knocking at her door after he had left her. She believed in Fate. She would never forget him, and she knew that he would become the greatest painter in the world. Now she must pack" (98). Don returns to the closet and kneels down only to discover that the familiar peephole has been plugged up "with a ball of wet paper,—the same blue note-paper on which her letter had been written" (99). Cather gives us our last vision of Don moments after this discovery:

> Tonight he had to bear the loneliness of whole lifetime. Knowing himself so well, he could hardly believe that such a thing had happened to him, that such a woman had lain happy and contented in his arms. And now it was over. He turned out the light and sat down on his painter's stool before the big window. Caesar, on the floor beside him, rested his head on his master's knee. We must leave Hedger thus, sitting in his tank with his dog, looking up at the stars. [99]

We will learn the last we are to know about Don at the story's very end, when Eden returns to New York and seeks out information about Don's success. How long did Eden know Don was spying on her? And what does it mean that she did know? That she posed for him—that, in effect, she engineered his art? Why has she plugged the hole only now? And, finally, what are we to make of the nature of the material she has used to block Don's visual access to her space?

It seems so unpoetic to call the peephole stopper a spit ball, but it isn't inaccurate. Eden takes a small piece of the same paper that she has used for Don's farewell note (does she perhaps rip off a corner, thereby trivializing it?)

gets it good and wet in her mouth—even chews it possibly since she can form it into a ball—and stuffs it into the hole. What seems striking to me here is the slight vulgarity of the act. It's a tiny bit indelicate, just on the edge of indecorous. It's ill-bred really, more what we might expect of Don the maculate than of Eden the pristine. But then Eden's mouth is intrinsic to her art-making.

ART MATTERS

Miss Bower didn't usually tell the whole story—about anything.

The matter of Don's art is paint. Its creations cannot be isolated from the turpentine-filled jars that hold his brushes, the paint-smeared jacket in which he works, and the charcoal stick he uses for preliminary sketches. The beauty he makes emerges from such sorts of unclean stuff. But Eden's art is generated by her body itself, and specifically by her breath. In other words, her art is made from the invisible aspirations of her body's interior whose relationship to its exterior Cather makes clear by having Eden exercise. By creating the female artist as a singer and the male artist as a painter, Cather provides a graphic basis for their oppositional representation of the dirty and the clean, as well as sets in motion a theory of artistic creation that contrasts male and female in a way that suggests her own fears of and pleasures in creation. Cather's art, as something linguistic and as the printed page, is composed of both breath and matter. It is, thus, apparent and yet invisible expiration. In this sense, Cather is like Don as well as Eden. Just as Cather resembles Don in her shared attraction to the female body, she is like Eden in having a female body and in necessarily, therefore, grasping after the "Fate" that Eden's farewell letter and the story imply is not to be turned away from if a woman is devoted not to romance but to her art.

In its necessary mess, Don's art seems to call for creative acts of excretion. But Eden's art seems more associated with acts of artistic custody, with the energetic retention and relinquishing of breath. Her art requires the discipline of her body's tremendous energy. While Don's unsuccessful housekeeping is the unfruitful redeployment of his inspirational excitement upon discovering Eden at her exercise, Eden's necessarily regulated breath is exactly what is needed for her creative production. Eden is continually depicted as active: she moves fast, she exercises and fences, she even rides in balloons. Her body is hardly lacking in vitality. Instead that vitality, her body's breath, must be controlled if it is to be aesthetic.

But breath is not necessarily unsullied. And there is the curious detail that Cather inserts in her description of one of Don's spying visions of Eden, that she is smoking a cigarette as she looks out over the rooftops (76). This particular episode is noteworthy because, in retrospect, it can be read as suggesting that Eden has discovered Don's closet habits and is now playing to him. Eden is constructing Don as audience when *he* believes himself to be spy. Eden's smoking suggests that even an art that is pure breath is nonetheless impregnated with a less clean residue. Richard Klein, in *Cigarettes Are Sublime*, points out that smoking can serve emblematically as the sign of refusal to live within provincial constraints of morality and gender convention.[6] If nothing else, Eden's cigarette declares her unwillingness to abide by a set of precepts that would control her inspiration—both what she takes in and what she exhales. Eden's smoking is a sign of her resistance to any desire but her own. Her cigarette's smoke exhibits her interiority as well as her refusal to be fully apparent to Don in even this most intimate of visual moments. She is, in a sense, regulating Don's intake even as she indulges her own. As a smoker, Eden controls her apprehension by another even as she displays the soiled origin of her own art. Her art's origins emerge as a confluence of the external, her cigarette, and the internal, her breath, which together produce smoky evidence of their union within the private "trunk" of her body.

Cather makes explicit reference to music's breath in a scene that takes place early in the story. Don and Caesar have gone to the roof one hot evening shortly after Eden moves in. The roof has always been Don's private space since he alone is strong enough to open the heavy trap door that allows entry. On hot nights, Don often sleeps there. This evening, there is a "slender, girlish young moon in the west, playing with a whole company of silver stars" and Don watches with delight as various stars "darted away from the group and shot off . . . with a soft little trail of light, like laughter" (68). This scene offers Don, and us, a playfully youthful, feminine heaven that, like the young goddess of the story's title, is more interested in celestial fun than duty. But Don and Caesar are diverted from the"glittering game" by a sound "not from the stars, though it was music" (68). What they hear is not the Prologue to Pagliacci that often arose from a nearby Italian tenement, "with the gasps of the corpulent baritone who got behind it; nor was it the hurdy-gurdy man, who often played at the corner in the balmy twilight. No, this was a woman's voice, singing the tempestuous, over-lapping phrases of Signor Puccini, then comparatively new in the world, but already so popular that even Hedger recognized his unmistakable gusts of breath" (68).

It is significant that Cather precedes her identification of the singer's gender as female by first pointing out that it is neither of the two, familiar, male voices. The description of the sky that Don sees is so obviously feminine that we should hardly expect a male voice to enter the scene, particularly since we already know that Eden is a singer. What is even more interesting is that the emphasis in this passage is not on Eden's breath but on Puccini's: it is Puccini's *"unmistakable gusts of breath"* that mark him as the recognized composer. This is noteworthy as yet another instance when Eden's body is guarded from Don, and from us, especially since Cather, just a few lines later, will pointedly describe Eden's voice as emerging from the roof's trap door's cloacal hole like a "strong draught" (68). The breath of her melody, but not her body, is allowed to enter this private male site. But something more appears to be going on here. As Cather has written this passage, it is as though the expected voice is male, as though the music of even those very feminine stars and girlish moon should be, and familiarly is, masculine. And even when the voice is not a man's but a woman's, it is nonetheless the shaping male's, the composer's breath, that is most noteworthy.

While both Don and Eden, as artists, are self-made, Eden's self-making demands that she not comply with the cultural norms that accomplish the creation of a gender named female. Eden has unsophisticated visual aesthetics and her equation of fame and wealth with artistry is clearly wrong. But in her refusal to conform to feminine standards of behavior that would deny her access to experience, and in her creation of standards for herself that cross the usual moral boundaries, Eden is the articulation of a transgressive ethical code. Don, too, steps past the usual social codes since he makes his art the primary value in his life. But Don is, after all, a voyeur—and he's a *hedger*. Don frowns upon taking foolish risks (83). Although Cather depicts as valorous the inspirational result of Don's spying, his discovery that Eden has blocked the closet aperture suggests that Eden rectifies gaps in the moral order—or, at least, in the gender system. That Eden is perfectly willing to abandon romantic love for a shadier alliance which might further her career suggests that "she'll get what she wants," as Molly Welch admiringly claims of her (85).

What the rooftop passage insinuates, therefore, is that the woman artist's breath will be heard as male, even when it is recognizably female. That only the presence of her body can certify it as something other than male and that even then, as two of Eden's smitten young dinner guests will comment, she may have a beautiful talent, but it is her "beautiful figure" that gives them pleasure (76). Just as Eden's art and her body are able to be separated in the minds of these two fellows, Eden's breath and her gender are not equally discernable to Don's thinking. Indeed, the scene seems briefly but intensely homoerotic since what is found desirable in the female voice is its figuring of the male. In this moment, Eden's breath is not soiled, not suggestive of physical debris as it is when she smokes her cigarette. Instead her breath is no longer her own but represents a male to a male. Her missing body becomes an aperture through which a male auditor and a male artist connect.

In writing a story about both a male and a female artist, Cather not only makes the demands of each's art different, but she assigns a bodily toll for those demands made of the woman artist. Eden's artistry calls for a denial of all life other than that of musicianship if her full potential is to be perfected. Although "Coming, Aphrodite!" makes it clear that male artistry also calls for utter dedication, Don's body remains safe from his art's tyranny. His painting emanates from his psyche, and moves beyond him, finding permanence upon the canvas. His flesh itself is not the matter of his art. But for Eden, her body is the "apparatus" for her creation. Thus, when we see her entering New York seemingly quite like the goddess whose role she will sing the next night, we realize that her performance requires that the apparatus of its production be concealed. She is not to so much produce her art as become it. Without the art, when away from whatever role she currently takes on, she is empty, nothing more than a plaster cast until she is again enlivened by her role. For Eden's art, there is no distinction between the "real" and the "performance." It is precisely when she dons the mask of Aphrodite that Eden comes alive.

By means of Eden Bower, Cather exemplifies the force of her own literary ambitions. But at the same time as Don's compulsive observation of Eden and his need for the creative stimulus she provides configure those of Cather's own aesthetic history, Eden's sexuality and its role in her own artistic energies give us reason to think about Cather's presence here in the story as well. Cather needed both a male and a female artist in order to create this narrative of apprenticeship, but not because she was interested in gender equity. Rather, the female body as art's erotic spur and the sexual female body as the artist's own medium are Cather's dual experiences as a queer author.

Notes

1. Willa Cather, *Youth and the Bright Medusa* (New York: Knopf, 1920; New York: Vintage, 1975); reissued in *Collected Stories* (New York: Vintage Classics, 1992), 63–101. All further references will make use of the 1992 Vintage Classics pagination and will be cited in the text. In 2005 the story was also available at *http://etext.lib.virginia.edu/etcbin/toccernew2?id=CatMedu.sgm&images=images/ modeng&data=/texts/english/modeng/parsed&tag=public&part=1&division=div1*.

2. I use the contemporary term "butch" as a kind of shorthand for those women who predated the last half of the twentieth century and whose identity seemed unattached to femininity, even in childhood. James Woodress, as well as other biographers, notes that even before she was thirteen Cather wore her hair cut as short as a boy's and signed her name as William Cather, Jr. or Wm. Cather, M.D. She continued to cut her hair short and took male roles in dramatic productions during her first year at the University of Nebraska, Lincoln. See James Woodress, *Willa Cather: A Literary Life* (Lincoln: University of Nebraska Press, 1987), 5, 69.

3. I am indebted to Esther Newton's description of the butch in her essay "The Mythic, Mannish Lesbian: Radclyffe Hall and the New Woman" in *The Lesbian Issue: Essays from "Signs,"* Estelle B. Freedman, Barbara C. Gelpi, Susan L. Johnson, and Kathleen M. Weston, eds. (Chicago: University of Chicago Press, 1985), 7–26.

4. "Readers of 'The Passing Show' [Cather's column in the *Nebraska State Journal* in 1886] who did not know must at times have wondered if Willa Cather really was a woman. So completely had she embraced masculine values that when she wrote about women writers, she sounded like a patronizing man" (Woodress, *Willa Cather*, 110). For a marvelous portrait of Cather's behavior when taking on her writerly mantle see Marion Marsh Brown and Ruth Crone, *Only One Point of the Compass: Willa Cather in the Northeast* (Danbury, CT: Archer Editions Press, 1980).

5. Eden's character is Aphrodite-like in a number of ways. She likes gaiety and glamour, and chastity is not her strong suit, as she is quite willing to admit to Don. For lots of wonderful information on Aphrodite see the following site: *www.pantheon.org/areas/*.

6. Richard Klein, *Cigarettes Are Sublime* (Durham: Duke University Press, 1993), 127–32.

Suggestions for Further Reading

Abelove, Henry, Michèle Aina Barale, and David Halperin, eds. *The Lesbian and Gay Studies Reader*. New York and London: Routledge, 1993.

Butler, Judith. *Bodies that Matter: On the Discursive Limits of "Sex."* New York: Routledge, 1993.

———. "Imitation and Gender Insubordination." In *Inside/Out: Lesbian Theories, Gay Theories*, Diana Fuss, ed. New York: Routledge, 1991, 13–21.

Case, Sue-Ellen. "Toward a Butch-Femme Aesthetic." *Discourse 11*, no. 1 (Fall 1988/ winter 1989), 55–73.

Castle, Terry. *The Apparitional Lesbian: Female Homosexuality and Modern Culture*. New York: Columbia University Press, 1993.

Goldberg, Jonathan. *Willa Cather and Others*. Durham: Duke University Press, 2001.

Grosz, Elizabeth. *Volatile Bodies: Toward a Corporeal Feminism*. Bloomington: Indiana University Press, 1994.

King, Katie. "The Situation of Lesbianism as Feminism's Magical Sign: Contests for Meaning and U.S. Women's Movement, 1968–72." *Communication* 9 (1986), 65–91.

Lindemann, Marilee. *Willa Cather: Queering America*. New York: Columbia University Press, 1999.

Martin, Biddy. *Femininity Played Straight: The Significance of Being Lesbian*. New York: Routledge, 1996.

Muñoz, José Esteban. *Disidentifications: Queers of Color and the Performance of Politics*. Minneapolis: University of Minnesota Press, 1999.

Newton, Esther, and Shirley Walton. "The Misunderstanding: Toward a More Precise Sexual Vocabulary." In *Pleasure and Danger: Exploring Female Sexuality*, Carole S. Vance, ed. Boston: Routledge and Kegan Paul, 1984.

Sedgwick, Eve Kosofsky. *The Epistemology of the Closet*. Berkeley: University of California Press, 1990.

———. *Tendencies*. Durham: Duke University Press, 1993.

Feminist Film Theory and the Problem of Liking Characters

Sabrina Barton

Sabrina Barton (1990) taught film and gender studies for nine years at the University of Texas at Austin. She currently writes and develops presentations on feminist visual literacy for a wide range of audiences, including secondary-school teachers. Her public presentations have focused on such topics as "Film Analysis in the Humanities Classroom" and "Image, Fantasy and Identity." Barton's recent publications include "Hitchcock's Hands" in *Framing Hitchcock: Selected Essays from the Hitchcock Annual*, Sidney Gottlieb and Christopher Brookhouse, eds. (2002), and "Face Value" in *All the Available Light: A Marilyn Monroe Reader*, Yona Z. McDonough, ed. (2002).

Sabrina Barton writes that "since the 1970s, feminist film theory has had a tremendous impact on the field of film studies. Inspired by the women's movement, feminist activists and scholars broke new ground when they examined how gender and sexuality were being represented by popular culture, and asked what the personal and political consequences of those representations might be. Women's studies has helped to keep gender issues on the table amid an escalating hostility among young people toward the very term 'feminist.' What seems most pressing in my field today is drawing the valuable insights forged by several decades of feminist film theory into closer contact and conversation with viewers both within and beyond the academy."

Nothing, of course, will ever take the place of the good old fashion of "liking" a work of art or of not liking it: the most improved criticism will not abolish that primitive, that ultimate test.

Henry James, "The Art of Fiction" (1884)

I thought the movie was good. I especially liked all of the hardship situations the main character was up against. It made her role more believable by going against all the odds and shows her as a phenomenal woman ☺.

Post from *Double Jeopardy* Internet chat room (1999)

Popular press film reviewers readily indulge in what novelist Henry James calls "that primitive, that ultimate test" of "'liking' a work of art or of not liking it."[1] So do moviegoers, who freely voice personal preferences based on their own personal likes and dislikes regarding both plot ("I especially liked all the hardship situations") and character ("a phenomenal woman").[2] Responses rooted in taste and feeling (likes and dislikes) carry little weight within much of academic feminist film studies, however, where critical prose about cinema and gender is expected to be rigorously analytical. In the classroom, too, students are often coaxed out of their "primitive" movie-viewing habits, above all their habit of liking or not liking characters, and trained instead to decipher textual form, cultural significance, and theoretical or political stakes, all elements of what James would call "the most improved criticism" of our time.

Feminist film criticism has had much difficulty in communicating with potentially interested viewers beyond, or even at times within, the university. I believe that this difficulty stems, at least in part, from the fact that *critiquing* characters has come to substitute for *liking* or *disliking* them. The substitution of critiquing for liking took hold through two major phases in the feminist film theory tradition: first, the "images of women" approach, which evaluated cinema's depictions of women as either positive or negative reflections of real women in the real world and, second, the "Woman as image" approach, which argued, by contrast, that cinema (along with other mass media) produces and reproduces the gendered representations that inescapably mediate and indeed define our "reality," including "Woman" with a capital W.[3] Together, *images of women* critique and *Woman as image* critique map a trajectory away from viewers who, feminist or otherwise, continue to feel passionately about liking and identifying with film characters.

This chapter will first examine feminist film theory's problem with liking characters and then will suggest a route toward reconnecting academic and popular viewing habits. I am specifically interested here in those female viewers who respond with pleasure and enthusiasm to suspense thrillers that feature a woman rather than a man occupying the hero role. What I will call the *woman's suspense thriller* is something of a hybrid, combining a traditionally male-centered genre with an active female protagonist. I am not suggesting that *all* female viewers "naturally" share the same taste in movies, much less enjoy this particular genre. However, there is evidence that genres centering on a woman and her experiences, from classic Hollywood's "women's films" to contemporary "chick flicks," have traditionally pulled in higher numbers of female viewers.[4]

Even genres such as horror, conventionally associated with predominantly male audiences, elevate their appeal to female audiences when the lead character is a woman. In her empirical study of female horror fans, the critic Brigid Cherry found that the films most frequently chosen as top-ten favorites, including *Alien* (1979) starring Sigourney Weaver and *The Silence of the Lambs* (1991) starring Jodie Foster, had major female characters, a fact participants drew attention to when asked to explain their choice. "Many respondents," notes Cherry, "felt that the representation of a strong, intelligent and resilient female was a major change from the vast majority of female roles they had previously seen."[5] The boundaries between horror and suspense thrillers are somewhat blurry. Elements from horror films that regularly turn up in women's suspense thrillers include a psychologically deranged male killer and a woman put into dire jeopardy. These then are coupled with a female protagonist who investigates, battles, and rescues. What has feminist film theory said, and what more can it say, about female viewers who identify with the strong women of suspense?

"SHE DOES THINGS"

> I was so busy applauding Genevieve Bujold [in *Coma*] that I forgot to be cowardly. She storms through the film undaunted and unstoppable, at last providing me with the heroine for which I've been searching, most of all she *does* things.
>
> Penny Hollow (1978)

The late 1970s witnessed a cycle of "independent women" films as Hollywood sought to capitalize on the feminist consciousness of the previous decade or so. One of the most commercially successful of these releases was *Coma* (1978), a medical thriller featuring Genevieve Bujold as Dr. Susan Wheeler, a gifted surgeon who singlehandedly uncovers a nefarious conspiracy at Boston Memorial Hospital: Healthy patients are being put into comas in order to auction off their organs. In the course of the film, Wheeler surmounts all sorts of hardships, obstacles, and life-threatening situations to expose the conspiracy and its perpetrators.

Reviewing *Coma* for a feminist publication in Britain, the critic Penny Hollow writes passionately about liking its female protagonist, whom she describes as "the heroine for which I've been searching."[6] Hollow's words suggest that popular culture's images of women have a direct impact on viewers. Consciousness-raising groups during the seventies spurred feminist reviewers and theorists to criticize mainstream cinema's images of women as overwhelmingly sexist and wholly inadequate to the complexity of real women's lives. In 1972, the first feminist film journal, *Women & Film*, declared that "women must be shown in a much wider variety of roles. Their characterization must have heroism and human dignity—expressed in fields besides homemaking, loving a man, and bearing children. Women must be shown as active not passive. . . ."[7] Without question, *Coma*'s protagonist fulfills *Women & Film*'s call for wider roles, heroism, and human dignity for women: Susan Wheeler is a top-notch surgeon who saves the day, taking an active position within the narrative. I will return in a moment to the strong implication here that viewers must not go on accepting, much less liking, conventional depictions of passive women.

Hollow's phrase "She *does* things" aptly summarizes Dr. Wheeler's response to a tragedy that occurs minutes into the film: Wheeler's best friend, Nancy Greenly (Lois Chiles), has checked into Boston Memorial for a minor surgical procedure and, to Wheeler's grief and bewilderment, inexplicably winds up in a coma. When Wheeler reacts to the shocking news by immediately trying to figure out what went wrong, her boyfriend and fellow surgeon, Dr. Mark Bellows (Michael Douglas), tells her that she's "tired" and "upset" and urges her to go home, to which Wheeler retorts: "You think because I'm a woman I'm going to be upset. I simply want to understand the variables" and "I'm not going to just stand here!" Wheeler pulls her friend's chart, studies it meticulously and notices that an unnecessary tissue-typing test was conducted. She proceeds immediately to investigate the lab, and next persuades a hospital employee to run an unauthorized computer search on all coma patients within the last year. Wheeler pays for this breach of authority the next day, when Chief of Surgery Dr. George Harris (Richard Widmark) sharply reprimands her. Wheeler's response is to reiterate her position as a woman who does things: "I wanted to do something, do you understand? To do something, right away. I couldn't just sit there . . . I wanted to understand what happened to her."

Dr. Susan Wheeler spends the first half of the movie "doing things" with her eyes, ears, and mind in order to figure out what happened: reading, interrogating, listening, investigating reports, and bending rules and regulations. Cinematography vividly conveys the female protagonist's intellectual "action" through a pattern of shots that emphasize her face as she processes information. For example, as the computer technician explains why he can't search for the data she needs, an extreme close-up fills the frame with Wheeler's intensely concentrating face (you can almost hear the wheels turning); suddenly, slight movements of head, eyes, eyebrows, and mouth signal that the female protagonist has hit upon a solution.

Gradually, Wheeler turns physically active, exhibiting strength, speed and nerve as she as pursues clues and tries to put the pieces of the conspiracy together, while fighting off a threatening stranger who has obviously been paid to put an end to her efforts. A series of tense, fast-paced action scenes show Wheeler climbing up ladders and through ventilation shafts, taking down her pursuer first with a fire extinguisher and then with an onslaught of frozen cadavers, and even making an escape by lying on top of an ambulance, holding onto its siren.

What differentiates *Coma* from the typical Hollywood suspense thriller, as so many of its reviewers remarked, is the active woman at its center. *Coma*'s images of a strong female protagonist mirror the reality of powerful women, thus providing an empowering viewing experience. This critical perspective assumes that positive and negative images have an immediate impact on audiences; in this respect, responses to movie characters matter. At the same time, although there is room for emotional response, individual viewers are not licensed to "like" whichever characters they happen to, well, like. Rather, they are expected to respond to characters through the filter of feminist critique, approving only what can be claimed as positive. In short, critique has gained the upper hand. Once it begins to displace liking in the arena of popular culture, feminist film theory becomes didactic and its non-academic audience leaves in droves. Sympathetic to feminism or not, viewers rarely come to the movies prepared to check their politically incorrect pleasures at the door.

"SHE IS 'WEAK'"

As a character [Susan Wheeler] is "strong" but as an actant she is "weak."

Elizabeth Cowie (1979/1980)

Not long after the release of *Coma* and Hollow's review, the British critic Elizabeth Cowie published a lengthy two-part critique of the movie in *m/f*, a feminist journal reflecting new developments in semiotics, psychoanalysis, and Marxist theory (constituting a theoretical orientation known as *structuralism*). Her essay surveys a number of reviews, including Hollow's, that voice a feminist appreciation for Dr. Wheeler as a strong woman protagonist. But Cowie does so to question the ostensible strengths of this character and the pleasure it yields to feminist viewers. Reversing the presumption that championing positive images constitutes a valid tactic for feminist critique, Cowie redefines mainstream cinema not as a reflective mirror but as an *apparatus* whose texts arrive with built-in systems of meaning. The claim is that viewers, now renamed spectators, cannot help but inhabit a film's encoded perspective, including its perspective on gender, since only from this vantage point will the overall story make sense.

Cutting through *Coma*'s superficial images of female strength, Cowie finds that although Wheeler "appears to be in a place of knowledge, agent of the discovery of knowledge," in truth she "is consistently displaced from this position" by the film's underlying textual system (118). Unlike the detective genre, *Coma* uses suspense techniques to regulate the flow of narrative and visual information in such a way as repeatedly to leave its female protagonist at a disadvantage. Cowie argues that despite a fierce determination to understand what happened to her friend, Susan Wheeler inaugurates the wrong sort of investigation, trying to untangle a medical puzzle rather than a criminal event, and then proceeds to focus on the wrong suspects. The female protagonist's authority is undercut when, on several occasions, she (but not the spectator) is excluded from furtive discussions of her possibly compromised mental state. In one such instance, after she has exited both the hallway and the camera frame, we overhear the hospital psychiatrist comment to Dr. Harris that Wheeler is "paranoid and upset." A different sort of undercutting happens midway through *Coma* when, late one evening, Wheeler discovers that her car won't start. The plot has her lose emotional control, crying and hitting the car, upon which the camera cuts away from Wheeler's perspective to that of a lurking assailant. In classic suspense form, an autonomous female character has suddenly been transformed into the vulnerable object of a menacing male gaze.

Adopting the psychoanalytic perspective developed in Laura Mulvey's essay "Visual Pleasure and Narrative Cinema," Cowie calls attention to another manner in which Susan Wheeler's authority is undercut by a male gaze. Mulvey's essay, which delineates the underlying structures of voyeurism and fetishism at work in classic Hollywood cinema, demonstrates how traditional framing and editing techniques have operated, again and again, to layer together three controlling "looks"—that of the hero, the camera, and the spectator—into a single gaze organized around Woman as a sexualized image.[8] Near the beginning of *Coma*, Susan and Mark, exhausted after work, arrive at the latter's apartment and begin arguing about who is responsible for dinner until Susan, much to Mark's irritation, manages to slip into the shower first. This narrative development seamlessly transfers the couple's feminist-flavored argument into a voyeuristic context involving images of a nude, bathing woman, her body only slightly blurred by the transparent shower curtain and framed from Mark's vantage point as he stands at the doorway to the bathroom. Three looks—those of Mark, the camera, and the spectator—are conjoined through the spectacle of the looked-at female figure.[9] The scene stands out in a film that otherwise offers a sensibly dressed and refreshingly de-glamorized heroine. The ending of *Coma* finds Susan Wheeler undressed once more, pinned by sheets, strapped down to a gurney, and drugged by her trusted Dr. Harris—the film's true villain—as he prepares to give her an unnecessary appendectomy in order to induce (through anesthesia) a fatal coma. From the collapse of the female protagonist, moreover, arises the male hero: it is Mark's role to stop the villain and saves the girl in the nick of time.

Such filmic practices, suggests Cowie, weave a familiar patriarchal subtext into a film whose feminist flourishes merely distract from its covert participation in wider cultural discourses about gender. *Coma*'s female protagonist falls "victim to the events she seeks to engage with": "As a character she is 'strong' but as an actant she is 'weak'" (125). While *Coma*'s ending startled and disappointed some of its feminist fans, for Cowie the film's textual patterns of ambivalence regarding the strong woman have pointed to this closure from the beginning. To "like" Dr. Wheeler is to be duped by the movie's signifying system, something for which Cowie has little patience. "[T]he feminist appropriation of Susan Wheeler's role as a strong woman," claims Cowie, "extrapolate[s] just this element from the narrative" in "a willful denial of the film's work" (125, Cowie's emphasis). Evaluating the strength, individuality, and psychological depth of characters, a mainstay in images of women criticism, here gives way to the analysis of textual and ideological effects, whose sum produces the illusion we call "character." Critique has not merely displaced liking; it has dismantled the concept of character altogether.

On the face of it, the images of women and Woman as image approaches of the 1970s and 1980s may seem to have little in common. The images of women approach called attention to the ubiquity of sexist images in the media, the impact such images have on perceptions of gender, and the need to promote positive images. The Woman as image approach, by contrast, uncovered how cinema's textual forms operate insidiously to position spectators within gendered structures of patriarchal ideology and desire, even when we think we are viewing "strong" female characters. When we look at these dueling paradigms from the present moment, however, two striking commonalities stand out. Both maintain an unwavering focus on *viewers and characters*, that is, on the effects, dynamics, and implications of how we interact with gendered film characters. Furthermore, for each paradigm, critiquing characters ultimately takes precedence over liking them. The case study of *Coma* reveals why: both critics take for granted the political necessity of classifying a film as either feminist or not feminist as a criterion for "'liking" a work of art or . . . not liking it" (James). Hollow regards *Coma* as feminist and embraces it; Cowie regards *Coma* as patriarchal and rejects it.

REVIEWING VIEWING

In a 1990 essay, Janet Bergstrom describes her experience of reading through the survey responses of nearly fifty prominent feminist film critics asked to discuss their views on "the female spectator" for a special issue of the feminist media journal *Camera Obscura.*[10] What Bergstrom discovered, amid the reams of commentary, were critics struggling to reconnect their personal viewing pleasures with their hard-won theoretical insights. Bergstrom describes this struggle as a shared desire among these critics "to rescue intuition and to interrogate exactly what it is that draws the feminist film analyst to these films (the woman's film, film noir, melodrama) with such a high degree of affect, in spite of what she knows in other ways" (193–94). Notice how this statement encapsulates the tension between *liking* ("a high degree of affect") and *critiquing* ("what she knows in other ways"), a tension at the core of the feminist film theory tradition. Can we, for example, embrace the female protagonist of a woman's suspense thriller even as we also acknowledge the genre's not-exactly-feminist conventions (such as placing its women in jeopardy)? After reading all these surveys, Bergstrom surmises that "[o]ne of the most urgent questions is how to reconcile personal experience with a theoretical orientation" (193).

Through the 1990s, feminist film theory progressively reframed its founding question concerning viewer/movie relationships: from "what are movies doing *to* viewers?" to "what are viewers doing *with* movies?" Exemplary among recent developments are race/ethnicity studies and queer theory, each of which emphasizes the differences in and variety among viewers and viewer perspectives. Jacqueline Bobo, for instance, explores black women's responses to *The Color Purple* from the point of view of black female history and cultural experience.[11] Meanwhile, queer theorists such as Alex Doty find that viewer desires and identifications, far from fixed by the text, cross the boundaries of gender and sexuality to find expression in and among a range of characters.[12] Gone is earlier film theory's limiting presumption of a one-to-one correspondence between a gendered viewer and her/his gendered counterpart on the screen (a woman and a female character, a man and a male character). Instead, the meanings and effects of movies were proving to be surprisingly multiple. The most decisive shift to the specific experiences of actual viewers has been prompted by cultural studies. Critics like Janet Staiger and Jackie Stacy began to make use of reception theory, using interviews, ethnography, and archival research to place viewers within their differing constellations of history, ethnicity, class, age, and sexuality in order to bring to light how audiences negotiate with, resist, and even appropriate film texts for their own purposes.[13]

Nevertheless, in all of these developments, we haven't quite arrived at a place where the individual viewer's thoughts and feelings are granted meaningfulness in their own right (at face value, so to speak). Even critical research into what a particular group of viewers "does" with a cultural text tends to set its sights on measuring that group's relationship—is it complicit? resistant?—to society's dominant ideologies. Moreover, as Judith Mayne astutely points out, data on real readers is highly susceptible to being drawn into the critic's own favored projection of an "ideal reader."[14] Thus, while the phenomenon of viewers liking characters may have been reinstalled as a concept and even as a key component of the viewing experience, critics still assume that its *significance* can be revealed only by reading between the lines, so to speak, of viewer response.

"GO, GIRL, GO!"

But Charlie from *Shadow of a Doubt* was the best: she really stood up to her psycho uncle.

Student from "Hitchcock and Gender" seminar (Spring 2000)

I realized that *Double Jeopardy* had struck a nerve with female viewers when during test screenings women began shouting "Go, girl, go!" as Ms. Judd began hunting down the villainous husband who framed her. . . . These movies are really about female empowerment.

Producer Sheri Lansing (1999)

What do the female protagonists of the two suspense thrillers, *Shadow of a Doubt* (dir. Alfred Hitchcock, 1942) and *Double Jeopardy* (dir. Bruce Beresford, 1999), have in common? Like the female protagonist of *Coma*, both characters are coded, visually and narratively, as strong: They *do* things. I have noticed, as a teacher of Hitchcock and a researcher of suspense thrillers, that films like *Shadow of a Doubt* and *Double Jeopardy*, whose strong female protagonists have "stood up" to threatening, even psychotic male characters, frequently do indeed strike "a nerve with female viewers."[15]

In *Shadow of a Doubt*, Charlotte ("Charlie") Newton (played by Teresa Wright) is the only member of her small-town family who has figured out that their popular, urbane, visiting relative, Uncle Charlie (Joseph Cotten), is in fact an anonymous serial killer identified in the press only as the Merry Widow murderer. The female Charlie, isolating herself from the family she wants to protect, actively pursues clues in secrecy, bravely confronts her once-beloved uncle, survives attempts on her life, and, in a violent final showdown, kills her uncle before he can kill her. In *Double Jeopardy*, Libby Parsons (Ashley Judd) has been framed and jailed for the murder of her husband Nick (Bruce Greenwood). Separated from her son and isolated from disbelieving friends and authorities, Libby manages a daredevil escape from her parole officer, Travis Lehman (Tommy Lee Jones), actively tracks down and bravely confronts the perpetrator (Nick himself!), survives attempts on her life, and in a violent final showdown kills her husband (with her parole officer's last-minute help) before he can kill her. Go, girls, go.

Despite some withering reviews from critics, *Double Jeopardy* was one of 1999's biggest hits, spending four weeks at the top of the box office charts and passing the all-important $100,000,000 marker of a blockbuster. (That figure is especially significant for a reasonably budgeted thriller with a female protagonist and minimal special effects.) Responsive to the millions of movie fans who keep up the "good old fashion" of liking characters, movie producers too grant pride of place to liking over critiquing. When women in a test audience for *Double Jeopardy* erupted into expressions of intense pleasure and engagement, producer Sheri Lansing eagerly used this reaction as a basis for making a feminist claim. Lansing's comment concerning "female empowerment" fits within traditional images-of-women criticism's celebration of strong female characters, but in reverse so to speak: Characters do not have to pass feminist muster in order to be liked; instead, characters who are liked by women can then legitimately be drawn into the orbit of feminist claims. A fan's thoughts and feelings about a female protagonist carry weight: "I especially liked all of the hardship situations the main character was up against. It made her role more believable by going against all the odds and shows her as a phenomenal woman ☺." The event of women liking strong woman characters is made primary. Lansing, in other words, relies upon what James called "that primitive, that ultimate test": "you're striking a chord here," Lansing insists, "some strong primal need where women are no longer the victim" (26).

Responding to 1970s feminist reviewers for whom *Coma*'s female protagonist struck a similar chord, Elizabeth Cowie described such pleasures as *"a willful denial of the film's [patriarchal] work,"* dismissing viewer/character relationships as a subject worthy of serious analysis. Cognitive film theorist Murray Smith sums up the sorry fate of characters within academic film studies this way: "Over time, the study of emotional response to character has come to be regarded as the area in which the hapless critic is most likely to wander astray into the slough of simplistic mimeticism."[16] Smith is referring to contemporary film theory's disdain for the notion that representation and reality directly mirror each other ("simplistic mimeticism"). Perish the thought that a critic should fall into the viewing public's habit of responding emotionally to fictional film characters (liking them, crying for them) as if these characters were real people. Undeterred, and with cognitive studies as his framework, Smith asks: Why are movie viewers, as well as movie narratives, so overwhelmingly centered on characters?

Cognitive scientists suggest that the brain relies on an organizing system of filters and categories whose purpose is to classify, at lightning speed, what we would otherwise experience as an overwhelming influx of sensory information. Central to this system, argues Smith, is the *person schema*, a cognitive filter that differentiates sensory information into either "human" or "nonhuman." Citing cognitive psychology and cognitive anthropology, Smith asserts that all cultures possess a concept of *personhood* that is, first, associated with "a discrete human body, individuated and continuous through time and space" and, second, expressed through attributes of human agency such as "thought, intention, self-awareness, self-impelled actions, and so on" (47–48, 17). These criteria for personhood ("basic capacities") inform and give shape to fictional character construction.[17]

Murray Smith goes on to say that specific expressions of a character's personhood are "learned and sustained within a given cultural environment" (50). Different cultures give rise to different expressions of, for instance, gendered personhood. The legacy of patriarchal individualism informs the "cultural environment" of Hollywood. No surprise, then, that numerous suspense thrillers privilege an active, goal-directed male hero who rescues a threatened female object. Mainstream cinema has a history of diminishing the personhood of certain characters, including women, non-whites, non-heterosexuals, and characters with mental or physical challenges.[18] This pattern helps to explain feminist film theory's commitment to critiquing, and even dismantling, the very idea of characters as autonomous individuals (as Cowie does with *Coma*). But as cognitive film theory demonstrates, characters—liking them and not liking them—are pivotal to how viewers engage with fictional worlds. Next, this essay will return to the female protagonist of suspense and consider what makes her so engaging to her fans.

What I want to ask is this: What happens when the Hollywood suspense genre's privileged attributes of personhood are gendered female?

WOMEN ON THE MOVE

The remarkable, audience-captivating achievement of cinema as a medium was to make images appear to *move*. Early in its history, as film became a supreme storytelling medium, ordinary constraints of time and space were defied with filmic techniques such as crosscutting—the back-and-forth editing together of two scenes that enables audiences to experience being in two places at the same time. Given the centrality of motion to the cinematic experience, it is perhaps not surprising that, as elements of characterization, movement and stasis are not gender neutral. The history of cinematic suspense abounds in images of women-in-jeopardy, bound, gagged, strapped down, confined to small spaces (*stasis*), alternating with images of men racing to the rescue, riding, running, fighting, climbing, driving (*mobility*).[19] Just for fun, try reversing these roles: imagine a suspense thriller in which a woman races to the rescue of a trapped, terrified man-in-jeopardy (played by, say, Mel Gibson? Tom Cruise?). Can you feel your imagination straining against Hollywood's "natural" gendering of the rescue plot?

In significant ways, *Shadow of a Doubt* is a suspense thriller that does position a woman as rescuing hero. The film's introduction of Charlie Newton connotes stasis: She lies listlessly on her bed during the daytime hours, complaining about the "terrible rut" into which she and her family have fallen. A surprise visit from Uncle Charlie (for whom she was named) seems to resolve her dilemma. Later in the film, however, after a disturbing conversation with a detective working on the infamous Merry Widow murders, Charlie makes up her mind to solve the mystery of her uncle's peculiar behavior. Why, for example, did he abscond with a section of her father's newspaper and later physically prevent her from retrieving it?

Shadow uses images of mobility to represent the female protagonist's pivotal decision to investigate, a decision expressive of "thought, intention, self-awareness, self-impelled actions" (Smith). That night, Charlie slips out the back door and down the back stairs of her house, racing to reach the library before it closes at 9:00 p.m. Charlie's journey from her bedroom to the library, door to door, is compressed by twenty shots into slightly under two minutes of screen time. A frenzied orchestral score heightens the scene's tempo and tension. When a cut instantly advances Charlie from her street to a downtown intersection, the elliptical editing style (which means that portions of time/space have unobtrusively dropped out between shots) intensifies the quality of mobility associated with Charlie in this scene. A real-time version of Charlie's trip would bring the story to a crawl, while a straight cut from bedroom to library would fail to dramatize visually Charlie's transition into a woman who does things. As the female protagonist strides down the sidewalk, the camera hastens alongside her; in this manner, cinematography emphasizes both speed and solitariness as Charlie's figure outstrips the more leisurely pedestrians on the sidewalk. After a final dash (awkward in heels), she manages to talk her way into the closing library.

Charlie hurriedly locates the newspaper in question and among its pages blares the headline, "Where Is The Merry Widow Murderer?" A close-up shot calls attention to Charlie's hands as she removes the gleaming emerald ring, placed there earlier by her uncle; she matches its engraved initials to the name of the Merry Widow murderer's most recent victim. Mystery solved. What follows is a famous Hitchcockian shot: Starting from behind Charlie's slumped back, the camera retreats, craning up, up, up, until its sharply downward angle, diminishing the young woman in the shadowy frame, creates a visual metaphor for the vast burden of horrific knowledge placed upon her shoulders. However, throughout the remainder of the film the female protagonist proves herself more than able to bear this burden. She will courageously confront, combat, and finally defeat her uncle.

Shadow of a Doubt's most pronounced theme might best be described as an innocent small-town girl's painful awakening to sordid evil, rather than her transformation into a woman who does things. But this by no means prevents the twenty-first century feminist critic from laying claim to Charlie Newton and reframing her as the active hero of a suspense thriller.

Cultural meaning-making is in perpetual motion, as new ideas and understandings eventually come to challenge or even shoulder aside old ones. In the cultural environment of the early 1940s, *Shadow* associates Charlie's heroic actions with her stalwart defense of home and family, and rewards her with romance: She ends the film engaged to the detective. Several decades after *Shadow of a Doubt*, the Women's Movement was making its mark and the cultural environment was shifting. As I discussed in the first section of this essay, Hollywood responded with a cycle of "independent women" films, including

Coma in which we actually hear feminist principles voiced on screen as Dr. Wheeler demands equality in her relationship and respect in her workplace. New cultural discourses—such as feminism—can open up new pathways for cinema's stories and characters. Although placing a female character within a traditionally male-identified genre, such as the suspense thriller, sometimes amounts to little more than a marketing ploy on the part of movie studios, this does not obviate its impact on an audience's gendered habits of perception and imagination. As Smith contends, "we are capable of expanding and adapting our existing conceptual frameworks through new experiences, including our experience of fictional representation" (52)

Arriving in 1999, fifty-seven years after *Shadow of a Doubt* and twenty-one years after *Coma*, *Double Jeopardy* participates in its own decade's pop-feminist discourse, female empowerment, as it focuses on a woman's transformation from victim to hero. Libby Parsons, paragon of feminine beauty and domesticity, begins the film as a passive spectator to her successful husband, Nick, watching with pride as he hosts a fundraiser at their beautiful home. The degree of Libby's obliviousness is measured by her utter shock and horror upon discovering (through a few well-placed calls she make from prison) that her husband has framed her for his own (ostensible) murder and begun a new life with her former best friend and Libby's son, not to mention her son's two million dollar trust fund. Trapped and helpless in prison (stasis), a depressed Libby Parsons is one day inspired during kitchen chores by another prisoner's comment that no one can be prosecuted for the same crime twice (the "double jeopardy" principle). The next scene tells us that Libby has instantly mobilized herself to get strong, get out, and get revenge.

A montage sequence begins with a shot of Libby's face, now steely and resolute, framed on each side by iron bars. When a weight pulls up into the frame, we understand that the female protagonist is not, after all, passively sitting in a cell; she is taking action or, better, turning herself into an action hero. The montage moves us rapidly through images of a woman in motion: fitness machines, knee lifts, solo sprinting around the prison yard in the middle of a downpour, all to the beat of a thumping soundtrack. Hackneyed though it may be, the fast-paced sequence exerts its pull on viewers who are stirred by these images of female strength, speed, grit, and determination.

It is telling of *Double Jeopardy*, and of the woman's suspense thriller generally, that the protagonist's resolve does not seem to extend to any of the other female characters. Watching Libby sprint around the yard is another prisoner, an African-American woman who stands in a raincoat smoking a cigarette and, as spectator, expresses her admiration for Libby's gumption: "I gotta hand it to you, honey, it's just sheer hate driving you on." From the time Libby arrives in jail, this woman and her ambiguously-ethnic friend are delegated by the film to initiate, teach, and support the naïve white woman.[20] The friend, a disbarred lawyer, was the one who informed Libby about the principle of double jeopardy. The movie expends no time or effort developing these two characters, for their function is to provide a backdrop against which the female protagonist's exceptional personhood attributes, her "thought, intention, self-awareness, self-impelled actions" and, one might add, her whiteness, accrue prominence against a backdrop of marginalized others. In their last scene together, the two female prisoners coach Libby on exactly what to say and how to act in front of the parole board to earn an early release. Why on earth have these two women not used their obvious resourcefulness and wisdom to effect a similar mobility for themselves? The answer is not rational but ideological: In keeping with the individualism typical of the suspense thriller (whether conventional or "woman's"), the two serve less as characters than props whose function is precisely to "set off" the star's strength and mobility.

Here are a few of the things that the woman who does things does after earning an early release from prison: surfs the Internet at the library (research in libraries and newspaper archives is a staple of women's suspense thrillers); breaks into a building to procure a crucial file; sprints across a beach outrunning winded police officers; drives her parole officer's car off a ferry boat (mobility) even though she is handcuffed to the passenger-side door; steals her parole officer's gun, knocks him unconscious, and swims to safety; maneuvers her truck like a stunt driver. After tracking Nick to New Orleans, she cleverly appropriates the name and room number of a wealthy patron to score an Armani gown at a hotel dress shop and makes a stunning entrance to a black-tie charity event that night, where she places the winning $10,000 bid on an eligible well-to-do bachelor up for auction, her newly named, newly accented, not-so-dead husband, whom she then proceeds to blackmail in order to get back her son. For all her forms of agency and resourcefulness, however, the female protagonist finds herself duped by her husband a second time: During their rendezvous at a cemetery (to reclaim her son), Nick manages to knock Libby out cold. The screen goes black, silent, until we hear the scraping noise of a lighter, once, twice. . . . The third time it flares, revealing Libby's tightly-framed face and shoulders, supine, and her trembling hand holding the lighter by her face, just inches beneath a satin-covered lid. Casting her eyes downward, Libby manages to glimpse her feet pressed up against the end of the box. Nick has imprisoned Libby inside a coffin (not buried but locked into a vault at the cemetery). Suffocating blackness returns as the flame expires. Flick once, twice, and the flame flares to reveal an extreme-close-up shot of Libby's thumb pressing firmly down on the lighter mechanism. The image tells us that, despite the primal horror of claustrophobic immobilization (buried alive, not to mention jammed alongside an ancient corpse), the female protagonist will continue to think and to act, and even light the scene for us. Instead of hapless hysteria or frenzied flailing while awaiting a rescuing hero, the suspense turns on exactly how the woman-in-jeopardy will escape this ultimate stasis (death) by rescuing herself.

Within the close confines of the coffin, the "action" of self-rescue finds expression through back-and-forth cutting between close-ups of Libby's face (registering thought and emotion) and close-ups of Libby's hands (exploring, pushing, and activating light). During one of the "face" shots, Libby's expression registers a sudden discovery: her backpack is lodged beneath her legs.

The camera alternates between Libby's hand inching down her side, and her face now contorted with strain and determination. Finally, fingers fumbling in fabric under her thigh, Libby extracts the gun she stole from her parole officer, the gun Nick obviously could not even imagine his helpless wife might possess. As a prop and a tool, guns in Hollywood movies have long operated as signifiers of phallic power. Here, a woman pulls that signifier of power from between her legs (more or less) and becomes her own hero-rescuer. After ripping away patches of satin lining and locating the coffin's metal hinges, Libby Parsons shoots her way out to freedom. The first shot tears a small aperture of light into the blackness, an opening into her future.

Without question, this scene has enacted the familiar trope of voyeuristically positioning the viewer to watch a woman trapped, confined, helpless, and in dire jeopardy; feminist psychoanalytic film theory is probably best positioned to explore the unconscious underpinnings that fuel this fantasy. In *Double Jeopardy*, the female protagonist will rescue herself because her agency in the narrative is singular: without her, the movie could not continue. In the end, however, as with *Coma*, *Double Jeopardy* finds it necessary to reintroduce a male rescuer for the denouement. Together, Libby and her parole officer face down Nick, although it is Libby who gets off the final shot that takes down the villain.

Suspense thrillers pit heroes and villains against one another; action and violence ensue. This essay has examined how the cultural categories of gender and personhood inform such scenarios. The empowered female protagonists of *Shadow of a Doubt*, *Coma*, and *Double Jeopardy* may fall into life-threatening danger, they may even at times require male rescue, but this does not undo or cancel out the essentially active roles they assume in defeating the villains and rescuing themselves and others.

AUDIENCES DO THINGS

There are compelling reasons to follow the trail of viewers who like strong women characters, and compelling reasons not to dismiss the deep appeal of female characters granted personhood, even when they appear in texts that express a cultural environment still shaped by patriarchy. Yet rather than invoking a fixed, reality-based content for positive images of women, we can examine the visual and narrative construction of these characters, and discover in what ways they repeat and reconfigure the gendered genres and conventions of mainstream cinema.

Underlying this essay's argument is my wish to see a more accessible and relevant feminist film theory. In part, I am responding to a recent upsurge of concerned public debate over popular media's impact on society, and to calls for improved education in visual media literacy. Feminist film theory has a great deal to contribute to that conversation, but only if it can make itself seen, heard, and understood. A genuinely feminist pedagogy of gender and cinema seeks to provide viewers with multiple (if not necessarily compatible) concepts and tools that can facilitate any number of explorations. I have suggested that creating a context for discussing why we like or dislike characters (heroes, villains, and everything in between) can help to establish a more flexible and accessible approach to feminist film analysis and can do so without sacrificing critical or theoretical sophistication. I would also suggest that differing critical approaches (images of women, Woman as image, cultural studies, and so on) be taught as differing approaches rather than as a one-way line of development in which better models outsmart and make superfluous what has come before.

Changes in how Hollywood and its audiences think about movies and movie characters are bound to be partial, halting, ambivalent. It is the work of feminist film analysts—critics, teachers, and students—to take note of small adjustments, articulate their significance, and indeed actively attach significance to them by drawing them into both intellectual and cultural conversations. Whatever the source—Hollywood cinema, independent cinema, feminist film criticism—developing and circulating discourses about strong female characters may pressure and prod the gendered habits of suspense thrillers. If a female character in a suspense thriller rescues herself, let us pay attention to how this gesture hints at renewed possibilities within the genre's longstanding conceptual framework. Have a discussion, organize a conference, or write a script that articulates and explores and broadcasts these new possibilities. The gendered habits of suspense, so embedded in the culture, may always be expanded and adapted through new experiences, through critical thinking, and through creative reimagining. Movies do things, and so do their audiences.

Notes

1. Henry James, "The Art of Criticism," in *The Art of Criticism: Henry James on the Theory and Practice of Fiction*, William Veeder and Susan M. Griffin, eds. (Chicago: University of Chicago Press, 1986), 176.

2. "Icnyasty," *Double Jeopardy* chat room; Internet post #76 (9/26/99). I researched postings in this chat room in June 2000 (there were a total of 537) but, not surprisingly, the Web site had vanished without a trace. In 2005, a site for *Double Jeopardy* (opened June 5, 2003) had 83 members, 95 percent of them female ("Innocent! The 'Double Jeopardy' Fanlisting," located at *http://www.milky-pancake.net/jeopardy*).

3. In their introduction to *Re-Vision: Essays in Feminist Film Criticism* (Frederick, MD: AFI/University Publications of America, 1984), editors Mary Ann Doane, Patricia Mellencamp, and Linda Williams describe the "displacement from 'images of' [women] to . . . the production of that image" (6). Shortly before going to press, I learned that Suzanna D. Walters's *Material Girls: Making Sense of Feminist Cultural Theory* (Berkeley: University of California Press, 1995) titles a chapter, "From Images of Women to Woman as Image." Whereas I focus primarily on relationships between viewers and characters, Walters looks in depth at numerous aspects of feminist film theory.

4. Melvyn Stokes, "Female Audiences of the 1920s and early 1930s," in *Identifying Hollywood's Audiences: Cultural Identity and the Movies*, Melvyn Stokes and Richard Maltby, eds. (London: BFI Publishing, 1999), 42–60.

5. "Refusing to Refuse to Look: Female Viewers of the Horror Film" in Stokes and Maltby, *Identifying Hollywood's Audiences*, 194. The two movies mentioned are themselves hybrids, joining horror conventions with science fiction (*Alien*) and with the woman's suspense thriller (*The Silence of the Lambs*). Regarding female fans, also see *Reel Knockouts: Violent Women in the Movies*, Martha McCaughey and Neal King, eds. (Austin: University of Texas Press, 2001).

6. Hollow's review is quoted by Elizabeth Cowie, "The Popular Film as Progressive Text—a Discussion of *Coma* (Parts 1 and 2)," *m/f* no. 3 (1979) and no. 4 (1980); my reference is to the reprint in Constance Penley, ed., *Feminism and Film Theory* (New York: Routledge Press, 1988), 108. While some U.S. reviewers acknowledged the appeal of this character, including Janet Maslin and Jay Carr, some deliberately trivialized Wheeler: "a plucky Girl-Surgeon out to solve mysteries. . . . Just the sort of thing your average young female surgeon is trained for and would do," Stanley Kauffman, *The New Republic* 178 (2/18/1978), 25; ". . . the Nancy Drewlike adventure faced by pretty, plucky Dr. Susan Wheeler," Vincent Canby, *New York Times* (2/2/1978). Canby uses the epithet "pretty, plucky Dr. Susan Wheeler" throughout his review.

7. Sharon Smith, "The Image of Women in Film: Some Suggestions for Future Research," *Women and Film* 1 (1972), 19. See also Marjorie Rosen's *Popcorn Venus: Women, Movies and the American Dream* (New York: Coward, McGann and Geoghegan, 1973) and Molly Haskell's *From Reverence to Rape: The Treatment of Women in the Movies* (New York: Holt, Rinehart and Winston, 1974).

8. Laura Mulvey, "Visual Pleasure and Narrative Cinema," in *Feminism and Film Theory*, 57–68.

9. Cowie, "The Popular Film as Progressive Text," 110. After Hitchcock's *Psycho* (1960), female shower scenes are never neutral, especially within the suspense genre.

10. Janet Bergstrom, "American Feminism and French Film Theory," *Iris* 10 (1990), 193–94; Bergstrom and Mary Ann Doane, eds., *Camera Obscura* 20–21 (May–Sept., 1989), special issue on *The Spectatrix*.

11. Jaqueline Bobo, *Black Women as Cultural Readers* (New York: Columbia University Press, 1995).

12. Alexander Doty, *Making Things Perfectly Queer: Interpreting Mass Culture* (Minneapolis: University of Minnesota Press, 1993).

13. Janet Staiger, *Perverse Spectators: The Practices of Film Reception* (New York: New York University Press, 2000); Jackie Stacey, *Star Gazing: Hollywood Cinema and Female Spectatorship* (New York: Routledge, 1994).

14. Judith Mayne, *Cinema and Spectatorship* (New York: Routledge Press, 1993), 82–85. I am indebted in my thinking about spectatorship to Mayne's fine book.

15. Sheri Lansing, *New York Times*, Sec. B (10/08/99), 26.

16. Murray Smith, *Engaging Characters: Fiction, Emotion and the Cinema* (Oxford: Clarendon Press, 1995), 188.

17. Ibid. Smith insists that these attributes of personhood—above all, human agency—are "not merely the product of the individualism of modern Western culture" (23). Though skeptical of such claims to universality, I find productive Smith's emphasis on *personhood* as a framework for making sense of the world.

18. Martin F. Norden, *The Cinema of Isolation: A History of Disability in the Movies* (New Brunswick, NJ: Rutgers University Press, 1994).

19. Silent movies offered a surprising number of female action stars. See Jennifer M. Bean and Diane Negra, eds., *The Feminist Reader in Early Cinema* (Durham, NC: Duke University Press, 2003).

20. The African-American character's name, Evelyn (Devenia McFadden), is mentioned only once in passing (by Libby as she seeks consolation). End credits identify the other character as Margaret Skolowski, played by Roma Maffia who is regularly cast for the ethnic "colorfulness" she brings to secondary characters.

Suggestions for Further Reading

Bordwell, David, and Kristin Thompson. *Film Art: An Introduction*. New York: McGraw–Hill, Inc., 1993.

Carson, Diane, Linda Dittmar, and Janice R. Welsch, eds. *Multiple Voices in Feminist Film Criticism*. Minneapolis: University of Minnesota Press, 1994.

Corrigan, Timothy. *A Short Guide to Writing About Film*. New York: Longman Press, 1998.

Erens, Patricia, ed. *Issues in Feminist Film Criticism*. Bloomington: Indiana University Press, 1990.

Grossberg, Lawrence, Cary Nelson, and Paula Treichler, eds. *Cultural Studies*. New York: Routledge, 1992.

hooks, bell. *Black Looks: Race and Representation*. Boston: South End Press, 1992.

Lapsley, Robert, and Michael Westlake. *Film Theory: An Introduction*. Manchester: Manchester University Press, 1988.

Modleski, Tania. *The Women Who Knew Too Much: Hitchcock and Feminist Theory*. New York: Methuen Press, 1988.

Mulvey, Laura. *Visual and Other Pleasures*. Bloomington: Indiana University Press, 1989.

Sklar, Robert. *Movie-Made America: A Cultural History of American Movies*. New York: Random House, Inc, 1975, revised 1994.

Tasker, Yvonne. *Spectacular Bodies: Gender, Genre and the Action Cinema*. New York: Routledge Press, 1993.

Thompson, Rosemarie Garland. *Extraordinary Bodies: Figuring Physical Disability in American Literature and Culture*. New York: Columbia University Press, 1997.

Turner, Graham, ed. *The Film Cultures Reader*. London: Routledge Press, 2002.

Walters, Suzanna Danuta. *Material Girls: Making Sense of Feminist Cultural Theory*. Berkeley: University of California Press, 1995.

Williams, Linda. *Viewing Positions: Ways of Seeing Film*. New Brunswick, NJ: Rutgers University Press, 1994.

Feminism and Art History: Past Achievements and New Directions

Susan P. Casteras

Susan P. Casteras (1975) is Professor of Art History at the University of Washington. The main focus of her current work is Victorian visual culture, on which she has written extensively. Among her publications are *Images of Victorian Womanhood in English Art* (1987); *James Smetham* (1994); *A Struggle for Fame: Victorian Women Artists and Authors* (1994); *The Grosvenor Gallery* (1996); *Richard Redgrave* (1998); and *The Defining Moment: Victorian Narrative Paintings* (2000). Her newest publication (2003) is an essay for the *Pre-Raphaelite and Other Masters from the Andrew Lloyd Webber Collection* Royal Academy catalogue and she is currently working on a book on Victorian religious painting.

> *As an undergraduate at Vassar thirty years ago, Susan Casteras had the privilege of studying with Linda Nochlin, internationally recognized as one of the luminaries of nineteenth-century art history as well as one of the founders of feminist scholarship. "It was in one of her seminars that the notion of divergent ways of representing women first struck me—with a power akin to that of lightning striking—and it was in her class that the seeds of my doctoral dissertation were planted and later grew to fruition. The face of art historical scholarship has been profoundly altered by the forces of feminism in the last twenty-five years. While some books have reassessed to some degree the contributions of women artists as well as critiqued masculine canons, there have been few attempts to provide a succinct personal overview of these major changes and how attitudes have significantly shifted over the years."*

The face of art history has been profoundly recast by the forces of feminism, as scholars in the field know.[1] Although numerous articles and books have recounted the contributions of women artists and scholars and critiqued masculine cant and canons, I offer my own overview of these upheavals and of

348

how attitudes have significantly shifted over the years from wariness to toler-ance to acceptance (and a mixture of all these). Since the 1970s, feminist art his-tory has proven its adaptability and strengths by intersecting with formidable forces such as Marxist theory, French literary criticism, new revisionist methodologies, imperialist and colonialist inquiries, and queer as well as gender studies. These major transformations in scholarship took root with differing rates of growth and absorption into the mainstream soil, but without feminism as the catalyst, few would be imaginable today in their current flour-ishing forms and potency.

It would be shortsighted not to mention at the start the obvious caveat that feminism in art history was and is not a monolithic body of ideas or personages. There are many strains of feminism, and as the scholar Katy Deepwell has succinctly summarized, feminism serves simply as a "broad umbrella term for a diverse number of positions and strategies amongst women involved in the production, distribution and consumption of art."[2] While instability of meaning is among the attributes feminism has endorsed as a valid, if not crucial, trait in sundry realms, an unstable coalition of many perspectives is paradoxically what feminism embodies in my own area of experience and expertise.

Feminism should, moreover, be construed not as a segregated occurrence that unexpectedly materialized but rather as a decidedly political phenomenon that proudly announced and promulgated itself with phrases championing "the political is personal." In essence, feminism has historically been an attitude as well as a political movement. The birth of late twentieth-century feminism during a particularly tumultuous era of protest and injustice in American history—intersecting with antiwar sentiments, abortion rights and birth control crusades, and civil rights demonstrations—was not coincidental, for all these causes fought diverse battles against exploitation, abuse, and exclusion. Along these lines the eminent scholar Linda Nochlin has described feminism as "a transgressive and anti-establishment practice, meant to call many of the major precepts of the discipline into question," and that definition serves as an apropos place to commence my own observations.[3] The subject itself is prob-lematic and complex, for there were various factions—some still embroiled in controversies—and my account might differ substantially from those projected by others. Nonetheless, I aim to address some seminal transgressions and is-sues in the field from my own sidelines, from the margins to the center and vice versa, remembering always that—as feminism has amply demonstrated—the edges of history turn out to be a very worthwhile place to traverse.

My approach to this vast subject is admittedly subjective, but that stance of self-expression and intimate involvement is something that feminism has adamantly endorsed. As Joanna Frueh has written, feminism inherently "belongs to an art criticism of overtly personal engagement" that forsakes objectivity and sustains "penetration of a sort into underlying assumptions about art . . . or its maker."[4] In brief, feminism helped me find my own voice, and it is still a vocal force that has empowered untold others to discover their own abilities and reasons to speak out.

As I initially outlined this chapter, I planned to expatiate on the transition from the state of art history before and after feminism's influence. I contemplated an analytical and annotated chronology and checklist describing pioneering articles, exhibits, books, periodicals, institutions, and ideas that had shaped the field and left indelible imprints upon it. These seminal works would certainly have included, for example, Linda Nochlin's famous essay "Why Have There Been No Great Women Artists?" and her co-editorship of *Woman as Sex Object*, as well as Eleanor Tuft's *Our Hidden Heritage*, Germaine Greer's *The Obstacle Race*, and Rozsika Parker and Griselda Pollock's *Old Mistresses: Women, Art and Ideology*. In terms of fledgling publications, *Women and Art* and the *Feminist Art Journal* were memorable entries, while at the College Art Association, the establishment of the Women's Caucus in 1972 marked a watershed event. In museums and galleries, besides significant one-woman shows, *Women Artists: 1550–1950* (curated by Nochlin and Ann Sutherland Harris) caused quite a stir in 1977, and in ensuing years group shows like one in 1997–98 showcasing Pre-Raphaelite women artists (co-curated by Jan Marsh and Pamela Gerrish Nunn) followed the lead by bringing to light rediscovered objects and artists for general viewers and specialists alike to appreciate.

However, I soon decided that list-making would serve as an insufficient and rather soulless way of delving into this vibrant topic. Instead, I believe it is more appropriate and revealing to discuss how my own career and research were directly affected by the advent of women's studies and feminist influence on art history. Indeed, the latter term has been superseded in many quarters by the more generic "visual culture," a more inclusive way of encompassing all types of art production as culturally determined and no longer just aesthetically bound. Through the process of my self-examination, readers will, I hope, be able to glean some of the main questions and obstacles that existed, how these were overcome, and how they differ from today's counterparts.

Thirty-plus years ago, as an undergraduate at Vassar College, I had the privilege of studying with Linda Nochlin (now the Lila Acheson Wallace Professor of Modern Art at New York University's Institute of Fine Arts), who has for many years rightly been saluted as one of the international founders/foremothers of feminist scholarship and a principal luminary in nineteenth-century art history. Then, as now, I remain dazzled by her incredible intellect and the innovation, depth, and passion of her ideas; her commitment to students was another of her qualities that inspired me throughout my career. Not surprisingly, when I was an undergraduate, I tried to take any and all of her courses, and it was a seminar in 1969 on women and art that proved a breakthrough not only to me, but more important, to the general discipline of art history.

It was then that I experienced a flashpoint, or what *Ms.* magazine would have termed a "click" moment, when I suddenly became aware of the oppressive pervasiveness of male-dominated preconceptions about women as both subjects and makers of art. In previous classes, I had often wondered, where were women in the proverbial big picture? Why were their art-making activities so absent, unvalued, and unexamined? Women seemed utterly invisible as artists in the mainstream, much less the avant-garde, and an awareness of their marginalization proved a turning point in my realizations that art history was sexist, not at all an impartial judge of worth, quality, and meaning. Contrary to what I had imagined, there were no universal yardsticks of measurement, and there was certainly no fairness in past assessments of women. Had I perhaps missed locating the parallel universe in which women were producing art along with the culturally dominant activities of men that had been foregrounded in recorded history? What were the myths and truths underlying why the contributions and place of women in Western culture had for so long been restricted and suppressed? All of these and more queries exerted a vertiginous impact upon me even as they fueled my curiosity. It was as if I had been struck by a bolt of intellectual lightning, one that galvanized my passionate interest in women artists, feminism, and ultimately, in trying to contribute to changing the conservative canons of art history. (I might parenthetically add that it was in this same seminar that the seeds of my doctoral dissertation were planted and later grew to fruition.)

Even as an undergraduate, as I read "Why Have There Been No Great Women Artists?" I had the sense that art history might never be the same after Linda Nochlin's essay appeared, and indeed, it never has been. Nochlin's article exploded the myths of male greatness, great art and the masterpiece, and genius and the conditions under which these were all spawned. Her essay caused an immediate uproar and paved the way for lively dialogue and debate for years to come and, as Thalia Gouma-Peterson and Patricia Mathews have pointed out, constituted a critical first stage or generation of treating this subject.[5] It was in this initial phase that I was fortunate enough to be trained, formatively influenced, and, in a sense "born," as a young scholar.

When I thereafter went to Yale for my doctoral training, I naively believed that all professors and learning environments would be Nochlin-esque in terms of their open-mindedness, brilliance, and reciprocity of intellectual exchange. As it happened, Linda had "spoiled" me and all her students by letting us imagine that this was the norm, but when we found otherwise we were even more indebted to her for the doors she opened (and those she continues to unlock for current students in the field).

In the intervening thirty years since my own entry into graduate school, the contours of art history have proven quite malleable and been significantly remolded and resculpted by feminism. From the outset, the elasticity of feminism has been one of its greatest assets, for it has the capacity to expand into multiple areas of investigation and often to profoundly alter each one. No longer could an object be counted on to possess a singular identity; feminism helped to propagate the notion that an object and its maker enjoy several identities, from the cultural, racial, and social to the economic. Not even its creator could control its impact, for each viewer had the power to interpret and create his or her own response. The empowerment of ambiguity and openness was itself liberating. This multiplicity and multi-directionality were also evidenced in the ways feminism embraced so many divergent periods and styles from realism, expressionism, and abstractionism, to postmodernism. In some respects this pluralism was a harbinger of post-modernism itself and the myriad developments and hybrids it has witnessed and ultimately absorbed.

My own work has reflected this multifaceted evolution, from the time of conceiving and producing a dissertation to the present. At the outset of my academic career, the Woodrow Wilson Foundation began giving doctoral dissertation grants in women's studies in the mid-1970s, and I was fortunate to be among the first recipients. My dissertation prospectus did not dare use the word "feminist," an omission my advisor had strenuously recommended, and there was no method or ideology at the time beyond the inspiration of Linda Nochlin's model to guide me. Had I fully realized then that I would be one of the trailblazers on a new—if off-the-beaten—track in Victorian iconology and cultural feminism, I would have been understandably intimidated. But I was blithely unaware and so undertook an innovative study of the representation of male and female behavior—and their underlying power dynamics—in the imagery of British Victorian courtship culture drawn both from "high" and "low" sources. While previous modes of art history would have rejected this iconological strand of imagery, not to mention the study of social practices and leisure behavior as codified in documents such as etiquette books, feminism embraced it. My work was primarily culture-driven, with its feminist aspects by post-modern standards perhaps more latent than overt or strident, but the results nonetheless portended new directions in the interpretation of a pictorial theme that would previously have been dismissed by many as frivolous or unimportant. The outcome of my research, beyond my nine-volume dissertation opus, was, in due course an exhibition at Yale, a book entitled *Images of Victorian Womanhood in British Art*, and numerous articles in anthologies and periodicals. Thereafter, I continued to embark on increasingly more adventurous iconological forays into spheres also nurtured by feminist beliefs: the representation of boy geniuses, maternity, sorceresses and witches, nuns, errant women, fairies, emigrants, childhood, and traveling women artists.

The first stages of feminist art history, as one might have been predicted, dwelt upon seeking legitimation, and I keenly felt the pressures of this in my early labors. Various art historical writings concentrated on the notion of (male) genius, and on (female) exceptionality, or how certain women who managed to succeed in the male art world qualified for various reasons as exceptions to the rule/norm of masculine supremacy. Some women artists, such as Rosa Bonheur, were, in effect, viewed as deviants and even quasi-males who "made it" either because their male sources of support or tutelage (by father, husband, or other relative) had accustomed them to producing like men or they were otherwise atypical/aberrant from the way most females lived. A fundamental component of this stage was the rediscovery process, unearthing "lost" or neglected women from history and reviving their accomplishments as well as struggles.

In 1973, I participated in this unofficial rehabilitation campaign by researching and writing a master's thesis and exhibition catalogue at Yale about the career of Susan Macdowell Eakins, who left a corpus of her own realism-steeped paintings executed mostly before she married Thomas Eakins. Some scholars have retrospectively maintained that the rediscovery or excavation of lost and ignored major and minor artists, although valuable to the original impulses of feminist art history, was quintessentially flawed and inadequate. Deepwell, for example, asserted that reclamation efforts were more archaeological in nature, or at least more "reformist than truly revisionist; for they exemplify scholars' interests in new subjects, but with a continuing employment of standard art historical tools."[6] Perhaps, in hindsight that is true, but I shall never forget the liberating excitement of tracing a forgotten woman artist's journals, paintings, exhibition records, and critical reactions by the press. If anything, this process triggered other, deeper and more long-lasting, responses and made me constantly vigilant about never accepting the obvious and always striving to pursue even remote clues in the hopes of discovering more about an artist, whether female or male.

In my own mind as well as in the collective consciousness, in the mid-1970s and early 1980s there was concurrently a burgeoning and acute sense of awareness and irritation that women continued to be so absent and underrepresented in current exhibitions, galleries, or books. (An apt example was how long it took H. W. Janson's *History of Art* tome to include female artists in its text.) The economics of women in the art marketplace became another related corner which feminism has contested. This ranged from outcry about the dearth of women exhibiting on the walls of the Whitney Museum or the Museum of Modern Art to concerns about why dealers represented relatively few women artists, gave them scant one-person shows, or didn't promoted them in the same ways as they dealt with men. In public and private, I lamented these lacunae and pledged it a priority to remedy this situation once I ascended the curatorial ranks. As Curator of Paintings and Sculpture at the Yale Center for British Art for many years, I actively strove to include women whenever possible in permanent and temporary exhibitions. I also purchased for the collection some outstanding examples by artists such as Vanessa Bell, Joanna Boyce Wells, Emily Mary Osborn, and the Claxton sisters, Adelaide and Florence. One of the compliments I cherish most was uttered by a British viewer who approvingly noted that there were more works by women artists on view at the Center than there ever were at the Tate or any other English institution she had visited.

Still another hurdle, despite the paths hewn by Nochlin and others, involved surmounting prevailing biases about the division between arts and crafts. This schism mostly affected women, whose production in realms such as textiles or decorative arts tended to be downgraded as mere "women's work." Judy Chicago's *Dinner Party* of 1979 was a landmark challenge to the glaring artificiality of that gap. The polarization within the hierarchy of art proved vulnerable to attack and underscored the state of tacit separatism that predominated. This was manifested not only in the unspoken ranking of art (women's art equals inferior; crafts or decorative arts are inferior, so women who made decorative arts or crafts were thus doubly damned), but also in the distressing tendency of past critics to disparage women's art as (negatively) unique and different from that made by men. These assumptions rankled many women, but soon what was seen as a disadvantage turned into an asset set to new purposes by feminism, which proposed that sexual difference and essential femaleness were positive traits that could not be overlooked or underrated. Feminists assailed the innate sexism of critics (mostly male) and of language itself, phallo-centric criticism that typically demoted women's productions as soft and imitative versus hard and innovative like "man's work." I recall my own wrestling with this problem when I read nineteenth-century reviews that either paid some women like Elizabeth Thompson, Lady Butler, the back-handed compliment of "painting like men" or denigrated them in loaded language as forever circumscribed by expectations that their works could only be charming, attractive, dainty, and sweet.

Into this turmoil and dissension, the first feminist art critics bravely stepped, Lucy Lippard arguably being the most notable practitioner in the United States. Feminist art history belonged to a proverbial new order and required articulate spokespersons, and Lippard eloquently filled this function. As one recent scholar has remarked about this period, feminist art criticism was specifically "criticism with a cause . . . committed to challenging the representation of women's work in a culture which continues to devalue, denigrate and ignore it."[7] Again and again, Lippard registered protests about the status quo and proclaimed that the notion of "fine art" (like male-defined genius) was atavistically chauvinist and irrelevant. Feminism helped to eradicate the chasm of distinctions between "high" and "low" art and even good and bad taste, forging new creative dignity both for the anonymous woman and the maker of crafts, thereby placing quilt-making on an equal level with the traditionally more exalted easel-painting. Along with these, it swept away assumptions that particular kinds of painting—for example, history pictures (usually painted by men)—were inherently superior to other types such as stillife or genre (realms to which women often contributed). As if this was not enough, feminism also introduced new empirical forms of criticism predicated on the significance of the gendered gaze of a viewer.

In such efforts to reform the hallowed halls of academe, feminism sought revolution, not mere accommodation, and as Nochlin wrote in the preface to her 1988 book *Women, Art, and Power and Other Essays*, this resulted in feminists running the (worthwhile) risk of being stereotyped as troublemakers. They were accordingly accused of a litany of alleged sins, the foremost being "neglecting the issue of quality, destroying the canon, scanting the innate visual dimension of the art work, reducing art to the context of its production—in other words, of undermining the ideological and, above all, aesthetic biases of the discipline. All of this is to great good: feminist art history is there to make trouble, to call into question, to ruffle feathers in the patriarchal dovecotes. . . ."[8]

All of these elements, revolutionary and otherwise, to one degree or another informed the direction and content of my own writings, whether by inspiring me to follow neglected thematic or iconological byways or spurring me on to seek more facts about a little-known woman artist and the conditions under which she toiled. Besides thriving on the rigorously investigative nature of feminist art history, I have enjoyed the camaraderie it fostered and the sense of purpose it bestowed. Feminist scholarship to me seemed less isolating and more supportive than other circles, and there was much mutual reinforcement when colleagues made new discoveries or wrote to expose the fallacies of patriarchal power and the perils of elitist value systems. Over time, however, feminism and its proponents were not satisfied merely to denounce the dominant hegemony of masculine bias and production and to reevaluate forgotten artists—and by the early 1980s, a subtle shift had evolved and the focus was on probing the nature of repression in terms of gender, class, race, age, sexual proclivity, and ethnicity. One of the major tenets of feminism was to identify the Other, and in doing so it renegotiated the nature of repression beyond that of women to encompass minorities, non-Westerners, members of the gay community, and other outsiders. In this respect too it was a harbinger of future areas of discourse and study—multiculturalism, imperialism, and queer theory. I welcomed this change and taught classes on representations of the Other, a topic that greatly interested students.

Exactly what the archetypal as well as the contemporary implications of "female" and "feminine"—and its obverse, "masculine"— communicate has obsessed feminism and its proponents for the last quarter century. From an acknowledgment and indictment of past prejudices and abuses, feminism proceeded to more sophisticated considerations and exegeses of patriarchal ideology and authority, shifting from acrimonious (if righteous) accusations to psychoanalytic approaches in which women were seen as signifiers of power and privilege, as Jacques Lacan postulated. Beyond Lacan and the equally influential authors Jacques Derrida and Michel Foucault, later feminism was drawn to the writings of European (mostly French) women intellectuals such as Luce Irigaray, Helène Cixous, and Julia Kristeva. From structuralism to intertextuality, these individuals generated an enduring impact on the content of countless articles, lectures, books, and classrooms. More important, their avant-garde vantage points offered new tools for analysis that fertilized several fields and proved, as one colleague has astutely noted, as "rich formally as they are sociologically."[9]

Among the most long-lasting achievements of feminism has been the degree to which it has linked previously separate and autonomous areas. In many ways it has mediated the gap between making art and producing art history. On other fronts, feminism encouraged continuous cross-overs and transfers over past boundaries, among disciplines as well as in university curricula and general theories and reception. For example, in film practice and theory, feminism has shone through with particular triumph. One of the best and most often cited discussions of narcissism and the female gaze was posited in a 1975 *Screen* article entitled "Visual Pleasure and Narrative Cinema" by Laura Mulvey, and it is still considered a classic in feminist interdisciplinary literature. Its impact is one that has filtered to the general populace, who today are far more likely to be aware—at least on some level—of the notion of gendered spectatorship and how men and women view the same subject in art, film, or television quite differently.

In terms of subject matter, feminism questioned and chose to override many of the prevailing taboos, provocative topics like female eroticism, poverty, rape, incest, homelessness, ageism, lesbianism, homophobia, illnesses like AIDS, and ecological or environmental issues. It validated the feminine experience in new dimensions and made the creation and discussion of art consciously subjective, from the intimate relation of autobiography to the subjective stance of the critic. In my own specialty of nineteenth-century art, I have benefited from this spirit of liberation and incorporated some of these topics into my research and writing, in articles on the portrayal of dispossessed single mothers and broken families, religious females, male desire and embowered women, and even androgynous fairy sprites and violent sexual acts in Victorian art.

The so-called first generation and its immediate adherents tended to focus more on social history and biography than on matters of theory. Even as it dismantled past stratagems of art history, feminism complemented and broadened the more traditional modes and borders and allowed for considerable interconnectivity. It has moreover survived, even prospered from, skepticism, since many scholars have been unwilling or slow to accept the more radical theories. This was true to some extent of my own work, for at times I too was hesitant to embrace European models indebted to Marxist, deconstructionist, or post-structuralist concepts, partly because I dislike the often unnecessarily dense and obfuscating, sometimes borderline intelligible, jargon.[10] Instead, particularly in my earlier work, I chose to inform my writing with more of a social history or sociological slant, choosing literary, historical, and cultural contexts in which to embed a work of art as my means of gaining access to and interpreting objects. Narrative and genre pictures cloaked in "realism" have always appealed to me, propelling me to study the conditions of everyday life, leisure, values, and other aspects that conspire, through the artist's imagination, to create a fictional, if beguiling, world for spectators to behold and judge. I have often utilized the original reception history of works of art— including the response of women whenever known—as a revealing index of taste and a starting point of inquiry. However, I recognized that social/cultural interdisciplinary approaches and monographs would not alone suffice to transform the canon and significantly advance the cause of feminist art history, so over the years I have consciously tried to adapt and grow, to learn something from each new stage and to reflect this in my writings with solid ideas and lucid prose that appropriately accord with my approach, style, and goals.

For the second and third waves of feminist art historians, the differences between the sexes enunciated in earlier pronouncements were channeled into different foci. These later scholars concentrated on divisions in theoretical approaches, speculating about new "unfixed" perspectives on women and placing them into a system of signification and psycho-sexual constructions.[11] Simultaneously, the very language of art history was becoming unfixed and morphing at what occasionally struck me as warp speed. Not content to stagnate, feminism joined forces with literary criticism and participated in the restructuring of a new aesthetic linguistic framework. Terms such as discourse, discursive constructs, deconstructionism, post-structuralism, signs and signifiers, psychoanalysis, binary oppositions, dialectics, scopophilia, and semiotics have all since become commonplace as they were incorporated into a new infrastructure and rhetoric of language and thought.

Another challenge that feminism encountered and squarely met was female sexuality, as a central theme in both past and current art. Hannah Wilke, Lynda Benglis, Joan Semmelths, Cindy Sherman, and Mary Kelly were among the many who upset reigning stereotypes by using their own anatomies and selves as a kind of "body politic" for inscription of meaning. Increasingly, feminist artists brought their own lives to their art, in the form of performance art, body art, video, and other hybrids. Topics that once were forbidden—lesbianism, pregnancy, incest, and rape—were also part of this resituation of what it meant to be female in gender and artistic production. This angle of inquiry has influenced my own work, and I have explored sexual as well as anatomical topics in my teaching and my writing, analyzing the creed of ugliness and deformity in face, body, and gesture in Victorian art.

The other role I have played besides that of curator is that of professor, for throughout my career I have made it a priority to teach even when I worked full-time at a museum. In these arenas, too, feminism has affected the fate of women employees. Just how dire was the situation before the rise of feminism? As Professor Alicia Craig Faxon, a colleague who witnessed firsthand the feminist march of history, recalled, "As a graduate student in 1970–71, I heard the chair of the art history department say to a group of faculty and graduate students that he would consider anyone as his successor 'except a woman.' This, of course, would be actionable today, but was accepted then. Two brilliant women art historians coming up for tenure were told to look elsewhere because 'we don't tenure women.'"[12] Despite these barriers, on the pedagogical front, feminism has expanded the boundaries of art history, and for at least two decades many art historians—primarily women—have integrated women artists into their mainstream courses as well as devised courses devoted exclusively to a history of female painters. In this way too, the frontiers of art history have been pushed to new limits and yielded new grounds for exploration.

In the halls of academe and museums the situation has improved, but the difficulties and discrimination have not totally disappeared. Although statistically women dominate art history departments in terms of raw numbers as teaching staff, fewer women are promoted to full professor ranks, receive tenure, or hold chairs than do their male counterparts. It is not much better in museums, where, in my experience, women often tend to stagnate in mid-level positions in curatorial or especially educational divisions and are thus, to some degree, potentially thwarted from staging the kinds of exhibitions and programs that might reflect feminist content or affinities.

In the end, three decades later, what is feminism's lasting legacy to the field of art history? Above all, it has debunked myths and stimulated an entire era of professionals and their scholarship, triggering new criteria and methodology that intermixed class, gender, race, and other factors into the perception of a work of art. Feminism was truly revisionary in several senses of that word. It has proffered new questions as well as innovative queries to pose. It has mediated the old and the new, offering new approaches to and critiques of objects, artists, and issues both traditional and radical. By comparison, the past before feminism seems one-dimensional and even boring. Feminism shook the foundations of art history by redefining patriarchy, rethinking representation and power, knocking authority figures off their pedestals, and renegotiating borders. It has created a resonant continuum that brings revitalized meaning, freedom, and stature to the phrase "women's work."

Feminism reenergized the field and its practitioners and proposed innovative ways of seeing that have permanently transformed the notion of "the gaze" in several media. I can honestly say that as a result, I "see" objects differently and reexperience even the so-called "great" works of art according to realigned angles of vision and lenses of perception. Feminism, in the best sense of the word, has "feminized" art history and made it a far richer discipline. Many colleagues share this appraisal. Julie F. Codell, Chair of the Art School at Arizona State University, remarked that once the canon was restructured, "paintings are now recognized as having rich content and in some cases social and political messages that had been entirely missed. Feminists do not simply suggest agitprop analyses but recognize how ideals and values are embedded in the very media and forms of art. . . . Both unexamined and overexamined art became objects of new questions about how aesthetics contains its own social and political ideologies, and how limited and presupposed was our traditional definition of art itself." [13]

Now, even by the most conservative standards deemed a part of mainstream scholarship, feminism has been prodigiously productive and is no longer treated as an unfortunate disease. But what about its future? The "missionary" phases, class-coded tensions, and internecine warfare have largely subsided and a sort of revisionist detente seems to have been reached. Militants and middle-of-the roaders will continue to coexist, and the valorization of the personal will probably still endure, but so too, inevitably, will detractors as well as backlash. But there are other possibilities, as my colleague Julie Codell has postulated. She believes—and I concur—that "feminism has been transformed by recent studies in masculinity which it has parented. These studies have extended feminism's critiques to include masculinity as constructed, fragile, and historical, opening up new studies of gender relations and ways in which gender is made palpable in culture to reflect and to shape subsequent cultural values and personal identities. In this form of gender studies, feminism's grandchild, a wide range of cultural expression has become scrutinized and expressed." [14]

Another expert in this field, Patricia Failing of the University of Washington, who focuses on issues of artists' sexual identity, cites among her own notes of influence the impact of feminist inquiries by Simone de Beauvoir, Foucault, Lacan, John Cage, Trinh T. Minh-ha, Elizabeth Groz, and more recently, Judith Butler and Virginia Beecroft. To Failing, "cyberfeminism and other articulation of the posthuman body" remain in the vanguard for future growth, for "the deep structural underpinnings of the male/female binary are now eroded, at least in theory."[15]

Feminism has thus proven itself not to be just a series of arguments, annexations, and admixtures but instead continues to evolve. It has, moreover, not only affected art history, but all the areas in which it operates, from criticism, language and theory, museums and exhibitions, and publications, to teaching. As Linda Nochlin has remarked, feminism has gone beyond "greatness" and continually alters itself and the world around it. In prophesizing future directions, she demarcates the past as well: "Feminist politics today is far more multivalent and self-aware; the battle lines are less clearly drawn. The binaries—oppressor/victim, good woman/bad man, pure/impure, beautiful/ugly, active/passive—are not the point of feminist art anymore. Ambiguity, androgyny, and self-consciousness, both formal and psychic, are de rigueur in challenging thought and practice."[16]

Notes

1. The single most useful article on the subject of feminist art history is Thalia Gouma-Peterson and Patricia Mathews, "The Feminist Critique of Art History," *Art Bulletin*, 69 (Sept. 1987), 326–57. The best books are edited by Norma Broude and Mary D. Garrard: *Feminism and Art History: Questioning the Litany* (New York: Harper & Row Publishers, 1982); *Expanding Discourse: Feminism and Art History*, (New York: Harper Collins, 1992); and *The Power of Feminist Art: The American Movement of the 1970s, History and Impact* (New York: Harry N. Abrams, 1994). Another worthwhile source is *Framing Feminism: Art and the Women's Movement 1970–1985*, Rozsika Parker and Griselda Pollock, eds. (London: Routledge & Kegan Paul, 1987).

2. Katy Deepwell, ed., *New Feminist Art Criticism: Critical Strategies* (Manchester: Manchester University Press, 1995), 1.

3. Linda Nochlin, *Women, Art, and Power and Other Essays* (New York: Harper & Row, 1988), xii.

4. Joanna Frueh, "Towards a Feminist Theory of Art Criticism," in *Feminist Art Criticism: An Anthology*, Arlene Raven, Cassandra L. Langer, and Joanna Frueh, eds. (Ann Arbor: UMI Research Press, 1988), 154.

5. On this positing of different generations or stages, see Gouma-Peterson and Mathews, "The Feminist Critique," 326, 346.

6. Deepwell, *New Feminist Art Criticism*, 1.

7. Ibid., 5.

8. Nochlin, *Women, Art, and Power*, xi–xii.

9. Sept. 13, 2003 e-mail communication to me from Prof. Julie F. Codell.

10. Another reason for my hesitancy was my concern that Americans were relying too heavily on European models and needed to create their own. A kindred opinion is expressed in Joanna Frueh, Cassandra L. Langer, and Arlene Raven, *New Feminist Art Criticism: Art Identity, Action* (New York: Harper Collins, 1994), xii: "Mainstream critics . . . spoke as though American feminist art critics couldn't be

trusted to voice their own insights about masculine authority and the discourse of 'others'—especially women."

11. Gouma-Peterson and Mathews, "The Feminist Critique," 346.
12. Sept. 10, 2003 e-mail communication to me from Prof. Alicia Craig Faxon.
13. Sept. 14, 2003 e-mail communication to me from Prof. Julie F. Codell.
14. Sept. 13, 2003 e-mail communication to me from Prof. Codell.
15. Oct. 20, 2003 e-mail communication to me from Prof. Patricia Failing.
16. Linda Nochlin, "Feminism & Art: 9 Views," *Artforum* (October 2003), 141.

Suggestions for Further Reading

Casteras, Susan P. *Images of Victorian Womanhood in English Art*. London: Associated University Presses, 1987.

Chadwick, Whitney. *Women, Art, and Society*. New York: Thames and Hudson, 1990.

Cherry, Deborah. *Beyond the Frame: Feminism and Visual Culture, Britain 1850–1900*. London: Routledge, 2000.

Deepwell, Katy, ed. *New Feminist Art Criticism: Critical Strategies*. Manchester: Manchester University Press, 1995.

Frueh, Joanna, Cassandra L. Langer, and Arlene Raven, eds. *New Feminist Art Criticism: Art, Identity, Action*. New York: Harper Collins, 1994.

Garb, Tamar. *Sisters of the Brush: Women's Artistic Culture in Late Nineteenth-Century Paris*. New Haven: Yale University Press, 1994.

Greer, Germaine. *The Obstacle Race: The Fortunes of Women Painters and Their Work*. New York: Farrar Straus Giroux, 1979.

Harris, Ann Sutherland, and Linda Nochlin. *Women Artists: 1550–1950*. New York and Los Angeles: Los Angeles County Museum of Art and Alfred A. Knopf, Inc., 1976.

Hess, Thomas B., and Linda Nochlin, eds. *Woman as Sex Object: Studies in Erotic Art, 1730–1970*. New York: Art News Annual XXXVIII, 1972.

Lippard, Lucy R. *From the Center: Feminist Essays on Women's Art*. New York: Dutton, 1976.

Marsh, Jan, and Pamela Gerrish Nunn. *Pre-Raphaelite Women Artists*. Manchester: Manchester City Art Galleries, 1997.

Mulvey, Laura. "Visual Pleasure and Narrative Cinema," originally published in *Screen*, 16 (Autumn 1975), 6–18.

Nochlin, Linda. "Why Have There Been No Great Women Artists?" originally published in *ARTnews* (January 1971), 22–39, 67–71.

———*Women, Art, and Power and Other Essays*. New York: Harper & Row, 1988.

——— et al. "Feminism & Art: 9 Views," *Artforum* (October 2003), 141.

Parker, Rozsika, and Griselda Pollock. *Old Mistresses: Women, Art and Ideology*. New York: Pantheon, 1981.

———, eds. *Framing Feminism: Art and the Women's Movement 1970–1985*. London: Routledge and Kegan Paul, 1987.

Petersen, Karen, and J. J. Wilson. *Women Artists: Recognition and Reappraisal, from the Early Middle Ages to the Twentieth Century*. New York: Harper & Row, 1976.

Pollock, Griselda. *Vision and Difference: Femininity, Feminism and the Histories of Art*. London: Routledge, 1998.

Raven, Arlene. *Crossing Over: Feminism and Art of Social Concern*. Ann Arbor: UMI Research Press, 1988.

Robinson, Hilary, ed. *Visibly Female: Feminism and Art Today*. New York: Universe Books, 1988.

Seigel, Judy, ed. *Mutiny and the Mainstream: Talk That Changed Art, 1975–1990*. New York: Midmarch Arts Press, 1992.

Tickner, Lisa. "Feminism and Art History." *Genders*, 3 (Fall 1988), 92–128.

Tufts, Eleanor. *Our Hidden Heritage: Five Centuries of Women Artists*. New York: Paddington Press, 1974.

Study Questions

1. Martha Nell Smith stresses the importance of making sources on women available on the Internet. As you read other essays in this book, examine the sources the author uses, including novels, diaries, letters, or poems, and look to see which of these can be found online. Given that these are "virtual documents," where are the actual documents located? Can you discover who decided to make them accessible online? Who put them there and how do they stay there? Are there feminist issues involved in the answers to these questions?

2. Using Michèle Aina Barale's essay on Willa Cather as a model, how would you reevaluate the literary style or aesthetics of one of your own favorite female authors?

3. Imagine yourself as a film critic. Watch *Coma* or *Double Jeopardy* or any recent film you prefer and write your review, explaining whether you find, as Sabrina Barton did, that liking or disliking a female character affects your judgment of the film. Explain what it is about these female characters that determines whether you like them or not.

4. Susan Casteras mentions several artists from several periods in her essay. You might want to locate a reproduction or a museum original of a work by one of these artists, or a work by another woman, and find critiques of that work written before 1960 and after 1970. How do the pre-1960 critiques differ in tone and approach from those written after the wave of feminist scholarship in the 1970s?

Index